An Artist Empowered

An Artist Empowered

DEFINE AND ESTABLISH YOUR VALUE AS AN ARTIST NOW

TRIUMPH OVER REJECTION

A PRIMER FOR CREATORS

Eden Maxwell

Copyright © 2007 by Eden Maxwell

All rights reserved.

This book, or parts thereof, may not be reproduced in any form, including information storage and retrieval systems, without permission in writing from the author, except for brief quotations included in articles and reviews.

For information write to: artist@edensart.com
Fair Lawn, New Jersey
USA

Publisher's Cataloging-in-Publication data

Maxwell, Eden.
    An artist empowered: define and establish your value as an artist - now: triumph over rejection / Eden Maxwell.
    p. cm.
    Includes bibliographical references and index.
    ISBN 978-0-6151-5095-6
1. Creation (Literary, artistic, etc.) 2. Self-actualization (Psychology)--Problems, exercises, etc. 3. Creative ability--Problems, exercises, etc. 4. Creative thinking. 5. Success--Psychological aspects. I. Title.

BF408.M328 2007
153.3520--dc22   2007904378

ART & BOOK DESIGN: EDEN MAXWELL
FRONT: *PRIMA DONNA* (DETAIL), 2003, PRIVATE COLLECTION
BACK: *BUDDHA UNWINDING*, 2007, STUDY FOR A SCULPTURE

INSIDE ARTWORK: ORIGINAL COLOR WORKS WERE MODIFIED TO GRAYSCALE WITH 80% TRANSPARENCY.
(PP. XV, 47, 79, 209, 223, 271, 333, 353, 413, 442, 479)

www.edensart.com

THIS BOOK IS DEDICATED TO ADELE, MY MOTHER, WHOSE LOVE IS THE WELLSPRING OF MY DHARMA AS AN ARTIST FROM THE SOUL.

CONTENTS

prologue 2

UPFRONT AND PERSONAL

Always Consider the Source

chapter one 8

CONVENTIONS

Liberating the Word

chapter two 12

I ACQUIT MY SELF

Serve Somebody

chapter three 20

OPENING THOUGHTS

On Sacred Ground

chapter four 32

NO SECONDHAND NO'S

Affirm Your Purpose

chapter five 36

A NEW POSTER CHILD
Artist as Hero

chapter six 42

THE GAUNTLET GUARANTEE
Disengaging from Mind Control

chapter seven 48

WELCOME BACK
My Dinner With Lawrence

chapter eight 54

REJECTION HQ
The Interview

chapter nine 60

THE RULES OF ENGAGEMENT
Power and Peril

chapter ten 66

THE CORE QUESTIONS
Revelation and Desire

chapter eleven 72

LORD OF ILLUSION
A Humility Primer

chapter twelve 80

THE EIGHTEEN BE-ATTITUDES
Indelible Markers of Character

chapter thirteen 88

THE UNDERSTUDY ISSUE
Getting the Part

chapter fourteen 92

MOZART OR MUZAK
The Gift

chapter fifteen 100

AWARENESS
The Arbiter of All

chapter sixteen 104

THE MAGNIFICENT TRUTH
Deliverance

chapter seventeen 110

THE LOTUS FLOWER
Petals of Freedom

chapter eighteen 120

THE FELLOWSHIP OF CREATORS
Only the Strong Survive

chapter nineteen 130

FACE-TO-FACE
Ego and Soul

chapter twenty 136

DIALOGUE DE JOUR
Kites • Color Pencils • Prophecy • Kachina Dolls

chapter twenty one 148

INTELLIGENT IS NOT SMART
Epiphanies in the Hood

chapter twenty two 152

TIERS OF REJECTION
The Crucible of Art

chapter twenty three 168

ART AND COMPETITION
The Jury

chapter twenty four 174

ART & PHYSICS
Earth | Space | Time

chapter twenty five 204

JACKSON, WE LOVE YOU
Pathos and Truth

chapter twenty six 210

BEFORE THE STORM
From Purgatory to Paradise

chapter twenty seven 216

THE GRAMMAR ENIGMA
Wanderlust & Money Laundering in LA

chapter twenty eight 224

WORDS THAT DEFINE
Mean What You Say

chapter twenty nine 230

EXISTENTIAL PINOCCHIO
Puppet With a Dream

chapter thirty 240

THREE PARABLES
Luck, Letting Go, Pill of Truth

chapter thirty one 244

PICASSO UNPLUGGED
Spinning Straw into Gold

chapter thirty two 258

INTUITION DETECTOR
An Open Channel

chapter thirty three 266

WORDS IN THE WAY
A Rogue's Glossary

chapter thirty four 272

THE PIANO MAN
A Solo Revelation

chapter thirty five 278

DHARMA, DESTINY, DREAMS
Avatars Among Us

chapter thirty six 288

INSTINCT / INTUITION
Formative Years

chapter thirty seven 294

ALPHABET ART
The Painted Word

chapter thirty eight 300

YOUR PAPERS, PLEASE
A Gatekeeper

chapter thirty nine 304

INTUITION
Bemused, No More

chapter forty 312

FULLY REALIZED
The Dynamic of Needs

chapter forty one 334
RESISTANCE / DISTRACTION
The Usual Suspects

Chapter forty two 340
DECODING THE IMAGE
Art for Art's Sake

chapter forty three 354
THE THRESHOLD
Drawing the Line

chapter forty four 358
TRAFFICKING IN ART
Acquire Within: Premodern to Modern

chapter forty five 384
A PREMONITION
Phantom In the Parking Lot

chapter forty six 388
BEYOND THE VEIL
Creation, Creativity, Imagination

chapter forty seven 392
IMMORTAL COMBAT
Disarming the Dragon and the Demon

chapter forty eight 400
DETACH AND CONQUER
The Law of Non-Attachment

chapter forty nine 414
NO WHINING
And I Mean It

chapter fifty 418
RORSCHACH'S INKBLOTS
What Might This Be?

chapter fifty one 422
LETTER TO MY MOTHER
Boulevard of Dreams

chapter fifty two 426
THE GESTALT
Children of Art

epilogue 432
HERE AND NOW
Art of the Covenant

bibliography 436
Recommended Resources

index 444

acknowledgment

I am thankful for all my teachers—a feeling of gratitude that flowers most fully in retrospect.

The gift of art comes with one condition: *DEDICATION.*

PROLOGUE

UPFRONT AND PERSONAL
Always Consider the Source

WHEN I DECIDED to write a book about kites in 1986, several authorities in the field and a half dozen literary agents told me that I was wasting my time. I was informed that everything important about the subject had already been covered, the market was too small, and no mainstream publisher would be interested.

After listening to this consensus concerto of advice, I felt opportunity calling and went with my intuition—which is the soul singing the divine song of the Creator. I did find a mainstream publisher.

Nearly two decades later, my book continues to sell both here and abroad, and a new, updated edition was published in 1998. What did I learn? The experts, who may even have been earnest with their doomsday advice, couldn't grasp the vision I had. Don't be deceived: sincerity is often totally wrong.

KARMIC DEBT

Having had some success in being published, people would occasionally ask my advice concerning their aspirations to write. Should I? Shouldn't I? My reply was, and still is, this: If someone can talk you out of it, then don't do it. After getting the usual puzzled then thoughtful look in return from the wannabe, it is clear the responsibility has shifted back to the seeker, and I have made a payment on the installment plan—one less coupon of karmic debt in my booklet.

I am a late bloomer engaged in my visual art life. I had spent years learning lessons on the front lines while purging myself of those aspects of social conditioning that didn't serve a creator. These forces that ultimately reveal my own self to me are tested daily; the lessons are never over. How many of us, stripped naked of our veneer, our material-based identity, would remain steadfast in our mission, with self-esteem and a sense of self left intact? For this is *the* question each true artist must ultimately confront.

Time is a dictator.
NINA SIMONE

When that moment of truth does come, you will be prepared by having an open mind to a new realization. This gives new meaning to the phrase: being honest to a *fault*. The alternative is unacceptable.

WALK THIS WAY

As an artist who has decided to go public, your goal is to find your audience. A gauntlet will be thrown down to challenge your dedication, spirit, and sense of humor. There will be tribulations that can trip up the most talented artist.

Without character, humility, and a fearless trust in the power of intuition, even genius can easily lose its way in the world.

Every life is a series of decisions.

You are the author of your own story—a declaration I have been writing about, advocating, and living for many years. You can be an extra in your reality programming or the main character. You not only have the green light to rewrite the script, you have one of the most sought after privileges in Hollywood—the director's artistic license of having the final cut. As a human being, as an artist, you have the power to expand reality with your art. The question is will you?

Remember, many are called; few choose to go.

There is a leap into metaphysical real estate involved here that no codex can ever explain. You must stake your own claim and work the 'promised land' yourself.

In your commitment to playing the protagonist on a quest to fulfill his dharma, you must be steadfast in your life as an artist. As in any story, however, the hero must experience encouragement—small perks of some type for enduring the hardships standing in the way of accomplishing the goal. Without such compensation, our hero eventually gives up only to wash up on the bleak beach of failure, like so much karmic residue.

But don't despair.

There is a simple and direct answer to keep the momentum going; and it is momentum that powers your dream from atrophying. Your perceived identity must come solely from the self; your soul needs no outside authority—including other artists—to validate its value; in turn, your soul rewards your earned autonomy with insight.

The decision to take responsibility for your worth demands a lifetime commitment that will be challenged daily. I wrote that the answer was simple, not that it was easy.

IN THE INFERNO

About soufflés, James Beard said: "The only thing that will make a soufflé fall is if it knows you are afraid of it."

Nearly a decade ago now, after I had finished writing an article for an art magazine, I began receiving positive feedback for my piece from readers across the country. As the magazine was pleased with my work, I surfed on my momentum and asked the editor if she would recommend a savvy New York City art dealer who could recognize talent when he saw it.

Selling known names is dealing in brands, established cachet, and commodities, not necessarily art.

Art and life are synonymous in this way: giving meaning to both completes the experience. If you can grasp this, then the whole thing falls neatly into place.

EDEN

I got a lead and went to a gallery in trendy Soho.

After more than a few decades, the art dealer was closing up shop. The rent was becoming prohibitive, and he had decided to leave for warmer climes. He was amiable enough. After looking at a selection of my slides, he suggested I visit another gallery a few blocks away.

Although I didn't like making cold calls, I went to encounter the other New York Soho art dealer, who had a large gallery. My primary interest when presenting my work to a gallery is this: Would you like to sell my work, or not?

I will decide if I want a critique and from whom.

After quickly examining a half dozen or so of my 35mm slides with his slim pocketsize slide viewer, this dealer had a need to volunteer a pompous remark about my paintings, which, in retrospect, turned out to be an unwitting compliment. And for that, I thank him.

This isn't the first time I have felt gratitude toward someone who has rejected my work. Although hearing *yes* is grand, it has always been *no* that has pushed me to go further in the right direction.

After I joked a bit about the dealer's commentary on my work, I then asked to see his pocket viewfinder. Not quite sure of my motive, he reluctantly placed the viewer in my palm. I popped one of my slides in and placed the viewfinder to my eye.

"My work looks fantastic," I said. "And this viewer fits in my shirt pocket, too. I'll get one of these . . . and it's so light even with the batteries. You've been helpful." I put my portfolio together, thanked him for his time, said goodbye, and left. On my way out of that Soho gallery, I remember stopping for a moment to look at the main exhibit: an installation of life-size five-foot tall reproductions of eight or more termite mounds made of elephant dung. I shrugged.

As I walked out and into the din and daylight of Soho, I felt apprehensive for a weak and transitory moment. I followed the busy street to a nearby Starbucks and, like a rider who had been thrown from his horse, got right back on. I did a fine ink drawing while having a cappuccino.

If I, forged by the fires of rejection many times over, could still get unsettled, what about the less seasoned soul? What about me? There was a lesson here to learn—a gem in the rough. My intuition directed me to check the bookstores.

Pablo was not only a great talent, he was fortunate enough to have a father who encouraged his son to become an artist, which is as rare now as it was then. Such approval and protection helped the seed of art grow untrammeled by society into what would become Picasso.

EDEN

THE SHELVES HAVE SPOKEN

Most how-to books for artists addressed art-making techniques, art marketing and business practices, psychological and creative block issues, and the fear artists have in creating art. There were also a number of excellent self-help titles on coping with life as an artist—but none tackled rejection as a primary issue—which would become, to my own amazement while writing this book, a surprising and intriguing avenue to enlightenment.

A compelling force tugged at me to tackle this often misunderstood subject of rejection. I went to work and wrote an article about mastering rejection, but I couldn't place it with the magazine I had in mind.

Eventually, I realized that my article on spec was the foundation for a larger work. With the passing of time, I came to appreciate the significance of my encounter with the gruff Soho art dealer. Buried deep within the words he had spoken, which I had initially deemed worthless, lay the seed from which this book would grow and flower.

HORTICULTURE

You are now holding more than the subject at hand. The existence of this book is a physical artifact, proof of metaphysical laws working independently and transparently behind the scenes. This revelation is tantamount to an intrepid ufologist uncovering indisputable proof of an alien encounter.

If you become attached to a specific outcome, you limit the possibilities for success. The seed for this book—as we have seen—grew out of a seemingly unhelpful remark by an art dealer, but not before germinating and disguising itself as a homeless magazine article.

Another factor in the equation is that *no* doesn't mean never. It simply means not now.

Relative patience is a virtue.

Talent is organic and needs the right soil, time, and climate to grow. A budding plant can easily get trampled. The seeds of success are firmly planted in every defeat; you need only be aware of them.

LEATHER SHOES

How can this book help me? Sri Ramana Maharshi, the Hindu sage, sets the stage: "Wanting to reform the world without discovering your true self is like trying to cover the whole world with leather to avoid the pain of walking on stones and thorns. It is simpler to wear shoes."

Instead of considering the impractical task of addressing every possible contingency in your art related interactions with others, it is much smarter and exponentially more effective to be aware, not of any particular thing, but of awareness itself—the direct source of original art. From this intuitive Zen perspective, you will over time develop the supreme advantage of vision with the strength of character to triumph over rejection, and, for that matter, any situation.

This book is about finding your walking shoes.

You can't ask someone else how to be original.
EDEN

Art is freedom borne of self-discipline, which also defines a great painting.

CHAPTER ONE

CONVENTIONS
Liberating the Word

IF YOU INTEND to pioneer new ground, you can't remain confined by convention, which includes stirring up the living invention we call language. The word 'art' is so heavily charged with opinion and confusion that what is accepted as art by a consensual society is ultimately reduced to consensus—the tyranny of the masses.

ART, IN A WORD

Art is a vision of God created in the material world. Do you feel the truth of it? No matter how I describe art, it is, for you, still secondhand information. Whether you are a graffiti artist, Mr. hip-hop, or you play the cello for a philharmonic, you engage your audience by a set of rules: Are you giving people what they need, want, or are you giving them your art unfettered by motive? This is a distinction, not a competition. Each one of us fulfills a purpose. Remember, it is finding your dharma, not another's, that is your purpose in life.

To appreciate art, you (artist and patron) must experience what you need to know. You must make it your responsibility to find out where art comes from; this is your leverage for knowing from firsthand experience instead of speculation. All questions about the nature of art can be found at its wellspring; as there is no map for that destination you will have to use your moral compass to get there, which is what this book is all about.

MAKE NO MISTAKE

This book is for the true artist. Anything less than true won't do. Half-hearted is exactly what it sounds like. To triumph over rejection you must feel—not think about—that divine fire in the belly, a flame that can only be extinguished by you; no one else has dominion over your work. Did you think otherwise? Remember, failure isn't when someone rejects your art; failure is when you give up on your own self.

When I write the 'true' artist, I am specifically designating the authentic artist whose work—in whatever form—is the direct result of finding her

---

When I asked Deepak Chopra what he would say to each artist about persevering over rejection, he told me this:

Every artist in the world should memorize and store this answer indelibly in their consciousness.

Rumi, the 13th century Sufi mystic and artist said: 'I want to sing like birds sing, not worrying who listens or what they think.'

DEEPAK CHOPRA

*Beauty is truth, truth beauty,—that is all
Ye know on earth, and all ye need to know.*

JOHN KEATS

Art for art's sake should not be misunderstood. It is first art for the artist's sake to fulfill a dharma in transit; and then it is art on its own for the sole purpose of being.

EDEN

dharma, or one's purpose in life, which is the grand prize of temporal existence. The true artist is self-referential. She needs no outside authority or show of hands to validate her art—which is absolute. Along the way, she has learned a valuable lesson: when you respect your intuition, the form of your art will follow.

For the true artist, art isn't a decision based upon an educated guess, an academic hypothesis, a subject to scratch off a to-do list, an aptitude test, or a career counseling session. Art is a mission, which can't be countermanded by any external force. Loyal to her vision, the true artist has no illusions about the nature and value of her work. Remember, 'you are on sacred ground when you know where you stand.'

The true artist knows precisely where she stands as a creator. She is in harmony with her soul because she has found her passion, her dharma. And to discover her dharma she was willing to commit to the adventure and pay the price, whatever that might be.

Are you?

There is no other way. Each artist must pass through the eye of the needle alone and on her own merit.

All art isn't from the soul. This isn't a point of separation or a comparison; it is a distinction that each artist must make for her own self. If you don't know where you stand, then you can be assured others will make that choice for you. The artist who creates art for art's sake paints an indelible line in the sand. She remains steadfast and unadulterated by the temperamental winds of taste, social conditioning, or cultural pressures to conform. While this artist may be politically active, or not, she is never complacent. Her art can't be co-opted or unsettled by the nonsense or agenda concocted by others. She uses her work for whatever reasons she desires; as long as it is her decision, her work remains pure—and that is the mission, which includes earning a living and staying healthy.

She is the vanguard.

TRUTH AND LOVE

When I write 'truth', I am referring to absolute truth, which is fundamental and can't be diminished over time by opinion, or overturned by any future revelation. This truth is never imposed; it is revealed. Some might shy away from using the word truth in their art, but you have got to take responsibility for your work sooner or later.

The truth isn't out there; it is within you.

These truths that concern us here are irreducible components of metaphysical forces; and these forces influence the course of our experiences as we live them across the invisible matrix known as the space-time continuum. These truths are self-evident through the eyes of firsthand experience. Truth isn't knowledge, which contains facts that change—in time—as more details are uncovered. Universal laws are immutable and eternal; this is also known as absolute truth.

You ultimately become that which you love, and the way to true love is through the passion that is your dharma. Universal laws have always been and will always be. They are natural endowments waiting to be discovered by each one of us—one artist at a time.

To know even one truth is to touch timeless beauty, the countenance of the Creator.

As the poet Rabindranath Tagore of India wrote: "When you feel beauty, you will know it as truth."

PRONOUNS

Let's liberate the self, reflexive personal pronoun and otherwise. I often write 'your self' and 'my self', which are 'correctly' written as compound words (yourself and myself), two-word concatenations in English. Where appropriate, I respectfully do away with this convention to more precisely and emphatically convey my meaning when writing about the self of the soul, which is the pure self as expressed by me. Your self is a soul entity, and we don't want to overlook one's self by failing to notice it because of misguided allegiance to a standardized grammatical rule.

After all, you would write let's discuss your body, not 'yourbody'; 'I will go by myself' is harmless enough and the meaning that you are going solo is clear in this context. But my *self* is my soul, never alone, and forever connected to the Creator.

To avoid the awkward repetition of *he/she* clutter and other such self-conscious pronouns, I use he and she interchangeably.

For emphasis, you will encounter the occasional 'no thing' and 'every thing' as well as 'some thing'. Keep in mind too that Buckminster Fuller advocated that God is a verb, not a noun. You decide.

God

Here is god's purpose—
for god, to me, it seems,
is a verb
not a noun,
proper or improper.

R. BUCKMINSTER FULLER

CHAPTER TWO

I ACQUIT MY SELF
Serve Somebody

ALL THE EXCUSES of every person on the planet wouldn't create a single work of art—or accomplish anything for that matter. Of course, the short answer is: *do it!* To arrive at this state of action and self-awareness on purpose, you must know how you got there in the first place; otherwise, all your efforts will forever be hit or miss.

The expressed purpose of this book is to:

- identify and elevate your sense of self;
- define the merit of your art;
- and fortify your character with an organic confidence based on awareness for all the seasons of your life.

Here is my lingua franca of sorts, my diplomatic way of further establishing a rapport, a connection with you that demands a fundamental baseline. The efficacy of this book relies upon a covenant between you and me, and that contract is based on trust. There is no fence sitting when it comes to trust: either it is there or it isn't. Trust is earned and demonstrated through action over time.

BOOK CREDENTIALS

An Artist Empowered is entirely the result of original research. Nothing was taken for granted; nothing was farmed out; nothing was accepted at face value; nothing was regurgitated, and, as a direct consequence, secondhand information is mercifully absent from these pages. You can't ask someone else how to be original. Each insight of self discovery is the result of having proven that lesson to my own self over an odyssey spanning thirty years.

I have to my own satisfaction engaged the often volatile forces of art, character, and dharma; I have done this to the highest standard that I could confront, which was and is significant.

> *Rejection, as it turns out, isn't the bane most artists believe it is; rejection is a mirror that reveals truth about your dedication; you are compelled to confront your own self and that is a moment of awareness.*
>
> EDEN

If a DNA-RNA genetic code programs the design of roses, elephants and bees, we will have to ask ourselves what intellect designed the DNA-RNA code as well as the atoms and molecules which implement the coded programs.

R. BUCKMINSTER FULLER

The only peace, the only security, is in fulfillment.

HENRY MILLER

This book will work with you on many levels and some may not be immediately apparent. But they will be when you are ready. This book is also a pathfinder that will guide you through surprising and provocative new territories, which are all somehow quite familiar.

A LION'S SHARE

The Savannah is hot, and the lion pride is hungry. A herd of gazelle is nearby. A lion has no identity problem and knows what to do. The hunt begins. After the kill, the big cats feed until they are stuffed.

The lions find the shade of a tree and roll onto their backs to sleep off the meal. But they cannot rest. Another bloodthirsty creature is tormenting them. Flies abound like locust. The lions are being pestered to death, pounded by swarms of bloodsucking flies that attack the lions' open wounds, causing considerable pain. These are Stable flies, also called biting houseflies. Although they resemble houseflies, they have a needle-like piercing mouth appendage folded below their head. Both sexes feed on the blood of warm-blooded animals, including humans, pets and livestock.

The flies are relentless and the big cats are traumatized. They try to hide, climb trees, and crouch in the long grass—with little relief. The bone-crunching lion can't kill or devour the insatiable hordes of insects. Who is the king of beasts? The jungle is unsentimental and takes no prisoners. Artists, do you hear me?

ATTITUDE IS ALTITUDE

To affirm our thematic standard and gestalt, conventions throughout these pages underwrite and extol the unwavering intention of the soul, firsthand knowledge, and the power of pure awareness, also known as the Creator.

To maintain our focus on the objective of persevering, I have assembled The Eighteen Be-Attitudes, a list of qualities that effectively constitute the psychological and spiritual makeup of an artist who—through an intimate relationship with his soul—has transcended the angst of rejection; and by implication this artist is living an authentic life in the present moment of fulfillment instead of future uncertainty, doubt, and hope. Our artist is steadfast knowing not all will be enamored of his work. He accepts this fact, which is a gift of awareness, a point of illumination, not a problem.

To provide further insight, I also include a selection of personal experiences, anecdotes, tales, perceptions, and tools for right action, which ultimately formed my philosophy. To tell you categorically that the answer to all your searching is connected to the number *eighteen* without providing a bit of history of how I arrived at that metaphorical number would be too minimalist if not cavalier and reductive. If you come to a conclusion, then you need to know *how* and *why* for it to have any lasting value. Otherwise, you are parroting the words of others.

WHY THE APPLE FALLS

I'm not asking you to believe in anything that you can't prove to your own self. I'm not explaining the reason for the universe or everything in the world. I am explaining a process of how an aspect of the universal machinery functions, nothing more. The ultimate purpose for the machine resides with its Creator. It then follows that the purpose of your art resides with you. Despite our science, we can only theorize about the most basic of natural forces. While we may be able to explain the physical effects of gravity in great detail and its influence upon celestial bodies millions of light years from Earth, we still don't know why this fundamental force, in its particular state, exists in the first place. The difference between how and why is the secret everyone in his heart is after. If I were to categorize art in scientific terms, it would be this: pure research.

While art may require an introduction, it doesn't need a translator. You don't need someone to explain the emotional impact of that which is prime, or universal.

Today, on the radio, I heard an American singer interpret a Russian folk tune written by the revered Soviet-era poet and songwriter Bulat Okudzhava. The music was bittersweet, a lament. Although I don't understand Russian, I felt the emotional highs and lows emanate from the wistful words as evoked by the singer and the melancholy as expressed by the accompanying plaintive guitar.

After the ballad was over, the singer explained that the words chronicled a traveler (Okudzhava) who rode the midnight trolley bus in post-Stalinist Moscow. To overcome his feelings of despondency, this traveler rides the bus meeting everyday people, those with misfortune and still others with good fortune. The words say that riding the midnight trolley takes the traveler's pain away. While this impromptu libretto by the singer supplied more details, I didn't need this information for the ballad to draw me in. Although learning the meaning of the lyrics and the song's history provided an additional layer of significance, such particulars are best filled in after your soul has been smitten.

ALL OR NOTHING AT ALL

Art is what it is. Can we say engagingly and democratically with hats off to political correctness that everything is art? Scratching deeper we see that if everything manmade were art, then nothing is art. Of course, anything, when done with love and attention to detail, can be elevated to an art form. But it is art, naked and alone that concerns us here. Each person brings his own experience, depth of feeling, willingness to risk, and level of appreciation to each art event, performance or painting.

When you hear or read someone translating what the art in question means for him, then it is what it sounds like. You are experiencing the rendition through the filtration system of another, which, even if sincere, is secondhand, and may not reflect your interpretation. Unless I have a specific motive, I don't look at reviews, preemptive or otherwise, of films, plays, exhibits, or other art offerings; I do enjoy hearing or reading a critique after I have witnessed the event. Otherwise, my perception might be adulterated by another. I don't want to be told what I am supposed to experience, which is antithetical to the advertising age we live in. I want to feel the art for my own self. Don't you?

Remember, advertising aims to please by communicating a specific and instantly recognizable message. Art is interpretative and all its dimensions, like a woman of mystery, aren't immediately revealed. Is a painting of

Be who you are and say what you feel, because those who mind don't matter and those who matter don't mind.

DR. SEUSS

Purpose of being:

It can all too easily be taken for granted that we have memory, the astounding ability to record our time in this incarnation; as there is a purpose for all creation, memories of a life, too, eventually transcend and merge into the sea of consciousness according to the purpose of the Maker.

EDEN

squares and rectangles intersected by a few black lines abstract high art, or is it simply an image of geometric forms? Would it make a difference if this painting were by your Uncle Bob, or Piet Mondrian? Don't give away your power; no one knows how you feel better than you.

A NEW MENU

I write about firsthand experience; secondhand knowledge is what it sounds like. I wouldn't ask of you what I haven't done. This approach fosters an effective and enduring medium of communion—also known as trust. Artists who have maintained unsatisfying beliefs, spurious understandings, and questionable commitments, the time and means for confronting your old decisions has arrived as challenges in this book.

The intrinsic nature of honestly facing your past assessments and heady rationalizations will begin to free your mind and your self of those things that don't serve you. I have, I do, I will always.

Rejection of your art can hurt because love is involved.

You love your art and when it is spurned, you feel passion rebuffed. When you learn how to view such rejection in the framework of non-attachment, when you are no longer a slave to a particular outcome, you have begun to liberate your own self on the journey toward becoming the self-sufficient artist you always knew you were.

HOW-TO BABYLON

Years ago, after I had written a how-to piece on building one of my award-winning kite designs for a major magazine, the editor told me that the publisher wanted to meet me, which was unusual. I sat in the publisher's office as he admired my flying sculpture. Tall with gray hair and a ruddy complexion, he looked like a publisher.

In an affable manner, he offered: "Do you want to know the secret of this business?"

I nodded eagerly in the affirmative.

"It's like this," he said. "After more than thirty years at the helm of publishing this flagship magazine, I've found that most of our readers never build a thing. It's hard to believe that they'd pay for something they will never do. They simply enjoy going over the plans and reading the directions. Getting a vicarious experience is all they want, and, of course, we give it to them. And, as you have no doubt found out working with our editors, we are sticklers for getting our plans absolutely correct."

It was one of those seminal moments that stick with you for a lifetime. This isn't a how-to-feel-good book. I don't want you to confuse reading this book with doing this book. I don't want you to use this book as a vicarious experience, and, as an artist, you would demand nothing less. I don't want you to feel good until you know why you should: this is a cardinal point to grasp. You must know why about this or that; if not, you are floundering.

One situation I come across now and then is this:

Someone will say, "What do you know … you don't have any problems. You have it easy."

Of course, if that person would take a moment, he would recognize the absurdity of his glib observation. It is important to understand the psychology

---

Do not dwell in the past, do not dwell in the future, concentrate the mind on the present moment.

BUDDHA

at work here. This person assumed that I don't have problems, annoyances, or issues to face because I don't make them a topic of conversation. But I am no different from him or you. I don't relish hostile showdowns either. I would rather paint and write. This brings up another all too prevalent martyr complex among artists that we will address here: no, you aren't the only person facing issues in your life as an artist, or otherwise.

When the dragon nears, what choice do I have? What choice do you have? What is the alternative?

JUMPERS WELCOME

I strive for a pure link—intuition—to my consciousness in all matters: this attitude and action produce a currency that is immune to depreciation or theft. Transcendental wealth is the one everlasting treasure that one can acquire in material reality, and, if you agree with the law of karma, not only can you—you do take it with you. I serve my relationships best the more in tune I become with creation.

To make great art, one must take great risks. But so what? You may have heard that when you make a leap of faith the net will appear—somehow, magically. Who knows precisely how or why? I don't subscribe to the sequence of that scenario. The net is already there, in place, a cosmic fabric awaiting a jumper into the space-time continuum. What seems to appear out of thin air is you, the brave self that defies social conditioning, not the net, which is grace rewarding you for landing on your feet—and then standing your ground at any cost to discover and fulfill your dharma.

Remember, your mission is to discover your dharma, your purpose, not mimic someone else's destiny. The past is ripe with a legacy of vacillating opinions: critics, museums, and other art evaluators are forever reassessing the contribution of some overlooked artist or the hyperbolic value of another. Perception, not the art, has changed. As you can't second-guess the future, you engage your art process in the present moment, leaving posterity to deal with posthumous reputation and art history. The aesthetic experience belongs to the individual, not a committee.

As an artist it is part of my inherent mission to press beyond known limits; and I am, of course, referring to my own self-imposed boundaries that restrict my access to consciousness. Despite any such limitations, I, as a living being, acknowledge that biology and survival are prerequisite requirements for realizing the evolutionary process of art making—which is the spirit reaching out to the Maker. Artists are akin to the salmon: intrepid creatures genetically programmed to fight their way upstream toward their spawning ground, which is the still nascent, cool waters found at the deep end of the gene pool.

To believe in someone because you have an intuitive faith in that individual is one thing. To believe or accept that something is true without proof is as tenuous in the metaphysical realm as it is in the empirical world of science. In the context of clarity, which concerns us here, it is unimportant what I believe or what you believe—that only matters in the land of make-believe and politics; and anything, including art, can be politicized.

Does unconditional truth—art—rest with the most persuasive rhetorician, media manipulator, or those who have returned from the trenches intact?

When your standard is challenged, don't be glib. Test the newcomer thoroughly without restraint.

EDEN

Once more with feelings.

Do you think you're hungry, or do you feel the hunger?

Do you think you feel good, or do you feel the good?

Do you think you're in love, or do you feel the love?

Feelings are more difficult to master than thinking, which is contrary to the popular misunderstanding.

EDEN

There is a difference. Let's not lean on that rickety fence of hope for truth and salvation; let's know and feel truth, and in its beauty, each artist, despite transitory rejections, will find purpose and redemption. You can only know truth firsthand and that is if you have the fortitude. No middleman can do the job for you.

I WANT PROOF

The most profound lessons often come from the most unlikely people and situations. I have learned that true faith is based on proof; not the other way around, which is the common impression. I strive for an open mind and heart—admittedly, most often difficult to do, but who said it would be effortless? I am interested in what you know, not what you believe. I'm not referring to what you have heard, memorized, or read in a book, but in what *you* have discovered about truth and how you have integrated this transcendental cognition into material evidence. When confronted by courage and purity of the soul, rejection quickly trumpets the call for retreat.

I want proof. Don't you? This book focuses on truths of eternal value. These insights are primal and emanate from the intuitive, or metaphysical realm beyond thoughts, prosaic deduction, induction, and reason. Since it can't be measured, weighed, or empirically established, how do you prove a metaphysical truth? Belief isn't the answer, and since true faith is based only on proof, do we have a conundrum? The answer is that no one can prove it to you. That isn't the way it works.

Since every aspect of the metaphysical is both unique and an enigma, it can't be studied under clinical conditions attempting to find conformity. You must do the work and prove the existence of the metaphysical to your temporal self, which is the prerequisite act for building the strength of character you desire for overcoming obstacles, including the rejections in your life as an artist.

Intuition is the carrier wave of my art. Can I prove that to anyone? The proof is in front of me and well in sight of you, and is no more complex than pure feeling, which is a capacity available to anyone willing to shed the straightjacket of ego for unfettered communion with creation. The proof *is* the art, the material evidence of the transcendent, which is the power of the metaphysical realm put to good use in the here and now, not the hereafter. It is up to each one of us as individuals to recognize this truth, and we do so by feeling it, which is a sensation also called beauty. If you can't feel the truth now, maybe someday you will. Once you touch the power of your own awareness, truth will eventually reveal its existence to you.

Yes, I want proof. This is the stance every artist, or anyone for that matter, must take to make smart use of his allotted and privileged time in this world.

COGS WANTED

The true artist leads the way because he is the risk taker who casts the light onto the darkness. There is a price to pay for leadership. When the battle is about to begin, any weakness in their field general is the last thing the enlisted men need to see. To command, you rise above your thoughts and feelings of self-doubt and fear. With your strength to persevere you inspire others to have the courage to engage and rout the enemy—the negative invader—in whatever form they may assume, including the rejection of your work.

Your spirit in the face of adversity doesn't imply immunity to misgivings, anxiety, or even dread. Courage means that you are, in daily practice, stronger than most—that is why you are the commander of your art. Without sacrifice, there can be no mission of value. Without earning it, the prize is meaningless. Dharma demands that you, the artist, won't quit—no matter what. It is up to you and me.

Excuses are what they sound like.

It is a difficult and demanding thing to find out who you are—your unique voice—in a vast sea of social conditioning where the dominant culture, to stay afloat and in charge, demands more cogs than unique parts, which have no apparent use in powering or steering the machinery, the ship of state. Our distinctness as artists is our contribution to the collective magic that is life on Earth. If you aren't aware of your own self and the responsibility you have for making life work, you risk getting soul wrecked—and, in the end, washing up on the shore of despair alongside the flotsam and jetsam of the disingenuous—those artists who were called but chose not to risk, not to go.

When someone once told me that I am a taskmaster, I replied: "What then would you like me to be?" What you perceive as tough is appropriate action. No thing of value comes easy. You must be resolute to persevere. You must be prepared to meet your public without, as my mother likes to say, folding up like a cheap accordion when things don't go your way.

As Jonathan Swift observed: "When a true genius appears in the world, you may know him by this sign, that the dunces are all in confederacy against him."

I am on your side.

As the master has said: art is unique.

But that doesn't preclude aberrations and posers from finding an audience.

Unique isn't a synonym for different; in the same way, being one of a kind doesn't imply awareness, only curiosity.

Unique for our purposes means original, which is the inevitable and extraordinary outcome of soul awareness.

EDEN

CHAPTER THREE

OPENING THOUGHTS
On Sacred Ground

CONGRATULATIONS FOR HAVING the courage to be an artist. If you have been doing your work, then you know what I mean.

As we come to realize: 'you are on sacred ground when you know where you stand.'

Although I make references to mostly artists and painters, the information provided here is equally relevant for all creators: poets, writers, musicians, dancers, filmmakers, actors, explorers, and innovators in any field. If we look beyond labels, it becomes clear that this book is for anyone with a passion for leading an authentic life. You must decide where you stand.

One of my preeminent and recurring realizations is this: that annoying self-defeating voice inside my head, the inner critic, is no stranger. I am talking to myself as you are talking to yourself. Until you witness and diffuse this demonic-prone aspect of the psyche—ego—you are prey to the fear and doubt that it feeds upon. Aware of this codependent relationship, you confront and then extrapolate to understand a fundamental dynamic: if I were to allow rejection (or even something truly serious) to defeat me, then I have lost faith in my mission. When the mission is clear, there is no ambiguity. Failure is when I abandon my gift. In turn, rejection exacts a degree of impact proportionate to the artist's lack of purpose. Rejection is a word, a reaction to action, not an eternal truth, or a life sentence.

FOR THE BIRDS

Another crucial point here from the get-go is that no one knows more about your art than you do. I find it both amazing and alarming to read books or articles by certain noted art teachers, critics, academicians, and other art aficionados who focus on the irrelevant instead of their subject's essence. Like kids with their noses pressed up against the window of the candy store, these mavens of art can see the candy beyond the pane, but the secret ingredients, how it is made, or how it tastes remain out of reach. Musicology isn't music. Art criticism isn't painting. Art history isn't art. Don't give your power away to anyone.

There is no room for God in him who is full of himself.

HASIDIC PROVERB

The ego for the sake of a label that concerns us throughout this book is not the mediator of the psyche as posited by Freud; this is the ego that has run amok.

EDEN

Politicians seek approval, not the true artist.

DEEPAK CHOPRA

The Art Form Question:

One can say this is a form of art, but what does it mean?

Anything accomplished with attention to detail, great care, passion, and love can be elevated from the ordinary to artfulness—from folding napkins, arranging flowers, cooking, serving tea, handwriting, or making tools—anything. The Japanese are especially adept in this area as everything in their traditional culture is artfully done.

The art that concerns us here requires no embellishments or training wheels.

EDEN

In his 1973 documentary *Painters Painting*, filmmaker Emile de Antonio interviewed many of the figures, including Barnett Newman, who, after the Second World War, had fueled the abstract expressionism movement in New York City. Barnett: "Yes, because many years ago at a conference in Woodstock that was held with a panel consisting of philosophers—esthetes, really, professors of philosophy, professors of esthetics—and artists, I declared that even if they were right, and even if they could build a system, an esthetic system that they could claim explained the activity, the creative activity, it would be of no value, because esthetics for the artist was as meaningful as ornithology must be for the birds."

NATURE'S WAY

After accepting responsibility for your thoughts and behavior, you can then advance by adopting and living with The Eighteen Be-Attitudes featured in this book. These Be-Attitudes, or attributes of character, will work faithfully and beautifully for you, but only after you have constructed a foundation of clarity based on tackling the core questions submitted to you. If you don't do the hard work now, when will you? Rejection is nature's way of weeding out the dilettantes. If this sounds stern, it is. But, it isn't my doing; I am passing along a universal law as I discovered it; and, after a time, you will also prove it to yourself.

The information in this book is concentrated. You don't have to memorize any sort of 'recipes for success' because this isn't a book about serving dogma as 'truth de jour'. The body and mind work in similar ways; the body needs a regular diet of wholesome food to maintain optimum health, and the mind needs a continuous flow of challenges to remain alert and pliable. Absorb the material in this book as you would any nutritious meal; your body (and your mind) functions best with small portions, which is more sensible than attempting to gulp down the whole thing in one gluttonous sitting. Yes, table etiquette does count. Don't be in a hurry; and don't get weighed down by dull thoughts and nonsense.

Stay light, agile, and receptive.

As previously noted, this isn't a feel-good book that you read today and forget shortly thereafter without getting what you have come here for. You need potent foods, the right proteins and carbohydrates, not empty calories to fuel your odyssey. To test your commitment to your art, these pages demand much—and you, as an artist, would demand no less. Remember, if you want to learn how to swim, you must get wet.

METAPHYSICAL LIPOSUCTION

Success is a subjective value judgment that for many, or more likely most, remains inexorably intertwined with sales, critical acclaim, an art fellowship or grant, a magazine cover, a museum exhibit or acquisition, a lead role in a major film, or performing at Carnegie Hall. A seemingly accurate picture of 'making it', but not the panacea as the struggling artist might envision. The popular notion is that it is *easy* to deal with rejection when your work is selling, and you can afford that ocean view from your Malibu beach house. Not so. Fear and anxiety exist irrespective of monetary wealth, and they can follow you no matter where you live. Celebrated artists aren't immune to self-doubt, negative reviews, positive reviews (Can there ever be enough to satisfy?), creative blocks, or feeling spiritually vacuumed, trapped in a style now demanded of them by their dealers and the tyranny of the art buying public. Remember the words of the 'profits': crowd pleasing comes at a price. Once you have an audience, are you going to be able to hold their interest? You see where this leads.

If you have been looking for metaphysical liposuction to remove the angst you have been harboring for years, I need to alert you now that a quick fix is what it sounds like. You will have to work and sweat your insecurities out naturally and permanently. *An Artist Empowered* has a goal, and that goal is for you to transform and evolve from the inside out; this is organic and will last for your lifetime without further corporeal or spiritual complications.

Now would be a good time to begin the education of your own self.

Developing a confident attitude toward rejection as early on as possible in your art life instills a winner's edge for sustaining yourself during the daunting process of materializing from obscurity into the glare of visibility. If you are going to ask for acceptance, prepare yourself for opinions and consequences—whatever they might be. Remember, to endure success you must first ride out rejection, which is a lifelong but controllable companion in the adjoining seat next to acceptance.

The challenges confronting the artist are formidable. To create and survive, he must take care of body and soul, most often under adversity; he must do this no matter what. He must live by his work, his wits, and a faith based not on belief, but on the material proof borne of his art.

NO BEDTIME STORIES

I often read, but don't accept the premise, that in today's world there is no universal agreement on what is art. To further finesse this point of view, the late Janet Flanner, Paris correspondent for *The New Yorker*, wrote: "There are no permanent criteria for declaring what art is and what it is not." Even artists, it seems, are suspect for discerning what is art. By implication then, can confusion in defining the artist be far behind? You will note that it is never a universal creator who declares this notion of the ambiguous artist.

Of course, the art in question here isn't the premeditated utilitarian art of business, decoration, design, or flattery. It is the art that takes us deeper into the meaning and purpose of our own lives: into consciousness. It is the art that can't be demystified or pinned down precisely because it is magic. It is the art that you must discern on your own. It is the art that transcends definitions and comparisons. This art isn't a qualifier (art therapy) nor is it the object of a modifier (commercial art). This art is what the French refer to as having that 'je ne sais quois'—an indefinable something, which for our purposes is art from the soul: art conjured into existence by the sorceress seeking truth and who isn't ambivalent or confused about what art is and what it is not.

Whatever the perception of art and artist was in the past, it is time for an unambiguous understanding now—in this present moment. When you know who you are, when you know your dharma, no one can confound you with bedtime stories.

I don't fear failure.
I only fear the slowing up of the engine inside of me which is pounding, saying, 'Keep going, someone must be on top, why not you?'

GENERAL GEORGE S. PATTON

Remember, the greatest will be replaced while the great remain timeless.

EDEN

Everyone has inside of him a piece of good news. The good news is that you don't know how great you can be! How much you can love! What you can accomplish! And what your potential is!

ANNE FRANK

To have faith is to trust yourself to the water. When you swim you don't grab hold of the water, because if you do you will sink and drown. Instead you relax, and float.

ALAN WATTS

You must establish a standard for art that can be concisely explained. If you don't, other parties will be pleased to pigeonhole you and your art.

If you have been showing your art, then you know what I mean.

Despite what is written and promulgated as fact about art and artists, the true artist throughout history has never needed any outside authority to define him or his work. Even those painters and sculptors who were patronized by the Medici and the Papacy during the Renaissance knew in their heart and soul that they were more than tradesmen, or members of a guild who could follow a set of artificial rules. Look beneath the surface; the underlying truth is in the pentimento.

Do you feel, for example, that Botticelli, Michelangelo, or Leonardo da Vinci didn't realize their gift had a purpose and significance beyond pleasing patrons? Far from being victimized, these and other artists of that age were patronizing their patrons.

Ultimately, responsibility for the quality of life falls on the shoulders of those who are conscious and aware.

A SHAMAN'S LIFE

It is all art, but attempting to define art solely by the result is a pedestrian approach to what is at its core a spiritual path. The mystique lies in the act of creation; the final work is physical evidence. Either you are a shaman, or you are not.

In his book, *Search for the Real*, Hans Hofmann writes: "Art is magic. So say the surrealists. But how is it magic? In its metaphysical development? Or does some final transformation culminate in a magic reality? In truth, the latter is impossible without the former. If creation is not magic, the outcome cannot be magic. To worship the product and ignore its development leads to dilettantism and reaction. Art cannot result from sophisticated, frivolous, or superficial effects."

As apprentice to the sorcerer, or not quite yet, you must, at the very least, be honorable enough to persevere in good spirit. The true artist has always been aware of the misconceptions that abound about art. This is why the artist must stake his claim as he avoids getting trampled in the rush for judgment in the badlands of taste. The artist must show his own self and the world that he does indeed have a nugget worthy of appreciation. He must do all this and create, too. As an artist, you must traverse this untamed territory.

Art existed ages before there were museums, galleries, critics, patrons, and art historians. Unencumbered by intellectual labeling and marketing motives, the birth of art was of the spirit and evolution was its mentor. Although I use the term artist to mean anyone who creates art for art's sake, the qualities of character I describe in The Eighteen Be-Attitudes for triumphing over rejection are equally pertinent for those in the applied arts. You, not a committee, must decide for your own self who you are as an artist. Where do you stand and why? One true artist recognizes another; the law of natural selection instructs that it takes one to know one. You must know thy self before you can be thy self.

Do the work and proceed with an organic feeling of inner calm and indestructible confidence known as authenticity.

EGOIST OR EGOTIST

In *The Devil's Dictionary*, Ambrose Bierce defined an egotist as: "A person of low taste, more interested in himself than in me." An egotist thinks and talks about himself excessively. An egoist, while he may also be a party to undue self-admiration, also espouses that all morality is based on self-interest, which is the opposite of altruism.

In *Practical Exercises In English*, written over a century ago, Huber Gray Buehler made this semantic distinction, which is relevant today: "Egotism, in the sense of self-worship, is preferable to egoism, since egoism also designates a system of philosophy." As a creator, you are charged with innovative expression and knowing the distinction of your tools, which includes nuance and the meaning of words you choose. An artist-egotist who voluntarily worships himself and is arrogant with nothing to be arrogant about has already broken the first rule: don't believe your own bullshit. If, however, we encounter an artist-egoist who is aware by way of a conscious reflex that is universal, then his self-realization is already neatly intertwined with our own self-interest.

As we have come this far, we should also include yet another perspective: there are those who feel that a consciousness, or more precisely a state of awareness purified of conceit reflects mortal perfection and the most potent and benevolent of powers—enlightenment. This orientation isn't only necessary for a Buddha; it is also a signpost in the right direction for an artist who strives to keep his ego from deterring him from his dharma. Do not fake something you aren't—a trap that befalls many an artist. As you will, I trust, come to appreciate, this book focuses on the soul self, which is on a mission that transcends any ego-based desire for self-fulfillment that can never satisfy. Why? Fulfillment of the self, like the birth of art, cannot be bought, sold, bequeathed, or traded like a commodity. It must be earned through tests of character, which is what this book is all about.

To a casual observer, however, the uncompromising commitment of the transcendental self can be mistaken for an ego orchestrated trip. It will be up to you to discern this difference in others and perhaps more important, in your own self.

> "Every morning when I awake, the greatest of joy is mine: that of being Salvador Dali."
>
> —*Salvador Dali* (egoist or egotist?)

The artist on his mission is often perceived as an egotist or an egoist at best, and to some degree, both are true. There are two fundamental reasons for this perception. One is based on image, the other on necessity. Insecure artists try to live up to and play a stereotype; and, to be fair—an artist must be self-centered as creation is ignited directly from the self—that is, the transcendental self.

A creator is a breed apart. He doesn't try to fit into any preconceived image, nor does he select a false mask of personality to appease; and, when it comes to his art, he is an individual who is unfettered by the motive to please dealers and collectors, which is an accomplishment in itself. This doesn't, however, preclude doing work for hire, which is in no way

---

I find working with glass meditative, almost therapeutic. I can leave the world behind, and focus. . . . The simplicity of form, the drama of rich, intense color, the joy of challenge, and the challenge of endurance. . . . The piece, when it is over, is not what is made, but how it is made.

ANDREW KUNTZ

Mission, Morale, Money:

This is the sequence for an organic confidence based on dharma. Acknowledge the merit and energy of the first; tend diligently and ground yourself to the second; and remain non-attached to the particular outcome of the third—releasing a flow of currency to complete the circuit.

EDEN

You can achieve what others may say is unachievable, if you will just embrace your intuition.

RON RUBIN AND STUART AVERY GOLD, ZENTREPRENEURS

Intuition Express:

'Is it or is it not my intuition?' This is the fundamental question involving action or restraint; if ego drives either, then results are self-conscious and open to distress; if awareness is the arbiter and driving force, then the intuitive results are grounded in reality.

Intuition follows universal laws of enlightenment, which includes do no harm.

EDEN

dishonorable or in conflict with the artist's primary mission. Independence in his art creation doesn't diminish this creator's never ending focus and process to have his work seen and acquired. This creator, this universal artist is by definition unique, and there can be no comparisons among unique. His individuality isn't a premeditated gimmick, nor is it a goal; it is a by-product of his vision, his dharma, his purpose in life, which has nothing to do with spin or ego-based labels.

Art is spirit, and spirit awakens in the fullness of consciousness. In this context, is the artist, egocentrism notwithstanding, his brother's keeper? This is a prime question you must attend to by yourself. In my experience, what is rarely portrayed or known is that the true artist, one who is both mentally and spiritually rich, is emphatically concerned with the well being of the world; the soul would have it no other way. This artist is no fool. He knows he must care for himself and his art first, which may well be an act of egoism, of necessity, while simultaneously coordinating and extending his art self to his family, friends, and acquaintances.

There is a dark side here as well. Sadly, anxiety-ridden artists are the most flagrant offenders when it comes to sabotaging their fellow creators. Familiarity when mixed with insecurity still breeds contempt. Remember, Buddha's first realization on his journey toward enlightenment was that of *compassion*—a deep awareness that is available to anyone who holds no grievances. Compassion is a direct result of self-fulfillment. No other special training is required. If talent is a gift from God, then it is the artist's manifest duty to impart that blessing upon the world. Imbued with this knowledge and sense of mission, the artist can then better serve his relationship with himself, others, and with his creations.

KNOCK TO ENTER

Not to be recognized for your art can be discouraging. It is not unusual for a degree in art from a prestigious institution to have more perceived clout than a body of original work from a self-taught artist—and to keep the record straight: all creators are self-taught. Art school teaches technique; you must find art on your own.

Do not be dismayed.

I've seen great art ignored, and mediocre art embraced. Haven't you? Art history is rampant with inequity. To chase after the why, fairness, or justice of it all is a red herring that diverts me from my mission—which is your mission—to create and sustain my own self by my own hand as an artist. Remember, the Great Creator is the door opener. You must still knock to enter.

As the word 'artist' itself can take on various meaning, expression, and purpose, debating and comparing the merits between disciplines is a trap. It is much simpler and accurate to agree that excellence in anything, including any art form—the applied arts and fine art—is rare. It is up to you to know where you stand. If you have to ask someone else about your status, you are lost. But this is not a calamity. You can always find the way back to your own self through dedication—a compass direction that will always guide you home. Remember, no matter how far your odyssey takes you, you will discover that the truth isn't out there; it is within you.

NO'S TO SUCCESS

While no artist wants to hear 'no' about her art, you will come to appreciate that you, like Pinocchio, the marionette who wanted to be cut free from his strings of conformity, must follow your no's to success, which is the unpredictable path, the sequence of circumstances, events, and decisions that allow you to continue creating your art, the work that is your purpose in life. The true artist is pragmatic and knows chasing rainbows is for wishers and hopers, not doers and achievers.

When worldly recognition, fame to whatever extent, is seen as a by-product of a healthy attitude toward creating the artwork, the artist doesn't go insane. Talent fueled by unfaltering persistence is what gives the master a fine and unbreakable edge. The master knows the value of her art and the divinity of her beating heart in the present moment—not out of fraudulent arrogance, pride, or bluster, but in humility, which is the artist's ally.

This book is the organic fruit born of an integrated process that came about through many years of cultivation and dedicated cross-pollination. No thing in the cosmos is stronger or more integrated than some thing that grows from within its own unique nature, also known as organic. This means the seeds of intuitive perceptions sown in your consciousness now will eventually sprout and blossom into perennial insights.

As any experienced gardener will tell you, seeds need the right soil, a quiet place, nutrients, care, and time to grow. The most strikingly beautiful flowers often bloom late in the season.

In The Eighteen Be-Attitudes, I have composed a set of attributes that an archetypal artist would require to engage and vanquish any debilitating perceived power, including rejection. Moreover, this book will also help you define and establish your value as an artist now, which is a prerequisite for prevailing while you are still alive. Let posterity deal with art history. Artists in the 21st century need a new and potent understanding for defining success—which is the driving paradigm of this book.

The once accepted image of the damaged and destitute artist is more than passé; it is dead.

Let's bury this destructive stereotype, light a candle, and release it.

Whenever I use the word rejection, it means that your art wasn't accepted by whomever for whatever reason. Rejection and failure aren't synonyms; failure is when you give up on your own self.

AN ECLECTIC EYE

I often refer to terms and concepts from various fields of study, belief systems, and faiths—from Humanistic Psychology and Jungian Archetypes to Judaism, Christianity, Hinduism, Buddhism, and Zen. Although these disciplines frequently seem to have conflicting viewpoints, an eclectic eye will see brilliant insights in them all.

When I encounter a new and higher standard from whatever source, I immediately adopt it as my own, and in so doing, I elevate myself to become more than the previous sum of my parts.

I also frequently cite the terms dharma, self, soul, and, as mentioned earlier, the true artist. In the context of this book, *dharma* is your purpose in life; *self* is the transcendental essence that is you; not the finite ego self,

You see things and you say, 'Why?' But I see things that never were; and I say, 'Why not?'

GEORGE BERNARD SHAW,
BACK TO METHUSELAH

Technique in art is akin to learning how to read; while the effort is useful and admirable, it isn't synonymous with being a creator or a writer.

EDEN

but the unadulterated self that, by being in direct contact with creation, is the communicator of infinite power and great art; *soul* is the bearer of intuition, which is the Creator speaking directly to you; and the *true artist* defies dogma, custom, and social pressure by creating for no other purpose than to create—and should the work edify or entertain, then so be it. Art and everyday existence are inseparable to the true artist.

Although I can provide characteristics that constitute and define an artist who has transcended the hurt of rejection, the question remains: Who precisely is a true artist?

ROOMING WITH VINCENT

It is simple. Better to meet the authentic article than read a library's worth of definitions. Don't confuse the true artist with madmen, charlatans, or posers. It is true. A great artist may be mad, but what then is the point? The notion that the artist must be mad to create anything worthwhile is an unfortunate legacy from ancient Greece where Plato had a misinformed premise of associating genius and inspiration with melancholy. While you may love Vincent van Gogh's art, would you want to live with him?

To be fair, the image of Vincent in the popular culture as the mad artist may be mostly misleading. In an essay on van Gogh's masterpiece *Starry Night*, art history professor Albert Boime portrays a different picture of the Dutch painter who would come to represent the epitome, or the cliché, of the deranged artist. At times lucid, coherent, and productive, van Gogh also endured delusions, hallucinations, blackouts, and he had also cut off his own ear—which seems good reason for concluding that he was mentally ill.

However, it appears that far from being the isolated lunatic on the fringe, van Gogh was a practical and methodical artist with a healthy sense of his times, coupled with an interest in science, astronomy, poetry, and literature. As Becky Hendrick, in her fine book, *Getting It*, puts it: "He was a great painter *in spite of* his mental illness, not as a result of it." Van Gogh wasn't mad when he painted or wrote letters, especially to his brother, Theo, which were clear, pragmatic, and mindful of his mission as an artist.

One could argue, as Boime does, that Vincent was less mad and more a victim; he suffered seizures that were most likely brought on by a form of epilepsy; he didn't recall cutting off his earlobe, and this frightened him. On July 27, 1890, van Gogh left for a nearby field (earlier that month in the fields he had painted vast stretches of wheat, crows, and turbulent skies) where he shot himself—which might be explained away by a seizure, but not why he had a pistol with him.

DEDICATION, NOT MADNESS

Vincent, who was goodhearted and a dedicated artist for an intense decade, had suffered bitter disappointments, including his art; he knew his art had broken through another veil of illusion, but nearly no one else did. Van Gogh loved Japanese art. In mid-September of 1888, he executed a self-portrait that gave his face a distinct Asian cast; he later dedicated this portrait to his friend, Paul Gauguin. Van Gogh wrote about this painting: "But as I also exaggerate my personality, I have in the first place aimed at the character of a simple Bonze worshipping the eternal Buddha."

Whenever I injure life of any sort, I must be quite clear whether it is necessary.

Beyond the unavoidable, I must never go, not even with what seems insignificant. The farmer, who has mown down a thousand flowers in his meadow as fodder for his cows, must be careful on his way home not to strike off in wanton pastime the head of a single flower by the roadside, for he thereby commits a wrong against life without being under the pressure of necessity.

ALBERT SCHWEITZER

We know of van Gogh's struggles and insecurities from his letters; he felt overlooked as an artist and a burden to his brother Theo who supported him.

But there was another overriding dark force powerful enough for Vincent to take his own life; he had lost his purpose, and that spelled disaster for a creator who said that he painted what he saw.

EDEN

Given his feelings for wisdom from the East, it isn't far-reaching to speculate that he was also exposed to the intuitive serenity of Zen Buddhism and the teachings of Hinduism, including the Law of Non-Attachment. While it might not have solved all his problems (he had no control over epilepsy, or mental illness), transcendental knowing and not being attached or a slave to the precise outcome of his desires would have most certainly provided him with a healing perspective and a buffer—to whatever degree—from his maladies.

Van Gogh certainly wasn't attached to the old school of European art; neither was he held hostage by the arbitrary rules of Impressionism, the modern art of his era. Vincent's enormous influence on Post-Impressionism, Expressionism, and Abstract art was the result of risk, not appeasing the crowd, or even Theo—his brother and patron. As fellow artist Gauguin wrote in a letter of 1889 to Emile Bernard: "What would you rather have? A mediocrity which pleases everyone or a talent which breaks new ground? We must choose if we have free will.... Attacks on originality are to be expected from those who lack the power to create and shrug their shoulders."

The price an artist must pay for divine fire is dedication, not madness.

BEYOND THE GATE

We come back to you, your dharma, and your life. Why not be an artist who is emotionally and mentally sound? And how can you tell whether the artist in you is genuine or some lustrous imitation? You can't find out by reading about it. Invest the time necessary to establish the difference, which is a discernment earned only from firsthand experience. If you can't recognize great art in another, how will you determine the magnitude of your own work? Asking others to ratify your worth is a slippery slope into the eternal pit of torment called self-doubt. Stay away. Remember Vincent.

My intention is for you to succeed in transmuting rejection in all its forms into resiliency. This is a formidable and necessary challenge. Before you can tackle this task, however, you have to understand that rejection is a surface issue; it isn't the heart of the matter as one might think.

Rejection is merely a gatekeeper; you are seeking the house beyond the gate. To triumph over rejection, the artist must first forge his sense of self until his identity is sufficiently tempered—hard, flexible, and resilient. To harden your mettle, you must be intimately familiar with how to integrate the precise mechanisms that underlie the concept of identity. Otherwise, you are playing with matches instead of harnessing divine fire.

Without absorbing the introspective knowledge that is packaged within your essential self, all you would get from this book is a pep talk and a kick in the pants—which may make you feel better for a few fleeting moments. Feel good when it is clear to you how you have earned it.

Instead of focusing on the seemingly never-ending psychological and fiscal side issues that orbit rejection, it is much simpler to pop open your awareness, the eternal umbrella of all that is. In so doing, you will see with unflinching clarity that which is the healthy and winning tempered edge you wanted in the first place. Blessed with this inner perception of purpose combined with dedication, you enter the world with the supreme confidence required for persevering in all that you encounter.

A caveat on success:

Even stronger than this is what Carlyle says: 'You know the glowworms in Brazil that shine so that in the evening ladies stick them into their hair with pins; well, fame is a fine thing, but look you, to the artist it is what the hairpin is to the insects.'

VINCENT VAN GOGH,
FROM A LETTER TO THEO

Instead of saying that was disappointing, say that was revealing; hear and feel the difference.

EDEN

The Brothers van Gogh:

Theo van Gogh was certainly ambivalent of his older brother's original talent. While providing a monthly allowance and art materials for Vincent, who routinely sent him paintings that would one day attain iconic status, he was also dismissive of his brother's art.

An art dealer of some note, Theo promoted and encouraged Pissarro, Degas, Renoir, Gauguin, Sisley, Signac, Toulouse-Lautrec and Monet; but he refused to exhibit Vincent's work on the pretext that they were not yet good enough.

In his assessment, Theo may even have been sincere, but that didn't make him right.

Vincent, who knew all this, ultimately accepted his brother's stipend for unfettered time to paint, but at a price: his work, especially during those last productive years, would end up collecting dust in a corner of Theo's apartment in Paris.

EDEN

SCRATCH THAT ITCH

From my earliest recollections, I have been drawn to both the how and why of things—in both the physical and metaphysical. If I could watch, not merely glimpse, how the metaphysical gears of the universe operate, I said to myself years back, I would have a chance of making the machinery of the cosmos work for me instead of being a mere cog at its mercy—instead of being a victim. While I may never learn why the machine even exists, knowing its fundamental rules keeps me in the game as a player.

After all, you can read a self-help book that encourages you to be more alert, aware, sensitive, inventive, patient, passionate, to follow your heart and heed your intuition. But when you put the book down, how specifically do you put these affirmations and words of advice into action? You scratch your head. But this isn't the itch that concerns us here. This book is that most flexible of backscratchers that will let you reach that most inaccessible spot called your soul, the harbinger of clarity. Remember, your soul is itching to work with you, as you are its sole purpose for being here. Hear the thunder, see the lightening, feel the rain. Use your senses as if they mattered and don't be deceived by glitter. Once you establish contact and a rapport with your soul, it will reveal all that you need to know and all that you need to do. This is called awareness.

I have provided specific things for you to do that will prepare and expand your awareness for handling rejection and disappointment in the trenches, where it counts. But there is more—a wildcard. Somewhere in this book you will find a word, a phrase, or a point that will spontaneously ignite as truth within you—which is what you want in the first place. How will you know it? You will know without question.

LOST AND FOUND

A truth is as much a feeling, or emotional intelligence as it is a quantifiable experience. I was at an art opening when someone asked me: "You talk about truth a lot. How will I know the truth, how can I recognize it?"

Have you ever been lost? I don't mean lost in the next town, or that you missed the exit on the freeway. I mean lost in the wilderness. You don't know where you are, and it's beginning to get late. You have no food, and you can feel the hunger coming. You have no water, and you can feel the thirst coming. You walk, and every direction looks the same; you don't know where you came from, you don't know the way out, and now it is getting dark. The wilderness comes alive with strange and wild sounds. The beasts are all around you; they seem to be closing in. You are sweating in the cold of night. You walk on, looking over your shoulder. Your heart is pounding.

Suddenly, in the final moments before the sun wanes and disappears, you spot a small house with a warm orange-yellow glow coming from the inside. You move closer. You recognize this house; it is the house you passed when you first entered the wilderness. It is the landmark for the way out. You know where you are. All anxiety dissolves.

That is how I would describe what it feels like to come upon the truth. You must find your own metaphor.

CAMP DHARMA

While having the courage to be an artist is admirable, persevering against the collective drag of disappointment, doubt, and hardship demands more: you must fortify—not coddle—yourself with strength of character if you are to fulfill your dharma, or purpose in life.

Today, artists can try to remedy the disappointment of rejection by seeking outside encouragement, seeing a therapist, changing their style, attending a workshop, reading a feel good book, or name your potion. If no solution presents itself, then anxiety and fear reign, or worse—the artist abandons the dream.

But, do not dismay.

With a fundamental understanding of the self, you will, over time, learn to replace hearsay with truth. Over time through self-discipline, you will identify, deflect, and thwart negativity in all its disguises. Once unmasked and exposed to the light of insight, the bane of rejection disintegrates like the vampire caught off-guard by the rising sun. In time, you will learn to heed the divine instead of those who don't yet appreciate your talent. Maybe one day they will. You aren't counting on their endorsement to persevere.

You *will* prevail if that is your mission.

Know the score. Compose the notes. Play your music. Art history is not art; musicology is not music; and the quest for the self is not ego. The artist must not only be self-reliant, she must also remain vigilant of those who would co-opt her fire from heaven to roast marshmallows.

You have now entered a cliché-free zone.

The secret of getting ahead is getting started. The secret of getting started is breaking your complex overwhelming tasks into small manageable tasks, and then starting on the first one.

MARK TWAIN

Don't waste yourself in rejection, nor bark against the bad, but chant the beauty of the good.

RALPH WALDO EMERSON

CHAPTER FOUR

NO SECONDHAND NO'S
Affirm Your Purpose

ALTHOUGH THE ACCOUNT described below is about writing, the point is vividly relevant for all creators. While reading about the travails of other artists, and how they overcame difficulties in their life quests is certainly inspirational, it is still, at the very best, secondhand information, which is exactly what it sounds like.

> "In 1969, *Steps*, a novel, by Jerzy Kosinski, won the National Book Award. Six years later a freelance writer named Chuck Ross, to test the old theory that a novel by an unknown writer doesn't have a chance, typed the first twenty-one pages of *Steps* and sent them out to four publishers as the work of 'Erik Demos'. All four rejected the manuscript. Two years after that he typed out the whole book and sent it, again credited to Erik Demos, to more publishers, including the original publisher of the Kosinski book, Random House. Again, all rejected it with unhelpful comments—Random House used a form letter. Altogether, fourteen publishers (and thirteen literary agents) failed to recognize a book that had already been published and had won an important prize."
>
> —from *Pushcart's Complete Rotten Reviews & Rejections*

When I asked Julia Cameron how she dealt with rejection, she replied:

My personal formula is this: Rejection becomes opportunity when 'Why me?' becomes 'What next?'

JULIA CAMERON

For my book to have the grounded impact of credibility, I write from the trenches, not the Ivory Tower. Like the provenance for an artwork of great value, I vouch for the authenticity of my experience. Still, it is my experience and I don't ask that you take me at my word alone.

You won't learn anything of lasting value that way.

Challenge and put each precept you read in this book to the test; investigate and prove them to your own satisfaction.

Do this and you will accomplish the intention of this book, which is what you are after in the first place.

Ever tried. Ever failed. No matter. Try Again. Fail again. Fail better.

SAMUEL BECKETT

If you think the price of the dream is too high, calculate the cost of the alternative.

EDEN

LIVING NOT LEASING LIFE

The shape of each soul is unique. Each person has a destiny to fulfill. It is up to each person to find out what her dharma mission is and then do it—this is divine fulfillment. Until your soul finds its tenor and direct expression in belonging to your work, there is angst, regardless of how much money you are making.

Hardwired methods, models, procedures, policies, and systems—society's cookie cutter approach for stamping out 'civilized' clones—are detrimental to the evolution of the individual. The recipe for the remedy has the simple and insightful aroma of Zen. When the work is you and you belong to your own self, you are whole, in sync with your soul—life flows along a natural course, including the uncertainty of whitewaters and hidden obstacles, with an unparalleled satisfaction of purpose.

Artists don't live in a vacuum. They make choices in life. Society all too easily and without question succumbs to the cult of consumerism where idolizing celebrities, blind-sided competition, and functional jobs are accepted as consensus reality. Functional as in practical isn't at issue here; a life lived mindlessly by the design of others is what it sounds like.

It is only when the system of the workplace breaks down that workers, often highly educated functional drones, awaken to see that they have traded the timeless wealth of their soul time for indebtedness to transitory symbols—cars, boats, and houses—that are all eventually repossessed by time, surviving relatives, and the tax man. Don't be deceived by sincerity. Many are called; few choose to go. Those who willingly play the dharma denied card know they are complicit in the bargain. This is an observation toward awareness, not a comparison.

What is left? The functionary never really owned anything—a devastating realization that is also liberating for those who choose to do so.

Fine art as meaningful work is mostly deemed impractical in contemporary society. This is, of course, a self-fulfilling prophecy for anyone who accepts the irreversible numbness of soul death. Are you willing to persevere against the torrential conformity of the mainstream to reach heaven's gate? Perspiration is reality. Still, those who do 'make it' in the arts are held in high and nearly reverential esteem by the same society that places little value on the artist. Mixed messages abound. The irony here is that every functionary dreams of being free, of being an artist.

WHAT'S THE POINT?

There is a hunger among people that no outside source or authority can ever satisfy. On the soul level, each person is born into the world with a gift; no one can express this unique talent better than the individual who recognizes that this is his 'dharma', or calling in life. Of course, a gift needs opportunity, which does show up for those who remain resolute. The equation is absolute; we want to belong and to share our gift. This dual desire with its implicit need for acceptance is strewn with obstacles. If you want to live your dream, there is a price—you must be awake and remain vigilant to opportunity. You must also know the rules and what you are buying into. To paraphrase Oscar Wilde, we know the price of everything and the value of nothing.

No thing ever stopped the true artist from living an authentic life. This is the immutable line drawn in the cosmic sand, the threshold that separates the artist from the dilettante. Whether you are prepared to expend the passion necessary to succeed with your gift is a matter that must be addressed before you stretch your head out onto the bloodied block of public opinion—there is no shortage of willing executioners. A diamond, after all, is a piece of coal that did well and magically metamorphosed under pressure over time measured in millions of years.

AGONY INTO ECSTASY

Rejection can destroy you, or you can use the resistance to evolve into the person you know you are, or can become. As Friedrich Nietzsche also observed: "What does not destroy me, makes me stronger." After all, what is the point of going through pain if you aren't going to transmute the agony into ecstasy, the hardship into strength of character? Use everything that comes your way to learn: this is economical and smart. What is the point of going through disappointment and anguish if you don't harness it to become stronger, more discerning, and more evolved?

Physical pain alerts us to danger and teaches us lessons; pain of the psyche does the same.

Use rejection and other hurdles to affirm your purpose and to develop your strength for completing the mission; this is the object lesson.

First, there will be questions about the quest for your dharma; then there will be many tests to fulfill your mission; and then there will be a life well lived—soul and all.

EDEN

CHAPTER FIVE

A NEW POSTER CHILD
Artist as Hero

THE ARTIST of the 21st century knows that while talent is the gift, genius is dedication.

Artists need a new model that defines success. As I said before when speaking about Vincent van Gogh, the image of the damaged and destitute creator who is alienated from society is more than passé; it is dead. So, let's bury it, release it, and move on.

The artist in this new millennium possesses an overall confidence supported by attributes or qualities that define his character. This indomitable and inner security is the direct result of the artist's hard work, heightened sense of awareness, and self-referential acceptance of his work—he has faced himself naked, without the false masks of personality; he knows why he is an artist and the intrinsic value of his art; and he allows no outside authority, whether receptive to his work or not, to validate his *dharma*, his purpose in life. This artist knows he is on sacred ground because he knows where he stands. He is a creator; let posterity work out the details.

This artist has exorcised victimhood from his being; he isn't a hapless by-product of social conditioning, nor has he traded in his soul, or his voice, for impermanent material trappings; he isn't a slave to any particular outcome, knowing that rigid attachment excludes every other possible opportunity. He is a fully realized human being who lives by his wits and projects a positive voice in this universe of souls. A fully realized person is one, while doing no harm, has the desire and the drive to express his unique dream at whatever the cost.

He isn't after perfection or self-indulgence; he is after self-realization. He has realized that there is a distinction between the ego, which is the self-important aspect of the mind, and the quest for the transcendent self, which is the soul—the courier of all great art.

This model artist in this new age has the correct posture and attitude to soar above his own fears and those naysayers who may dismiss or deride his art. He has made the commitment to locate the source of what matters and to find out things on his own; he won't give up his power to the agenda of others; he knows secondhand information is what it sounds like.

> *The act of rejection, as well as acceptance, is based on subjective criteria and has nothing to do with your value as an artist, or as a human being.*
>
> CAROLL MICHELS

Genius always finds itself a century too early.
RALPH WALDO EMERSON

TWENTY-TWENTY

This artist sees life clearly as it is rather than from some biased viewpoint. He is a creator who is healthy in mind, body, and spirit. His perception isn't distorted by desires, anxieties, fears, hopes, wishes, false optimism, or pessimism.

Seeing beyond illusion is what Buddha called this penetration of reality. This artist is decisive about what is right and wrong. He knows that compassion is a combination of compass, or moral direction, and passion from the soul. He sees more efficiently, and his unique sense of discernment extends not only to his art, but also to all areas of his life. This integrated artist realizes that true success is based on a holistic experience of life.

He says: 'Everything I do is my art.'

This artist of the present-future is flexible, spontaneous, less inhibited, more expressive, simple and natural; he is willing to make mistakes. He welcomes new ideas and readily admits ignorance and error. He compares his work to no one, for making comparisons in art is a trap. He doesn't fear the ridicule of others because his sense of self is immutably positive.

To maintain his strength, dignity, and clarity, he brushes off rejection and negativity like mud from his work boots.

This artist is willing to forego popularity for truth. After all, the ability to be recognized is a function of exposure, which isn't necessarily synonymous with talent or fulfillment. He knows that this is a meaningful universe and that life is a spiritual escapade, which is a faith borne not out of belief, but out of proof, out of knowing. He realizes creation demands courage, the ability to stick his neck out, the ability to ignore criticism, and the inner resolve to resist the influence of his own culture.

Our artist of the 21st century has proven to himself that self-discipline, which is the rejection of a lesser action for a superior one, is freedom.

ARTIST AS HERO

As I have suggested elsewhere in this book, the artist embodies both the protagonist and antagonist—he either gets it done or does himself in.

It is an internal affair.

If we could see the artist's life from how God might see it, we would witness the canvas in its entirety. We would get a clear construct of what is right and wrong action for the play to unfold in the hero's favor.

From our omnipotent point of view, we would certainly see the dead ends and the opportunities.

We would observe that when the artist rises beyond the box of self-imposed limitations, he then perceives things and events dispassionately, and that invariably leads to right action.

There are plot elements, pivotal scenes, costs, and rewards that move the story forward in every drama, in every life as it gets played out on this worldly stage—with deference to Shakespeare. In every story there is a hero with a mission and that goal must be clearly understood by the character and the audience.

The artist must know his own objective; if it is not clearly defined, he will flounder and the audience will lose interest.

Think about it.

ADVERSARY

For the hero to succeed, he must overcome not only the apparent obstacles but also the hidden traps within subtle temptations, which are the most insidious for setting up interference between the hero and his attaining the prize.

To break through these barriers, which most often include the potential seduction by fame, sex, drugs, and money, is what makes for a compelling story. For the artist as hero to make good, he must confront various degrees of adversity as his story unfolds. Rejection qualifies as an internally conjured adversary. Every hero needs a worthy antagonist for the story to grip us with suspense. I didn't make it up; drama breaks down that way. To defeat your opponent, you must know who he is, and more important, who you are. For the artist to keep on going, however, he must also receive some manner of reward for enduring hardships along the way. These rewards don't need to be grandiose; they can be simple as long as they confirm that the artist is moving along the right path—that he is making progress for moving the story forward.

The artist hero, for example, can be drawing in a café. A mustachioed well-dressed old man, a stranger, walks over to him and comments how much he loves what the artist is making, and that it reminds him of the ancient art from his county. The old man then asks the artist if he'd be willing to sell him a piece. This acknowledgment without ulterior motive injects a dose of satisfaction and fulfillment into the hero's veins; this perk gets his adrenaline pumping to take on whatever comes next in the story that is his life—your life.

COURSE CORRECTIONS

It is as simple as this: If the artist doesn't receive some benefit, some incentive to sustain him along the way toward his quest, he, no matter how brave, steadfast, and single-minded of purpose, will eventually reach that point of diminishing returns, and ultimately give up—and then, go ahead, feel free to finish the final act—the story becomes a tragedy. But this is not a tragedy in the Greek sense where the hero, after winning the spoils of war, is undone by a character flaw. Nor is this the story of Job who, as a pawn between the powers of good and evil, suffers unrelenting tests of *faith*. This scenario is a tragedy because the artist, now impotent, has defeated himself into anonymity; he has given up on his gift; he has failed to complete his mission.

The true artist, the hero who concerns us here, categorically denies failure. He is a creator who finds a way to maintain momentum. Usually, and through his efforts, it is some external element that provides him with encouragement—breathing room between scenes dealing with overcoming the 'bad guys' in whatever form they take in the story.

While the true artist as the hero faces daunting obstacles, he does not see himself as a victim; the artist, like the consummate entrepreneur, does not identify with failure.

Why, after all, should the hero wait for a chance offer of a scrap here and there?

He doesn't.

> *I cannot give you the formula for success, but I can give you the formula for failure—which is: Try to please everybody.*
>
> HERBERT B. SWOPE

Learning to make films is very easy. Learning what to make films about is very hard.

GEORGE LUCAS

Counting your blessings isn't an unrealistic bromide for optimism. Better yet, truly feel grateful for what you do have; then you are like King Midas with the touch, but not the curse.

EDEN

A more direct approach, which may be less dramatic, yet no less effective, is for the hero to reward himself as he strives to fulfill his stated mission. If one thing doesn't work out as planned, he can detach and move on, taking another course toward his dream.

While external support is welcome, the artist does not count on it or let its absence deter him. There is a powerful drama in the life of every true artist and that story is as unique as the artist living it.

REEVALUATING REALITY

The question then becomes: How do you reward your own self so that you remain resolute until the prize is at hand? This is how I do it; this is my construct for success now. Having found and earned my passion, my dharma as an artist, I have already won the cosmic lottery. I know where I stand and that gives me strength. The future is but prologue, which I must create as both the positive and negative strands weave throughout the fabric of my story.

I will my thoughts to coincide with my emotions; this is the attitude I have set up for myself. I feel grateful for each day; I feel thankful for my blessings; I don't take my art for granted for that misstep places me on that well-trodden and seductive slope into ego hell; I heed my intuition, which, in turn, expands my awareness and opens up my canvas to the 'field of all possibilities'; no thing in this material world is more awesome than the creator force within. I acknowledge these points daily, and rewards reveal themselves in forms I couldn't have predicted.

Remaining resolute is the sign of dedication, genius, and mastery. When the hardships and disappointments of life, the sufferings of pain and illness, and the masks of death in the last act do show their faces, I am compelled to confront my own philosophy. Don't we all?

The question then becomes: Does my model for living an authentic life hold up against the inner demons of angst and agony? In those moments on the 'razor's edge', I realize that I don't have to reinvent the old wheel of karmic understanding.

I need look no further than what Buddha revealed ages ago: anyone can make peace with self-inflicted pain and suffering through awareness, which snaps the perceiver out of illusion and into seeing reality as it is in the here and now. In this way, I keep my story lively while living in a state of evolving self realization, despite the cycle of obstacles, denseness, nuisances, nonsense, and all the dire and petty things that desperately want to derail me from my mission, my dharma to make art—and I do so daily.

Nirvana is reality as it is.

BEARING THE STANDARD

As the master from India had said: "It is better to live in fulfillment than in hope." I embrace the artist as hero because this creator embodies emotional intelligence. I know that the attainment of the goal is but the outward manifestation and confirmation of what I already understand—which didn't come cheap. When someone doesn't 'get' my art, I am not incensed or devastated; I know that person would appreciate the work if he had the dharma to 'see' it. I make this statement with soul authority, knowing where I stand because I have answered the core questions in this book.

Mind-numbing social conditioning engenders a world mostly 'comfortable' and in step with mediocrity, at least from a creator's point of view; this world, however, must run to catch up with excellence in whatever visionary form it takes.

As my standards are tested, and while waiting for the future to catch up with me, I am eternally painting and writing because my mission parameters allow me to have relative patience.

FORENSIC EVIDENCE

Strive for clarity and understanding, which is the goal. However, we should not ignore our relationship to needs. In the late 1950's, Abraham Maslow and a few others advocated what he coined The Third Force of Psychology (the first two forces were Freudianism and Behaviorism). The term 'Third Force Psychology' has also become synonymous with humanistic psychology.

In Frank G. Goble's 1970 book, *The Third Force: The Psychology of Abraham Maslow*, we read: "The esteem needs: All people in our society (with a few pathological exceptions) have a need or desire for a stable, firmly based, (usually) high evaluation of themselves, for self-respect, or self-esteem, and for the esteem of others. By firmly based self-esteem, we mean that which is soundly based upon real capacity, achievement and respect from others. These needs may be classified into two subsidiary sets. These are, first, the desire for strength, for achievement, for adequacy, for confidence in the face of the world, and for independence and freedom. Secondly, we have what we may call the desire for reputation or prestige (defining it as respect or esteem from other people), recognition, attention, importance or appreciation."

After much original research, it was clear to Maslow that satisfying the esteem needs leads to self-confidence, usefulness, and worth; and, in turn, ignoring these needs produces a sense of weakness and inferiority. There is a caveat here to remember: to enjoy the respect and appreciation of others is no vice; to evaluate your worth by those same external reactions is the trap.

Art is forensic evidence of the transcendent, the metaphysical, the spirit in the physical world.

Peace of mind is that mental condition in which you have accepted the worst.

LIN YUTANG

When artists speak of their work as being simpatico with Buddhism, keep in mind their interpretation may not be your own.

EDEN

CHAPTER SIX

THE GAUNTLET GUARANTEE
Disengaging from Mind Control

THE INSIDIOUS THING about social conditioning is that you are unaware of it.

There is something required of you before proceeding. If you have already skimmed ahead, consider it a worthwhile detour into the future where nothing has been lost.

THE CHALLENGE

You must make it through an entire day, while conversing with others, without using these three common tick words: 'just', 'hope', and 'wish', or uttering a single cliché. I call them 'tick' words because they are merely marking time, nothing more.

Another reason that tick words are annoying and imprecise is that they are indirect, whereas direct is more powerful. Instead of 'just do it', say 'do it', or even 'do it, please'. The tick word challenge is equally effective for all artists, regardless of form. And it is the prehistoric invention of painting after all that led to speech and the written word.

You have got to loosen up before you can adjust yourself to a new understanding.

If you feel this assignment is much too easy and you are game, up the ante by not saying 'I', the most personal of pronouns on that day of word fasting where less will turn out to be a whole lot more.

WHY?

There is no point in reading what I have written without first establishing a rapport based on a common understanding about our own selves. In addition, I offer you a reward for your effort. Complete the assignment and your perception will be forever and unalterably improved. I guarantee it. I don't make this claim lightly. Giving advice can be a dicey business. If something doesn't work out, who are you going to blame? I am confident in my field-tested approach. I don't suggest anything I haven't proven to my own self. We are all in this together.

I'm a painter. What do I have to know about words and writing?

What do you have to know about speaking? Test the theory. Choose a few well-known creators and you will note that whether speaking or writing, they were at the very least cogent and clear. Don't infantilize yourself into mediocrity.

Remember, as the master instructed: an artist has no medium.

EDEN

It is a mistake to look too far ahead. Only one link of the chain of destiny can be handled at a time.

WINSTON CHURCHILL

How can your work be original if you think, speak, and act in clichés? Once your ear is attuned to this disability, you will mend your ways and your art will naturally become authentic.

EDEN

The goal of this challenge is to invigorate your receptivity to the information in this book. There is no more effective way to accomplish this than for you to prove to your own satisfaction how social conditioning hardwires our thought patterns, undermining the limits of our potential. After you consciously confront the rigidity of a mindset firsthand, you will have a significant insight into your own psychology that will serve you well in tackling rejection.

I want you to experience instant gratification. This exercise is something you can do right now. You don't have to believe anything, or even have faith. You need only do it—now—to prove this mental challenge to yourself. What more can you ask?

Being diligent about these tick words by not using them is mental alertness and discipline. This is a way to focus. You need not agree with me or be concerned about the exact meaning or the ultimate fate of 'just', 'hope', and 'wish' in the lexicon. You need only be alert enough not to use them. You are in control of your mouth.

HONOR SYSTEM

A reliable test to see whether you have summarily discarded a tick word from your vocabulary is this: You are asleep. The phone rings and you answer, not yet fully awake. Someone on the other end says, "Come on, let's go. We'll be late." Even if you did regress by saying, '*Just* a minute,' don't despair. The only important thing is that you realize you said the verboten word. You caught yourself in the act of slipping into a mindless preconditioned pattern. This momentary relapse is a heads up for how we can so easily fall back into old and familiar patterns that keep us prisoners of social conditioning. Of course, other tests will come to see whether you have removed these life force sucking ticks from your speech.

Be alert. Tick words usually resurface, and to your own amazement, again when you are tired or under pressure.

This assignment is, of course, on the honor system. Although the common words 'just', 'hope', and 'wish' speak for themselves (and you), you will have to be diligent in ferreting out the clichés, trite expressions, and hackneyed phrases on your own. I have confidence that you will ultimately rise above parroting the words of others.

How else then can you be original?

Once you gain an awareness of your habitual use of these common terms in everyday speech, you will soon catch the word before it leaves your lips. You won't say 'just' even if roused from a deep nap. When it involves clichés, one thing I do for motivation is this: The first cliché of the day is on the house—free. For each cliché thereafter, as the master had instructed, I fine myself fifty cents. Of course, I allow myself the occasional cliché with the understanding that I use it only for effect, and on purpose.

MIND CONTROL

There is power in words. Recall George Orwell's dire vision of the future in his 1949 novel *Nineteen-Eighty-Four* where *Newspeak* (the politically correct speech of Oceania) manipulated the language and, as a direct result, controlled the minds of its citizens—where 'reality' meant white was black and black was white, and where 'thoughtcriminals' received their final form of punishment as dispensed by the Ministry of Love.

Mind control, which is rampant throughout history, is nothing new.

Consider post Renaissance Italy where, in 1633, the Church Inquisition threatened the mathematician and astronomer, Galileo Galilei (1564-1642), with torture and death if he didn't recant his conviction that the Earth was in orbit around the sun. Galileo's findings threatened the Cosmology of Christendom, and the absolute power of the Papacy.

Galileo knew he was right, but abjured, knowing what his fate would be if he did not.

The Inquisition had burned the Dominican Friar Giordano Bruno (1548-1600) alive at the stake for his 'heretical' views of the heavens. Galileo lived on for a time under house arrest only to die a broken man, but not before recording his groundbreaking experiments on motion that a hundred years later would help Isaac Newton establish modern physics.

Subsequent discoveries of gravitational law in the 18th century by Newton, who was born the year Galileo died, gives a proper explanation of the elliptical orbits of the planets, and of the Earth's motion, confirming Galileo's (and that of Nicolaus Copernicus and Johannes Kepler) observation.

MEA CULPA ... SORT OF

There is a recent postscript along the historical timeline to the Inquisition of Galileo worth noting. In October 1992, a Vatican commission conditionally admitted that the Galileo affair had been mishandled, and concluded that the Inquisition had, indeed, treated Galileo too harshly. However, the commission added that Galileo was partially to blame by insisting he had absolute proof of the heliocentric system of astronomy that Copernicus had envisioned.

It was true. Galileo's argument, based on the ebb of the flow of the tides, didn't prove the Earth's motion. To prove the validity of Copernicus' theory would take centuries more of scientific study. The Vatican of today decreed, in summation, that the actions of its predecessors were overzealous, although not wrongly motivated.

But let's not be too critical of the ignorance from the past.

As mentioned throughout this book, there is truth, knowing, and firsthand information. If I see a sign that reads: POISON—DO NOT DRINK, I will take their word for it and accept the printed conclusion as a fact, the truth.

There is another kind of knowing which is based on authority and belief. For example, you might hear an astrophysicist say: 'Yes, we know the Earth moves around the sun.' But could you empirically prove it if you had to? Very few people living on the planet today could. So, you take someone else's word as proof that the Earth moves around the sun—which is another form of secondhand information that passes for 'knowing' based on authority, not firsthand experience.

Apparently, the average citizen of the 21st century, despite his 'knowing' that the Earth orbits the sun wouldn't have fared any better with the Inquisition than Galileo.

You get the point. The truth is powerful, and often dangerous. Remember, truth is conveyed most reliably through action.

A man of genius has been seldom ruined but by himself.

SAMUEL JOHNSON

It's only a detour if you don't stay.

EDEN

WE THE PEOPLE

In English, the ubiquitous words 'hope' and 'wish' have particular meanings that are imbedded in the American and British psyche. 'Hope' and 'wish' are passive words; once informed, a creator wouldn't willingly use them.

In the Declaration of Independence, we read: "We hold these truths to be self-evident, that all men are created equal, that they are endowed by their Creator with certain unalienable Rights, that among these are Life, Liberty and the pursuit of Happiness."

Thomas Jefferson didn't pen: We *hope* these truths are *obvious*. To its credit, there isn't a single utterance of 'hope' or any other passive word in this magical document that the Founding Fathers bestowed upon posterity.

OTHER LANGUAGES

Other cultures may not use 'hope' or 'wish' in the vernacular. The conspicuous absence of these words says as much of that culture as the culture that uses them to the hilt. If your native speech is other than English, you will have to substitute equivalents for these trite and weak common tick words, including 'just'; and clichés are rampant in all tongues. Readers who are deaf or mute may substitute equivalent tick words that show up in sign language.

If this book has survived into the far future and these tick words no longer apply in the spirit of this exercise, then you will have to substitute tick words and clichés in whatever form from your own time.

When you have completed this assignment, I will be waiting for you in the following chapter: 'Welcome Back'. It will be a day you won't forget.

We will discover the nature of our particular genius when we stop trying to conform to our own or to other peoples' models, learn to be ourselves, and allow our natural channel to open.

SHAKTI GAWAIN

NINA'S NIGHT

CHAPTER SEVEN

WELCOME BACK
My Dinner With Lawrence

NOT SO EASY. Or, was it? If you had a difficult time, then you got the message and I have your attention.

I chose 'just', 'hope', and 'wish' because, as previously mentioned, they are weak words taking up valuable space. And clichés don't speak for themselves; they represent you as you regurgitate the words of others. The object lesson here isn't that you eliminated these words in your first attempt, but that you have become aware of how difficult it is to overcome ingrained social conditioning—in this case, words.

PERILOUS VIEWS

You might have noticed that the assignment didn't include these annoying verbal ticks: 'um', 'eh', 'like', and 'ya know'.

The reason for this is that editing out the hardwired reflex words in the Gauntlet challenge will spontaneously and organically begin to eliminate other ticks. If you are an abuser of 'obvious', then I urge you to drop this dangerous word from your vocabulary. The true artist once informed knows that no thing is obvious—if it were, wouldn't you have already been acclaimed for your genius?

Keep a sharp ear and hear how many otherwise intelligent people use 'obvious', a reflex, holier than thou word meaning that everyone would come to the same conclusion—which is a perilous view apparently overlooked by so many.

How insidious covert coercion can be as it attempts to manipulate our lives as artists, especially when dealing with rejection or acceptance. If you control your language, you will define and give meaning to a reality of value where you have authority.

STANDARD BEARER

Of course, while conscious word choice isn't a panacea, it is light years ahead of the alternative. If, however, you accept existing paradigms, you choose to live by the standards of success and failure designed by others.

Insofar as it's possible, this is the best response to every rejection:

The work wasn't wanted there; where will it be wanted? You peer out into the world as wide a world as you can manage and give your work its tenth or fiftieth or thousandth shot at connecting with someone.

ERIC MAISEL

It is much smarter to discover and develop your own set of standards—in doing so you will be the standard bearer of your art. If you won't, who will? Although I write 'your own set of standards', this doesn't exclude others who are also striving for clarity from discovering the very same standards, which are universal. The inherent beauty of excellence lies in its availability to anyone willing to achieve it.

Passion eventually leads to truth.

Now that 'just', 'hope', 'wish', and whatever clichés you have come to rely on are on your hit list, I trust that you will begin to hear and feel how much more power there is in your thoughts, in your speech, in your relationships, and in your work.

DINNER WITH LAWRENCE

When we begin to discard the irrelevant, the tick words and their ilk, we begin to empower our communication with our own selves and with others. Words can evoke beautiful feelings, make a baby laugh, heal a relationship, or they can do malicious harm at worst or show our ineptness and insensitivity at best.

Let me tell you about my dinner with Lawrence. It went like this.

I was living in the Cow Hollow section of San Francisco. My hill street was steep enough to overlook the Marina straight down to the Bay. The Golden Gate Bridge was a few long blocks away. I would often walk down to the Marina Green, a grassy expanse between Fort Mason and the Presidio, with my Yorkshire Terrier, Larry, who was a pup at the time.

As we followed the Marina Green, Larry and I would eventually end up on Crissy Field, which ran along the bay on the north side of the Presidio. Beyond the field lay a long narrow beach that skirted the coast westward toward the base of the bridge. I would spend hours near the beach training tiny Larry to sit, heel, come, and stay. Despite his toy size, he was still a stubborn terrier. But his eagerness to please was the key to discipline. He quickly caught on to both my voice and hand signal commands from a distance. Knowing that people had a tendency to spoil this breed, I had decided I would treat Larry as if he were a big dog; he would learn big dog commands. My philosophy was this: he could do anything he liked as long as he listened to me.

PARTY IN MARIN

My raven-haired girlfriend of the time, Hanna, told me we had been invited to a party in Marin County that weekend. One of her longtime girlfriends had parents who loved to throw a yearly bash that was always fun with lots of people, plus there would be excellent food.

Saturday came around. What choice did it have? We drove north across the Golden Gate into Marin County. We had to park a few blocks away as cars lined the country road leading to the party. The night was black, and there were no streetlights on this rural lane. Hanna and I walked toward the blues, jazz, and chatter that streamed out into the night air from the huge old house in the woods. From the front porch, we peeked inside through large windows. People were enjoying appetizers, including caviar canapés, and mingling with drinks in hand.

All growth is a leap in the dark, a spontaneous unpremeditated act without benefit of experience.

HENRY MILLER

You either capture nature or release nature.

Consider this polarity to see where you fit in. This is a point of discretion, not a comparison.

EDEN

Hanna and I entered. The hosts, Lawrence, a man in his seventies with a short gray beard, and his friendly Rubenesque wife, Frieda, were setting up to serve dinner for some fifty guests. They had several dutiful helpers getting things ready for the feast. After Hanna introduced me to the host and hostess, we walked about the roomy house, talking, and mingling, too.

THE BOHEMIAN

Lawrence sat down on an old wooden chair at the head of the enormous table set for thirty people. Several smaller tables had been set up to accommodate the overflow. Hanna and I managed to get two chairs at the main table. Suddenly, as people were taking their seats and getting comfortable, Lawrence's chair collapsed out from under him. He dropped out of sight below the table as if someone had yanked him to the floor. While those near him were helping him up someone brought in another chair. Lawrence laughed, composed himself, and then made a toast to the well being of all in attendance.

After a sumptuously prepared and well-served meal, the dinner party spread out into every crevice of the old house. Hanna was catching up with her old friends. I didn't know anyone. I went into the living room where I found a comfortable love seat near a wall with an impressive library of books from floor to ceiling. The lights were muted. Music reverberated to a constant buzz of talk circulating through the air. As I took a deep breath, I felt the seat bounce. Ah, I thought, Hanna had returned.

Lawrence was sitting there with an impish smile. He began speaking to me. It turned out that he had for many years owned a bookshop in the San Francisco section called North Beach. Tucked between Chinatown and Fisherman's Wharf, North Beach, at one time, was known for its avant-garde population that included artists, plus a diverse ethnic mix. This eclectic neighborhood was often compared to Paris' Left Bank partly due to affordable rents for artists. Lawrence was a Bohemian and a literary man who had been part of the 1950's Beat Generation. He knew them all: Jack Kerouac, Lawrence Ferlinghetti, Allen Ginsberg, Charles Bukowski, William Burroughs, and others of that era. He had sold their books and they would stop in to see him now and then.

MY FAUX PAS

As Lawrence spoke, his voice subtly shifted in cadence to the jazz coming from the CD player. His words flowed in poetic imagery as he described the people in the room and what they were doing. Then, within this flow of words and artful gesticulations, he began speaking in various accents, French, German, British, Italian, Australian, with impeccable panache and in perfect dialect. He was a master.

He painted marvelous pictures of life with words strung together like luscious pearls. Humor, tragedy, and a range of emotions came in waves—the ebb and flow of his existence. In an uninterrupted stream of consciousness, he told me of his life. Lawrence also had a beautiful singing voice, and his repertoire flowed effortlessly from opera, folk, and pop to jazz and reggae. He spoke directly to me, seamlessly shifting into song,

Any fool can make a rule, and any fool will mind it.

HENRY DAVID THOREAU

With due deference to Jack Kerouac, we are no longer dharma bums.

EDEN

It took me three, four years, to get from my first film to my second film, banging on doors, trying to get people to give me a chance. Writing, struggling, with no money in the bank, working as an editor on the side.

GEORGE LUCAS

Is there something better than your art beyond that far horizon? I leave you to your own conclusion based on the three core questions in this book.

EDEN

confiding a lifetime of living. His tone and intensity were mesmerizing. Soon, the buzzing activity of the party and the other guests faded into the background, leaving Lawrence and me to our own devices.

Then, after nearly an hour of magical prose, poetry, and a cappella vocalizing, Lawrence's voice, in perfect tune with a jazz piece resonating within the room, filtered back slowly and nearly imperceptibly to normal, until, suddenly, we were back in the din at the party in the present moment. His improvisational performance to his audience of one had ended.

He said quietly: "What did you think of that?"

"Not bad," I said, immediately knowing in my gut that my response was inadequate—lame.

Lawrence winced. "You can do better than that," he said. "Not bad. That's what you say about a fast food hamburger. I must admit it was fucking brilliant. I haven't performed like this in years. My writing was wonderful, too, but no one noticed."

He was right without being arrogant. He was awesome and brilliant, and I had let him down with a weak acknowledgment of this talent.

RISK AND RECOVERY

"You're right," I said. "My apologies. It was magnificent. I've never heard anyone do what you magically did this evening [nor since for that matter]. Bravo, Lawrence." I meant every word. I saw in his old eyes that he knew I was no sycophant.

Lawrence stood up, took a theatrical bow, and moved off into the party among his other guests, leaving me dazzled on the love seat.

After a few minutes, or so it seemed, I realized what had happened. Lawrence was an unknown genius who somehow had fallen between the cracks of renown. He had been part of the Beat Generation, but no one had caught on to his superb gift. Although bitter, he wasn't completely destroyed knowing his work had been overlooked while lesser talents were glorified. I didn't know all the facts. I didn't need to. Lawrence's performance that evening had given me volumes of his life to consider between the lines of his poetry and prose.

I was fortunate that he had singled me out to hear and witness his art. Lawrence knew the scope of his abilities. He had no doubts about it and knew were he stood in the pecking order of talent. He taught me a few other things of value that night. If you feel it, acknowledge the talent of another with enthusiasm. Don't be stingy with your praise. Don't end up a rejected or overlooked genius.

There has to be a better way to cope with talent, I thought, and I was determined to find out.

I left that soiree a richer young man.

When the artist realizes her dharma, in that timeless moment, she finds herself high above on a tightrope spanning the cavernous gap from the past into the future. This is a situation.

Fortunately, the choice is clear: she is already halfway across; turning back makes no sense.

CHAPTER EIGHT

REJECTION HQ
The Interview

ARTISTS NEED a new model that defines success. As I said before when speaking about Vincent, the image of the damaged and destitute creator who is alienated from society is more than passé; it is dead.

So, let's bury it, release it, and move on.

Brevity, as we again confirm, is still the soul of wit, which is the expressed confidence of self-discipline.

ARE YOU TALKING TO ME?

It would seem a book for artists that confronts rejection would include an armory of salvos primed with effective retorts aimed at those rejecting their work. What to say to whom and under what circumstances isn't something you have to read about in a book. Such an approach is far too ponderous and pretentious. There is, however, a code of conduct you may expect from yourself and others, which I write about in more detail in the next chapter: 'The Rules of Engagement'.

Proper responses to specific situations are a matter of discretion that can only be learned from firsthand experience. Anyone can be bold until the moment of confrontation arrives. The quality of how you handle yourself in any situation is a function of character, not a result of memorizing a canned rejoinder.

NO DRESS REHEARSAL

This book isn't about he said, she said. Such an approach is far too narrow and of no value to any artist unsure of himself and his art. It is only after you have done the grunt work of knowing your own self as an artist that the right response to naysayers will come to you spontaneously with no need for planning.

You don't have to rehearse being you, do you?

Because you feel the truth of the moment in your being, the wit on your tongue will lilt off your lips should the occasion require it. As it turns out, the most effective response in nearly every situation where your work isn't

> *No is not forever. A plan for rejection is this: retreat, reevaluate, and re-approach.*
>
> SAM HORN

wanted is this: disengage graciously from the rejecting party. Although not to parry when your blood is on fire may seem weak, it is, in fact, a sign of inner strength, a wondrous by-product of self-discipline—a quality this book will help you confront and develop. And, after all, what is there to say? Really?

The path you must walk toward triumphing over rejection has nothing to do with anyone but you. Being a victim over what you can control is simply not tolerated; dire circumstances are, of course, another matter. The category of blame doesn't exist in the gestalt of the true artist. It is all about you, and therein lies the secret for living a life of fulfillment in the present moment instead of hope in a world where nature takes no prisoners.

FULL FRONTAL REJECTION

Rejection is based on three fronts: personality, taste, or a situation. A chronically disagreeable personality will most likely remain that way until he dies. Unless you thrive on self-abuse, stay away from inveterately negative people. "Ah, good taste!" Picasso reportedly said. "What a dreadful thing. Taste is the enemy of creativity." Taking it a bit further, Thomas Hoving, former director of New York's Metropolitan Museum of Art, observed: "The only true enemy of art is good taste."

So, be flexible and know that taste, like all fashion, is often perfunctory, self-conscious, and transitory while great art is timeless. If the rejection is situation-based, then the timing might not have been right and there is potential for acceptance at a later date. For every reason you can think of and for every reason you can't, the gallery owner, the potential patron, the museum director, the art magazine editor, or the critic couldn't appreciate your art in that instance. There is still no law against bad taste, or poor judgment in art.

Remember, a 'no' can often simply mean not now. Keep the situation room door open with civility and even charm if you can muster it. You won't be sorry, you have nothing to lose, and possibly much to gain—albeit in delayed gratification. But so what?

Knowing you are the creator of your experience has great liberating power. If you don't know this yet, I trust you will, at least, know it is true by the time you complete and integrate the information in this book.

THE INTERVIEW

There is no question that others can smell your fear. For all our intellectual and technological meanderings, we are still pack animals on the hunt with iPods.

When I was in the corporate world, including publishing, I would often interview prospective job applicants for my department. I would first lay out the challenges to see who squirms and who perks up at the opportunity. This approach saved both the job hunter and me lots of time. I learned the merits of this tactic early on when I had been on job interviews.

I was in my twenties at the time. After passing the screening process of the personnel department, I was introduced to one of the partners in the company. He told me about all the others who had failed in this position

---

Art shrouded with ideas is easier to think about because its source is conceptual; art of the soul must be felt with feeling—emotional intelligence. There is no other way.

EDEN

and why the job was so difficult. He did his best to discourage me. I listened quietly until he was finished.

"Don't you have any questions?"

I told him, "No."

"Why?" he said.

"Because I understand the nature of the job, and why it didn't work out for the others."

"Why?" he asked again.

THE DEAL

Not one to give away secrets (see Brunelleschi's *The Radical Egg* in 'Trafficking in Art') prematurely, I said: "You'll have to hire me to find out. I see it this way and I feel that you'll agree. If you haven't given me a substantial raise within six months, you were right. If I get the raise for an amount we can agree upon now, then I'm worth it and I'm right, which is what you really want in the first place."

I got the job.

Six months later. Everybody, including me, knew I had excelled expectations. I opened my paycheck to see the increase in my take home pay. The raise was not there as we had agreed. I called the personnel department to see whether an increase in my salary had been put through. They confirmed that it hadn't. I walked into the partner's office and told him that I wanted to show him something. He looked up as I placed my check on his desk. He wasn't sure what to make of this scene.

"It's been six months, I said. "I'm still here, but the salary increase isn't. You remember our agreement?"

He fumbled a bit, then said, "Oh, yes. It's been six months already ... has it? Well, I can't put this through now. I have to discuss it with the other partners who have to sign off on it, too." The two other partners were both out of town.

I told him that while I can appreciate protocol, what was there to discuss? I said, "I want the raise as we had agreed." He kept insisting that I be patient and wait until his partners returned from their business trips.

If you are going to make a stand, know your value. I politely informed the partner that if I didn't have my increase by the end of the day, I would regretfully be leaving the company. I had nothing to lose. If you let someone con you and you know it, then you are complicit in your own misfortune. I had kept my word; now it was the partner's turn to pay up. When you draw the line, be prepared to walk.

Confidence exudes a chemical into the air that is palpable.

If, however, your action is driven solely by bravado, you may end up defeating your own self.

THE ENVELOPE, PLEASE

At first, he thought I was joking. A moment later, the smile on his face dropped off into a pursed lip serious mug. He knew I wasn't bluffing because I knew I wasn't. He, of course, bristled, knowing that I was no slacker. I left my paycheck on the partner's desk and returned to my office.

Once I was working with a woman who had been struggling for days with her own judgment and doubt, disliking her painting immensely.

Finally she took a break for a cup of tea, and she was sitting on the far side of the studio, looking through the central glass atrium at her painting without realizing that it was her own. Enamored, she said to me, 'If only I could paint like that. That painting is so beautiful!'

STEWART CUBLEY

On his deathbed in response to a priest asking that he renounce Satan:

Now, now my good man, this is no time for making enemies.

VOLTAIRE

It was two o'clock in the afternoon. I went about doing my job and the hours passed—slowly. As five o'clock loomed up, one of the ladies from personnel appeared in my office and handed me an envelope. This could be my severance pay here, I thought. I opened the envelope. Instead of a pink slip, I found a check that now reflected my pay increase and note from the head of payroll that read: Our apologies for this oversight.

Each artist must acknowledge the difficulties ahead; your response to these obstacles, not the form they take, is relevant. When the moment is right, confront anyone who would sap you of your talent and merit. When you feel the truth of the situation, the 'right' words will come to you magically and seemingly without effort. You must be willing to walk.

POST-911 PAYCHECK

Rejection is an equally relevant issue for all creators: painters, poets, writers, musicians, singers, fashion designers, dancers, filmmakers, actors, explorers, innovators in any field, and anyone involved in an original enterprise that cannot be reduced to a prosaic formula. Those seeking new ways to better themselves must prepare mentally, knowing that confronting difficulty and disappointment are part of the cost of doing business.

While artists may seem to get most of the press when it comes to challenging mainstream values, there is also a growing psychologically and spiritually aware sector of the workplace that yearns for a life worth living. In a post-911 world increasing numbers of individuals are reevaluating their lives; mindful, they sense their unique purpose and that there is a better way; and some are ready to risk action, no longer willing to sacrifice their dharma for a paycheck that can't sustain their souls. They desire a means of fulfillment that will nourish their higher self and pay the rent.

Fortunately, a life of regret is an avoidable tragedy—knowing this outcome in advance has great liberating power because you can act now to alter that possible future. A life well spent is an art. The intuitive lure, appeal, and the dream for leading an authentic life is universal. Remember, 'you are on sacred ground when you know where you stand.'

There is a point of no return, critical mass, where a second before there was doubt and a second later there is universal knowledge of a truth; no one can dissuade you from knowing this aspect of the absolute.

Having the truth reflected in your work is not enough; you must understand the mission parameters and why you are an artist; this is leverage for overcoming adversity.

CHAPTER NINE

THE RULES OF ENGAGEMENT
Power and Peril

WHEN YOU GO public with your art, you are asking for reactions for which you must be prepared.

You are an artist, a partisan for the 'evolution'. You follow the Rules of Engagement. You adhere to a code of conduct that describes the circumstances and limitations under which you will present your art. While you trust that your trips into the field will be, at least, civil, there will be times when you may encounter less than honorable folk, and even hostility. Remember, adversity is a teacher you can trust.

Keep the ROE close to your vest at all times:

- Treat others with equal respect and expect the same in return. It is a code of conduct that is simple.

- If someone attempts to demean you, or your art, remove your self from that situation—physically, emotionally, and spiritually.

- How you conduct your self as a human being is no less important than the art you create; if you think the two are mutually exclusive, look into it again. If you have a gift for a higher calling, then behave accordingly. Your friends, family, and audience will notice.

- While you can't control the behavior of others, your deportment has a great influence over how others perceive you, and your art. Conduct yourself with dignity: the consequence of respect and recognition will come over time.

Remember, there are ways to reject or accept someone's art on the one hand without stabbing him to death with the other.

Going into any situation, it is imperative to know in advance where you stand with your own self. Answer the core questions.

Change.

It has the power to uplift, to heal, to stimulate, surprise, open new doors, bring fresh experience and create excitement in life. Certainly it is worth the risk.

LEO BUSCAGLIA

You use up everything you've got trying to give everyone want they want.

NINA SIMONE

To discover your dharma is the elixir that gives meaning to life.

EDEN

Do you have a healthy dose of self-esteem? Knowing whom you are dealing with in advance is also a supreme advantage. But, if that isn't possible, your contact will reveal himself to you soon enough. If you don't have a clear understanding about the inherent value of your work, then you are choice fodder for anyone who would exploit your weakness.

Fortunately, you have adopted The Rules of Engagement (ROE) as your standard, which gives you a decided advantage on the high ground. Knowing what you want is the force that engenders respect. Remember, those who may not overtly acknowledge your self-discipline and good conduct, secretly admire it on a soul level.

POWER AND PERIL

When you show your work, a power play dynamic comes into existence. Since you are asking someone for some thing, that person may feel he has power over you by either rejecting or accepting your work. Who will have the upper hand in the exchange? Do not become a victim artist and you will emerge from any encounter feeling proud. You know a person more by how he handles 'defeat' than by how he manages victory.

Do not be deceived by how power is portrayed in the media. Power, as with other sought after prizes, is not what it appears to be. While a celebrated artist may be able to pull strings and seemingly call his own shots among an entourage of ass-kissers, this show of force dangles on a mighty thin power line called *in vogue*.

Creation is power. Power is energy. Power need not be ruthless, which is the mentally disturbed model. Power and compassion represent the evolved model, and that's why the hero wins in the end. As an artist, you wield the desirable power to create. Ironically, many artists experience a lack of power in the world, a symptom of not being recognized for their contribution; this situation is further aggravated by a lack of awareness about what it means to be an artist. And who is responsible for that scenario?

Daydreaming of 'what if' or 'if only' has no dominion in this realm. The power of self-discipline must be experienced firsthand. In doing so, you will get to know thy self and the mettle of your character; and, as the master affirmed: character answers all questions. Whether your work is rejected or accepted, this affirmation, which is stated throughout this book, underscores the right response to any situation.

Power takes different forms. Exercising the power of compassion over your ego is perhaps the ultimate strategy of self-control, also known as freedom because it is power based on naked identity, which, by universal law, must reflect the truth about you in this moment. Power over others involves perceived status: stronger, more intelligent, more talented, better looking, richer—name your 'poison'. I didn't include smarter in this example because smart is a function of the soul, which is here to complete its mission, not compete in petty rivalry. If you create art, then you already know the power and responsibility of freedom.

NO TANTRUMS, PLEASE

Feeling powerless isn't what it seems to be; not being in control fosters the illusion of helplessness. But control over what? It is power over yourself—not others—that matters most. Power is within your grasp, despite any outside barometer. The truth of your art is timeless and invincible. Is it not? Think about it. If it isn't, reconnoiter and answer the core questions in this book; you must first face yourself naked before your self and others will take you seriously. If you lack the strength of conviction when you are unknown, then the power you may feel when someone does take notice of your work is based on fleeting flattery, not the sustainable intuitive power that will make you a dynamic force as a creator—and that is what you want in the first place. Suckering your own self with false pride is exactly what it sounds like. Regain your potency—be decisive, honorable, and grateful.

Power is responsibility and with it comes danger. That is why most avoid it. But the peril comes not from where you might think. Having been in positions of overt power, I know how it can corrupt fresh meat. The unprepared and unseasoned person who is not alert to power's seductive heat and wiles is in peril. He may well succumb to its insidious subtleness, which can enamor like the most provocative lover. Power is more intoxicating than any drug or aphrodisiac, and a catalyst for revealing self-awareness, or not. Power must be earned absolutely, and when it is, power transmutes into intuition, which is the direct link to consciousness—the Creator.

An *enfant terrible* who throws 'artistic' tantrums—which exist only because others indulge them—doesn't add anything worthwhile to the show. Like any other group, artists are distinguished primarily by their temperament. I have seen artists who made good art fall into the ego trap of treating others with contempt. But to place the entire blame on these artists for acting out deplorably would be a miscalculation. Partners in codependency empower unacceptable behavior at best and the dark side at worst. Browbeating has no place in a creator's handbook for living. And for that artist with poor people skills, I say this: How much greater your art and quality of life experience would be if you excused your ego and didn't believe your own public relations.

CRISIS MANAGEMENT

When I was working in the corporate world, a successful and acid-tongued senior executive told me with great pride that under his watch the company had done five hundred million dollars in sales. I thought to myself: Under my watch, we would have done a billion. I wasn't bragging. I had a grander perspective of what was going on in the company. The fear in people's eyes made him feel powerful. He felt that things were getting done. His dense approach blinded him; he was unaware. He didn't see the valuable talent going to waste, which were the very employees he domineered so well into mediocrity and crisis management.

True power is quiet and still, and yes, the strong silent type. It doesn't have to shout to be heard. Remember, your soul whispers; your ego yells.

Bullying people to perform tasks is as ancient as humankind and a poor model on the evolutionary scale of consciousness. It is much simpler, smarter, more productive, and more powerful to lead by example and treat those with whom you work and encounter with courtesy.

Remember, there is always time to set someone straight should the situation demand it.

A true master doesn't tell you that he knows, and he's going to explain it to you.

The master says: I know something, and now it's for you to find out. Be alert, aware, and resourceful, and you will learn.

EDEN

Because it's judgment that defeats us ...

COLONEL KURTZ,
APOCALYPSE NOW

BEING COMMON

While you mostly work alone as a painter, poet, writer, or in some other solo activity, engage everyone with equal respect. This makes you a common man or woman, and a rare individual who will be acknowledged now and remembered later as a liberated artist, a fully realized human being. If you manage people on a sliding scale of respect depending on their status, you not only don the false masks of personality, you will be forever lost in a mire of motive that harbors pretense and pettiness. If you have somehow harnessed the magic of creation and remain a lowlife, then what is the point?

Your behavior here isn't limited to the impact you have on others; your self-control over power directly influences the evolution of your art, life, and the resolve to rise beyond pettiness, the confines of self-imposed limitations, and being overlooked by those who could not yet read or understand your work.

Strength of character in both adversity and victory is the power (also known as yoga) that will see you through the perils of disappointment as well as success. As any conqueror will tell you: the hardest struggle comes after the war is won.

Remember, the world is not out to get you. Only your ego would devise such an inflated self-important fabrication.

Pretty Baby:

On the most basic survival level, approval from others is absolutely necessary. As a baby, you must have approval from your mother so she will take care of helpless you. You must get approval from your father and others of the village so that you can grow up into adulthood.

In the same way as you will outgrow your baby teeth, you can shed this need for approval from outside sources to move onto the next level. While the need for approval is built into the entire biological system, into the genetic code for survival, it remains a formula for sameness.

Through right action in each moment, a creator breaks free from routine programming where, in rising above weakness, he touches divine fire.

CHAPTER TEN

THE CORE QUESTIONS
Revelation and Desire

MAKE NO mistake. It is your life; it isn't a dress rehearsal. It is about the survival of the gifted, and you will need abilities you might never have considered for the journey.

Ever feel like this?

> "I have come to an unalterable decision—to go and live forever in Polynesia. Then I can end my days in peace and freedom, without thoughts of tomorrow and this eternal struggle against idiots."
>
> —*Paul Gauguin*, 1894

When I asked writer Michael Blake, who had overcome many trials both before and after his success with Dances with Wolves, for a thought, he gave me this quote, which he said, fit best with his own feelings:

> '*The proper function of man is to live, not to exist. I shall not waste my days trying to prolong them. I shall use my time.*'
>
> **JACK LONDON**

As artists we empathize with Gauguin's frustration.

He had conviction and intuitively knew the merit of his art, and yet, despite sporadic acceptance from collectors, art dealers, critics, and even other artists, he experienced mostly words of rejection. Not only was he accused of plagiarism, his work was also categorized as: crude, coarse, clumsy, grotesque, and primitive in the pejorative sense.

Although he felt unappreciated in his lifetime, Gauguin, the master who would become a Post-Impressionist icon, had worked to the end with no salvation in sight—a self-proclaimed martyr to the cause of painting.

Let's get our bearings for the duration. One of my standing mottoes is: No thing is obvious.

You have made an unwavering commitment to your art. Haven't you? Withdrawing to an island paradise in the South Seas isn't on the itinerary, yet, and as Gauguin learned, not a panacea either. Freedom is self-discipline, which is about restraint not mindless action.

Secure in your unique vision, you have produced a body of work. Mindful of conscious intention, you have also set a course, a destination called your audience—you may even have tasted a seductive morsel of recognition.

The rite of passage from being unknown to public awareness can feel as if you are trekking uphill through an endless minefield of hardships strewn with rejections. You are not alone.

Only when we touch each other do we find realization. It's not a thought in my mind or a thought in your mind.

—SO SAID THE MASTER

*No thing is obvious,
a self-evident observation made by Edgar Allan Poe in The Purloined Letter.*

EDEN

FRUIT FOR THOUGHT

Fortunately, there is good news. If you are wise to the spurious myths and booby traps, you can get there from here without becoming another emotionally scarred casualty of the art business. How to deftly diffuse the impact of rejection and build confidence is a skill—like drawing—that can be acquired by anyone motivated to learn. Practicing this skill every day over time strengthens character; and, as the master said, character answers all questions.

In her book, *Initiation*, Elizabeth Jenkins recounts her mystical experiences in Peru with Juan, a priest in the Andean tradition. Speaking of acceptance, Juan tells her: "Look at it on a simple level. When you appreciate someone, you are giving him or her some of your living energy. Receiving your energy, they will have more and be better able to give you some back later. This is a natural self-sustaining process of interdependence. When fruit ripens it wants to be picked and eaten by animals and people." The fruit sustains the fruit eater, the seeds then find their way back into the soil, and the fruit lives on. By eating the fruit, you help keep the fruit alive. This metaphor is especially potent for the artist whose fruit is intuitive energy transmuted into art. Good fruit will be eaten when the season is right.

Acceptance is like a magnet that works in beautiful polarity with the Law of Attraction, which we can sum up as follows: We, our soul selves, are attracted to what gives us life, acceptance, and energy, in the same way the leaves of a green plant reach upward to face the sunlight that gives it nourishment. In opposition, however, if we turn away from the light, we falter in the darkness of our weakness and stumble about misguided by our myopic egos.

There are tiers of rejection from childhood onward, from lost loves, lost jobs, lost elections, lost friends, lost desires, to lost face. No one wants to feel devalued, devastated, or worn down by rejection.

Richard Bolles, author of *What Color Is Your Parachute?*, explains that the dream job goes to those who know how to get it, not necessarily to those most qualified for the job. It isn't enough to know what you want; you must find a means of straddling the hurdles.

While intuition guides, you must do the grunt work yourself. Art can't come into being without sweat. Studies of savvy job hunters show that those who repeatedly succeed depend upon effective methods to accomplish their goals—and that goes for artists, too. Rejection in art involves overcoming the vicissitudes of getting seen, then once seen, enduring both criticism and praise.

THE CORE QUESTIONS

Use everything to your advantage; let nothing be wasted on you. All conscious change begins with awareness and assessment. Self-doubt, the bane of many an artist, is also a useful yardstick for measuring truth against rationalization—the endless onionskin of excuses. Are you on your life's mission (dharma), or is it an aimless joyride?

Trying to bluff your own self is self-sabotage that is ultimately harmful. Remember, while you might be deluded by your ego, you can't lie to your own self.

Psychotherapist Eric Maisel, in his book, *A Life in the Arts*, points out that artists without clearly defined answers to fundamental issues about their work are likely to flounder. The key here is fundamental, which is the indivisible and underlying bedrock each artist must mine for answers about himself. Although we are all different with diverse experiences, there are certain fundamental things we need. It isn't that we want them. We need them. These are the basic things like food, shelter, water, and so on—which psychologist Abraham Maslow studied in his work on the hierarchy of needs. Instead of focusing on pathology, Maslow, a founding member of Humanistic Psychology, felt it was far more illuminating to scientifically study, explain, and understand the behavior and values of healthy individuals who possessed a natural ability to persevere.

As far as the artist is concerned, his needs go beyond living a life according to a template; he must carve out a unique life for himself in this world. There are fundamental questions each artist must answer if he is to prevail where it counts. These questions and the answers to them are no less essential than the need for water and food—for the artist doesn't live by bread alone. If life were relegated to merely staying alive, there would be no transcendence, no heroes. These fundamental questions are the core questions. When you can answer each one truthfully, your awareness expands; it doesn't contract. Less is more. This should not be misunderstood.

Many years ago, a master artist asked me: "Why do you want to be an artist?" This is, of course, *the* question; in time, I added the other two.

- Why am I an artist?
- Where does my art come from?
- What is the intrinsic value of my art?

The presumption made throughout this book is that before you present your work to an audience, you have answered each core question to your own satisfaction. Your answers are private; you don't need to inform anyone else, unless you have a reason, for them to have the desired impact.

Everything that matters emanates from your responses, which determine your self-inspiration, discernment, and relationship to your work. If your replies are truthful, focused, passionate, self-sufficient, and integrated, then you express a secure and resolute foundation that supports the strategy for routing rejection. Indomitability of spirit is the unconscious message you project with your art into the world. Answers that are fragmented, glib, self-effacing, or unconvincing reveal an underlying weakness that is best addressed before stretching your artistic neck onto the public block that is home to the sharp tongues of opinion.

There is no shortage of willing executioners.

REVELATION AND DESIRE

Not to know why you are an artist bores an ever-expanding and debilitating hole in the whole story.

To know why you are an artist *is* the blessing.

And, while you are being introspective, you may also want to ask yourself: 'Who validates my art?' Do you rely on outside authority to confirm that

God gives you life; you give meaning to your life.

BAUDELAIRE

Machination:

If you went to the art mecca of New York City to make your mark as an artist, you would find, in time, that many would offer you advice on how to proceed, or that it was impossible to succeed in this market.

Do not take anyone's word as gospel—because, in truth, the path toward recognition is always unique and unknown. Otherwise, everyone would already know the route, and that wouldn't be so bad.

EDEN

To have that edge when you're on it is one thing; to keep that edge when things are outwardly working in smooth transition is quite another.

EDEN

your work is art? Are you certain in your soul that you are making art and not a bogus approximation that may still be revealed for what it is? While you might have persuaded some to believe in your art, acquire your art, and to even champion your art, are you for real, or have you succumbed to breaking the first rule: don't believe your own bullshit.

How tenuous is your dedication to your art? Knowing this has great liberating power.

Would you make your art if there were no one else to appreciate it? Would you perform if there were only an audience of one? Do you aspire to be a celebrity or a creator? Which is it—the lure of stardom or the fulfillment of dharma, which doesn't preclude fame?

Can someone talk you out of your destiny, or not? Of course, there is only one person who can pull the plug on fulfilling your dharma, and you are already quite familiar with this individual.

Remember, if you want depth, you must dig deep.

Note: non-artists reading this book aren't left out; simply substitute your 'work' for 'art', and what it is that you make, sell, or contribute—and then take it from there.

Time for art:

You may hear from somewhere that it's important to have a life outside your art as a balance. Let's dig deeper: it's life inside your art regardless of what you are doing; it's all your art no matter what you are doing in the moment: cooking, walking your doggie, reading, marketing your work, and everything else. If you start segregating your art from life, you will fall into trouble, and frustration. That's when you begin to feel guilty that you may not be spending enough time with your art, and that's a misstep.

If you're doing your art all the time, then that's the harmony and balance you are looking for.

CHAPTER ELEVEN

LORD OF ILLUSION
A Humility Primer

SOME YEARS back, I was in an art gallery nestled in a charming garden-like courtyard situated off a fashionable avenue in San Francisco. The gallery had a large glass front window with a view of who was coming and going. My artist friend had recently opened the gallery to showcase his paintings. There were no regular hours as it was by appointment only. He was a superb creator, and his work was no less original than Picasso's art. He was articulate with his brush, writing, and the spoken word. He also had a short fuse. Although never the aggressor, he was an unstoppable and lethal counter puncher.

As the artist and I were talking, a man and a woman entered the gallery. My artist friend smiled and his eyes gleamed with perhaps an acquisition twinkle from an unscheduled walk-in patron. By their dress, fattened rosy cheeks, and the prerequisite camera hanging from the man's neck, it was clear the couple were out of towners who had come to see the sites of the City by the Bay. One thing I had learned is not to prejudge. I have seen the most unlikely people acquire fine art. And you never know who will love your work.

The couple walked up to the artist. The man spoke up, saying: "Maybe you could help us out?"

The artist nodded, yes.

"We wanted to know if you knew where we could buy some art," said the man, rubbing his beer belly. His wife looked on eagerly for the response.

In my mind's eye, I saw blood on the walls and what was left of a camera shattered on the floor. This unfortunate yokel had come to the wrong place. I felt that the artist would explode into a rage that would blow them back to Kansas, or wherever they hailed from. There the couple stood, surrounded by magnificent art, and oblivious to the masterworks on the walls. I waited for the detonation as the seconds ticked off.

Silence.

I watched the artist. His face transformed from a blank stare to a pleasant countenance, as if he had run into a long lost old friend. He put his arm around the man and began moving him and his wife toward the

When I am working on a problem I never think about beauty. I only think about how to solve the problem. But when I have finished, if the solution is not beautiful, I know it is wrong.

R. BUCKMINSTER FULLER

If your art isn't speaking to you, then you can pretty much finish this sentence by yourself.

EDEN

door, saying: "You people need to go down there. See?" He pointed in a direction. "You make a left at that street and follow it all the way down to the wharf, the tourist area, and you'll find your art there. Maybe even some paintings on velvet."

"Why thank you, sir," said the man.

The couple left the gallery with great enthusiasm, as if they had learned some great secret. When the couple turned back to look at the gallery, the artist stood at the door smiling and waved them off.

I don't think I had been breathing the entire time of that encounter. My body suddenly took in a deep breath. The artist came back to the rear of the gallery, looked at me, and simply shrugged. His behavior with the couple had taken me by surprise, but that is when you learn the most provocative lessons.

Did I ever get the message, I thought to myself. I knew then that I would remember this lesson forever. If this master artist could display such disarming self-control, humility, and humor in the face of overt ignorance, then I, too, would adopt this standard as my own—which I did.

This was humility borne out of great strength and character, not meekness, which was the smart approach. You don't have to be famous to test your humility—which I learned then, is the artist's ally.

LORD OF ILLUSION

My artist mentor friend in San Francisco had shown me that conscious humility was the way to balance when confronted by extremes. Knowing the way and walking that tightrope of negative tautness daily was another matter entirely. Negative and positive were also, in a sense, 'out of towners' taking up residence where they could with whomever would have them.

Negative is the polar opposite of positive. One can't exist without the other; they are codependent in a world of extremes, of duality, which also represents our three-dimensional universe—right and left, up and down, back and forth. To integrate ourselves with the one consciousness and rid ourselves of many temporal ills, Buddha instructed that we release our attachment to duality: you and I, pain and pleasure.

As the legend goes: Gautama Buddha gave his first sermon in the Deer Park near Benares in northern India. There, he spoke of The Fourth Noble Truth, which is the Middle Path between extremes that leads to the cessation of suffering. Buddha taught that this path produces insight and knowledge and leads to peace, wisdom, enlightenment, and Nirvana.

The Enlightened One explained that the two extremes of vulgar pleasure (debauchery) and denying the needs of the body for spiritual attainment (self-mortification) are not to be practiced by one who is enlightened. This path of moderation shouldn't be misconstrued as a synonym for indifference, mediocrity, or a quick fix for manic depression. Keep in mind that Siddhartha, the one who would become the Buddha, had lived a life of extremes: he was born a prince who renounced a life of privilege to become a Samana, a wandering ascetic.

Gautama, according to tradition, came to the Middle Path after being confronted by Mara, a personification of death, delusion, and temptation. While Siddhartha sat under the sacred Bodhi tree of awakening, Mara assaulted him with doubts and temptations such as hunger, sensuality, fear, and sloth to dissuade him from pursuing the path toward enlightenment.

But all temptations failed and the Buddha attained Nirvana. The Lord of Illusion couldn't seduce Gautama from his mission to see reality as it is. This parable is a favorite among Buddhist artists and teachers as it illustrates the pillars of character and spiritual striving: discernment, truth, renunciation, and calm.

Resolve or great art can't exist without tests of character.

How then can we apply the Middle Path specifically to strength of character? If one of these extremes would be the absence of character, a lowlife, then the opposite would be as gratuitous, an attitude corrupted by self-righteousness, as in holier than thou. Remember, character is the prerequisite vessel for holding The Eighteen Be-Attitudes and the hallmark of an empowered artist.

Far from fence sitting, this path, this noble truth, demands vigilant discretion in questioning the mainstream through self-discipline—which is the one true freedom each of us can attain. To find that path—that rhythm of yin and yang between negative and positive—is the sweet chord of harmony, and of art.

To be a slave to any extreme demeans the individual into delusion, which is precisely what it sounds like. Test this observation.

NO PASSING FANCY

You may have read or heard how essential it is to avoid negative thinking people and circumstances. Even if you have given the destructive power of negativity some thought, it is worth mentioning the value of deflecting negativity again, over and over. Negativity in biology is entropic, representing disorder and a wasting away.

If not dealt with, negativity saps your life force and your energy to create, and it will eventually destroy you. Negativity is disagreeable, nasty, and resists evolution. This is not new age hysteria; it is reality. Negativity is no less harmful than a deadly pathogenic virus. Negativity is always sniffing at the door; it can lie dormant waiting patiently for a moment of weakness, an opening, so it can enter and infect the host.

To succeed as an artist in the public arena, confronting negativity is all encompassing, and that includes the trials engendered by rejection. Negativity is not necessarily blatant. It is much easier to confront the overt. It is the insidious form of negativity that can bring down anyone who takes any thing for granted.

MOLEHILLS NOT MOUNTAINS

Rejection of your work is not inherently negative. The art dealer or panel of jurists, for example, may have bad taste, no taste, dislike your work, or they simply don't recognize a unique talent, which is not yet a cardinal sin—or, as Tevya of *Fiddler on the Roof* might put it, 'no great honor either'.

You want an immediate and visceral reaction based on feeling, not intellectualizing: I love your work; wow; yuck; awesome; awful; I don't get it, or even I hate it. *Interesting* as a reaction will not do as it is fence sitting, cerebral meandering, and of no consequence.

Like all dreamers I confuse disenchantment with truth.

JEAN-PAUL SARTRE

If you've never heard 'no,' then 'yes' has no meaning.

EDEN

An artist is valued for his personal interpretive insight and not for his conformity to traditional patterns.

So it is always an indication of uncertain knowledge if, when judging a work of art, one compares the work of one artist with that of another.

Quality is quality wherever found. The artist must follow his inner urge, independent of fads and fashions.

HANS HOFMANN

You can most certainly detect condescension or a rejection armed with a nasty cutting edge in all its overtness. You know when someone is verbally skewering you, don't you?

Negativity can be imperceptibly subtle, inconspicuous, and can come from anyone, including family, friends, other artists, and worst of all—your own self. You already know this: you are your best ally, or worst enemy. As an artist on a mission, you must be vigilant. No negative thing is too small to overlook. Keep your eye on the horizon, knowing that folk stumble, trip, and fall over molehills, not mountains.

ON THE FLY

Thoughts are like sub-atomic particles. No one has seen these particles; they are too small for any device to make them visible. We only have evidence of them from the trails they leave behind in particle accelerators. We see this 'evidence' of their existence because we are looking for them. Thoughts are of the same phenomenon. A thought, like the invisible theoretically proven sub-atomic particle, exists only if you give it your attention, and in so doing, bring it into reality. You are your attention.

Thoughts can pass through any object. Thoughts of all kinds are this instant whizzing here, there, and everywhere. A great thought can fly across a crowded room completely unnoticed. But when someone becomes aware of it, then that thought blinks into existence because someone—the receiver—is expressing it. Thoughts in themselves can do no harm or good without a corporeal outlet; even wise men have bad days.

As you are an organic conduit, being aware of your thoughts gives you the power to control the positive and negative ebb and flow through you. An over exposure of negative thoughts will eventually harm living matter.

Remember, you are harboring the thought; the thought has no power if you aren't a coconspirator. You are the fulcrum that permits the positive and negative to swing in balance, or not. The beauty behind the design, which is constantly at work whether you know it or not, is that it is entirely up to you. As the pivot point, you are the constant within a system, while circumstances remain the variable.

This information is power for the artist to persevere in a fickle world where chance of the draw is also a player. Luck favors a prepared soul. Luck can be made as it a function of intuition.

THE JAR LID

One day, I watched a friend trying to unscrew a stubborn lid from a glass jar, and couldn't, no matter how hard he tried. Finally, out of frustration, he said: "The lid is on way too tight and I don't want to break the glass."

I noticed that he had been choking the lid. I motioned for him to give me the jar. I grabbed the lid, squeezed until I had a firm grasp, not a death grip, and then turned until it began to unscrew. My friend, who was physically stronger than I, looked at the opened jar, then shrugged. I saw more than a stuck lid. I saw someone who had defeated himself with his own strength. Instead of applying a vise-like pressure, which kept the lid from turning, to overcome resistance, he needed to apply finesse. Valuable lessons can be found everywhere, and most often in the most mundane of tasks; you need only be aware of them. Not too hard, and not too soft gets the job done. As noted, Buddha observed this universal truth, which he called the Middle Path between extremes, some 2,500 years ago.

SMOKE AND MIRRORS

The best defense is still a smart offense. As in Aikido, get out of harm's way by letting the 'enemy' use his own energy to defeat himself. If not, you will spend your invaluable currency of time battling the density of the world, and you won't win playing against the house.

There is no need to become paranoid, either. Awareness will handle it all for you. As the proverb goes: keep your friends close, but your enemies closer. Of course, this doesn't mean that you see enemies everywhere who are out to get you. It does mean for you to be aware of illusion.

Due diligence and scrubbing negative residue off the brain are good housekeeping habits for keeping your vessel pure. The point is this: while you can't control negativity in the world, you can let it pass through you so it does you no harm. In this manner, you acknowledge the negative without giving it dominion over you. This is the smart thing to do. I didn't say easy.

There are times, however, when direct confrontation is necessary, and you must stand your ground. This is always the moment of truth for you as an artist and a human being. Can you overcome the demons of fear, anger, and hatred is the issue? Can you? One way to overcome inertia or fear, for example, is to make an unalterable decision, and mean it. The instant you make the decision, you can feel the palpable release. The universe then begins to accommodate you.

Yes, *the universe will help you*. You might have seen this declaration plastered in all sorts of new age media. In practical terms, you may well ask, 'what does this mean?' Who or what is the universe and why should it help me? Keep it simple. A true friend will help. When you acknowledge that there are forces at work beyond what your physical senses can detect, you are opening a door to a universe of all possibilities.

When you are resolute, in dharma, and make a choice, you become aware of opportunities that will support your effort. This is the 'law of attraction' at work. The creator force of the universe, God, is on your side.

Of course, you must do the work and become alert to these opportunities as they arise. Embrace your intuition and release preconceived notions.

Do this and you will persevere in the most astonishing way, one that you could not have planned or predicted. It is a miracle.

THE KARMIC BULLET

Dressed in well-worn robes, the master and his student were walking along a dirt road one late afternoon toward the next village; they were on a pilgrimage of enlightenment. They decided to stop and rest for a while in the shade of a huge sacred fig tree.

The student, who had a somber disposition, was deeply troubled by all the pain and suffering he had witnessed in every village and city they had visited over the past years. Finally, he asked his teacher: "Master, how do you explain this world?"

Law of Attraction: We are attracted to what gives us life, acceptance, and energy, in the same way the leaves of a green plant reach upward to face the sunlight that gives it nourishment.

If we turn away from the light, we falter in the darkness of our weakness and stumble about misguided by our egos.

EDEN

Often enough painted in poverty, it [art] has come to symbolize wealth.

JANET FLANNER

Without hesitation, the master replied: "What do you expect from so much karmic residue?"

For many moments, the student felt stunned, disappointed, and thought: 'Why such a callous answer?'

As they continued their journey in silence, the student suddenly realized the beauty of the master's insight, and in that instant his face lit up knowing he would start doing his part. To clean up the residue, he would begin with making someone laugh in the next village.

As the pair resumed their journey, the master said: "You are in good spirits. Ask me any question."

"Master," said the student, now backpedaling in front of his teacher, "please tell me a tale."

"I'll tell you one that my teacher told me many ages ago. It goes like this: Disciples are always asking about truth and proof. One truth is time, and in time we have another truth known as the sun to us and a star to others; as this star brings life, it too is alive—life in karma is only another form of 'being' in the here and now."

The student listened, and realized that his upbeat demeanor had brought him the gift of the master's tale of great understanding.

Here, the open-minded disciple intuitively grasped the Zen moment: no one gets to dodge the karmic bullet. Remember, it is you who must change, not the world. For courage to matter, you must muster it up across the board, not only about your art form—for that would be disingenuous. You are either in or out; there is no safe house.

The Buddha understood that the real enemy of man is ignorance.

His last words were: "All composite things pass away. Strive for your own salvation with diligence."

There is no fence sitting when it comes to character.

A CUP RUNNETH OVER

Nan-in, a Japanese master during the Meiji era (1868-1912), received a university professor who came to inquire about Zen.

To welcome his guest and set the stage, Nan-in served tea. He poured his visitor's cup full, and then kept on pouring.

The professor watched the overflow until he no longer could restrain himself. "It is overfull. No more will go in!"

"Like this cup," Nan-in said, "you are full of your own opinions and speculations. How can I show you Zen unless you first empty your cup?"

From this teaching of Zen, we can appreciate that unique art is the product of an empty cup or mind. If we extend this metaphor further, we also come to understand that a smart and organic solution to a problem flows from a mind uncluttered by preconceived notions; insight means that no preceding thought led up to the realization at hand. Grasp this perception now, break free from linear thinking, and the cornucopia of art will reveal itself.

CHAPTER TWELVE

THE EIGHTEEN BE-ATTITUDES
Indelible Markers of Character

WITHOUT THE PROPER attitude, you will never get off the ground, let alone fly. This is as true for a kite, airplane, sailplane, jet, and the space shuttle as it is for you.

It is step by step that we evolve, and I have been using this ever-evolving model of self-empowerment successfully for years. I didn't create these qualities, these Be-Attitudes; I discovered them as a direct result of experience—becoming more aware of my own self. Each quality is an integrated gear of a dynamic perpetual self-sufficient and self-maintaining gyroscope that will keep you on course and afloat during the worst of storms. Should one concept seem in contradiction with another, it isn't. You are an active participant on this voyage. You must do your part. You must apply discretion and balance to each situation as it occurs.

As a seasoned poker player will tell you: know when to hold 'em and when to fold 'em.

If you don't posses a natural immunity to a disabling disorder, then the remedy resides in building up resistance under controlled exposure—an inoculation. Consequently, the most direct way to get around rejection is to go through it with a positive mindset along the way.

Let's be clear, thinking positive thoughts is admirable, but it is a temporary bandage at best if you are secretly harboring doubt and fear in lieu of awareness. What is the point of polishing an apple that is rotting from the inside out?

TIMING

There is a helpful and important distinction to be made here about getting the most out of a positive mindset. It's not 'thinking' positive; it's 'being' positive. One is externally segregated in the head while the latter is a healing emotion, soundly internal and holistic. To understand what this means, you will have to dig deep and feel the truth of it for your own self.

Fear and passion are our two most powerful emotions. Fear is endemic to the adventuring world because it contributes to our survival. Indeed fear and our learned coping mechanisms are important regardless of our vocation. Passion contributes to our forward motion.

When we're feeling at our worst, when we see no clear path ahead, when we are fearful, our passion reminds us of why we persist. With a healthy recognition of our fears and passions the roads less traveled lead to the roads of richest reward.

ERIC PHILIPS,
EXPLORER

See me, feel me, touch me, heal me.
See me, feel me, touch me, heal me.
See me, feel me, touch me, heal me.
See me, feel me, touch me, heal me,
heal me, heal me.

TOMMY, THE WHO

If you don't understand now, then maybe one day you will. After all, does a person of character, civility, thoughtfulness, and of good nature think he is so, or is he being so? You get the picture.

You are human. If you got a 'no' about your art, feel free to be disappointed, but for no more than five minutes, then move *on*—which is 'no' transposed and poetic at that. Honestly dealt with, adopting these attributes will, over time, replace rejection with resiliency, allowing you to move forward until your talent connects with the right opportunity—also called timing.

INTIMATE DETAILS

Wrap your comprehension around the word fundamental, as these indivisible qualities are the bedrock of a healthy creator. The Be-Attitudes are magical ingredients. The artist blends them in his crucible to concoct a spiritually harmonious life in the here and now. Let posterity work out the details.

The Be-Attitudes define the shape of your character because character is the vessel that contains them. Remember the adage from the master: character answers all questions. It is as straightforward as that.

Make a commitment to know these attributes from personal experience by utilizing them, not memorizing them. Remember, rote will get you naught in this realm. If you have been chasing after divine fire to merely roast marshmallows, then it would have been simpler to light a match. Knowing these Be-Attitudes intimately is the only way they will work for you.

And true intimacy doesn't happen overnight. But, you might say, how can I find these attributes?

Be patient. There is no requirement to comprehend everything all at once. You don't have to seek out these Be-Attitudes; they will come to you naturally. Over time, you will see that the potential power of each quality enters your life in a direct response to a complementary situation, as a test—an opportunity to show your mettle.

If you are dedicated, strong, and don't give in to fear, each trusted attribute will join to support you on your mission.

THE EIGHTEEN BE-ATTITUDES

As these Be-Attitudes indelibly form your character, you will sense that you will prevail. Say it out loud: 'I will prevail!' If you don't feel it and say it, who will? Remember, fortune favors the brave artist.

1. **aware**: Awareness is intuitive perception without thinking. Pure awareness is the protective mother; she includes everything and comes before all else. Sentience of the self is often the last thing learned before you can nudge open the door to self-realization.

    You have personal knowledge of the mother spirit that protects the universe, also known as pure awareness. What is pure awareness? While you don't need to be an ascended master to dip your toe in the ocean of awareness, you do need to appreciate that life is enriched by transcendent experiences. Without spirit life is sterile. Awareness is the all seeing eye of the Creator, and who better to be in contact with than the Artist and Patron of all there is, or will ever be. You have learned that you can't proceed toward awareness without confronting and mastering the first rule: don't believe your own bullshit. The second rule is that no thing is obvious; and the third is that no thing goes without saying. You are aware because you can discern between what is pertinent from what is irrelevant. If you can't, then how can you create art?

Note: For those who claim to have never experienced the power of creation or the Creator, it is time to take your pulse now before it is too late.

2 **dedicated**: You don't give up on your self. You are capable of wonder. You know where your art stands in the universe. You say nay to the naysayers. You know that while talent is the gift, genius is dedication.

3 **grace**: You feel blessed for all your gifts. You are in contact with the Great Creator through your intuition. You feel gratitude, not necessarily about any single thing, but for the state of gratitude itself. You focus on what you have, not on what you don't—that is a fool's errand. You have the world by the oysters because you have cast out the irritants called greed, envy, and doubt. Only the pearl of goodwill remains.

4 **independent**: You think and feel for your own self. You don't relinquish your perception or power to experts. You don't rely on reviews, critics, and other secondhand sources to make up your mind for you. Of course, when you see a sign on a bottle of lye that reads 'Poison, do not drink', you accept the warning without having to taste it for yourself. Independence without discernment is a flaw.

Committed to firsthand experience, you decide the merit of things on your own. Despite the unrelenting gravity that society exerts to control the rigid flow of the mainstream, you know redemption and conformity for the artist don't mix.

5 **fair witness**: You are accountable. You can see the forest for the trees. In the instant you realize it, you confront and admit your mistakes and weaknesses and then move on, knowing that you are evolving. As a creator, your own self isn't diminished by error events, which you transform into life lessons, strength and compassion.

If you see it, then you own it. You are God's eyes in this incarnation.

6 **confident**: You know who you are and where you stand. Confidence can't be bequeathed. You must earn it. Although sense of self takes time to grow and to flower, you have always known you had a purpose in life beyond the mundane. You are confident because you have a vision of value. Remember, 'you are on sacred ground when you know where you stand.'

Unconscious. Conscious. Consciousness.

For our purposes, let's define our terms: The wellspring of art flows from the unconscious in the Jungian sense; conscious is an awareness of the soul self; and consciousness itself is the source of all that is, or will ever be.

Given this understanding, we see that the prize of temporal existence is higher awareness; consciousness is already divine and requires no improvement on our part.

EDEN

When Harry Cohn, the notorious—and much despised—head of Columbia Pictures died in 1958, Hollywood crowds at his funeral prompted this famous response: 'It just goes to show you … if you give the people what they want, they'll come out.'

RED SKELTON

Let's take this concept further. If you give people what you think they want, and you're right, then you have an excellent chance for financial success. But, when you present people with original work, then it's another matter entirely. There is a price to pay for standing out from the crowd.

EDEN

7 **discerning**: You know opinions are six billion strong and growing. Everyone has them. You don't rule out tradition, but you ultimately rely on your own cognition to know the value of things. You have learned that negative judgments are as lethal as the assassins responsible for the hardening of the arteries. You concentrate on distinctions, not the artificial, not the competitive crazy making of good, better, and best. You know that comparisons in art are a trap. After all, there is no way or need to compare the unique. Knowing this distinction has great liberating power.

The views that intrigue and influence you come only from those whom you respect—and it is essential that you know why you hold such people in esteem, otherwise, you are merely a fan.

8 **discretion**: You own your actions with no need to check with external influences, or opinions. Because you have come to trust your intuition, you have developed insight and sound judgment. You aren't perfect, but that isn't your claim or intention. You are aware and you do things on purpose. You are deliberate, mindful, and passionate. You are discreet. Because you can do something doesn't mean you do it. You have taken control of your own self, and while this isn't easy, it is the path to freedom as an artist.

9 **authentic**: You have discarded manipulative motives; there are no hidden agendas up your sleeve. Since you can be trusted, so too can your art as the pure manifestation of the Creator and her power. Your art is original, a unique representation of your authenticity. You use your own words, brushstrokes, and actions. You have learned that simple isn't quite so simple. To speak in your own voice and to be your own self takes a master—and that is a truth.

10 **gracious**: You accept consequences without getting derailed, most especially when things don't seem to go your way. You have removed the barbs and stings from your repertoire because you are a lady, or a gentleman. You know it takes time to reassess.

You don't deride those who don't appreciate your art. You know that the more personal the art, the more challenging it is to find an audience. This is the ambitious price you pay for creating original work.

You don't give up on your art because generosity of spirit also means being good to yourself.

Despite adversity, you will always make a next time, you will always find a way to create and sustain yourself.

11 **self-esteem**: You know who you are because you have arrived at this point in the journey as the result of self-discipline. You appreciate the dignity of living an authentic life based on firsthand experience. Your sense of identity is the direct result of having discarded the trappings

and weaknesses of conformity. Your worth, tempered by many tests, emanates from an inner value immune to the whims of any outside authority. You triumph whether your work has been rejected or accepted, knowing that this polarity of experience can't derail the true creator from his mission.

12 **spontaneous**: You are in the present moment, and you behave without over thinking, or second-guessing your self. When you feel compelled, you act in harmony with the situation. You don't say or do the same thing twice in precisely the same manner. You improvise. You create with whatever you have. You don't have a laundry list of prerequisites before painting or taking action. You have learned that the true artist has no medium. You know that you can't plan or rehearse creation, which arises from spontaneity, not the size of a studio space, the availability of only certain materials, meetings, consensus, the right light, or other self-limiting preconditions for working.

13 **integrated:** You grasp that integrity is the galvanizing force that holds the elements of your character together. You are a fully realized human because you have discovered the purpose, and consequently the meaning of your life—and it is from meaning that you learn how to live. United as a whole individual, it is your earned integrity that gives you the inner strength of metal forged and tempered in the furnace of creation.

Without the quality of integration, you are fragmented, disjointed, disconnected, and incomplete. Even awareness, to be effective and useful, relies on the integrity of universal laws or truths. You have infused the Be-Attitudes into the fibers of your life to the point where they are indistinguishable from yourself. You weave all that is positive into a magic carpet that transports your self-awareness to the realm of consciousness, the source of courage and great art. You aren't a part-time artist because there is no such thing. While there is nothing inherently wrong with being a dabbler, it is as far from being a true artist as Earth is from the far edge of the known universe.

You have made a defining decision, and it is this: each thing you do is your art. Through the power of integration, you have liberated yourself from compartmentalizing your talent and your life. You invest the family farm in your character, knowing no thief can ever rob you of what matters most. Your strength of soul communicates through your art and its unquestionable reflection of a creator's force. You know, despite all the Be-Attitudes one must harness, you are dealing with aspects of the same guiding force. The pieces have come together and the puzzle is now complete. You are your art to this extent: the art reflects how well and how truthfully you have integrated everything.

14 **self-reliant:** You are resourceful. You find a way, not an excuse, a response that separates doers from wannabes. You turn less into more. You are sure because being unsure inspires no one. You are the man or woman; and you are a creator who makes things happen because you

The best and most beautiful things in the world cannot be seen or even touched. They must be felt with the heart.

HELEN KELLER

Frame the question correctly and you will get the right answer.

It's never should I trust my intuition over reason, logic, or practical considerations. Since intuition is infallible and thinking is not, you have your answer.

The question then becomes do you have the courage to live by your intuition. Remember, many are called; few choose to go.

EDEN

are in control of your own self in a world of circumstances and ambiguity. When confronted by adversity, you are reminded to see that the problem is the lesson, which is that you can do what is necessary yourself. You understand that self-discipline, which is true freedom and the crown jewel of freewill, is ultimately acquired on your own.

15 **self-inspired:** You could be self-motivated, but that would imply that the fire goes out from time to time. You are in love and that implies an eternal flame of purpose and inspiration, a divine fire that burns brightly from within. Although self-induced motivational talks once served the cause, you no longer require them. Now that you have moved your self to a perpetual state of inspiration, you appreciate that despite all the wonder inspiration can bestow, you aren't a pawn or dalliance for a fickle muse.

Waiting for inspiration is a romantic notion, a truly dramatic artifice, and not how a body of work is created. While inspiration may ignite the passion, you are still left to fuel and keep the desire alive through dedication. You paint shape and form or dance the whirlwind in the fury of uncertainly when others have already forgotten the dream.

You create with inspiration that flows from your core with every breath. No longer do you wait for external motivations to get you going. An artist doesn't rely on any single thing as a condition to create. That wouldn't be smart. You don't need a pep talk to work because that fire in the belly is a steady reminder of your mission. You live by your wits, on the frontier beyond social conditioning, something every artist must do. You are unconventional by necessity, not out of any strategy or spin designed to impress—this implies personality, which is one of many false masks or veneers, not the authentic self that is your art.

16 **will to prevail**: You continue in the compass direction of your soul despite setbacks or even victories. You don't identify with failure. No one, most especially yourself, can talk you out of your passion, and you don't look back.

The past is dead, the present moment shines, and the future beckons with marvels waiting to born through your art form. Some might call you stubborn, but that isn't an insult.

It is clear to you now that to be stubborn on purpose for a conscious cause is simply another way of describing the will to prevail despite the 'common' wisdom, which is rarely common, or indeed wise. When you reach for the stars, they become that much closer.

17 **dignity:** You respect others in equal measure—busboy or museum director or patron. In turn, you earn and expect the same. You treat all with consideration despite their station in society, or whether they can do something for you or not. As a true artist, you are a common man, and while that is no easy task, this insight liberates you from

---

Always ask if you want something and give when you are asked. That makes life easier for everybody.

ANTOON SAUVÉ,
FARMER'S KNIGHT

Soul and purpose:

When you have found your purpose, you have found your soul, as they are one in the same.

This is also called balancing the equation—from this point you can evolve.

EDEN

ego-based constructs: the false debilitating masks of personality. You have one authentic face that reveals your true self in all your activities. This is liberty.

18 **humor**: You have a keen sense of it; more important, you are capable of laughing at your own self and at your own expense, which is the cost of doing business in a healthy environment.

THE BLUEPRINT

Now, that you have had the opportunity to familiarize yourself with these attributes and the qualities you must adopt, it is worth repeating that this approach to routing rejection and its minions is organic. You can't apply these Be-Attitudes like makeup; they must radiate from inside of you.

Initially, you may succeed with some attributes and less so with others. When you are called to make the hard choices, to stand your ground, you will choose the honorable path because the alternative is dreadful: a life of superficiality and mindless conformity. At the very least, you will know where you have slipped up and why because you now have in your hands the DNA of a creator, a transcendental genetic blueprint for success that dispels any notion of being a victim. Let's be clear: awareness isn't a form of idealism; it is pragmatic. Awareness allows you to see your faults. How else can you fix them?

Why eighteen? I wrote down these attributes in one sitting without thinking about how many and the quantity coincided with Hebrew numerology where the number eighteen stands for life—and 'life' as an artist is what this book is all about. If you were to add other attributes to this list, you would soon realize that they are all aspects of the same thing. Or, as my mother often observes: the same bride in a different wedding gown.

ALCHEMY AND ALL

These are The Eighteen Be-Attitudes and the miracle is this: they come into existence only when you acknowledge them. These forces of character and creation are here to serve you with honor. This knowledge has great liberating power.

As an artist, a creator in the midst, it is my mission to elevate my character whenever I am confronted by a new and higher standard despite its source. Is this not your mission, too?

Not being an 'official' Buddhist living in a monastic tradition, for example, doesn't prevent me from being a lay appreciator who advocates the universal beauty of this philosophy.

In the spirit of the Awakened One and to see how far you have come, don't forget the classic Buddhist teachings of loving kindness, compassion, joy in the attainment of others, and equanimity. This implies that you are a gentleman or gentlewoman, not a doormat.

The truth comes in two varieties, the source and everything else.

Bravo!

I don't know of any innovation in art that was generated by a grant or a fellowship.

I'm not referring to ideas or concepts; I am talking about innovation.

EDEN

CHAPTER THIRTEEN

THE UNDERSTUDY ISSUE
Getting the Part

THE MASTER from India said: "There *is* no problem." And from his declaration, we conclude that the preponderance of our problems is of our own manufacture.

Resolving difficulties intuitively and, at the very least, thoughtfully permanently elevates our awareness, giving each of us more self-control over the quality of our lives.

> "I'll have these players
> Play something like the murder of my father
> Before mine uncle: I'll observe his looks;
> I'll tent him to the quick: if he but blench,
> I know my course. The spirit that I have seen
> May be the devil: and the devil hath power
> To assume a pleasing shape: yea, and perhaps
> Out of my weakness and my melancholy,
> As he is very potent with such spirits,
> Abuses me to damn me: I'll have grounds
> More relative than this: the play's the thing
> Wherein I'll catch the conscience of the king."
>
> —*Hamlet, act ii, scene ii*, by William Shakespeare

Still, no one is exempt from resolving complications of varying magnitudes that shamelessly seek to upstage us. This means, although your ego would say otherwise, you aren't the only artist who must confront issues in his life, and work.

Some problems loom larger than the rest to command a leading role at any given moment.

Sure, the problem is real, but to what degree of importance is it in the grand scheme of things? To punctuate what the master said, the problem is mostly you.

And you are the main character, aren't you?

> *I don't measure a man's success by how high he climbs but how high he bounces when he hits bottom.*
>
> **GENERAL GEORGE S. PATTON**

Even faith based on a miracle can falter; be alert, witness any fearful thought for what it represents—the ego breaking through to expose weakness.

Immediately address yourself to the truth of your lapse, reaffirm your faith and mission, and create.

EDEN

CENTER STAGE

If, for example, one of your artworks wasn't chosen as a winner in a competition that would have landed a body of your work in a prestigious museum exhibit, then you may well feel the weight of yet another rejection and opportunity for recognition lost. Then, when you do see the artworks that did win the competition, you are further devastated. Not that the winning artists were awful, but your work was brilliant. Is there no justice?

The disappointing museum incident now takes center stage, consuming your thoughts and feelings, playing out its role in endless and pointless 'what if' scenario loops that your inner monologist and critic so generously provides. You can't shake that judge inside your head who vociferously and unrelentingly voices disapproval over your 'failure', once again. You feel possessed by evil spirits. Fortunately, a few days later the inner critic begins to subside. You are beginning to get through the fog of the museum let down, and you are ready to move on when you suddenly trip while getting out of the shower and black out.

You wake up in the hospital. Looming over you is the doctor who spells it out: you broke your neck in the fall and you may never regain sight in your right eye or walk again—cast down in your prime. Is there no justice?

THUD. A NIGHTMARE.

Like an anxious understudy, this dreadful news leaps upward, primed from inception to be a star problem that mercilessly upstages the previous issue as the leading antagonist in your drama. The contrast of severity between these two problems is so extreme that the museum exhibit debacle, which was of Greek tragedy proportions a few days ago, now fades into the shadows of insignificance from whence it came. Our problems adhere to a pecking order based on the rank that we assign to them. Don't forget it.

And so it goes. Problems will forever be waiting in the wings, eager to take center stage with you. Solve or release one problem and another invariably leaps forward to take its place. It is the Myth of Sisyphus all over again. You can't beat the odds if you play the problem game because, in the end, the negative house always wins. If you insist on playing against the house, the torrent of problems will eventually overwhelm you and wear down your passion to create. The pertinent question is this: How will you respond to the never-ending parade of problematic understudies disguised as rejection? While every artist may well have what it takes, not every artist will take his own standard into fray.

WE'LL CALL YOU

When you accept that rejection is merely a force that demands constant feeding to survive, you will take a stand: you won't give these problems speaking parts in your play, an action that now promotes you to producer as well. You won't become demoralized or brought to the brink of suicide by *your* problems because instead of being metaphysically myopic, you move back for a perspective of the larger picture. You won't venture down that angst-ridden road toward perdition. As the main character in your life's play, you will remain focused among the distractions, harmonious amid uncertainty, and ready to take on all comers, which represent but a gaggle of issues when you can see with both eyes, breathe unattended, and walk under your own power. Remember, to get the part, each problem must audition for you. Now that you are wise to what gives the problem its power, you conclude with: 'We'll call you.'

You can't fight with problems or make believe they don't exist. Denial will also get you into deep red pastel doggy do. Handle each confrontation as it occurs with courage knowing the wings are filled with understudies who will defeat you if you give them the part, the authority—your indecision and weakness will do it. This knowledge has great liberating power.

AN EXISTENTIAL DANISH

Like Prince Hamlet, know your course and that conscience is the soul speaking the truth. When you create and live from the soul, there is no existential problem.

One day, you will boldly hold the skull of all your disappointments in your hand and say: 'Alas, poor Rejection! I knew him … a fellow of little jest, of most dreary fancy: he hath borne false witness upon me a thousand times … where be your gibes now?'

Remember, the problem *is* the teacher.

You have to know how to accept rejection and reject acceptance.

RAY BRADBURY

CHAPTER FOURTEEN

MOZART OR MUZAK
The Gift

DON'T COMPARE your own self to any other artist. Doing so plants and nourishes grievance seeds with long roots that sprout suffocating weeds for a lifetime of envy, ultimately stifling the dharma for which you have been born. Don't concern your self with the seeming accomplishments of other artists. To covet has no place in a creator's handbook for living.

Focus on the present moment and leave art history to posterity. Mind your own business and create.

ENVY

In the 1984 film, *Amadeus*, adapted from the play of the same name by Peter Shaffer, the playwright dramatizes a popular urban legend in the world of classical music: the alleged rivalry between two composers in the late 18th century court of Austrian Emperor Joseph II, the musical king. There is the official royal Italian-born composer Antonio Salieri; and the newcomer, the Austrian prodigy Wolfgang Amadeus Mozart. Although the film is fiction, the story is portrayed in such a convincing narrative that many take it as being historically accurate—which it isn't.

More important, Shaffer's poetic fabrication (in close collaboration with director Milos Forman) makes for an allegorical object lesson worth etching into the psyche of every artist. The story portrays the ultimate of rejections—by God himself, who seemingly and capriciously bestows the gift of great art upon those who may not 'deserve' it.

In the movie, Salieri is a composite of the artist as a victim who derives his value solely from the approval of others. He secretly loathes Mozart, whom he 'sees' as a selfish, spoiled, and vulgar little man. Mozart isn't unaware of his own behavior. He acknowledges that while he may be vulgar, his music is not.

Despite feelings of animosity, Salieri is simultaneously in awe of Mozart's magnificent music—a gift from God. And despite his own success at court, Salieri feels his work is mediocre by comparison, and is, in today's parlance, mere Muzak, while Mozart is Mozart—musical notes from heaven.

Listening to, trusting, and acting on your intuitive inner guidance is an art.

Like any other art or discipline, it requires a certain commitment. It is an ongoing process in which we are always being challenged to move to a deeper level of self-trust

SHAKTI GAWAIN

What is an artist? You need to know. If you can't satisfactorily answer this question, then what you produce is open to speculation by others, including yourself. There's no power in that!

This is shaky ground.

EDEN

PACT WITH GOD

But Salieri suffers yet another rub. The entire film is told in a series of flashbacks. A young priest has come to hear the confession of an old Salieri whose residence is now an asylum. He recalls a vow he took when he was twelve.

Salieri: "Whilst my father prayed earnestly to God to protect commerce, I would offer up secretly the proudest prayer a boy could think of. Lord, make me a great composer! Let me celebrate your glory through music, and be celebrated myself! Make me famous through the world, dear God! Make me immortal! After I die let people speak my name forever with love for what I wrote! In return I vow I will give you my chastity, my industry, my deepest humility, every hour of my life. And I will help my fellow man all I can. Amen and amen!"

At first glance, this is an idealistic-sounding pledge, but when examined carefully, this prayer is riddled with egocentric motives destined for ultimate doom should it ever happen.

After such 'pure' devotion on Salieri's part, how could God have bestowed His heavenly gift of genius upon crude Mozart? This is Salieri's hell on Earth. He recognizes Mozart's immense talent while at the same time he is consumed, blinded with envy in the face of brilliance. How such wondrous music could come from one as boisterous as Mozart drives Salieri insane and to thoughts of violence. He is convinced God is personally playing one of the cruelest possible jokes on him. Salieri, who had made a vow of chastity for the gift of music, now recants and declares war on God.

WORKING THE ROOM

The grievances are so compelling that it is almost easy to overlook the truth. Who, after all, could possibly be more deserving of God's love than Salieri? He loved music, but loved himself more. What if Mozart hadn't been a skirt chasing self-assured upstart, but a genteel and pious man? Would Salieri have hated him any less? Based on what Salieri felt he was lacking, his grievances are contrived and self-destructive. You pray for awareness, not a gift. Salieri's angst comes not from God's malice; his grief is born from within himself and from not knowing where he stood. He wanted to be something other than what he was, and his ego diligently served him up agony. Instead of appreciating his respectable position at the royal court, giving thanks for what he did have, he degenerates into despising the very thing he claims to love—God's eternal art, music. His love of music is on a self-serving sliding scale. Salieri, feeling inadequate, a musical fraud in Mozart's shadow, lets his ego do the humming, not his art felt soul. Step back and see the situation for what it was. While Salieri played to the audience, Mozart played for the audience—of course, you would have to hear the distinction to know and appreciate the difference. While Salieri worked the room, Mozart was working the notes. While Salieri lived up to provincial expectations, Mozart delivered universal surprise.

CROWD PLEASING

Ultimately, Salieri is driven to poison the instrument of his pain—Mozart. He is getting revenge on God. But God doesn't strike him dead. For his audacity, Salieri gets to live a long life into senility, only to see firsthand how posterity orchestrates the final movement of this requiem. Old Salieri tries to commit suicide, but *God* won't let him. While Salieri and his works of the Classical period fade into obscurity, Mozart's timeless music lives on into the Age of Enlightenment and the Romantic era. Salieri says that while God may forgive Salieri, he won't forgive God for giving him dreams of an art he couldn't fulfill. Is this God's fault? If Salieri would have only done more listening and less talking, he may have heard those immortal notes that he so desired from God's voice instead of his own. While Salieri was whining, Mozart was hard at work and listening to heaven.

Continuing his role as a victim, Salieri, now pathetic and feeble, rambles on about Mozart, art, and God. This is the anguish of comparison and the eventual payback for pettiness and jealousy. It is Salieri, after all, who has rejected himself. Intent on blaming God for not blessing him with enough talent, he doesn't confront himself. It isn't God who is capricious; that flaw belongs to man. As the chief court Kapellmeister, Salieri was consumed with writing operas to please the Emperor and his court—and crowd pleasing comes at a price. Salieri was a fixture at the court while Mozart was more of a novelty—at least, at that time. If Salieri had been bold, progressive, and indifferent to pleasing others, then he may have surprised and even surpassed himself. But in writing less traditional music, he might have lost and given up his status and audience at the court. This is the price of catering to taste. Taste in popular art changes with the times. Trends flow in and then flow out into amnesia. While taste may be the enemy of art, it is timeless art that ultimately endures.

While Mozart certainly composed with his patrons in mind, he also took risks. Not all of his works and 'modern' themes where immediately embraced as the enduring wonders they have become. Ultimately, Mozart was more interested in pleasing himself. Salieri was the court portrait painter while Mozart was the abstract expressionist of notes. Listen, for example, to Wolfgang's string quartet (1785) in c major, also called the Dissonant Quartet, and hear why this piece of chamber music lives on into the 21st century. This was one of his most sublime works, featuring two violins, one viola, and one cello. The first movement begins—adagio, very slow. To compose a musical piece comprised of mingling discordant notes took someone willing to take brilliant risks. First, Mozart intoxicates the ether with a phrase of the strings. Suddenly, the sound drops steeply, dangerously, a whole step, before the phrase repeats, building again from the cello up through the first violin. Then, while the cello continues its pulsations, the viola plays a mournful, rising, chromatic line, luring the violins and cello into imitative responses.

Now, listen to a work by Salieri and you will hear not unpleasant harmony from a conservative, safe approach of that era.

A VOW GONE SOUR

As the old and bitter Salieri, seeing his music forgotten while Mozart's music only grows in popularity, confides to the priest in the asylum: "Yes, Father. Yes! So much for my vow of chastity. What did it matter? Good, patient, hard working, chaste—what did it matter? Had goodness made

If a man does not keep pace with his companions, perhaps it is because he hears a different drummer. Let him step to the music which he hears, however measured or far away.

HENRY DAVID THOREAU

Buddha.

Siddhartha was a young, handsome prince who renounced his wealth in the pursuit of truth.

After much self-denial and testing the meaning of enlightenment, he found himself sitting under a sacred Bodhi tree where, once and for all, he would face Mara, the Lord of Illusion who would seriously tempt him with women, riches, vices, and threats of death.

In the end, after a fantastic and frightening night of confronting himself and his place in the universe, Siddhartha awoke as the Buddha, the Awakened One who had compassion for the whole world.

In that moment, the world was at peace.

EDEN

me a good composer? I realized it absolutely then—that moment: goodness is nothing in the furnace of art. And I was nothing to God…. All I ever wanted was to sing to Him. That's His doing, isn't it? He gave me that longing—then made me mute. Why? Tell me that. If He didn't want me to serve Him with music, why implant the desire, like a lust in my body, then deny me the talent? Go on, tell me! Speak for Him!"

To further make his case against God, old Salieri tells the priest of an event that happened when he was twelve years old; at that time a six-year-old Mozart was already playing for kings and emperors, even the Pope.

Salieri says: "I admit I was jealous when I heard the tales they told about him. Not of the brilliant little prodigy himself, but of his father, who had taught him everything."

ART AND OPPORTUNITY

Here, the court composer brings up a relevant point about art and opportunity. Would Mozart have discovered his musical prowess if his father hadn't been a music teacher?

Would Picasso have discovered his talent if his father had been a butcher instead of an art teacher? Talent is no different from any other valuable gem. It must first be discovered, then unearthed and unleashed before it can be cut to shape to expose its true brilliance.

"My father did not care for music. He wanted me only to be a merchant, like himself. As anonymous as he was. When I told how I wished I could be like Mozart, he would say, 'Why? Do you want to be a trained monkey? Would you like me to drag you around Europe doing tricks like a circus freak?' How could I tell him what music meant to me?"

Salieri, after conveying that his life without music would have been a disaster, adds: "And do you know what happened? A miracle!"

We see the flashback scene of twelve-year-old Salieri and his family at dinner. His father chokes to death on a fishbone.

"Suddenly he was dead. Just like that! And my life changed forever. My mother said, 'Go. Study music if you really want to. Off with you!' And off I went as quick as I could and never saw Italy again. Of course, I knew God had arranged it all; that was obvious. One moment I was a frustrated boy in an obscure little town. The next I was here, in Vienna, city of musicians, sixteen years old and studying under Gluck! Gluck. Father, do you know who he was? The greatest composer of his time. And he loved me! That was the wonder. He taught me everything he knew. And when I was ready, introduced me personally to the Emperor! Emperor Joseph - the musical king! Within a few years I was his court composer. Wasn't that incredible? Imperial Composer to His Majesty! Actually the man had no ear at all, but what did it matter? He adored my music, that was enough. Night after night I sat right next to the Emperor of Austria, playing duets with him, correcting the royal sight-reading. Tell me, if you had been me, wouldn't you have thought God had accepted your vow? And believe me, I honored it. I was a model of virtue. I kept my hands off women, worked hours every day teaching students, many of them for free, sitting on endless committees to help poor musicians - work and work and work, that was all my life. And it was wonderful! Everybody liked me. I liked myself. I was the most successful musician in Vienna. And the happiest. Till he came. Mozart."

THE ANSWERED PRAYER

Salieri says it all: He went from obscurity to fame, and that was still not enough. Fame never is. Of course, Salieri had been living a self-congratulatory life before Mozart came to the court. Salieri, the court composer, had no gratitude in his heart for what he did have, which was considerable by any standard. You are an honorable petitioner at best; and making deals with God is a self-delusion. The Creator offers only one binding agreement—a fifty-fifty partnership that you must negotiate in good faith, not demands. And what did happen when Mozart came to Vienna? Salieri was confronted with Mozart's music, a new standard of purity. Instead of embracing and adopting this new standard as his own, and in the process elevating himself and his work, his ego went to work, engaging envy and jealousy as allies in a struggle than never won any war.

Poor Salieri felt cheated by God for not having enough talent. However, as the film unequivocally depicts, Salieri did get what he had prayed for—a musical life and celebrated for his work in his lifetime. He did go too far in asking for immortality for that is posterity's domain. It was Salieri who most appreciated the genius of Mozart. It was Salieri who could tell, could feel, the difference between hackwork and God's work. To recognize art is as much a gift as the art itself. The art appreciator completes the circle. After all, the connoisseur must work as hard as the artist to grasp the essence of what is true art without having to consult a committee on what is what. Secretly coveting Mozart's talent, Salieri couldn't appreciate his own life in the present. It is, of course, a wonder to play God's notes; to hear and know the source is no small blessing, either; to hear anything at all is a gift.

Salieri doesn't concern himself with Mozart's problems of living. Even the most gifted artist has troubles to deal with; this is life. And, after all, how could any of Mozart's difficulties in the film compare to Salieri's feelings of betrayal by God? If Salieri had known where he stood and why, he would have aged gracefully with a deep appreciation for the talent God did give him. To know why you have a specific gift is a personal triumph of empowerment that completes an odyssey. The quality of Salieri's music would certainly have benefited from this insight and his compositions may even have soared well into the future.

DIVINE COMPREHENSION

How do you want to live your life as an artist? Don't reinvent the cello. Use the sublime example of Salieri and Mozart showcased in the film as a dynamic crucible to better comprehend your own self. Be grateful daily for some thing, remove pettiness from your being, and know intuitively the value of your work as an artist. Your art isn't something you ask God for, but something (as a blessing not a sacrifice) you offer up to God.

If you feel that another has more talent, then that is a red flag to address your dharma. Be aware of where your attention is taking you. Envy is a form of mental illness, a neurotic manifestation that transforms the richest

I was awfully curious to find out why I didn't go insane.

ABRAHAM MASLOW

Among the notes I made while writing this book [Exhibition: art in the age of intolerance], I find this comment: If you spend any amount of time looking at paintings or talking to artists you quickly realize how far you are from art.

Art is not merely another language ... It is another world of relationships—to objects, to ideas, to life's priorities.

Nonartists can painstakingly describe works of art and even record every word an artist says. But, in the end, the only thing that can fully explain great art is the work itself.

LYNNE MUNSON

of men into despicable husks. Because he has created a life worth living, no true artist is envious of another. What else do you want? When you cast out resentment, your unique talent flourishes. You don't need psychotherapy for this, either. The other artist doesn't have more talent; he has another talent. The other artist you may call gifted understands something most artists do not: Genius is dedication. This is divine comprehension.

To appreciate genius is also a great gift; this is what composer Salieri in the film didn't know. You can't create that which you don't hear, see, feel, or sense on some level. But let's not be excessively impressed with genius. As wonderful as Mozart's music is, there are times when his notes can be annoying, especially with the flute. Can't an adult become a prodigy, too? Or, perhaps, that adult had been a child prodigy all along but without opportunity. Then again, if Salieri knew the real score, there would be no artistic angst for the drama to unfold as a film and as a profound example of discerning the difference between Muzak and Mozart. Remember, Mozart wasn't born famous; neither was Picasso.

PLANETARY ALIGNMENT

Note: With deference to Marshall McLuhan, master of aphorisms, the medium isn't only the message—it is the *message*. With no 'stars' and over two and half hours of reel time, a film about classical music isn't a likely candidate for earning big box office—that is if you went by the common wisdom espoused in Hollywood where art and film are like oil and water, and where the tyranny of marketing, test screenings, and focus groups dictate the vision, cut, and the finale. With yet another deference, this time to *Ars Gratia Artis* (art for art's sake) that banners Leo, the MGM Lion, if you mention that your screenplay is art to the major film studios in Los Angeles, you will be shortly shown the exit, and don't slam the door on your way out.

In Hollywood (the Petri dish for the general audience), the reductionist formula for success is reaching the lowest common denominator as it represents the widest possible audience. The major studios are right: art and committees don't mix. Independent films are called that for a reason. Despite the collective combination of three seemingly 'negative' noncommercial elements, *Amadeus*, like the subject it confronts, transcended genre, formula, attention span, running time of 180 minutes (and the bladder) to become an award-winning (8 Oscars) cinematic achievement with considerable audience appeal. Of course, the film was based on a successful Broadway play, but that was no guarantee either. You can't second-guess art or the public. No thing will stop the events from unfolding when the planets are in alignment and the heavens want it to happen. All you have to do is show up with your art.

Original art can't be accomplished by consensus.

Regarding wealth consciousness:

I recall visiting a millionaire land developer in his home. We were in the kitchen. He asked if I would like a sandwich. Sure. He got up and went to the sink. He picked up one of those plastic containers with dishwashing liquid. It was down to a molecule or two of soap. He filled the container with water and shook it until he could see some measly suds. Satisfied, he began washing a couple of plates.

Instead of tossing the empty container, he diluted the soap to make some weak suds, which in no way could have cleaned much, and perhaps saved half a penny in the process.

I wondered if this compulsive thrift was the means he used to build homes for what seemed reasonable prices. After all, once the home is built, you can't tell if the work is substandard until there is a problem.

CHAPTER FIFTEEN

AWARENESS
The Arbiter of All

IS THAT all there truly is?

When you dive into the ocean, you take a deep breath and leave the realm of air for the domain of water that now surrounds you. You can't know all that is under the ocean, but you are unquestionably aware of being submerged in a purely different element that seemingly defies gravity as it fully supports your body. You are weightless. You can float and fly in this new world of aqua. Entering the sublime environment of pure awareness shares this metaphorical transition from air to water. You are either in or out, and you know it.

From a practical stance, how do you gain this personal knowledge of pure awareness . . . of God? Although only you can answer when, the mechanism for how is the same for everyone. At some point, you have a transcendental experience: there is something palpable and greater than your own self. Whether through meditation, a spontaneous event, or creating art, you are welcomed into a realm of clarity that exists without the clutter of incessant thinking and intellect. For a treasured time, you become buoyant and adrift on the sea of consciousness, free from the constricting minutiae and entrapments of social conditioning. You know beyond all doubt that you and a power from the cosmos are in communion. You may even sense that you have tuned into the right frequency and that intuition is the carrier wave.

Everyone has heard their intuition; everyone has also had the experience of ignoring its counsel and paying the price. 'If only I had listened' is the common lament.

THE MASKS OF EGO

Whenever I become aware of awareness, I am drawn to the teachings of Zen Buddhism, which is the art of awareness. Not awareness of something specific (also known as attention), but awareness itself—being awake, alert, and in emotional touch with what is happening in reality now—not the past, or future. It is about relying on the immediate experience of this

Deeds of kindness are equal in weight to all the commandments.

TALMUD

Given the vast inequalities we are daily confronted with, the most notable feature of envy may be that we manage not to envy everyone.

There are people whose enormous blessings leave us wholly untroubled, even as others' negligible advantages become a source of relentless torment for us. We envy only those whom we feel ourselves to be like—we envy only members of our reference group.

There are few successes more unendurable than those of our ostensible equals.

ALAIN DE BOTTON

present moment. It is about exploring the most basic questions of life. It is about freedom from mind. It isn't about belief, doctrine, rules, dogma, ritual, formula, or tradition. For this 'truth', which is Zen, I can in good conscience substitute 'art'.

WHISPERS SOFTLY

In his book, *Creating Affluence*, Dr. Deepak Chopra explains the difference between timeless awareness and time-bound awareness.

"Time-bound awareness occurs when we relinquish the self for the self-image. The self-image is the social mask, the protective veneer behind which we hide. In time-bound awareness our behavior is always influenced by the past and by anticipation and fear of the future. Time-bound awareness is burdened by guilt and sorrow. It is rooted in fear. It causes entropy, aging, and death. Timeless awareness is the awareness of the self.

"The Vedic seer says, 'I do not worry about the past and I am not fearful of the future because my life is supremely concentrated in the present, and the right response comes to me, to every situation as it occurs.' This is also the state of bliss. The self is not in the realm of thought. It's in the gap between our thoughts. The cosmic psyche whispers to us softly in the gap between our thoughts. This is also what we call intuition. Time-bound awareness is in the intellect; it calculates. Timeless awareness in the heart; it feels."

THE BOOBY PRIZE

You are no stranger to the power of creation. A piece of music, a lyric, an image, a painting, a performance, a touch, or a defining moment has moved you to where your skin tingles with energy from a higher sphere, and your emotions soar to places as yet uncharted in your soul.

You realize awareness is the key for knowing every thing else that comes into your life. Awareness is that magic mirror born in myths and fairy tales. It reflects the truth of every thing that you hold up to it.

Once you know awareness exits, you know it forever, and you spend your life drawing upon its supreme and consistent essence. However, this doesn't mean you are forever exempt from the issues that arise in daily living. This does mean you always know, no matter what is happening, that there is a higher standard to which you strive.

You aren't seeking perfection, an island that doesn't exist in this world. As the British art critic and social commentator of the Victorian Age, John Ruskin, wrote: "No good work whatever can be perfect, and the demand for perfection is always a sign of a misunderstanding of the ends of art."

To be aware is the prerequisite for experiencing life beyond illusion, your own, or the cumulative self-consciousness amassed by society. You see things for what they are because your awareness is the ultimate solvent for dissolving the veil of mass social conditioning.

Pure awareness is the source of all great art. You are sentient. You have learned what the ancients knew.

As Lao Tzu observed: "Knowing others is wisdom, knowing yourself is enlightenment."

This is the Tao of understanding.

And, as the master from India revealed: Understanding is the booby prize. Go ahead. Think about it. If you don't get it now, don't despair; maybe one day you will. As an artist, you have stripped your self naked of personality, social conditioning, and ego for an expressed purpose. You want to see your own self without interference, which is also known as art.

THE ARBITER OF ALL

You move freely between understanding and the mindless traffic jams that all too often clog the mental thruways of society. An enlightened soul can move more freely among the barbarians, but not vice versa. You have learned there is a difference between awareness of a particular thing, and awareness itself.

To be aware of a single thing means you have your attention on it, which is the first step toward doing anything. You also realize attention exists within the larger sphere of awareness. While attention is mandatory for completing tasks, it is more important to remain aware. You could be engrossed in your favorite piece of music while your house was burning down. It would be smarter to be aware that the house is on fire instead of paying attention to the music.

This feeling of pure awareness allows you to function in the world, even observe customs while remaining connected to your transcendental self, which is the arbiter of all that is of lasting value, including your artwork. Your knowledge of your self provides you with the moral amplitude to persevere; you aren't dismayed, or hardly so these days, for any meaningful amount of time by negative outside influences. You have faced the issue at hand: rejection can't defeat you because you are no longer codependent.

All external bravado pales in the glow of self-awareness, which is a direct conduit to consciousness.

Remember that you are an actor in a drama, of such a part as it may please the master to assign you, for a long time or for a little as he may choose.

And if he wills you to take the part of a poor man, or a cripple, or a ruler, or a private citizen, then may you act that part with grace!

For to act well the part that is allotted to us ... that indeed is ours to do, but to choose it is another's.

EPICTETUS

CHAPTER SIXTEEN

THE MAGNIFICENT TRUTH
Deliverance

LET'S GET to it. If we don't confront the important questions now, then the consequences will play themselves out soon enough.

'Truth' is a charged word that many feel is too hot to handle for fear of fallout in whatever form—from political ideology to religion, to love, to family matters, to philosophy, to getting that fellowship or grant, to origins of the species and the universe, and to art.

As apparent as it might seem to be, we must first acknowledge the existence of truth—that, in fact, there is such a thing. Different forms of truth exist as topics of heated conversation, and buying into any version without due diligence is akin to purchasing an all natural food, only to discover that 'all natural' in this case doesn't necessarily imply nutritious, or healthy. When truth—art—is presented as the vanilla truth, then it is what it sounds like. The true artist is concerned with universal truth, which is the enlightened, provocative, irreducible, and practical application of creation that enhances the quality and evolution of life. Enduring truth isn't about democracy, social equality, or anxiety, nor is it ever dictated. This timeless truth is revealed through art one person at a time.

Even if we weren't dwellers in a politically correct and pluralistically charged environment, the question of *whose* truth rises up like an indignant dragon spewing fire, which instantly, evenly, and indiscriminately melts the unique along with the commonplace into a dull lump of mediocrity. Truth is power, and power can be dangerous; but only to those who fear it, or are afraid they will lose it. Zealots who believe they have found the truth and want to forcibly convert everyone are no less a grave threat to universal truth—and art—than those who mindfully enforced the Spanish Inquisition without impunity.

WAGGING THE DOG

The relevant truth for our needs here is the universal paternal non-coercive truth that loves everyone equally. This is the truth that will set you free to explore your art with confidence despite rejection—which will show itself

Works of art, in my opinion, are the only objects in the material universe to possess internal order, and that is why, though I don't believe that only art matters, I do believe in Art for Art's sake.

E.M. FORSTER

Knowledge is what is both true and believed, though not all that is both true and believed counts as knowledge.

PLATO

in some form sooner or later. This is the truth you must find out for your own self. Proselytizing isn't acceptable; and missionaries need not apply for assignments to this realm. Universal means absolute truth, which has nothing to do with facts or human agendas, nor, like some temporal rules, does it bend, break, or have any exceptions. You can rely on this rule: The truth won't come after you; it is you who must go after the truth, woo it, and in the end you will find that it resides within you. This is a signal. If the truth doesn't fit this picture, if the truth is chasing you, pressing you, then something is wrong—run, don't walk, and don't look back.

If, at this moment, your mind is throwing up a salvo of questions and defensiveness, you are already thinking too much and will miss the point. Don't get ahead of yourself if you want a new vision. You want to know how to overcome difficulties, get on with your art while making a contribution and a living. That is why you are reading this book. To endure and ultimately triumph demands that you dig deep—for it is in our darkest hour that we find our true selves. You must dig as deep as necessary and wherever necessary to find meaning, the truth, your dharma, your purpose for being here. If you don't, then contemplate the alternative: you have cast your karmic ballot for living a life of approximation, never quite in focus, and in 'quiet desperation'. How can you expect others to respect your passion if you don't?

EYE SEA

This book, like meditation, isn't about relaxing; it is about transcending the mindless and mundane; it is about discovering your own self in a sea frothing with 'I' pronouns; it is about winning the war against yourself.

In the Zen metaphor of the master's fingers pointing at the moon, if your attention is on the fingers, which are pointed in the right direction, you won't see the moon, the object of truth. Universal truth is transcendental, which, by definition, is beyond the potential interpretive and often loosely hinged trapdoors of thought and reason. Universal truths, laws, and rules are all one in the same; they aren't abstract concepts; they are the values of God who is consciousness.

In a world littered with misinformation, it is beautiful to comprehend that you can't break a universal law, topple a universal truth, or bend a universal rule—immutable ideals not open to interpretation.

And to this end, Buddha stressed right action, which is synonymous with the transcendent; and those with an awareness of right action don't require legislation to inform them that larceny is immoral, or, in an almost anticlimactic sense, against the law.

As we eventually learn, the conquerors end up writing the history books. Since the creation of art demands integrity in the work, the artist must know the truth of his work if he is to endure and prevail while successfully fending off rejection.

I can't stress this point enough. If you are going to get rejected, knowing what is getting overlooked is more important than why. If you don't know the inherent value of your art, who will? Applying this knowledge will liberate you; your sense of freedom and power—your life force—will reside in your work. Over time, others will notice.

THE WEATHER REPORT

If there is one common thread neatly stitched into the genetic fabric of all humanity, it is our quest for the 'truth'. However, there is more to the truth than verifying a fact. The truth, or certain subjective truth, can be interpreted. In Akira Kurosawa's metaphysical 1950 film *Rashomon,* each of four eyewitnesses describes the same event with different eyes, and no two versions quite agree. That is why lawyers love eyewitness testimony. With deference to Buddha and Jesus, the question then becomes: can any one person know absolute truth, or does temporal perspective keep the holy grail of ultimate perception out of reach? Of course, the artist must grapple and come to terms with this question of truth for her own self, or she will be at the mercy of a dizzying array of alternative narratives supplied by others of what her art is *really* all about—that is if she can get anyone to notice her work.

Your relative truth may not be my truth if, for example, we are on the phone talking about the weather. The sun may be streaming into my California studio while raindrops are dancing on your roof in Seattle. We are both right; we are both describing the transitory truth as we experience it. A certain type of truth can be a variable fact depending upon location or some other factor.

HERE AND NOW

I told someone the other day that: 'Enlightenment is about the quality of life in this world, not the hereafter.'

Is my declaration about enlightenment an absolute (objective) truth, or a relative (subjective) truth? Whether you read this statement as a truth at all isn't at issue here. The artist who can discern the difference between relative and absolute avoids getting caught in the crosshairs of rejection or acceptance—either one can be lethal in time. The opinions of others about your art are relative—like the weather. Your comprehension of your art, however, must be absolute—like a force of nature, like the constant of physical matter that is the speed of light. Answering the three core questions in this book will reveal any fundamental weakness of character or self worth you may have as an artist, which is the first step in getting tough—a prerequisite for perseverance.

But wait, some person might ask: "How can you be objective about your own work?"

If you fall for that red herring of a question, you will forever be on the subjective defensive about your art. Say to this inquiring mind, if it is true: "Because I can." This definitive statement is true when you are grounded in awareness, most especially of your own self, not floundering in bias, or on the bleak beach of uncertainty. The truth that concerns us here can only be described in poetry.

"But how can you?" is a response you might get, followed with "I don't understand."

You now know to disengage from an argument you can never win. "Maybe one day you will," you say gently, and that is that.

As I only have firsthand knowledge of this life, I must, for the benefit of the construct, categorize my statement about enlightenment not being

> *The Law of Non-Attachment shouldn't be misunderstood. I strive to have no attachment in how a particular outcome manifests.*
>
> *I work; I create; I have faith in fulfilling my dharma; and my evolving strength tells me the Universe is handling the details.*
>
> EDEN

How did I think up my drawings and my ideas for painting?

Well I'd come home to my Paris studio in rue Blomet at night, I'd go to bed, and sometimes I hadn't any supper.

*I saw things,
and I jotted them down in a notebook.
I saw shapes on the ceiling ...*

JOAN MIRÓ

Overall, to paraphrase Voltaire, one universe is as miraculous as countless multiverses.

EDEN

for the hereafter as a relative truth, one based on my experience in the here and now. Although I can't empirically prove it, nor should I have to, I intuitively grasp that my statement about enlightenment is absolute. I can only bring this perception into your sphere of awareness. You, in turn, must prove any metaphysical conclusion to your own self.

GIVING AN INCH

Is there one ultimate truth for everything? Albert Einstein thought it is possible and spent his post-relativity years trying to develop an insight that would explain it all in a formula that measured a linear inch or so (roughly double the length of $E=mc^2$)—a tall order for a short equation, even for Einstein, who never did discover the complete and concise mind of God, which wasn't a shortcoming. No one will ever be able to comprehend the total mind of God—also known as consciousness.

When quantum mechanics entered the world of theoretical physics, the game was afoot. Up for grabs was the prize that would explain the supreme mysteries of the universe, or multiverses. Although I won't get into Superstring Theory here, this view of creation, with its vibrating strings as the fundamental instruments orchestrating all that we call matter, integrates Einstein's linear space-time continuum of general relativity with subatomic particles, hidden dimensions and universes.

In reality, by nature's law, every thing exists in contrast and in relation to the other. If, for example, you paint every area on your canvas using the same color, how would you know what you are doing, and how could your viewer see it? What a waste of paint and canvas space.

What relationship is there between theoretical physics and a book for artists on rejection? To see a painting without comprehending its source is like seeing the façade of a great palace and never going inside. In turn, the same is true for looking at the cosmos. Physicists are attempting to formulate every conceivable contingency in nature's blueprint. The artist does the same intuitively.

Art is the elusive formula of creation that transmutes itself into an infinite possibility with each work. The true artist experiences no less than painting such an equation (what Einstein was seeking) for creation on every canvas. The internal logic, visual syntax, and integrity of the piece is what holds it together—a force alternately known as symmetry, balance, or harmony. While this art equation, in whatever expression, may take up more space than Einstein had envisioned for his formula of God, it is no less elegant for this knowledge is pure and has great liberating power.

Meanwhile, truths build upon truths as the mortar of one's character, which constructs a quality of life. Knowledge can be changeable; cosmic truth is immutable. When you sense a probable universal unalterable truth, immediately put it to the test. That is why it is there. Don't dismiss such an opportunity.

Firsthand knowledge is power that brings you in contact with truth. In this fashion, you will know instead of having to guess or believe—which is most often an aggregate of what others have planned for you.

Each true artist confronts, challenges and tests the truth of his art every day—not through laudatory acceptance, but against the hard face of rejection.

Otherwise, what is the point?

TRUE GRIT

A magnificent truth can be written down in a word, a sentence, a poem, a glance, a melody, a dance, a symphony, a painting, a performance, a selfless act, or as an equation in physics that is symmetrically elegant. It can't be beautiful—true—if it doesn't add up. A truth can appear in a dream or on a baby's face. To realize the truth of a statement in whatever form, however, the artist must overcome the inertia of common wisdom, be in motion and in sync with the information revolving around him. If not, the transcendental truth will spiral away beyond his grasp like a far-flung galaxy hurtling through space. The artist must be on alert, which is that critical mass point of readiness to discover the truth of an observation on his own. Secondhand information, no matter how brilliantly penned, is exactly what it sounds like—indirect and despite the reference to 'second', it may be any number of steps removed from the original event.

I have more than one motive in writing this book. Of course, I want you to succeed by experiencing that rejection is a test and a consequence of action, not failure. There is more. What is the point of learning anything if you can't pass the torch along? This is how we evolve beyond mere propagation, which takes no special acquired talent. My desire is for artists to develop more quickly and assertively into fully realized human beings, not the suffering, lost, and misunderstood icons of art history who are so often popularized in the media. Like a meat tenderizer, it is art that breaks down the density of human ignorance—beginning with the artist and all those he touches. Art is deliverance. Concise and apt, the Zen proverb goes: 'When the student is ready, the teacher will appear.'

MORAL COURAGE

What is truth? Who is the true artist? Truth, with homage to Buddha, is the absence of illusion. To see things as they are is revelation, which is what the artist does. The truth exists only in this moment, in reality, not imagination—which is beneath creative, and creative we come to understand is subordinate to creation. The true artist isn't self-indulgent, nor does he have delusions about the nature and value of his work. You must know where you stand in the space-time scheme of things; or what is the point? This is awareness; this is dharma; this is deliverance from the throes of rejection.

Of all the truths out there, knowing the truth about your own self is what matters most—this is the threshold from where you have the invincible power to dismiss rejection and mean it. If you don't yet subscribe to the introspective understanding of truth, maybe one day you will.

As J. Lawton Collins had observed: "No matter how brilliant a man may be, he will never engender confidence in his subordinates and associates if he lacks simple honesty and moral courage."

In the end, if the truth be told, let your art do the talking.

> *It is through Art and through Art only that we can realize our perfection … through Art and Art only that we can shield ourselves from the sordid perils of actual existence.*
>
> OSCAR WILDE

> *The true artist is the cause, not an effect.*
>
> EDEN

CHAPTER SEVENTEEN

THE LOTUS FLOWER
Petals of Freedom

IF THE TRUTH were self-evident, then, by God, wouldn't it and the genius of your art be *obvious*?

What is the back-story about universal truth? In 'The Magnificent Truth', we looked at the distinction between subjective and objective truth. As with all simple understandings, there is always more. Truth has nothing to do with institutional dogma that is marketed through organizations and doctrine. Whom or what can you trust to know the truth? Can you trust your own self? If you have to think about it, then you have already answered the question.

Truth will remain elusive if you allow others to not only lead the way, but to also demand that you accept their pointing finger (doctrine) aimed at the moon (truth) for the truth itself. Fortunately, you can get there from here without the long leash attached to dogma. To glimpse the vista of enlightenment you must make the journey, which involves action and momentum, not words. You can't delegate this trek of personal experience; there is no other way. I can't stress this point enough. You must experience the clarity of truth for your own self. If not, all is but hearsay and blind obedience, and it is what it sounds like. Truth, like a diamond, is where you find it; and someone in a hurry going nowhere can easily overlook a truth in the rough.

WHOM DO YOU TRUST?

You can honestly feel you know the truth, but that may not be the case. Truth isn't a synonym for honesty. Truth as it concerns us here is an indivisible principle. Honesty, which is a laudable function of one's character and judgment, and the trademark of a fully realized human being, isn't an absolute truth—nor should it be.

Some things must remain flexible and adaptive to be of use, and expediency can often be the right choice. You might, for example, have to lie to save your life. Because you chose not to tell the truth under duress in no way diminishes your dependability as a reliable witness. The situation

What one has not experienced, one will never understand in print.

ISADORA DUNCAN

Don't worry about the rejections. Everybody that's good has gone through it. Don't let it matter if your works are not 'accepted' at once. The better or more personal you are the less likely they are of acceptance. Just remember that the object of painting pictures is not simply to get them in exhibitions.

It is all very fine to have your pictures hung, but you are painting for yourself, not for the jury. I had many years of rejections.

ROBERT HENRI

Process vs. Product:

When you know the value of your process you can stand confident knowing the value of the product. Not knowing what or why you are doing some 'thing' is the breeding ground for insecurity and discontent.

Rejection and its minions are at the door, ready to cause havoc for the unprepared.

EDEN

dictates the wisdom of telling or volunteering the truth, or not. A prisoner of war who lies to the enemy is a hero; a prisoner of war who provides his interrogators with the 'truth' is a traitor. Remember that discernment is the master key in all things.

ZEN TO GO

I am not a joiner per se, but that doesn't preclude me from being an advocate. Over time, I have developed a strong affinity for the introspective simplicity of Zen Buddhism and its direct approach to truth, which is the way I make art—the mind is quiet, imperturbable, no longer clinging to concepts, ideas, petty desires, or illusion, which leads to no thinking, to emptiness! There is no confusion when the mind is quiet.

Why bring up Zen ('meditation' in Japanese), or other exotic-sounding systems from Eastern philosophies? A good idea is a good idea no matter where it comes from; this is my approach to learning. Because its teachings work without conflicting with your present comprehension of the world, Zen, in a real sense, is the do-it-yourself 'religion'. Since you must prove things to yourself, and to your own satisfaction, Zen eliminates the middleman from the process. If you remove the politics from organized religion, you discover that the pure tenet of the faith challenges you to find the spirit that is God for yourself. This is divine emancipation, not heresy.

Zen is a proven system for dissolving rigid construction and moribund beliefs that no longer inspire or serve you. You don't have to give up any baggage until you feel the weight, the truth of it. Zen can loosen the anvil around your neck, but you must cast if off. Zen empowers you to expand beyond rejection, which is one of the qualities you are after.

Let's be clear, I am not attached to Zen being your philosophy for deliverance. Whether your door to the truth is Yoga, Buddhism, Taoism, Judaism, Christianity, Islam, humanism, the mystical invocation by the shaman, the sweat lodge, Sufi dancing, or name your religion or philosophy, you are still after the same thing—to connect with the source of creation. If you have a system of preference that will help you break free of weakness and pain, then embrace it before answering the core questions in this book. Your life as a creator begins when you know that it is you who has the insight to discern truth from deception. Tom, Dick, or Swami Gee can't do it for you. There are no shortcuts to firsthand experience. When you are at that moment of truth, that pivotal moment of weakness or strength, don't give your power away. Weakness is no great honor.

Like most every other prescription in this book, it is essential to understand that truth—about yourself, about your art, about your dharma—is the healing antidote for fending off rejection. Observation without the smothering and defensive filter of the ego is the mechanism for seeing truth. I am referring to the truth as *you* find it; power lies in self-discovery, not in gossip. Rather than obsessing over rejection in its endless forms, it is smarter to expand your awareness toward truth, which must be felt on your skin, in your heart, and throughout your soul searching. Faking this experience is akin to faking an orgasm. Who are you kidding, and why? Hearing about a truth from another is a beginning, and may even be engaging, but it isn't the truth. As the Zen master instructs us: the truth can't be explained; you must see it for yourself. Instead of attempting to grapple with an overwhelming number of issues as to why your art wasn't wanted, you simplify. You address only the truth that you have discovered so far, which, in turn, is the one reliable reality checker that will in time answer all your other questions: this metaphysical leverage isn't only brilliant, it is both efficient and economical, saving you time, the rarest of temporal commodities.

For all our respect for an esteemed master, let's not get caught up in undo worship. A master is human and doesn't know everything; it is enough that he knows everything about you and what you need.

DEGREES OF TRUTH

What is truth? Let me restate: you won't 'know' it by asking anyone else; truth is no different from art, as no one can 'know' it for you, either. No one else can have an epiphany for you. The truth is that you must find out for your own self, which may sound abstract but is completely grounded in experience. I can only refer to timeless truth obliquely, which is also how it is experienced, as a witness to a result of some action that overcame inertia. A truth, or universal law, always comes first at some cost, a price, where some perceived loss occurs. Then, if you have learned your lesson well, this law proves itself as true to you the next time with a gain, and a gain thereafter if you don't forget the truth of that lesson. This is the economical universe at work.

The whole truth, or reality as it is, can't be perceived directly through reason or observation. When you look at your face in the mirror, is that the whole truth? What about the other 359 degrees that circumscribe your head plus all conceivable and observable angles and points of reference available in three-dimensional space? Each degree of freedom is but a part of the whole truth. When you can grasp the whole, the absolute—intuitively, then you have bypassed the cognitive for the transcendental; the benefit to you then is that the inherent power of such truth endows you to create and to persevere within a cultural system bent on shaping you into a living cog: common or specialized, a cog's a cog.

Truth, whole truth, absolute truth is passed along only in aesthetic silence, in that moment between thoughts; after all, what is there to say?

You don't have to be a monk living in a monastery to be virtuous, to know right from wrong and to behave accordingly. There are, of course, those who would argue that there is no universal right or wrong, and that virtue is relative. How can one culture judge the values of another? How can we say the beliefs of one group are bad and the mores of another are good?

Look around. The world is the product of manifest destiny.

A cultural relativist would say that each culture is separate but equal. Each culture, the relativist would argue, makes sense in its own context; and to know the context explains behavior and why the people are doing what they do.

Imposing a set of universal, or absolute, standards would, in conclusion, not only be impossible, but wrong, as all cultures are equally valid under the sun. Then again, whose standards would be imposed on all the other 'lesser' cultures? Who would say what is right or wrong for everyone?

One afternoon I heard a radio interview about Buddhism in the arts. One guest, a painter and sculptor seemed to have strong feelings for Buddhism.

She said: "Yes, Buddhism was a good way of working in the arts since artists must face failure upon failure in their lives."

This was yet another bit of misinformation streaming into the minds of other artists and the public. Perhaps well intentioned and sincere, this artist would have better served if she had said difficulties instead of failure—as we know, failure is not a synonym for rejection; failure is when you give up on your gift, your dharma.

EDEN

Zen does not confuse spirituality with thinking about God while one is peeling potatoes. Zen spirituality is just to peel the potatoes.

ALAN WATTS

Do not get stuck in dogma-doo of any kind, which includes any system, including interpretations of Buddhism that rely on rote.

EDEN

MISSIONARY POSITION

The cultural relativist reasons that it's much better to allow each community to set its own moral standards. While this may sound credible and even democratic, it is a specious position.

What assessment can there be about countless atrocities throughout human history? These cultures had 'values' and 'reasons' for their actions. Were these merely cultural differences, or aberrations—tragedies of human ignorance, hate, greed, or evil incarnate? Is sacrificing a life to the gods okay with you? There existed people of conscience within these societies who knew better. Would you have spoken out against the regime's repugnant policies if it meant your torture and death? According to cultural relativists and their pluralist machinations, a Buddhist, a slave trader, a cannibal and a headhunter represent social groups that evolved 'naturally' within their environment, making them all equally legitimate. Who would you rather meet along a lonely path in the deep forest?

Those who feel all cultures must be viewed as equal within their pre-defined context come from the same school still trying to measure God with a ruler. Attempting to confront such anthropological largesse would seriously entangle anyone suckered by such holier than thou sophistry, which is often accompanied by any number of philosophical examples spouting egalitarian principles—all spurious. Avoid cultural apologists who don't know right from wrong, and don't get distracted by those who would adulterate your art with nonsense, for they would be among the first to reject your work, or worse yet—co-opt it.

Remember, as an artist, it is your dharma, your evolutionary calling to lead the way with your art—not as a missionary, but as a visionary.

MEMORIES STIRRED

Is it not the grand purpose and gift of consciousness to raise the bar of human awareness so that behavior is enlightened rather than a mindless reflex capitulating to the mob? We should not overlook that Western culture in the 21st century is no stranger to blood sport or cultural abuses either. If Buddha knew the truth of right action and right livelihood more than 2,500 years ago, what excuse can modern day humans have for not embracing a universal standard that empowers every other human being? It isn't a question of which culture is best, or hosing petty doctrines and traditions off the great unwashed; understanding is the goal; and when enough (critical mass) people—from wherever they are on the planet—lift up the lotus flower, superstition, ignorance, and animosity will dissolve, leaving awareness of the absolute, which will gently transform the world for the better; it is knowing that the power of transcendence here and now will set the present moment in the direction of right action.

There is magic in truth. You can apply truth from anywhere to where you are right now. I have been in opulent mansions that were devoid of spirit; I have been in one-room flats that were rich with generosity and gratitude. Remember, the true master teaches you nothing, nothing but to see the truth on your own. He awakens and unleashes what you already know to be absolute. Otherwise, how would you recognize truth when you felt it? A cord is struck, the vibration within you is exquisitely pitched, and the truth reveals itself without question, without fanfare. This is art and the power of communion that will see you through the worst of times. There is a simple test. If your truth, your soul at work, doesn't engage with intuitive prowess to protect you when you feel the most vulnerable, you have been deluding yourself. But don't dismay.

You can get back into the game at any time by will alone, knowing that your character gains in strength more from the negative habits you can discard than from the qualities you can acquire; this is also called balancing the equation. Remember, no rejection, no rejecter, can discourage the artist who knows what is what. After all, what is the point of learning a lesson if you aren't going to have the guts to use it?

ZEN, AGAIN

Steve Hagen, in his book, *Buddhism Plain and Simple*, explains: "Zen Buddhism is about awareness. Not awareness of something in particular, but awareness itself—being awake, alert, in touch with what is actually happening. It's about examining and exploring the most basic questions of life. It's about relying on the immediate experience of this present moment. It's about freedom of mind. It's not about belief, doctrine, formula, or tradition. The observations and insights of the Buddha are plain, practical, and eminently down-to-earth. They deal exclusively with here and now—not with theory, speculation, or belief in some far-off time or place. Because these teachings remain focused in this moment, they remain relevant, and of profound value, to every culture and every person who investigates them seriously."

In Zen, there is no duality within appearances; there is no 'I' or 'you' of the ego variety; there is no separation; there is only the one Buddha-nature, which is eternal existence outside of time. It is looking in the mirror and seeing the whole picture, all 360 degrees of freedom—a truth we can prove to ourselves. Given this view of unconditioned beingness, Zen doesn't articulate God, the self, or the soul, which are, of course, fundamental tenets in the Judaeo-Christian tradition as well as Hinduism, and many other belief systems.

But don't get trapped by labels or doctrine of any kind, including any that might have crept into Zen. Tradition can be good; mindless tradition isn't. Don't dismiss the child of God because she isn't wearing sanctioned clothing. Don't dismiss the avant-garde out of ignorance. Creators can see themselves transparently in terms of 'I' with no harmful after effects.

As an unwavering proponent of individual achievement, I experience no conflict with the teachings of Zen. I am part of a power greater than myself; I know my dharma is to assert my truth, my art as a testament to the spirit in this world. No committee ever produced a single work of art.

Be eclectic and savor the sweet cream no matter who is pouring. Adopt great insights and teachings from wherever they come; there are no contradictions, complications, or competitions among universal truths.

For this reason, Zen remains an authentic system for conveying direct truth, which includes its literary pathways of: *haiku*, the shortest form of poetry; *koans*, impossible riddles; and *sutras*, the ancient sayings of Zen masters. In Zen there is also *chado*, the way of tea; *kado*, the way of flowers, *kendo*, the way of the sword, *kyudo*, Zen archery; *judo*, Zen self-defense;

Appreciation is a wonderful thing: It makes what is excellent in others belong to us as well.

VOLTAIRE

Knowing the true nature of any single thing is redemption.

EDEN

Zen:

Not reliant on the written word,
A special transmission separate from the scriptures;
Direct pointing at one's mind,
Seeing one's nature, becoming a Buddha.

BODHIDHARMA

If that dark hour comes upon you, acknowledge and confront it knowing this: that nefarious cloud of time lost will soon depart if you remain strong.

EDEN

and *shodo,* Zen calligraphy. All these forms and teachings depend on first-hand experience and personal responsibility; these disciplines stress the dynamism of the here and now, the beauty of clarity, and the apparent truth found in the present moment.

While tales, stories, parables, proverbs, and anecdotes made by Zen masters point toward the truth, the statements themselves aren't it. Truth itself, like the soul and your art, is beyond words and thoughts.

When you do hear the truth, there is nothing more to say. The word 'chair' or a painting of a chair isn't the chair. The artist Mark Rothko painted his floating abstracts of vertically aligned rectangles large enough so the viewer could step in and feel engulfed, to have a transcendental moment. Is art the truth itself or the doorway? As the Japanese Zen priest, Shunryu Suzuki-roshi, said: "When I raise the hand thus, there is Zen. But when I assert that I have raised the hand, Zen is no more there." That moment is gone. When you call attention to the moment with thinking, the truth of it is already gone.

From *The Little Book of Zen*, edited by Manuela Dunn Mascetti:

"Zen traces its origins of enlightenment directly from Buddha. According to legend, the birth of the understanding of what was to become Zen occurred at a single moment of great significance in one of the Buddha's discourses, 'The Sermon on the Mount of the Holy Vulture.' Buddha was preaching to a gathering of his disciples. He sat upon the podium and remained completely silent for a long time, and, instead of resorting to words in order to explain his point that day, he lifted a single lotus flower and held it up in his hand for all to see. The disciples were baffled and could not understand the significance of his gesture, except for Mahakashyapa who quietly smiled at Buddha to show that he fully grasped the meaning of his gesture. Buddha, seeing his smile, declared, 'I have the most precious treasure, spiritual and transcendental, which this moment I hand over to you, O venerable Mahakashyapa.' Bodhidharma, who brought Zen Buddhism to China, was a direct spiritual descendent of Mahakashyapa.

"Zen followers generally agree that this incident is the origin of their doctrine, for by raising the flower, Buddha symbolically revealed the innermost mind of Buddha-nature. The essence of Zen is revealed in what happened to Mahakashyapa, who, by letting the silence of the master penetrate to the very core of his being, understood its deep significance and attained enlightenment. The master is silent, the disciple smiles, the two minds are one. For the nearly two-and-a-half millennia that date the history of Zen, enlightenment has been the way of transmitting the message from one generation of Zen monks to the next. This direct line of experience resembles a transmission of the lamp that was first lit by Buddha so many centuries before. The sayings of the masters are thus an invaluable recording of wisdom traced through the centuries, wisdom that is as timeless as it is poignant and pertinent to us today."

Understand what Buddha had done. He lifted up the lotus flower in silence. After all, what could he have said about the flower that any of his disciples couldn't grasp on their own through firsthand experience. The universe of truth is inside of you and in front of you. Don't doubt your courage to feel the truth.

TWO ZEN SCHOOLS

For all its insights and instruction against dogma, Zen isn't beyond having traditions about proper meditation, breathing, posture, and other observances. Still, anarchy rules without some form of tradition. Tradition isn't evil; it is only detrimental when no one questions its history, validity, or usefulness. Zen isn't above interpretation, either. There are different approaches to Zen. Two main Zen schools arose (*circa* 1200 CE) in Japan. One was *Rinzai*, and the other was *Soto*. Each contributed alternate means for reaching enlightenment. The Rinzai School believed they would find enlightenment through spontaneous flashes. Followers of Soto attempted to reach enlightenment through lengthy sessions of meditation.

Meditation isn't about relaxing; it is about transcendence. Meditation is about nothing, nothing but connecting to the present moment, and then the next in a continuum while being in that moment beyond enlightenment, or what followers of Zen call *satori*. Or, put another way, once the mind reveals itself, the mind is quiet, which is the awakened state of the master who is beyond the concepts and judgments of her senses. What is left is timeless being; the traps of illusion that form clouded perceptions no longer entice.

The art is pure in this state of awareness.

Let's be clear. I'm not suggesting that you take up the robe of a Zen disciple and devote yourself to a monastic life for grasping the ineffable and brilliant simplicity of Buddha nature—which is a profound dharma if you are called. I am suggesting that, by any means necessary—from contemplation to action, you grasp the truth of your own incarnate self, which is an essential character building understanding for persevering in your life as a creator. The important thing to comprehend here is that by connecting with reality as it is, the big picture, you inherently step of out of the box that diminishes you.

By rising above self-consciousness, you distance yourself from the psychology of rejection, which in turn provides you with the insight to see rejection for what it is—merely a word, a reaction, not an eternal truth, or a life sentence.

Remember, it is your ego that is drowning in anxiety and fear—debilitating emotions that give rejection its power over you.

Embrace any form of right action, accomplishment, for it and its future reverberations may be more profound than you can know. While it is essential that *you* know the value of your work, art thrives in the face of an audience. If one other soul comprehends your art, then it is no longer the Tower of Babel; it is the communion of two—it is the lotus flower.

While there are different schools of Zen with various methods on how to reach enlightenment, they are all engaged in knowing the same thing: the fundamental concept of intuitively grasping the truth. The teachings of Zen aren't about retreating from life, but rather your full immersion in it. Those who practice Zen reject the phantom world of dogmatic beliefs, pointless ritual, and hardwired concepts; you are capable of perceiving the world directly.

Zen masters choose not to indulge in lengthy discourse because it involves enlisting the intellect. This doesn't mean that Zen is against reason, which can be no more than a rationalization; instead of layers of thinking,

So come the storms of winter

And then the birds in spring again

I do not fear the time

For who knows where the time goes? Who knows where the time goes?

SANDY DENNY

Time:

Who indeed knows where the time goes?

Does it go anywhere? Is time alive? You cannot see time. You can only experience it indirectly, like truth, by its effects. Time itself is invisible and weightless. This is proof of the metaphysical.

EDEN

truth is tackled head-on through intuition, which can't be subverted by motive. Zen teachers don't emphasize verbal methods; their technique is more direct. The object lesson in Zen is that you don't need to vocalize that you 'got it!' Your subsequent behavior will tell all. The master's work is to awaken the power of consciousness within the student who, in turn, develops intuitive understanding and confidence. Beautiful!

The more you temper your ego, the more you perfect your own character to attain freedom from illusion, not perfection—which is a fool's errand. Remember, as the master artist said: character answers all questions.

BETWEEN THE SANSKRIT

What happens when what you previously knew as being totally true suddenly becomes untrue? How do you handle such a revision of reality? Your world can be turned inside out.

Down is up and up is down. Can you accept the new standard, or do you wallow in the shallow remains of the old contradictory belief system? This is a fundamental issue you must confront—now would be a good time—in order to triumph over attachment and its palpable potential to defeat you.

Making a significant change in your perception of what is true demands discarding that which is familiar no matter what the cost, a process that is ultimately more liberating than psychologically traumatic. Everything of value comes at a price. And if you are aware, you will get what you pay for because you know the value of what you are acquiring.

To dismiss what you believed in the face of unequivocal and contradictory evidence is the enduring path of the brave artist.

What choice do you have?

Dr. Deepak Chopra, who seamlessly melds Eastern philosophy with Western sensibilities in his book, *Creating Affluence*, writes that the ancient text from India known as the *Veda*, says: "Know that one thing by knowing which everything else can be known."

What a beautiful expression. But, as important, what does it mean? What is that one thing?

The *Veda* is referring to *Brahman*. The *Upanishads*, one of the later written (*circa* 600 BCE) and introspectively radical philosophical Vedic texts, defines Brahman as Absolute Reality, Pure Being, Pure Consciousness, Pure Bliss, the truth. Brahman is in all things and is all things, but Brahman is also beyond all things. Brahman transcends our understanding, our definition, our naming. Brahman is '*neti, neti*'—not this, not that. While Brahman transcends quantitative analysis, you can paradoxically merge with it. As Dr. Chopra explains: "And there is a Sanskrit phrase '*Brahmavit brahmaiv bhavate*,' which means to the extent one knows Brahman, one becomes Brahman."

The intuitive truth is infallible.

You may be asking: So, what has Brahman to do with me?

Read between the lines.

What the Veda is saying is this: Which is smarter? Trying to overturn every conceivable rock in search of the truth; or reading hundreds of books with millions of words in a desperate attempt to know what is authentic,

---

Attachment to spiritual things is ... just as much an attachment as inordinate love of anything else.

THOMAS MERTON

What is art?

Aside from the aesthetics, which can be forgotten the minute one leaves a museum or gallery, art educates and instructs both the artist and art appreciator to feel and understand.

EDEN

what is eternally absolute; or to find that one thing that reliably reveals the truth of everything else—that one thing that could never be coerced into betraying you?

Having the courage to discern truth from artifice empowers your art and strengthens your backbone. This is what Buddha meant. Now that we are both inheritors of enlightened knowledge and fortunate to have been born beyond superstition, we are blessed with the power to overcome, which is the genius of consciousness in 'the field of all possibilities'.

You decide.

ONE FOR ALL

My art and Brahman are one. My art mirrors my authenticity; it is the galvanizing force behind my perception. Is the same true for you? Put it to the test. Find your Brahman; find the truth for yourself in the Zen mode of intuitive knowing. No classes, no workshops, no dogma and no kidding. Begin by answering the core questions in this book, and you will be pointed in the right direction, knowing that the signpost isn't the destination.

One day, your dedication will be rewarded as a truth reveals itself like the most elegant and beautiful of flowers. In that moment you will know to be silent, to smile, and to raise the lotus—knowing how Buddha had felt all those ages ago. A timeless transcendental moment. A miracle.

Although we may not agree with many of his philosophical and political views, Arthur Schopenhauer did get this part right: "All truth passes through three stages. First, it is ridiculed. Second, it is violently opposed. Third, it is accepted as being self-evident."

You will note that Schopenhauer, like Thomas Jefferson with the Declaration of Independence, also chose self-evident for clarity, avoiding the pitfall of *obvious*—my verboten word. If truth were obvious, then stage one and two wouldn't exist.

The reason Baudelaire was one of the most penetrating art critics of his time was that he analyzed less what he thought than how he felt about art.

JANET FLANNER

Don't be dogmatic.

Not all social conditioning is negative. We accept such values, conventions, and behaviors as: don't kill each other; respect one another; don't litter; red means stop; and green means go.

EDEN

CHAPTER EIGHTEEN

THE FELLOWSHIP OF CREATORS
Only the Strong Survive

NO PROBLEM ... it is in the vernacular. Dig deeper; there is more going on here than a polite reply, an accommodation, or cluelessness. As the revered and practical master from India had impressed upon me: "There *is* no problem."

You are still in bed in the morning, or it is late at night before falling asleep, and your mind is pursuing all the issues, which invariably involve the past, the future, your art, finances, fantasies, other people, personal possessions, or, most likely, all of the above.

TICK TOCK, TICK TOCK

Stop through self-discipline. Suspend the inner incessant monologue for a moment; see the absolution in disarming angst with gratitude; see the world beyond the box containing your problems. There is no honor in being metaphysically challenged. You can transcend your to-do list. As Dr. Deepak Chopra points out, you are where your attention takes you. What does this problem want to teach me? In the act of asking the question, you remove the psychic thorn that hooks you into the issue. Alleviating knee jerk pain then allows you to recast the problem as a lesson that benefits you.

Here is an example of confronting rejection and the ensuing subtext that evolved as I was working on this chapter. Don't get stuck in the insidiously preconceived fabric of routine, of attachment. Follow the thread, any thread, into the intricacy of the weave, and let the tapestry tell the tale of live and learn, not kiss and tell.

THE POET AND THE PAINTER

While researching and writing this book, I contacted a short list of people whom I respected—from the internationally known to others below the media radar—for an insight about persevering that would serve the artist. Nearly all were generous with their time, experience, and a quote.

But, and there always seems to be that nefarious *but*, there was one author and poet of some note. I had sent him a letter plus a postcard invitation

A person who doubts himself is like a man who would enlist in the ranks of his enemies and bear arms against himself.

He makes his failure certain by himself being the first person to be convinced of it.

AMBROSE BIERCE

If you know someone who seems to have everything going for him and is still nervous, then you know the importance of the soul.

EDEN

from one of my past art exhibitions. I wrote a personal dedication to him on the card, which featured one of my artworks on the reverse side. While my name might not have been on the tip of his tongue, we had corresponded before and he did have one of my books, so I wasn't a nonentity.

And, even if I were, so what?

We must all begin somewhere.

In my letter, I described the intention of my book and requested a pertinent quote that I might use. Although I could have most likely found a suitable passage about rejection from his bounty of published works, I felt compelled to contact him, feeling *sure* he would take the opportunity to provide other artists with a personal observation about confronting rejection and other tribulations. No response. Then, after a few months, I emailed him with the same request, and got no reply from that attempt either. Since I couldn't assume my correspondence had reached him, I dialed his number, and the poet picked up. He had no recollection of my letter or email. Okay, I thought, let's start again. After briefly explaining the purpose of my call, I heard only dead air from the other end. After many long seconds, he said: "I'm not going to bite on this one."

WRONG. WRONG. RIGHT.

Not only was his response a seeming non sequitur, it was jaded, especially considering the subject matter of my book. Have the courage to know right from wrong; don't give those whom you admire more wiggle room than anyone else. Otherwise, you are caving into fear. Fence sitting is for the birds.

I had to suppress my tongue. Although I could have come back with any number of rejoinders, I wouldn't place myself in an adversarial position. 'No' is bait that conceals a sharp hook, and I wouldn't bite either. After all, this wasn't the reception I expected from a poet who ostensibly lived by sacred energies and by the impact of words upon others. I did want to add: Does this mean reading my manuscript for a book jacket blurb is out of the question? But even humor needs an opening. There was nothing left to say. I thanked him for his time and got off the phone.

Rejection comes in all forms, and from other artists, too. And, as this book extols, there is opportunity concealed within each problem, within each rejection. Take a few moments and role-play. What would you have said to the poet who had turned down your simple request? Play out the scene with different replies to their logical conclusions and you will see what I mean. You end up a salesman, or sounding defensive, or you put your self in an unfavorable situation. Of course, there are those dire and demanding times—when your character is being assailed—when one must speak up. Mostly, however, restraint is best. Knowing when to do one or the other comes with experience and self-discipline.

There is irony lurking out there waiting to happen when you least expect it. I may encounter this poet again in some other context. Should a meeting ever occur, I would know that my decision to maintain dignity had been the right one and well worth the price one pays for self-control. You might be thinking: What if the poet reads this account? Won't that cast a negative fog over any future interactions? It would be my pleasure if the poet did stumble upon himself in this narrative, and I stand my ground. Remember, mouthing off without conscious purpose is a losing game. You give the other person control, convincing him that he was right to do what he did in the first place. Not on my watch, and I trust, not on yours.

FELLOWSHIP OF CREATORS

Here was the poet whom I felt had a thought, a verse, something of value to offer on the subject of rejection. I am respectful of another person's time, and I realize he was under no obligation to contribute a vowel. However, this wasn't about obligation; this was about the fellowship of creators. If we let each other down, what else is there? I call it fraud. Live up to your word; nothing else will do. You have got to give to get; it is so written. By quoting the poet, I would have also introduced his work to a new and appreciative audience. Instead, he blew me off as if I were a telemarketer trying to sell him swampland in Florida. While he might have had many other things to do, he could have simply said he was too busy and sent me off with a good thought, but he didn't. Rather than offering a word of encouragement, he came back with a 'biting' salvo. Can you sense the edge, the barb—the negative implication in his reply? No, I'm not too sensitive. Be still. Trust in your own self. Hear the subtle vibrating truth of words as they are spoken. As you may have heard, it isn't what you say; it is how you say it that matters. This was no way to treat a fellow creator. There are ways to say 'no' that do no harm—artist or not. I know. I receive such equivalent requests for my time and experience from others, too.

If we dropped the above scenario from further investigation, it remains but a façade, nothing more. There are deeper strata to mine in the layers of communication between the poet and my self. The power of intent is stronger than any resistance you may encounter, including rejection. If the poet had said that he merely had no time, as I initially proposed, it would have been the 'wrong' answer for me. His reply was, in fact, the 'right' response as it was a direct reaction to my intuitive intent, which manifested itself from a dimension beyond cognitive thinking, beyond the poet's control. No one can resist the force of unfaltering intent. The poet had no choice but to help me, as you will see. Intention is more powerful than the resistance of any curmudgeon. Remember, if you want depth, you must dig deep.

FARMER'S KNIGHT & HAIKU

One of my email pen pals in the Netherlands, who shares my delight in kites, told me what his father, Antoon Sauvé, a former farmer's knight, had taught him. "Always ask if you want something and give when you are asked. That makes life easier for everybody."

You might say: 'Well, maybe the poet was having a bad *haiku* day.' Never fall for feeble reasoning or excuse bad manners. If you do, then you have earned the consequences. No conscious individual brings the past into the unspoiled purity of the present moment. Such behavior is unacceptable, and I don't need an act of congress to enforce this rule for my own self. If you are in a foul mood, don't answer the phone and spare the caller your bile.

It seemed that my request of the poet had been a bust. I sat at my desk while Larry and Beau, my two Yorkshire Terriers, lay blissfully asleep on

I take rejection as someone blowing a bugle in my ear to wake me up and get going, rather than retreat.

SYLVESTER STALLONE

Remember, like in Edgar Allan Poe's tale of The Purloined Letter, you could be looking at it right now and not see it.

EDEN

the nearby couch. After enough moments had passed, I disengaged from my ego and attachment; after all, if I'm smart ego will exist to serve me.

As the density and heat of my letdown faded from opaque into translucence, the significance of my interaction with the poet began to reveal itself. Unwittingly, his spontaneous response exposed a chink into his underlying nature, which was exceedingly more relevant for my book than any possible quote he could have provided. What did I—once again—discover about rejection? Be persistent. Listen to what people say, and you will learn.

Whether you like what they tell you or not is irrelevant. Be dispassionate. Artists aren't above reproach, stupidity, pettiness, or nastiness.

The poet incident instigated yet another issue, an important subtext on the page of rejection that you too must address when it occurs. My rule is to only concern myself with the opinions of those whom I hold in high regard. How does one then confront disappointment in someone he had previously respected? This is a major hurdle; how you handle the situation draws your character into play; you don't want to lose respect for yourself. How can I reconcile my own rule with what had taken place with the curt poet? I can't have it both ways; double standards cut in either direction and won't do. I either value this person or not. Do I throw the poet out with the 'prose-water' or not? Of course, the short answer is that even the most exemplary among us isn't without failings.

I had been on this precipice before where character, respect, and where I stood converged as the issues at hand. To enhance my meaning, let me describe two examples, one from recent history, and one from trenches of firsthand experience.

WAR OF CURRENTS

We associate Thomas Alva Edison with being the great man who invented the incandescent electric light, among other things. Contrary to popular belief, however, he didn't 'invent' the light bulb, but rather he improved upon a fifty-year-old idea. Edison's achievement was packaging electric light. His invention included not only an incandescent electric light, but also a system containing all the necessary elements for making the incandescent light a practical technology.

'Tesla who?' Although seemingly overlooked for years, there is a current renaissance of interest in the eccentric man who understood electricity. In the mid-1880's, Nikola Tesla, a lanky twenty-eight-year-old Serbian immigrant and eccentric genius, nervously laid out his plans for alternating electric current (AC) to his hero, Thomas Edison. However, Edison was already heavily committed to direct electric current (DC), a delivery system that was both cumbersome and inefficient. Edison gave the eager and penniless Tesla a job, but not why you might reason. He hired Tesla to keep him from further developing AC, which was clearly the superior technology. After a brief time, Tesla quit working for Edison over two primary reasons: the AC issue and Edison's failure to pay him a $50,000 premium for a select number of innovations he had developed for DC power.

In what was to become known as the 'war of the currents', Edison, desperate to convince his customers that AC was dangerous, sponsored public circus-like spectacles where AC power was used to electrocute dogs and old horses.

A realization is like having a mini-reincarnation that burns up undesirable karma.

EDEN

In 1887, Tesla filed for seven U.S. patents in polyphase AC motors and power transmission. These innovations would turn out to be the most valuable patents since the telephone. Soon after, George Westinghouse, head of the Westinghouse Electric Company in Pittsburgh, bought the patent rights to Tesla's system of alternating-current dynamos, transformers, and motors. There was a power struggle between Edison's direct-current systems and the Tesla-Westinghouse alternating-current approach, which ultimately won the war.

Tesla's system of power distribution became the industry standard, and although the industrialized postmodern world wouldn't exist without AC power, the brilliant Tesla remains far from being a name associated with household current. When it came to research, Edison was the self-taught dogged trial and error man, the technology scribe who saw invention as five percent inspiration and ninety-five percent perspiration. Tesla, who had a formal European education, was a poet of technology. He perceived many of his innovative inventions in precise detail before moving to the construction stage. Genius in whatever form can't be contained; genius is, after all, dedication.

After learning about the friction generated between Tesla and Edison, I was disappointed in avuncular old Alva who wanted to monopolize and saddle electricity with an inferior distribution system. Here we had Edison, the Genius of Menlo Park and a giant of his age, looking quite small in contrast to the more autonomous leaning Tesla, whose share of idiosyncrasies didn't include greed. He believed energy should be free for all, and gave away a fortune in patent royalties to keep Westinghouse Electric from going under. Besides AC electric current, Tesla's inventions include: neon light, florescent light, self-propelled rockets, laser beams, radio, and, among others, designs for a perpetual motion (energy) machine.

Although Edison recognized Tesla's brilliance, he was ready to bury the AC competition, which was the superior technology. Edison too, it seems, betrayed the fellowship of creators. If he had embraced Tesla's work, Edison could have taken a short-term loss and would have come out smelling much better, and richer in both character and finances in good time. But ego can destroy the visionary as well as anyone. While we can't and shouldn't ignore Edison's contributions, we can learn a lesson from his sanctioning of cruelty to animals to his shortsighted behavior in this affair—clearly tainted by avarice and no doubt jealousy of the young Serbian, who had an intuitive grasp of electrical power. When you recognize a new and more powerful standard, bid it welcome and immediately adopt it as your own.

WHEAT FROM THE CHAFF

The other instance of putting respect in perspective is firsthand, involving a great painter and myself. We met many years ago. At the time, he gave me—his student—the fundamental canon. He said: 'Take all that is good from me, and forget the rest.' I followed his direction, and it has ultimately led me to rare and wonderful understandings about art and life. He was someone I respected—perhaps the most of anyone I had ever met. But there were aspects of his behavior I couldn't reconcile. When you are in the presence of a force of nature, it is often difficult to distinguish art

Rejection is the other side of accolades—and both balance us out, and twist our perceptions. We wish we could get along without them both, but someone keeps seeking the honors, which lead inevitably to the possibility of rejection.

I always remember about the artists who were jilted in their lives.

RODIN

What does it mean to have as much trust in our failures as our successes?

DAVID WHYTE

Someone who has talent knows it; what he may not yet know is what that talent is.

EDEN

from foible. Although a Promethean creator, he had issues that made him, in some instances, petty, too. *Taking* from him as he had instructed me wasn't like a shopping spree at the mall. I had to shed my ego to receive. I gave my mentor what I could in return, as nothing valuable is free. The exchange rate for greatness is non-negotiable.

I also learned that being a formidable artist isn't necessarily synonymous with sainthood.

While some great men may have serious flaws, how much better it would be for them if they didn't. I'm not referring to perfection as no one can be accused of living on that flawless isle in the sea of panacea. While an artist may be gifted and unstable, he creates despite his affliction. It is equally true that an artist can be gifted and stable—for his own sake. I had listened well to my teacher. I took the good, culled the rest, and eventually disengaged, now a free agent creating a universe of my own. The student must know when it is time to move on. As an artist, you must decide your history for your own self. I had to learn this one-on-one.

Individuals from my past who had 'disappointed' me had also provided me with a great service—lessons of a type appreciated only in retrospect. Keep the lens on hindsight clear and free from bias. Did you act honorably, or did you deserve that kick in the ass? Holding no regrets or grievances allows you to grow, evolve, and to move on.

THE POET'S BARB CONTINUED...

While I don't dismiss the poet's literary contribution, he convinced me it was time to reevaluate, time to reduce his stature from eminent and distinguished to a 'Planck length' sized bard on a scale only a quantum field theorist could measure. This is extreme, but I am exercising poetic license. On balance, however, the poet's 'unhelpful' remark galvanized my understanding that even heroes must be held accountable for less than admirable behavior; veneration is best left for the Creator. Don't lionize, idolize, or make celebrated figures (this list includes all those who may reject or accept your art) into icons of perfection who you deem as essential to your work; this corrupts both you and them.

When, for example, I was in Hollywood, I saw worthy film projects fall apart because the producers, attempting to obtain financing, made a 'name' actor (or director) an indispensable part of the package. This was an unrecoverable mistake in leverage; talent isn't always available when you are ready, and it gave too much power to the actor and his agent. Although attaching specific talent is a well-worn formula for making a film costing many millions more attractive to a studio or an independent group of investors, it doesn't insure success and can queer the deal.

An astute approach for most deals, including your own, is to couch things for flexibility. In the film deal, one might say: In the lead role, we will have an actor of so and so's caliber. This perspective takes the edge off the egos involved and permits maneuvering room for unanticipated contingencies, including breaks for as yet unknown talent.

With much of the attention focused on bankable A-list actors or directors, style can easily overtake substance. The quality of the screenplay, the star of any film, can and often does suffer, which is why good films are rare.

While negotiating contracts, if the 'essential' actor bailed for whatever reason, the producer had no deal.

Remember the Law of Non-Attachment and its inherent flexibility for creating new opportunities. Artists, stars, prima donnas, museum directors, gallery owners, art publishers and poet laureates, are people—not infallible avatars—after all.

As Mark Twain observed: "Keep away from people who try to belittle your ambitions. Small people always do that, but the really great make you feel that you, too, can become great."

MISSION ACCOMPLISHED

At the core of every problem, there is a perennial kernel of knowledge that you can harvest to use now and for the next time your soul needs a bit of trail mix on your journey as an artist. Problems are oddly effervescent. They defy gravity and want to rise to the top of your thoughts where they can burst onto the scene called home base—where your ego resides. If you try to repress them, you keep them alive and bubbly as in a closed bottle of soda pop. When you release the pressure of ego, which wants to control everything, you open the cap, liberating the problems until they have no choice but to fizzle off into nearby flatland according to the laws of bubbles and physics.

All great art is self-taught for this reason: no one can teach you to be original.

EDEN

In the realm of problems, I rate my skirmish with the poet on an order of magnitude I will call: mission accomplished.

Do I throw the poet out with the 'prose-water'? No. Take all that is good and discard the rest. If this sounds calculating, remember everything in the universe does add up. I can discern what is useful from what isn't because the poet, who was a word miser, provided me with a useful sentence; in so many words, he reminded me of the freedom of self-control and the rewards of introspection. He, like the sought after A-list actor, wasn't an indispensable part of my deal.

The poet's self had spoken directly to my self because of the power of my intent. I can't emphasize this enough. Every artist must at some point intuitively know when she has outgrown her guide—whether a mentor in proximity or teacher from afar. Savor the morsels of brilliance and leave the crazy-making negative shenanigans behind.

Of course, to discern the difference between art and nonsense, she must be an artist who has found her dharma, her purpose in life, which is her pillar of strength.

QUESTIONS AND PATTERNS

In her book, *Awakening Intuition*, Dr. Mona Lisa Schulz writes: "Why am I here? This is the plaintive, fundamental question voiced by men and women since the beginning of time. What is our purpose for being? Why do we live? We want to know not only the collective purpose of the human race on earth but also the meaning and reason for each individual life, the purpose for which you and I and the man next door and the woman down the streets exist. All of us, as we go through life, need a sense of our own life's purpose. The failure to connect with our purpose affects us profoundly in the seventh emotional center."

Physics is delighted with the math—the equation must balance and the result is black and white for all concerned.

Art regales itself with ambiguity, for that is the beautiful nature of a painting—a metaphysical equation of infinite subtlety each one of us must interpret for ourselves.

EDEN

As Buddha taught, it is our work to discover our work, and then embrace it with passion. The question isn't why are we here; the question is why are you here.

Inextricably woven into the web of our desires is a pattern, a universal gossamer glyph easily interpreted by any dedicated individual. The pattern reveals a sublime structure known as the Law of Non-Attachment, which is an aspect of self-discipline cited throughout this book. Becoming attached to a specific goal or outcome narrows the field of opportunity. With the poet, for example, if I had remained fixated on getting *the* quote about rejection from him, my narrow field of attention would have remained frozen on disappointment and rejection; and I might not have realized that my desire and intent had taken an unanticipated turn, which presented me with a prize, an insight, supremely more valuable than the one I had asked for. Feel the truth of this statement: when you become attached to a particular outcome, you become its slave—impotent to awareness and blind to serendipity.

A TIME TO SPEAK

What is the problem? Is it a tragedy, a nuisance, or something between? Is it causing angst, anxiety, disappointment, frustration, grief, anger, or pain? What is the point of going through any of these experiences if you won't use them to get stronger, smarter, and intuitively savvy? We are mortals, and these emotions abound within us. As I write these words, I am confronting issues that involve two people who refuse to fulfill their commitments to me. What can I do? Phone calls haven't worked. I drive over to the place of business of one of these slackers, and I confront him with the issue. Although he eventually agrees to resolve the problem, he is also reluctant and the resentment in his voice is palpable. Why bother to make good in a halfhearted manner? When you decide to make things right, do so graciously and liberate your own self. This makes for positive feelings and goodwill for all concerned, and it is the way to keep your customers—who are patrons after all. While the perpetrator here may not yet see the wisdom in this, it is yet another lesson I won't forget. When you are ready to make good, mean it.

The other person is intractable and won't budge. I can't persuade him into doing 'the right thing'. After all, he has something I need that is of extreme value, so he might feel that he is in charge. What I can do and decide to do is this: I choose to control my own self, my own response, my own behavior, and that puts me ahead—in all ways. I let this individual know that I am disappointed in him, which is an exceedingly effective tactic that sets the stage, giving the other person room to make good or not. In the end, I told this person that I released him from his debt: I took the responsibility away from him. I don't need to carry the extra weight of this psychic negativity around my neck either. A few days later, I applied myself to a complex task and completed the project on my own. In a significant way, the obstinate person had done me a favor. He reinforced my sense of self-reliance, an essential quality for the artist as a creator, and one who will triumph over rejection.

If I become undisciplined and tell someone off, which may feel 'good' for a transitory moment, I pay the emotional toll for my momentary lapse in judgment. If, however, I give someone a shakedown on purpose and not out of haste, then the consequences are understood and I am on steady ground. Once said, it can't be unsaid. Before mouthing off, I want to be sure I know all the facts; I don't assume anything; it is possible *I* am the one who hasn't been clear. And isn't it exceedingly better if I make that discovery on my own instead of placing myself in an untenable situation? There is a time to speak up, and you know it intuitively: you are compelled to do so with courage and awareness. There is also a time to remain silent until you can see dispassionately. The art here, as you can appreciate, is when to speak up or not. Intuition guides me through the maze of such decisions. Speaking up may provide you with an adrenalin boost of some instant gratification. The alternative of keeping quiet, however, demands patience. The benefits of silence most often take time to reveal themselves.

When dealing with a problem that includes a person to whom you are attached, it is much simpler and more powerful to state your expectation without editorializing or ad hominem remarks—that is, attacking someone personally instead of their performance, which is the issue you want resolved. No matter how much I need a person's contribution, I refuse to let them hold me hostage if that is their game. In fact and in retrospect, such awkward and at times infuriating situations have consistently and unerringly catapulted me toward better opportunities.

YOUR TEACHER

The problem may want to teach you patience, introspection, art, candor, clarity, assertiveness, humility, perspective, morality, ethics, or some other aspect of character. At the heart of each problem is your lesson and the lesson plan is to, as my mother likes to say: 'Nip things in the bud'. All the issues you face and your responses to them are a reflection of you in that moment. Looking at a problem in the lucid mirror of awareness, you eventually confront the liberating truth as expressed by the sage from India: "There *is* no problem." This isn't Orwellian doublespeak, or a new-age slogan blended in panacea-mango juice. The 'problem' is mostly an external event; all the feelings and thoughts about it reside within you. This dynamic is neither good nor bad; it is a relationship for you to use, for you to explore, and ultimately for you to master. The 'problem' isn't having a bad day, *you* are. In this sense, you are the problem. Our problems depend solely upon us for their existence. We are referring here to manageable challenges, not dire circumstances.

You excise yourself from victimhood when you accept responsibility for how you feel; and, as a direct result, you learn to persevere over rejection as well as acceptance, for it too has pitfalls. Look at the pathos of a fading star or the angst of a 'successful' artist who has sold out. To acknowledge and then practice self-control over your problems has unlimited emancipating power that can only be appreciated from firsthand experience.

As Jerry Butler so eloquently and prophetically evokes in song: 'Only the strong survive'.

No problem!

It is dangerous to be right in matters on which the established authorities are wrong.

VOLTAIRE

I did not set out to be an artist. I set out to find some truth, and I found one: that artist and soul were one in the same.

EDEN

CHAPTER NINETEEN

FACE-TO-FACE
Ego and Soul

ART WITHOUT SOUL, or spirit, isn't alive. The spirit in art is the quality of life. Do you want to be that ubiquitous cog in the wheel of eternity, or a creator who presses on through difficulty and rejection as if you had purpose? A creator contributes original work to reality. A creator has a clear sense of her self worth without having to resort to flagrant pride or prejudice.

In his book, *Anam Cara: A Book of Celtic Wisdom*, John O'Donohue writes: "The Bible says that no one can see God and live. In a transferred sense, no person can see himself and live. All you can ever achieve is a sense of your soul."

No one can convince you that your soul exists. You can't know your soul through hearsay, dogma, or thinking about it. I don't like compartmentalizing the integrated whole individual into facets as if these facets were capable of independent action. After all, the various aspects of ourselves that we love to label still add up to being ourselves. With that said, it is still helpful to acknowledge the role of the ego and the soul. You must know where you stand with this duo. Neither the ego or the soul can be seen; they are, however, recognizable by the consequences of their actions, the trails they leave behind.

EGO IN SPACE-TIME

The ego self is a basic survival construct. While it can be cordial to others, as Freud noted, the ego is primarily a function of the mind as in 'I am separate and distinct'. But this isn't separate and distinct as in unique. Ego is mostly deluded by fear, self-importance, and pointless competition; it is never fulfilled—never. To understand the ego and its power over you, you must experience the moment when you first become aware of what the ego (you) is doing, and in that searing moment of insight and shock you realize: 'Aha, this is it. This is the thing preventing me from learning. It is myself. Not my own *self*, which is the soul, but myself, the ego-based self of rigidity that is rooted in anxiety, envy, and doubt.' Fortunately, there

I'm a rebel, soul rebel. I'm a capturer, soul adventurer. I'm a rebel, soul rebel. I'm a capturer, soul adventurer.

BOB MARLEY

To get a bearing on the mysterious ego, you need only listen to that incessant monologue, that chatter inside your head, you know, the one you would want to stop.

On balance, the voice of the soul is something you could listen to forever.

EDEN

is also an upside: a healthy ego devoid of neurosis provides stability for your independent instincts to adapt to reality and interact with the outside world. When the ego confines itself to the well-being of your temporal identity, as in pinpointing your individual presence on the space-time grid, as in remembering your name, address, phone number, email address, and other personal data, then all is in harmony. Remember, the ego isn't the enemy here; the ego is a function of your state of awareness. Anything unrestrained, no matter how beneficial, can spell disaster: a little sun is good; too much sun can cause painful sunburn, or worse.

SOUL POSSESSION

The soul self is the metaphysical masterpiece of existence; the soul is immune to negativity and rejection, and it is the galvanizing force of truth and great art. All properties of the metaphysical are available to anyone dedicated to discovering the absolute truth of that 'thing' at all costs; nothing less will balance this equation. Truth that is absolute, indivisible, timeless and eternal goes for a fixed daily rate of exchange paid out over the time necessary to acquire it—possession occurs when you prove this truth to your own self. Everyone, in equal measure, must pay to play—and this cost is whatever it happens to be in the moment, which includes anything you possess or can barter, including ordinary cash. The truth will promptly meet you halfway once it senses you are willing to go all the way. When the moment of truth does come, you won't flinch, Will you? If you are on that mission you feel is your purpose in life, and somewhere you have a hidden backdoor, a way out, what do you think will happen?

You will become that which you contemplate.

To quote again from *Anam Cara:* "Sometimes our spiritual programs take us far away from our inner belonging. We become addicted to the methods and programs of psychology and religion. We become so desperate to learn how to be, that our lives pass, and we neglect the practice of being. One of the lovely things in the Celtic mind is its sense of spontaneity, which is one of the greatest spiritual gifts. To be spontaneous is to escape the cage of the ego by trusting that which is beyond the self. One of the greatest enemies of spiritual belonging is the ego. The ego does not reflect the real shape of one's individuality. The ego is the false self born out of fear and defensiveness. The ego is a protective crust that we draw around our affections. It is created out of timidity, the failure to trust the Other and to respect our own Otherness. One of the greatest conflicts in life is the conflict between the ego and the soul. The ego is threatened, competitive, and stressed, whereas the soul is drawn more toward surprise, spontaneity, the new and the fresh. Real soul has humor, irony, and no obsessive self-seriousness. It avoids what is weary, worn, or repetitive."

SELF-RELIANT

Film director Ridley Scott said that: "You get clever with a little amount of money because it makes you think. There's a big lesson in there."

For instance, Scott described a situation that came up while he was directing his second feature film, the 1979 critical and box-office success, *Alien.* One of the last things on the production schedule to shoot was discovering the alien spaceship relic on the planet. After seeing the miniature model of the planet and the spaceship, Scott realized it wouldn't work; no one in the audience would be fooled by this miniature set piece. This was years before computer-generated imagery (CGI) became widely used for creating incredible digital visual effects. In any event, the production was also out of money.

Scott borrowed a consumer video camera, then, holding the camera in hand along the ground, shot footage as he tracked his way toward the spaceship on the miniature set. This was the scene that made it to the screen. The reason he could get away with using a twitchy poor quality video image was that it fit into the natural environment of the scene: the audience was seeing the approach to the alien spaceship relic through the eyes of Ash, the science officer. Ash was sitting in front of a monitor on the *Nostromo* (the crew's spaceship) watching these grainy and noisy images as they were coming through cameras mounted on the headsets of the crewmembers on the planet's surface. Not only did Scott turn a potentially negative situation into a positive solution, the overall otherworldly feel of the improvised shot was incredibly effective because of the context. No one would guess that this critical scene had been entirely jury-rigged out of necessity.

Many established Hollywood directors had turned down *Alien*. But Scott, who at the time had directed only one other film, read the script, and agreed to direct it. He had a clear sense that this material could be enticing in the right hands—his. Not all directors are created equal, and Scott is among those who can pull off a unique vision. He attended London's Royal Academy of Art where, among others, David Hockney, the painter, was one of his contemporaries. Scott made excellent use of his art-school background in developing the realistic sets and intense atmosphere that distinguished *Alien* as an original work. Of course, conceptual art is integral to filmmaking, especially in genres that use fantasy and science fiction to tell the story. Scott had supplanted ego with the elegant necessity of self-reliance, which is the soul of invention and a hallmark characteristic of the true artist.

REALITY FOR SALE

On the other extreme, it isn't enough to throw money at a problem. There is more to developing character and knowing the truth than parting with the legal tender of your particular realm; if it were merely a matter of moolah, every person with a million dollars in the bank would be above reproach and in bliss, and every movie costing many tens of millions of dollars would be a critical and box-office success. This non-negotiable fee for acquiring the truth is based on an exchange rate of universal currency that is minted only with the stamp of direct experience and honest action; this fee is based on freeing you from the illusions your ego has provided for you. These illusions are fabricated constructs—delusions—accomplished only with your tacit consent.

When the opportunity surfaces, and it will if you are seeking the truth, you must reassure your ego that it is merely time for it to embrace humility—which is a life-enriching incarnation, not a death sentence. With this newfound self-imposed detente, you will rise beyond the limitations

How strange a thing this is! The Priest telleth me that the Soul is worth all the gold in the world, and the merchants say that it is not worth a clipped piece of silver.

OSCAR WILDE

Remember, the devil of lore is not after your home, your car, your swimming pool, your job, or any of your temporal acquisitions; he is after the one thing you truly own and that you do take with you: your soul.

EDEN

Every artist dips his brush in his own soul, and paints his own nature into his pictures.

HENRY WARD BEECHER

you had boxed yourself into. In the same way your ego knows facts, your soul knows universal law. Ego works with relative facts; soul works with absolute truth.

When you sense the unmistakable quality of your intuition for the first time, the presence of the Creator in your blood is also self-evident; it is the moment of truth when the metaphysical steps over and becomes visceral; it is when the spirit becomes manifest; and it is the instant when you snap out of your dullness to take responsibility for confronting that inner self-defeating voice inside your head, which is none other than thyself. You need no one else to confirm the epiphany. Nothing less than such firsthand experience will ignite that fire in the belly that takes on all comers, defeating rejection where it stands—not in hostility but in soul awareness.

Do you feel the heat?

In whatever form it takes, intuition is straightforward, not cryptic or psychologically obtuse. The soul is a beautifully polished mirror, accurately reflecting the reality of your life, and of your art. When you see your own self for the first time without the veneer of self-indulgence and ego, the old and harried stereotypical you fades like a shadow in the clouds, and the soul in you emerges. You realize that there is only one reality and that you are now seeing more of it. Temporal matters can't intimidate the soul; this is your strength to persevere.

VOLUME CONTROL

To be reborn—the transmigration of the soul—is a recurring motif of salvation in many belief systems, from Hinduism to Christianity. To see your own self as you truly are is also a theme in literature. In *The Metamorphosis*, for example, Franz Kafka wrote a timeless short story about a man who wakes up one morning to the nightmarish realization that he is an insect. Kafka's allegorical tale is outlandish and a mirror for seeing yourself as you are without the dense cloak of illusion that causes atrophy, disappointment, and pain; lifting the seductive veil of illusion and ego is also a pillar of Buddhism and its later incarnation, Zen.

Fortunately, there is good news: you don't have to die to be reborn.

The reincarnation of your existence from being asleep to wakefulness and awareness can happen in one spontaneous moment when the awareness of consciousness is palpable. But don't get too cocky. Remaining awake can't be taken for granted. The true rebel has learned that freedom is a synonym for self-discipline, for mastering himself.

When you achieve that intuitive sense of your soul, you will know the meaning of passion: rejection, or any obstacle, can't rob you of your talent, character, or your dharma. In time, your ego, no longer feeling isolated or in fear, will shed its adversarial identity. The inner critic in your head will fade away as you lower the volume on its need to exist. For the first time, you will no longer hunger for distractions—in whatever form—from the present moment. You will look in the mirror and know what it means to experience a quiet mind, to be healed, to simply 'be'.

Remember, every piece of art is redemption.

To persevere you cannot falter, no matter what. If this sounds adamant, then the meaning is clear.

Since you are asking for a lot, you must do whatever is necessary. Otherwise, you are being disingenuous with your self. This is a distinction not a judgment. Nothing—except you—can prevent you from living an authentic life.

If your desire to create is fueled on less than a fire in the belly, then fully realize your situation: to be self-aware is the goal.

To live your dream, you must wake up and remain awake.

CHAPTER TWENTY

DIALOGUE DE JOUR
Kites • Color Pencils • Prophecy • Kachina Dolls

IN THE ART of conversation, it is essential to know when to move silently and when to speak up.

Here are several encounters that compelled me to engage, teaching me a thing or two about my art and my own standards. If the moment is right, and you trust your feelings, go ahead, articulate your perception and confront the issue. As Dr. Seuss reportedly reminded us: "Be who you are and say what you feel, because those who mind don't matter and those who matter don't mind." Listen dispassionately. Hear and learn how well you express and distinguish your self. Can you do better?

Remember, in nature, sheep flock together while eagles soar alone.

STAND BY YOUR KITES

After my book on kites had been published, I was surprised to see how quickly my cachet in this realm garnered attention. I immediately began receiving invitations to judge kite contests, write articles, appear on TV and radio, and give kite workshops. Among the offers, one jumped to the top of the list. The executive editor (I will call him Fred) of a well-respected and large circulation science magazine contacted me through my publisher. Would I write a major piece on kite technology for the magazine?

I met with Fred in the magazine's spacious New York City office to go over the scope of the project. He told me they had been thinking about doing a kite feature from a 'what's new in technology' point of view for some time. It was winter, and the publisher wanted the article to run in one of their early summer issues. Taking their lead-time into account, this gave me about three months to research and write the piece. We discussed the basic elements for the article. They would also assign a photographer to travel across the country; he would visit various kite builders of my choosing and take photos of their designs.

This project had a professional budget. We shook hands on the fee, and I left the office flying over what was a plum assignment. The contract arrived in the mail a few days later. I went to work and completed the piece on my

The worst thing I can be is the same as everybody else. I hate that. That's why I went into bodybuilding in the first place.

It was the idea of taking the risk by yourself rather than with a whole team.

ARNOLD SCHWARZENEGGER

To see beneath the surface of things is a gift and a responsibility. A graphic example of this ability as metaphor is a key element in the 1999 film, The Matrix.

Characters in the story who have been deprogrammed to see the 'truth' can then also see material reality as it is—in this case, the form of a man, a woman, a child, or anything is composed of nothing more than endless streams of computer machine code that is invisible to the uninitiated.

Reality isn't all that different.

EDEN

due date. Fred was totally pleased, and the accompanying photos turned out great—from incredible kites in action to kites as art.

I was ready to move on to another assignment, but hadn't yet anticipated what it would be when I learned that my sister would be having surgery. She lived in the Washington, D.C. area. I had volunteered to help out, as my sister would need bed rest for a couple of weeks. While her husband was working, I would handle things in their home as needed.

Before flying off with my five-pound Yorkshire Terrier, Larry, I called Fred and gave him my number in Maryland in case he needed me.

Everything went well. My sister was soon on the mend, and Larry enjoyed romping in his new country setting. Days on the calendar flipped along at a quick pace. It was Friday on my last weekend there. I had come back from food shopping when my sister told me Fred called. He wanted to speak with me.

Now what? I thought the piece had already gone to bed for the upcoming issue. I called. Well, Fred told me, the publisher wanted to cut the piece from six full color pages to four, and they wanted to know what to cut.

Okay, I saw red. Not good.

Without thinking, the words came out of my mouth as if they were inevitable: "I'm sorry to hear that Fred, but you can't do that."

Silence. Of course, the magazine held all the power. If they didn't want your piece for whatever reason, they would pay you the agreed upon kill fee and your work would never see the glory of the newsstands.

"Why not?" Fred asked.

Okay, I said to myself. I am still in the game.

"The piece is tightly integrated," I said. "It's a whole concept, and every element is necessary. If I cut something, the power and range of the article are destroyed and it wouldn't do your magazine justice. You told me you wanted a piece that no one would forget. Remember?"

Fred said: "I don't know. They're pretty set on cutting it, and they will cut what they want if you don't tell them what to edit out. The publisher has never given so much room to a kite article. I mean a full six-color page spread. Four wouldn't be so bad."

By this time, my mouth was totally dry, and I knew I was right.

"You can't cut the piece, Fred. It won't work. Would you trim the Mona Lisa so it could fit into a smaller frame?"

I was stretching it, but I knew I couldn't back off. I was in no position to tell him what he could do, but I was in the position to live up to my standard.

"Okay," said Fred. "Let me think about this over the weekend. I'll get back to you. Will you be at this number?"

"I'll be here Monday morning, but I'm flying home that afternoon."

A long weekend loomed ahead, and one that I would have to sweat out. Why do these things always seem to happen on a Friday? Although being a contributor to this magazine held prestige, I had decided to stand my ground knowing there might be a price to pay. But I was prepared to walk.

It was late Monday morning as I was getting out of the shower, when I heard my sister call up to me, saying: "Fred is on the phone."

"So, Fred. What's the good word?" I said.

"I wanted to catch you before your flight. Well, you've got the six pages as we discussed," Fred said, sounding genuinely pleased and surprised simultaneously.

A definitive 'y-e-s' flowed silently from my lips.

"That is definitely a good word. What happened?" I said. It is always a good idea to hear how the mechanics of success work. There will be a next time.

Fred explained that he thought about it over the weekend, and the image of cutting the Mona Lisa stayed with him. He decided that early Monday morning he would show the full six-page spread to the publisher, who, up until then, had only heard six color pages without having seen the piece. After a few minutes of reviewing the text and photographs as a complete concept, the publisher told Fred to run with it as is.

The executive editor and I said goodbye for now, and the air was ripe with confidence. At the time, however, I didn't know it was my intuition that had once again led me on a bold tack, which I had followed to reach the shore of success.

As an artist, if you back off when you feel you are right, you will wash up on the lonely beach of despair. Do the right thing and you will ultimately persevere through the worst and best of times.

CRANKING IT OUT

Let's take a deep metaphysical breath before diving deeper yet into the gene pool of evolution where you must jump in to get wet if you are to become self-aware.

If your art is a job with a predefined outcome, then finding an audience means giving people what they want. The financial success rate in this category is good. If your art is the result of spontaneous creation without motive, then you reveal the authentic you—fair game for all too see. To find an audience of patrons who will embrace self-referential artwork takes a valiant artist who is undaunted by the challenge.

I love working with color pencils, especially while having a cappuccino at my local Starbucks. The color pencils fit in my art bag, and I can set up my portable studio almost anywhere.

Occasionally, someone will come up to me, look at my art in progress, and then ask me about the work.

In this case, the question was: "How often do you crank out one of those things?"

Since I sense the person isn't malicious, only ignorant, I respond in a factual manner: "I don't crank out my art. This is not a production line, or a factory, and I'm not involved in piecework in that sense."

Mostly, folks of this sort invariably force a smile, look elsewhere, withdraw, and dematerialize. But that is their limitation. If they wanted to know more about the process of creating art, I would be pleased to explain a bit of what I do and then give them my website address—so they can see my work and my views on art at their own pace.

Occasionally, however, a person, instead of disappearing, will want to go to the next level. It is remarkable how pushy folks can be about my private business.

Doubt, indulged and cherished, is in danger of becoming denial; but if honest, and bent on thorough investigation, it may soon lead to full establishment of the truth.

AMBROSE BIERCE

The only way to get rid of hard-wired social conditioning is to unplug.

EDEN

Even if you have the gift, something has to take place to unleash it.

Finding your dharma will do it.

In that instant, you will come home.

EDEN

This person will continue with: "Hey, do you sell any of that stuff?"

I'm quiet for a moment. "You mean my art," I say.

"Yeah, your art," the person says.

I nod in the affirmative.

"Who do you sell it to?"

"Collectors," I say.

"Your friends …"

"No, not my friends."

"Who do you sell it to?" the persistent person asks again. "Aren't your collectors your friends?"

"No," I reply. "Collectors are my patrons. Although it could work out that a patron could be a friend."

"So, you sell your art to collectors," the person sums up.

"Yes," I say.

I bid them a good day and go back to my drawing, which has quietly elevated itself in the person's vocabulary from stuff to art, which is all in a good day's work. You can often learn the most about yourself and your art from the most seemingly disinterested parties. Don't dismiss anyone; the most unlikely people can end up acquiring your work.

LIES AND WHISPERS

One evening, I ran into an artist friend at my local Starbucks. Since it was dinnertime, the caffeine delivery café was sparsely populated. After getting my cappuccino, I sat down at table. As I took out my pad of heavy vellum paper and color pencils, the other artist, an affable fellow, joined me and opened his newspaper to the art section.

"You know," he said. "The art market had been down for a long time and I read here that the market is making a comeback."

"I didn't know that the art market had been in trouble," I said, while working the paper surface with the pencils.

"Oh, sure. It has. Definitely."

"Yes," I said. "According to whom? The galleries, auction houses, articles by experts, artists, and publishers?"

He nodded, yes.

"You bring up an important point, here," I said. "When I hear that the art market has been in a slump, I look at who is reporting this information. This reminds me of my days in Hollywood hearing that a studio reported disappointing box office for a particular movie. What they were saying was this. 'We expected to make $250 million, but only made $180 million domestically, in the USA.' The studio isn't closing down for business; and the executives are not going hungry or trading in their expensive cars to take public transportation. The box office figure, of course, will increase substantially, when the distributor factors in sales to Europe and other international markets. What they're saying is not that the movie didn't make a hefty profit, but they didn't make as much as they had expected. Greed is usually behind such statements."

My artist friend laughed. "I see."

"Let's look beneath the veneer here," I said. "It's important that artists understand the business and politics of art."

"Oh, yes, sure. It is important," said my friend.

"The art establishment is no different than the Hollywood studios. When the auction houses report that sales are down, they may be accurate while being misleading at the same time. They are saying they didn't make as much as they'd like to make. And they are selling art as a commodity. You won't see the work of an unknown artist in the auction catalogs. This type of art trading is in the realm of investment and as symbols of wealth. The galleries also have it in their interests to support this view: the art market is narrow and it can only support a limited number of artists. Of course, it is true that there are a limited number of galleries. But so what? Good work will find an audience. The question is in what timeframe. I always advocate the importance of acquiring the works of living artists. You see where I'm going here?"

My friend looks at my drawing pad and then at me. "Well, go on. Let me follow you."

"Listen to the overt if not subliminal message to the artist. There are simply not enough art collectors to support all the artists. When I hear that there are millions of artist out there from a gallery owner or other art sales organization, there are times when I'm compelled to call them on their ploy: 'Really? True artists? Where are they? I'm not tripping over them in the street, and I don't see them falling out of the trees.' Hearing that the art market is up, down, getting worse, getting better are all red herrings. This type of reportage makes the insecure artist feel powerless like a victim in the snake pit. The galleries, auction houses, and publishers are then in the position they want to be … you know, on top while manipulating the art market and the artists who create their product. Do you see how insidious this is?"

"Ah, I'm beginning to see … yes … yes," my friend claimed.

"Good. I'm glad to hear it. Misinformation keeps the artist off balance. It is essential for the artist to create and continue creating, despite marketing forecasts. You can't be a fair weather artist. It is essential that artists be aware of how the art market works. Artists are, after all, entrepreneurs. This knowledge of business is far from being beneath the artist. It is his duty to be informed. Instead of the artist as a misanthropic nebbish, we have a new model—a savvy artist who knows talent will ultimately prevail. This is power. This is why I don't give any credence to pronouncements on how the art market is doing. I do listen carefully to everything, and I found that truth is on a distinct vibration that resonates … and when I'm clear, I hear it. So, what I do is this. I close my ears to all negative whispers, whether it is pillow talk or on the news—no matter where they come from. I listen to how I'm doing. I depend on me. It's smarter."

"Ah," said my friend looking at my pad. "I see your piece is starting to take shape. I like it."

"Thank you," I said. "So, is the art market getting better?"

He laughed. "You have me thinking about this one."

I'm not sure if he completely understood what I had said. I trusted that it would make sense for him at some point in his present incarnation. I looked around. The after dinner crowd had descended upon the café in large numbers with a thirst for java. I said ciao to my friend, then walked past the throngs of folks awaiting their jolt of caffeine.

I learn by going where I have to go.

THEODORE ROETHKE

If you are to learn from rejection, use the experience as a moment of reflection, not a pool in which to drown.

EDEN

> *To be angry about trifles is mean and childish; to rage and be furious is brutish; and to maintain perpetual wrath is akin to the practice and temper of devils; but to prevent and suppress rising resentment is wise and glorious, is manly and divine.*
>
> ALAN WATTS

In the parking lot, I lifted my head upward. Gray and white diffused light formed a crescent moon that looked like a distant croissant painted onto the evening sky. I thought to myself: There is unlimited room for the artist who knows his place in the universe, the showcase of all creation.

The art market has never been better than this instant, the present moment in which you are alive.

PROPHECY

Some time ago, I had met Peter, an artist of some note. He had one of those meteoric rises to fame straight out of his master of fine arts education, but, as of late, interest among the public had been waning for whatever reason.

One late afternoon, we were in his studio loft sitting on a large old couch where he kept on complaining about what a 'curse' art was for him. He spoke of the 'burden' that had been thrust upon him—not unlike Cassandra. In the Greek legend, Cassandra, the Trojan princess received the art of prophecy from Apollo. Because she wouldn't accept him as a lover, he changed her blessing to a curse, causing her prophecies never to be believed. Artist, do you feel a direction connection to this myth?

Peter went on with his laundry list of the problems that art was causing him—from being stuck in a style, financial woes, losing his wife and kids, to the bleakness he saw as his future.

I didn't see it that way, I told him. "Art is a blessing, a gift, not a burden or a curse." He didn't or couldn't hear me. This was by no means the first time I had listened to an artist bemoan his talent—and such whining came from artists known to unknown.

"How long have you been painting?" I said.

He shrugged. "Ever since I can remember. I was in grade school ... a long time."

"You've lost perspective," I told him. "You now take your art for granted and it knows it." Who was I to second-guess him? He had been making and selling art for ages and knew much more about the art scene than I. But he had become jaded by experience, which wasn't serving him now.

He shook his head from side to side. "What are you talking about? You just don't know," he said.

And what could I know? From his perspective, after all, he was known, he was in museums, and I was this younger upstart yet to be 'discovered'.

I decided to ignore the self-pity and condescension in his voice. How could he know what I knew? If you don't complain, others, those pathologically self-absorbed, often misinterpret your attitude for a seeming absence of problems.

I said, "TEE GEE EYE F."

Peter looked at me, one eyebrow arching upward. He couldn't figure out what I was getting at.

"What? TEE GEE ..."

"You know what that means?" I said.

He sat upright. "Sure," he said. "You mean that restaurant chain, TGIF. You want to grab a bite there? They've got some action there I heard."

"Close," I said. "I do mean the worker's proclamation: Thank God It's Friday."

Peter, the artist, dropped down and slouched even more deeply into the couch.

"When was the last time you thought about that?" I said.

After searching his memory, he told me, not for a real long time.

"I would call that quite a payoff," I said. "People who rally around TGIF are mostly those serving their time at a job they certainly would rather not be doing, or at a job some may even hate."

"Your point," he said, pressing, rubbing, and massaging his head against the couch.

"I don't think about it either. Monday, Wednesday, Friday, they're all days that flow from one into the other and blissfully would be my choice. I am not a slave to society … to the machine that civilization has constructed. And I don't think you are. Are you?"

He sighed. The weight of the solar system was upon him; it seemed from his posture that life was more than he could endure.

One of my adopted rules is no complaining or whining. If you truly see your art as a curse, you would be an idiot to continue. But, if you are simply being histrionic, then I don't know why you would enter that melodrama either. I am not discounting the events. The artist must pay his dues, and not everyone understands the passion—which sometimes and most especially includes wives, husbands, and other family folk.

"TGIF," he said, nodding as if something was clicking within him. Then, without a word, he stood up, went over to several easels with a canvas in progress on each. He picked up a brush loaded with oil and went to work on the largest piece.

I watched for a while, saw that he was in a better place, then got ready to leave.

"Don't go," he said.

"I've got to. There's a canvas waiting for me, too."

"Eden … my friend, listen … please use one of mine here. I started it. Why don't you finish it?"

I felt that was a good idea and accepted.

We both went to work—two artists transforming paint against canvas as evening light seduced the studio with an even natural cast. With divine fire in our hands, we were immune to muses and vengeful gods. Creation was in the air, and we were breathing, inspiring, its essence. We could, I thought, in this heavenly ether, predict a future that we both could live in and one that we could believe in ourselves.

In all the subsequent times we ran into each other, Peter would smile and say 'TGIF brother'—which became his code expression for the freedom that art bestowed rather than it being a curse. He didn't complain, at least not to me. He was looking fit and his wife for some reason wanted to try again, and life he told me was now much richer.

I had done my karmic work. Remember, if you see it, you own it.

ART, SACRIFICE, MISSION

There is an important postscript to my talk with Peter that brings up another widely held misconception underlying a life in the arts and rejection that is worth addressing here. Do you know what sacrifice means? If you haven't

Everything comes gradually and at its appointed hour.

OVID

The artwork is an artifact of truth—those moments recorded in time when the artist knew where he stood.

EDEN

If you think you've finally got it, you're only partially right because there is always a new and deeper realization around the corner.

EDEN

experienced it, then the word is abstract. To sacrifice, you give up something of great value for something else that you deem to be of even greater value—your art in this case. The word sacrifice is all too often misused by many to describe an inconvenience, a petty desire not materialized—not suffering, or an act of heroism.

Before you decide to sacrifice for your art, take the time to address the three core questions in this book. You are satisfied with your answers. You are grounded in your faith as a creator. You have removed yourself from the 'haven't you heard', or 'woe is me' mentality that thinks small, gossips, and huddles in like groups.

Is it then fair to say that you must sacrifice, even suffer, for your art? Is it then fair to say that you will do whatever it takes to do your art with such unflinching resolve that nothing can deter you from your mission? And, make no mistake, as an artist, you are on a mission; and the only way to stop a person on a mission is to kill him.

It is a matter of life or death.

If the artist is to prevail, he must find his own way with conscious intent and perseverance, avoiding the pitfalls of negativity and doubt along a path strewn with the mangled bodies of wannabe artists who floundered instead of flourished.

Sacrifice bites deeply and to the core. Are you willing to put all else aside—family, home, friends, security, social pressures, you name it—so that you can make your art? This is, of course, *the* question—and universal test. You will be held accountable to see whether your desire is truly a passion or an impotent wish to be famous. When you know the inherent value of your work, neither rejection nor acceptance has dominion over you.

There is no reason or requirement for an artist of passion to live in squalor in the 21st century. If the artist is a creator, then he must also create the context for his life. He must create and make his prophecy manifest, or what is the point? The artist can prosper with a wife, children, friends, and anything else he desires—but only if he has first made the journey to find his dharma; then, having found his purpose, the courage to live that life, which may be against the odds from society's point of view, he does so with the grace of God.

Remember, it is often and erroneously repeated that an artist must suffer for his art; the way it works is this: one suffers the trials of authenticity until he finds his voice, his art (purpose), his dharma, not afterwards.

Now you know, too.

KACHINA DOLLS

I love surprises along the way. Don't you? This mind-expanding adventure has subheads.

When I was living in Brentwood, California, a writer friend who had worked with Oscar Janiger on a book had invited me to meet the well-known psychiatrist. Among other accomplishments, Oscar was a pioneer in the study of LSD's potential for liberating the intellect and creativity. He gave LSD to some 1,000 volunteers (1954-1962) before it was made illegal. Oscar wanted to know whether LSD could juice up creativity, tune in consciousness, or be a valuable tool in therapy. During the late 1950's, he had also given the philosopher Alan Watts his first dose of mescaline as part of a research study.

Oscar had a comfortable home in the Santa Monica Canyon area and one of the largest personal libraries I had seen—nearly 20,000 volumes and he seemed to know the location of every title.

On this night, it was pouring rain.

I met Oscar. He shook my hand and then said to us: "Let's go."

MYSTERY TRIP

My writer friend and I followed Oscar who was wearing a trench coat down a long dark street as the hard rain fell. We made it to a building that housed the large and leaky studio of Tom, an artist of some note. I learned that he and Tom hosted a weekly art class where they would invite about a dozen or so artists over and hire a shapely model. I had my color pencils with me and joined in. After a while the model got up to stretch her legs. She came over to look at my pad.

"Oh, you abstract artists. You don't need models," she said.

"Look closer," I said. "And let your eyes relax."

"Oh, my God! I do see my body inside all of that stuff," she yelped.

A couple of hours had passed quickly. I thanked Tom and Oscar for letting us join them for an evening of life drawing. My writer friend and I left; it was still raining in Southern California.

DOUBLE HELIX

After that introductory evening, I visited Oscar a couple of times. Oz, as many friends called him, suggested I read certain books, which he would pull from his vast library to show me. He also told me many stories, from his fascination with Dolphins to his early research with LSD. Oscar had incorporated LSD into his therapy using guided sessions for volunteers including several notables: Anaïs Nin, Aldous Huxley, Cary Grant and Jack Nicholson. Having well-known personalities partake in such a dramatic study would certainly attract media attention to the project.

Although Oscar wasn't an artist, he impressed me with his remarkable understanding of art as a connoisseur, and student of the mind and soul. He was particularly interested in the possibility for artists to access a state of altered consciousness using this 'creativity pill'.

Oscar took LSD a number of times. He said it showed him that many things were possible, but what that was is unclear. There is a rumor (the only one mentioned in this book) worth noting here—not for its veracity but for what it implies about perception. According to believers, 'Francis Crick, the Nobel Prize-winning father of modern genetics, was under the influence of LSD when he first deduced the double-helix structure of DNA more than 50 years ago.' Whether this questionable and anecdotal account took place or not is irrelevant. Regardless of how it happened, we do know this discovery was the result of ingenuity coupled with passion: a circumstance of a prepared mind meeting intuitive information.

We thank Crick and his research associate, James Watson, for being sufficiently aware in March of 1953 to 'see' what was in the genie's bottle: the molecular structure of DNA. Unless you were looking for it, how many

Mastery of nature is not the only possible relation to it for a scientist.

ABRAHAM MASLOW

would have recognized the double helix, the genetic instructions, or blueprint of life, if they saw it standing on their kitchen table? How many in the presence of an innovation in art would recognize the breakthrough for what it was before it was sanctioned by the powers that be?

During the days before California made LSD illegal in 1966, Oscar had invited mostly artists, writers, and musicians to take part in a creativity experiment. He asked the volunteers to paint or draw an American Indian Kachina Doll before taking the LSD and then again one hour after taking it. Some 250 paintings and drawings were created during those sessions.

In 1988, Oscar cofounded the Albert Hofmann Foundation, a nonprofit organization, originally chartered to preserve the earliest records of psychedelic activity. Hofmann is the Swiss scientist who in 1943 accidentally discovered the hallucinogenic properties of LSD—his 'problem' child.

THE STRIP MALL

One late evening, as I was showing Oscar art from my portfolio, he looked for a few moments, then nodded as if he understood something. Great, I thought, an admirer, and who knows what would come next.

One afternoon, a few days later, Oscar called. He said he had some paperwork to do at the Hofmann Foundation and would I like to see the art he had there. I jumped into my car, picked him up, and we were off.

As we were driving down a busy street in Santa Monica, he said, pull in there, pointing to a strip mall.

"In there?" I said.

"Yeah, it's on the second floor above the shops. We didn't want anything conspicuous."

He had definitely succeeded. Once inside, he showed me around. There were some Kachina dolls on display. He went to a flat drawer cabinet and pulled out a few portfolios.

"Here, take a look," he said, placing the art on a huge desk.

I sat down, and I took my time taking in the art experiments of all those years ago. All the before and after pieces of art were there: without LSD and then with. Quite a few of the volunteers had been artists, but I recall that some were not. After perusing more than a hundred artworks, it was clear that all the pieces done during LSD were definitely much looser and perhaps even expressive because of it.

Inner perception of the outer world had definitely undergone some alteration. After a couple of hours, we were ready to leave.

"You see," he said, neatly placing the art portfolios back in the cabinet. "I do."

Oscar didn't ask me what I saw, and I didn't volunteer what either. It was palpable that something good had happened. He locked up, and we drove away from the strip mall toward his home. In the car, the wizard who was Oz confided that he didn't feel LSD would somehow magically transform anyone into a full-blown artist. He did, however, feel, at least in the early years of his research, that it might give an artist another tool to work with, which, for my part was a dubious conclusion, especially after having viewed the inconclusive evidence—the before and unremarkable after images of the Kachina dolls.

To observe how art reveals the underlying reality of things, we need only watch the documentary, The Mystery of Picasso. He's not painting from imagination. Watch the artist's hand as it searches, finds, and reveals the shapes and forms that are already there, but the eye can't yet see. These images are aspects of the unconscious unveiled.

EDEN

IN RETROSPECT

Fast forward: Here are my thoughts about my experience with Oscar. As I said, it was evident that looser lines or more intense colors après LSD did not an artist make. And those images created by the volunteer artists were not significantly unleashed, either.

Having no direct experience with LSD, my information is secondhand. But, based on my conversations with Oz, and what people have said and written about their acid-induced trips of cognitive shifts and waking dreams, I intuitively understand this: while painting I am experiencing an organic version of such a synthesized trip naturally—not as uncontrollable hallucinations but as revelations of reality. This phenomenon takes place in concert with trusting the cosmic mind to guide me. Taking this sort of guidance may seem effortless to an onlooker, but it isn't an easy thing.

The upshot: the topic of drugs and art is a volatile one; and we know that many an artist has, with disastrous results, turned to drink or substance abuse to cope with feeling blocked, rejected, or even accepted. If you think that ingesting substances will make you a better artist or give you courage, then you don't yet see a clear picture of what I am writing about in this book. An artist in dharma is already 'perfect' because he acknowledges the source of his gift. Nothing from the outside can improve upon the inner harmony that already exists. If you have a gift of art, you are then also charged with a duty: you must protect that gift from any vice that would destroy it. And, have no doubt, the dark forces are forever attempting to seduce a creator from his mission, as we know from Buddha and Jesus; each had to confront the lord of illusion in their inner journey toward Nirvana and the Kingdom of Heaven.

BENEATH THE MATRIX

There is no more important or powerful a 'substance' than intuition, which is the conscious tool each artist can use to cultivate his gift in the garden of culture. Intuition seems abstract when you can't hold it in your hand. But this makes perfect sense as we are engaging the metaphysical. Remember, intuition is first experienced as a sensation, a feeling, or a vision, not as thinking in words.

Somehow, intuition, which is potential but not yet inevitable, opens a direct pathway into the fabric of consciousness that is otherwise unavailable. This live and healthy connection is a behind the scenes look into the raw data, the cosmic mosaic and language of information as it is—in the quantum mechanics model of primordial matter—without the selective but necessary filters for survival of our subconscious mind; in the realm of intuition, both perceptions and thoughts are purified of nonsense to reveal and manifest themselves as shape and form, design and color—art and poetry, or the double helix.

This 'sermon' is over.

Oz did tell me one late afternoon in his library that he was intrigued and interested in acquiring a work on paper painting. I was thrilled. Although the transaction never took place for a number of reasons, his enthusiasm and warm engagement made it feel as though it had.

Just as it is pointless to stand in front of a Mondrian or Pollock, for instance, and ask what the painting is of, so it's pointless to ask what the electron under quantum mechanics looks like. Neither question has an answer ...

ARTHUR I. MILLER

It's not what it looks like; it's what it feels like.

EDEN

CHAPTER TWENTY ONE

INTELLIGENT IS NOT SMART
Epiphanies in the Hood

GOD IS THE door opener. You must still knock to enter.

Intelligent and smart are two words that are all too often used as synonyms when they aren't. There is a definite distinction. Since I often mention smart in this book, here are a few words of clarification. We must get our terms straight if we are to communicate.

While intelligent and smart aren't mutually exclusive, the two don't inevitably dwell together. While smart presupposes intelligent, a person can be intelligent without necessarily being smart. When put to the test, you will discover this assessment isn't only accurate, it is liberating.

What is smart? And, please, leave out all that highfalutin academic stuff. Smart is how you process information differently from others in the mainstream. Smart is how you see opportunity when others see through the eyes of the socially conditioned. Smart is a direct function of intuition that is expressed through awareness moment by moment.

Example? Here's one.

The common idea that success spoils people by making them vain, egotistic, and self-complacent is erroneous; on the contrary, it makes them, for the most part, humble, tolerant, and kind. Failure makes people cruel and bitter.

W. SOMERSET MAUGHAM

HOLDING THE DOOR OF PERCEPTION

I was in my neighborhood Russian specialty food market looking for a hearty-made bread. I went to pay at the cash register, which was near the front door.

As the clerk was putting my bread in a bag and getting my change, an elderly black man and a much younger big Russian fellow arrived at the door at the same moment.

The older man held the door open so the younger man could enter the shop. The younger man said in a half joking manner and in a heavy Russian accent: "Oh, you are holding door for me because you are doorman?"

Without missing a beat, the black man said: "No, I'm holding the door for you because I am a gentleman."

This was a moment of truth. The gentleman had surpassed intelligent with a reply that could only have come from smart. Do you see it? Can you hear it? Can you feel it? With a leap from his awareness, he knew where

Your soul isn't in your body; your body is in your soul.

ALAN WATTS

There is another form of sign language; it is perceiving how seemingly random events are connected, and then acting upon this exclusive information in the here and now.

EDEN

he stood. He completely and gently reversed the perception of his action to everyone near him. He made an indelible impression I will have with me always, and that is another clue for recognizing smart. While you may forget an intelligent remark, you will never forget a smart one.

Smart is from the heart. This is fundamental. It flows from intuition with compassion; intelligence is rooted in intellect, which is calculated through thinking. You can be more intelligent than someone else, but not necessarily smarter than that someone else.

As a species, we were intelligent to invent language and develop civilization. We will have to be smart not to destroy ourselves with the instruments of global annihilation devised by the intellect. We will have to be smart not to destroy what we have created. The more humanity is involved in art, the better our chances are for surviving our intelligence. Rejection loses its grip on you in direct proportion to how smart you are, and how well you have learned to disengage from negativity with grace. The beauty here is that you can get smarter at any time, which is a function of the soul.

THE RUSSIAN BEAR

The revelation of the 'doorman' wasn't my only foray into intelligent is not smart through the generosity of the Russian front of illumination.

To more fully appreciate the meaning and proof of synchronicity in the Jungian sense, please read the section 'Art & Physics' before continuing with the following episode.

I'm working to finish this book. I'm fine-tuning my tome of a chapter that weaves through art, physics, space-time, and absolute truth.

My five-pound rakish Yorkies, Larry and Beau, are pawing at my feet.

It is late and time for a break. I get the leashes. I am walking them along a dark and deserted street on this frigid November night when a bear of a man appears before me like an apparition.

He stops and says with a distinct Russian accent: "I want to let you know I'm not afraid of dogs."

I laugh. He then tells me that he stops and talks to everyone.

I say, "Oh."

"Say," he says, as he begins to walk along with me. "Do you know what absolute truth is?"

Of course, I can't believe that this question is coming at me from out of nowhere. "Excuse me, but what was it that you asked?" I say, as Larry and Beau sniff their way along the frozen grass.

"Do you know anything about physics and the laws of motion?"

"A little," I say, walking and watching all the time that my diminutive doggies haven't gotten caught up in the bushes.

"Well, if people would listen to the laws of physics, thermodynamics and up to Einstein and relativity, we would have a better world. Don't you see? Since most people can't understand the absolute truth of physics, they have religion."

Okay, I say to myself, let me see what this is about.

Suddenly, he asks, "What do you do?"

"I'm a writer, a painter."

"Ah, I could tell you stories about my life, my growing up alone, an orphan, and my experiences with the KGB, my life in the gulags. This would make a great book."

"I don't doubt it," I say. "Why don't you write it?'

"Yes, others have suggested the same. But, I'm feeling depressed. I speak six languages … I'm a teacher, but I don't have a woman or family in my life. I keep thinking of my past, the mistakes … there were many. It brings me down. So, I don't write."

"Listen," I say. "The past is dead. There is now and perhaps tomorrow. Write and you will feel better. You will liberate yourself." There are no more absolute truths than these.

He scratches his head. "I speak six languages, you know. How many do you speak?"

"English."

"That's it?"

"Yes," I say. "Remember, the past is dead. Write your story. Be well, good luck and *dos vedanya*."

I walked off with the Yorkies toward home and waved goodbye to the man who could speak of absolute truth in six tongues. There is a lesson in here I think to myself. If this bear of a man truly knew one absolute truth, he could have added smart to his intelligence, and he would be able to overcome feeling depressed.

Absolute truth is on the street where you live.

You have to experience what you need to know.

HENRY BUTLER,
MUSICIAN

You can get infinitely smarter through awareness; you can't, however, become more intelligent, which is a finite aptitude.

EDEN

CHAPTER TWENTY TWO

TIERS OF REJECTION
The Crucible of Art

INSTEAD OF BEING at its mercy, use rejection as grist for the mill. Prove to yourself that your art is a thing of value.

The line forms here.

Remember, failure isn't when someone rejects your art; failure is when you give up on your own self. Rejection is nature's way of weeding out the dilettantes and dabblers. Rejection most often implies getting to that first line of resistance in your quest to arrange a forum for your work, to get your art onstage, exhibited, and sold.

Rejection is a scavenger that all artists, whether known or as yet unknown, encounter in the jungle of art marketing at some time and on some level in their lives. Don't be under the impression that an artist whose work is selling doesn't experience rejection—if not directly from the public, then from other entities. You might suppose it is a lot easier to deal with rejection when your work is selling. This form of thinking may sound logical, even reasonable. Of course, one can't discount the complacency that the flow of money brings with it. But while it may be difficult for a struggling artist to appreciate it, the initial high of economic success is quickly reduced to a jaded trickle in the bloodied pool of critical rejection. Angst is an equal opportunity employer. Your book has been published, but now what if the reviews aren't stellar? What then?

If you aren't solid at the core with your work, then money in any amount or any other external force, pleasure, or social credit will assuage the demon that lurks within.

EMOTIONAL INTELLIGENCE

The sooner you realize that rejection is the underside of the same springboard that will eventually catapult you into the arms of those who will appreciate your work, the sooner you will become a formidable player; but to be a player you must be in the game. I can't say it any other way. You need to trust that you can feel, not think, your way toward the light called your own unique self.

Flops are a part of life's menu and I've never been a girl to miss out on any of the courses.

ROSALIND RUSSELL

God talks to us through pure emotion; the dark side can only squeeze through as doubts and fearful thoughts.

EDEN

As Deborah Haynes, author of *Art Lessons*, writes: "To contribute toward the future, the artist must have a keen intellect, strong body, and compassionate spirit, as well as a developed inner vision and far-reaching outer sight. Keep your eye simultaneously on your next step and on the long horizon. Cultivate stamina, for the artist's vocation is strenuous. It is not for everyone."

Look at the job description. If you can create art, why not simply extrapolate your ability? Create your life in the shape and form of prosperity. Draw upon the creator force within. You have the power to do what no one else can. Do *you* know it? Like a floating decimal point, you can instantly move the dot—your own self—over to the right and raise the ante at any time. And the point is this: to build your world, you must begin; you must start somewhere, anywhere. Now!

To create you must feel deeply; you must also possess a unique palette of emotions and a passion matched by courage to express them. I'm not suggesting an out of control emotional state here, but a natural and healthy diversity of balanced feelings that ebb and flow in your life of experiences—from exultation to sorrow, from birth to bereavement, and from empathy to compassion. Dr. Richard Cytowic, author of *The Man Who Tasted Shapes*, takes us further toward the philosophical and neurological high ground when he suggests that not only are emotions another form of intelligence, but that consciousness itself is a type of emotion. While Cytowic's proposition initially sounded radical, neuroscience has since swung around to appreciate that no decision is made without the input of emotion. Either too little or too much results in poor choices. Cytowic says, "Learning to live with oneself and to manage our constant doubts is the height of emotional intelligence." And, it is pure feeling after all that informs us all as to what is *really* going on.

ESPRESSIVO—WITH FEELING

When I write feelings, I'm not referring to saccharine sincerity, self-pity, sentimentality, or, with deference to Ophelia in *Hamlet*, a woe is *me* mentality. Melodramatic and dubious concerns insidiously weave their sticky traps of self-indulgence and victimhood for the unwary. Remember, one can be as sincere as a saint about something and be totally wrong. You must learn to discern the difference between indulgences posing as intuitive feelings and authentic vibrations that elevate your awareness—a subtlety achieved through the finesse of firsthand experience. As Robert Henri writes in his book, *The Art Spirit*: "Art is simply a result of expression during right feeling. It's a result of a grip on the fundamentals of nature, the spirit of life, the constructive force, the secret of growth, a real understanding of the relative importance of things, order, balance. Any material will do. After all, the object is not to *make art*, but to be in the wonderful state which makes art inevitable."

A creator creates from emptiness; he makes something from nothing. Let's be clear. When I paint, I am revealing my intuitive emotional connection to the Creator. I'm not expressing my mood. As long as I keep my feelings honest and my canvas free from pretense, I can invoke a receptive and indestructible vessel to hold divine fire. Pure feeling is a high vibration that cancels out debilitating mind chatter and other forms of nonsense. This state provides the space to create and to live a life based on fulfillment, not hope. In life, we remember facts more than we do feelings, which are ephemeral. Art is a symphony of feelings frozen forever in time; art brings us back to trusting our feelings, intuition, and to the present moment called life—a blessing that is all too often overlooked.

Feelings are connected to color. When you mix certain colors on your palette, you get depth, richness, and luster; when you mix others, you get mud. How I feel is irrelevant; the painting has its own life apart from mine, and the work appears spontaneously according to its own intuitive emotion and merit. You must know where you stand with your feelings for them to work with you instead of against you. Remember, in its purest form, you can't think how you feel or feel how you think. Of course, you could be analytical about anything, but then you would miss the point, the aesthetic moment. There is a difference between breathing and holding your breath. When you are in dharma, fulfilling your life's purpose, nothing can stop you from communicating the wonder of your inspired work.

GETTING SATISFACTION

I am writing for you, the artist who has come to a conclusion based on the varied elements of your life; this conclusion culminates in the act of creation. You create. You aren't hampered or blocked when it comes to your art. Presenting your art to the world is another matter entirely. You are leaping from the act of unfettered creation into the required morass of marketing, into finding a home for your work, and into transmuting art into sustenance.

You have made a decision: you have incontestable faith in your work and the inherent value of your art; and you are committed to earning a living from your artwork. Is it possible to achieve such an elusive way of life? Others, many others, have done it. Picasso wasn't born famous. Why not you? Those artists, well known and less so, who prosper with a healthy attitude, aren't smarter or more gifted than you. What they do have is an uncompromising sense of self, an unwavering commitment to their art, and the awareness to recognize opportunity, which often shows up well disguised when it does finally present itself. Do you possess the attributes described in The Eighteen Be-Attitudes? These aren't mystical qualities that are beyond your reach; they are practical qualities attainable by any artist willing to adopt them. If you don't measure up to your own self, then even if the quality of your art is good, the internal fulfillment you desire will elude you—with or without your audience.

In his book, *Status Anxiety*, Alain de Botton writes:

"It was an American, William James, who, a few decades after [Alexis de] Tocqueville's journey around the United States, first looked from a psychological angle at the problems created by societies which generate unlimited expectations in their members.

"James argued that one's ability to feel satisfied with oneself does not hang on experiencing success in every area of endeavor. We are not always humiliated by failing at things, he suggested; we are humiliated only if we invest our pride and sense of worth in a given aspiration or achievement

I did it my way.

FRANK SINATRA,
LYRICS: PAUL ANKA

The artist creates meaning, not status.

EDEN

Of course, we know that whoever commands the media controls the popular reality. Consider the conglomerates that own the television and radio stations, magazines, and newspapers.

Fortunately, the unexpected is evolution's ace in the hole. The Internet and World Wide Web as a counterweight to social conditioning arrived to level the playing field.

EDEN

and then are disappointed in our pursuit of it. Our goals dictate what we will interpret as a triumph and what must count as a catastrophe. James himself, for example, as a professor of psychology at Harvard, took a great deal of pride in being a prominent psychologist. If he should discover that others knew more about psychology than he did, he would, he admitted, feel envy and shame. Conversely, because he had never set himself the task of leaning ancient Greek, the knowledge that someone else could translate the whole of Plato's *Symposium* whereas he struggled with the opening line was of little concern to him.

"He [James] explained: 'With no attempt there can be no failure; with no failure no humiliation. So our self-esteem in this world depends entirely on what we back ourselves to be and do. It is determined by the ratio of our actualities to our supposed potentialities, thus; self-esteem equals success divided by pretensions.'

"James's equation illustrates how every rise in our levels of expectation entails a rise in the dangers of humiliation. What we understand to be normal is critical in determining our chances of happiness. Few things rival the torment of the once-famous actor, the fallen politician or, as Tocqueville might have remarked, the unsuccessful American."

BAGGAGE CLAIMS

There are seemingly different levels of rejection, each with baggage that carries a distinct set of inherent weighty obstacles to unload. And while it may seem a daunting task to take them on all at once, the solution is much simpler. Instead of peeling back each issue of rejection like countless thin layers of an onionskin, you can cut to the core, as Alexander the Great sliced through the Gordian Knot, by taking your own self to task; and you do this by digging deep until you strike the wellspring of intuitive knowing that will quench the thirst of your desires. All this will happen when you are firmly standing on the bedrock called your soul, which is the immutable harbinger of all material and transcendental events in the human story. You won't have to ask anyone if you have arrived. This isn't hubris since no one but you can corroborate your dharma. Once you are free from negative deadwood and you set foot in this marvelous territory of soul, you will know it because you have gone where you had to go and you have done what you had to do—this is fulfillment in the here and now.

After a time the piercing thorns of rejection soften into nothingness, leaving only rose petals—soft, colorful, and fragrant, yet mortal nonetheless. Both thorn and petal are temporal, impermanent, and in the end, illusion. This isn't new-age doublespeak; this is the wisdom of the fully realized human being. You punish or reward your own self. If you doubt the veracity of this declaration, consult Buddha, and then ask your own self again. It isn't that you are immune to rejection; you have built up a resistance to it over time; you are human and an artist; you have feelings; you also see rejection in all its forms for what it is; you fight the war between dark and light inside you every day; you see beyond the maya, the illusion of social conditioning and self-delusion. Getting a 'no' doesn't stop you from creating or showing your work. The 'no' is merely a momentary detour, not your desired destination. When you see rejection for all its smallness, you and your art can't help but flourish since the source of your spiritual nourishment is your eternal soul—and it loves your work.

FLY ON THE WALL

If you have ever been present at a closed meeting of a museum's board of directors, or have spoken with a museum director, art curator, art consultant, art critic, or a well-known artist at a gallery opening for that matter, you would have seen the performance, the art world on stage. What tickles the public's fancy is most often well orchestrated in advance, and in true homage to Machiavellian form. Remember, it is the art business, not the art ashram. Despite spin, marketing, and persistent behind the scenes manipulations by a persuasive informal cabal, it is still the art buying public who ultimately accepts or rejects the artist's work—known and unknown. Being included, for example, in a museum show, which is welcome, doesn't guarantee anything else. It is still the aware artist who underwrites himself physically, spiritually, and emotionally to persevere while he is alive.

Furthermore, if you had the opportunity to speak candidly, one-on-one and off the record with any of these art world players (or their counterparts from another art form), the inside experience would ignite and illuminate your power to succeed as a fully realized human being who is an artist. In your tête-à-tête, you would learn firsthand what lies in the bellies of the other beasts. An art dealer may have a savvy pitch for selling art, or a curator may have an impressive command of art history and the names for various art-making techniques. But so what? Such information doesn't bring you into the secret chamber of what art is. I recently read in the paper that a certain group of curators from a well-known museum were interested in showing artists who have specialties. Decipher at your own risk.

After a time, you would quickly get wise to the following: experts, while they can and do influence the public, don't know more about art than you do. They might know more about fads, trends, and styles, which are copy-cat movements that last for a time—that is, until the novelty fades and the trendoids pursue and coagulate over what is in vogue at the moment. As for other artists, they know what they know. If they have managed to garner an audience, so can you, but only if you know what you are doing as an artist and know where you stand. If this precept strikes you as oblique, you must 'confront the core questions'—an admonition repeated throughout this book.

BETWEEN THE CRACKS

After all, who decides what fine art is or what a painting is worth? If you, the artist, don't know that your work is art, then you are lost—even if your work is selling. Value is what your art is worth to you now. Don't undervalue your work or price it out of the market either. Your confidence helps build the demand. Find a balance and hold your ground in whatever the situation. If you made the art with the consumer in mind, then you are a manufacturer. If you created the art for the magic of it, then you must still deal with economics, sooner or later.

The more art world folk you could meet in candor, the more you would discover how art, the product, all too often succumbs to: idiosyncratic

Describing how her early shows on TV were produced:

'Live on tape.'

JULIA CHILD

Save your rejection letters for tax purposes as proof of your dharma: you are a working artist.

EDEN

taste, lack of taste, self-interest myopia, art of the deal, fashion, decoration, self-indulgence, so-called experts, and ignorance—the least of deadly sins in this instance. The true artist must not hide from these banalities and realities. You are an entrepreneur and you want to sell your work. Say 'I will sell my artwork' out loud. Now, say it again as if you mean it, as if you have a purpose. Are you keeper of the flame, or not? Are you convinced? Good. The next steps are right in front of you. I have created art. Where is my audience? Does anyone want to acquire my work? You must admit to yourself that you are in business, or you will flounder on that well-known tacky shore of disappointment.

While non-artists have been manipulating and brokering the business of art for centuries, artists must make it their responsibility to know how the current marketing system works and persevere in spite of it. There is nothing charming about ignorance or gullibility.

Here is a list of significant categories that constitute the multilayered construct of an artist's life. The impact of each layer varies according to the artist's spiritual condition and his temperament. If you don't adequately answer the core questions posed in this book, you abdicate your mission by handing your power over to everyone else. These layers rule with the double-edged sword of acceptance or rejection; in either case, don't get bloodied in the process.

THE TIERS

The following list of layers is populated with entities. Some can say yea or nay about your art while others might be more influential as they can either support or undermine your mission; you will confront most if not all of them in your life as an artist.

A **self**: The self stands alone; the unadulterated cosmic self is firmly connected to the Great Creator. The self thrives when engaged in creation regardless of approval from others. Self-acceptance based on character, honesty, and truth is the template upon which all other layers rest. If your sense of self is bogus, then your life as an artist is a house of cards. Handle the self, and all else falls beautifully into place—which is what you want in the first place.

B **peers**: A peer is an equal. When you find one, please let me know. Artists should look out for the welfare of their comrade creators, but do they support one another?

In Shakespeare's *Othello*, the treacherous villain, Iago, speaks this line to his master, Othello, the Moor of Venice: "O, beware, my lord, of jealousy! It is the green-eyed monster, which doth mock the meat it feeds on." The betrayal here is all the more insidious as Iago lies to Othello and eventually drives the Moor to murder his innocent wife.

It is unquestionably ironic and tragic that artists are the most flagrant offenders when it comes to undermining other artists. It is among this anxiety-ridden lot that you will find those who are the cruelest to their

All the realizations in the world have no meaning without trust.

EDEN

fellow creators. This behavior, which appears across the spectrum of known and unknown artists, stems from insecurity and manifests itself in unworthy ways—from rejection to worse. After all, what true artist would envy another? The concept itself is ludicrous. You must ask your own self that question, and answer it.

No matter what you have read or heard about the most well-known of artists, those among them who are weak, unsupportive, and resentful of their fellows as rivals are petty. The public's attention is drawn to the artist with a platform. But simply because an artist is known doesn't mean he knows any more than you do, perhaps even less. Great art doesn't come from small minds and miserly hearts. And even if it did, what is the point? By great art I am referring to substance, which is the artist's experience of creation—not where the artist has merely mastered a technique. If artists permit jealously to infect and trivialize their existence, what good does their talent do them? Worrying about what the other guy is doing is a bad habit that is best shed quickly. When you have touched heaven, what more do you want? When you are on a mission as an artist, the good news and bad news is that you have no competition other than your own self.

C **family**: You might be fortunate enough to have a mother, father, wife, husband, brother, sister, cousin, uncle, aunt, some family member, or friend who does see and acknowledge the merit of your work and the courage of your spirit. Having a single patron is an achievement, and no less significant than Buddha holding up the lotus flower that gave birth to Zen. It means at least one other individual to whatever degree understands your art language. Family members who don't share your vision or way of life most often unleash their disapproval in passive aggressive behavior. If that is the case, the smart gardener knows that it's time to prune the deadwood.

D **gallery**: Gallery owners are merchants with shops, overhead, and rent to pay. They can also be like Ambroise Vollard, who, as an impresario, recognized early on the value of Cézanne, Gauguin, Picasso, and many others who would lay the foundation for modern art.

Galleries are not shrines to art. A gallery owner may pass on your work for a variety of reasons. The preeminent motive for saying no is that he doesn't think he can sell your art to his clientele, and he may be right; he may also be oblivious to the magic in front of him because noticing new talent isn't his job. Remember, loving art from the past, or reconstituted work is no great stretch. Discovery is the domain of the connoisseur who is as rare as great art. When a gallery owner is also an impresario, then the unknown artist has a chance.

Generally, high-end gallery owners, those shakers and makers of what is new, swim through artists' studios, museum exhibits, and art shows hunting for fresh blood and that reprehensible concept in art—the next big thing. While seeking out new talent is admirable, choosing the artist

What marketers, promoters, and advertiser have known for ages: to create demand, a product requires consistent exposure over time to penetrate the public's already saturated psyche. Now, there you have it—a simple model to work from.

EDEN

flavor of the month has much in common with the Hollywood star system that is buoyed by hype and shameless pandering to the crowd. There is also another parallel between the art world and the Hollywood Studio system. The independent filmmaker, the auteur, has a vision he wants to bring to the screen. The major studios, however, mostly want cookie cutter movies based upon an accepted formula (box office sales) that works for the lowest common denominator; these films with predictable patterns and audience acceptance are often edited even further based on the opinions of focus groups—and changing the theme or even the ending in an attempt to satiate the audience isn't uncommon.

Of course, when an independent filmmaker has a breakout hit, the majors are more than eager to throw money at him for his next film without fully grasping the merit of the first movie. I'm generalizing here, but only slightly, to make a point.

Whether the gallery is garden variety or high profile, don't second-guess why the owner said no thanks. There is no point in trying to prove a negative—which you can't do in any case. If you are ambivalent about your place as an artist or the quality of your art, then why are you showing your work? Not answering the core questions in this book places your credibility on the line with your own self. It is enough for the master artist to suffer fools when showing his work. Know where you stand so you don't get tripped up by the subjective nonsense of others who would like you to believe they know more about your art than you do. If you don't set the stage according to your vision, you can be assured someone else will. Remember, 'you are on sacred ground when you know where you stand.' If you do value someone's opinion (a person whom you respect), then listen up, but never forget that no one knows more about your dharma than you do.

E **art publishers**: Art publishers make their money distributing art reproductions in quantity. Because they sell for substantially less than an original painting, reproductions can make your artwork more accessible to a wider audience. More of your works in the marketplace means broader name recognition for you. Read the fine print in the publisher's agreement (in all contracts for that matter) to make sure you are getting a fair deal. You are negotiating with business people, not Albert Schweitzer or Mother Teresa.

If your work is perceived and classified as commercial, you may score with a publisher. Art publishers are aiming for specific art markets, including the mass market. Here is something you can do for your self. Place a reproduction next to an original work of fine art and then look at them. One is alive, the other isn't. Serious collectors want to own originals. You must develop a sense of who would love your work.

F **art grants**: Getting a grant or fellowship to pursue your art can be glorious, and it can add academic prestige to your curriculum vita. If you apply to the right granting institution for your work, fill out the

---

Alexander the Great didn't include the option of giving up in his handbook for conquering the world, and perhaps even himself. Are you on any less of a mission?

EDEN

forms correctly, and if your timing is right, you might be chosen. Not applying guarantees not being selected. Most grant and fellowship-giving organizations have websites where you can view previous winners and the quality level of their work, which is an eye-opener—you will have to come to your own conclusions.

Getting rejected by a review committee here barely qualifies as a letdown because the aesthetic of the jury, or their consultants, is most likely unknown to you, making such awards arbitrary in most respects. More often than not such selection committees are swayed over by previous endorsements, awards, and residencies that the artist can muster rather than the inherent quality of art without a pedigree.

Other funding sources are after ideas, which, of course, must be supported by previous experience and sanctioned exposure. One such grant funding agency included this description in their guidelines: "Artists must demonstrate innovation in their work. Projects that do not make a case for innovation of form and content will not be funded." You would have to see examples of what they mean by innovation, which may not be your assessment. See the section Feasting on Innovation in 'Fully Realized'.

Grant recipients hail the funding source as perceptive; those disqualified may have another adjective or noun in mind. If you said that they simply didn't understand, you would be right. I have noticed a trend which is this: a majority of art funding sources, including those that fund individual artists, select those who can conceptualize and tailor their work into a 'community' project of some sort: rebuild the city; help cure that disease; save the environment; save the world; and so on. This isn't an inherently diabolical scheme if such grants were going to advertising; when the artist is clueless, co-opted through the lure of bucks and what sort of art should be made, then, well, I feel that you can pretty much finish this sentence. Keep in mind that a 'no' now doesn't mean a 'no' forever. Endeavor again.

Grant me strength.

G **museums**: In ancient Greece, the fine arts were presided over by the Muses, hence the word museum—a place where the fine arts are displayed. The ancient Greeks had no muses for painters or sculptors. Depending upon the mission statement of the museum, most museum directors and curators are interested in artists who have a publicity machine already in place, or, at the very least, a public buzz happening. Discovering unknown talent isn't what museums do; these institutions are in the exhibition business to showcase 'acceptable' artists, attract traffic, members, and the grease behind the machine—money. Although museums aren't in the impresario business, you might be included in an exhibit de jour, or get caught up in a wide net for a biennial type show eager for diversity and experimentation. I love museums; where else can you see such collections of art? I also find museum people bright, and willing to help you out if you can make your case. Fair enough.

On balance, art funding resources have budgets, and they do want to award grants and fellowships to artists.

Of course, if they want oranges, don't send them apples; if you can insinuate yourself into their program organically and you do so on purpose, you are still on sacred ground; however, if you start thinking solely in terms of what funding sources demand, then you have been co-opted because someone else has dictated what type of art should be made—even if it was your idea.

EDEN

Keep this in mind:

Apply for a grant; it will teach you valuable lessons about your art, whether you receive the award, or not.

Grant funding institutions are run by consensus; this show of hands format is looking at what can first disqualify you.

If there are any seeming chronological gaps, lack of previous awards, or other perceived weaknesses in your art-making life, address them in your application before the judges do.

EDEN

H **critics**: Most art criticism that I have read has nothing to do with art. This doesn't preclude a shining insight from a smart critic or an art lover now and then. I choose not to have anyone else to tell me what I am looking at. I can't stress this enough for you and for me. If you need someone else to tell you how to feel, consider revamping your approach. You have to decide to trust your own emotional intelligence or the art viewing experience is dogmatic and devoid of any significant meaning. Who knows better how you feel than you?

Criticism in any form surfaces when the artist's work reaches the public sphere. Having people survey the art—in a gallery, museum show, or other venue—is a supreme achievement for most artists as it validates their work in the public eye, the art world establishment, and themselves. Now that the art is on view in a 'properly' sanctioned space, an art critic might emerge to critique the work. Although a review may laud the work as high art, or pan it for not being art at all, the art may still receive public acceptance because it now has a forum. While a positive review can certainly evoke interest and sales, a negative review often does no harm either. The bottom line premise of a critique is that the reviewer will save the reader time and money—a dubious notion. What good is saving time and money if you give your power of feeling away to another? Isn't it much better to love it or not on your own terms? For the artist, it is about getting noticed, making sales, and paying the rent. The yea or nay from critics is part of the art market crapshoot. Ultimately, there is no empirical marketing formula to predict if an artist will score, or not, as that is up to providence. In the end, however, talent plus dedication will equal genius.

I **collectors**: Of all the people who might reject or accept my work, collectors are the most guileless. Most artists don't want to be involved in directly selling their work to collectors. Dealing directly with a small group of dedicated patrons and have my work represented as well works for me. Of course, everyone concerned wants a piece of the action; be generous with all who support your work.

Good balance is keeping in touch firsthand with what your collectors are saying about your work without having their feelings and thoughts filtered through others. Such commentary is for your personal enjoyment; a creator listens to the opinion of another, or not, but doesn't let public opinion dictate the course of his art. To hear the joy of your patrons is God speaking directly to you. But to hear disappointment in a patron's voice is yet another test of vision colliding with commerce.

You will be steadfast.

There is a difference between a patron and customer; a patron personally knows the artist; by acquiring work on a regular basis, a patron plays a significant role in his life; a customer buys the occasional piece. A true patron also supports the artist through various stages of development of his art-making career; and customers are always appreciated.

Unless you have a studio set up for receiving potential buyers and critics, and a primed pipeline bringing them to you, selling directly is not feasible for most artists. With that said, I have sold my work to people whom I had met while walking Larry and Beau, my Yorkshire Terriers. Of course, if you become too well known (Is there such a thing?), personal contact with each patron becomes a welcome impossibility that you can manage when the time comes. There is also an undeniable psychological edge to having someone else showing and selling your work. Others can toot your horn better than you can. While it may take a genius to create great art, it also takes one to sell it.

In many cases, wealthy collectors buy and display art as trophies, status symbols of their wealth, not necessarily of their culture. The closest you can come to buying culture is the type found in yogurt. Another thing to keep in mind is this: collectors come in all wallet sizes. A patron doesn't have to be loaded to acquire art. There is a rich variety of original art available for all types of pocket books. To all collectors I say this: Do your own legwork and support *living* artists, which will enrich your soul and improve your quality of life. The artists of the past no longer need your patronage.

J **public**: The buying public of original fine art is relatively small, but not insignificant. If the artist is well known, then the art is expensive. If the art isn't well known, then only someone who knows what she is looking at will buy it. It isn't uncommon for the buyer to have an art advisor counseling her to buy it now before the artist gets famous. Buying art on speculation is suitable for those who like to gamble, not for those who love art. If you are buying and selling art like a trader, then you are in the commodities business, which has nothing to do with the intrinsic value—the self-awareness of the artist—of fine art.

In *Art and Investing*, a perceptive piece by Robert Donahue, a freelance writer, art critic and collector of work by emerging artists, writes: "A collector who approaches art with the mentality of an investor needs to have either a great deal of luck, or the capability to purchase works by artists that already have a solid market value, like Rembrandt or van Gogh. Many speculators purchasing art in the 80's art boom were in the end sorely disappointed. Artwork that was purchased for tens of thousands at so called 'important' and trendy galleries cannot be resold today on a street corner for fifty bucks. These galleries, designated 'important' by *The New York Times*, are now obscure memories, lost to an unrecorded history, and the 'important' art dealers who ran them and authenticated the value of the art are now, if they survived the epidemic, selling burritos or working at computer stations in graphic design and website houses."

Let's not be too hard on the public. They aren't the enemy here. The public is in enough trouble when it comes to reading, let alone the visual arts. The public responds to trends and advertising, which are concepts they have been weaned on. Remember the success of Pop Art?

There is no such thing as an omen.

Destiny does not send us heralds. She is too wise or too cruel for that.

OSCAR WILDE

Speaking for your art:

Of course, the buyer must do some work; but don't miss an opportunity to explain how your art came into being, why you make art, or some other relevant information, which could result in an acquisition.

EDEN

We are sick with fascination for the useful tools of names and numbers, of symbols, signs, conceptions and ideas. Meditation is therefore the art of suspending verbal and symbolic thinking for a time, somewhat as a courteous audience will stop talking when a concert is about to begin.

ALAN WATTS

Is it art? Go ahead and backtrack to the answer. If he or she is an artist, then the outcome is art.

EDEN

ABSENTEE ARTIST

A recent report in *Vanity Fair* stated that as many as one in six works by the late Andy Warhol is a fake. According to the expose, works that Warhol "discussed or produced in the company of Factory assistants have been denied (as being authentic by the Warhol Estate), despite multiple affidavits from those assistants."

The question in many fence-sitting minds remains: Was Andy even present when those art pieces were made in his New York studio. Of course, this is the wrong path of inquiry. Andy's atelier was known as the Factory, which to my mind, gives those assistants the right of authentication. They all get my vote of confidence. The president of a company doesn't have to be in the factory for the product to be genuine.

Andy Warhol, in a similar yet quite different fashion, chose the model made by Henry Ford, who reduced craft to the dehumanizing yet highly profitable assembly line. Andy, of course, didn't have to dehumanize the populace; they had already caved into seeing advertising and in-jokes as great art. He and his gang of intrepid searchers made art an innovative co-op or factory enterprise—recasting iconic and mundane images for mass consumption. Since the public mood could be cowed and corralled into buying ad space as art during the 50's and 60's, Warhol, and others of that era, gladly sold it to them as Pop Art—a style of art that explores the everyday imagery—as if there were some shortage—of contemporary consumer culture where unique has lost its value. Common sources for such images included advertisements, consumer product packaging, celebrities, and comic strips.

POP THE QUESTION

Was Pop Art offensive, evil, anti-abstract expressionism, or a joke? No, no, no, and maybe—and an artful one at that. The issue is none of these reactionary labels. But is it art? This is also the wrong question.

Pop Art is art. The question is: Where did the art come from? Does Pop Art feed the soul, or is it conceptually and outrageously expensive empty calories?

I am drawn to art that is magic, art that doesn't need ideas, imagination, or is eager to make a clever statement—which is a staple of advertising. This is a distinction, not a comparison. There is room for all types of art and there is an art to knowing what you are looking at. Or what is the point?

To all those disgruntled Warhol art patrons, I say: Next time, dare to feel for yourself and invest the time necessary to know what art is before plunking down all that moolah for what could fool *ya*.

In reality, this brouhaha, this tempest in a silkscreen factory has little to do with Andy, and a lot to do with greed, ignorance, and stupidity. After all, if you feel—or were snowed into thinking—that the art is good, what does it matter who did it? You are loving and enjoying it.

Buying a name, or a perceived cachet for its own sake and for yourself with no emotional involvement is snobbery in this fashion: an 'art' collector having premarital sex with himself—much more than half the thrill is still missing.

MULTIPLE EXPOSURES

In the larger world of rejection, there is a myth propagated by certain marketers that you are likely to encounter: There are *too* many artists. Then, to further fan the flame of disinformation, we are exposed to the absurd rumor that there are millions of artists; and, by implication, the message is who needs yet another one. Art marketers and galleries in general would have you believe that artists are falling out of the trees, and you can't but bump into at least a dozen of them each time you go out and about.

Certainly, gallery owners, for example, do see many artists because artists approach them to sell their work. In a practical sense, this gives gallery owners an edge since they have more experience in dealing with artists than artists have in negotiating with them—an astute point made by Caroll Michels in her fine book, *How To Survive & Prosper as an Artist*. Marketers would like to perpetuate the premise that any 'artist' can make a work of art, but it takes a genius to sell it—a premise that is admittedly not without some merit.

By perpetuating this myth of 'too many' artists, such marketers get the upper hand in a psyche out manipulative game that creates a false sense of competition and puts the unwary artist on the defensive. The savvy artist, however, knows better than to fall into such traps because there is no honorable reason for anyone to bring up this myth in the conversation. Even if there were millions of artists flowing from some magical and veritable cornucopia, quantity isn't an indicator of quality. There is no shortage of space for the true artist because there is always plenty of room at the top, and elsewhere.

One response in good humor, if you know where you stand, is this to the offending party: 'No, no. Millions of artists are not falling out of trees. Nuts fall of out trees, not artists.'

As the master said: It is better to be the bottom of the top than the top of the bottom. Now, that you are informed, don't get bamboozled when you next hear this or any other ploy from someone who wants the upper hand. Remember, unless you are asking a gallery owner (anyone for that matter) for a critique of the work you would like him to sell, the only appropriate and acceptable replies are: yes or no, good luck, or perhaps a recommendation to another gallery. Anything else is superfluous and suspicious. Another response from you, which I would use sparingly, in this instance to test the intention of the eager purveyor of the 'too many' artists myth or any other condescending comment designed to diminish the value of your work is: 'Why are you telling me this?'

Then, wait in silence.

Of course, each new meeting is an opportunity in awareness and character where the ante is an open mind and heart—then you can take it from there.

THE CRUCIBLE OF ART

Without an unbending will to create and to continue creating, the artist is lost, and no one can save such a victim from himself. Carl Jung wrote: "The artist's life cannot be otherwise than full of conflicts, for two forces are at war within him—on the one hand, the common longing for happiness,

Painting, n.: The art of protecting flat surfaces from the weather, and exposing them to the critic.

AMBROSE BIERCE

Catch yourself in the act and you will be saved.

EDEN

satisfaction and security in life, and on the other a ruthless passion for creation which may go so far as to override every personal desire. There are hardly any exceptions to the rule that a person must pay dearly for the divine gift of creative fire."

With all the misinformation at best and disinformation at worst about 'too many' artists, it is essential to dig deep within your own self for clarity and purpose. Where and how is an artist forged? You—the artist—must be able to answer this question succinctly and clearly for your own self. If not, don't expect help from anyone else. You are the only one who can supply the answer to this fundamental question. I don't mean is an artist born or made. While you may have been born an artist, this doesn't mean you have discovered that being an artist is your dharma, or purpose in life.

A gift must be acknowledged, proposed to, and then developed. There are many distractions.

In the main, family and society follow a pattern of conformity, a form of unrelenting pressure that doesn't support the artist and his work. An artist must not only possess talent, he must have the courage to manifest that talent in a world that might be indifferent to his work. What is the ordeal that transforms one from a spectator into a creator? You can't plan the circumstance; the events choose you and you must be up to the test. If not, the self-imposed purgatory of regret beckons until you are ready to try again in good faith; a contract that is never denied.

THE POSTMORTEM

You applied for the grant, fellowship, or museum show, and the letter arrives in the mail. You are apprehensive as you open the decision. If it's a yea, then you begin planning for that event. If it's a nay, then what? You sense some level of frustration. How could that jury overlook the quality of your work? This is why 'obvious' doesn't belong in your vocabulary.

Of course, this is yet another opportunity to test your mettle dressed in the tattered drag of rejection. You take a deep breath. For whatever reason, the panel of art jurors failed to appreciate your gift, which you know is original. You feel the disappointment. Your heart pumps through your body like an escalating tsunami; fortunately, you, like an Aikido master, let the rejection run its course unchallenged until it expends all its energy, washing out through and out of you.

Now, in its wake, you are left fortified, and to your own amazement, feeling more whole and with added conviction than before. You have faced the moment of truth, passed through the existential hurdle, and you have gotten stronger in the bargain.

Remember, 'you are on sacred ground when you know where you stand.' Knowing this real estate has great liberating power.

JUDGMENT DAY

The artist must also be aware of acceptance and its demands. The moment has finally come when a high-powered gallery owner and an influential critic embrace your work. Suddenly, your art rises in value. Your stature in the art world swells. Your cachet seems secure. Or is it?

To learn, understand, and appreciate a new language, including an original visual idiom, takes time, repetition, motivation, interest, unbending intent, perseverance, and so on. This is how you develop your audience.

EDEN

Has your art improved based on such endorsements? What happens if they sour and reject your new work? If you have bought into the public relations about yourself, then the commercial aspect of your talent is at the whim of others. There are those art critics and gallery owners who write and speak about art with such authority that it sounds as if they know what they're talking about. The true artist will not be misled.

Remember, there is a steep balloon payment if you aren't prepared to stand your ground, knowing the intrinsic value of your art without the trap of serving outside adulation.

DO THE MATH

To become art aware takes a commitment of time and energy that is no less rigorous than what is required to be an artist. Would anyone expect to speak a foreign language or work out equations in quantum mechanics without first mastering the fundamentals? Why would anyone think that 'getting' art would be any different? How can you appreciate something without taking the time to know its true nature?

You aren't born with culture; you acquire this innate but not inevitable potential through dedication.

Knowing the various tiers of rejection described here and any other tiers that may exist for you is no reason for dwelling in the murky shadows of any of them. Collapse all the tiers into one convenient layer, knowing each is a manifestation of the very same thing; put it aside now with a head clear of distractions; and then go about creating your art. The more art you make contributes gravitas to your commitment; people feel better knowing that art is your dharma, your lifelong passion, and not a fling.

With so much focus here on the artist's individuality, and on the self, it shouldn't be overlooked that the true artist engages the world one on one; he doesn't turn his back on his fellows.

This is the way.

There are enlightened thoughts and there are base thoughts; in the same way, there are enlightened feelings and base feelings.

EDEN

CHAPTER TWENTY THREE

ART AND COMPETITION
The Jury

IF YOU SUCCUMB to the syndrome that my brush is bigger than your brush, not only have you missed the point about art, you will forever look over your shoulder with anxiety, fear, and doubt as your partners.

Art for art's sake isn't about indulgence. Art for art's sake, which is created without motive, isn't a competitive activity, despite what you may have heard or read. Picasso may have felt that he was in competition with Matisse, but it wasn't about art. Of course, the performing arts or other activities requiring auditions are another matter. I don't make art to compete; I create art because that is my destiny, my dharma, and when you are in dharma, no one does what you do better than you.

There is no such listing in my creator's handbook as healthy competition among artists making personal art because you can't 'compare' unique, which is a contradiction in terms. Is Cézanne better than Kandinsky? Is Beckmann better than Schiele. Is Bonnard better than Mondrian? Is van Gogh better than Gauguin? Is Matte better than Pousette-Dart? Is that other artist truly better than you? Unique by definition has no equal and is incomparable. How then can something that is unique be in competition? Which is the most original work of art among a group of original pieces? You know the answer. Art from the soul stands alone because it is metaphysical accomplishment that can't be measured as one gauges achievement in sports.

THE ENVELOPE, PLEASE

Of course, there can be robust discussions, opinions, even discourse, and agreeable disagreements among artists. And yes, panels of jurors award commissions and grants based on the competition model; going in, the artist knows the score; and you will find such contests mostly elicit conceptual works rooted in some particular theme that suits the people handing out the money.

While a grant or fellowship may certainly enhance the resume and the potential for exposure, does the award in any way improve the essential quality of the winner's art? The decision-making process in such cases

While you might prefer the work of one artist over another, this does not imply that one is better than the other. It simply means one speaks to you more clearly, for whatever the reason.

EDEN

Acceptance, not rejection, is power.

EDEN

When you feel the heat, you know that the light is on the way.

EDEN

is anonymous. However, let's not get sidetracked by the self-evident; this isn't what concerns us here. Competition in art is the fabrication of promoters and marketing people—not artists; this doesn't negate that some artists do feel competitive with others. This 'my brush is bigger than your brush' syndrome is a non-issue and is none of my business. Let's be clear. Competition isn't evil. It serves as a great catalyst in the realm of ideas, innovation, and invention. And, after all, can prayer be competitive?

In recent memory, I have read a number of views on art for art's sake, and it isn't difficult to discern from the interpretations of these declarations what agenda is being touted. Bypass all intellectualizing and you will know that art for art's sake means one thing only to the true artist. The art wants to be born for no other purpose than to be here now in the present moment and take its chances—which is precisely the same incentive for each soul. Art for art's sake is alive. That is why living energy exists in abstraction. That is why connoisseurs collect original works that are directly imbued with the depth and spirit of the artist's awareness and soul.

Remember, to create without motive, without concern for an audience is liberation, which is a decision each artist must make. Art for art's sake, however, isn't born to compete; it is born for no other reason than to be here now, which is its material destiny, the goal of the yogi, and the nature of Buddha, a prince who became an ascetic and found that the middle path—the path between extremes—was the way to Nirvana. Buddha's farewell admonition to his students (relevant to all artists) was: "Be lamps unto yourselves, and strive unremittingly."

Art for art's sake doesn't exist in a vacuum, either. Making pure art doesn't in any way diminish the inherent excitement you experience when someone loves your work and is willing to acquire it for money. After all, the artist must sell his art to fulfill his dharma. Acceptance is power. Money is power. Art is power. When these three converge in organic harmony, they confirm the artist's cachet. This is a good thing provided the artist doesn't let the attention gorge his ego. But should recognition and money elude for now, the true artist finds a way to make art each day, knowing that art is the galvanizing force. It is overcoming adversity that makes a life of art worth creating at all costs. When the moment of acceptance does come, all previous rejections mercifully fade into oblivion where they belong. Savor your rewards, made all the more sweeter by rejection, for being true to your art.

Although the true artist creates with no motive and for no other reason than for the art to be born, he can have a clairvoyant vision in his mind's eye of the art about to enter the fray in this world.

A VOICE THAT MATTERS

When you do find your art being scrutinized for whatever the reason, be aware. Within the melee of words, watch to see who is speaking and what, if anything, this person has created. But don't stop there. Even if this person is an artist who has a body of work to speak of, what about his temperament, his values, his level of awareness beyond himself? These qualities are no less important than the art itself. Don't let the aura of art overshadow character; otherwise, you will pick up bad habits.

Each true artist's work forms and articulates a unique vision; pure in essence, such art challenges the art lover to perceive it. Are you this artist? Are you this art lover? But don't think about it. Be the artist you know you can be and the world will change for the better, one soul at a time; there is plenty of elbowroom for you to pass through this eye of the needle called truth.

Remember, to create without motive is liberation; it is freedom.

THE ART JURY

When you are exposed to a judgment, you are better served when your first reaction is this: Who is doing the judging? Otherwise, what possible significance could this opinion have on you and your work?

After you find your way to the belly of the beast, let's talk.

Your art must be made public through some means for you to sell your art. What works for one artist may not be the way for another. You must find your own path through the maze of the art-buying world. Galleries, patrons, museums, and grant committees want to be reassured you are an artist committed to your work. Keep in mind that as the artwork increases in value, patrons are most often buying status more so than acquiring the intrinsic value of the work in the bargain. Unique works need constant exposure for their impact to develop a presence in the art-buying world. But you have an edge. With the understanding of the core questions in this book and intuition as your mentor, realizing your dream will become reality and that you will prevail in your success.

In a mid-summer some years ago, I got a call from a gallery owner who asked me whether I would like to participate in a juried show. Although pure art can't be quantified, art competitions are nevertheless ubiquitous. Already familiar with my work, he told me I could bypass the 35mm slide route and submit three framed artworks directly to the jury. Through unconventional circumstances in the past, I had won prizes for my work; and I had also been a judge in various competitions. I knew from both sides that winning and 'losing' was an arbitrary and momentary circumstance.

TOO COMPLEX, TOO BIG

While winning a prize for your art can certainly make your day, it doesn't ensure immediate acceptance and success. Gaining critical acclaim cuts both ways, and most often does.

History is replete with great art being rejected in its time. Around 1785, when Mozart started composing for himself instead of the public, his audience began leaving him and his 'too' complex music. Mozart, who was in desperate need of money, soon began writing more familiar notes to win his audience back.

In 1909, Wassily Kandinsky became a member of the influential New Society of Munich Artists. In time, other members of the Society became increasingly at odds with Kandinsky's abstract work. Some derided his art as being the work of a madman, or someone under the influence of drugs. Two years later the Society rejected Kandinsky's masterwork, *Composition V*, for an exhibition because it was too big, an infringement of the Society's rules. Kandinsky resigned in disgust.

You can't cheat an honest man.
W.C. FIELDS

Be ready to walk, or you are lost.
EDEN

Man is free at the moment he wishes to be.

VOLTAIRE

Be gracious in rejection.

Thank them for their time. Rejection is only momentary. You will have another opportunity—that is, if you are dedicated. And, if you had been less than courteous in your moment of angst, you will say to yourself with deserved regret: Why didn't I behave well instead of stupid, jejune or weak?

EDEN

Has anything changed in nearly a hundred years? In the popular culture of today, for example, films that impress a critic often do poorly at the box office; and conversely, films that are panned can become blockbusters.

THE FINE PRINT

There would be, the gallery owner explained, a special four-week showing in the fall of all participating artists. I was waiting for the other shoe to drop, and it did. He added that there was a fee for each artwork submitted to cover various costs. I winced at this news, not that it was anything new.

Many art juried type affairs require fees to be paid by the artist, which seems unsavory. It would befit the situation if galleries and institutions would secure a sponsor to foot the bill for such expenses; the artist is already providing his talent, his blood on a brush. Paying to have your art judged is like asking each actor auditioning for a part to pay a fee for being auditioned, or having a literary agent charge reading fees for submitted manuscripts, which some do—writers should avoid such entanglements.

I had never been interested in seeking out art competitions since you can't compare works that are unique. It is like saying this shoe is better than this chair. Over the years I have seen extraordinary artists overlooked while mediocre artists were embraced for whatever the reasons. It was time to see how this gallery competition would work out. The gallery was less than an hour's drive away. I delivered three fine pieces and my check. The winners would be announced on the opening day of the exhibit.

Summer gave way to cooler days in early October and the weekend of the exhibit had arrived. I had no doubt that I would win; this was self-confidence in the quality of my work, not hubris. Oscar Wilde, having exhausted the inheritance his father had left him, needed a new source of income. He accepted an offer to lecture in the United States. In 1882, when a custom's agent in New York City asked the great Irish wit if he had anything to declare, Wilde purportedly replied: "I have nothing to declare except my genius."

PANEL OF THREE

At last. The day had arrived. The gallery was crowded with potential patrons as well as nearly thirty artists. My three pieces were prominently displayed. I wove through the flocks of cheese eaters and wine drinkers to see the other artworks—my 'competition'. The range of art went from mediocre to powerful—my work. If I don't feel my work is awesome, who else will? Have I telegraphed the outcome by now? I didn't win and, despite all my understanding and time in the trenches of rejection, I pouted, especially when I saw the gallery owner awarding first, second, and third prizes to art that wasn't particularly good or original.

When my head and feelings cleared the way for meaningful analysis, I asked myself: How could this be possible?

To remain objective, non-attached, when your work is being shown the door is what will keep you centered and unfettered from ignorance and stupidity at best, and jealousy at worst.

The expert panel of three who had juried the show was absent from the opening. Two of the members were gallery owners who were also artists, and the other was an art professor at a nearby college. Who were these people? After the exhibit ran its course, I called on the galleries of the artist judges. The art professor was away on a sabbatical and unavailable. He would have to remain an unknown factor. More important, visiting these judges in their environment refreshed my eyes to the informative gestalt of art juries—from gallery competitions to curated highbrow museum selection committees.

As it turned out, both judges were less than remarkable artists. How could they recognize a piece of original work even if they were looking for it? Nature's law is that you have to be one to know one. It was clear my work was in another realm, one that was alien to them both. After my reconnoitering mission, any lingering angst over not winning had evaporated. And, after all, what had been my motive for entering? Winning. Diligent as ever, my ego had been on the job. Again, I proved to my own self that you must know who is looking at your work before taking anonymous opinions to heart. As I have written: I am interested in comments about my work exclusively from people whom I respect. Be sharp and alert to learning from letdowns. When you weed out the deadwood, rejection releases its death grip on your spirit; in turn, this frees up the space to create and to find your audience—which is what you want in the first place.

ORANGES AND APPLES

I'm not mounting a crusade against art competitions per se; and I send good thoughts to all who partake. If you are so compelled, I encourage you to investigate competitions where you will learn about the scene firsthand and come to your own conclusions. If the competition is about draughtsmanship, then be sure you know how to draw; if the competition has abstract work as its focus, then be sure your work is abstract. Don't give them oranges when they want apples. Although winning doesn't guarantee making it into the big time, it can't be denied that careers have been launched from the aesthetic combat of art competitions.

For example, while a student at Oxford, Oscar Wilde won the prestigious Newdigate prize for his poem, *Ravena*, which was subsequently published by the university. When Wilde published his first play *Vera*, however, it was poorly received and rejected by a succession of theater managers. A year later, in 1881, Wilde published a collection of poems, which didn't please the critics. These transitory rejections couldn't suppress the irrepressible Wilde from becoming a popular world-class 19th century man of letters, and a legend to this day.

If you choose to enter the fray, do so knowing who the players are; if that isn't possible, winning or losing can be viewed as a capricious outcome and, while being chosen is momentarily satisfying, you learn nothing about your art from either decision.

As for competition in art, some may say the jury is still out; I know that competition among artists is a scheme promoted by marketing entities. The true artist is in competition with no one.

Remember, there is no redeeming value in being gullible.

Good luck.

To be a great artist, you don't have to be better than Picasso; you need only be your own self.

EDEN

CHAPTER TWENTY FOUR

ART & PHYSICS
Earth | Space | Time

"WANNA TAKE A RIDE?" The industrialist S.R. Hadden asks the question of SETI researcher Elly Arroway in the film *Contact*. Hadden is offering our heroine the opportunity to be humanity's representative on a machine built to transport its passenger light years away to a superior alien civilization.

Does the artist not ask the same question? Does the artist not accept the challenge?

Contemplating and engaging the arts and sciences raises the awareness of each participant in direct proportion to the energy and dedication expended. This is a fact, not a theory. Please read on and follow the universal evolving thread that weaves through art, physics, space-time, and the quanta information that is you.

TAKING TIME

With an old pair of sterilized pliers, I crunch up the hard dog food. One by one the nuggets break into the right consistency. I do this for my Yorkshire Terrier, Larry, who is now going on nineteen, a senior citizen.

While I fracture the kibble within the mouth of the pliers, I look over at Larry who is standing on the far side of the room. Although still a spry five pounds, his hearing and eyesight are failing, and his teeth are a memory. From my point of view, the experience of time for Larry and me is different. A couple of decades for him represent a generous life cycle. But in another time context, he and I are equals; our time here is impermanent.

As I place the broken nuggets in Larry's bowl, Beau, my other Yorkie, who is much younger and has his canines, meanders over. Instead of eating the full nuggets put aside for him, Beau goes directly after the broken tidbits in Larry's bowl.

Is Beau plain lazy or is he going with the flow, following nature's path of least resistance, like an electron seeking the fastest route to wherever it is going?

A fair question.

Why all this information about physics and quantum theory in a book for artists on how to persevere?

While no one can show you how to be original, you can be challenged with concepts that may prove ambitious to comprehend intellectually, but not intuitively—which also follows the path of art. If you engage your intuition for the truth of things, from theoretical physics to painting, you will add gravitas to your palette; remain steadfast and you will glimpse the consciousness behind the mystery of the universe.

If you don't challenge yourself now, if you don't free your mind and heart, how will you innovate, how will you create original work?

— EDEN

The task is not so much to see what no one yet has seen, but to think what no body yet has thought about that which everyone sees.

ARTHUR SCHOPENHAUER

By now, Larry somehow senses there is action near his food. He saunters over and dives into his overflowing bowl of morsels.

For the moment my crunching up chore is done. I would use a food processor to break up the kibble, but the machine grinds up the hard meal into powder instead of the proper consistency of granules, which must be done by hand using the retro-technology of pliers.

When I was about eleven years old I used to think that if you can break something in half, then in half again, and so on, you could do so for infinity. If things could get infinitely small, I wondered, couldn't things also get infinitely big? I would later learn that such infinite and successive divisions or increases in number were as much a philosophical matter as it was a theoretical mathematical one—no one knows because it is impossible to demonstrate these polar opposite theoretical possibilities in physical reality. Infinity, up or down, is after all a concept, an idea, not a number. I also use to question time. How, for example, could it be noon on the East Coast when it was nine o'clock in the morning in California? Still, as a kid I felt these 'monumental' thoughts about size and time were unique—mine alone. I didn't know Albert Einstein had gone beyond 'daylight savings time' by formulating an astounding relationship between space and time or that quantum mechanics had been successfully predicting the mysterious and strange interactions among the very small, such as electrons and quarks.

POLISHING NEWTON'S APPLE

Although my adolescent speculations and questions about the very small, very large, and relative time may seem like kid's stuff, seemingly simple images and thoughts can lead to astounding insights. When Einstein was 16 years old, he painted a 'thought experiment' for himself. He tried to imagine what it would be like to ride on a beam of light. Could he travel as fast as light? Would light become motionless? Would time itself stop? Could he travel faster than light? From this mental image, nearly a decade later, while Einstein was employed as a clerk at the Swiss Patent Office, he was also pondering the nature of light; in 1905, he published an article that proposed his special theory of relativity, which shook the foundation of science by replacing Isaac Newton's notions of space and time—which was tantamount to moving from art of antiquity to modern art of the 20th century. The rules of the game had changed, and dramatically at that. It was Newton after all who in the 17th century founded modern physics by giving the world his laws of motion and his theory of gravity.

For centuries, it was known that space had three dimensions, and time only one. But it was Einstein who formulated them into an integrated four-dimensional system where space and time can't be separated or viewed independently—as it had been in Newton's universe. Impressive as special relativity was when Einstein first proposed his radical view, it was mostly ignored by the establishment that comprised classically trained physicists who held Newton's laws as sacrosanct. The evolution of art is no different; for example, impressionism and expressionism were once considered crude, unskilled, amateurish, abominations, ugly, and meaningless by the long forgotten sensibilities of those stuck in the classical forms of the past—the status quo. Although Newton's theory of gravity unified the celestial with the terrestrial more than 300 years ago, his equations, which still make accurate predictions, were sufficient to plot the course for astronauts to land on the moon. While Newton could calculate the effects of gravity on Earth and on the planets, he did not know what gravity was.

Einstein would resolve all that.

THE PATENT CLERK

In time, the unknown twenty-six-year old patent clerk's theory would come to revolutionize our understanding of space and time; and even gravity would be explained. In Albert Einstein's universe there are four dimensions: length, breadth, width, and time. While objects in space occur in three dimensions, these three dimensions are not constants. Einstein called the three dimensions (length, breadth and width) 'space' and considered 'time' as a fourth dimension that interacts dynamically with the other three. (Prior to Einstein's view of time as a dimension, many believed that the discovery of the fourth dimension would be one of space.) Einstein determined that all four components (length, breadth, width and time) of his cosmology were not constants but variables depending on velocity, or motion. Einstein needed a cosmological constant to measure the shift of the structure of space, time, and matter. He needed a miracle.

Einstein's great insight is based on the profound recognition that the speed of light (186,000 miles per second or 300,000 kilometers per second) is a cosmological constant. He postulated that nothing physical could go faster than light. We experience an example of this speed every day. It takes sunlight 8 minutes to traverse 93 million miles—the distance from our sun to reach Earth. If the sun were to disappear this instant, people on Earth wouldn't know it until 8 minutes had passed. According to Einstein, light always travels at this constant speed no matter how fast you are moving when you measure it. Special relativity also limits the speed of an object to be less than the speed of light; this means the theory predicts that you can never catch up with light.

Since the speed of light is a universal constant, it always moves at the speed of light relative to an observer. No matter how fast an object is moving, light emitted from that object will always move away from that object at the speed of light. In special relativity, one could approach the speed of light but never attain it—which may seem an absurd concept for us on Earth where our everyday experience tells us that if you go fast enough, you can catch, and even overtake any moving object. Keep in mind, however, that as with all factual-based knowledge, a future discovery may surpass this cosmological speed limit. As it turned out, ten years after special relativity, Einstein did concede faster than light travel (which opened the door to the possibility of time travel), but under certain conditions in his more comprehensive 1915 general theory of relativity.

While no person has yet traveled as fast as light, it has been empirically proven that Einstein was right. When a starship nears the speed of light, 'strange' things begin to happen. An observer would see the starship begins to shrink in size in the direction of motion and that time for its passengers would begin to slow down—from the perspective of the passengers on board, however, everything would appear normal. Special relativity also

In recent years, an astonishing and baffling observation was made by researchers. In a laboratory experiment, a pulse of light emerged from a cloud of gas before it even entered. The end result was a beam of light that moved at 300 times the theoretical limit for the speed of light.

It was Einstein who said nothing physical could break the speed of light barrier because, among other things, to do so would also mean traveling back in time.

Of course, this brings up metaphysical time travel.

EDEN

predicts an event called time dilation: time passes more slowly for moving objects than for stationary ones. With this revelation, space and time were no longer the fixed and unrelated absolutes as described by Newtonian physics. Time was relative to the observer's frame of reference.

To an observer on Earth, a clock traveling at the speed of light ticks more slowly than a clock at rest. Scientists have already demonstrated that an atomic clock traveling at high speed aboard a jet plane ticks more slowly than its stationary counterpart—a finding that presents us with a time difference of no real consequence at the relatively 'slow' speed of a jet, but with extremely significant time dilations when speeds start approaching that of light.

THREE STARSHIP TROOPERS

As the classic twin paradox proposed by Einstein goes in its most basic form: If you were a young man who had a twin brother and he took off in a starship to a distant sun in the Milky Way at near light speed, and then returned to Earth, you would have aged many years (stationary clock), or perhaps even have died of old age, while, for your still young stellar traveling counterpart, all but a few days (moving clock) had passed for him. (There are subtle and complex contradictions within this paradox, which I won't get into here; but feel free to investigate the whole matter and indulge yourself.) Time can't exist without velocity, or motion; in the same way, your success as an artist depends upon your momentum; inertia is rejection's cohort.

Another way to look at time is to see time and mind as one; you can't pin down either because they are a nonmaterial essence; time, it seems, is an artifact of consciousness; we all agree a second is a second; and what we do have is windows into time, which includes the past, present, and future.

Here is a reference example for lightspeed travel: physicist Michio Kaku, in his book, *Visions*, describes a hypothetical fusion ramjet starship that left Earth and is approaching the speed of light: "But since time slows down aboard the starship, according to Einstein's special theory of relativity, the crew could reach the Pleiades star cluster (M45), which is 400 light-years away, in as little as eleven years, by the clocks aboard the starship. After twenty-five years, such a ship could even reach the Great Andromeda Galaxy (although over 2 million years would have passed on the Earth)."

Such astronomical speeds and stellar distances are not part of our everyday life. We earthbound folk walk at about 5 mph and are still driving along the freeways at 65 mph. It is no surprise then that those seemingly 'counter-intuitive' concepts of space and time as being separate yet codependent can be admittedly mind-boggling. But difficulty in whatever form does not stop the true artist from getting his head wrapped around the provocations of nature, including her riddle of space and time.

If Larry, Beau, and I were on that advanced light speed starship, we would all age very slowly; moments, days, or years to us could represent many years, many generations, possibly hundreds or thousands, or even millions of years passing on Earth. It is also theoretically possible that my doggies and I would remain forever young, and not age at all as long we could attain and maintain true light speed through the vacuum of space.

By exploring a subject that you might not otherwise tackle or at least become somewhat familiar with, you elevate your awareness; this can only be a good thing for your work, your confidence, and your relationship with others.

A creator strives for excellence; there is no other way.

EDEN

Recall Einstein's thought experiment: What would you see if you could travel along with a beam of light? Einstein held that if you could catch up with the speed of light, you would see that length (of matter) would contract to zero and time would stop. Since time is a measurement of motion, without motion there is no time. The answer to Einstein's thought experiment of his youth was that you couldn't make this trip. Of course, no one knows—and even the most brilliant physicist changes his views based on new information. When you approach the frontier, doors not previously possible, become available—perhaps we will find such answers beyond space-time in hyperspace, which theoretically and quite seductively may contain many more dimensions, shortcuts to other galaxies, and even parallel universes where you not Pablo Picasso altered the history of art.

PHYSICS AND ART

As an artist it is essential to be awed and amazed, to question dogma and authority, and to wonder with a purpose about what is beyond. If not, how will you keep yourself honest? How will you innovate? If you take things for granted, then this attitude will show up in your work and life; and some form of rejection will always be at your heels. How will you recognize art that is awesome and wondrous, including your own?

When you are feeling down turn your attention upward and outward into the workings of the cosmos—the manifest artwork of the Creator. You can't know the meaning of faith without having first experienced the awe of some miracle, which is evidence of transcendent beauty in temporal life. This is the nexus where faith first begins.

Until then, it is all hearsay.

Remember that you are where your attention takes you, in space and time: good thoughts or unproductive thoughts in the past, present, or future. Lift off from petty details and transitory setbacks. Of course, you would rather not confront any weakness you might have, a rejection, or any other negative situation.

But so what? If you are a player, you must ante up; if you intend on winning, you must stay in the game for the duration. Look into the mystery called creation and you will feel much better.

Although Mother Nature is not interested in the individual per se, she can be wooed and will disclose her deepest secrets to the ardent suitor or confidant willing to step into the unknown—a region on the itinerary that Einstein knew was essential for the scientist. We can add the artist to this travel plan.

To the casual observer, including the artist and the physicist, the relationship between physics and art may not be immediately evident, or seemingly important—especially when your work is getting the shaft. I don't recall undergraduate physics students hanging out with the art majors in college. But to dismiss the connection shared by these two disciplines would be a rush to judgment. You might ask, 'what does this have to do with overcoming rejection, my art, or me?'

Based on his comments about modern art, Einstein didn't appear to grasp the connection between art and physics, either. The relationship between these two disciplines underscores one of the major underpinnings

I do not believe in a fate that falls on men however they act; but I do believe in a fate that falls on them unless they act.

G.K. CHESTERTON

If it isn't unique, it's not art.

—SO SAID THE MASTER

Einstein not only had talent, he also possessed another gift: relative patience.

EDEN

of this book: Intuitive knowing is not only infallible it precedes factual, or empirical knowing. And it is no secret that for thousands of years, art and philosophy have organically and unerringly predicted and anticipated scientific discovery. When you look up into the heavens, do you see equations or poetry, or perhaps both? Physics describes the universe with the nomenclature of symbols; art from the soul is the thing itself, not a symbol of a thing. It is the innovator who first sees the connections between seemingly disparate concepts and things; it is the innovator and embracer of intuition who is light years beyond the insidious gravitational pull of planet dogma. When you discover a kindred spirit in any form, embrace that other perspective, which is also after the truth.

And the artist needs all the help he can get.

In his fine book, *Art & Physics: Parallel Visions in Space, Time & Light*, Leonard Shlain, writes: "Art and physics are a strange coupling. Of the many human disciplines, could there be two that seem more divergent? The artist employs image and metaphor; the physicist uses number and equation. Art encompasses an imaginative realm of aesthetic qualities; physics exists in a world of crisply circumscribed mathematical relationships between quantifiable properties.... Yet despite what appear irreconcilable differences, there is one fundamental feature that solidly connects these disciplines. Revolutionary art and visionary physics are both investigations into the nature of reality."

Like arrows shot from the same cosmic bow, physics and art aim for the fundamental truth of the matter. Physics is after the elementary building blocks of the universe and how they work; art reflects transcendence as the material manifestation of the spirit. Physics and art are both reductive, forever seeking the underlying truth by equation or pastel. Both dig deep for the individual gem buried within ultimate truth.

In physics, we search for the indivisible component and its unifying secret that constitute all matter and energy. In contemporary art, it is the quest by the individual artist for truth and the inherent reward bestowed for unbending commitment to her unique vision. To find one's own voice, one's purpose, or dharma, is no less a feat than discovering the essence of reality. This isn't an abstract metaphor; the artist's work is the quantifiable experience. Art is about the world that we can perceive all around us with our senses—which includes our intuition; and physics is about imperceptible realms we can only detect and validate with machines and technology.

It is no accident that some of the most gifted theoretical physicists describe creation in spiritual terms. Einstein said, "I want to know God's thoughts ... the rest are details." The former patent clerk wasn't referring to a personal God as he clarified: "I believe in Spinoza's God who reveals Himself in the orderly harmony of what exists, not in a God who concerns himself with fates and actions of human beings."

Einstein intuitively sensed that awe coupled with dedication would one day lead him to awesome revelations of the natural world. While Einstein wasn't a prodigy per se, he had an admirable knack for sticking with a problem for years until a resolution would present itself.

THE THEORY OF EVERYTHING

Discovering the building blocks of nature has been an evolutionary process. What is fundamental in matter, including art, has changed over the eons. Ancient peoples believed that earth, water, air, and fire were nature's most primitive elements.

During the Classic Greek period in the 4th century BCE, the pre-Socratic philosopher Democritus proposed that all matter is made up of various imperishable and indivisible elements which he called atoms. More than two thousand years later, 20th century physicists believed neutrons and protons were the indivisible constituents of an atom's nucleus. Then, in the late 1960's, experiments in particle physics revealed that protons and neutrons are made up of quarks, still smaller subatomic particles thought to be elemental and indivisible.

In the 21st century, physicists have a lot riding on a tantalizing solution to explain the fundamental unit of all matter. Known as superstring theory, this revolutionary model proposes that the particles that make up all matter in the universe, including all the forces that allow matter to interact, consist of incredibly small vibrating strands of energy. In recent years, a brilliant new theory has evolved called M-theory, which may one day explain the origin of strings and the true nature of our dimensional universe.

But, when it came to the theory of everything, it was Albert Einstein who had set the bar higher than ever before. In the 1920's, Einstein, after having already changed our perception of space-time and gravity, embarked on the construction of a grand vision, his unified field theory that would explain the fundamental underlying relationship of everything. Einstein spent the last 30 years of his life working to formulate this elusive theory within a single equation—perhaps an inch long—that could explain the four known fundamental forces that govern the universe: gravity, electromagnetism, and the two nuclear forces (weak and strong).

Unfortunately, the young man who in 1905 wrote: '$E=mc^2$ had arrived in the world' was unsuccessful in establishing a unified field theory; his time had run out.

In the end, Einstein felt the real significance of his work would not be understood for a hundred years—a not uncommon prediction among avant-garde artists. Einstein was right. While he didn't come up with the right answer, he did put into motion the right question, which is equally impressive when you think about it.

In his book, *Einstein, Picasso*, Arthur I. Miller writes:

"The corpus of Einstein's fourth paper entitled 'On the Electrodynamics of Moving Bodies,' the so-called relativity paper, is at first glance no different from other scientific papers of that era.

"Yet first glance deceives: It was daring in both style and content. Today no leading physics journal would publish it because of its complete lack of citations to the literature."

If this is so, then art and physics are allies in the description of truths: physical and metaphysical. Nearly a century after Einstein drew his line of chalk in the fabric of space-time, the quest for the Theory of Everything has become the holy grail of advanced theoretical physics. The equation of the millennium would explain the elemental relationship of matter and energy, gravity and light.

Taste is the enemy of creativeness.
PABLO PICASSO

A prudent question is one-half of wisdom.
FRANCIS BACON

Yet some of Einstein's subsequent work became an integral part of quantum mechanics. In 1916, he formulated a new theory of how large numbers of atoms interact with light, which became the basis of the laser ...

ARTHUR I. MILLER

But the 'theory of everything' is not limited to theoretical physics.

Getting at the magnificent essence of a thing is also the nature of universal art, which is the transcendental manifestation of God—personal, of Spinoza, or otherwise. All the bases are covered.

STRINGS AND DICE

Brian Greene, author of *The Elegant Universe*, writes: "The fundamental particles of the universe that physicists have identified—electrons, neutrinos, quarks, and so on—are the 'letters' of all matter. Just like their linguistic counterparts, they appear to have no further internal substructure. String theory proclaims otherwise. According to string theory, if we could examine these particles with even greater precision—a precision many orders of magnitude beyond our present technological capacity—we would find that each is not pointlike but instead consists of a tiny, one-dimensional loop. Like an infinitely thin rubber band, each particle contains a vibrating, oscillating, dancing filament that physicists have named a string."

On the cosmic scale of Einstein's general relativity, everything warps, curves, and flows smoothly in space-time; in the subatomic scale of quantum mechanics, the world of the infinitesimally small is seemingly chaotic where events can only be predicted as probabilities. Einstein, who would not accept quantum mechanics, said: "God does not play dice with the universe." Of course, he meant the universe was created with an underlying order based on reliability, not one based on chance and anarchy. Einstein and quantum mechanics couldn't be both right. Our universe wouldn't have two different sets of natural laws to accommodate the big and the tiny. There must be a unifying theory that would explain it all. Is string theory the answer? Are strings the end of the line?

In the theoretical cosmos of strings, the previously incompatible and divergent theories of general relativity (an orderly universe) and quantum mechanics (a chaotic universe) would be elegantly unified. From a physicist's point of view, if you can't verify it, then it is philosophy, not science. If, however, superstring theory can eventually be verified (which could take decades or more, or perhaps never), then Einstein's general theory of relativity (big things) and quantum mechanics (tiny things) will finally wed to beautiful music perfectly scored and conducted by the strings that make up everything under, and including, the stars.

Whether there is an even smaller constituent than theoretical vibrating strings remains to be seen. And, while the pursuit to explain everything is exciting, the indivisible essence of creation can never be quantified because it is consciousness itself. This is not a limitation of science, which is still mostly concerned with measuring experience in the due course of cause and effect, not speculating on the ineffable, the absolute—which is the domain of art and philosophy.

DIVIDING GOD

But let's speculate on behalf of a theoretical physicist in the far-distant future where the bygone age of particle accelerators has long been passé.

Using a quanta-extractor, our physicist once again calibrates the search pattern. Unafraid, she gazes into the ultimate lightness of being that is the micro-universe of the infinitely small. Suddenly, she gasps in disbelief to the rhythm of her pounding heart as the elusive quanta has been realized. Overwhelmed with wonder, she is speechless. The more profound the emotion, the less there is to say.

For the first time, a child of stardust looks bravely and in awe upon the eye of the infinitesimally intelligent as it floats in space-time with no need to move since it is everywhere in the cosmos simultaneously. She has, by some synchronicity of converging forces, observed the absolute, the sweet spot of reductionism where it is no longer possible to divide the subatomic structure of matter and energy.

What treasure has our heroine discovered? Intuitively, she knows that she has made the discovery of all time: God is *the* fundamental element. 'I see … it's all so clear now,' she says to herself, 'there can be no temporal equation for ultimate reality, the nonmaterial timeless essence that is God.' Art, science, and philosophy converge into one comprehensive moment: God is emotion, which is not an equation. This find is meta-empirical evidence for the existence of the Creator—a 'proof' no advanced class in theoretical physics could have anticipated. You can't divide God any further with quantum mechanics, or any other discipline. God *is* the irreducible matrix that imbues absolutely everything—again, personal, of Spinoza, or otherwise. Our physicist has seen the sublime countenance of the Creator. She knows because the indivisible mote of pure consciousness looked back with the absolute understanding: Truth *is* God. Of course, this revelation is not the end; it is the beginning.

Truth alone is eternal, everything else is momentary. It is more correct to say that Truth is God, than to say that God is Truth … All life comes from the one universal source, call it Allah, God or Parmeshwara.

GANDHI

The breakthrough made by our physicist heroine is still fiction, or is it? It is clear. The essence of the Creator can't be detected or measured with instruments; art, a manifestation of spirit, can't be quantified for the same reason. You can't put God in a bottle as if the divine were some exotic specimen worth preserving. You can, however, measure artifacts of the Creator's consciousness, or what we call reality. Proof of the Creator's existence doesn't require a 'star trek' into interstellar space or a 'fantastic voyage' into the subatomic realm of quarks and strings. Your being and everything around you in this moment is more than 'probable cause' for the Maker. If there is a painting, then there must be a painter. You can't co-opt pure art. You can't dissuade the true artist from her dharma. Your existence is irrefutable evidence—personal, of Spinoza, or otherwise.

Remember, true faith in the transcendent is based upon proof—not the other way around, which is the common misunderstanding. The existence of the transcendent isn't beyond our senses; the metaphysical can be felt in your heart, soul, and even in your bones. Memories of your creation, call it DNA, are in every cell of your body, not only in your brain. You can't measure or divide God, love, or courage because they exist irrespective of size and are perceived—like truth—only and indirectly as the result of action.

QUANTUM SOUL

When I contacted physicist Fred Wolf, author of *The Spiritual Universe*, about his thoughts on the relationship between physics and the soul, he summed things up as follows:

Quantum teleportation:

Although experiments in quantum physics tell us that physical information can't travel faster than light, we do, in fact, experience this amazing phenomenon every day; we know it as intuition, which is the instantaneous transmission of information without physical contact—from the Cosmic consciousness directly to you.

EDEN

"I no longer see quantum physics as a 'proof' of the soul. The notion of quantum physics proving the existence of anything spiritual is problematic at best and impossible to accept at worst. However, having said that, let me speculate: The existence of the soul is deeply implied by quantum physics simply because the universe and self-reflecting sentience play a role in the evolution of the universe. Quantum physics shows that an unobserved universe would not be anything like the world we do observe.

"Consciousness seems to be deeply involved in the process of observation in that it changes what was possible to an actuality. According to quantum physics possibilities in the world can be shown to influence our observations. If two or more possibilities are present, one of them can interfere with another producing no possibility for either at all or an enhancement of either when the two are 'close' or yielding a similar 'pattern' in an abstract nonphysical space. But all that occurs without the action of an observation. Once consciousness starts, an observer seeks to see something, it suddenly ends with an actual outcome and the interference magically vanishes.

"I see this as evidence of the existence of a soul entity—the ultimate observer present at the Big Bang and throughout the universe. I also see the process of observation can be self-reflecting and hence the soul can be 'caught' in the physical realm through its desire to make something happen and 'see' the physical world. Since even it can't control outcomes, both 'good' and 'bad' things can and do occur.

"So my speculation above is not a proof of anything; it is a model of one aspect of the spiritual domain of our fragile existence … Keep in mind that science and spirituality, like cultures from opposite ends of the earth, have a difficult time dealing with each other. Words like 'proof' have different meanings depending on whether or not you are a scientist. I believe that quantum physics is rapidly approaching a time where the soul and our spiritual existence can't be denied."

NO PRISONERS

Revolutionary findings in quantum physics seem to demonstrate the need for an observer (a witness) to be present for a potential outcome to manifest, to become real. After all, why should our presence affect the range of potentials from one value to another? While it may be difficult to grasp this implied series of events because it seems to conflict with common sense, is this sort of dynamic truly weird? Maybe not.

If the act of our observation alters the outcome of events on the quantum scale of the infinitesimally small, what about our actions and activities on the human scale? Where one person sees nothing, another sees nothing but opportunity. Where one viewer sees seemingly random splashes of paint on a canvas, another sees a breakthrough in art. Meaning is a function of observation, which is how you make a reliable case. The perception of the painting alters its potential significance, value, and destiny. And, as we have heard, beauty is in the eye of the beholder.

Given a broader perspective the mystery of the observer influencing a quantum event of fundamental particles no longer seems as remote or enigmatic from our everyday experience of life. As the Zen-like riddle goes: Does a tree falling in the woods make a sound if there is no one present to hear it? Rather than barking up this perennial chestnut for a solution, it remains amazing to me that there is a tree, the woods, sound, and a someone asking for an answer to this question—which, in the end, relies not only on a philosophy but on one's definition of sound.

If you desire proof of the transcendent, you won't find it in a book, as the 'unknowable' exists exclusively as a potential ready to be realized in the presence of a reliable witness. If you see it, then you own it. Transcendence is accessible to the artist, physicist, and anyone with the passion to engage the existential quality of life through firsthand experience, not hearsay. Nature, mother that she is, takes no prisoners. She doesn't claim perfection because that isn't her plan. Nature, with no overt sympathy for pain and suffering, is willing to sacrifice the expendable in the pursuit of survival, adaptation, and evolution. As an artist, to persevere, you must be no less resolute than nature with your art while still following a path guided by your moral compass.

Remember the first rule of awareness: don't believe your own bullshit.

Ah, but a man's reach should exceed his grasp. Or what's a heaven for?

ROBERT BROWNING

INSTINCT OR INTUITION

Rejection is nature's way of weeding out the dilettantes. Gather and toss with abandon all your crippling thoughts and beliefs into your own bonfire of the vanities. Get rid of them, now. If you don't know what they are, then begin to write them down when they appear. Remember, intuition is the soul whispering the song of God—the indivisible truth—directly to you. Of course, science may differ with my definition of intuition.

I asked theoretical physicist Brian Greene if he meant *instinct* when he uses the word *intuition* in his writing. He replied: "Yes, I would say that science intuition refers to an 'instinct' for what physical principles underlie what we experience and measure." Intuition in the science sense is based on our ability to quantify and categorize our perceptions of the physical world—all that possess mass and dimension.

When I use the word intuition I am not referring to instinct, which is inborn, or some other inherent aptitude like parenting, language or swimming. Intuition, which is non-material, is beyond the limits of reason, including all orders of magnitude involving the progression of future technologies. Intuition is one resource for your art and life that, remaining forever loyal, will never let you down; this form of direct knowing without the clutter of thinking is an integral aspect of Zen Buddhism.

It is not by chance that Einstein biked and took long walks to free his mind. Through these physical activities, he knew, on and intuitive level, that his thinking mind would disengage, making room for intuition to resolve some elusive problem conscious thought couldn't. Arthur Miller also points out that as a high school age student, Einstein was a pupil (1895-96) at the cantonal school in Aarau, Switzerland. In this progressive environment under the tutelage of the educational reformer Johann Heinrich Pestalozzi, Albert the teenager absorbed the importance of intuition, visual imagery, and independent thought—elements that would make him one of the great 'conceptual' thinkers of the 20th century.

Think about it. Haven't you experienced the free flow of thoughts, feelings, and perhaps an intuitive knowing of the world around you while riding

Nothing can so pierce the soul as the uttermost sigh of the body.

GEORGE SANTAYANA

There is nothing admirable about being gullible or naïve.

EDEN

your bike, walking along the beach, or even when driving your car solo? Of course, if you are attached to your cell phone or listening to your iPod during these times of locomotion (traveling through space and time), you may relinquish a transcendent communication for a temporal one. While Einstein might not have expressed the mind and intuition relationship precisely in these terms, the mechanics as presented here are the same for everyone—you, Einstein, and me.

This timeless power labeled intuition, which is only a word, is more than a biochemical reaction in the brain, or a biological adaptation, or a gut feeling, or even the collective sum of these manifestations. But I don't mean that these are merely phenomena to be dismissed. The very existence and experience of these natural functions are miracles of biotechnology in themselves. Intuition is the door opener to the perception of everything in both the temporal and transcendent realm. For those who know there is a soul and for theoretical physicists who want to empirically explain the underlying secrets of nature, God is alive—personal, of Spinoza, or otherwise. Although science can measure artifacts of creation, it can't measure the Creator. Temporal technology can tell you how, but not why. This isn't a problem. It is a distinction. Consider all the marvels science has discovered and will reveal on this ultimate odyssey for truth.

MIDNIGHT OIL

Eventually, truth, like rich cream, rises to the top. This is not a *hope* or *wish*; it is a universal law in perpetual motion. Physics attempts to explain the unification and workings of matter and energy using equations; and art is the transcendental canvas of mixed media connecting us to that same objective reality. Does one put his faith in physics or in art to unravel the mystery of creation?

If, for example, I want to understand what $E=mc^2$ means, I have to make an unwavering commitment. While I might be able to appreciate Einstein's equation as a historical breakthrough on a purely abstract level, I have to work hard to comprehend its underlying significance as a concise description of a natural law containing awesome power—nuclear energy. In other words, how can knowledge of this equation be applied in the real world? Art is no different. Why would anyone take for granted that it takes less effort to comprehend the soul of art than to understand the symmetry of physics? Art and leisure don't belong on the same page. If the painter must learn to grasp the equation, then science must commit to appreciating the irreducibility of the painting, which can be quantified through appreciation, not machinery.

Without transcendence, life is reduced to mere propagation and sterility of purpose. Remember, meaning is your contribution to life.

GOSPEL OF ART

As mentioned elsewhere in this book, the ancient text from India known as the *Veda*, says: "Know that one thing by knowing which everything else can be known." And what is that one thing? The *Veda* is referring to Brahman, which is Pure Consciousness. Instead of poring over volumes of data and dogma, it is smarter to know one thing that, like a magic mirror, reflects everything you need to know. That one thing for me is my art; it not only reflects the gospel of the moment, it, like a trusted lieutenant, reverberates the truth of all those around me.

Physics is seeking out the one underlying truth to explain matter and all the forces in the universe. This truth is also Brahman. In Zen, there are intuitive understandings beyond words, paradoxes of existence, and the profound comprehension of awareness—which is not awareness of any particular thing, but of awareness itself. What a Zen master would call awakening to ultimate unification, or Buddha enlightenment, a theoretical physicist might describe as discovering the one indivisible component that forms all matter and energy—like the revelation that God is that indivisible entity as witnessed by our heroine physicist from the future. On this level, reincarnation, transmigration of the soul, the redistribution of matter and energy into sentient life, is not a theory, but a practical reality.

It wouldn't be a stretch to call the quest for the theoretical indivisible and vibrating quanta (strings) used to construct our universe an ambitious undertaking. This drive to attain the unknowable is also a function of art, of Zen, of Brahman, of getting to know God—personal, of Spinoza, or otherwise. This is the drive that rolls over rejection wherever it stands.

Physics, art, philosophy, and pure spirit without dogma are describing aspects of the same thing. Transcendental truths that can't be empirically demonstrated are grist for the mill for those willing to tough it out. Are metaphysical experiences real, or not, even if they can't be duplicated under clinical conditions?

Keep in mind that you can't duplicate unique experiences. Nothing is more profound than direct personal experience of a thing, which is the point of Zen and art. Remember, Buddha, who predated as well as inspired Zen, saw no separation in reality; he took up residence inside Nirvana—in a word, the unified field envisioned by Einstein.

Everything is connected. This ancient view becomes less philosophy and more science with each new breakthrough made by modern physics.

Do not lose sight of awareness, which teaches us that intuition needs no outside source or authority (physics or otherwise) to validate its authenticity or purpose. Not all truths can be measured with instruments. The only people who would believe that instrumentality is the only way of knowing truth are those who rely solely on instruments and those who build them.

If there is any doubt concerning the existence of the uncertainty principle in quantum mechanics, remember this concern the next time your computer won't do what it normally does—despite appearances where everything seems to be working properly.

EDEN

NO HALF THOUGHTS

Thoughts are true in the sense that they exist. You have them. There are heavy thoughts and light ones. Haven't you experienced them? But do thoughts have weight? Where is a thought? When you forget and then remember, where did that truant thought go? Can you find a lost thought? While we may take thoughts for granted because they are ubiquitous and seemingly happen spontaneously out of thin air, their nonmaterial (you can't cut an idea in half like a cantaloupe) existence is no less mysterious and wondrous than the source of all existence—consciousness. If it is mind over matter and energy ($E=mc^2$), then an equivalent equation harnessed by your thoughts alters as well as contributes to reality.

Human nature is not nearly as bad as it has been thought to be.

ABRAHAM MASLOW

You cannot divide or weigh God in the same way you cannot divide silence or courage; they are already indivisible.

EDEN

You can prevail over feelings of rejection at any time of your choosing, with one stipulation: you know where you stand under the sun by having conscientiously answered the core questions posed in this book. The gift to choose is irreducible, eternally beautiful, and experience of its eventual payoff is a great liberating power.

Most folk don't give space much thought. Take a moment and look around the space you are occupying at this moment. You exist both in space and time. We live on a small planet in a universe defined by three spatial dimensions: height, width, and length. We can travel along these three perpendicular paths and only these paths.

Artist, can you envision another spatial dimension?

The other necessary element in our universe is a fourth dimension, not of space but of time. Nothing can happen without time—the past, present and future.

Artist, can you envision any other way that time passes?

Some theorists propose that time flows like a winding river; others, like Einstein, hold that the past, present, and future exist side by side simultaneously. Every event that takes place in three-dimensional space (from your appointment with a museum director to a supernova in deep space) must take place at a particular moment along a timeline conceptually defined by yesterday, today, or tomorrow. Despite our personal agendas, we all live by the celestial clock. Lunar and solar cycles affect us deeply, and our bodies naturally respond with sleep at night and activity during daylight. Upsetting this biorhythm can have serious health-related consequences.

Even the most sublime mysteries of the universe eventually reveal themselves for the intrepid soul who has ditched the heavy baggage of his ego to find his dharma, or purpose in life—this is the fundamental equation you must formulate, calculate, and then balance for your own self. No one else can make this computation for you. There is only one way to validate your dharma and that is you must prove it, first to yourself.

If you say you are a painter, then paint; if you are a writer, then write; and if you are a musician, then play, and so on. When you are in dharma, which is transcendental lightspeed, you are in timeless awareness; rejection, no matter how much it strains, with deference to Einstein, will never catch up with you.

When you are the vanguard, nothing can prevent you from fulfilling your mission, your destiny—the purpose of your life. When you are living life in dharma, you are in concert with the Zen master, the Nobel prize-winning physicist, and the Creator of all that is and will ever be. You are in tune with the strings of creation. This is beautiful music. While theoretical physics may initially appear daunting, it is fundamentally concerned with questions that ultimately matter, which is not beyond the reach of any motivated student. Even if superstring theory turns out to be *the* theory, it will invariably lead to more questions because even the most erudite physicist will admit that although he may now be able to explain *how*, he still can't explain *why*. The physicist seeks the explanation for the primal forces of nature; the true artist formulates the equation for the theory of everything in every painting. Like physics, art is after the same thing and will settle for nothing less than stripping away stubborn hardwired illusions to reveal the fundamental picture that is the experience of life and the indivisible code—universal truth—of creation.

This desire and tenacity to understand is the trait of a creator.

THE FOURTH DIMENSION

Einstein did for physics what Pablo Picasso did for the evolution and promotion of modern art. Of course, their genius was to integrate what had been done before into an original way of seeing, seriously challenging the mainstream perception of reality. Keep in mind, however, that they did not do it alone. Einstein's route to his breakthroughs in physics is more clearly delineated as his work is based on a well-documented history of previous mathematical discoveries; once a mathematical problem is solved, it is solved for everyone—art follows a similar pattern.

Picasso's route to invention, while it had its share of self-evident influences, leaves much out, as there were contributions of other great painters of his day, plus those who did not make it big in the art history books and nameless antecedent creators who were also keepers of the flame. Posterity chooses its messengers.

The year 1905 and thereabouts was a magical time for art and science. Einstein was postulating that space-time is a single fabric, warped and rippled, and bound together by the three dimensions of space and the single dimension of time—later called the *space-time* continuum, which may well be the fourth dimension. Einstein's brilliant deductions about the geometry of space-time didn't arrive out of thin air. His innovations were built upon the discoveries of other luminaries who preceded him.

Einstein's friend and founder of quantum theory Max Planck saw that energy didn't flow in a steady continuum but moved as discrete energy packets (quanta); and, James Clark Maxwell who, with four elegant equations, had unified electricity and magnetism (electromagnetism).

CRUMPLED PAPER

Picasso (in collaboration with Georges Braque) jettisoned the confines of three dimensional art for a fourth dimensional perspective through Cubism—where the viewer could see the object from multiple points of view simultaneously—like a being might from a fourth dimension.

Although they are forever intertwined historically, Picasso didn't 'invent' Cubism (*circa*, 1907) out of whole cloth by pulling it fully formed out of a hat. He developed Cubism, which was a bold self-styled 'imagined' experiment, through the effort of investigation and original research, in much the same way that Andy Warhol instigated pop art or Jackson Pollock adopted drip painting. Proffering art based on readymade objects, pop icons, or even household items was hardly new, and although dripping wasn't the sole invention of Pollock, he used it to 'paint' purely intuitive nonobjective works, something Kandinsky had surely done before him.

The consensus in art history books is that other artists and motifs directly inspired Braque and Picasso who were both influenced by Paul Cézanne, African sculpture, El Greco, Dominique Ingres, Georges Seurat, and the Fauves; and, Picasso, as some theorize, was excited by the early 20th century

Georges Braque, like his father and grandfather, first trained as a house painter and decorator.

He also attended art school for a couple of years, but that experience didn't prevent him from innovating and creating a personal style.

EDEN

Yet another theory goes that Picasso's inspiration for Les Demoiselles d'Avignon and cubism came from a camera with a cracked lens; the resulting portrait photos he took had fractured planes and distorted features.

Regardless of what had influenced Braque and Picasso, the salient point is that it was they who had first put the pieces of cubism together.

EDEN

mathematical zeitgeist of physics, space-time, and the lure of what was on everyone's lips: the realm of possibilities called the fourth dimension.

How were they influenced, exactly, is *the* question? Aside from conjecture, no matter how plausible, how did this duo arrive at Cubism? Was it some idiosyncratic moment or a sublime convergence of perception? What truly brought it on? Of course, Braque's Cubism was different from Picasso's. One minimalist theory is that Cubism was born when the artist picked up a work on paper that had been crumpled; the 'shattered' art now exposed on facets of different planes was self-evident. Another goes that Cubism was the result, or a by-product, of absinth, hashish, or opium. But that can't be so. If it were, then we would be inundated with art innovations every day. But, no one knows, except Picasso and Braque.

In The Museum of Modern Art exhibition catalogue, *Picasso and Braque: Pioneering Cubism*, William Rubin writes of Braque:

"Late in life he observed: 'During [the Cubist] years, Picasso and I said things to one another that will never be said again … that no one will ever be able to understand … things that would be incomprehensible, but gave us joy.…' 'All that,' he insisted, 'will end with us.'"

In *Einstein, Picasso,* Henry Miller writes: "The general line of argumentation among art historians is that the roots of cubism are in Paul Cézanne and primitive art. This view discounts completely how astounding developments in science, mathematics and technology contributed to the very definition of 'avant-garde.' It has long been known that the roots of science were never totally within science itself. Why then should the roots of the most influential art movement of the twentieth century lie totally within art? By widening our viewpoint of the origins of Picasso's *Demoiselles* to include science, mathematics and technology, we gain deeper insight into Picasso's monumental struggles."

The ongoing mystique surrounding Cubism should be a source of inspiration for your own work. After all, Picasso did stop short of pure abstraction, leaving plenty of room for everybody else, including you and me. And, more important, you know as much as the artists mentioned throughout this book; you need only have faith in your own dharma.

Focus on your work, let nothing hinder your daily creation, and the stars will eventually line up for you as well. Every great artist owes a debt to another.

BREAKING THE SHACKLES

As Michio Kaku writes: "Artists have been particularly interested in the fourth dimension because of the possibilities of discovering new laws of perspective. In the Middle Ages, religious art was distinctive for its deliberate lack of perspective. Serfs, peasants, and kings were depicted as if they were flat, much the way children draw people. Since God was omnipotent and could therefore see all parts of our world equally, art had to reflect His point of view, so the world was painted two-dimensionally. Renaissance art was a revolt against this flat God-centered perspective. Sweeping landscapes and realistic, three dimensional people were painted from the point of view of a person's eye, with the lines of perspective vanishing into the horizon. Renaissance art reflected the way the human eye viewed the world, from the singular point of view of the observer. In other words, Renaissance art discovered the third dimension."

Then, as things would unfold, Cubism broke the shackles of three dimensions for four. Marcel Duchamp's Cubist masterpiece *Nude Descending a Staircase* (1912) explored the same figure shown in some twenty successive points in time as it might be seen coexisting in the fourth dimension. Despite it being a sensation, *Nude Descending* was quickly acquired for $350 in 1913 by a San Francisco art dealer. Duchamp, in a 1938 interview, said that the *Nude* was not a painting at all, but 'an organization of kinetic elements, an expression of time and space through the abstract expression of motion.' But motion from another realm had already been on the move.

In 1878, Eadweard Muybridge photographed the first successful serial images of a trotting horse, proving a long-debated argument among horsemen—there is a moment of suspension where no hooves are touching the ground. Muybridge's kinetic images of animals and humans in motion inspired scientists Thomas Edison, Etienne-Jules Mareym, and others who, during the late 1890's, went on to develop and refine what would become the motion picture camera—film as art and business was born.

SWAN SONG

As art of the avant-garde moved decidedly forward, deconstructing accepted sensibilities in its wake, movement by movement in its time, expressionism, nonobjective art, and abstract expressionism continued to anticipate the future of reality. While art may anticipate the future, the true artist knows that it is much smarter living a life in the present moment of fulfillment instead of future uncertainty and hope.

Neither Einstein nor Picasso was born famous; creators never are; you can't bequeath fire from heaven. Both men proved that genius is dedication. Picasso not only confronted rejection and poverty in his early years, he had to continually reinvent his art, which is no small challenge since it must sprout organically. Einstein too faced rejection, felt misunderstood, and as a young man confessed to his sister that he was a failure who would never amount to anything; then, in the latter part of his years, Einstein, the man who had changed the world, felt the pressure of the 'what have you done lately' syndrome from the scientific community and younger physicists.

Although Albert Einstein, who we should recall showed no apparent genius growing up, didn't live to complete his final grand symphony—the unified theory of everything—his work continues to challenge scientists. Many aspects of his theories and equations have yet to be fully explored and proven empirically. While I was writing this book, for example, NASA astronomers confirmed one of the effects of gravity on space-time predicted by Einstein's theory of relativity. Picasso, as I say, needs no more publicity from me; he has left a legacy that every artist can learn from. Once the public anoints you (or you do so yourself) as the *greatest*, there is only one direction to go from there. If you want to top yourself, keep it a secret until you are ready.

RIPPLES IN REALITY

Everything in the universe, Einstein said, exists within the space-time fabric. If gravity could affect the direction of light, then space itself must

To succeed in the world it is not enough to be stupid, you must also be well-mannered.

VOLTAIRE

Physics: The truth that is matter.

Art: The matter that is truth.

EDEN

You might want to include Beethoven in your book on rejection. He proposed marriage to Magdalena Willmann in 1794 and was rejected. Then he proposed marriage to Therese Malfatti in 1810 and was rejected yet again. And his deafness prevented him from hearing his Ninth Symphony when first performed in 1824.

Erskine Caldwell's struggles with rejection are detailed in his autobiography. He failed and failed and failed until he finally rewrote Tobacco Road for Broadway where it was performed for seven years.

And also, Melville did not achieve fame for Moby Dick until after his death.

MAURICE BASSETT,
PUBLISHER

warp, too. Einstein's breakthrough general theory of relativity, which he proposed in 1915, showed space-time can be visualized as a fabric that becomes stretched and distorted by the presence of matter and energy. This great insight allowed him to redefine our understanding of both time and gravity. To illustrate the point, here's a commonly used example: Picture a bowling ball in the center of a stretched rubber sheet. The heavy bowling ball naturally causes a depression in the sheet's surface. If we then place a baseball on the edge of the sheet, it will travel forward into the depression toward the heavier bowling ball. (The bowling ball is our sun and the baseball is Earth.) Einstein reasoned that smaller masses travel toward larger masses not because they are 'attracted' by a mysterious force (as Newton had erroneously theorized), but because the smaller objects travel through space that is warped by the larger object.

In other words, gravity is something we notice when we happen to be traveling within a particular configuration of space and time—a resilient 'fabric' that can bend and ripple. Earth is in orbit on the cusp of the dimple created in space-time by the enormous mass of our sun. The sun's gravity (sphere of influence in the fabric of space-time) holds all the planets in their stable orbits. Planetary orbits are a balance between gravity and the motion of the planet. If the planet weren't moving, it would fall into the sun. If you were Superman, you could throw a baseball fast enough and high enough so that it would go into permanent orbit around the Earth. It is this warping or curving of space-time that creates what we feel as gravity. Einstein rightly reasoned that gravity was not some powerful force, but a function of geometry.

For the artist, art is born of gravitas in both receiving and giving. Rejection or disappointment has no hold or influence on an artist whose mass is dignity, one of the Be-Attitudes; and like the sun, dignity attracts complementary objects into its sphere of energy and opportunity.

Remember, don't take the road to rote by memorizing anything you read in this book; read the words until you do understand; then, with this new understanding, you must act when you are called; only then can you metabolize the meaning into your being as an indestructible thread woven directly into the evolving fabric of your character—and character, which thrives on truth, the antidote for rejection, isn't an inexplicable force acting at distance, but a power of mass appeal borne of the unique and local displacement of the space-time energy being that is you.

This is the material of superheroes.

Work this concept until it is yours. I did write in so many words that this book wasn't light reading, which is what it sounds like.

MORE THAN A PEEPHOLE

With homage to Einstein who replaced Newtonian physics with his own, I experience a similar sense of space-time. Of course, I can't empirically prove my observation since each person can only experience it for himself.

As space is the infinite canvas stretched over the known universe, life energy flows outward along the continuum called time. This stellar cosmic tableau is the birthplace of not only celestial events, but also art for art's sake, which is an organic force of nature—evolution.

Self-referential art comes into being like the spontaneous birth of a star; while it can glow content and alone in the vacuum of space, the sun becomes more than simply another nuclear furnace (there are some 200 billion stars in our own Milky Way galaxy) when its energy warms life on one of its orbiting satellites, or planets.

Since *the* beginning, people have sensed there is something more going on than what can be seen in our three-dimensional universe of width, height, and length. Science continues to prove what has already been anticipated by philosophy and art for thousands of years: we are looking at the universe through a tiny peephole.

Although electromagnetic waves exist in a vast range of wavelengths, the retina in our eyes can perceive only a very narrow band that we call light and color.

This narrow band of wavelengths is called the visible light spectrum.

Visible light waves are the only electromagnetic waves that we can see. We see these waves as the colors of the rainbow. Each color has a different wavelength. Red has the longest wavelength and violet has the shortest. When all the waves are seen together they make white light. Every scientist since Aristotle had believed that white light was a basic single entity, but it was Newton who concluded white light isn't a simple entity at all.

When he passed a thin beam of sunlight through a glass prism, Newton noted the light had dispersed into a rainbow of wavelengths, or the colors of the visible light spectrum. This is how light behaves. But what is light? Is it a wave or a particle? It has characteristics of both. This question baffled scientists for many decades.

Light is information.

Information, like energy, or mass, can't be destroyed. In a sense, this means that every event is immortal as light; reflections of each living thing and action on the planet speed out into the universe forever.

Beings with special telescopes on planets thousands of light years from Earth could at this very moment be observing Siddhartha evolve into the Buddha under the Bodhi tree, or a boy in ancient Egypt playing with his sacred cat in the shadow of the Great Pyramid as it is being built.

EDEN

THE LIGHT CONUNDRUM

Then, in 1905, Einstein, building upon the work of Max Planck, advanced a radical theory of light when he explained that light is a stream of particles, or energy packets of quanta (later called photons). Light, he proposed, had a dual nature. Until then, the accepted idea was that light was a wave. Einstein's insight established the theoretical basis for the photoelectric cell, or electric eye, which made sound motion pictures, television, and many other inventions possible.

Our modern way of life with all its fantastic electronic gadgets is a reality because of the theory of quantum mechanics and how things interact on the subatomic level.

But is light ultimately a *wave*, or a *stream of photons*? Physicists have two valid ways of looking at light: 1) as individual particles called photons, and 2) as a wave. Modern physicists believe that light can behave as both a particle and a wave, but they also recognize that either view is a simple explanation for something more complex, or to say that light has a dual nature doesn't fully explain the paradox we call light.

Despite our advanced technology, seeing light for what it truly is remains debatable. Still, we do talk about light as waves because this provides the best explanation for most of the phenomena our eyes can see.

Light, depending upon which tests are applied, appears to be either a wave or a particle—which remains a conundrum. In his book, *QED, The Strange Theory of Light and Matter,* Richard Feynman, the brilliant and

If you look at the myths of a culture, then that pretty much explains everything.

EDEN

iconoclastic physicist, who, like Einstein, was partial to light being a particle, describes how the wave-particle duality works: "Nature has got it cooked up so we'll never be able to figure out how She does it: if we put instruments in to find out which way the light goes, we can find out, all right, but the wonderful interference effects disappear. But if we don't have instruments that can tell which way the light goes, the interference effects come back! Very strange, indeed!"

This gives new meaning to out of sight, out of mind.

What is the point? As this experiment suggests, the presence of life, of an observer alters the pattern of reality, which is what art is all about. In recent years, cutting edge science has already proven that feelings and thoughts affect material reality. This is, however, hardly news for the artist. So, in what remains an unexplained phenomenon, the mind, or perhaps the soul of the observer as physicist Wolf suggested earlier, directly influences the outcome of the light experiment. We see what we expect to see, and that is a habit. The perceiver completes the painting or the performance.

Remember, visible light is only a fraction of the electromagnetic 'wave' spectrum. We don't really know how or why light works, yet. How can it be two things at the same time? This is a humbling reality. This is art.

Einstein labeled space-time as the fourth dimension—which is a component of reality still under debate. The fourth dimension has both inspired and perplexed artists, writers, mystics, and scientists for thousands of years. For our purposes that elusive 'something more going on than what can be seen in our three-dimensional universe of width, height, and length' is, of course, art, which, like our life-giving sun, exists in time through motion only in relation to everything else, an observation that does not go unnoticed by the bold artist who places his hand into the crucible of divine fire, the source of creation, which is best expressed as poetry.

When I write that art is magic, I am not talking about mumbo jumbo or sleight of hand. I am referring to the transcendental nature of living art, which, by direct implication, occupies a palpable dimension in space-time that can be felt but never compared or measured because, being unique, it can't be duplicated. If you can't recognize what is unique in the works of other artists, how then can you do so for your own self?

PAST, PRESENT, FUTURE

Far from being a resident life form in accord with Mother Earth, we are a technologically infatuated species clinging to destructive patterns even as we claw our way toward 'progress', which is currently a precariously steep and erratically conceived Tower of Babel.

With no common language, enlightened sense of values, or a worldview obligation for planetary stewardship, the tower of many tongues remains pointless as paradise on earth remains a lost horizon.

Where does the necessity of art fit into such a volatile context? Where do you fit into this political maelstrom as an artist?

Are you on that slippery slope of dull density lubricated with societal hubris? Or, are you a sanguine artist committed to designing and building a more enlightened tower of your own? Do you know? Ignorance here is no virtue.

To route rejection and its negative brethren you must peer through the looking glass lens for a perspective only made visible from your unique tower of power. For clarity and to scrape off any pettiness I may have stepped in, I often do this: I move back from the circumstance, the issue, and most important—my own self. Yes, you can be too close to a problem in the same way that you can be too close to an artwork. Go ahead. Press your nose up against the canvas. What do you experience?

Approach art or a challenge first from a distance with subtlety as if it were an alluring stranger. Do not get too familiar or too close too soon.

There is no revelation without trust, and no trust without time. And trust only those whom you respect from firsthand knowledge.

Yes. It seems something hasn't gone my way.

A rejection or some other disappointment threatens to destroy my day, my time. Have the gods abandoned me, or have I forgotten my power of perspective? I am distancing myself from the problem.

I move back further … further … further … further still and then for as far back as I can hold the image. Some might call this technique a form of guided imagery, or prayer; I call it my time dilation machine. Even Einstein's general theory of relativity, which describes the ebb and flow of space-time, allows for the possibility of time travel. Recall too as previously mentioned, Einstein learned early on that the power of guided imagery was a key to unlocking the mysteries of the universe.

Of course, time travel as portrayed in science fiction novels and films where the hero visits a bygone era or future civilization isn't yet feasible, even for artists.

Knowledge of transcendence is beyond the limitations of known physics. The further back I can go, the more clearly I can distinguish my self within the timeline of events that constitute the past, present, and future. Pulling back from inside the box I inhabit provides me with a perspective I can use to my benefit. I don't want to fit in; I want to make the box bigger, and if I am clear, I can move beyond the confines of the box altogether.

As Einstein purportedly said after a close friend had died: "Now he has departed from this strange world a little ahead of me. That means nothing. People like us, who believe in physics, know that the distinction between past, present, and future is only a stubbornly persistent illusion."

Buddha had come to the same conclusion thousands of years earlier.

Remember, when you pull back far enough, you become bigger than any disappointment, any momentary rejection, which becomes but a loose speck in the grand mosaic. You can see the forest for the trees.

THE HIGH GROUND

Let's say, for example, you are standing on the floor of a valley. You can see only the nearby flat terrain and the mountains above in the distance. If you moved to a strategic hilltop in that valley, you could survey what is taking place for 360 degrees, including the valley floor below. From your vantage point, a train is coming into view as it heads for a deserted train station on the valley below.

At the same time, you spot a wildly speeding car tearing along a dirt road toward the railroad crossing. The red lights are flashing their warning

Perception is the point of art.

EDEN

Fear is the mind killer.

FRANK HERBERT,
DUNE

as the crossing gates begin to descend. It doesn't appear the driver of the car cares about the oncoming locomotive, which isn't slowing down for this whistle stop.

Intent on crossing the tracks before the train gets to the station, the car rips up the road, dust flying in its wake. You note that the train is moving far too fast to stop for any reason. Although repeated whistle blasts from the train are deafening, the car continues to accelerate toward what now seems inevitable. Having an unobstructed advantage, you can see the convergence: what is about to happen, what will happen, and what will most likely happen. If nothing alters the course of the train or car, then you will witness the past, present and future as it collides in a calamity.

Your life as a human being and as an artist, which are indistinguishable labels if you have done your work, is tantamount to either being up on the hilltop or down on the valley floor. If you have the vision and guts to make it to the high ground, you have an edge; you can anticipate the 'disasters' and make your moves accordingly.

Remember, finding a quick and safe exit out of a maze is much simpler from a bird's eye view.

When you pull back you shed the ego; released from your attachment to any specific outcome, you experience yourself within an infinite range of possibilities; then, suddenly, as if by magic, disappointments lose their grip on your psyche as their claim on you withers from neglect.

You have chosen to be strong in the dour hour of doubt. Now, rejection no longer spells the end of the universe—as you know it.

CULTURAL CHICKEN

But not even the vantage point of the high ground will help you unless you know precisely what to look for. To survive physically and metaphysically, you must learn how to see and feel your way in both realms. You must know what a diamond in the rough looks like to find it; you must know what art is before you can make it. If you are guessing, then so too is your audience—a dangerous game of chicken on the cultural highway. The right and wrong decisions may not be as apparent as in the scenario with the suicidal car and unstoppable train. From your advantage on the hilltop, where you can take in everything for as far as the eye can see, you will have to discriminate between relevance and irrelevance. Otherwise, a lack of focus leads to trawling after red herrings, which represent more than smoked fish and like mirrors. Chasing the irrelevant sets a course for hazardous rocks on the sea of illusion where the shipwrecked souls of unwary artists meet their fate. Remember, if you see every *thing*, you can't see any *thing*.

This, of course, brings us back to your mission.

You haven't forgotten, I trust. Have you answered the core questions posed in this book to your own satisfaction? Are you on sacred ground? No advantage will do you any good if you haven't discovered your dharma and the inherent freedom of purpose that it bestows.

Even intuition, which is your guiding partner not your slave, doesn't function in a vacuum. You must do your part. If you don't, who will?

There will be challenges not only to the merit of your art, but the reason for your art. While rejection can take on many faces, it is essential that you emerge with a single authentic you without pretense and the false masks of personality. You treat the waiter and the museum director with equal dignity.

CAMELS AND NEEDLES

Some tongues, for example, argue that contemporary art should have a social obligation beyond being intrinsically self-referential, dismissing modern art and art for art's sake as a failure. Art, some tongues say, should, for example, address the degradation of the environment, which will most assuredly do us all in if left unhealed. If an artist feels the call to save the world through his work, then he should. But not because his art has been co-opted by the pressure of misinformed others; in such a scenario, the artist becomes a dupe instead of a creator.

It is smarter and far more strategic for the artist to redeem herself first; then, by universal decree, one soul at a time helps humanity lean toward the elusive yet inevitable critical mass that will one day transform the experience of life on earth from a planet of karmic residue into an enlightened dream worth dreaming.

The true artist knows that he must work with what he has. This is not a limitation. All the materials and resources required for the Promised Land are available—now, in the present moment. To politicize art for religious or secular agendas is what it sounds like. Words and images can heal or incite the devil to spread like a virus, destroying the perpetrator while infecting an unsuspecting but perhaps not entirely innocent public. When and if we have the courage to knock on heaven's door, we would all like to enter. Jesus said, "It is easier for a camel to go through the eye of a needle, than for a rich man to enter the kingdom of heaven."

You can't fully draw upon the force of creation while coveting values devoid of virtue. I often hear: 'Can great art come from a madman?' I might say: 'Yes, but so what?' I often hear: 'Are there no more great artists?' I might say: 'First, what do you mean by great?' And yes, there are great creators living among us now who are all but 'unknown' to the larger art world. I know. But, more important, such leading the witness questions prepossess a bias; these types of inquiries of questionable motive are still more red herrings, which I have no intention of chasing.

Don't get derailed by the wrong questions. Remember, 'you are on sacred ground when you know where you stand.' And that holy ground is found in every corner of the universe. There is plenty of room for everyone.

THE DOOMSDAY CLOCK

Before we get heady about our advanced status at the top of the food chain, we need to stop and realize that it's the 21st century. Now is what was once touted as the gloriously anticipated future. We have yet to evolve from a world demarcated by nation states, petty disputes, divisiveness, and deplorable planet management skills; as a species we continue to cannibalize the Earth. The fact that there is a need for 'The Humane Society' speaks volumes about our culture and society at large. As H. G. Wells prophetically

If there is any confusion as to the importance, or more important the existence of the soul, consider this: The dark forces, no matter their origin, are after only one thing from you.

These forces aren't after your social status, riches, possessions, or anything else you can acquire through inheritance, or buy with money. These forces are after your soul.

EDEN

When the 13th-century mystic and poet Rumi wrote 'The Field' he anticipated what science would discover eight centuries later.

There is a field 'out beyond ideas of rightdoing and wrongdoing' and it is consciousness, the matrix where all creation takes place.

Yes, Rumi, we will meet you there.

EDEN

put it: "Human history becomes more and more a race between education and catastrophe."

According to the Bulletin of the Atomic Scientists, "February 27, 2002: Today, the Board of Directors of the Bulletin of the Atomic Scientists moves the minute hand of the 'Doomsday Clock,' the symbol of nuclear danger, from nine to seven minutes to midnight, the same setting at which the clock debuted 55 years ago. Since the end of the Cold War in 1991, this is the third time the hand has moved forward."

In 2007, the clock remains at the seven-minute mark; the clock does not anticipate events or trends; it responds to them.

A GALACTIC PRIMER

Since I did write that pulling back gives me the power of perspective, let's up the ante with a stellar yardstick. Where do we stand on a galactic scale? This is a question I would often discuss with a master painter who was in league with the great creators. What relevance does such an astronomical question have to do with art and rejection?

As art is about creation, the far reaches of our galaxy, The Milky Way, and beyond are of absolute concern to the universal artist. One look at photographs of celestial formations in deep space is all that is required to witness a timeless exhibit of the first abstract Painter of all creation.

If you don't know awesome firsthand, then how can you create awesome work? Everything arises out of a need to exist; and that thing must conform to the laws of nature. When you learn to think, feel, and see on a cosmic scale, you will also evolve to disarm rejection by handily engulfing it with your largesse. Remember, by becoming bigger than any problem, you diminish it into irrelevance.

While we don't yet have *The Time Machine* that Wells made famous in his 1895 novel of the same name, we can do a fair amount of speculation about the future. Note too that in this novel, Wells used the literary form to anticipate Einstein's (who did the math) breakthrough understanding of the space-time continuum.

Art predicts reality.

"Clearly," the Time Traveler proceeded, "any real body must have extension in four directions: it must have Length, Breadth, Thickness, and—Duration. But through a natural infirmity of the flesh, which I will explain to you in a moment, we incline to overlook this fact. There are really four dimensions, three of which we call the three planes of Space, and a fourth, Time. There is, however, a tendency to draw an unreal distinction between the former three dimensions and the latter, because it happens that our consciousness moves intermittently in one direction along the latter from the beginning to the end of our lives."

TYPE I, II, III

The future, including yours, is being formed now. Using hypothetical extra-terrestrial civilizations and the way they would most likely control energy as a barometer of technological superiority, Russian astrophysicist Nikolai Kardashev devised a simple yet enduring classification system that labeled these advanced cultures into three types: Type I, II, and III civilizations;

these well-defined categories are based on the natural progression of energy consumption derived from their planet, star, and then the galaxy, which sequentially corresponds to the Type I, II, and III civilizations.

On Kardashev's scale of technological evolution, we note that a Type I civilization has mastered global weather and all forms of terrestrial energy. While they still face extinction by natural disasters such as impacts from meteors and comets, a Type I civilization has made impressive progress.

As Michio Kaku writes in his book, *Visions*: "By the time a civilization has reached Type I status, it has reached a rare political stability. A Type I civilization is necessarily a planetary one. Only a planetary civilization can truly make the decisions that affect the planetary flow of energy and resources. A Type I civilization, for example, will derive much of its energy from planetary resources—i.e., from the oceans, the atmosphere, and from deep within its planet. It will modify its weather and mine its oceans, using planetary resources that are only a dream today."

A Type I civilization has mercifully worked out most of its unproductive nationalistic and religious squabbles.

A Type II civilization can extract stellar energy from its own sun and that of neighboring star systems where it has established a number of colonies. This civilization is, for the most part, immune from extinction. Earth of the United Federation of Planets as portrayed in *Star Trek* would qualify as a nascent Type II civilization.

A Type III civilization is a galactic colonizer that controls the power of billions of star systems. An early depiction in science fiction of a Type III civilization is the galactic empire of Isaac Asimov's *Foundation Series*. Taking thousands of years traveling at the speed of light to reach other star systems is impractical on many levels. For example, the center of our Milky Way galaxy is in the constellation of Sagittarius, which is about 26,000 light years from Earth. Even if you were on a starship traveling at near the speed of light with time passing at a mere fraction of that on Earth, you might still not live to reach your destination.

According to Einstein, however, no time would pass for anyone traveling at the speed of light; this traveler wouldn't age. Everyone else on Earth, however, would have become ancient history. But there still may be a better way.

Instead of moving along a limited linear route at the speed of light, Type III space farers would take a cosmic shortcut, crossing stellar distances through a network of wormholes. These wormholes are, in simplest theoretical terms, tunnels, or tears in the fabric of space-time that would act as gateways—instantly teleporting a Type III starship from one location in space to another on the other side of the galaxy. Or, perhaps, this civilization has learned how to warp or fold space itself—making trips across the galaxy a mere walk in the cosmic park. If space-time can be thought of as a fabric, as Einstein suggested, then it follows, metaphorically at least, that the fabric—space—can be folded so that the starting point merges with the destination, making stellar trips across vast galactic distances possible.

In more recent years, the ancient races of science fiction who built the wormhole technology featured in the TV series *Farscape*, the *Stargate* franchise, and in the book, *Contact*, by Carl Sagan, qualify as Type III

Arrogance is not exactly an admirable trait; but when someone is arrogant with nothing to be arrogant about we have something much worse—self-deception.

EDEN

Do you want to copy nature, or do you want to be a force of nature? There is a distinction.

EDEN

civilizations; and the mythic empire of the *Star Wars* universe is slowly approaching Type III status.

For a humbling perspective on this grand scale of energy prowess, let's travel back to Earth. Currently, we haven't yet made the grade to even be in the running. We are a Type 0 civilization that, for the most part, still powers its machines by burning dead plants (oil and coal). While we are not presently a galactic player, our descendants may yet make the team.

Freeman Dyson, former professor of physics at the Institute for Advanced Study in Princeton, estimates that we should attain Type I status within 200 years. Wouldn't you love to be around to see it? Kardashev estimated that it would take 3,200 years to reach Type II status, and 5,800 years for us to develop into a Type III civilization. Remember, the industrial revolution is but a couple of hundred years old and humans have been flying in powered craft for a scant one hundred years. Thousands of years are mere micro-ticks on the cosmological timepiece.

Of course, this hierarchy in broad brushstrokes of extraterrestrial progress and civilization types is intelligent conjecture. Whether advanced civilizations are out there remains a mystery.

As the late Carl Sagan once asked: "What does it mean for a civilization to be a million years old? We have had radio telescopes and spaceships for a few decades; our technical civilization is a few hundred years old . . . an advanced civilization millions of years old is as much beyond us as we are beyond a bush baby or a macaque."

COSMIC BOOSTER CHAIR

What does all this otherworldly conjecture have to do with me as an artist? Not to take notice of creation itself would be a lost object lesson. A creator creates not only his art, but his whole life as well. To see and appreciate your relationship to the whole (as in the high ground) places you on a cosmic booster chair for a rarefied view of things as they are. Having the inner strength of awareness precludes rejection from invading your space. While we are hardly masters of the universe, we can become masters of ourselves—in the Zen sense of intuitive knowing.

The more people on the planet pondering space, other galaxies, advanced civilizations, and the mystery of creation, the closer we edge toward what I will call a Type A civilization. In this future culture art and technology co-exist as equals to avoid sterility; art is the reflection of the everlasting truth and the triumph over ignorance; and art portrays the material face of the metaphysical, which can't be poked, prodded, or measured with hardware. So, how does the artist find her way in a cosmos of many twisted tongues, motives, and wormholes? After all whom and what can you trust? In the universal language of mathematics, for example, one might use prime numbers (nations do agree what they represent) as a way of initiating a meaningful dialog based on science sans rhetoric—an effective technique used by an alien civilization to contact Earth in the film *Contact*.

For our purpose, to carry the metaphor over, there is also a metaphysical prime constant: art, which is unwavering transcendental truth, represents fundamental experience that is divisible only by itself and not in conflict with any future discoveries—including those made by a Type III civilization that has mastered the space-time continuum, exceeded the speed of light in its galactic travels, and may at this very moment be traveling back and forth through time itself.

Back on *terra firma*, when something is not working out, do not fall from that inner space called grace. Resist finding fault with others. Consider your relationship to the big picture from the high ground. After all, any yahoo can have a knee-jerk reaction, but not everyone can have a winning response. Anyone can blame another for what has gone wrong. Those so and so's didn't appreciate my art. Well, do you love the work of every other artist? Few are sufficiently introspective to explore what they could have done better—a lesson that can be applied when a similar situation comes up again. Be part of this relevant minority. With that said, the fault may have been with another. But so what? It is your mission as an artist and as a self-realized human being to anticipate events—and, being honorable, you stand on sacred ground. Your mission parameters instruct as follows: do everything in your power to maintain forward momentum without getting dragged backward by pettiness, which is the limited 'worldview' as perceived by the ego. That is why you aim for the high ground. Remember, blame will forever be a victim's game. Now, when faced with a difficulty, you will pull back from it all and witness more than the immediate upset; see how 'letting go' is the resolution for freeing your mind from the death grip of your own ego; see your art for what it is; see rejection undressed and naked for all its absurdity, and smile. When issues come down like acid rain on your parade, don't get unnerved even if you get wet for these tainted drops can't erode your soul. Proceed with the cosmic view and persevere; this is the secret of all healthy creators.

Finally, there is another aspect to the high ground that you can use for the benefit of all. When you can speak with people in universal terms beyond your ego and theirs, you distinguish yourself from others. Even though they might not be able to express it, they will feel your power as a creator on an intuitive level. But you are not counting on anyone else's validation—as warm as that does feel. Sense your strength of character pumping through your being; it feels clean, good, and robust; and in time the cosmic picture will include you as a worthy player in this life.

Remember, art is the cosmic conduit connecting the artist from one point in space-time to another unknown point in creation. This is the journey worth taking. If you don't challenge yourself, you are lost in space.

MIRROR, MIRROR

In this chapter, you have joined me on a voyage that traversed the physics of space-time, art, and to the heart of matter itself; we have touched on many free-flowing concepts, some baffling, and streaming ideas that I trust to whatever degree expanded your sense of wonder. If you felt challenged by difficult constructs, then we have both done our jobs. For your effort, I offer another insight into what art is. Forget all intellectualizing and pretense. What is art? Art is alive. Art is the doorway to truth, if not the truth itself. Art is consciousness. And how do you know whether you have created a work of art? The art, like your magic mirror, looks back and acknowledges you; this is not a metaphor.

The modern artist is working with space and time, and expressing his feelings rather than illustrating.

JACKSON POLLOCK

Destiny grants us our wishes, but in its own way, in order to give us something beyond our wishes.

GOETHE

The art *does* recognize you, its creator. This palpable acknowledgment supports intuition as being your infallible barometer for knowing your value as an artist, which, in turn, will keep the black hole of rejection many parsecs away from your life in this space-time continuum.

THE END IS COMING

Our Milky Way and the Andromeda galaxy are 2,500,000 light years apart; they are hurtling toward each other at 120 kilometers per second. Astrophysicists predict that in 5 billion years these two spiral galaxies will collide, causing Milkomeda—a stellar event spanning many millions of light years across. This merger will most likely destroy everything on the outer rim of the Milky Way, including Earth, our solar system, and any other dwellers in the neighborhood. How then does temporal dharma fit into this cosmic plan of impermanence?

There are some 50 billion galaxies in the universe of consciousness. In less than one hundred years after the Wright Brothers lifted us into the air, we stood on the moon and are now sending probes to the planets—and into deep space. Extrapolate. Should we have been sufficiently wise, alert, and aware to create a world of conscious coexistence, we would, when the time came, be capable of personal intergalactic travel to a 'safer' quadrant of the cosmos: via starship, teleportation, or devices yet to be conceived. The dharma chain of life remains vital, relevant, and unbroken in the arms of our evolving universe.

THE YOGIS

Larry and Beau have finished their meal of hearty kibble; of course, I had also carefully supplemented the hard fare with moist tidbits of human food containing proteins and carbohydrates.

With full tummies, these Yorkshire lads have now taken their sleeping positions—Beau on the couch and Larry on a large easy chair. As I watch them drift off into the sleep of the innocent, I remember a moment in time years ago when I had an art party in my Laurel Canyon studio high up on Wonderland Avenue near the top of the mountain. It was a mixed LA crowd: directors, producers, writers, actors, neighbors, artists, and known art collectors.

One thirtysomething collector in a fashionable short black dress was on the floor playing and doing her best to communicate with my Yorkies who cocked their heads to the side as if they understood baby talk. She looked up and asked me: "Who are these little doggies?"

Then, as if on cue—the jazz, chatter, wine drinking, and the sampling of hors d'oeuvres stopped; the soiree was suddenly quiet. From out of nowhere, it seemed, a writer friend without hesitation filled the silence with: "It's self-evident, isn't it? They're reincarnated yogis who chose Eden to pamper them in this incarnation."

My friend was right.

Today's Fare:

Let us transcend our transitory attempts for defeating negativity and rejection with ego.

While bravado may be fast acting, its effect is temporary, and soon fizzles. Feeding the ego will never satiate our hunger for fulfillment.

Instead, let us draw upon the power of the soul for strength, right attitude, and awareness to fulfill our dharma as artists—in the here and now, not the hereafter.

CHAPTER TWENTY FIVE

JACKSON, WE LOVE YOU
Pathos and Truth

IS IT ART because I say so, or because they say so? To be seen you must be bold.

An underlying and profound reason for having difficulty with rejection is that we are, to a significant extent, products of social conditioning. We grow up with a skewed perspective of what is already a narrow view of the world. We are mostly judged by our possessions, which feeds a consumer-driven society into excess, into gluttony, into mindless growth, and into the relentless worship of materialism.

If you are insecure about your inherent value as an artist, then even trappings of material success won't soothe your anxiety. The upside is that you can expand your perception—at any time of your choosing—to see a more unadulterated worldview without the blinders imposed by yourself and the powers that be.

The truth isn't out there; it is inside of you.

If you don't come to terms with successfully confronting rejection, you will miss the magic of your life, develop angst, and you may eventually fizzle out as an artist. What then? Remember, self-confidence is a learned trait earned by taking risks. There is no other way. This is the line drawn in the sands of karma.

TIME OUT

While you may get savvy advice on how to market your work through networking, socializing with the right collectors, moving to some metropolitan mecca with an art beat, meeting influential gallery owners and curators, designing a website presence, generating press coverage, and other grunt work involved in establishing a reputation, none of it will matter if you don't have a grasp of your unique identity as an artist—a fundamental understanding that begins by answering the core questions in this book. Everything emanates from the core to your advantage. Be alert. Know whom you are dealing with. I can't stress this enough. Since you don't exist in a vacuum, engage. You will need to weave your way through both

> *With the deepest admiration and with no little historical sense, [Willem] de Kooning says: 'Every so often, a painter has to destroy painting. Cézanne did it. Picasso did it with cubism. Then Pollock did it. He busted our idea of a picture all to hell. Then there could be new paintings again.'*
>
> RUDI BLESH,
> MODERN ART USA

Are you one-of-a-kind or one-of-many? When you're one of a kind, there is no competition.

SAM HORN,
POP! STAND OUT IN ANY CROWD

Art and leisure do not belong on the same page.

EDEN

supporter and detractor to learn what is going on. Otherwise, you become a pawn instead of the king or the queen. When things don't go your way, you have permission to sulk, but not for more than five minutes. Regroup and recommit. Don't be dismayed; and most especially don't be discouraged out of ignorance—yours and otherwise.

WALLPAPER ART

There is yet another level to look at here. Why do certain artists receive a disproportionate amount of attention? Exposure, exposure, and more exposure, until art critics, dealers, patrons, museums, and magazines, eventually conclude that here is a serious artist whose talent is now 'self-evident' and his art is worth collecting after all.

Talent by itself isn't enough. Talent needs opportunity.

It isn't uncommon for an artist, no more gifted and perhaps less so than others, to become well known and collectible. You must also add God to this plan. Despite all your efforts, it is the Creator who is the door opener for opportunity; don't forget this divine law, and don't forget to knock. If you do, then you qualify for having what the ancient Greeks called hubris, a reliable indicator that a fall from grace is in the making. Those crowned as breakthrough artists most often have the hardest road to pave.

Jackson Pollock's (1912-1956) rise to fame and subsequent self-destruction tells a story.

In the 1940's, art collector and dealer, Peggy Guggenheim, arranged for Jackson Pollock's first one-man show, which was a success; she also provided him with a monthly stipend of $150, and gave him a commission: a mural for the entryway of her New York apartment, a painting some called expensive wallpaper. The American art critic Clement Greenberg, who saw truth in Pollock's paintings, was one of the first to champion the artist's work.

Despite being taken seriously by these and other makers and shakers in the art establishment, Pollock wasn't an instant hit. He endured severe personal doubts and hard financial times for most of his life.

BREAD AND CIRCUSES

The public is fickle; and even art critics can change their mind in your favor. Eventually, others began to 'catch on' to what Jackson was creating. Then, in 1949, the stars aligned for Pollock in a sequence that no one could have predicted. Greenberg had already crowned Pollock as America's greatest living painter. To have called Pollock a great American painter wasn't good enough for the press Greenberg envisioned. After all, it was Alexander the *Great*, not the *greatest*, and we still remember his achievements quite well to this day. Those art world denizens who paint themselves into a complex competition motif demand a palette of the month—what is new heralds both the rise and fall of someone.

Remember, it isn't the great, but the greatest show on Earth. It isn't good in show, but best in show. After 2000 years, Western society at the core is still the mob in the Roman Coliseum reaching out for 'bread and circuses'. If you proclaim to be the greatest, you assure yourself of living under the Sword of Damocles, and eventually being dethroned.

If someone else anoints you as the greatest and you buy into the coronation, then the outcome is the same. If you, in your heart, can sense and appreciate the external achievement of great or even good, you remain unsullied and in that realm forever.

The Pollock spin machine was splattering gobs of action painting rhetoric on the art world as fast as the painter was dripping and pouring his abstract works. Pollock was working on huge canvases rolled out on the floor of the garage in his rural home on the remote end of eastern Long Island. Building on Greenberg's proclamation about Pollock, *Life* magazine profiled the artist in 1949 with the headline: *Is he the greatest living painter in the United States?* The rhetorical headline was a coalescing force that pummeled and primed Pollock into fame in his own lifetime. This by itself would seem to have vindicated and liberated Jackson from any further angst.

Keep in mind, however, that basing your credibility and worth as an artist on any external validation is a recipe for disaster.

In the end, recognition for his work couldn't compete with Pollock's demons—bipolar, or otherwise. The painter and alcoholism were a self-destructive brew as the tragedy of a fatal car crash in 1956 played out killing Pollock and a female passenger.

It is unfortunate—a tragedy—that the pathological myth requiring an artist to be tortured as payment for divine fire persists to this day. Remember, a true artist can unleash the force of creation while being aware, sane, and fulfilled. The painter creates great art not because of his personal difficulties, but in spite of them. This is the paradigm for the artist in the 21st century as portrayed throughout this book.

DRIPPING BULLETS

Pollock rightly recognized that his work came directly from the unconscious, in the Jungian sense; and while this might have been comforting to him on some level, the unconscious, the wellspring of humanity's symbols and collective dreams, by itself was still far too abstract and impersonal to do his mental health any good. If the unconscious was the well, then who owned the land? Despite a pithy quote from Pollock here and there, ultimately, he was more in touch with his judgmental ego than in sufficient contact with what made his art outstanding; this was the harbinger of his insecurity.

Letting the critics and public decide for you is giving away your power. The public didn't make his art great; the Creator did. Knowing this, not merely giving lip service, would have brought him a sense of peace and healing. The problem was that Pollock didn't know why he had become successful, which was like having one hand dripping paint while the other held a pistol playing Russian roulette.

If you don't know where your art came from, then you may feel that your current success is a fluke and that you may not have any talent at all. This describes the tyranny of public opinion as fueled by the artist's angst and uncertainty. If an artist is sure of himself, he is perceived as arrogant. If he is weak, befuddled, and angst-driven, he is fair game and fodder for exploitive books and films. If he is assertive, mentally sound, and caring, then he is an empowered artist—the one who concerns us here.

Technique is often mistaken for art, which is free from premeditation.

EDEN

Abstract art:

When it's done right, abstract work is efficient and succinct, like language or an elegantly balanced equation in quantum physics.

EDEN

Realization is unlike any of the thoughts that preceding it; this is art.

EDEN

WALKING THE PLANK

Despite all your efforts to become known, realize that your control over circumstance is limited. It is the Creator, the artist of all creation, who is the source of all great art and the door opener for all opportunity. If you don't agree now, then maybe one day you will. Meanwhile, if you rule out this knowledge, then you may well end up suffering from insecurity at best or at worst, hubris—a reliable indicator that tragedy is inevitable and on the way.

Whether Jackson Pollock's work excites you isn't at issue here. His persona as a tortured genius is more than art history; it's an object lesson for anyone who creates. Don't let the pathos of his life go unnoticed. This is why I feel: Jackson, we love you.

Answer the core questions in this book.

If there are any loose planks supporting your platform as an artist, now is the time to mend and tighten them up—before you step out into the world of art and opinion.

PRETTYBOY AND FRIENDS

CHAPTER TWENTY SIX

BEFORE THE STORM
From Purgatory to Paradise

AS SIR ERNEST SHACKLETON, the great Antarctic explorer points out: "If you're a leader, a fellow that other fellows look to, you've got to keep going."

There is a price to pay for standing out from the crowd. Are you willing to pay up? Are you willing to prepare and toughen up? Are you?

NOTHING EXISTS ALONE

Every thing exists in relation to the other. A blank piece of paper is empty. Draw a line on it and you have created a position. Draw another line and you have created a relationship. Draw another line and you have a witness.

Why must the artist make a living from his art? Why do people acquire art? Where is it written? There is no job description for the unknown artist because he is a nameless invention that doesn't yet exist in the public eye. Why is one artist embraced and lauded by the critics and perhaps the public, too, while another of equal or greater talent is marginalized, or, worse yet, ignored? Given that both artists have done their utmost for exposure, there is no satisfactory answer other than the taste of the times and the serendipity of being in the right place at the right time—also known as synchronicity, which Carl Jung defined as: "a meaningful coincidence of two or more events, where something other than the probability of chance is involved." Instead of focusing on why or why not, the essential thing is for the artist to keep on creating despite the fickle variables that ricochet throughout his world.

ART FOR ALL SEASONS

The artist and his work are inexorably linked. In return, to complete the circle, the art must provide the artist with sustenance. Although not a clinical necessity for life, art, as the psychologist Abraham Maslow would no doubt agree, is no less essential than food for a healthy, evolving society. If art is his dharma, his mission on Earth, then he can trust in the universe to handle the details—and the details are all those meaningful coincidences,

Success is the ability to go from one failure to another with no loss of enthusiasm.

WINSTON CHURCHILL

Don't hit the snooze button when you get the wake-up call.

Sometimes the call is coincidence.

Aside from it being meaningful (it can look like luck, or a premonition), coincidence has another purpose: to remind the one experiencing it that there are grand transcendental forces at work, which leads to the goal—understanding.

EDEN

the synchronicities, and luck beyond his control. Remember, when a patron sustains the artist, he gives sustenance to his own soul in the bargain.

The trap that trips up many an artist is this: they isolate and segregate their art from the rest of their lives, or from other work they might do. To counter this seeming fragmentation, I realized that everything I do is my art; this insight allowed me to continue as an artist uninterrupted while living an integrated holistic life. When I paint, this is my art; when I write, this is my art; when I illustrate, this is my art; when I walk my dogs, this is my art; when I interact with people, this is my art. You get the picture. This isn't a new perspective. Leonardo da Vinci's art and science, for example, aren't separate, but belong to the same lifelong pursuit of knowledge.

Instead of fracturing my art into painful self-mutilating shards, I include my art in everything, which makes for a healthy approach to opportunities as they arise. When you are confident in your art, then doing other work for hire—art related or not—makes you no less the artist. For a painter, doing an illustration, making a poster (or even hanging posters as Gauguin had done to earn a few francs), designing a brochure, driving a cab, or waiting on tables, isn't threatening or beneath him. When you do whatever it takes, which you must, good fortune magically appears as a doorway where none had existed before. It is still up to you to knock.

I can't stress this distinction enough: in its purest form, you can't feel how you think and you can't think how you feel. Thinking and analyzing about the experience of feeling isn't the experience itself. Each of us must find the truth of this for himself. Although I had the art patron in mind, this statement is as relevant for the artist who either feels art or thinks art—two different palettes.

When your work is the result of an idea, then it is conceptual and driven by a thought. If this idea is rejected, then it is the thought that wasn't needed or wanted at that moment in time for whatever reason. When your art is from pure feeling, the soul, then your work, your manifested energy, is transcendent. Art from the soul isn't an idea. Although creation and thinking coexist, they aren't synonymous. Creation is divine improvisation; and in time thinking is an after thought.

BUDDHA'S REPLY

Art from the soul is free to soar beyond conceptualization, purpose, motive, or pleasing a contemporary public that has been breastfed on squirts of advertising and predigested media pablum. Never have so many been overfed with mass consumables while simultaneously suffering spiritual malnutrition and soul starvation. This is reality as it is, an assessment, not a judgment. This is the world that the artist must live in if he is to thrive. However, this isn't a bleak picture at all as fortune favors the brave. A painter doesn't have to garner the acceptance from millions of people, unless, of course, greed gets in the way. The patronage of a hundred or so loyal collectors will sustain the artist quite well. The caveat here is, of course, not to rely on any one patron, which most often leads to unwelcome entanglements. To assemble this cadre of patrons, the dedicated artist must successfully get past the rejection of everyone else.

It is precisely because of the artist's relationship to his art that rejection can sting his being, or even devastate him upon meeting the 'mob' of art buyers. Without a clearly defined sense of self and a strategy, the artist is asking for unnecessary difficulties. Prepare yourself to successfully weather out the coming storm by answering the three core questions and then working to adopt The Eighteen Be-Attitudes in this book.

While art is the essence of the artist's self, it is the artist who must deftly trim the taut sails controlling his reaction to acceptance or rejection without being at the mercy of either tempest. This is self-discipline.

A seeker asked Buddha: "Are you a God?"

Buddha replied: "No."

"Are you an Angel?"

"No."

"Then what are you?"

"I am Awake."

Remember, rejection is nature's way of thinning out the herd to separate the posers from those on a mission.

DANTE'S VIEW

To become an artist of might doesn't come without a price. To reach in and touch the eternal flame of divine fire, the artist must first purge himself of social conditioning, smugness, personality, ego, and self-deception—hindrances that stifle and smudge the spirit. The artist must strip himself bare of veneer to reveal the soul self—only then will the power of creation partner and work with the artist, whom we shall now call true.

If the artist hesitates when the challenge to test his mettle appears, then life becomes fraudulent—a form of purgatory that the artist can live in—or leave, if he successfully grabs the brass ring when it comes around again. Opportunities for artistic redemption are unpredictable, but they do circle back like returning comets from the cosmos—you need only be aware of them. You don't want to be among the crowd that did too little too late as the cliché goes. And if I were a cliché abuser, I would add—or those who are consistently 'a day late and a dollar short'. If you've lost your way, humility—as in shedding hubris—is the attribute that will faithfully guide you in the right direction.

In Christianity, Purgatory is described as a place of temporary suffering and punishment where penitent souls are purified of sin prior to entering heaven. As a symbolic construct, Purgatory is the main stage and central grist for the mill of man's fall and redemption in poet Dante Alighieri's (1265–1321) great allegorical work, *The Divine Comedy*—101 Cantos that describe the Inferno (Hell), Purgatory, and Paradise—and, in the process, we are exposed to the questions of love, freewill, and destiny.

Dante, intending this poem for his contemporaries, foregoes the Latin of Academia and writes in the popular vernacular Italian of the time. With the poet Virgil as his guide, Dante tells us of his delight in arriving before dawn from the infernal regions to discover the pure air that surrounds the isle of Purgatory. Dante continues the narrative. The author relates how, in turning to the right, he beheld four stars never seen before, but by our first parents. On their left, Dante and Virgil then meet Cato of Utica,

Any fool can criticize, condemn, and complain— and most fools do.

DALE CARNEGIE

What is awareness?

It's similar to driving a car on the open road. You are aware of everything around you, yet of no particular thing.

If you become attached to a particular thing, say a sign, then it means you are now paying attention to it and have taken your eyes off the road ahead where they belong. Do not lose sight of the horizon.

You must consider what is happening now in the present moment. This is reality as it is; this is awareness; this is power.

EDEN

who, having warned them of what needs to be done before they proceed on their way through Purgatory, vanishes. Then, the two poets go toward the shore, where Virgil cleanses Dante's face with the dew, and girds him with a reed, as Cato had commanded.

In the opening of Purgatory, Canto I, Dante wrote:

> "O'ER better waves to speed her rapid course
> The light bark of my genius lifts the sail,
> Well pleased to leave so cruel sea behind;
> And of that second region will I sing,
> In which the human spirit from sinful blot
> Is purged, and for ascent to Heaven prepares."

BIPOLAR HERESY

As an artist, do you feel blessed, or not? Do you feel that you must sacrifice and suffer for your art? Do you torment yourself by the intensity of divine fire, or do you use the heat to forge a new world evolution? While others may have sold their souls to the company store, you have kept true to yours at all costs—not as in the prosaic ends justifying the means, but as an individual of character who knows the heavens don't penalize mortals; men punish or reward themselves. The price for divine fire is dedication.

I have known artists who felt not quite damned and were rarely in heaven. I knew why they were in turmoil, but most could not hear me. They thought too much about their work and even more about prestige and themselves. They were conceptualizing when they needed to evacuate thinking. It might sound paradoxical, but thinking defuses original spontaneous work.

You can't have one foot in Purgatory and the other in Paradise—that would be bipolar heresy. Of course, the concept of purgatory is self-induced real estate by the artist who turns his back on his dharma, his purpose in life. But such artists need not dismay. Purgatory isn't forever, and redemption through courage under fire is always at hand.

To know heaven, you would have to know hell—and what pure, rare, and subtle colors would then grace your bold palette.

The public is a ferocious beast—one must either chain it up or flee from it.

VOLTAIRE

Your grand reward is the art; the rest is marketing.

EDEN

Truth is ambidextrous:

In one system, snakes are evil. In another culture, as in Greek mythology, the snake is a wise creature. In some systems, being born left-handed is a curse, while in another it's a blessing from the gods. Other than a cultural bias, neither is universally true.

Christy Brown, the Irish painter and writer, was born into a large family in a Dublin slum. He was a spastic quadriplegic seriously afflicted with cerebral palsy; his only functional limb was his left foot. For the first 10 years of his life, he was considered retarded—a diagnosis his mother did not buy; where others saw a vegetable, she saw intelligence, and humanity trapped in a body at war with itself.

Eventually, Christy persevered. He learned to use his left foot to write and paint.

CHAPTER TWENTY SEVEN

THE GRAMMAR ENIGMA
Wanderlust & Money Laundering in LA

"TEACHING WITHOUT TEACHING ..." said the young Zen disciple. "Is that truly possible?"

"Yes," replied the master. "When the student learns without learning."

There is more than one way to gain knowledge, and that insight alone is enough to get things going. I sat in the class with what seemed an acute case of acid reflux. This was English 101, and I was a college freshman. The bushy bearded Professor Fulton had a reputation for being aloof and tough, which spelled a major problem for me.

PROVIDENCE

For some unexplained reason, I couldn't grasp English grammar. Somehow, I had squeezed through high school with my grammar block intact. But now the syntax was about to hit the fan. After a few classes, I saw the chalk on the blackboard: this professor expected me to know grammar basics, which wasn't altogether unreasonable. He wasn't sympathetic to my plight as my first and second assignments came back with the F seal of disapproval.

I was certain that I would fail this course, and passing was a prerequisite for graduating. Providence had other plans. A month into my freshman year, I was in a serious car accident. The other driver had run a stop sign and broadsided my tiny Fiat, which rolled over and over and over. I lost consciousness after the third tumble. I woke up in a strange bed, a bed with railings on either side.

I was in the hospital. My doctor informed me I was lucky to be alive and that there would be a long recovery.

"What about college?" I asked the doctor.

"Not this year, son."

I leaned back against the pillow in total disbelief. I would have been disappointed or even depressed, but the pain was my immediate problem. I passed out—most likely from shock, and the news of losing my first year in college didn't help me, either.

> *It is not more surprising to be born twice than once; everything in nature is resurrection.*
>
> VOLTAIRE

Science is organized knowledge. Wisdom is organized life.

IMMANUEL KANT

SAME TIME, NEXT YEAR

Nearly a year later, I was back in English 101 with a new group of freshman. This time I had the dapper Professor Edwards, who also had a reputation for being hard on his students. It was inevitable. Before the end of the period, the professor was handing back our first blue book assignment, a short story, along with our grades. I had been dreading this moment, and here it was.

Professor Edwards walked along the aisles, handing the blue books over to each student. I looked at him, and he looked at me with a gleam in his eye. I stared at the cover of my blue book and saw something I had never seen on one of my English assignments. There it was in red pen—a glorious A for content, and alongside, an F for grammar that reflected my lack of understanding the rules of punctuation. But I already knew that. More important, he had acknowledged that I had something to say.

DECIPHERING THE SEMICOLON

I remember leaving the English class, and as I walked across the campus to my demanding biology course, a miraculous thing was taking place. I suddenly began to understand where and why to place a comma in a sentence. Punctuation marks and fragments of code swirled overhead like asteroids around Saturn. I wasn't thinking about punctuation; somehow, the rules of grammar were surfacing into my awareness from some unknown abyss. By the time I reached my biology class, even that 'bane' the semicolon made sense. What had been a frustrating puzzle a mere hour earlier was now becoming clear, with seemingly no effort on my part. The gates had opened into grammar heaven, and this time I had my foot in the door. I knew I could get grammar now. Nothing could stop me! For future reference, this is the feeling you want to remember whenever rejection appears and tries to write you off.

Within two weeks, I was no longer intimidated by grammar. I now understood the rules because for the first time I could see what was wrong with the punctuation of a particular sentence. After all, you can't fix something if you don't know what's wrong with it. I not only made peace with grammar, but also wrote my way to the highest grade in the professor's English course. My enthusiasm spilled over as I scored exceedingly well in biology, too, and, with my newfound power over the written word, I went on to make the dean's list. With one smart action of rejection tempered with acceptance, Professor Edwards had unleashed the confidence that I needed to lift the veil of grammatical confusion—my nemesis for far too long. Without saying a word, the professor, in Zen-like fashion, had done his job. He taught without teaching.

NEAR DEATH EXPERIENCE

I have written this elsewhere: you can easily forget an intelligent action, but you will never forget a smart one, for smart flows from infallible intuition. Artists—listen up: keep the lesson of this tale close to your palette. Although my auto accident seemed like bad news at the time, let's dig deeper beneath the surface of pain and disappointment. Providence was busily at work behind the scenes of this drama and dharma.

As fortune mercifully played out, I had dropped my mother off at her job minutes before the collision. As the passenger riding in the shotgun seat she would have been most assuredly and instantly killed. I had escaped an early departure from this world with a concussion compounded by a banged up body.

Although I tried boning up on grammar during those long months of convalescing, my attention span was frayed and didn't serve me. But not only was I alive, I had confronted a near death experience in that crash. While there was no telltale light beckoning me at the end of a tunnel, I did note that the universe has a sense of humor. When you believe you are about to die, you discover the authentic realm within.

There is more. If the 'unfortunate' accident hadn't happened, I wouldn't have met Professor Edwards, the teacher who freed my self-confidence to learn, process, and master the rules of grammar.

Remember, a tempered rejection from an enlightened soul will open up opportunity as surely as a period punctuates the end of this sentence.

MONEY LAUNDERING

Getting a foothold inside the realm of grammar was something that moved my story forward. Having some talent as a writer and the ability to see beneath the surface of things, I felt that one day these attributes would lead me to fulfillment if not riches. Let me describe several substantial encounters with moolah and my lessons about legal and tender.

People without money think that having lots of it will solve all their problems; people with money think if only it were so.

The artist is in the same financial boat with his fellow humans. He needs money to live.

Fine art, however, is far from the thoughts of most consumers who can more actively engage in conversations about cameras, computers, electronics, movies, clothing, homes, children, schools, and vacations. To carve out a life based upon a personal art that isn't part of the popular culture takes guts and the conviction to keep on creating. Money isn't inherently evil, nor is it magnanimous. Money is the grease that moves the wheel. And art is the destination known as truth. When these two energies converge, the artist reaps his material reward. Over the years, I have had opportunities to face money for what it is and for what it isn't—and to confront myself, which is what these episodes were about.

If you've never had much money, you most likely think about money all the time. You might envision what it would be like to have enough money so you don't have to think about it—so that you could do your art without worrying about the rent and the relentless need for patrons or customers. You might think money is the answer to your problems—most of them at the very least.

ANOTHER SHOPPER IN NEW JERSEY

It was three years after I had put writing my science fiction novel aside. I was now married to a beautiful woman. I had landed a well-paying job as director of public relations for a mid-size agency and things seemed to be okay. I was wearing tailored suits and looked sharp.

The dumbest people I know are those who know it all.

MALCOLM FORBES

My mother, Adele, would often remind me of a Jewish proverb: When a fool throws a stone in the garden, ten wise people cannot find it.

EDEN

Knowledge is of two kinds: we know a subject ourselves, or we know where we can find information upon it.

SAMUEL JOHNSON

Treat evil with awareness.

EDEN

One evening, as I was driving home, I realized that working late nearly every night had somehow become a habit. Getting home as fast as possible was no longer a priority. I passed a huge shopping center off the highway and pulled into the parking lot. I went into the mall and began walking among the crowd. The chain stores and specialty boutiques were all lined up in garish lighting as if in some surreal dream. Although I was a consumer, a feeling of alienation fell over me. I poked about in a few shops.

While I wasn't a millionaire, I could buy most any item I wanted. But the desire to acquire was gone. I didn't want anything. Despite having all this disposable income, I suddenly came up short. I had longed to be in this position of consumer power, to buy what I want when I want it. I realized for the second time in my life that this power of the purse had no lasting meaning or value. I had confronted this issue years back when I left the perks of a Fortune 500 company position to begin writing my novel.

But now, I was inside a sunglass boutique in the mall where I looked in the mirror, adjusted my tie, and combed my hair.

I drove back to my luxury high-rise apartment and my wife, knowing one thing for sure: going out to dinner that evening wouldn't satisfy a growing hunger, or make everything all right.

WANDERLUST TO LA: A FEW YEARS LATER

My perfect superficial life had dissipated. I couldn't shake this feeling of wanderlust. I wanted to write; I wanted to hang-glide; I wanted adventure. She wouldn't budge to a new place unless she had a doorman, and I had a good job waiting. I shed my job in public relations, the middle class trappings, the wife, the doorman, and drove west to Los Angeles.

The San Andreas Fault and I were linked. We both needed to relieve pressure; my stress was a strain on a restless heart. I knew I was something more but didn't know what—grist for self-discovery. To say that my intuition was right is redundant. Intuition is infallible because it is a direct communication from the soul, and the soul is direct contact with the Great Creator. In order to grow and thrive, a living thing needs the right climate.

The Golden State, the geologically turbulent youngster of the continental USA, was the eclectic real estate essential for my rite of passage. I had grown up on the mean streets, learning firsthand about the lower depths and my own dark side.

Without temptation, you will never know your self. This is the story of Buddha, of Jesus, of every true teacher who has faced the lord of illusion with grace and courage. The past is old, cold, and dead. There was more to know, more to experience, more tests to encounter.

California beckoned.

There, I would confront my character—life lessons I had to discover for myself as a man, as a writer, as an individual who had traded in the illusion of the American Dream for reality of life on 'the razor's edge'. In Los Angeles, I accumulated exciting and unique experiences, as one would collect fine works of art.

Among my adventures, I became the editor of a magazine run by a playboy who threw in a new Corvette as part of my compensation package.

After my first day on the job, I drove off in my muscle machine along Santa Monica Boulevard and parked in front of the trendy boutiques that faced Century City. I leaned against the gleaming cherry red sports car and watched the late afternoon sun bathe the skyscrapers in a brilliant and shimmering soft orange. I had everything: money, a girl, a car to reckon with, and a plum job. I could buy whatever I liked and I had chucked the corporate world to boot.

This was it.

I was on top of the world. At least, it seemed that way in the twilight as neon lights from the sidewalk shops reflected off the Corvette.

But suddenly, my reverie fell flat; my challenging and creative job felt like a burden. I sensed all this apparent power and the money to live well in LA was subterfuge. While my car had a full tank, I was still riding on empty. Whatever I was looking for was not for sale.

I leaned back against the car's fender and saw my reflection in a boutique window. There was something missing from this picture, something that I would have to find.

THE LOTUS EATERS

Some time later, I was in another situation with a partner who had big bucks. There was plenty of money, a house in the Hollywood Hills with all the accoutrements that smacked of wealth, including a pool, Jacuzzi, maid, and a harrowing emptiness I had not planned on. In those days, I was keen on saving the world; I later realized that I needed to save myself first.

You might think that having access to money gives you freedom. In a sense, it does, but at price.

What do you do when you don't have to think about survival? It is a real question and the answer is not the idyllic scene you may have dreamed about. You may find out that you are not the person you thought you were; you may find out that you did believe your own bullshit.

If you don't have a clearly defined purpose, then money acts as the most seductive of drugs, as a buffer, which can be effective for a time, and that time is fleeting. A dramatic drop of diminishing returns is in the wings no matter how well-heeled you are as you have no place to go. You can wrap yourself in a fabricated cocoon of your possessions, but it's a shallow, veiled, and cold experience. A butterfly can't emerge from such a wrapped trap. It is not that the money was corrupt.

Although I had brought a wealth of experience to the partnership, it wasn't enough. This money came not with strings but with a sticky oozing gossamer web, and once caught, escape is nearly impossible. The corrosive nature of the money in this circumstance was that I had not earned it by way of my true purpose in life—as an artist.

Easy money, which is a contradiction in terms, is a guaranteed harbinger of disaster. This was expensive money. Money without earned value and positive purpose is dangerous; the enemy is often disguised as leisure, or pleasure, or invincibility. You begin to lose touch with what is real, organic, and healthy, and at a certain point you may become that lost soul who overdosed—that tragic artist who makes for sensational and exploitive copy in a tabloid, book, or fodder for a film.

We know what we are, but know not what we may be.

WILLIAM SHAKESPEARE

In art or spirit, there is no closing of the canon, which pretty much explains the world as it is.

EDEN

WILLIAM HOLDEN AND I

Leaving those many millions of dollars and a lifestyle so many would 'die' for in the hills of Hollywood wasn't easy. If left unchallenged, my ego would have held on to the lurid lure of glitter. But, then again, I had no choice in the matter. Because of various unstable characters in this drama of mine, I sensed that I might end up floating face down in a swimming pool like poor William Holden does in *Sunset Boulevard*—the film eerily traced my own storyline as a writer.

The only way out from the dark side was to run, don't walk, and don't look back, either. This decision, which was gut-wrenching and unnerving at the time, would catapult me upward and into a far-flung and wonderful art situation that I couldn't have planned, or predicted. I had broken free from my entanglements with the monied black widow and the lotus-eaters who fed off each other in that harrowing web of conceit.

I was now on my way toward finding my dharma, and those thoughts of running on empty during my Corvette days would soon be a distant memory. At least, it seemed so at the time.

Remember, I was looking for my passion, my purpose in life, and there are no readymade convenient maps for such a journey. You must carve your own path to the territory of your soul. If you won't complete your mission, then who will?

When you earn your daily bread through your art and soul, no one is wealthier than you.

BETTY

CHAPTER TWENTY EIGHT

WORDS THAT DEFINE
Mean What You Say

WHATEVER FORM your art takes, you are also a thinking and linguistic entity. Distinguish yourself by being clear through expression. Clarity isn't an accident.

Take your time, avoid artificial deadlines, and know that intuition, once identified, is infallible.

Words have precise meaning, which is their genius. The collective meaning of words trickles down through the brain matter as thoughts, influencing your perception of the world and your art whether you are aware of it or not. If we are still, if we have a quiet mind, we feel the motes of meaning settle on the bottom of our awareness—it is then that we arrive at clarity.

LINGUISTIC ANARCHY

Definitions of things are word symbols and not the thing being defined. Still, since we must start somewhere to establish common ground in a complex world, readers will find no shortage of definitions in this book.

Language, for example, to be explicit and powerful, must have agreed upon rules—otherwise, we have linguistic anarchy and confusion. Comprehending the meaning and distinctions of words that you use will empower you as a communicator—in the art of being understood. Depending on context, words often have more than one meaning, or an incorrect meaning if you are guessing.

The word descriptions here are meant to enhance and clarify your lexicon as an artist who is far from clueless: she knows what she is talking about. Open up the full throttle that is your awareness and test-drive the accuracy of the words in this list for a while; you will soon experience improved handling in understanding your art, your own self, and, as a direct consequence, others.

Rejection is not a synonym for failure. Note also that rejection is a word, not a universal truth, or a life sentence.

Giving up on your art is like giving up on your baby.

ADELE RICHTER,
MY MOTHER

If facts are the seeds that later produce knowledge and wisdom, then the emotions and the impressions of the senses are the fertile soil in which the seeds must grow.

RACHEL CARSON

Success means that you determine whether you have accomplished your purpose. If you let others define fulfillment for you, then they and not you are controlling your art.

Acceptance is a synonym for success if the artist has chosen to please the crowd as her priority. This artist makes and tweaks her art based on a show of hands, which is understandable for an art that must satisfy a group, and necessary for a performer playing *to* the room—but even then, the artist-performer who plays *for* the room knows to give the people her inner need, what she has, not what they want because then there will be nothing left of her.

Self-acceptance is a synonym for success if the artist gauges value and fulfillment by her priority of standing naked and risking honesty in creation: this art is born free without motive, external pressures, or preconceived notions.

While maintaining her integrity, she must also have an audience that appreciates her individual vision.

If earning her daily bread is at hand, there is no subterfuge in dharma when creating works for hire: give the customer what he wants. The limelight doesn't blind her nor will she fall victim to depression and doubt should the wattage flicker and wane.

Ignored some would say is worse than rejection. As Oscar Wilde had observed: "There is only one thing in the world worse than being talked about, and that is not being talked about."

Clever can be a desirable quality, but not in art.

Criticism, whether yea or nay, isn't my business.

Passion is my business.

Obsession is irrational and not part of my makeup.

Compulsion is an out of control urge that isn't part of my makeup.

Note: Obsessive, compulsive, or both are all too often used to describe the artist; and many artists are also culpable as they too describe themselves in these pathological terms. To manifest an unhealthy preoccupation that is against my will or intention is no great honor. The healthy artist suffers from neither of these irrational out of control syndromes. Anyone can feign crazy, but few can create great art.

Madness is an affliction.

Divine fire comes at a price, which is dedication, not madness.

Art is truth, a relationship, the spirit made manifest, which means the experience of art can't be adequately described. You can't demystify art or pin it down precisely because it is magic.

One can't fully appreciate the product without understanding the process. Art doesn't illustrate; regardless of form—objective, abstract, or nonobjective—the art itself is the subject.

Personality is the interchangeable array of false masks that are presented to different people based on motive. It is façade. The true artist has one authentic face for all. Beautiful.

Freedom is self-discipline, which is the one true freedom, and the crown jewel of freewill.

Self-expression is, for our purposes, the mechanics of art—as it is the self, the soul, and its infallible connection to the collective unconscious that is being expressed.

Self-indulgence is me, myself, and I—not art.

Unconscious is, for our understanding here, the mind of God.

Awareness is intuitive perception that transcends attention; it is the quality of knowing without thinking. When you are running, you gaze at the horizon, not your feet.

Art therapy is a tool for healing; it is not, however, the art that concerns us here, which is the self-inspired art of the artist who, to be clear, knows each piece is a work of deliverance.

Art for art's sake is divine manifestation in the physical realm.

Talent is the gift, an endowment from the Creator; if its currency isn't spent, it has no value.

Character answers all questions, so said the master.

Temperament is the characteristic mental, physical, and emotional aspect of an individual. Tantrums have everything to do with ego, but nothing at all to do with talent or art.

Compassion is the combination of compass, or moral direction, and passion from the soul.

Predisposition is an inclination based on genetics, environment, or a combination of both; it is not, however, inevitable.

Want is an external desire that can be mostly expendable.

> *The creative process is not a form of psychotherapy, even though many have talked about it in that manner.*
>
> ALBERT ROTHENBERG

Knowing is not enough; we must apply!
GOETHE

Need is uncompromising. The artist needs his art as he needs food. The art is a prerequisite for a fully realized life.

Belonging, in league with being understood, is an innate sense of feeling part of something greater than your own self. To belong is to feel at home.

Mixed feelings have no place in art.

Identity is the fundamental true self that governs all behavior. Remember, lions don't have an identity problem.

Followers include those of the herd mentality. By surrendering their individuality and power to create, members of this group are free to live as devotees by rote and clueless in Babylon.

Advocates are individuals, not fans or followers, who support some cause, idea, or movement.

Down to earth is often used to mean pragmatic and realistic, which I take as a compliment. It also means without pretension or affectation—an essential freedom and quality for creating universal art. This homespun earthy perspective is organic, practical, and sensible like Zen philosophy, where having an awareness of things as they are is enlightenment. And how are things, really?

Stress is often artificial, self-imposed psychological pressure that threatens the individual's physiology, health, stability, or functionality. While not immune to every possible strain of stress, including those that are genuine, each artist must compose himself to thwart this drain on life energy.

Motivation is powered by desires and needs that instigate behavior, which leads to action. A fire in the belly fuels the self-motivated artist. While it is possible to motivate someone else for a brief period, such external incentive is like the latest fad diet. To lose weight and remain fit, you must forever change what, when, and how much you eat. For it to matter as passion, each person must motivate himself. Better still, move beyond motivation into the higher realm of self-inspiration—the eternal flame that never needs fanning or a pep talk.

DON'T GUESS

I encourage you to expand upon this brief glossary with suitable words and phrases that may also require clarification on your part. For language to work in a meaningful way, you must know what the words represent before using them; choose the wrong colors and they don't harmonize, or worse yet, turn to mud.

Don't guess. Otherwise you remain a willing inmate in the Tower of Babel where misuse and abuse still reign supreme.

The note in the bottle—reread:

It's not that you can be anyone you want to be; it's that you can find your dharma and be who you are—that is the message.

CHAPTER TWENTY NINE

EXISTENTIAL PINOCCHIO
Puppet With a Dream

WHEN I DESCRIBE this artist without strings, I am not referring to a musician who has lost his cello.

As I was writing this book, I awoke one morning with *Pinocchio* on my mind. It was a curious feeling, and I have learned not to dismiss seemingly unrelated or passing thoughts that come my way. Although I hadn't read the children's book and I hadn't seen the Disney animated feature of *Pinocchio* either, it seemed to me that whenever I came across a reference to *Pinocchio*, it was universally accepted that he wished to become a real boy. However, this convention of wishing no longer seemed right, even for someone who only knew *Pinocchio* by osmosis. Of course, the word 'wish' is on my hit list. I was off on an adventure like a sailor harnessing the wind by tacking into it.

I have repeatedly proven to my own self that remaining unattached to a specific outcome is the route to opportunity. So, I followed the puppet to see where he would take me for the moment. As it turned out, *Pinocchio* led me to a literary triple crown, beautifully touching on and integrating intuition, word choice—meaning, and firsthand knowledge: three forces for routing rejection as explored in this book.

WHEN YOU DREAM UPON A STAR ...

We begin with intuition, the source of all brilliance. Although intuition brought *Pinocchio* to my attention, it was still up to me to dive in. The only way to demonstrate that you trust your intuition is to prove it to your own self. No one else would know one way or another. I read *Pinocchio* for the first time, and then watched several film adaptations. Intuition isn't something you think about. Although it seemingly appears out of nowhere, intuition is your direct connection to the Creator, and all you will ever need to know. Ultimately, intuition is of no value if you don't go for it. Remember, if you want to learn how to swim, you must get wet.

Certain words such as 'wish' and 'hope' are so thoroughly encoded in the infrastructure of our brains that we are unconscious of how often we

We are stardust, billion year old carbon.

JONI MITCHELL,
WOODSTOCK

The universe is full of magical things, patiently waiting for our wits to grow sharper.

EDEN PHILLPOTTS

use and mostly misuse them. A word can soothe and heal, be benign, or attack like a pathogenic virus. The word 'wish', in its ubiquitous capacity as a noun or verb, has been imprinted upon us since our earliest recollections. Happy Birthday … blow out the candles … and now make a wish. Hope springs eternal. Where there is life, there is hope. How can we resist? And I mean it.

There is a question that goes deeper still. Do you want to live in a world populated by wishers and hopers, or doers and achievers? If you intend to press through rejection and other obstacles to fulfill your destiny, then you realize on which side of the equation you must make your stand. I'm not suggesting that wish and hope be summarily stricken from the dictionary. I am saying that these impotent words by definition are cumulative obstacles in moving your story along in the direction of self-determination. Whether this claim is true or not becomes a windmill for the Don Quixote in each artist. Life is sterile without romance.

A PUPPET WHO WOULD BE HUMAN

Carlo Collodi (1826-1890) was the pseudonym for Italian writer, Carlo Lorenzini, who is best known as the creator of *The Adventures of Pinocchio: Story of a Puppet*. First published in serialized form in 1881 (the same year Pablo Picasso was born), the story about the wooden boy puppet that came to life has inspired hundreds of translations around the world, and many theatrical interpretations for both the stage and screen.

Most English-speaking people, especially Americans, know *Pinocchio* exclusively from the 1940 Walt Disney animated film that features a personable cricket named Jiminy who sings *When you wish upon a star*, lyrics that set the tone for this musical fantasy and morality tale. In their book, *Pinocchio Goes Postmodern: Perils of a Puppet in the United States*, authors Richard Wunderlich and Thomas J. Morrissey argue that Americans know a trivialized, diluted version of the tale, and one such source is Disney's perennial classic. The authors also note that when adults are introduced to the 'real' story, they often deem it as unsuitable for children. This isn't altogether surprising. In Collodi's book, Pinocchio suffers some scary moments: he gets his feet burnt off; he gets chained up like a dog; and he gets hanged from a giant oak tree and left to die. And, in the manic-depressive department, a few chapters into the adventure, Pinocchio, in a fit of rage, kills the talking cricket.

Although it is a sugarcoated version of the original story, Disney's *Pinocchio*, where wishes come true, dominates the popular culture. Do you believe that wishes come true? Jiminy lets us know that he does and it is Pinocchio that makes him a believer. We get the distinct impression that we too will believe after watching this tale. For anyone not even marginally familiar with *Pinocchio*, the marionette had a special attribute: his nose grew longer when he told a lie and returned to normal size when he told the truth, which is a visual cue forever connected with Pinocchio and the merits of veracity. In the original work by Collodi, Pinocchio's nose was far more impertinent and unpredictable, and not always a divining rod for truth telling. But telling the truth as a virtue begs the question of whether we should always tell the truth? There is a quantifiable difference between truth based on opinion and truth that tests and reflects your character. Not only is always telling the truth not a virtue, it is a social hindrance that can be downright dangerous. Events occur when lying is the right action for getting yourself out of a life-threatening situation. Bribing a customs agent to get out of a hostile country may be simply expedient and doesn't taint your character. The ethical person, the artist, must live by a higher standard than that of society, which is governed by law books, not embedded God consciousness. Pinocchio finds the world as it is, not as it should be. He must behave accordingly or suffer the consequences.

To appreciate the gestalt and impact of *When You Wish Upon a Star*, here are the hummable lyrics from the Disney film:

>When you wish upon a star
>Makes no difference who you are
>Anything your heart desires
>Will come to you
>
>If your heart is in your dream
>No request is too extreme
>When you wish upon a star
>As dreamers do
>
>Fate is kind
>She brings to those who love
>The sweet fulfillment of
>Their secret longing
>
>Like a bolt out of the blue
>Fate steps in and sees you through
>When you wish upon a star
>Your dreams come true
>
>—lyrics: by Ned Washington, music: Leigh Harline

Now there is one outstandingly important fact regarding Spaceship Earth, and that is that no instruction book came with it.

R. BUCKMINSTER FULLER

It is a wonderful song about longing and wish fulfillment, and it seems harmless enough. But the metaphors are a goulash of concepts without Hungarian paprika that leave my taste buds unsatisfied. The interwoven themes about wishing, making dreams come true, and, as the fairy decrees, earning what you desire through action crosses wires, short circuiting the impressionable neurons of little children, their parents, and artists who grew up wishing instead of dreaming and doing. Wishing is a delusional gesture as one would pine for a thing. Should something happen simply because *you* wish it? Dreaming lives in another realm as it ignites ambition, and within the desire a structure for attaining the goal is formed; and action means what it sounds like. Wishing (more like commanding) things into existence is God's prerogative. Dreaming is man's privilege and purpose. When you dig down deep, wishing is the height of human conceit. Don't be sentimental when it comes to booting out words that deserve it. If you want the truth, you must journey to its source. Everything else is hearsay.

> *The possession of knowledge does not kill the sense of wonder and mystery. There is always more mystery.*
>
> ANAÏS NIN

PINOCCHIO'S DESIRE

When it comes to truth telling, Walt Disney's adaptation dispenses with subtlety and context; the truth here is black or 'snow' white. Pinocchio's nose grows with every lie and dutifully retracts with every truth. If we extrapolate from this premise, Pinocchio will never learn that there are situations when telling the truth is counterproductive and times when not volunteering the truth is the smarter thing to do. Truth telling must be tempered with tact on a case-by-case basis. When it comes to art, however, there is no penalty for honesty—although honesty doesn't necessarily reflect truth or understanding. While tact is a sign of refinement for getting along with others, it is of no consequence in art. The artist strives for truth in each artwork.

Wunderlich and Morrissey write: "In the Disney film, and some other Pinocchio spin-offs, the puppet's nose grows whenever he lies, but not in Collodi's book. First, in the novel, Pinocchio's nose grows twice before he ever tells a lie, first while he is being carved, and second when he discovers that the fireplace and bubbling saucepan in Geppetto's cottage are just painted and that there is no food for the starving puppet. These spontaneous and irrepressible nose-growings have nothing to do with lying; in fact, they have a lot to do with the truth about who Pinocchio is, a mobile newborn with unmet needs and insatiable desires … there are three instances in the novel in which Pinocchio's nose does not grow even when he is not truthful."

The truth as currency is a valuable variable when used wisely—to know when to speak up, when to be silent, and when a white lie does no harm is a sign of maturity. When the truth is directly related to taking responsibility for your actions, lying in this regard is usually—but not always—a sign of weakness. This form of lying, or denial, is the most self-destructive and Pinocchio's nose is the barometer for lies that matter. And yes, the truth can liberate: you admit your shortcomings to yourself and to others, but only on a need to know basis. The object lesson here isn't to become an inveterate confessor, but to become aware. As we don't yet live in a Utopia, teaching children about the value of telling the truth demands finesse, which is a fact of life Collodi understood and passed on to his younger and older readers.

Far from being the guileless innocent of the Disney adaptation, Pinocchio was a brat and a borderline sociopath (remember, he killed the cricket) who had to learn the price of self-indulgence the hard way. The Italian literary critic, philosopher, and historian Benedetto Croce said that: "the wood out of which Pinocchio is carved is humanity itself." Like *Alice in Wonderland* and *The Wizard of Oz*, the original *Pinocchio* is more than a fairy tale. Collodi's text is rich with symbolism, social commentary, and characterizations that reflect the mood of late 19th century Post Unification Italy where a nation growing up had great interest in active citizenship, conformity, and the need for education.

How did the author of *Pinocchio* frame the puppet's desire? It didn't seem to me that Collodi would leave such an integral element to chance. Did Pinocchio wish, hope, pray, or want to become a real boy? Why did Pinocchio want to become a real boy in the first place? Was this even his idea? These things were worth investigating. I wanted details from the source, not from adaptive works—which, of course, can be worthwhile in their own right. Word choice is an important issue since Disney's Pinocchio has for generations ingrained wishing upon the collective unconscious. Pinocchio is, after all, a worldwide phenomenon.

As it turns out, many people wrongly recollect that Pinocchio's greatest ambition in life was to become a real boy. In Disney's version, it is Geppetto, the kindly old woodcarver, who first wishes that his beloved and lifeless puppet Pinocchio could become a real boy. While Geppetto sleeps, the lovely fairy descends from the wishing star to the quaint village where, after she transforms Pinocchio into a living marionette, lays down the ground rules: for Pinocchio to become flesh and blood as Geppetto wishes, he will have to earn it by being brave, truthful, and unselfish. You see? Here, we note that Pinocchio not only comes to life for the desire of a lonely artisan, he must also complete a mission by living up to an ideal if he is to become real. And, is this not the same for each artist?

THE REAL PUPPETMASTER

You didn't sprout full-grown overnight. You grew up, and over time you learned how the world works—that is, if you were alert—from experience, parents, siblings, teachers, friends, co-workers, and others who ostensibly knew what was what. I am referring here to subtleness and nuance, not facts. The art of living is passed down from mentor to student—one-on-one—or in groups through storytelling. You also derived critical perceptions from other sources—from the top down as it were.

Be honest, you accepted many conventions without due diligence or challenging their veracity. You memorized but didn't understand. A preponderance of this questionable baggage by rote came your way courtesy of the media. And there is no doubt that he who controls the mass media controls the pliable mind of the people.

The power of the media crawls into your home and into your mind, wielding enormous influence, communicating sundry values and how things presumably get done in this age of information. While the media can enlighten, it most often does not. Movies and television programming saturate society with images that reflect the times and mythology of our age; and while myths and fantasy are especially effective teaching tools because they are also entertaining, a thoughtless pivotal word choice spells disappointment in the real world, and spins what could have been gold into lead for generations to come. People do, after all, naturally digest what they are fed; this applies to ideas as well as food. Feed the public garbage and you get back mediocrity at best and psychosis at worst; feed the public kernels that edify and you enrich the quality of life.

The dumbing down of our culture is no myth.

WISHING WELL

In 'The Gauntlet Guarantee' you experienced (Didn't you?) that certain words constitute a linguistic felony. Words can evoke great feelings, even action. Words can incite the mob, make peace, melt your lover, or make a baby smile. As any grade school child will tell you, words can also cut. Recall the mantra of 'Sticks and stones may break my bones, but words (names) will never hurt me.' While this well-intentioned manifesto for

What is a weed? A plant whose virtues have not yet been discovered.

RALPH WALDO EMERSON

I prefer to be true to myself, even at the hazard of incurring the ridicule of others, rather than to be false, and to incur my own abhorrence.

FREDERICK DOUGLASS

The pitfall of obvious is this: If the inherent quality of your art were obvious, then wouldn't everyone recognize your genius?

EDEN

thwarting bullies might have helped a few unfortunate young people buffer verbal abuse or worse, the reality remained: words *can* hurt you. Words are most damaging not so much when hurled at you from others, but from the words *you* yourself use, the words that define your level of awareness, and how you honestly feel about your own self, which your inner critic will confirm.

A wish isn't a dream sounds like a lyric from a hit country and western tune. If only the distinction were that popular. Who, after all, doesn't use 'wish' in their vocabulary? World leaders, heads of state, media people, artists, royalty, and rich people, too, use 'wish', 'hope', and even 'obvious'. Will it ever stop? When your ear is keyed into these insidiously assuming abstract words, you will be amazed to notice how many people, influential and otherwise, unconsciously use these verbal crutch (or tick) words—and when you hear them being used, they will sound as if someone is dragging their nails across a blackboard. Wish, a paradoxically anemic word that keeps on living, is endemic in our culture. The question then becomes decidedly medical: Can you remove the crutch words without harming the patient? Of course you can. Not only will the patient not suffer, she will express gratitude for becoming aware, wish free, and more powerful. Somehow, I can't envision Julius Caesar or Winston Churchill abusing the use of 'wish' or 'obvious'. And Martin Luther King, Jr. had, after all, a dream.

If, for example, you convince people, through your own ignorance at best, or manipulation at worst, that wishing is a viable means for attaining a specific fulfillment, then you set the stage for frustration and defeat. As an artist you know wishing, or hoping for that matter, doesn't create a single work of art. There is good reason for calling it a 'work' of art. If wishing won't create art, then what makes anyone think it will create anything else? If you free the genie from the bottle, you get three wishes. Who hasn't heard this magical premise for grand storytelling? But the fable of *Aladdin and the Magic Lamp* ultimately doesn't serve the audience in the long term. People who continually wish simply blow out more and more candles until they get old. People who have a dream generate an intention, which leads to a way of creating the dream—no matter what. This world is about making dreams come true. If the artist doesn't understand this, then what can you expect from the rest of society?

Of course, everyone to some degree identifies with Pinocchio as he searches for identity in his rite of passage from pinewood to flesh. Although the Disney movie about the puppet has a film noir quality that reflects the dark and more dangerous side of the original, most remember the music, superb animation, and the well-defined characters. And the word 'wish', in its entire insidious innocent splendor, continues to weave its trance upon an unsuspecting audience.

DIGGING DEEPER

I contacted Rebecca West of the University of Chicago and Nancy Canepa of Dartmouth College; both are professors who teach Italian literature and have an affinity for the puppet. Dr. West wrote an online seminar called *The Persistent Puppet: Pinocchio's Heirs in Contemporary Fiction and Film*. And Dr. Canepa recently translated a new English version of *Pinocchio*. According to both scholars, Collodi had written 'want', not 'wish' to describe Pinocchio's desire to become a real boy. I looked at several other English translations, including an edition published in 1916, and found that all had rendered Collodi's adamant want into the weak wish. Who knows why?

A careful reading of the original story also revealed that it was never Pinocchio's idea to become a real boy. In the second half of the book the mysterious fairy plants this notion of becoming a real boy into the marionette's head. But why did Pinocchio want to become a real boy? As Dr. West succinctly put it: "I suppose it has something to do with the fairy's general moral influence on the puppet, her lessons of self-sacrifice and the like, which make his carefree and fundamentally selfish puppet existence begin to seem inferior to the role of a real boy and responsible son to old Geppetto."

Dr. Richard Wunderlich also gave me his thoughts about the marionette's quest: "My take on why Pinocchio wanted to become a real boy is influenced by Bruno Bettelheim's *The Uses of Enchantment* (1976), where he discusses Grimm's Fairy Tales (he doesn't talk about *Pinocchio*). Bettelheim felt that in 'normal' childhood, one comes to a point where one is tired of being a child and wants to grow into an adult (though he makes clear one cannot actually make that happen), almost like a biological development. I think he did understand, of course, that there are apparently many adults who never really make that transition (and, of course, consumer culture today discourages them from doing so). In my own reading of *Pinocchio* I recall him actually saying he is tired of being a puppet and wants to know when he will grow; the Fairy points out that he cannot grow because puppets don't do that. So the Fairy may have been some influence here, but I think the real factor is that Pinocchio reaches a natural stage where he wants to move on (a necessary, but not sufficient condition, for doing so); and as Bettelheim discusses in a different context, he cannot do anything to make it actually happen, but one day awakens to discover it actually has; which is how I interpret the transformation of Pinocchio that occurs inside the Shark and is later certified by the Fairy."

Is there a price for growing up? Ask Peter Pan. In the introduction to her translation of *Pinocchio*, Dr. Canepa writes: "We can only wonder if the new, 'respectable' Pinocchio will have much chance to cultivate his best qualities in his life as a boy." This is an insightful observation as all children are born artists. The artist in most of them gets leeched out through social conditioning—as in *Pinocchio*—to become socially useful members of society. But to remain a citizen-artist despite the pressures of becoming a good little conformist is the challenge for every creator.

MORE PINOCCHIO IN CINEMA

In more recent years, *Pinocchio* has been adapted into several feature films: *The Adventures of Pinocchio* (1996), directed by Steve Barron, an inventive reinterpretation with new characters, a love interest for Geppetto, live-action and digital wizardry, and plot twists; *Pinocchio* (2002), directed by Roberto Benigni, a live-action film mostly faithful to the original text, with sumptuous set design; and *A. I. Artificial Intelligence* (2002), directed by Steven Spielberg, a computer graphics tour de force that uses the *Pinocchio* theme

We do not believe in ourselves until someone reveals that deep inside us is valuable, worth listening to, worthy of our trust, sacred to our touch.

Once we believe in ourselves we can risk curiosity, wonder, spontaneous delight or any experience that reveals the human spirit.

E.E. CUMMINGS

as the underpinning for a dark story about the nature of love in a robotic future. When it came down to it, the films by Benigni and Spielberg opted for wishing as a means to an end. In Barron's film, however, a welcome voice in the wilderness comes through with not a single wish in the entire film, not even a want. Pinocchio longs to be a real boy in Barron's vision where a *dream* comes true based on *love*, and a *miracle* made in the *heart*. These are power words I can live with.

As director, Barron, who also co-wrote the script, told me, not using wish was a conscious decision: "The word 'wish' is often connected to fairy dust magic. The thing I didn't want to do was repeat the fairy dust theme from the Disney movie. I felt this Pinocchio came from the magic of love. Wish is probably too connected with want for my liking, which is too closely related to greed. I therefore decided to keep the Blue Fairy out of our story, replacing her with Geppetto's lost love."

FOLLOWING YOUR NO'S

As I write throughout this book, words are chisels that shape our reality. When I listen to someone speak or read what she has written, I immediately get a sense of how this person views her experience in this world, the same real estate I inhabit. If you had been born a feral child with no language or words to conceptualize and categorize your experience, what form would your thoughts take? Images? Sounds? Smells? Images and dreams, after all, are the precursors of art, and art is the mother of language.

When you realize that the words you use unquestionably fabricate the quality of your existence, you also realize that you have a choice in the matter. Remember, it was Disney who made wishing the key to his adaptation of *Pinocchio*. You can see how both overt and subliminal programming that says wishing makes dreams come true becomes hardwired into our being.

When you question the status quo, you must expect hardships.

A LEXICON COLONIC

To undo years of social conditioning requires an unrelenting dedication. You can't extract wishing from your own self because it isn't localized; it inhabits you on a cellular level. Fortunately, there is a less invasive way to get at the wish syndrome. After prolonged abstinence from using wish, the body naturally identifies what it no longer needs and flushes out the atrophied word along with other waste.

In general, children as well as adults often repeat what they hear without much further investigation. Let each one of us replace the passivity of 'wishing' with the dynamic force of 'dreaming', and in so doing, with deference to Carlo Collodi, become 'real' artists.

And, like the existential Pinocchio who will never grow old and who well understood the pitfalls of attachment, no puppet strings will ever manipulate you on your journey, as you follow your no's to your dharma and success.

The hero is one who kindles a great light in the world, who sets up blazing torches in the dark streets of life for men to see by.

FELIX ADLER

Routing rejection is not something you accomplish and then forget.

You must defeat rejection daily or as it comes. Your triumph is the beginning, not the end.

As all conquerors know, the hardest part comes after the war is won.

CHAPTER THIRTY

THREE PARABLES
Luck, Letting Go, Pill of Truth

PARABLES ARE A WAY for giving us perspective by illustrating a truth in an entertaining way that we can see in others, but perhaps not yet in ourselves.

GOOD NEWS, BAD NEWS

I read a variation of this popular Chinese folktale many years ago and the theme has stuck with me, as would a true friend.

A man named Wem Shu owned a magnificent mare, which was praised far and wide.

One day this beautiful horse disappeared. The people of his village offered sympathy to Wem Shu for his great misfortune. Wem Shu said simply, "Who knows what is good luck and what is bad luck."

A few days later the lost mare returned, followed by a beautiful wild stallion. The village congratulated Wem Shu for his good fortune. He said, "Who knows what is good luck and what is bad luck."

Some time later, Wem Shu's only son, while riding the stallion, fell off and broke his leg. The village people once again expressed their sympathy at Wem Shu's misfortune. Wem Shu again said, "Who knows what is good luck and what is bad luck."

Soon thereafter, war broke out and all the healthy young men of the village, except Wem Shu's lame son, were drafted and were killed in battle.

The village people were amazed at Wem Shu's good luck. His son was the only young man left alive in the village. But Wem Shu kept his same attitude: despite all the turmoil, gains and losses, he gave the same reply, "Who knows what is good luck and what is bad luck."

STREAM OF CONSCIOUSNESS

Here is one of my favorite Buddhist tales.

An old monk and a young monk were walking along the road when they came to a rushing stream. It was neither too wide nor too deep. They were about to wade across when a beautiful young woman, who had been

Education is an admirable thing, but it is well to remember that nothing that is worth learning can be taught.

OSCAR WILDE

Let me tell you the secret that has led me to my goal: my strength lies solely in my tenacity.

LOUIS PASTEUR

waiting on the bank, approached them. She was elegantly dressed, and she fluttered her fan and batted her eyelashes, smiling at them with big eyes.

"Oh," she said, "The current is so swift, the water is so cold, and if my kimono gets wet, it will spoil the silk. Won't one of you please carry me across the stream?"

And she edged invitingly toward the young monk.

Now the young monk thought the woman's behavior was disgusting. He thought she was spoiled and shameless and ought to be taught a lesson. On top of that, monks are not supposed to have anything to do with women. So he ignored her completely and waded across the stream. But the old monk gave a shrug, picked up the young woman, carried her across the water and set her down on the other side. Then the two monks continued on their way down the road.

Though they walked in silence, the young monk was furious. He thought his companion had done entirely the wrong thing by indulging that spoiled young woman. And even worse, by touching her he had broken the monk's rule. He raved and ranted in his mind as they walked over hills and through fields.

Finally, he could stand it no longer. Shouting loudly, he began scolding his companion for carrying the woman across the stream. He was beside himself with anger and completely red in the face.

"Oh, dear," said the old monk. "Are you still carrying that woman? I put her down an hour ago." He gave a shrug and continued down the road.

BLUE PILL OR RED PILL?

Modern parables can also be found in films of vision that capture a universal truth for all to see, hear, feel, and think about.

The boundary between a perceived reality and the truth is often blurred, which is the subject of the 1999 film, *The Matrix*, a messianic cyberpunk parable written and directed by Andy and Larry Wachowski. Symbolically rich with both style and substance, the film effectively dramatizes the pivotal choice of confronting the limits of social conditioning.

There is a crucial decision each one of us must make that involves two options: when the wake-up call comes we either hit the snooze button and remain asleep or opt for learning the truth, which is the beginning of a grand adventure.

Neo, the main character, has been leading a double life. He is a hard-working nine-to-five computer programmer for a major software corporation. In the privacy of his home, however, he is a hacker guilty of almost every computer crime. Dissatisfied and groping for a meaning to his life, he has been searching for an answer: he wants to know what the *Matrix* is. One night he is contacted by an elusive computer presence known as Morpheus. Suddenly, on his computer screen, he reads: 'Wake up Neo … The Matrix has you … Follow the white rabbit.'

Eventually, a face to face is arranged. Neo and the mysterious Morpheus meet in a rundown hotel room. Although he doesn't yet know it, Neo is about to confront the choice of his life.

Morpheus: I can see it in your eyes. You have the look of a man who accepts what he sees because he is expecting to wake up. Ironically, this is not far from the truth. Do you believe in fate, Neo?

Neo: No.

Morpheus: Why not?

Neo: Because I don't like the idea that I'm not in control of my life.

Morpheus: I know exactly what you mean. Let me tell you why you're here. You're here because you know something. What you know you can't explain. But you feel it. You've felt it your entire life. That there's something wrong with the world. You don't know what it is but it's there, like a splinter in your mind driving you mad. It is this feeling that has brought you to me. Do you know what I'm talking about?

Neo: The Matrix?

Morpheus: Do you want to know what it is? The Matrix is everywhere. It is all around us, even now in this very room. You can see it when you look out your window or when you turn on your television. You can feel it when you go to work, when you go to church, when you pay your taxes. It is the world that has been pulled over your eyes to blind you from the truth.

Neo: What truth?

Morpheus: That you are a slave, Neo. Like everyone else you were born into bondage, born into a prison that you cannot smell or taste or touch. A prison for your mind. . . . Unfortunately, no one can be told what the Matrix is. You have to see it for yourself. This is your last chance. After this there is no turning back. You take the blue pill, the story ends, you wake up in your bed and believe whatever you want to believe. You take the red pill, you stay in Wonderland, and I show you how deep the rabbit hole goes. . . . Remember, all I'm offering is the truth, nothing more … [Neo takes the red pill] Follow me …

Neo is soon confronted with the truth of an existence that is so outside the box, so surreal, there is no way he could have predicted such a reality nor could he have been prepared for it.

The Matrix graphically portrays one of the fundamental 'tenets' in this book: no one can tell you about the truth; you must find out by seeing it for yourself. This is a fateful understanding for the popular culture to embrace since it can only enhance the appreciation and inherent value of art and the artist.

As Morpheus said: 'You have to see it for yourself.'

The artist paints truth over the face that is illusion.

Presented with the opportunity to confront the truth of his life, the artist has no choice but to enter the unknown. Every artist is a Neo.

Knowing that there is no going back, which will you choose: the blue pill, or the red pill?

When I dare to be powerful, to use my strength in the service of my vision, then it becomes less and less important whether I am afraid.

AUDRE LORDE

CHAPTER THIRTY ONE

PICASSO UNPLUGGED
Spinning Straw into Gold

REMEMBER, PABLO wasn't born famous.

In the year 1881, the world of art and literature was enriched as it welcomed both Pinocchio and Pablo Picasso into its midst. These two figures—the marionette and the artist—would become international symbols, and in their own *lifetime*. The artist, who would become fascinated by puppetry, shared not only the same year of birth with the marionette, but a common bond in their quest to invent a life worth living, to search for the soul, and what it means to be a creator. But unlike his living puppet confrere, who remains forever young as written by his author, Picasso was, after all, human—living out his life; then, as do we all, he exited from this incarnation to the next exhibit.

As I have often written, Pablo Picasso doesn't need any more publicity from me. Legends are fabricated, not born, and Picasso, the institution, is no exception. Over the years, Picasso's life has been scrupulously chronicled and dissected, but this doesn't mean all the information is accurate, something that becomes apparent as facts, dates, events in one book are often in contradiction with another source. He has been both idolized and vilified, from adoration to animus, from lover to monster; he has been portrayed in various roles that run the gamut from artist-shaman to destroyer of women to disloyal friend. Picasso might not have been the most evolved human being either. Whether he was generous or miserly depends upon who is doing the talking—perhaps he was both. However, since I wasn't present with Picasso at any of these interpersonal exchanges—good, bad, or ugly—all is hearsay, which, despite the reputability of a particular source, remains secondhand information.

URBAN LEGEND

While we have to begin somewhere, due diligence is our guiding light through the morass of 'facts'. Fortunately, there are biographical sources who seem more or less impartial in their assessments; these observers, who are also sometimes participants as well, provide us with more truth than

I sing to people about what matters. I sing to the realists, people who accept it like it is. I express problems. There are tears when it's sad and smiles when it's happy.
It seems simple to me, but to some, feelings take courage.

ARETHA FRANKLIN

Nothing is so strong as gentleness. Nothing is so gentle as real strength.

FRANCES DE SALES

those who might have been motivated more by self-serving prejudices than aiming toward the bull's-eye of objectivity. Generally, those who feel victimized are rarely innocent since they wouldn't have taken part in a relationship that didn't serve them in some way. Be wary of those crying exploitation. Remember what W.C. Fields observed: "You can't cheat an honest man." If you are an artist, then you know from reading this book that no whining is allowed. In the presence of someone who can mirror truth, any weakness one might have is immediately brought to the surface, and perhaps even exploited by complicity. If you give someone power over you, then you are no longer standing on sacred ground.

Our concern here, however, is to not praise Picasso, the painter, or to judge his foibles, insecurities, or imperfections, or to dethrone him from his accomplishments, but to learn, with the clarity of retrospect, from Picasso, the person, which can only be to our benefit. While we can regurgitate what others have said or have written about him and even quote the man himself, we still don't know him. But after a while, we can see patterns begin to emerge. From all the resources (books, articles, films, websites, and art) about Picasso's extraordinary life, I have chosen several events that boldly underscore—not unlike the artist's distinctive signature—a few primary observations made in this book: the hidden danger of negotiating with God, the sanctity of firsthand information, and liberation as manifested through the Law of Non-Attachment.

A 'MATADOR' IS BORN

Norman Mailer, in his book, *Portrait of Picasso as a Young Man*, describes little Pablo's unforgettable and prescient entrance onto the world stage:

> "Picasso, delivered at 11:15 p.m. in the city of Málaga, October 25, 1881, came out stillborn. He did not breathe; neither did he cry. The midwife gave up and turned her attention to the mother. If it had not been for the presence of his uncle, Dr. Salvador Ruiz, the infant might never have come to life. Don Salvador, however, leaned over the stillbirth and exhaled cigar smoke into its nostrils. Picasso stirred. Picasso screamed. A genius came to life. His first breath must have entered on a rush of smoke, searing to the throat, scorching to the lungs, and laced with the stimulants of nicotine. It is not unfair to say that the harsh spirit of tobacco is seldom absent from his work."

If the incident is factual, and even if it isn't, what a psychologically rich vein of hyperbole and myth-making open to mining. Picasso, born not quite alive like his puppet contemporary, Pinocchio.

Lord, if you do this thing for me, then I will do that thing for you. Even you may have made this supplication in your hour of need. But making such deals with God leads to disaster, not because your heart wasn't in the right place, but because it isn't your place to set the terms of the bargain; and such a pact, regardless of which way it goes, is one that you can't possibly live with in the end. Do you think the Creator makes deals? God does accept win-win contracts; the universal rule that governs all divine agreements, including physics, demands that everything exist within a balanced equation. If you doubt this conclusion, now is a good time to ask yourself why. With deference to Job, God doesn't expect you to relinquish your talent, your loved ones, your life, or character as the price for divine intervention since the implementation of your unique genius, your dharma, is your gift to the Creator.

THE BARGAIN

In 1895, when Picasso was thirteen years old, his younger sister, Conchita, came down with diphtheria, a highly contagious disease that was fatal in those days. While Picasso's family waited for an experimental serum from Paris to arrive that could possibly save her, the young artist apparently took a left turn toward his faith, forever connecting death to his art. According to John Richardson, author of *A Life of Picasso, Volume I, 1881-1906:* "In a burst of adolescent piety he vowed to God that he would never paint or draw again if Conchita's life was spared. Jacqueline [Picasso's second and last wife] told me this 'dark secret' some years after Picasso's death. She had no idea, she said, whether the vow had been made to a priest, at the instigation of his parents or out of some inner urge. If it was preemptive, Pablo might well have given way to temptation and painted. All the more reason for guilt. Another myth? Unlikely; Picasso seems not to have told [Jamie] Sabartés, his principal legend-monger. He confided it only to wives or mistresses."

The serum arrived a day after Pablo's sister had died. His youthful and naïvely inspired pact with God was assured. Pablo, the teenager, certainly could have interpreted his sister's death—the sacrifice—as an endorsement by God for him to continue painting. Of course, making such an ill-advised deal with God may well have led to all forms of psychological issues. According to several sources and apparently the artist himself, the relief young Pablo must have felt upon Conchita's death—liberating him from his renunciation of art—left him with a lifelong guilt, which may account for his insatiable search for love and his escalating ambivalence about God. In his later years, as Richardson tells us, Picasso claimed to be an atheist, but his last wife, Jacqueline, if we are to believe her, said that Picasso was capable of being more Catholic than the Pope.

Although Picasso prevails upon us—through his selective confessors—to feel the pain of his guilt, he didn't, to my knowledge, endow a hospital for children in need—in life or in posterity, as he didn't leave a will to his fortune. Although he did paint canvases that portrayed suffering, and in the early 1950's, one of his dove images was selected for a peace poster, these hardly seem commensurate for the angst seeded by such self-declared culpability over his sister's death. To feel regret without an act of contrition that addresses remorse in some meaningful way is disingenuous and a victim's game.

If, as Picasso alleged, he suffered through a lifetime of guilt for his doomed bargain with God, then you now know that such contracts are self-induced, self-fulfilling entrapments. Avoid them. Making questionably motivated deals with God invariably leads to misfortune.

I am comforted by life's stability, by earth's unchangeableness. What has seemed new and frightening assumes its place in the unfolding of knowledge.

It is good to know our universe. What is new is only new to us.

PEARL S. BUCK

To exist is to change, to change is to mature, to mature is to go on creating oneself endlessly.

HENRI BERGSON

THE RITE OF PIGEONS

When Picasso was about fourteen, his father, José Ruiz y Blasco, an artist and art teacher, attempted to steer his son toward a financially lucrative future in painting traditional religious art; but that would have been like trying to stop the Earth from spinning while basking in the glow of the sun. Don José would find out soon enough that the future cubist possessed a gift that far outshone his own.

But for now, there is yet another related albeit apocryphal account involving the father that has become an integral part of the Picasso canon, as Richardson explains:

"When don José's self-esteem was at its lowest, an event took place that would have as profound an effect on Pablo as the loss of Conchita. One evening don José asked his son to help him finish the painting of a pigeon that had been giving him trouble. His eyesight was no longer sharp enough for the intricate bits, he said, so he chopped off the claws, nailed them to a board and set Pablo to paint them. [Picasso would later evoke a similarly grotesque image of dangling severed body parts with *Seated Woman in an Armchair* (Eva), a 1913 portrait of his then ailing girlfriend, Marcelle Humbert aka Eva Gouel, who most likely had breast cancer; in this painting, Picasso depicted two hacked off little pointed breasts that are nailed to her body.] When don José returned from his evening stroll, he found the claws had been painted with such skill that there and then he handed over his palette, brushes, and paints to this prodigy of a son. He declared that he would never paint again.

"Biographers have taken this story of renunciation at its face value and come to some curious conclusions: Sabartés and [Roland] Penrose both see don José's gesture as a form of religious penance. Sabartés compares don José to his late brother, Canon Pablo, who 'offered his mortifications up to God, while he [José] offered his up to the devil.' Penrose [Picasso's friend and biographer] sees his self-denial as 'not unlike similar gestures among his pious Andalusian ancestors.'

"These pious interpretations might carry more weight if don José had in fact renounced painting, but he went on wielding his feeble brush until well into the twentieth century, portraying the pigeon of the year for Barcelona's Colombofila Society, of which he was president. Was this gesture of self-denial an empty one? Or are we confronted with yet another legend? Some small incident seems to have been magnified by Picasso, embroidered by Sabartés and taken much too seriously by one credulous biographer after another—ultimately by the artist himself. Whether or not it actually happened, don José's gesture loses much of its luster when seen in the darkness of his failing vision. Any lingering doubts are dispelled by Manuel Pallarés, who met Pablo a few months later and remained a lifelong friend both to him and to his father (Pallarés and don José later taught together at La Llotja [an art school in Barcelona]). Pallarés always maintained that the father never renounced painting in favor of the son. 'Made up out of whole cloth,' he said. And when informed that Picasso himself had recounted the story, Pallarés 'accused Sabartés, whom he disliked—the antipathy was mutual—of being responsible for the Picasso legends.'

"This story is the more revealing for being founded on fantasy rather than fact. Pablo's love for his father evidently had a patricidal tinge to it.

Like the vow that put Conchita's life on the scales with his art, it suggests why Picasso's art and life involved successive sacrifices: the sacrifice of man after man in commemoration of his father's. By dint of charisma and charm, Picasso had no difficulty in disarming and enslaving (and sometimes destroying) one not very gifted man after another: Pallarés, Sabartés, Casagemas, his son Paulo and a host of minor figures would all end up his besotted and only very occasionally resentful victims. Picasso's tyranny was the more effective for being tacit. He never forced anyone to sacrifice a wife, mistress or career. They were the ones who insisted on doing so. [Some accounts would have us believe that Picasso was no less than a volcano god, and to appease him, these lemming-like sycophants were compelled to hurl themselves or loved ones into the fiery maw. Or, we can believe Picasso, who said he was hard on his friends because he wanted them to be 'perfect', which doesn't seem to be the right word choice either.]

"That the myth of don José's renunciation of his brush should have been perpetuated by Sabartés is ironical. It was Sabartés who renounced his career as a journalist to become Picasso's secretary; it was Sabartés who thenceforth subordinated the loyalty he owed his beloved wife to the loyalty he owed his beloved master. And it was Sabartés who resigned himself to the humiliation and conspiratorial closeness that being a stand in for don José entailed.

"Picasso kept the story of his debt to his father very much alive. In the 1950s, when his dove of peace became a world-famous icon, he claimed to 'have repaid him in pigeons.'"

There is nothing like a dream to create the future.

VICTOR HUGO

MASTER AND APPRENTICE

The account of Picasso's father forsaking his own art is reminiscent of another famous artist who has come to epitomize the Renaissance. In 1550, Giorgio Vasari, the Florentine painter and impresario, published *The Lives of the Most Eminent Painters, Sculptors and Architects*, perhaps the first Western book of art history, in which he detailed the lives and works of all the major Italian artists of the previous two hundred years. In his book, Vasari tells us that when the master Andrea del Verrocchio saw that the work of Leonardo, his young apprentice, far surpassed his own talent, he reportedly gave up his career as a painter. Leonardo is quoted to have later said that, "poor is a pupil that does not surpass his master."

While this vignette as brought down to us by Vasari may be true or apocryphal, Kenneth Clark, in his monograph, *Leonardo da Vinci*, provides us with an alternate and a more likely insight: "Leonardo in his master's workshop held a position not unlike that of a head cutter in a small but distinguished firm of tailors, and it was natural that the proprietor, though himself a capable *homme du* métier, should leave to his gifted assistant that part of the work in which he himself had least interest. Here again we can find a core of truth in Vasari's story of how Leonardo painted the angel in Verrocchio's *Baptism*, 'which,' he says, 'was the reason why Andrea would never again touch colours, being most indignant that a boy should know more of the art than he did.' Possibly Verrocchio, when he saw such striking evidence of the pupil's skill, did give up painting, not so much from motives of jealousy or shame, as from expediency. It was enough to

Man has been endowed with reason, with the power to create, so that he can add to what he's been given. But up to now he hasn't been a creator, only a destroyer. Forests keep disappearing, rivers dry up, wild life's become extinct, the climate's ruined and the land grows poorer and uglier every day.

ANTON CHEKHOV
UNCLE VANYA, 1897

Reason is always fair game for rationalization and self-deception; but, when reason is led by aspirations of the soul, the equation is balanced as creation, which is another word for art.

EDEN

have one good painter in the firm: in [sic] future he could confine himself to his favorite arts of sculpture and goldsmithy."

Like the Leonardo and Verrocchio anecdote, the perpetuated envy and frustration of don José over his son's talent is but one of many tales about Picasso, which he encouraged, that romanticize his life but don't always hold up as true. When it comes to your mission as an artist, don't accept secondhand information, which is what it sounds like.

Even people who love you can't know the odyssey you must take toward the fulfillment of your unique dharma. Of course, there are times when you must take someone's word for something, and under the best of conditions it must be from someone you trust; I'm not talking about those instances. I am talking about acquiring specific information from the world at large that is integral to your success as an artist.

Others can easily lead you in the wrong direction if you follow along like a lost puppy. Even if their intentions are heartfelt, sincerity can, and often is, completely wrong. To get at the truth takes no less work and dedication than your art; you can't pass this responsibility off to another. When you find out for yourself, no one can tell you any bedtime stories.

DON'T TALK TO THE DRIVER

Picasso, as far as I know, didn't have official students, nor did he instruct others on how to create art. He did, however, leave us the *Mystery of Picasso*, the 1956 film by director Henri-Georges Clouzot that shows the seventy-four-year-old artist painting a series of works in front of the camera.

During his life, which included an extensive interchange with collectors, gallery owners, critics, and friends, Picasso wasn't much for writing about art, and discussing art seriously or at great length wasn't his forte either. When the conversation would get too heavy-handed about art, his reported favorite phrase was: "Don't talk to the driver." Aside from its purpose for lightening things up and perhaps changing the subject, this quip is no doubt an admonition for standing your ground as an artist.

As Norman Mailer writes in his book, *Picasso*: "In his last years at the Bateau-Lavoir, he [Picasso] had put up a sign pilfered from the cabin of a tourist boat on the Seine: Talking to the Pilot is Forbidden." Le Bateau-Lavoir (the laundry-boat) was the nickname given ('apparently by Max Jacob') to a block of squalid, one-story buildings in the Montmartre section of Paris. At the turn of the 20th century, artists lived and rented studios there. A small number of these artists would become famous, including Picasso, who not only painted *Les Demoiselles d'Avignon* while a resident at the Bateau-Lavoir (1904-1909), but reputedly hatched Cubism there as well. *Les Demoiselles*, Cubism, and even his later mural, *Guernica*, were first coolly received at best and trashed at worst. But the flow of criticism or rejection didn't deter Picasso, who was piloting art upriver through uncharted territory not meant for the meek. 'Don't talk to the driver.'

In his 1974 documentary, *Picasso: The Man and His Work*, Edward Quinn (1920-1997) had the rare opportunity to photograph and film Picasso in his everyday life, at home and at work. Quinn's intimate legacy chronicles Picasso's career from the beginning to his last years, and his passion for working until his death at the age of ninety-one on April 8, 1973 at

Notre-Dame-de-Vie (Our Lady of Life), his hilltop villa at Mougins on the French Riviera. Although the film was released a year after Picasso's death, we may speculate that he did see a rough cut. In return for exclusive access to the artist, it isn't unlikely that Picasso might have retained control over content and the right to sign off with his approval on the documentary.

Early on in the film, we learn that when the Spaniard Pablo Picasso was a young man in Paris, he met the art dealer Ambroise Vollard, who owned a progressive gallery. In June of 1901, Vollard included some of Picasso's work in an exhibition, which, according to the film's narrator, was a financial disaster—not a single painting sold. Then, we are told that not long after, as little interest was being shown in his work, Picasso felt he would suffer the same fate as van Gogh, who never sold anything either.

SELECTIVE PERSISTENCE OF MEMORY

Based on the 'inside' information gleaned from the film, I began writing about Picasso's difficulties with rejection in Paris that would be helpful to other artists reading this book. I began writing as follows: Fortunately, Picasso didn't let early rejections stop him from acquiring his destiny. He didn't create by consulting any outside authority to validate his work. Of course, Picasso would go on to not only sell his work, but to become rich and admired during his prolific lifetime—and become arguably the most famous artist of the 20th century.

Now that I had completed this introductory paragraph, which seemed to present an excellent example of how this world famous artist had survived despair, it suddenly seemed to me that this 'total' rejection of Picasso's early work as presented in the film was excessively melodramatic. While there is no doubt that Picasso endured poverty and rejection as a young artist, the Vollard show needed looking into. After researching this matter further, it turned out that the episode of Picasso feeling dejected over his 'failure' at the Vollard exhibit is yet another urban legend—one certainly not discouraged by the artist himself.

Quinn could have been listening to Picasso recount a tall tale or two of his early struggles in Paris, which the filmmaker then repeated in the documentary. Or, Quinn might have relied on available biographical notes for this dubious recollection of the Vollard exhibit. I contacted the estate in Switzerland handling the Edward Quinn Archives, but they couldn't tell me who, if anyone, had fact-checked the film. Regardless, Picasso didn't correct Quinn. And why should he? The drama of the event as told added more pathos to the ever-evolving fabrications and cachet of the artist's image. Pablo Picasso was also a master of branding. Several corroborating and reliable sources agree that the Vollard exhibit was a success, Picasso's work sold, and several critics gave the nineteen-year-old artist a positive review. In later years, Picasso also commented that the exhibit had been a success, a contradictory tidbit that had been overlooked in the film; but Picasso is known for having contradicted himself more than once.

A successful show in Paris was certainly a step up for the young artist who, only a year earlier, had been entrusted to design menu cards and promotional flyers for Els Quatre Gats (The Four Cats), a tavern in Barcelona that was well-known for attracting avant-garde artists.

Getting ahead in a difficult profession requires avid faith in yourself. That is why some people with mediocre talent, but with great inner drive, go much further than people with vastly superior talent.

SOPHIA LOREN

When you discover your mission, you will feel its demand. It will fill you with enthusiasm and a burning desire to get to work on it.

W. CLEMENT STONE

PROMOTERS AND PORTRAITS

In his book, *Making Modernism,* Michael C. Fitzgerald, Associate Professor of Fine Arts, Trinity College, Connecticut, writes: "Indeed, from the beginning of his career in France, Picasso applied his art and his social talents to the cultivation of those who might develop his reputation and make his fortune. Picasso's first show at Vollard's gallery in 1901 demonstrates the degree to which he consciously promoted his career in these early years. If Picasso chose Parisian scenes as his subjects and painted in broadly brushed, vivid colors to present himself as the successor of the post-impressionists, particularly Toulouse-Lautrec (see, for example, *At the Moulin Rouge,* 1901), he also painted three pictures that curried favor more directly. These were portraits of the three backers of the exhibition: Pedro Mañach (his agent, who convinced Vollard to hold the show), Gustave Coquiot (the critic and collector who wrote the laudatory preface to the catalogue), and Vollard himself. Picasso gave two other works to critics who wrote complimentary reviews (Félicien Fagus and Pere Coll). Thus, even in the desperate poverty he suffered at the beginning of his career, Picasso's actions reveal his understanding of the relationship between commercial success and critical commendation. His work, particularly the portraits, reflected this worldly approach for many years to come. So when his work began to command thousands of francs and receive public validation at events such as the auction of La Peau del'Ours, Picasso may have viewed his success as at least in part the result of diligent cultivation over the previous years."

While Picasso was surely a perceptive young man, he did have help in learning the 'reward' system of favors. John Richardson peels back the motivational rind a bit further: "Mañach and Vollard obliged Picasso to give a painting to each of the three critics who wrote enthusiastically about his show: Coquiot, Fagus, and the Catalan Pere Coll."

BRAVURA PERFORMANCE

Marilyn McCully, in her book, *A Picasso Anthology,* includes what Picasso's friend and aspiring poet, Max Jacob, wrote in 1901 about their meeting in Paris. "As soon as he had arrived in Paris, he had an exhibition at Vollard's, which was a veritable success. He was accused of imitating Steinlen, Lautrec, Vuillard, van Gogh etc., but everyone recognized that he had a fire, a real brilliance, a painter's eye. I was an art critic at the time; I expressed my admiration and I received an invitation from a certain M. Mañach, who spoke French and who managed all the affairs [sic] this eighteen-year-old boy . . . I went to see them, Mañach and Picasso; I spent a day looking at piles and piles of paintings! He was making one or two each day or night, and selling them for 150 francs on the rue Laffitte [Vollard's and other galleries were on this 'street of pictures']."

Richardson also confirms that the Vollard exhibit was far from the bleak failure expressed in Quinn's film. "Nevertheless, the Vollard exhibit was a stunning bravura performance for a neophyte, and it included some brilliant tours de force. Mañach's insistence on saleability paid off: the show was not only a *succès d'estime*; it was, in a modest way, a financial success. Well over half the items sold. '[The Vollard show] went very well,' Picasso said many years later. 'It pleased a lot of people. It was only later, when I set about doing blue paintings, that things went really badly. This lasted for years. It's always been like this with me. Very good and then suddenly very bad. The acrobats pleased. What I did after that didn't please anymore.'"

Some years later, when Ambroise Vollard wrote in his 'recollections' that the exhibition wasn't a success, it wasn't an excuse for his inexplicable lack of vision by not following up with a second show, nor was it about his reluctance to support the artist during the ensuing Blue period. The 1901 show didn't 'fare well' simply because Vollard didn't make as much money as he had expected. What occurs and its significance is often lost in the fray of personal opinion and plain old bias.

Small matters become big matters when you become famous.

"Vollard," as Richardson goes on to tell us, "had no faith in the saleability of the melancholy blue paintings Picasso embarked on after the show."

So, can we lay this episode to rest? As I discovered, apparently not.

MINING AT THE MET

The Metropolitan Museum of Art held a stellar exhibit, *Cézanne to Picasso: Ambroise Vollard, Patron of the Avant-Garde* (2007), that unveils yet another layer regarding this event. Not only did this show promote Vollard as a key figure in the shaping and marketing of modern art, it offered a bit more information that concerns us based on 'the wealth of previously unpublished material from the newly available archive of Vollard's documents.'

Curator Gary Tinterow provides us with a fresh and astute observation in the *Cézanne to Picasso* exhibition catalogue: "While Picasso and Mañach must have been thrilled with the effusive press and promising sales, Vollard, accustomed to the steady movement of paintings by Cézanne and Gauguin at substantial prices, understandably thought little of the effort.... From Vollard's perspective in 1901, the Picasso–Iturrino exhibition was no different from any of the fleeting exhibitions he hosted that were devoted to other artists to whom he had no personal commitment ..."

We also learn that 'Vollard bought many of Picasso's Blue Period and Rose Period paintings, and new research has shown that he purchased Cubist paintings as well, among them Picasso's memorable portrait of Vollard,' which the impresario of 6, rue Laffitte subsequently sold.

See the contradiction. The history of art and art appreciation is fluid, not static. One source says Vollard didn't warm to the Blue paintings, while another comes along with contradictory new information claiming that he did. Whether Vollard did or didn't have faith in Picasso's Blue Period paintings or how well the 1901 Paris exhibit had fared is a matter for another context. For our needs, we have a richer vein to mine.

It is your mandate as a creator to work from firsthand information in all issues of consequence; secondhand, as you see, falls into intelligent speculation at best, which simply won't do. Our excursion into art history illustrates that digging deeper does give you depth. While facts are open to revision based on new information, universal law, or truth, which includes your art, is indivisible, immune to hearsay, and can't be stretched, bent, broken, or altered by any future discovery. This is the truth Einstein was after.

It's faith in something and enthusiasm for something that makes a life worth living.

OLIVER WENDELL HOLMES

The stronger the emotion, the less there is to say. I rest my case.

EDEN

Is it so bad to be misunderstood? Pythagoras was misunderstood, and Socrates, and Jesus, and Luther, and Copernicus, and Galileo, and Newton, and every pure and wise spirit that ever took flesh.

RALPH WALDO EMERSON

WEALTHY AND POOR

Fitzgerald provides us with a vignette about Picasso's business sense that was evident a year before the Vollard show:

"[André] Level was exactly the type of buyer Picasso had in mind, admitting that he had made the work to sell: 'I was living on the rue Champollion [in 1900]. I wanted to do something to make some money. I'm a little ashamed to admit it, but that's how it was. So I did this pastel. I rolled it up and carried it to Berthe Weill. She lived in Montmartre, at the other end of Paris. It was snowing. And me with my pastel under my arm … she had no money … so I went away … and left the pastel.' A year passed before she hung it in a show and sold it to Level. [Level would go on to champion Picasso's work.]

"Picasso's frank acknowledgment of his commercial goal may shock those who were trained to believe that, at least among the avant-garde, art was created without concern for financial gain, but such idealism clearly does not correspond to Picasso's motivations. (Nor does it reflect the judgment of many critics at the later auction of La Peau del'Ours that commercial success could substantiate the importance of art.) To Daniel-Henry Kahnweiler, after all, he said that he had always wanted to be rich, 'to live like a poor man with a lot of money.' Picasso's enthusiasm for making money appears to have been moderated only by his desire to reject the social conventions that the bourgeoisie attached to wealth: his aim was to employ money to create freedom of action in his life and art. It is hard, therefore, to credit the claims of some recent scholars that Picasso was deeply sympathetic to radical politics in his early years. Instead, his acceptance of art as a commercial instrument places the avant-garde artist solidly within the tradition of entrepreneurship."

RUIZ, I PRESUME

Soon after the success of his Paris debut with the Vollard exhibit in the summer of 1901, Picasso, who would turn twenty in October, began receiving offers to do posters and magazine illustrations, which he was tempted to turn away since he saw such jobs as mostly hackwork that might compromise his status as a serious painter. He also remembered wasting several months in Madrid the previous winter doing illustrations for a friend's art journal.

However, Gustave Coquiot, his friend the critic who had written the preface for the Vollard exhibition catalogue, persuaded him to do otherwise, pointing out that Toulouse-Lautrec and Théophile Alexandre Steinlen (artists who Picasso admired) used such commissions to their advantage. Picasso did make some drawings of dancehall performers for a magazine called *Frou-Frou*.

As the Picasso name was beginning to get attention in Paris, he signed these commercial drawings with his father's name, Ruiz, which he had dropped from his signature a year earlier—leaving only Picasso (his mother was María Picasso y López). Some illustration work, however, held more clout. When Josep Oller, the Catalan impresario of the Moulin Rouge, offered his kinsman Picasso the opportunity to design a poster to publicize one of his other cabarets, he accepted. This poster was signed 'Picasso'.

Whether signing off as 'Ruiz' or 'Picasso', Pablo's sense of self-worth merged with the practicality of living to fuel both his ambition and stomach; he was a young man willing to do whatever it took—hackwork notwithstanding—to make a name for himself as an artist of some note. There is nothing inherently wrong with using a pseudonym for your work if the assignment calls for it, or for maintaining a mystery about yourself for that matter.

You must use discretion, as each situation is unique.

Ultimately, if Picasso deemed the work highbrow or lowbrow, or used an alternate signature to protect his image or not, he didn't disdain the work itself.

If you were able to successfully petition the oracle of art, you would hear that the only thing truly beneath the artist is for him to stop creating. Since the most famous of artists have worked for hire, you are off the hook—you can do so as well when necessary without losing your soul in the process, for that is the everlasting issue each artist must confront. While a painter can illustrate, the inverse might not be so.

Remember, everything you do is your art; this knowledge has great liberating power. Now you know, too.

GLOVED HAND

Instead of turning out to be an object lesson about rejection, the Vollard exhibit affair of 1901 and my subsequent investigation into the facts turned up two main themes mentioned earlier in this book: the necessity for firsthand knowledge, and how the Law of Non-Attachment can benefit you.

Since I did want to use the apparent rejection of Picasso's work at Vollard's (which seemed suspiciously over the top in Quinn's film) as an example, I, like any conscientious reporter, had to corroborate the information, which led me to other sources and evidence that set the record straight.

Without due diligence, I would be perpetuating misinformation, which already abounds in great quantity without my help. And, as we have seen, the Vollard exhibit was a success, not a failure at all.

Our perceptions are formed by what we hold to be true—and these perceptions lead us to triumph, or not.

The misinformation about the Vollard exhibit in the Quinn documentary, which nevertheless remains a superb piece of work, is a myth that does us no immediate harm. But if you let one myth slip through, and then another, and so on, how will you ever discover the truths you need to learn?

How will you?

If you accept things at face value, then the superficiality of your judgment may well end up slapping you into a rude awakening. If you want depth, you must dig deep. Yes, this is grunt work, but then again, no great art is done without sweat. If you take someone else's word for it, then you have given your power away.

When you abdicate your responsibilities, what then can you expect? You must find out what you can on your own. You will never touch the truth with the gloved hand of secondhand information.

The other theme associated with the Vollard affair invokes the Law of Non-Attachment. Instead of becoming attached to the outcome—that is,

Gratitude is not only the greatest of virtues, but the parent of all the others.

CICERO

Like any other human activity, art can be politicized, co-opted, and trivialized.

In the melee, art's grand purpose, freedom based on awareness, right action, and self-discipline gets lost in translation.

EDEN

disappointment in learning that the Vollard exhibit had been a success and no longer available as an illustration of how Picasso handled rejection, I let it go.

I wasn't let down.

If you become rigidly attached to a particular outcome, you also become blind to the field of all possibilities. Stepping back and releasing my initial plan to use the Vollard exhibit to make a point about rejection produced an alternate and greater outcome than I had first envisioned. This chapter is the result of seeing opportunity instead of disappointment; and this perception allowed me to discover hidden teachings within the anecdotal Picasso material.

'PINCH' OF TALENT

How you feel about Picasso or his work isn't at issue here. The object lessons generated by the urban legends about him as described within these pages are universally relevant and at your disposal: extrapolate, integrate, and instruct yourself as required.

In the end, no one can deny Picasso's contribution to the development of modern art.

When you look at the avant-garde works of his predecessors, Manet, Cézanne, and El Greco, for example, and his older contemporaries, Matisse and Kandinsky, it becomes clear that Picasso's innovations were as daring as they were inevitable—but only so because Picasso trusted his dharma and possessed self-confidence with a 'pinch' of talent.

PABLO'S REQUEST

Note too that all through his life Picasso surrounded himself with people who believed in him—and to be sure, they all had their own reasons. Picasso couldn't have achieved fame by himself.

You have got to give to get.

'Drink to me; drink to my health' were purportedly among Picasso's last words.

In exchange for his gift of experience that we can use to our betterment as artists, let's honor Pablo's request the next time around.

Let us rise up and be thankful, for if we didn't learn a lot today, at least we learned a little, and if we didn't learn a little, at least we didn't get sick, and if we got sick, at least we didn't die; so, let us all be thankful.

BUDDHA

Remember, we all—including babies—laugh and cry in the same language.

EDEN

Arthur Jacobs, producer of Planet of the Apes (based on the book Monkey Planet by Pierre Boulle), was rejected and ridiculed over and over when he was pitching the script to the major Hollywood studios.

Eventually, Richard Zanuck, who was running 20th Century Fox, saw the potential and the film was released in 1968, garnering both critical and box office acclaim.

CHAPTER THIRTY TWO

INTUITION DETECTOR
An Open Channel

THE BIG BROADCAST is always on the air.

I don't believe in intuition. I *know* intuition in the Zen sense through firsthand experience. Do you believe in your home address, or do you know it? I am interested in what an individual knows, not what he believes, unless we are in speculation mode. While empirical knowledge changes with new discoveries, knowledge based on intuitive awareness is universal, timeless, and doesn't become obsolete. Intuition is instantaneous knowledge from a transcendental source.

The question is this: How do I know it is my intuition and not a rationalization, a hormonal imbalance, a bad hair day, or some other fabrication based on a mental or base emotional bias?

GOD, THE VERB

Fundamentally, if the compelling force is for the good of all, then it is, indeed, intuition. If the feeling reeks of pettiness, self-pity, or any pitiful cohort, as in unscrupulous acts, then it is what it sounds like. Remember, intuition is your soul feeling the direct voice of consciousness—God. For those who can't wrap their sensibilities around the concept of the Creator, Buckminster Fuller, polymath, inventor, and social observer on spaceship Earth, maintained that God is a verb, not a noun.

Of course, scientists studying intuition continue their struggle to find out exactly what intuition is and the precise mechanism by which it works. Is intuition some as yet unknown function of the brain within a mind-body relationship? While neurobiology can reveal increasingly amazing insights into the biomechanics of the brain (the body's localized computing hardware), the source of intuition, as I write throughout this book, is transcendental and beyond the laboratory of physical measurement.

Although no one has ever seen the ego, which is an abstract concept, it is discussed in our culture at great length as if it were something that you could hold in your hand. Has anyone ever seen a mind for that matter? Intuition is, after all, only a word, a symbolic invention attempting to

A good idea is a gift, not an inconvenience. If your writing plan doesn't let in any light or leave room for a fresh idea, then change it.

PATRICIA O'CONNER

describe an event that can only be experienced—with tangible results such as art, which is the topic that concerns us here. Intuition can't be adequately defined for intellectual consumption because its source is metaphysical.

If you don't understand the source of a thing, you can't fully appreciate it. When the artist finds her intuitive voice, the soul joins to form a duet, and rejection, which is doomed by harmony, withers from neglect.

What a glorious mourning.

DRAGONS OF DENSITY

Dr. Mona Lisa Schulz, a psychiatrist and neuroscientist, asserts that intuitive insights involve emotions and that intuition is a language of the soul that speaks through our bodies. In her book, *Awakening Intuition*, she writes: "Whether we call them hunches, gut feelings, senses, or dreams, they're all the same thing—intuition, speaking to us, giving us insight and knowledge to help us make sound decisions about any number of actions we take. Intuition occurs when we directly perceive facts outside the range of the usual five senses and independently of any reasoning process … Intuitive insights involve emotion. They're hard to describe in words, or more accurately, they reveal themselves first as gestalt, as hunches that are difficult to put words to. The left brain, however, quickly begins to fill in words and details, making the intuition marketable and easy to communicate. Intuition is also associated with empathy."

Intuition isn't malicious, holds no grievances, and won't tolerate whining. You get the drift, if not the avalanche. Of course, the question must be this: What is the good for all? Isn't this subjective? It is. But it is a philosophical perspective borne of character, the pillar of strength that empowers great art, and your ability to fend off negativity and rejection. What about confronting malevolent people? You don't have to rely on your intuition to know that, as any seasoned field commander will tell you, choosing your battles is far superior to letting battles choose you. However, there are times when you may have no choice in the matter. Intuition is about persevering in this world; let karma deal with the next incarnation. While intuition won't instigate malice, intuition is a formidable counter puncher that has the innate power to defeat the dark side of others, and yours. Intuition will unerringly direct you to do what is right in the moment. There is a time to act and a time for restraint. Trust and you will allow yourself to experience the divine luck we know as intuition; you then establish true faith because you no longer have to blindly believe. There is another benefit to consider here as well. Inherent in the act of creating art is the dissipation of the dragons of density—those troubled incarnations that project humankind's self-inflicted woes onto this world. Don Quixote would be proud of your spirit—we all have our windmills.

To bring us full circle, intuition is a partisan of the soul that I willingly and lovingly embrace each day.

FEELING BEAUTY

There is nothing complicated about heeding your intuition. Mistaking intuition for some other manifestation with a hidden agenda beyond the grasp of your awareness is the result of trying to press intuition into service

---

If there is any doubt about the significance of feeling over thinking in society, consider this: governments, most especially oppressive and fascist regimes, to maintain power, are more concerned in controlling how you feel than in how or what you think.

In the same way, fearful thoughts unrestrained can imprison your most awesome intelligent emotions, drying up the supply line to innovation and your dharma.

EDEN

when intelligence will do. Intuition is a resource, not a lackey. Confusion, doubt, and uncertainty emanate principally from over thinking, which is interference generated from listening to the insecure inner voice of ego, which produces dense thoughts; and dense thinking is what it sounds like, a mind trapped in the gas pains of cerebral constipation. Intuition is a lively impulse of energy: a force that can transmute itself into a pure feeling in your heart, a clear image in your mind's eye, or a thought inside your head. Enlightened thoughts are based on great feelings; some may call it a divine hunch.

As the poet Tagore wrote: "When you feel beauty, you will know it as truth." Note that Tagore wrote feel, not see. The eyes can be fooled, but not the soul self. You want to access your intuition because you are born knowing that it is infallible, and your self desires to do the right thing, whatever that might be. Let's not forget that it took eons of evolution to place us all in the enviable position of recognizing intuition, which is innate, but not inevitable.

A smart attack is intuition at work.

AN OPEN CHANNEL

There is still ample maneuvering room for an analog example in a digital world. Anyone who has ever tweaked a radio dial has had this common experience. As you turn the dial on a crowded waveband, you hear static between stations. When the dial pointer nears the desired frequency, the broadcast from that station magically begins to filter out the unwanted radio noise that fills the invisible airwaves. You fine-tune until the station comes through static free. Of course, to receive a clear signal your radio must be within the range of the station's broadcast tower. And isn't it remarkable that a travel radio bought in the United States also speaks Spanish in Spain, Italian in Italy, and so on.

Fortunately, your intuition is broadcasting on an open channel with the call letters E-T-E-R-N-A-L, which you can receive no matter where you are—on Earth, on Mars, anywhere. Intuition requires participation. As the receiver it is up to you to let your internal selector tune into your intuition, a heartfelt frequency, which means doing less (as in not interfering), not more (as in second-guessing). In that moment of symmetry when you lock onto your intuition, the disconcerting static (uncertainty) produced by your incessant inner monologist ceases; you feel strong; and you know that the feeling, knowledge, or emotive intelligence you are experiencing is your intuition singing the song of God softly and directly to you. Does God sing? Why do you think humankind invented music?

In an apt transition, there is an intriguing theory in quantum physics that all matter isn't made up of tiny particles, but of unimaginably small vibrating strings.

Brian Greene writes in his book, *The Elegant Universe*: "String theory alters this picture radically by declaring that the 'stuff' of all matter and all forces is the 'same.' Each elementary particle is composed of a single string—that is, each particle is a single string—and all strings are absolutely identical. Differences between the particles arise because their respective strings undergo different resonant vibrational patterns. What appear to be

He is the wisest who seeks God. He is the most successful who has found God.

PARAMAHANSA YOGANANDA

Intuition is a feeling, like love or hunger; you can't mistake it for thinking.

EDEN

Intuition is first a feeling, an evolved emotion that communicates to us the thoughts of the Creator.

EDEN

different elementary particles are actually different 'notes' on a fundamental string. The universe—being composed of an enormous number of these vibrating strings—is akin to a cosmic symphony."

There is another essential element here to remember.

A while back when I had decided to change my dial-up connection to the Internet to a much faster Digital Subscriber Line (DSL) connection, I encountered a situation that is directly analogous to intuition. DSL is a type of telephone line that is a fixed end-to-end connection, a technology that is always on—like intuition. I received my new DSL modem and the instructions. After following all the steps, I couldn't connect to the Internet. I reread the instructions to make sure everything was set up correctly, but the modem refused to connect. I called my Internet Service Provider (ISP) for help.

The technical support person had his checklist for isolating connection issues. I spent many hours disconnecting all my phone jacks and tracing all my phone lines to see whether there was a break or loose connection somewhere along the lines. Everything seemed to be okay. Finally, the tech person told me it was probably the fault of my local phone company, the one providing my DSL connection.

After many more wasted hours going over my inability to connect problem with my phone company, they assured me that my line was 'live'. However, the modem, despite its activity lights flashing on and off, would still not connect.

I let the problem go and went back to painting.

The next day I called my ISP again and asked to speak with a support supervisor. As it turned out, they had shipped the wrong type of DSL modem to me and to, no doubt, thousands of other customers. Although information from the Internet was streaming through the phone line, no matter how *on* my DSL connection was, the wrong modem (receiver/sender) would keep me off line forever.

Of course, when the right DSL modem arrived a few days later, I connected to the Internet instantly. Everything had been in place all along awaiting the right piece of hardware.

I feel you get the picture.

Since you are essentially the DSL modem that receives your intuition emails, you are responsible for keeping and maintaining the connection channel open—and the right model modem is clearly labeled with an open heart and an open mind.

KANDINSKY, HOUSE PAINTER

While intuition is infallible, human beings are not. There may be times when you missed the cue, acted on some thing, and it wasn't your intuition guiding you after all. When you learn to trust your self without the agony of self-doubt, such missed cues rarely occur. And if a glitch in the cosmic plan does get through, you can always apologize later, if that is in order, to make things better.

The point is not to hold back because you might not be right about your intuition. When you act on your pure feelings, you will gain confidence in direct proportion to your boldness—this doesn't mean you have license to be rude, or obnoxious. Pure feeling is the vibrational magic that cancels out mind chatter, thinking, and nonsense. The more intensely you know how you feel, the better you become at comprehending and communicating that feeling. Intuition is the audio stream that provides proper instruction for your art and for engaging the people who can support you in your life as an artist.

So, the question still lingers.

Despite the examples, poetic imagery, and tips, you ask yourself: How do I know it is my intuition? You don't need your intuition to remember to brush your teeth; that is a function of memory and good early personal hygiene training. Since intuition is metaphysical legal tender, it can't be squandered on mundane matters because the exchange rate is incompatible.

In his book, *The Divine Matrix*, Gregg Braden tells us of an experience he had with a Buddhist abbot in the highlands of central Tibet. Braden wanted to know what the monks were experiencing internally as they chanted, and, of course, through the external artifacts of prayer in the "bells, bowls, gongs, chimes, mudras, and mantras." Braden writes: "A powerful sensation rippled through my body as the translator shared the abbot's answer. 'You've never seen our prayer,' he said, 'because a prayer cannot be seen.' Adjusting the heavy wool robes beneath his feet, the abbot continued, 'What you've seen is what we do to create the feeling in our bodies. *Feeling is the prayer!*'"

Feel your prayer without thinking and you will understand art, see the challenge, and the abbot's point, which is significant.

Attempting to expend your intuition, your conduit to consciousness, on nonsense would be tantamount to meeting Wassily Kandinsky, a master of nonobjective (purely abstract) art, and then imposing upon him to paint the exterior of your home with two coats of off white. Or, while we are freely jumping about in time, trying to coerce intuition would be akin to making an appointment with Einstein and then asking the great theoretical physicist to fill out your tax return forms.

Not only would such requests waste the natural gifts of these two men, you would have missed the opportunity of a lifetime by not discussing their insights into art and the mystery of matter, space, and time. Of course, these extreme examples are meant to get your attention. You don't need an intuitive flash to have the judgment or the presence of mind to make such metaphorical encounters worthwhile instead of lame.

If you want to be great, don't be mediocre.

Remember, intuition is a resource that responds in direct proportion to the merit and circumstance of the moment. Intuition is there for your good conscience. Intuition is 'off line' to nefarious plots.

BALANCING ACT

Elsewhere I have written that there is always a relationship. Things happen because of interaction, which can often be so subtle that only your intuition can decipher what has taken place and why. Your mission as an artist is to be aware of cause and effect, a universal law and the seed for humankind's wonderful discoveries, including the source of great art.

Gratitude is the fairest blossom which springs from the soul.

HENRY WARD BEECHER

Let us be grateful to people who make us happy; they are the charming gardeners who make our souls blossom.

MARCEL PROUST

Here, we must go further. You, as the artist, are cause and effect; you act to get results; you create; and you must test your self, or no thing beyond the mediocre will appear on the canvas of your art form.

Choose some test from the past.

How, for example, did you know you would be able to ride a two-wheeler bike for the first time? The training wheels were off, and your cycling destiny beckoned. You didn't know for sure, but you went for it. As your feet pedaled in earnest, you quickly discovered, to your amazement, that stability and control improved the faster you went. In turn, there is no way to adequately describe this sense of balance called intuitive knowing, which must be experienced firsthand. Once you do, you don't forget the sensation of 'cycling' through the universe.

Remember, intuition isn't a panacea for everything either. You must be the moderator, or what is the point? Intuition is about the present from where your future is shaped. Meditation and art making provide access to the present moment, and, for some, intuitive insights.

EMOTIONAL RESCUE

My intuitive knowing is continually challenged by outside forces, a dynamic that is an inherent part of learning to trust your own self. If you can't stand your ground, it is what it sounds like. Standing your ground isn't about rigidity; it is about the commitment to your soul, which will protect you from negativity and dissolve self-imposed limitations you thought couldn't be surpassed. Intuition is the guiding energy, information, and emotional intelligence of my art.

Once you experience your distinct intuitive voice, you will never forget the timbre of that sound or the heartbeat of that feeling.

Remember, if you put off action waiting for one hundred percent certainty, or even perfection, you won't do or achieve neither.

Lost in Translation:

What I said: 'I'm writing a book about how to triumph over rejection.'

What the person heard: 'So, you're writing a book on how to accept failure.'

No way.

CHAPTER THIRTY THREE

WORDS IN THE WAY
A Rogue's Glossary

THERE ARE THOUGHTS toward awareness, and then there are thoughts about everything else.

The words we use in both conversation and writing not only reflect our state of awareness, they define our expressed consciousness, and by direct implication our quality of art and life. Language can either liberate or imprison the user.

When was the last time you did some lexicon housekeeping?

Certain words and phrases are beyond extraneous since they insidiously clutter our minds and defeat our communication in the process. The words we use or misuse define our reality.

WORDS THAT RIPPLE

Most of us are familiar with how a dedicated bodybuilder can transform an average build into a muscular physique. You can redefine your body and your own self if you have the reason and passion to do it.

The subtle yet powerful influence of words on how we behave, think, see, and even feel is also a form of body-mind building. In comprehending what you are saying, you will exude self-confidence and avoid ambiguity; you will be clear to your own self and to others. You will communicate directly, which will set you apart.

You will elevate the standard instead of conforming to the lowest common denominator.

By absorbing this approach to words, expressions, and phrases you will, by removing linguistic fat, sculpt your psyche into a lean and formidable essence. Your awareness of mindless words and phrases is a significant and organic step toward possessing the attributes of the Be-Attitudes expressed in this book.

Context is your guide.

The point is to be aware of communicating your meaning; don't be dogmatic. It's okay if one of these words or phrases slips through the mist—that is, as long as you are aware of it.

It took me a long time to figure out that rejection and failure were different things. Once you learn that, rejection can be the greatest motivational force that you have.

TONYA HURLEY,
FILMMAKER

Gratitude unlocks the fullness of life. It turns what we have into enough, and more. It turns denial into acceptance, chaos into order, confusion into clarity … It turns problems into gifts, failures into success, the unexpected into perfect timing, and mistakes into important events. Gratitude makes sense of our past, brings peace for today and creates a vision for tomorrow.

MELODIE BEATTIE

The artist does not want to fit in; he wants to make the box bigger; and should he attain this goal, he then realizes that there is no box.

EDEN

STILL MIGHTIER THAN THE SWORD

In the preface to his book, *The Alphabet Versus the Goddess*, author Dr. Leonard Shlain writes: "There is overwhelming archaeological and historical evidence that during a long period of prehistory and early history both men and women worshiped goddesses, women functioned as chief priests, and property commonly passed through the mother's lineage. What in culture changed to cause leaders in all Western religions to condemn goddess worship? Why were women forbidden to conduct a single significant sacrament in these religions? And why did property begin to pass only through the father's line? What event in human history could have been so pervasive and immense that it literally changed the sex of God?"

Shlain, who is a vascular surgeon, proposes that the process of learning alphabetic literacy rewired the human brain, with profound consequences for culture. He engages us to consider the premise that literacy reinforced the brain's linear, abstract, predominantly masculine left hemisphere at the expense of the holistic, iconic feminine right side of the brain. As Shlain asserts: "Of all the sacred cows allowed to roam unimpeded in our culture, few are as revered as literacy. Its benefits have been so incontestable that in the five millennia since the advent of the written word numerous poets and writers have extolled its virtues. Few paused to consider its costs. Sophocles once warned, 'Nothing vast enters the life of mortals without a curse.' The invention of writing was vast; this book will investigate the curse."

THOU SHALT AND SHALT NOT

The literacy shift upset the balance between men and women initiating the disappearance of goddesses, the abhorrence of images, and, in literacy's early stages, the decline of women's political status. Patriarchy and misogyny followed. Dr. Shlain contrasts the feminine right-brained oral teachings of Socrates, Buddha, and Jesus with the masculine creeds that evolved when their spoken words were committed to writing. The first book written in an alphabet was the Old Testament, and its most important passage was the Ten Commandments. The first two reject any goddess influence and ban any form of representative art.

If the evidence, which is admittedly circumstantial, indicates that the written word could alter God's gender, then that is a clue, if not a warning for appreciating the power of language in more prosaic and insidious terms. As S.I. Hayakawa noted: "We are the prisoners of ancient orientations imbedded in the languages we have inherited."

By developing a new alphabet and a personal language unencumbered by age-old bias and conformity, the true artist breaks free from mindless tradition and social conditioning—and in this act of creation, we are compelled to live courageously by reevaluating the syntax and grammar of our visual and linguistic narrative, which both describes and enriches our experience of reality.

ROGUE'S GLOSSARY

You can think positive and lucid thoughts to your heart's desire, but thought must be tempered with action. Using words simply because 'everybody' else does is no excuse; this instruction is as relevant for the common language as it is for slang or jargon, which may connect you to the urban street, generation 'whatever', or a subculture, but it won't communicate your unique voice as a creator, if that is your mission. You can use the 'rogue's glossary' of linguistic felons below to begin invigorating your vocabulary. As you embark upon ratcheting up your thought patterns to free your mind from clutter and the catchall words and phrases of the moment, you will experience an immediate improvement in your conduct with rejection, authenticity, acceptance, relationships, and your art.

I encourage you to expand upon this short list with other words, expressions, and phrases that could use pruning from the vernacular. If we are to understand one another, then clarity and individuality are a matter of semantics. When you begin feeling the power of speaking as your own self, there is no turning back, nor would you want to.

1. **clichés** are verboten—unless used on purpose. A creator is original and doesn't parrot the words of others. When you catch yourself using a trite phrase, the first one of the day is on the house; but for each one thereafter on that day, as I suggested earlier, fine yourself fifty cents. Of course, a cliché is a brilliant observation suffering from overexposure.

2. **obvious**—one dangerous word. The true artist realizes that no thing is obvious. What if the artist himself is an abuser of 'obvious'? Once the pitfall of 'obvious' is brought to the true artist's attention, he will never (unless used on purpose or for effect) utter the word again. If the wonder of your art were 'obvious', then wouldn't all who see your work acknowledge your genius and your achievement?

3. **hope**—one weak passive word. Remember the Greek legend of Pandora and the box she was warned not to open? When her curiosity prevailed, she opened it and unleashed all the ills of the world upon mankind. But Pandora opened the box a second time and released hope, which was to heal man's ills. If the gods had included well-being in lieu of impotent and deceptive expectation, we could then all live in fulfillment instead of hope.

4. **wish**—one weak pathetic word. No wishful thinking, please. A man in the parking lot with a shovel told me, "There's more snow on the way tomorrow, but maybe it won't be so bad. There's nothing wrong with a little wishful thinking . . . right?" Not so, I thought to myself. Such seemingly harmless remarks expose the insidiousness of weak thoughts, weak character, and mundane art.

5. **just**—filler word, self-effacing and annoying.

6. **just** my luck! See how negative this is when referring to an unwelcome outcome.

7. **just** married. Okay, and good luck.

8. **just** cause. Okay, in the sense of justice.

Power takes as ingratitude the writhing of its victims.

RABINDRANATH TAGORE

Discernment and decisiveness are the keys for moving forward; and it is momentum that quiets your inner monologist from dragging you down and driving you crazy.

EDEN

Saying thank you is more than good manners. It is good spirituality.

ALFRED PAINTER

9 **It goes without saying**. No thing goes without saying, which is my third rule of awareness.

10 **interesting**. This ubiquitous remark is vague enough to tell us nothing. It smacks of ignorance at best and snobbery at worst; and is akin to 'whatever' as a dismissive response, which is completely non-specific and non-committal. Is this the ideological decay of the Western world? Ya know, like I mean, whatever. Interesting—as a reaction to art—is fence sitting, or a defense mechanism for the insecure. You want a direct visceral response, not a circuitous analytical one, which misses the aesthetic experience entirely.

11 **I don't care**. This is an ego at work, which is snobbery, passive-aggressive, full of bile, or plain nasty. Better to say, I am not curious about this or that, or I leave the decision to you, which, in most cases, is more accurate and user-friendly. A creator always cares on some level.

12 **Why don't they do something?** Who are 'they'? Why not you? Yes, pilgrim, it is that 'there ought to be a law' mentality. Perception comes at a price; if you see it, then you own it.

13 **In my opinion**. This is an extraneous lead-in phrase. Who else's opinion is it? 'In my personal opinion' is a phrase that adds insult to injury, twice guilty of redundancy.

14 **How is life treating you?** This isn't the question. This is another casual victim-based inquiry that is of no value. The question is: 'How are you treating life?' Educate yourself by listening to how people respond to this question.

15 **You don't understand**. How can another person know what I understand? This is a victim's position. Be understanding and, if it is there, remove this obnoxious phrase from your repertoire.

16 **That's how I am** or **this is who I am**. So, who are you, really? Let us know—that is, once you know what you are talking about. Avoid these defensive phrases as they do you no justice.

17 **Nobody's perfect**. Has anyone accused you of perfection lately? A deplorable excuse that is unworthy of a creator.

18 **Everybody else does it**. Certainly, this excuse for shameless and mindless behavior isn't in the creator's handbook of phrases.

By now you get the idea and I trust you have been properly stimulated. Once you are in tune with words and phrases that don't work, you will do your due diligence with original work and become a much improved communicator and artist.

Sculpting a lexicon in words, pastels, or phrases in a melody are all part of the beautifully interwoven invention called art.

THE SORCERER'S WIFE

CHAPTER THIRTY FOUR

THE PIANO MAN
A Solo Revelation

THE ANSWER in the broadest brushstroke is this: It is all art.

To consider the answer properly, one must first ask, what is an artist? The creation is the extension of its creator. The true artist is the manifestation of the soul merging with consciousness. The art that concerns us here is art from the soul. Once the soul is found, the form follows—painting, music, dance, literature, and so on. Isn't all art from the soul? No. Muzak isn't Mozart.

Let me tell you about the piano man.

DEBUSSY IN THE AFTERNOON

I was living in San Francisco at the time. It was in the early afternoon when a superb artist, several of his patrons, and I, were gathered in a large three-story stone mansion in the Cow Hollow district that overlooked the Marina. I looked around and saw that the entire first floor that had once supported many walls and rooms had been gutted to make space for an imposing ballroom. In the dimly lit inner sanctum there were some thirty pianos, each covered with a soft white sheet. Our host, a wealthy piano collector, told us various virtuosi and composers had owned these pianos.

He asked us if we would like to hear a piece. Yeses and nods. After carefully removing the cover draped over a grand piano, he ran several fingers along the mirror-like luster of the wood. As he sat down, our host mentioned that this fine instrument had belonged to Arthur Rubenstein and that Vladimir Horowitz and Igor Stravinsky had once owned the pianos to his right.

The piano man began playing from memory.

Suddenly, Debussy's *Clair de Lune* swept up all around the piano mausoleum. After about five minutes, the piece was finished and the air stopped vibrating. We applauded. There was no doubt our host had classical concert ability. Yet there was something missing from the performance of the otherwise haunting melody. While the piano man demonstrated remarkable technical proficiency, the music had been strangely sterile. Our

In my own compositions, no conscious effort has been made to be original, or Romantic or Nationalistic, or anything else. I write down on paper the music I hear within me, as naturally as possible ... What I try to do, when writing down my music, is to make it say simply and directly that which is in my heart when I am composing.

SERGEY RACHMANINOFF

At times our own light goes out and is rekindled by a spark from another person.

Each of us has cause to think with deep gratitude of those who have lighted the flame within us.

ALBERT SCHWEITZER

pianist had played the work as the notes ticked off unerringly by rote inside his head. It was accuracy without virtuosity, without passion, like hearing a detailed description of two people making love in clinical terms.

To know and appreciate the difference between technique and spirit makes for elevated awareness. Otherwise you are stuck in that eternal vanilla waiting room with Muzak for company. Each original artwork contains the soul of its creator; that is why the connoisseur wants to own original art; the life force that resides within the work is undeniable. From this understanding, you can enrich your ability to discern art from advertising, soulful from commercial, good from bad, and reality from pretension.

Discern not in rhetoric as in proclaiming this is better than that, but in awareness that this is this and that is that. Each true artwork enters the world alone and alive—as do we all.

COMPARISON TRAPS

From the dim twilight of human evolution, there was art before there was the spoken word of language. Human 'modern' culture is more than 40,000 years old; our ancestor not only survived, they made art—necklaces and carvings that transcended the utilitarian. Cave painters during Paleolithic times of 30,000 years ago didn't attend art school in the modern sense to produce their masterpieces, their representational systems for connecting to the spirit. Using words to describe art is conceptual and antithetical to feeling its nature. Of course, writing about art has its place as historical interest. How would you describe awe? No matter how beautifully or poignantly expressed, can words truly describe the feeling of love? It can only be described tangentially and metaphorically via simile. No matter how well I express the deepening orange hues and modulations of a setting sun to a blind man, he still can't see it—but he might feel something from the passion of my expression.

Writing about art isn't it. Viewing a piece of art hanging on a wall tells little about the art itself—oblivious to the process that created it, the viewer sees a finished work and not the force behind the art. How did the art come into existence is the quintessential question that completes the picture.

You can't know what art is from art history books or critiques; and you can't know what love is by reading the most heartfelt of poems or romance novels; while the words might bring tears to your eyes, the emotion is vicarious, which is secondhand.

Don't confuse sincerity or sentimentality with awareness.

FACING THE BULL

There are two fundamental questions to consider about a piece of art: What is the quality of the art and how did it come into the world? If the art came into being through an inexplicable power that reveals an original view into the realm called reality, then the art is born of creation. And by reality, I don't imply copying nature, which is creative, but an adding to nature, which is creation. Everyone has imagination, and creativity is the rearrangement of existential things. Neither imagination nor creativity, however, resides in the domain of creation. The art that concerns us here can't be demystified or pinned down precisely because it is magic.

Questions invariably persist. How is the spectator, the art patron to know whether the work is magic? How is the artist to know whether her art is magic? For the artist, it is a matter of lucid introspection without self-deception. The art patron has no less a challenge, as she must educate and dedicate herself to become a connoisseur.

You can't know the full depth of the magic until you see it forming in front of your eyes and in the presence of your soul. You can't know what art is until you taste its dewy essence on your own cultured palette. For this sensation, you have to find an artist who creates from the soul and who would invite you into his studio where you can become a reliable witness to creation, to the spirit made materially manifest. To find and know such an artist is the beginning of a great adventure. The reward of discerning what is what is in direct proportion to the energy invested in finding out what one is looking at. This each person must do for himself through direct experience.

Secondhand information won't do. We learn to identify something by first finding out all the things that it isn't. Can you know who God is because someone else told you to believe? If you have found God, you have found art; if you have found art, you have found God.

Although finding such an artist at this moment may not be possible, you can be present during the creation with a master at work. Pablo Picasso didn't like to get into heady discussions about art or speak much of the soul or God. However, watching him paint opens doors. In Henri-Georges Clouzot's 1956 film, *The Mystery of Picasso*, the director filmed Picasso as he created some twenty works, which were allegedly destroyed after the film was completed. Here, in this brilliant documentary about painting, Picasso draws himself and us from the 'outside' into the inside of the Unconscious. In the film, as Picasso worked on an image of a matador and a bull, he was more than familiar, in an intimate sense, with every angle of every line of every part of the body of the matador and the bull.

How would this drawing or that painting be different, in what context, in what narrative? You can see his hand searching for the unique, for another solution. While Picasso doesn't need any more publicity from me, remember that Pablo wasn't born famous.

If we could see the miracle of a single flower clearly, our whole life would change.

BUDDHA

FROM WHERE IS ART?

The art I am talking about is art that comes into being for no other reason than to be—art from the soul, art from the inner artist, which must be felt to be created, to be seen, and to be appreciated. Art from the soul comes into being from intuition; such art by definition is transcendental to thought and doesn't come from thinking or conceptualizing, which are cerebral pursuits. The art that concerns us here isn't a qualifier (art therapy) nor is it the object of a modifier (commercial art). Art from the soul is art without motive. This is what is meant by that familiar and much misunderstood proclamation: art for art's sake.

Remember, you can't fundamentally, in its purest form, think how you feel or feel how you think. While you can appreciate the mastery of technique, as seen with the piano player, such skill is sharpening the pencil for effect and, like drawing, is based on measurement, which is precise and finite. Beyond the veneer and headiness of technique and taste lies the force behind the power of art; here, in this pristine territory, you will discover that uncrowded window, the open one with a view of bountiful eternity, which contains all the indelible scenes that create your life.

FIRST DATE

At its essential nature, the answer to what is art is this: If the artist is certain he can do it again, then the edge of creation has been dulled by routine into a thing reproducible, refined again and again—and to what purpose? It is the artist copying himself. Reproduction in this sense shouldn't be confused with the artisan—a master of a specific craft who represents and understands his work for what it is. For the artist, it is better to copy someone other than himself.

If the artist is unsure of the outcome as if going out on that first date and is fully aware that the next set of improvisations, should they transmute into harmony, is a gift, then it is art—the art I am talking about, a unique product of creation that spirals ever upward toward evolution where the quality of life is engaging and 'quiet desperation' is but an archaic term.

And who better to model yourself after than the Creator, the Artist of all existence?

In the end, the piano man couldn't use his music to free his mind to the possibility of the spirit made manifest, which is this: Art is a vision of God created in the material world.

Adagio ... Fortissimo ... Adagio

There are as many nights as days, and the one is just as long as the other in the year's course. Even a happy life cannot be without a measure of darkness, and the word 'happy' would lose its meaning if it were not balanced by sadness.

CARL JUNG

Pollyanna Redux

If dear Pollyanna would come back to us reborn from an ashram in the East wearing a robe, beads, and sandals, then her cheerful optimism, expectation for people to act decently, spirit of forgiveness, and unflinching gratitude for what did come her way would identify her not as a fool or a naïve unfortunate, but as a master, or even a bodhisattva.

Eleanor H. Porter would be proud.

CHAPTER THIRTY FIVE

DHARMA, DESTINY, DREAMS
Avatars Among Us

WE YEARN for the unknown; we fear the unknown; something has to give. In perspective we have depth. Although the Sanskrit word 'dharma' has no precise equivalent in English, an appropriate understanding of the word in the context of this book is from the French phrase: raison d'etre, or reason for being, which is your 'purpose in life'. Your dharma then is the reason for which you have come here.

For what concerns us here, it is essential not to confuse the concept of dharma with the politics surrounding it over the ages.

FOUR CASTES

Information that is complete and holistic is useful; bits, pieces, and hearsay lead to inherent dangers of misuse and misinformation. Some might think dharma sounds inevitable, and in conflict with freewill. Paradoxically, the opposite is true. While we are all capable of learning how to swim, it isn't inevitable, especially if you grow up in the desert.

It is important to ask yourself: How much freewill I am exercising in my life right now? Freewill is the path to dharma.

Of course, an argument can also arise that the rules of dharma corrupted Hinduism in ancient India by enforcing the caste system, which divided humans into four rigid social classes (priests, warriors, traders, and laborers). Not all men were created equal since birth dictated your station and obligation in life. Upward or downward mobility for body and soul had to pass through the gates of reincarnation. The caste system was eventually absorbed into Hinduism, given religious sanction and legitimacy and has continued to function right up to the present.

The Buddha—himself born into the warrior caste, was a severe critic of the caste system. He ridiculed the claims of superiority made by the priests, he criticized the theological basis of the system, and he welcomed into the *Sangha*, or community of monks, people of all castes, including outcasts: the untouchables. His most famous saying on the subject is: "Birth does

Life is not easy for any of us. But what of that? We must have perseverance and above all confidence in ourselves. We must believe that we are gifted for something and that this thing must be attained.

MARIE CURIE

not make one a priest or an outcaste. Behavior makes one either a priest or an outcaste."

DHARMA SANS POLITICS

Buddhism, however, sees dharma in another light—and yet, the light is always coming from the same source.

Steve Hagen, author and head teacher at the Dharma Field Zen Center in Minneapolis, Minnesota summarized dharma for me: in essence, while Dharma in Buddhism has a multitude of meanings, the main three are:

- Reality or Truth (as it is, i.e., not relative)
- Teaching
- With a small 'd', the 'elements of experience'

Given this understanding by Hagen, I can accurately and in good conscience combine all three meanings to arrive at my purpose in life, for what good are these definitions individually if not to fulfill your mission on Earth.

NOBLE TRUTHS

As I have stated elsewhere, while I am neither a Hindu nor a Buddhist, I adopt universal truths, or standards from whatever the source to help me become more aware. While a debate about differences between Brahman and Buddha is beyond the scope of this book, a point or two about Buddhism is appropriate.

All the teachings of the Buddha center on the Four Noble Truths, in the same way the rim and spokes of a wheel center on the hub. They are 'Noble' because they ennoble one who understands them; and they are called 'Truths' because, corresponding with reality as it is, they are true.

Buddha's Second Noble Truth states that craving causes all suffering; this perception is worth the attention of each artist. When we desire something that we can't attain, we feel frustrated. When we expect someone to live up to our expectation and they don't, we feel disappointment. When we want others to appreciate us and they don't, we feel hurt. When we do get something we want, this most often doesn't lead to a lasting satisfaction either. We soon become bored with that thing, lose interest in it, and eventually begin wanting some other thing as the cycle begins again.

While getting (earning) what you want can be an admirable achievement, it doesn't necessarily secure happiness. Finding your purpose in life ensures what the master had said: "It is better to live in fulfillment than in hope."

Rather than constantly struggling to get what you want, it is much smarter to adjust and examine all your wanting, and your reaction to the outcome of your desires. If you become addicted to a particular outcome, you not only set yourself up for a fall, your inflexibility will blind you to other opportunities. If you make your happiness contingent upon one thing, then inherent in the psychology of reaping this possibility is the seed for disappointment. If, however, you can witness your self-induced

Character answers all questions

—SO SAID THE MASTER

melodrama objectively, you open your mind to possibilities that had been previously blocked out by you.

Do you acknowledge or feel the truth of this understanding? Unbridled craving, which can never be satisfied, deprives us of contentment from one moment to the next.

JEWEL IN THE CROWN

Dharma isn't fatalism where human beings are powerless to alter the events, predetermined and otherwise, of their lives. On the contrary, dharma is what every soul is seeking—its destiny. Is destiny inevitable? No. It demands your participation with action. No thing exists without resistance. Far from being at odds, freewill and dharma are kindred. Freewill demands perseverance: the reward is finding your purpose in life. Keep in mind too that such disciplines in psychology as the Freudians and the Behaviorists don't recognize freewill as an independent force in the complex study of human behavior.

For those shouting the loudest about freewill, what have they to show the world? Exercising freewill is a quiet affair. Those who have arrived have no need or desire to shout. As part of your discipline, you base your decisions on what *you* know, not on secondhand information. Self-discipline, which is true freedom and the crown jewel of freewill, is ultimately acquired on your own. Every master needs an apt pupil, and every astute student knows when it's time to be on her own. You don't need anyone's permission to assert self-discipline. This isn't to dismiss that artists living under repressive regimes don't have hardships. Despite the purges of cultural revolutions and political censorship, no thing has ever stopped the true artist, the survivor, from overcoming seemingly insurmountable odds to live an authentic life. Or what is the point?

You can certainly carve out a life based on cerebral decisions alone. However, as every introspective person ultimately asks himself: Was this the right choice, was this a life of no regrets, and was this a life worth living? When your life is in dharma, nagging doubts peel away like so much karmic residue as destiny beckons and fulfillment is reality.

HOW IT WORKS

You must make a crucial decision and a distinction sometime after your birth and before you depart this material realm. The decision is what will you do with the currency of your life (this is your true birthright, fortune, legal tender by your actions), and the distinction is the difference between a job where you are doing time and a passion—a divine calling—where you are creating in time, which is available to anyone willing to step away from the mainstream and enter uncharted territory. Remember, fortune and fulfillment will always favor the brave artist.

Where will you go?

When you go somewhere, it is presumably for a motive, Do you know why you went there, or not? You did go there for some purpose, didn't you? Life, too, is a destination and no different from going to that somewhere place. You have come here for your unique purpose in life, your dharma.

Success is counted sweetest
By those who ne'er succeed.
To comprehend a nectar
Requires sorest need.

EMILY DICKINSON

Everyone is a genius at least once a year. A real genius has his original ideas closer together.

GEORG C. LICHTENBERG

Don't take anyone's word for it since no outside authority can advise you about your dharma. You must discover this phenomenon for your own self.

When I first encountered the concept of dharma, I immediately knew that I had stumbled upon an eternal truth about one's self, fully articulated for anyone willing to listen. In Hinduism, the self is central. Buddha, however, defined the self as "that yearning which seeks pleasure and lusts after vanity whereas Truth is the correct comprehension of things, which is the permanent and everlasting, the real in all existence and the bliss of righteousness." Buddha, who was self-awake, took it further by refining his explanation: The very existence, or concept of self is an illusion since self denotes separation from only the one, which has innumerable manifestations—like you and me and every other living thing, including primordial matter. Is the self then the cause of all your earthly problems?

Remember, I use self to mean your direct link to consciousness, your soul. While Buddha didn't specifically concern himself with the soul, his practical teachings are no less divine.

Reading about the self, the soul, and dharma is a good step. But reading about these metaphysical components isn't the transcendental experience, which is beyond reason—a concept that can't be clarified or resolved by thinking. Buddha encouraged everyone to discover things for themselves, which is the trademark of a true teacher. I experience my *self* in the form of my soul; having found my soul, I now strive to fulfill my dharma. Remember, if you have the courage, you can ultimately meet your self. As for the self, Buddha had also observed: "When I die, the world dies with me."

A WISH IS NOT A DREAM

Dharma is determining your purpose in life, which isn't in conflict with your freewill. You embrace your purpose in life, and from your dharma you create your dream, your destiny, with your actions. There is a significant distinction between a dream and a wish. A dream implies action toward its realization. A wish, like hope, has no supporting structure and is based solely on a yearning that some desire will be fulfilled. Dreams are assertive; wishes are weak. Once informed of this distinction, you decide on how to frame your thoughts.

The concept of a 'wish' is embedded in society, into human culture worldwide as my chapter 'Existential Pinocchio' reveals. From myths, fairy tales, lyrics, poetry, books, and films, we are exposed to wishing and its kin, hoping—where there is life, there is hope, and so on. Sigmund Freud, in his book, *The Interpretation of Dreams*, wrote that certain dreams were an outlet for wish fulfillment. Of course, Freud was describing the dream state when we are asleep. As Freud noted: "It may be observed how conveniently the dream is capable of arranging matters." In our sleeping dreams, which are symbolic constructs set free to roam about the psyche, we can defy gravity and fly, and dispense altogether with the concept of Einstein's breakthrough in physics and the rules that govern 'space-time'.

Then, there is Lucid Dreaming, which means dreaming while knowing that you are dreaming. Frederik van Eeden coined the word 'lucid' in the sense of mental clarity. Lucidity usually begins in the midst of a dream when the dreamer realizes that the experience isn't occurring in physical reality; the experience is but a dream. In this freeform reality, you can do as you please, control the 'world' according to your values—which provides a revealing image of who you are, which may be in contrast to who you think you are. In this sense, lucid dreaming is an apt metaphor for the waking world where the true artist as alchemist or as shaman transforms his energy into priceless art in a leaden world all to easily bedazzled by the ordinary glitter of gold.

FLYING FOR REAL

While wishing randomly arranges nothing, wishing upon a star makes for dramatic imagery, giving one 'hope'. It is the waking dream, however, with its conscious intent that has the prowess to alter matter and the course of your own evolution, which is your history in the making. The Wright Brothers, for example, had a waking dream and solved what had stumped the greatest minds through the ages—from Leonardo da Vinci to Alexander Graham Bell. Wilbur and Orville Wright didn't wish or hope to fly. They had a conscious intention and inspiration that they could build a powered flying machine, and that is how humanity got off the ground.

"Persistence, a belief in themselves, and a healthy dose of engineering smarts led the Wright brothers to succeed," says Tom Crouch, Senior Curator of the Division of Aeronautics at the National Air and Space Museum in Washington, D.C.

How many times have you heard this remark: I wish she'd do this or that. Can you sense weakness, the victim mentality, and why such a request goes nowhere? Alas, our poor yokel ponders, I must suffer to avoid a confrontation.

To discover your dharma isn't the end, but the beginning. And doors will open. You must have the strength and awareness to know what to do and when to do it. God is the door opener, but you must still knock. As great minds throughout history have surmised: life is but a dream, and what is life about if not your transformation—making your marvelous dreams come true.

While it is generally positive to think things through, plan, set goals, and then go after them, this conceptual boulevard is populated with preconceived notions that may or might not be creative. This approach can be successful, even wildly materially prosperous. But it is a temporal success of the mind, which is limited, impermanent, and fickle, not the triumph of the soul—the eternal identity of the self. The eternal self incorporates the mind, but not vice versa. This is simply the way of things. I always look for the largest container to place things in true perspective. From the soul, you know from intuition without reasoning, which is at the heart of Zen Buddhism where faith is replaced by direct intuitive insight. In other words, as I write throughout this book, you don't take anyone else's word for what is doubtless the most important decision of your existence—your dharma.

THE SNOOZE BUTTON

Before launching into a career, it is astute to find your dharma first, and then go on from there. This approach is contrary to what most of us have

The future is something which everyone reaches at the rate of sixty minutes an hour, whatever he does, whoever he is.

C.S. LEWIS

In the middle of every difficulty lies opportunity.
ALBERT EINSTEIN

grown up with, where you decide your occupation based on various factors, such as status, security, aptitude tests, and society's demands—none having to do with dharma. When I was in high school and college, I remember a slogan that was hyped on TV and billboards: 'If you want a good job, get a good education.' Although this self-fulfilling prophecy seemed well advised and harmless at worst, it was, in retrospect, insidious propaganda, and especially misleading for the artist who must educate herself. This promise of a well-paying position bolstered by the security of a pension was rampant among the baby boomer generation that grew up believing in a dream focused entirely on material acquisition that was bogus. During my school years, I had never heard or read that finding your purpose in life came first. My intuition, however, had provided me with an empty feeling to get my attention. You have to wake up to realize you have been asleep. Don't hit the snooze button when you do get that wake-up call.

Although the dharma path is the mythical odyssey our soul needs to complete its mission on Earth, this rite of passage goes mostly unsupported in Western society where fabricating human cogs takes precedence over individual necessity. This is why so many who attain their goals and even their ardent aspirations, sadly discover emptiness instead of fulfillment. They have fulfilled society's collective dreams, not their own.

These successful people, drones nonetheless, construct an image of life that is supported solely by society-approved tokens of material goods. External elements, which are transitory, will never completely satisfy because there can never be enough to adorn a house or a body for one who has dismissed her soul. These achievers haven't attended to the soul because the outcome of finding their dharma is a choice that can't be quantified in advance, nor is it in encouraged by society.

No one suddenly tapped you on the shoulder, insisting that you must be an artist, or else.

If you buy into a system by rote, you are a coconspirator in your own disappointment, which is inherently inevitable within the system. Look around and truly see your circle of friends, family, and acquaintances. You don't realize that the system you are part of is flawed until it fails you. The aware artist rejects a preordained way of life that has been designed by some committee for their own ends.

Your spirit, your dharma, is like a burning candle in a jar. Cover the jar and the flame suffocates.

AVATARS AMONG US

The decisions you make about what you will do with your life are influenced from the moment of birth. Choosing a mission that is your livelihood based on aptitude tests, or sincere advice can't reveal your dharma. Taking whatever comes along is what it sounds like. Rolling with the wind, however, is organic for the tumbleweed, and even then this wandering plant is scattering its seeds. Harnessing the wind is superior to casting your fate to it. Decisions to be this or that in life are most often externally biased. Those who choose a life in the arts for the wrong reason may be as unsatisfied as an accountant who knew in his soul that he should have been a jazz pianist. Think about it. There are far easier ways than art to pay the rent and make your fortune. Who would willingly choose a life of hardship, rejection, and swimming against the current values of the mainstream?

There are artists who become emotionally crippled by rejection, a fully loaded noun that carries with it clinging relatives: dejection, fear, isolation, ostracism, and even death. Then, there are artists who use 'no' as a switch for igniting metaphysical plasma, an energy state conducive for transforming dreams into physical reality. Why? Is the combustible group born with some unique rejection-proof gene? The answer lies not in an inherited predisposition, but in her passion, her dharma, or purpose in life—her soul work, which is eternal and won't take 'no' for an answer. The universe, the ineffable manifestation of the Creator, calls you to persevere despite 'no' and well beyond 'yes'. Don't get complacent in either case.

While dharma takes on different meanings and nuances depending on its source, I use dharma in this sense: the reason for which you have come into this life, which is destiny on its way toward fulfillment. Great insights about the fundamental essence of consciousness are ancient; wisdom is often lost only to be rediscovered anew by receptive still evolving cultures.

A sobering thought: what if, at this very moment, I am living up to my full potential?

JANE WAGNER

THE GITA

Universally renowned as the jewel of India's spiritual wisdom, the Bhagavad-gita (see also 'Detach and Conquer') is considered by eastern and western scholars alike to be among the great spiritual books of all time. Spoken by Lord Krishna, the Supreme Personality of Godhead to His intimate disciple Arjuna, the Gita's seven hundred concise verses provide a definitive guide to the nature of consciousness, the self, the universe and the Supreme. Lord Krishna, the avatar of Vishnu in Hinduism, reveals transcendental knowledge to man, including this: Everyone has a path they must follow in order to uphold righteousness, and that leads to their individual salvation, which is the purpose and goal of human existence.

Lord Krishna, teacher of the world, says: "Be equally poised in success and failure; this is called yoga . . . Therefore, always perform actions which should be done, without attachments; for, by performing action without attachment, man attains the Supreme."

You don't have to be a Hindu adept to adopt the wisdom of Lord Krishna, who describes the science of self-realization and the exact process by which human beings can establish their eternal relationship with God. In terms of pure, spiritual knowledge the Bhagavad-gita is unique. Its intrinsic beauty is that its knowledge applies to all human beings and doesn't postulate any sectarian ideology, or secular view.

The primary purpose of the Bhagavad-gita is to illuminate for humanity the realization of the true nature of divinity. Within its epic poetry, the message is clear: the highest spiritual conception and the greatest material perfection is to attain the love of God.

There is no higher standard. Knowing and aiming toward achieving this realization sets the artist free to prevail in material reality. Many great souls such as Albert Einstein, Mahatma Gandhi, Albert Schweitzer, Henry David Thoreau, Ralph Waldo Emerson, as well as Madhvacarya, Sankara and Ramanuja from bygone ages have all contemplated and deliberated upon the Bhagavad-gita and its timeless message.

First say to yourself what you would be; and then do what you have to do.

EPICTETUS

ANCIENT RHYTHMS

In his masterwork of a book, *Anam Cara: A Book of Celtic Wisdom*, John O'Donohue writes: "If you can awaken this sense of destiny, you come into rhythm with your life. You fall out of rhythm when you renege on your potential and talent, when you settle for the mediocre as a refuge from the call. When you lose rhythm, your life becomes wearingly deliberate or anonymously automatic. Rhythm is the secret key to balance and belonging. This will not collapse into false contentment or passivity. It is the rhythm of a dynamic equilibrium, a readiness of spirit, a poise that is not self-centered. This sense of rhythm is ancient. All life came out of the ocean; each one of us comes out of the waters of the womb; the ebb and flow of the tides is alive in the ebb and flow of our breathing. When you are in rhythm with your nature, nothing destructive can touch you. Providence is at one with you; it minds you and brings you to your new horizons. To be spiritual is to be in rhythm."

The source of all great art is this rhythm of destiny. When you are in rhythm (dharma) you can engage the universe, which is a great instrument, and from your horn of plenty comes the wondrous notes of your art.

You may still be asking: How do I find my dharma?

There are those who know their dharma from birth. Others, most of us, must seek it out later in life. There is no map as this journey is unique for each person. You find your dharma by making the commitment to finding your passion with unfaltering intent. You have vision and there is no going back. Why would you want to? You are resolute. Your intention is a conscious choice to find your passion, which is your soul, for your soul holds the key to the purpose of your life, and to the material form of your art. Your intention is fluid and engaging, not dogged, stiff, or blind. The Law of Non-Attachment beautifully tempers your intention. You can't dictate intention in the same way that you can't plan or order great art into existence: attempting to manipulate either organic process results in missed opportunity. Intention isn't 'in tension'.

Loosen up.

Intention means being ready when the call comes to move ahead. After all, you asked for it.

THE MOUNTAIN BECKONS

How will I know it is my dharma when I meet it? Once the commitment is made, and only you know if it is genuine, one day something will pull you aside from the somewhere of everyday madness. Only you will recognize that this is the moment of clarity. You will feel it; no one can feel it for you. You must trust the truth of your feelings: this is the key for understanding yourself.

There is no other way.

A true creator doesn't accept anything by rote. You can't memorize the act of creation because it is spontaneous cause and unique effect. Reading scriptures and the wisdom of the ages, while a good direction, remains dogma if not put to the test and metabolized.

You, like the Zen master, must know a thing from self-discipline and the intuitive illumination that can only be known from firsthand experience.

After you have made the journey to the mountain, no one with a misleading agenda can dispel your direct experience of truth. Once you have a worthy dream, you will find your dharma; then, if you stay the course, destiny will be satisfied.

Be grateful and fully appreciate what you do have, and your humility for the gift will create a path to God, who is waiting to meet your soul halfway—which is the cosmic means for balancing the equation.

DIRECT FEED

There are ageless core longings that run deep among artists that include the quest for the soul, meaning, expression, and purpose in life. Of course, as noted elsewhere, these aspirations are found in all groups despite age or socio-economic status. Seeded liberally throughout this book are the underlying principles that form an organic primer for all creators.

I could not have planned or predicted that after embarking upon my journey I would awaken one morning a quarter of a century later to an amazing realization: I was an artist. The miracle did not end there. I had also acquired a spontaneous and indelible understanding of art as a gestalt—what it is, what it isn't, where it comes from, and how to create it. This was direct instruction in the Zen sense: information as truth gained intuitively from the source, bypassing any need for rote or the traditional cognitive learning process.

Amen, Shalom, and *Om shaanti shaanti shaanti*

One needs something to believe in, something for which one can have whole-hearted enthusiasm.

One needs to feel that one's life has meaning, that one is needed in this world.

HANNAH SENESH

CHAPTER THIRTY SIX

INSTINCT / INTUITION
Formative Years

WITHOUT GUT REACTION to sublime revelation you are still operating out of hearsay, which is what it sounds like.

Indiscriminate usage often blurs the distinction between instinct and intuition. They aren't synonyms. And as I write throughout this book, discernment is an essential quality that characterizes an empowered artist who has granted herself immunity from rejection through humility in acceptance. This artist isn't a slave to any particular outcome.

INSTINCT

Instinct is of the body and biological; it is physical. Instinct is metabolic and immediate. These sensations can be measured, if not always quantified. You know when you are thirsty, threatened, smell bread baking, or feel the heat of sexual arousal. You don't need a fact-finding committee to vote on what your basic instincts are directly telling you. When you are hungry and cold, you crave food and shelter.

Will painting have to wait until a sequence of needs is met? Creation blossoms out of necessity, which often includes the crucible of deprivation. Remember, while the true artist is an egalitarian, he is no ordinary man.

Pioneer psychologist Abraham Maslow reasoned that all people are motivated by the same hierarchy of needs, metaneeds, and self-actualization: physical survival, psychological, and then, when these requirements are satisfied, another gene kicks in, and the quest for a life worth living becomes more than a filling appetizer; it is a raw hunger as essential as the need for sustenance. Maslow also wrote that 'self-actualizing' people tend to experience life in a more harmonious and even more transcendental way.

INTUITION

The Zen Buddhists have known for centuries that while intuition can be understood, it is difficult to express. Writing about intuition is even more arduous, and at best opaque. The wisdom of Zen lies in this inexpressible knowing that reveals itself solely through firsthand intuitive experience.

In painting from intuition, the edge is in not knowing.

EDEN

Solidarity is not a matter of sentiment but a fact, cold and impassive as the granite foundations of a skyscraper. If the basic elements, identity of interest, clarity of vision, honesty of intent, and oneness of purpose, or any of these is lacking, all sentimental pleas for solidarity, and all other efforts to achieve it will be barren of results.

EUGENE V. DEBS

Both metaphysical and visceral, intuition is the soul whispering God's guidance directly to you—a process that defies academic or scientific quantification because it is beyond the scope of reason, thought, and probing instruments. You can't weigh, measure, or test intuition with a piece of equipment because it is transcendental. Intuition is the means your spirit uses for accessing consciousness. Without honoring the spirit, one's quality of life is tepid, a walk-on bit part in lieu of a memorable leading role.

SELF-DENIAL

With deference to Maslow, how do artists confront the inherent psychology of what is considered normal human needs? Artists don't represent a monolithic block. Although temperament distinguishes one artist from another, it is the true artist who knows he, despite circumstances, is blessed to have no choice but to create. While good and bad events will always whirl around his temporal self, the artist learns that he can and must keep his balance. He must be both agile and aware to remain steadfast within the calm eye of the hurricane. To exist near the fury of the storm without getting destroyed by it is life on the edge, the jumping off point for all creators.

However, being on a perilous odyssey isn't punishment for the artist's bad karma. It is his dharma and good fortune to be an artist. To make the time to create, it isn't uncommon for artists to deny themselves food, adequate shelter, material goods, security, love, or a family life—things that society values most. At first glance, such sacrifices don't seem to support a well-integrated life. It may sound self-destructive and even delusional.

Remember, if you want depth, you must dig deep.

Self-denial is necessary for the artist to be authentic. I didn't write self-destructive. There can be no journey of value without sacrifice; and while the rewards may take time to arrive, the artist recalls the words of the master from India: "It is better to live in fulfillment than in hope." This understanding has great liberating power for your day-to-day existence, which is how life plays itself out—one solar day at a time.

THE PRICE

To know balance, you must experience extremes. To the outside world, which often includes family and friends, self-seeking (at their own expense) artists who deny themselves the 'good' things seem to be 'crazy' at worst, or, at the very least, outsiders with a skewed value system.

Even a saint was a sinner who developed a well-defined motive. I have yet to meet an achiever who isn't self-absorbed on some level and in some direction. They might call such an artist obsessed, which he might be. But hanging the tired and old obsession label on the artist is trite.

The aware artist is passionate, in control, not obsessed, which implies out of control—a mental state that superficially seems to make for more dramatic copy than writing about a healthy artist who is a model to emulate. Behind every sanguine creator, there is a lesson, far grander in scope than obsession, for each artist who has the will to persevere.

The artist knows sacrifices must be made; divine fire comes at a hefty price. You are, after all, dealing with the 'gods'. Ask Prometheus. This doesn't mean the artist must live in stereotypical squalor to paint. On the contrary, the artist who knows the intrinsic value of his work is free to paint and live well in a creature comfortable environment without getting corrupted by complacency.

It is up to each artist to create the structure of his world with the same passion he uses to make his art. Intuition can't lie; trust it with your life and you will feel the magic freedom that is your soul. The price for divine fire as it turns out is dedication.

Good art requires instinct; great art demands intuition.

FORMATIVE YEARS

I was in my local Starbucks one late afternoon with Adele, my mother. At this time of day there would be at least one barista on duty that I already knew who would make a cappuccino the way I liked it—the milk deftly poured on top of the espresso must be thick, rich, and creamy, not full of air and foamy.

As I began drawing with my color pencils, the topic of taking a stand came up and the importance of right action. This sparked a memory that took me back to when I was a senior in high school. "Here's a story about a bully I never told you," I said. Mom perked up. Here it is:

I was at a senior dance in high school with some friends, including Bob, a tall, lean, amiable fellow. I recall asking a girl to dance and by the time I got back to my tall friend, the school bully, his gang watching eagerly, was ready to beat the hell out of him.

This bully was mean and crazy. After school, he would go around punching his fist through car windows in his rages. I didn't know what had set the bully off to focus on my friend. I did know that this 'tough' guy would definitely hurt Bob.

Some force greater than I came over me. My instinct for self-preservation was overwhelmed by a clear feeling of quiet gentle power.

I placed myself between the bully and my friend who was clearly scared. Although I had grown up on the mean streets where both fist and firsthand experience of drawing the battle line were no strangers, I was no brawler.

Without hesitation, I looked the bully in the eye and said in a voice that was adamant: "You don't want to do this."

There was silence among the teenage crowd that had gathered, a rowdy crowd eager for carnage, for blood sport. His eyes blinking rapidly as if he were having a fit, the bully looked at me as if I were the crazy one. I didn't know what to expect. Then, the bully abruptly turned, began muttering to himself, and walked away.

His gang followed.

Bob began breathing again and hugged me. Although the bully could have easily taken me on as his target, he didn't. I can't prove it, but I feel the reason he had backed down is that I told him the truth in a non-threatening manner—and fortunately the sane part of him had agreed. 'You don't want to do this.' These words had soothed the savage.

My mother sighed. "I'm glad you didn't tell me about this then. I would have passed out."

Nothing organic is more formidable than a steadfast person who is on a mission. Although I didn't know it at the time of that high school

A rut is a grave with the ends knocked out.

LAURENCE J. PETER

You've got to go out on a limb sometimes because that's where the fruit is.

WILL ROGERS

confrontation, it had been my intuition that intervened with the power to deflect an immediate threat to body and soul. I had listened, and two lives were spared lots of pain, or worse.

In retrospect over the years, each time I stood up for my own self, I was in training for my life as an artist where survival of the conscious in an urban jungle is nature's way of weeding out the frauds, imposters, and dilettantes. I have also learned that the formative years never end. No one chooses to be a hero, an icon, or a world famous artist. That perception is in the eyes of others. Labels of this kind are always thrust upon the individual who has no control over such events. The smart artist, however, knows enough to have control over himself. To become a hero, icon, or a famous person can be a fickle affair.

If the adulation is suddenly taken away, where do you, the artist, find yourself? Knowing the answer isn't living the answer. Remember, 'you are on sacred ground when you know where you stand.'

Others may say your art is awesome, or that you are a genius.

Great!

But it is you who must truly know why your art has value, not them. If not, you will forever be insecure, potential roadkill on that fast lane to art city.

Instead of bemoaning a 'breakthrough' artist like Picasso, Kandinsky, or Pollock (name your artist), embrace this artist for living up to his dharma and broadening the awareness of what art is.

Remember this: If your art is original, then you are not in competition with anyone. In simplest terms, when someone opens the door for you, what do you say? You say, thank you, like a gentleman or gentlewoman.

CHAPTER THIRTY SEVEN

ALPHABET ART
The Painted Word

SKIMMING OVER a work of art is like trying to speed-read the Rosetta Stone. You get the picture. There is no rush.

When I began to earn a living as a writer, I used to think how much easier it must be for a painter. After all, the patron looks at the art as a gestalt. Point and click in the mind's eye. With writing, an editor must read, a time-consuming effort that all too often falls on tired eyes that don't comprehend.

MEASURING TIME

As fortune would have it, years later I would learn that my presumptive thoughts about writing and painting had been totally off. It wasn't any easier for a fine artist than it was for an author with an original voice. Getting noticed and being understood had nothing to do with measuring time or paying attention: it had to do with the awareness of being and seeing.

If you were producing commercial art, the type readily understood by a public weaned on advertising, then your chances for acceptance were much greater than if you were an artist making personal art. Fine art challenges the viewer to participate in both the meaning and the creation, which is no less demanding than making the art itself. If a viewer looking at a painting in a gallery doesn't know, sense, or remotely understand what he is looking at, then seeing it all at once has no relevance, and time is definitely not of the essence. This gallery scenario translates into book publishing where an editor spends hours reading and then rejecting a manuscript that is a work of literature. This isn't unheard of.

GETTING NOTICED

Whether paintings or words, an instant or a lifetime, in neither case is it about time; it is about seeing and feeling; it is about who is doing the looking. The viewer observes and completes the painting experience.

To appreciate some thing, you must know what you are looking at. Otherwise, what is the point? Taking it further over the years, I not only

A true photograph need not be explained, nor can it be contained in words.

ANSEL ADAMS

discovered that getting noticed as an artist wasn't easier than the written word, it was, in many ways, far more difficult.

LANGUAGE OF THERMOMETERS

In his book, *The Language of Vision*, Gyorgy Kepes, the Hungarian-born American painter, designer, and theoretician analyzes the effect of visual language on the structure of human perception. The semanticist and U.S. Senator, S.I. Hayakawa, contributing an introductory essay to the book titled 'The Revision of Vision', writes, in part:

"Whatever may be the language one happens to inherit, it is at once a tool and a trap. It is a tool because with it we order our experience, matching the data abstracted from the flux about us with linguistic units: words, phrases, and sentences. What is true of verbal languages is also true of visual 'languages': we match the data from the flux of visual experience with image-clichés, with stereotypes of one kind or another, according to the way we have been taught to see.

"And having matched the data of experience with our abstractions, visual or verbal, we manipulate those abstractions, with or without further reference to the data, and make systems with them. Those systems of abstractions, artifacts of the mind, when verbal, we call 'explanations,' or 'philosophies'; when visual, we call them our 'picture of the world.'

"With these little systems in our heads we look upon the dynamism of the events around us, and we find, or persuade ourselves that we find, correspondences between the pictures inside our heads and the world without. Believing those correspondences to be real, we feel at home in what we regard as a 'known' world.

"In saying why our abstractions, verbal or visual, are a tool, I have already intimated why they are also a trap. If the abstractions, the words, the phrases, the sentences, the visual clichés, the interpretative stereotypes, that we have inherited from our cultural environment are adequate to their task, no problem is presented. But like other instruments, languages select, and in selecting what they select, they leave out what they do not select.

"The thermometer, which speaks one kind of limited language, knows nothing of weight. If only temperature matters and weight does not, what the thermometer 'says' is adequate. But if weight, or color, or odor, or factors other than temperature matter, then those factors that the thermometer cannot speak about are the teeth of the trap. Every language, like the language of the thermometer, leaves work undone for other languages to do … We are the prisoners of ancient orientations imbedded in the languages we have inherited … The language of vision determines, perhaps even more subtly and thoroughly than verbal language, the structure of our consciousness. To see in limited modes of vision is not to see at all—to be bounded by the narrowest parochialisms of feeling."

FOUND IN TRANSLATION

Despite the limitations of words, we do have a common denominator known as the written language. With art for art's sake, art that has no motive other than to be born, we have, as Hayakawa suggests, an image of comprehension and communication transcending the linguistic, the cerebral. The artist

---

Money is like manure; it's not worth a thing unless it's spread around encouraging young things to grow.

THORNTON WILDER,
THE MATCHMAKER

speaks in a personal language using a unique and spontaneous alphabet. You are invited—and challenged if the artist has done his work—to see, translate, and interpret that new idiom. Is it visual poetry or pablum? To understand the artist you must be motivated to learn her alphabet; you need some way to discern visual literature from gibberish. Comprehending art doesn't come without great effort. Why would anyone think it isn't so?

BACKPACKER IN LONDON

Years ago when I was in London I saw the Rosetta Stone, a compact basalt slab (carved about 196 BCE) treasure that is housed in the British Museum. Discovered in July 1799 in the small Egyptian village Rosette (Raschid), the Stone was to become the missing primer in deciphering one of the ancient world's great mysteries—Egyptian hieroglyphs. After looking at the Rosetta Stone in person, it was clear to me that if I had dug it up, I would have sensed it was an artifact, but I wouldn't have immediately appreciated its rare and intrinsic value.

Despite the Rosetta Stone containing three inscriptions in the form of hieroglyphs (script of the official and religious texts), of Demotic (everyday Egyptian script), and Greek, the experts of the day were still baffled as to the meaning of the hieroglyphs.

By 1822, the representation of a single text of the three mentioned script variants enabled the French scholar Jean Francois Champollion (1790-1832) to essentially decipher the hieroglyphs. Four years earlier, with the aid of the Coptic language (spoken by the Christian descendants of the ancient Egyptians), he had realized another breakthrough.

While some hieroglyphs were strictly symbolic, many glyphs had a phonetic value of an alphabet—proving that 'silent' hieroglyphs had not only symbolic meaning, they also served as a 'spoken language', which was a necessary component in making the complete content within these symbols accessible.

The purpose of a writer is to keep civilization from destroying itself.

ALBERT CAMUS

LEARNING ABC'S

In a significant sense, art and ancient Egyptian hieroglyphs share a common bond. Both remain a marvelous mystery and it is the viewer who must decode the language of each. There is also a distinct difference. Art is interpretative; hieroglyphs are conceptual and have a specific message to convey. Until one understands the alphabet of the artist, the art remains a lost language like the ancient hieroglyphs had been for thousands of years.

Remember, before you can read to access meaning, you must know the alphabet—visual or linguistic.

Is there a Rosetta Stone for art? Everyone could then decipher and comprehend what is being said, or not said? There is a link in this sense. Champollion needed the Rosetta Stone to decipher the secrets of the ancient Egyptian hieroglyphics. For your Rosetta Stone, however, you need only trust your feelings to unlock the individual language of each artist—and, that is, one artist at a time. If your feelings are buried, then of what use are they? Your feelings will tell you whether there is magic in her art or not. You need not and cannot comprehend everything immediately—art is complex in the sense that it is alive. Once you feel the wonder of the

Anyone who believes you can't change history has never tried to write his memoirs.

DAVID BEN GURION

alphabet symbols, the language of the artist will over time reveal itself and its secrets to you—the lover of the art.

FOR THE LOVE OF IT

Here is an insight into creation. If you took all the individual letters, which are fundamental elements, of an alphabet that composed the text in a book and threw them up into the air, the odds are that perhaps some letters would fall onto the ground and align themselves together to form words. Most of these letters, however, would drop into a pile of symbolic nonsense, unconnected to any meaning. When a painter paints, the same dynamic is going on. All the visual letters or symbols of his palette are suspended in a maelstrom beyond thinking. As the brush swoops onto the canvas, the strokes fall into place in a way that the artist could never have predicted. This is intuitive comprehension, not an accident.

Even a tightly composed work by Johannes Vermeer has elements of spontaneity. And, unlike the book analogy, *all* the visual letters, the brushstrokes in the painting interact to provide meaning within the internal logic of the artwork.

Champollion became a scholar for the love of it. There is nothing preventing you from becoming an expert in anything. You become an impresario and patron for the love of it. You are an artist for the same reason, aren't you?

In art, the only rule and question is this: Does it work?

The arid plains of the art landscape are strewn with bodies of those artists who dropped out because they couldn't take the heat or the lack of attention—a decision they regret for the rest of their lives.

Make no mistake: the casualty rate among the misinformed is high. But, do not be dismayed. Integrate the information in this book, and you will galvanize the power to overcome obstacles, including rejection.

You will be the true artist because you made it happen.

You will be a cause, not a casualty, of art.

CHAPTER THIRTY EIGHT

YOUR PAPERS, PLEASE
A Gatekeeper

AN ASTUTE OBSERVER will appreciate and recognize that your art is your resume. This talent of perception is associated with the impresario or the connoisseur who senses talent before any of the votes have been cast.

To paraphrase Duke Ellington: if it looks good, it is good.

AN ART OPENING

Santa Monica, California: Despite its location inside an industrial park, the trendy gallery got plenty of traffic. Two friends, a writer and a master painter, and I had come for the early evening opening of a one-man show featuring the work of Harold, an abstract expressionist painter from New York City.

One hundred or so people were drinking wine, eating cheese, and talking, talking, and talking. Harold, in his seventies, wore a beret confidently and was holding court with people here and there.

The gallery owners were a married middle-aged European couple. The wife, Greta, was petite; she was the dealmaker. The tall husband, Fritz, took care of the books and other gallery matters. Contemporary and uncluttered, the gallery had lots of wall space.

"Your paintings and drawings would look great in this space," said my writer friend to me.

At that moment, Harold had made his way toward us. We spoke a while about art. He was friendly, unassuming and handled the exhibit of his work matter-of-factly. He had been through this scenario many times. Harold moved on to other people waiting to speak with him. We took in his art and mingled a bit. My artist friend looked around and didn't say much that evening.

Before leaving, I introduced myself to Greta and Fritz. I told her that I'd like to show her my work.

"Of course, please do. Call me," she said with lots of teeth showing, and then flitted off to work the room.

From the start of my career, the issue I found the hardest to fight—harder than the opposition of sundry leftists—was the blind, malevolent stubbornness of men who kept telling me that my work was too intellectual and that 'the public doesn't think.'

For years, I have been arguing that the general public is much more intelligent that its alleged leaders give it credit for; that people do care for ideas and are searching desperately for the spokesmen of reason; that only reason can work, though not always immediately; and that the evidence of it, on a historical scale, is that fact that no dictatorship can last without the help of censorship—because, in a free marketplace of ideas, truth and reason will always win.

AYN RAND,
THE AYN RAND COLUMN

Writing is a solitary occupation. Family, friends, and society are the natural enemies of the writer. He must be alone, uninterrupted, and slightly savage if he is to sustain and complete an undertaking.

JESSAMYN WEST

Art, after all, doesn't sell itself.

A few weeks later, I was in the gallery again with my portfolio in hand. All was quiet. Greta greeted me. Fritz was on the far side of the gallery unpacking paintings for the next show. And the art from Harold, the New York City artist, was gone.

I met with Greta in her office.

She pored over my work and said, "They are quite good. Where did you go to art school?"

The question hung over me like an ax.

I explained that I hadn't gone to art school. I was self-taught as is every true artist.

She winced and didn't appear to agree.

I said: "Van Gogh and Gauguin, after all, taught themselves."

She sighed, knowing she had to concede the point.

"Well, then, let's see your resume."

"You're looking at it," I said. "My portfolio is my resume."

"Yes, I understand that," she replied, pretty much dismissing what I had said as she flipped through my paintings again, eyeing several in particular. "Good, good, but I also want to see your resume, the one listing all the shows you've been in and the awards you've won."

"This would be my first exhibit," I said.

Greta's eyes opened wide. "No shows? No awards?" She quietly closed my portfolio.

I shook my head, no.

"Why not?" she said.

"Because now is when it's come up. I'm an adult prodigy. It's that simple. I don't know how else to explain it."

Greta clearly had no clue as to what I was explaining to her. "Well, then, I'm sorry, but all the artists we work with must have a history. You must have papers so we can show our clients. They expect it."

I said: "Why not be the first then to begin my history? Why not discover me? You said you like my work."

Greta became rigid, dense, and fidgety. She was an art dealer, not an art connoisseur, or impresario. She wanted my papers. She must have papers. She wasn't selling art; she was selling papers. It didn't matter to her that she saw the pedigree in front of her. She had to have third-party corroboration. She needed my art institute background to validate the art I had shown her. She was looking for the provenance, or history of ownership, of my art. She was looking for my participation and awards in juried exhibits as if I were a Pomeranian. I had no curriculum vitae specific to my art. Without the proper papers, my art had turned invisible to Greta.

It was clear. I would get no further with Greta. In her eyes, I was an 'unaccredited' artist without art academic credentials and the prerequisite laundry list of shows, ribbons, and collectors.

I thanked Greta for her time, left the gallery, and walked to my car.

While driving up Santa Monica Boulevard that late afternoon toward my place in the Hollywood Hills, I knew I had met a representative gatekeeper and that I had learned an essential lesson. Greta was a cog in an art-marketing machine that has been grinding along over the centuries (since about the second half of the 16th century in Italy to be more precise) to this very day. The mainstream gallery business is a hierarchical component of a dogmatic caste system perpetuated by institutions, self-appointed and in some cases self-important experts, patrons, and a distinct form of incestuous art nepotism. The 'impenetrable' wall Greta represented was a veneer fabricated to intimidate and keep out the meek—a tactic that wasn't new to me.

I had met gatekeepers in the publishing world and knew from past successes in writing that the front door wasn't the only way into a house. On balance, having exhibits in mainstream galleries or getting work shown in museums doesn't mean the artist becomes an overnight success. No one can predict the magic of timing commonly known as luck.

As I drove along Sunset Boulevard where the manicured lawn street divider ran through Beverly Hills, I looked over at the mansions on my left. I had been in some of those homes and had seen million-dollar art collections on the walls. I thought: my work could grace those walls of fine art in good form as well. How to get 'there' from 'here' was the metaphysical question my soul would have to answer.

I had the uneasy yet oddly calm and confirming feeling that I would be seeing a lot more Gretas in my life as an artist.

English usage is sometimes more than mere taste, judgment and education—sometimes it's sheer luck, like getting across the street.

E.B. WHITE

CHAPTER THIRTY NINE

INTUITION
Bemused, No More

WHILE THE LITERARY device of the muse and her godly gifts may sound romantic, it isn't my model for inspiration.

The Greek Muses were born to inspire the arts and learning—noble pursuits. They were the nine daughters of Zeus and Mnemosyne: Calliope (heroic poetry), Clio (history), Erato (love poetry), Euterpe (music and lyric poetry), Melpomene (tragedy), Polyhymnia (eloquence and sacred poetry), Terpsichore (dance), Thalia (comedy), and Urania (astronomy).

MISSING: A MUSE

In the Hellenic Greek model, the muses for both painters and sculptors are conspicuously absent. The Greek word for a painter or a sculptor was *banausos*, meaning a mechanic, a term that describes their modest social standing in that worldview from antiquity, which was based on a contempt for manual work and getting one's hands dirty—unless, of course, you were killing someone in battle. Supported by this bias, the ancient Greeks erroneously concluded that neither the painter nor the sculptor could be 'inspired' or work according to instinct or follow intuition. Given this enduring yet misguided Greek mindset, low-ranking painting and sculpture were segregated from poetry, music, dance, and theater, which were highly respected and deemed divinely inspired art forms that stood outside the rules governing mundane activity.

Remember too that the Golden Age of Greek democracy and citizenship flourished in a large part on the backs of slaves who did the menial labor. This ancient prejudice to a significant degree is still with us: white collar versus blue collar; decorative versus utilitarian; and fine arts versus crafts. For those artists feeling left out, take heart: the Apostle Luke is the patron saint of painters and sculptors.

The allegorical nature of the muse is certainly appealing, which is why these sisters of the pantheon persist into our time. The buildings that house art collections are, after all, called museums. While the muses of myth could inspire artists to great achievements, collectively these goddesses

If things are not happening the way you want, it may simply not be the right time. You may mistakenly be pushing. At such times we tend to accuse ourselves of inadequacy—of not taking the right actions or of not being clear enough about what we want.

If the universe has its own timing—which it does—you may do better to relax and accept the situation and yourself just as you are. Keep your focus on creating positive energy in every moment, recommit to attracting positive change, and surrender to the idea that a greater intelligence than yours is at work. Surrendering allows Spirit to have a free hand to create for us.

CAROL ADRIENNE

lacked a certain grace called humor. The muses were often jealous, vain, vindictive, nasty, and out for mortal blood. While you can cater to and tickle the fickle muse to inspire your work, it is much smarter (and safer) to go direct: trust your intuition for divine guidance and avoid any muse motivated hostilities.

THE CHOSEN

At the first stirrings of my art life, I thought I had heard the muses calling, beckoning me to write, enticing me to live a life independent of the suits and boots world of business and the imposed banality and routine of brunch on weekends.

Was I a walking advertisement for bourgeoisie superficiality, or was I an individual of discretion with a mission and a destiny to fulfill? Only my actions would answer this question.

After many years of heeding a voice, a feeling really, that only I could sense, I eventually had a realization: the goddess who encouraged me to swim upstream against the torrent of tradition and dogma wasn't a muse at all; that voice of challenge and encouragement had been my intuition, not an ancient and misguided construct from Greek mythology.

Although intuition is a faculty that has an assortment of definitions, varied interpretations generally agree that intuition is a form of knowing that transcends the rational process.

I have proven to my own self that intuition is the divine communicating directly to me—not because I am chosen, but because I choose to listen.

Still, my description remains abstract until you hear the song of intuition for your own self. And when you do, there is no need to define it further because you have struck bedrock; then you, like the painter and sculptor, have gotten your metaphysical hands dirty in the trenches of epistemology.

KNOW THY SELF

I have learned firsthand that intuition is this: the song of God singing through the soul to anyone willing to listen. Intuition is direct knowledge without cumbersome cognitive foreplay or a need for any type of filtration through the rational process—thinking. The preeminent question is this: How do I know it is my intuition and not some poser, aberration, or a psychological manifestation?

In the same way that you can't teach anyone to be an artist, you can't teach anyone to recognize his own intuition, which is ironic since intuition is the carrier wave of your authentic voice. You must discover intuition for yourself; and you will if that is your mission. After all, if you can't trust your own self, then no outside authority can do it for you. Your level of awareness is entirely up to you—as it has always been and as it always will be.

A parallel situation makes the point. How do you know that someone you had recently met is your friend? You don't. Friendship develops over time like a healthy garden. Eventually, a bond takes place and you begin to trust that person because he consistently proves his intention, veracity, and loyalty. Intuition employs precisely the same dynamic. While intuition may, as some report, surface in dreams, it is an open channel that is present at all times—asleep or awake.

If I had to give young writers advice, I would say don't listen to writers talking about writing or themselves.

LILLIAN HELLMAN

Zorba came upon an old man planting an apricot seedling and asked why he, an old man, was planting a new tree.

'I live life as though I would never die,' was his reply.

'And me, I live as though I might die tomorrow,' said Zorba, 'which one of us is right?'

NIKOS KAZANTZAKIS,
ZORBA THE GREEK

AN HONEST NOTE

Intuition isn't a thought; it is an impulse of energy that you interpret into feeling, into language, and then into a verbal instruction. Intuition is a truth, not a fact subject to modification. First, you listen. You feel the vibration, the magical pulse beating inside you about something from somewhere. Then, you act on what you sense is intuition.

Should you delay until you are one hundred percent certain, you will never act or develop this desirable and personal relationship, which depends upon spontaneity—not recklessness. If it pans out, you know you are in tune—no symphony yet, a single honest note will suffice for now. You must be brave to befriend intuition because you must have faith in your own self. To find that self takes dedication and a willingness to err in the process. As you come to trust in this relationship, the stronger you will become. Then, at some point you know it isn't mindless chatter or ego nonsense; you recognize intuition because you experience its infallibility. Your intuition communicates with you in direct proportion to your awareness; this is an immutable law you will grow to respect, love, and fully appreciate firsthand and over time.

IN NO TIME

The instantaneous transmission of information from the Cosmic Mind to you is transmitted through intuition; it takes no time at all, meaning that intuition is timeless, beyond reason, and the laws of known physics. You can't measure intuition with a ruler because it is transcendent.

Although intuition and thought are of a nonmaterial essence that can't be seen or weighed, they aren't synonyms. Intuition is proprietary, pure feeling, emotional intelligence for your soul only; intuition isn't a function of thinking. Intuition is God speaking exclusively to your higher self; intuition doesn't involve itself in ego-based desire, self-pity, deception, or nefarious plots. Thoughts are of a different order; they are utilitarian and democratic; they are swirling all around in the ether of potential; they aren't exclusive or meant for a specific individual as thoughts belong to any receptive mind that can snatch them into reality and practical application.

When people contemplate they sometimes come up with useful thoughts that are destined to be conceptual as they dwell to serve the world of ideas; thoughts, like quantum events in theoretical physics, take time to manifest, even if such time is measured in infinitesimal amounts that we are incapable of noticing let alone comprehending. As Dr. Deepak Chopra writes: "For what else is a thought but an impulse of energy and information?" Thoughts manifest themselves as language that you hear inside your head; they also appear alongside feelings in our dreams as images and sounds that aren't bound by limitations or the physical laws of our waking state. In our varied nocturnal scripts, we experience through our brains the animated pictographs of a dream as reality: we can fly, travel through time, alter history, resurrect loved ones, solve problems, and visit other dimensions.

The outer world is a symbolic reflection of our inner comprehension of consciousness and the self-imagery we cultivate in our dreams, everyday life, and art. Our response to both acceptance and rejection defines our inner truth, emotional solvency, and level of awareness.

The best index to a person's character is (a) how he treats people who can't do him any good, and (b) how he treats people who can't fight back.

ABIGAIL VAN BUREN

Emotional solvency represents metaphysical currency earned through self-discipline.

EDEN

Parents can only give good advice or put them on the right paths, but the final forming of a person's character lies in their own hands.

ANNE FRANK

QUEUING UP

We take vision for granted having forgotten that learning to see and making sense of the world is a complex evolutionary process that takes a lifetime. Thoughts are forceful as they find a way of surfacing despite perceived limitations. A person blind from birth, having no visual cues, has thoughts based on his available sensory experience of the world as well as dream narratives that reference a heightened awareness of taste, smell, locomotion, and the tactile. A feral child raised by wolves might think in keen sensory imagery, but his thoughts would be devoid of a human language and the words we take for granted. Do you recall when a certain fragrance triggered a memory of some important event in your life? While thoughts might congregate in the same transcendental space, you can't have—or be aware of—more than a single thought at a time. Think about it: although your thoughts seemingly flow without interruption in an endless fluid stream, they do so only in single file one after the other, which is our space-time experience of memory. Try thinking or talking about two things simultaneously. Try feeling two emotions at once. In its purest form, you can't feel how you think or think how you feel. Otherwise, both words would be redundant.

I am an artist, you say. Why should I concern myself with the difference between intuition and thought? It is too philosophical and not important to my work, you might also think. But it is important, and only your ego would attempt to steer you away from a philosophy that would keep it in check. To the point: freeing the mind of thought through whatever means creates the space for intuition to enter, which is the source of strength that defeats both rejection and gloating. As we know from practical experience, material things in our universe don't occupy the same space at the same time. Still, how often have you felt one way and responded with an opposite thought? 'Oh, yes, that dress looks great on you.' Is this remark hypocrisy, cowardice, or good people skills? Of course, such political largesse doesn't belong in art.

PATIENCE, NOT INERTIA

You have come this far. Resist your temptation to memorize things here as the quest for your dharma demands fearless dedication, not rote. Take the time now to digest new concepts in small bites until you comprehend them—experience the cause and effect for yourself. You can't put a rush on getting it. Why is intuition ethereal? Why isn't intuition more direct like feeling hunger? While these might be valid questions, let's be grateful for learning *how* to harness the direct power of intuition. Only the Maker knows *why*.

While intuition is instantaneous and infallible, you are not. Depending on your receptivity and ability to be still, intuition may take time to form as a complete picture, or instruction. Cream eventually rises to the top because it is rich, and it does so more easily when the rest of the brew is calm. With lots of stirring and agitation the cream will get lost, diluted, homogenized, and adulterated. You must be silent inside for the cream, the intuition in you, to surface. If you are disturbed and doubtful, intuition will confront the blockade of resistance that your demons have constructed with your own mortar. There is grace in relative patience. So, be patient. Knowing when the intuitive impulse of information has been delivered in its entirety takes practice and faith in your own self. To be patient and still doesn't imply inaction. Based on my own intuition, which was far from a complete message I could grasp at the time, I traveled far and often, and to many places during my more than twenty-year-long walkabout to discover that I was an artist. Both art and intuition require discretion—a quality earned through courage under fire, a test of character that can't be inherited, purchased, or taught academically.

You might still be thinking: Intuition. Thoughts. Ideas. What is the difference? I want to paint. I want to write. I want to act. I want to sing. I want to play the saxophone. I want to triumph over rejection. I'm not interested in labels, you might add, and defiantly so. If you aren't aware of the source of your talent, then it is unlikely that you will find fulfillment in it—and that is the reason to preemptively delineate these distinctions now, before going public, or to revitalize yourself if you have already embarked on the high road to selling your art. Benedetto Croce, the Italian critic, philosopher, politician, and historian believed intuition was the main source of artistic creation. In this sense, art is borne of intuition, which exists in the mind of God before an individual artist apprehends it. According to Croce, a poet realizes his intuition verbally, through the inner process of writing; poetry is emotion, an expression of the soul at the precise moment of intuition, which is beauty made manifest. Intellect serves intuition, not the other way around.

Genius in art is the result of emotional intelligence, which is our innate link to intuition, not a score on a mental abilities test where aptitude is measured as performance in an allotted time like a horse race.

MIND THE GAP

I discover the irrepressible truth about intuition each day, as it is my moral compass and the carrier wave of my art. However, for intuition to manifest itself requires a transition from the metaphysical to the physical: the intuitive strokes of my paintbrush must first pass through my awareness, down my arm to the hand that holds the brush, before making its mark on the canvas. All this happens without thinking and in nearly no time.

Intuition doesn't build to a crescendo like a thought struggling and stumbling toward clarity; intuition is suddenly there—boom—perfectly formed and fully realized. All this takes place in the nonmaterial space that exists between thoughts, or what Dr. Deepak Chopra describes as the gap—"the window, the corridor, the transformational vortex through which the personal psyche communicates with the cosmic psyche."

The gap is the incredible field where intuition resides, and possibilities thrive without limit. Releasing our attachment to a particular outcome in the gap frees us to cultivate and tend to our dreams as they blossom in the 'field of all possibilities'.

It is true. Intuition is instantaneous. But our bodies, our physical receivers need time to process this direct feed of information; and, as you may appreciate, thinking not only bogs down the intuitive process with hesitation,

Patience and perseverance have a magical effect before which difficulties disappear and obstacles vanish.

JOHN QUINCY ADAMS

If I have seen farther than others, it is because I was standing on the shoulder of giants.

ISAAC NEWTON

it corrupts the information with bias. In tennis or Kendo, for example, if you have to think about your next move, then you have already lost.

Returning a dazzlingly fast serve, or landing an effective sword strike demands a direct and unwavering reflex borne of natural ability, dedication, and training. In these physically intense activities, thinking not only inhibits reaction time, it discourages the impulsive grace of spontaneity. Art is no different.

If Picasso had saddled himself with thinking about and painstakingly planning each one of his canvases, he might have become yet another painter of religious scenes, which his father had envisioned for him, and not the prolific innovator that we know today. Let's not take art history and appreciation for granted either. Would a Stone Age protoartist have comprehended the work of Leonardo? Would Rubens have appreciated the nonobjective compositions of Kandinsky? Or is the evolving language of art understood only in retrospect?

ALIVE AND UNPREDICTABLE

My mission isn't only to make art, but also to ensure that ideas, thoughts, and concepts don't insidiously intrude upon and pose as intuitive creation, which will usurp the purity of the work. Art isn't a cerebral enterprise, which is why you can't instruct anyone on how to be an artist.

But why are ideas, thoughts, and concepts antithetical to creation, you might ask. Is a galaxy, a solar system, a supernova, a planet, or a moon an idea? These celestial events are aspects of spontaneous creation, a need to be born, not conceptualizing. Intuition is the instantaneous conduit for creation. And, thoughts, as we have seen, while suitable for certain tasks, are far too ponderous for others. If our bodies weren't equipped with an autonomic nervous system that bypasses thinking altogether, we would be unable to function. The larger universe is no different.

Art flows from the wellspring of creation to a destination as a form no one can predict; and it is the true artist who holds the divining rod. It took eons of evolution to place us in the enviable position of recognizing intuition, which is innate, but not inevitable. Without distinctions, there would be desert but no dessert. As the painter and teacher Hans Hofmann wrote more than half a century ago: "The creative process lies not in imitating, but in paralleling nature—translating the impulse received from nature into the medium of expression, thus vitalizing this medium. The picture should be alive, the statue should be alive and every work of art should be alive." God embodies the universe with life; the artist infuses his art with soul.

The next time you feel you are hearing the divine song of insight wafting through the ether, take a moment to identify the source. Don't become bemused by the cult of those archaic and fickle goddesses, for inspiration is the gift of your intuition. This knowledge has great liberating power.

Remember, the Creator speaks to us all in the same voice of feeling. In turn, we all laugh, smile, and cry in the same language.

A genuine audience of one is not to be taken for granted; it is a significant accomplishment and a welcome confirmation of your dharma.

In discussing the artistic collaboration between painters and poets, Visual Arts Professor Archie Rand feels that poets offer a parallel reaction to art that painters find extremely validating.

If one other person understands what a painter is doing, Rand says, the painter has created a viable language.

CHAPTER FORTY

FULLY REALIZED
The Dynamic of Needs

ANOMALY OR NOT, you are an artist who is part of the system. You can approach the system as a compliant cog, or as an independent force of nature capable of penetrating beneath the layers of subterfuge. If you want depth, you must dig deep. The system, whether it is cognizant of it or not, is either prejudiced or liberated by the psychology of the day.

While the great age-old ideological debates between philosophy and science, between cause and effect, and between feeling and thinking continue to shape, fold, spindle, and sometimes mutilate the public's perception of art, the values you hold as true depend solely upon your dedication for their existence.

> "I suppose it is tempting, if the only tool you have is a hammer, to treat everything as if it were a nail."
>
> —from *The Psychology of Science* by Abraham H. Maslow

As an artist whose work is innovative, and perhaps most susceptible to rejection, it is both wise and practical to have an informed perspective about the current zeitgeist, which may or may not be receptive to your philosophy, your art. While our society is far from utopian, we are nonetheless privileged to be alive in this age of wonder where ignorance and superstition can't survive prolonged exposure to the radiance of reason, communion, awareness, and truth. Information, however, has its dualistic downside counterpart: mass amounts are susceptible to disinformation and misinformation.

GOD BY THE YARD

Despite this potential for data corruption, the artist remains steadfast in his accountability: he takes responsibility for his behavior knowing it is the sole barometer of character. Truth, and it is universal truth that concerns us here, is where you find it. Not everyone, however, would agree that

> *It is always with excitement that I wake up in the morning wondering what my intuition will toss up to me, like gifts from the sea. I work with it and rely on it. It's my partner.*
>
> *When I worked on the polio vaccine, I had a theory. I guided each [experiment] by imagining myself in the phenomenon in which I was interested. The intuitive realm . . . the realm of the imagination guides my thinking.*
>
> *Intuition will tell the thinking mind where to look next.*
>
> JONAS SALK

The acid test regarding mental illness has to do with the processes directly responsible for creations. If mental illness were to impinge on these processes or, even more pertinent, if these processes had psychopathological roots, we could—with relief or celebration—demand that the question be closed.

But the specific creative processes I have described are not psychopathological in origin; they are at the opposite end of the spectrum.

ALBERT ROTHENBERG

the individual is responsible for his actions, or that universal truth exists. Most mainstream behavioral science limits its field to empirical data; if it can't be measured, it doesn't exist. This calculating approach excludes transcendental experience from the human equation. There are those psychologists who argue that as yet unexplained phenomena or unusual experiences, which include variously described examples of psychic, coincidental, supernatural, magical, and intuitive events are either somehow precursors to their theories at best, or symptoms of a mental disorder at worst. Such wholesale thinking, as sincere and as economical as it might appear, erroneously dismisses the innate value of the metaphysical, and the spiritual that manifests itself as art.

Fortunately, not all scientific disciplines are in agreement. What if you raised the bar for what constitutes empirical data? Could we then liberate the mystique of the transcendental experience from the asylum? Could we then see that an artist need not be 'mad' to create? Could we then see that a troubled artist creates in spite of his madness, not because of it? Of course, we could, but will we? Will you?

UNCONTAMINATED EYES

Evolution of the individual is a basic concept of Humanistic Psychology and what one of its principal founders Abraham Maslow (1908-1970) called the fully realized human being. In his book, *The Psychology of Science*, Maslow wrote: "Long ago I learned from my artist-wife of her irritation with some of my scientist's obsessional classifying ways. For example, I asked always, in a kind of conversational tic, for the name of the bird or the flower or the tree that I admired. It was as if I were not content to admire and to enjoy but also had to do something intellectual about it." Maslow had realized that analysis was no substitute for the aesthetic experience.

Maslow also describes how much more he appreciated a drawing before he knew who the artist was. His preconceptions weren't in play to cloud his experience, which is the way to explore art and life. Experiencing with uncontaminated eyes and feelings opens up the dialog between the artist and the participant—your audience. Maslow concluded his confession with: "This fresh and defamiliarized experiencing becomes easy for any person as soon as he has sense enough to realize that it is more fun to live in a world of miracles than in a world of filing cabinets and that a familiar miracle is still a miracle." To classify in lieu of perceiving is as Maslow observed, "a form of blindness."

It takes passion to pierce the veil of social conditioning. If you are too busy to discover art for yourself, you will think that you had an experience, which is a thought about the experience, and not the aesthetic experience itself. Remember, in its purest form, you can't feel how you think, and you can't think how feel.

NEEDS ARE NOT WANTS

When your work isn't accepted and you feel down, then you need to understand the score. Throwing your hands up in the air while invoking that the world doesn't understand or appreciate you is a delusional lament only an ego would invent. Self-pity won't do you justice. You discarded victimhood the moment you picked up this book. When your art is rejected, your needs aren't getting fulfilled. The letdown reaches beyond a missed payday as your soul has been exposed to the fallout of rejection.

If you intend on prevailing, comprehending the dynamics of *needs* is in order; some understand this dynamic intuitively while most do not. There is no glory in self-imposed shortsightedness or ignorance. Needs aren't *wants*; this is a distinction that must be learned. While you may want a car to take you somewhere, you need your feet to take you anywhere.

To counterbalance rejection, a reward system of achievement must be in place. Trustworthy information and knowledge are a good beginning. While the Law of Non-Attachment is your metaphysical writ to freedom from lingering angst, you can't deny your psychological makeup, which seeks out recognition—if the truth be revealed.

As in every story, the hero (Isn't that you?) must have a sense of intermittent accomplishment along the way toward fulfilling the objective; if not, he will eventually quit, and the aborted mission will end in tragedy. Every journey of discovery needs a port in the storm, and a means for gauging progress through adversity. This is the myth of the hero.

If you are climbing a mountain, you need respites along the way; you also look down occasionally to confirm that you are farther from the bottom and nearer to the summit than when you had begun your ascent.

LIFE AS A TURNIP

In 'The Eighteen Be-Attitudes', I describe the attributes of an artist who has acquired the means to overcome rejection, acceptance, or any other potentially destabilizing event that confronts his character and the integrity of his work. This artist understands the distinction between needs and wants. To succeed in a healthy way, choosing a model worthy of your commitment is essential. The operative word here is 'model', an exemplary model that you can live up to and be proud of.

Each age has had a model, or archetype that represented the zeitgeist of the times—from the hero, the saint, the martyr, the knight, the renaissance man, the explorer, the gentleman, the mystic, to more recent media-spawned phenomena in the guise of the film or rock star who is more admired than the humanitarian; and, to further reveal society's conceit, the cult-worship of youth and surface appearance has become the mainstream idolatry. This is the climate of prevailing values in which you must persevere.

In the wilds of untamed nature, working together in groups for survival is essential. After the physical and biological necessities are fulfilled, including food, shelter, and sex, what then? 'Is that all there is?' is the lament, with deference to Peggy Lee, in any language.

Once the perception of community (marriage) and continuity (babies) is met, the only thing left is to evolve, to transcend, to make the best of your lot, to seek out truth (art) and create meaning in this existence. Otherwise, you might as well have been born a turnip. However, to be an edible root has its place, too.

Everything in the here and now begins or ends with the availability of energy, food, or fuel—this is a truth, or universal law that nature exacts to the letter.

I start with the premise that the function of leadership is to produce more leaders, not more followers.

RALPH NADER

There are no rules. That is how art is born, how breakthroughs happen. Go against the rules or ignore the rules. That is what invention is about.

HELEN FRANKENTHALER

Keep your fears to yourself, but share your inspiration with others.

ROBERT LOUIS STEVENSON

Everywhere I go I find that a poet has been there before me.

SIGMUND FREUD

ALL IN A MAZE

Sometime in the late 1930's, Maslow had a surprisingly original insight: modern psychology is based on the study of the abnormal and the ill. To provide a better picture of the human mind and what constituted positive mental health, he was convinced that it was fundamentally more illuminating to study healthy people. He was keen to explore why things work, not why they don't—this wasn't the common wisdom then, nor is it now more than a half-century later. No slave to clinical dogma, Maslow built upon scientific tradition while discarding the irrelevant. There is an art to observing behavior; rigid thinking can easily edit out the spirit of a meaningful conclusion. Commenting on the individual as an integrated entity, an organized whole, he said: "When a man is hungry he's hungry all over; he himself wants food, not just his stomach." Maslow's theories not only helped formulate the direction psychology would take into the 21st century, they influenced other traditional fields, including the law, education, and management.

In his 1954 book, *Motivation & Personality,* Maslow proposed that all humans are motivated by the same species-wide set of core human needs. Taken on this proposition alone, this wasn't scientific heresy; but Maslow, the brilliant loner, was reaching further: he suggested that since consciousness was an integral source of human behavior, it *was* a category for scientific exploration. Maslow pressed beyond himself and what had preceded him. His integrated humanistic approach was avant-garde and certainly not part of mainstream psychology. At that time, most psychologists and psychiatrists could trace their inclinations to either the Austrian neurologist Sigmund Freud (1856-1939) or the American psychologist John B. Watson (1878-1958).

Freud believed man was in constant conflict with society; a virtuous person represses his impulses while a sinful person enjoys them. Watson, who experimented with rat behavior, extrapolated his findings to describe human behavior. Watson felt that under the right conditions he could train any human to fulfill any task. Realize that these two men also had influences that formed their outlook on human behavior and life. Accept nothing that doesn't *feel* right. While there are many theories about the process of thought and feeling, your intuition is a metaphysical instrument for divining temporal reality and transcendent truth.

LADDER TO SELF-ACTUALIZATION

The centerpiece of Maslow's worldview was man's hierarchy of needs, which, when taken as a gestalt, was a deceptively simple and innovative tool for baring the bones of human motivation.

These sets of needs were broken down into five sets of goals, which Maslow arranged on a ladder in order of importance: physiological, safety, love, esteem, and self-actualization or self-fulfillment. On the bottom rung were the physical and most basic needs: air, water, food, and sex. Safety needs such as security and stability came next; then came psychological, or social needs for belonging, love, and acceptance. At the top rung were the self-actualizing needs, the need to fulfill one's self—what I refer to as dharma in this book. (Respect your intuition first, and the form of your purpose will follow.) Maslow felt that unfulfilled needs lower on the ladder would inhibit the person from climbing to the next step. Someone dying of thirst quickly forgets their thirst when they have no oxygen, as he pointed out. Those who reached the higher needs were what he called self-actualizing people.

Maslow also cautioned against viewing the hierarchy of needs too precisely. One must not assume that needs don't emerge out of step or overlap or become a secondary issue, as in someone risking his life to save another. Although art fits neatly on the pinnacle rung of needs, let's not forget the creator who denies himself certain lower needs to make art. By being productive and self-referential, the artist satisfies his self-esteem needs; self-respect takes precedence over accolades others may provide.

To enjoy the respect and appreciation of others is no vice; to evaluate your worth by them is the trap.

Maslow concluded that self-actualizing people tend to focus on problems outside of themselves, have a clear sense of what is true and what is phony, are spontaneous and creative, and aren't bound too strictly by social conventions—characteristics which you must embody to defy rejection.

Remember, while tags may be useful for isolating needs and subsequent behavior, a person isn't a label—unless, of course, he becomes a brand like van Gogh, Picasso, Andy Warhol, or Jackson Pollock where the work is acquired as much, or perhaps more so, for the name as for the art.

FREUD'S UNCONSCIOUS

To Freud, who was primarily interested in the mentally disturbed, man's essential behavior was the uninhibited expression of the animal drive for survival. Freud held that values weren't innate or divinely inspired 'shoulds' and 'should nots'; our sense of right and wrong was the result of evolutionary-based instinctual drives of associative learning; morality was the result of hard-earned human experience, not the word of God; and, given this theory, values were a variable not appropriate for consideration in scientific research.

In addition to man's conscious mind, according to Freud, there is an unconscious mind that influences his behavior.

Man, who is frequently controlled by unconscious conflicts, is also most often completely unaware of them. To gain access into the unconscious realm of his patients, Freud introduced two techniques: free association, where the patient reveals whatever thoughts enter his mind while he is relaxing, and the analysis of dreams, where the unconscious mind reveals itself in a disguised manner.

Today, such Freudian terms as ego, repression, the unconscious, projection, Oedipus Complex, inhibition, neurosis, psychosis, resistance, Freudian slip, and sibling rivalry continue to infuse not only the study of human behavior, but also literature, education, sociology, and the law. Agree with him or not, Freud also experienced many disappointments and rejections in his life. When his opus, *The Interpretation of Dreams*, was first published in 1900, it was a flop. Not everyone agreed with Freud then, or now. He was desperate; he had a family to support.

Still, he continued. That is the lesson.

The very essence of leadership is that you have to have a vision.

THEODORE HESBURGH

We can appreciate Freud's conclusions about human behavior; after all, history is a timeline mostly strewn with fear, doubt, anxiety, and aggression.
Fortunately, this self-defeating view of existence can be altered through awareness in the Zen Buddhist sense.

EDEN

Leaders aren't born they are made. And they are made just like anything else, through hard work. And that's the price we'll have to pay to achieve that goal, or any goal.

VINCE LOMBARDI

JUNG'S COLLECTIVE UNCONSCIOUS

Carl Jung (1875-1961) was one of Freud's younger colleagues who broke away from Freudian psychoanalysis over the nature of the unconscious mind. Freud said the unconscious was a reservoir of repressed sexual trauma that causes all neuroses. Jung felt the terrain of the unconscious was far richer and more positive, and not limited to personal issues. Jung said the unconscious wasn't "… a cauldron of seething desires, a bottomless pit of perverse and incestuous cravings, a burial ground for frightening experiences which nevertheless come back to haunt us." Jung had a lifelong interest in mythology, religion, and philosophy. He was also well versed in the symbolism of complex mystical and occult practices of his culture, including similar traditions in Hinduism and Buddhism. To more precisely understand human behavior, he contributed the holistic terms 'synchronicity' and the 'collective unconscious' to the modern lexicon.

Synchronicity, which is acausal, explained "meaningful coincidences" while the collective unconscious, which contained the universal archetypes of man, was, among other things, the wellspring of art. Jung's notion of the self-realized person has much in common with the self-actualized person as Maslow described him.

As the self-described alchemist of the human soul, Jung wasn't without his detractors since he couldn't empirically prove many of his assertions. According to the establishment, mysticism, the occult, and pseudoscience have no place in science. While Jung could be criticized for his 'unfounded' claims, his contributions in broadening our collective understanding of human behavior can't be dismissed. Among the short list of innovators in psychology, Jung especially understood art and the artist on an intuitive level, a distinction and comprehension appreciated by those who realize transcendental knowing isn't theory, science, or pseudoscience; practical metaphysical experience is no less existential than facts gleaned from the empirical world. In the 1940's, Jackson Pollock, in an attempt to confront the demons of his alcoholism, underwent Jungian analysis and produced a series of drawings that would later divulge aspects of his unconscious process. About the same time, the painter Mark Rothko, who was interested in expressing "basic human emotions—ecstasy, tragedy, doom" was profoundly intrigued with symbols and felt his paintings were reflective of the collective unconscious.

As Jung concluded: "Anyone who wants to know the human psyche will learn next to nothing from experimental psychology. He would be better advised to abandon exact science, put away his scholar's gown, bid farewell to his study, and wander with human heart through the world. There in the horrors of prisons, lunatic asylums and hospitals, in drab suburban pubs, in brothels and gambling-hells, in the salons of the elegant, the stock exchanges, socialist meetings, churches, revivalist gatherings and ecstatic sects, through love and hate, through the experience of passion in every form in his own body, he would reap richer stores of knowledge than textbooks a foot thick could give him, and he will know how to doctor the sick with a real knowledge of the human soul."

Of course, as profound as Freud's theories are, they isolate a human being into various psychological realms while focusing much on what happened in the individual's past to explain his present behavior. Freud saw psychology as a science of the interior mind that was useful for diagnosing and helping people deal with neuroses, or mental and emotional disorders. Even though Freud's premise is ingrained in our culture, we are also free to conclude that he might not be right. After all, given Freudian treatment over all these years, is the community of psychologically troubled people better off in any way? Once accepted, a theory of the mind, a political ideology, or a painting becomes, for better or worse, part of the establishment.

REJECTING CONSCIOUSNESS

The Behaviorists felt that man has no inner self directing him to act in certain ways; all behavior is externally motivated and reinforced through punishment and reward; and the goal of psychology was a means to an end in removing man's antisocial behavior and to improve the species through social conditioning and behavioral engineering.

To Behaviorists like John B. Watson, man's behavior could be reduced, measured, and explained by chemical and physical phenomena; like Freud, the vast majority of behavioral scientists considered values as completely outside the scientific study of human nature; they stressed the importance of external and environmental influences while deeming subjective desire and purpose as irrelevant. The world according to the Behaviorists wouldn't include the soul or that there was a transcendental meaning to life. Watson and his followers rejected the idea that consciousness could be studied scientifically. If psychology were to be a science, the Behaviorists concluded it must limit itself to the study of overt (observable) quantifiable behavior. Tossing and turning in your sleep, for example, is behavior, but a dream isn't behavior. The Behaviorists weren't interested in what people thought; they were only interested in what they did. In this regard the Behaviorists and I have common ground to this extent: a person's character is the result of his actions. Since mental processes are private experiences that can't be seen or touched, the Behaviorists decided that values and feelings couldn't be examined scientifically. In turn, they limited themselves to observing muscular movements and other bodily activities that can be seen or measured or detected with instruments.

Freud and Watson represented a manifestation of the collective thoughts, feelings, and aspirations of their age. They had a platform because they eventually found an audience. Despite their overall dismissal of values in the study of human behavior, this doesn't mean a Freudian or Behaviorist didn't feel or express love or grief or wonder; it meant these experiences as values or preferences couldn't be scientifically measured. Freud and the Behaviorists did want to expand man's knowledge of himself and, in turn, improve the 'quality' of life. But their convictions, as sincere as they might be, didn't make them right. They were looking out at the field of human behavior from their own windows. What was needed next was to get out of the house of bias and limitation, and climb on the roof to see what was what.

SPURIOUS NOTIONS

Prior to 1900, psychology had been primarily a subject for religious and philosophical debate as it confronted the mind, body, and soul. Then, as

Nobody made a greater mistake than he who did nothing because he could do only a little.

EDMUND BURKE

If I am a thinking being, I must regard life other than my own with equal reverence, for I shall know that it longs for fullness and development as deeply as I do myself. Therefore, I see that evil is what annihilates, hampers, or hinders life …

Goodness, by the same token, is the saving or helping of life, the enabling of whatever life I can to attain its highest development.

ALBERT SCHWEITZER,
PHILOSOPHY OF CIVILIZATION, 1923

psychology grew from philosophy into 'pure' science, anything that sounded scientific could still be easily embraced for particular motives, including those that were less than pristine. In the 19th century, for example, phrenology had its audience as did, to a lesser degree, the ethically spurious notion of eugenics, which the Nazi's later co-opted and politicized as a race purifier during the Second World War.

The science of human behavior in the early part of the 20th century represents a great leap forward from the dark ages of religious dogma and superstition; unfortunately, the scientific study of human behavior also, as we have seen, relegated transcendental human experience to the irrelevant bin. In addition, the secular schools of thought as expressed by Freud and Watson ignited the great debate between science and feeling, and what made knowledge and truth possible; and this would include the meaning of art. As you might suspect, these two scientific views of man as a creature driven solely by animal-like impulses wouldn't embrace the concept of spirit, dharma, freedom, personal responsibility, the existential theist, mysticism, or Zen, which instructs that absolute knowing, or truth is beyond reason; truth is gained directly from intuition.

While the scientific method sincerely espouses that empirical evidence is the only way to knowledge, it is yet another form of dogma wearing a different collar and white coat. The ongoing argument between science and feeling—intuitive knowing—is a red herring in this sense: those who truly know don't try to convert those who think they know.

Don't get caught in the crosshairs of this no win argument. Those who can't yet acknowledge universal truth, self-determination, meaning, soul, and the significance of virtues in the realm of human behavior must pay to play by their own rules; they may be so inured to the miracle that they will never accept the truth. Your mission as an artist is to remain aware, and to avoid seduction by any form of social conditioning that would imprison you and taint your art. Remember, Freud and Watson theorized a point of view, not the gospel. Jung, to his credit, invited you to investigate and see the human condition for your own self.

Man had little to say about his own fate, so say the Freudians and the Behaviorists. The system of dharma escaped them. In general, they saw mankind as a creature who, despite his evolved nature, was a biological slave to the stimulus-response model of life; and, to a meaningful extent, there is no denying that this is so. In their psychology, however, there is no inherent good or evil, only survival—nothing more. This is a cold view of the world, and perhaps even an accurate one, but to a point. After all, some children are born with a developed conscience in place while others need to learn right from wrong. While man is presently on the top rung of the food chain, he has more than a capacity to rise above his primeval instincts; he has over many millennia developed the need to make art, to meet his Maker as an evolving spirit. Otherwise, what is the point?

ONLY WHEN I LAUGH

There is more than one type of pain; there is physical and psychic suffering. Artists who surrender to the throes of disappointment and rejection succumb to uncertainty, fear, regret, and the inevitability of failure.

Age, too, is the great equalizer, a degenerative force that is inescapable, unless, of course, you can stop time. (If you could travel at the speed of light, it is theoretically possible that you wouldn't age and would exist forever.) Conversely, pain is also useful as the body's early warning system; pain warns you that your fingers are in the fire. Angst tells you that you are in the belly of the beast—in the midst of a life lesson.

> "God does not reward or punish you. He has given you the power to reward or punish yourself by the use or misuse of your own reason and will power. If you transgress the laws of health, prosperity, and wisdom you must inevitably suffer from sickness, poverty, and ignorance. However, you should strengthen your mind and refuse to carry the burden of mental and moral weaknesses acquired in past years; burn them in the fires of your present divine resolutions and right activities. By this constructive attitude you will attain freedom."
>
> —from *The Law of Success* by Paramahansa Yogananda

Why do bad things happen to good people is the flip side of why do good things happen to bad people. Neither one is the right question. The vanguard question is this: Why does joy, pain and suffering exist at all?

In his book, *Siddhartha*, Hermann Hesse writes: "Some Samanas once passed through Siddhartha's town. Wandering ascetics, they were three thin worn-out men, neither old nor young, with dusty and bloody shoulders, practically naked, scorched by the sun, solitary, strange and hostile—lean jackals in the realm of men. Around them hovered an atmosphere of still passion, of devastating service, of unpitying self-denial."

Over 2,500 years ago, the twenty-nine old prince Siddhartha renounced a life of privilege to fulfill his destiny, his dharma, which was to find the true keys to the kingdom—to solve the questions of the four sufferings: birth, old age, sickness and death. After six years of living life as a Samana, he realized, when it came to the needs of the body, the answer was the 'middle way', the path that lies between the 'two extremes'—that of asceticism, ignoring pain and self-mortification, and that of sensual self-indulgence, which is vulgar and laced with insidious repercussions.

On that day when the sun set as the moon rose, Siddhartha attained enlightenment under the Bodhi tree; he awoke to become the Buddha; he awoke from the stupor of illusion to the truth of reality as it is; he didn't explain the reason or the why of pain, which is unknowable; he saw the intuitive truth of suffering: everywhere there is pain, suffering, uncertainty, impermanence, death, and karma. Suffering is part of life in the everyday world, and the only thing we can do is to have less of it. The middle path was the enlightened path for living.

As Zoketsu Norman Fischer teaches: "And seeing all of that he understood how the world was. He understood that the nature of all conditioned things is suffering, and that the root cause of this suffering is mistaken, misplaced desire based on the foundation of ignorance about who we really are. And he saw that once this foundation crumbled suffering would end and there could be peace in the warmth of awakening. And he saw stretching before

I have always believed, and I still believe, that whatever good or bad fortune may come our way we can always give it meaning and transform it into something of value.

HERMANN HESSE

Evil is within us, so why not ignore and defuse it with the amazing brilliance of awareness.

EDEN

Everybody can be great ... because anybody can serve. You don't have to have a college degree to serve. You don't have to make your subject and verb agree to serve. You only need a heart full of grace. A soul generated by love.

MARTIN LUTHER KING, JR.

him the path that led to this awakening. He could see all its byways and bends and twists. And after that he could see the pattern of causation—how things came to be the way they are and how people mistook the freedom that is the nature of our real life for the binding quality of attachment and ignorance and how this went on and on and on and on and how it could be undone and undone and undone. And this is what the Buddha saw the night of his awakening. And he looked up and saw the morning star and his path was complete."

THE GOLDEN PATH

To avoid long-term suffering, and artists are especially prone to this form of sustained agony, one must dutifully examine his actions daily. The 1957 film *Wild Strawberries* from Swedish director Ingmar Bergman drives this point home in indelible black and white. Bergman's film is essentially a road picture about disillusionment and redemption. Every artist would do well to see this cinematic masterpiece. If you examine your life near the end, then you might realize it would have been much smarter to self-adjust your decisions along the way to avoid the trap set by regret. In this film, auteur Bergman explores the disenchantment of Professor Isak Borg, an elderly physician who reflects upon his life and mortality. As the doctor travels to Lund for an honorary award after fifty years of medical practice, he finds himself repeatedly haunted by dreams and hallucinations that expose his darkest fears. He comes to realize that the choices he made in the past have created an empty life, devoid of meaning or value. Similar themes of alienation, self-deception, and 'quiet desperation' were also explored in the 1886 novel *The Death of Iván Ilych* by Leo Tolstoy where the main character confronts the painful meaning of a life misspent, which is *the* tragedy. Ultimately, Bergman's story isn't one of total misfortune. Professor Borg achieves redemption through forgiveness and the love of his family.

In the Four Noble Truths, Buddha identified the reality of suffering; then, in the Noble Eightfold Path he described how to free oneself from suffering. It is seeing things as they truly are combined with compassion that leads us to this golden path—and to art. The remedy Buddha offered for suffering and pain is the disillusion of self-centered (ego) craving and the release of attachment. It is often and erroneously repeated that one must suffer for his art; the truth of it is this: one suffers until he finds his art (purpose), his dharma, not afterwards.

As Buddha taught, unfulfilled desire causes pain; the cure then is to fulfill these desires with awareness and tranquility, not worry and restlessness. Appreciate then the wisdom of the Law of Non-Attachment where you emancipate yourself from any particular outcome; no longer a slave to rigidity, through right action you allow the desire, like a seed, to fulfill its purpose spontaneously, organically, and when it is ready. After all, what is the point of enduring pain if you won't use it to connect with consciousness by getting smarter, stronger, and more resilient? Unfortunately, pain teaches, joy doesn't. If there is anything that separates us from one another, it is different states of perceiving consciousness, not artificial borders. Art portrays consciousness in physical form; art is real estate.

LEFT BRAIN OPERATIVES

Of course, while Freud and Watson might resonate with the pragmatic cause and effect teachings of Buddha, his 'awakening' to the truth wouldn't be entered as supporting evidence for anything. Science demands repeatable, observable, and measurable facts. This is certainly understandable when you are dealing with physics, chemistry, or biology; but, as you might already suspect, transcendental matters march to a beat that can't be orchestrated in advance.

If I told a group of researchers, who were analytical left-brain operatives, that this painting of mine is the result of my intuition and not thinking, they wouldn't accept my process. The painting, the finished *observable* object would still not be proof enough; the description of my experience wouldn't be proof enough. An experience or a feeling expressed by an individual has no weight in a world that would measure the meaning of existence and God with a ruler; but miracles do happen despite naysayers, studies, or rhetoric to the contrary. When you witness a miracle for your own self, you realize faith isn't blind; it is a function of proof. If you accept hearsay as evidence, then it is what it sounds like. If you doubt the miracle of life, it is time to take your pulse.

ON THE COUCH

A Freudian psychoanalyst might say art is a manifestation representative of neurotic excellence, perhaps an ongoing portrait of some inner conflict, or even a form of therapy, which does contain a point: art as an act of creation is a conduit to the soul, and contact with the soul heals. But art prescribed to exorcise one's demons or improve one's sense of self-worth is therapy, and another topic entirely.

Researchers from the behavior school of psychology wouldn't be interested in what I thought at all since thinking, or not thinking, and feeling can't be neatly measured with instruments. Should our psychoanalyst in this case work from his assumptions and relegate the transcendental experience of accessing consciousness for making art to be a learned behavior, he would be in error.

This we know: you can't teach anyone to be an artist; you can't teach anyone to be herself, but a great teacher can unleash the power of creation in a worthy student. Think it through, free your mind, and see that this is so. The soul of art is uniqueness, not conformity, which places it outside the realm of 'predictability'.

It is *art*, after all, not science.

To analyze art means to miss the point of art. One appreciates the art, not the analysis. Telling a Freudian or a Behaviorist that I experienced a miracle isn't sufficient; they wouldn't accept my word, which would be classified as a value judgment; they are either looking for defined mental disorders, sexual urges, dream analysis, or repeatable results and clinical trials that would neatly confine miracles inside a box of quantifiable certainty, which is impossible in the quantum world of chance and synchronicity. No universal art would exist without this force we call passion, which is measured from the heart chakra. Without passion there is no dedication, and without dedication there is no genius.

> *Art is unique; art also never becomes obsolete, which is one test that artists can apply to the truth of their work; art lovers are welcome to this parity of understanding.*
>
> EDEN

As Zen Buddhism masters over the ages have so clearly and beautifully demonstrated: The realm of intuition and the human spirit is not subject to dogma, theories, or finite empirical measurements of the laboratory.

THE NEED FOR BEAUTY

Maslow wrote in his 1966 book, *The Psychology of Science*: "When my work [1935] in psychology led me to explore nonpathology—psychologically healthy people—difficulties came up that I had never had to face before, problems of values and of norms, for instance… The study of these relatively healthy people and their characteristics opened up dozens of new problems for me both personally and as a scientist, and it made me dissatisfied with dozens of old solutions and methods and concepts that I had taken for granted. These people raised new questions about the nature of normality, of health, of goodness, of creativeness and love, of higher needs, beauty, curiosity, fulfillment, of heroes and the godlike in human beings, of altruism and co-operativeness, of love for the young, protection of the weak, compassion and unselfishness and humanitarianism, of greatness, of transcendent experiences, of higher values."

While the Freudians were psychoanalyzing, the Behaviorists were running their animal studies, each determined to make their case about the sum total of human behavior by dissecting it; neither discipline, however, despite their far-reaching influence into the 21st century, incorporated the value of man's transcendence, or acknowledged a higher power.

As two influential forces of the day, Freud and the Behaviorists did, however, pave the way for Humanistic Psychology, Maslow's 'third force' for championing a more holistic approach, which holds that the whole is more than the sum of its parts, also known as synergy. Maslow had an expanded vision beyond man's primordial nature; you might say he also recognized that man had a soul, even if he couldn't extract it from the body like an organ and say, 'here it is.'

Although the Behaviorists saw in man no innate or instinctual need for beauty, Maslow surmised to the contrary. He felt that by becoming exceedingly pragmatic, psychology avoids the human experience of pleasure, fun, play, beauty, art, joy, love, and happiness.

He found that the need for beauty in some individuals was so deep that ugliness made them sick. His experiments showed that the effects of ugliness were dulling and stultifying.

According to Maslow, you need beauty as much as you need calcium; beauty contributes to one's better health; and aesthetic needs are related to one's self-image. Those who aren't made healthier by beauty are limited by low images of themselves.

As the poet Tagore observed: "When you feel beauty, you will know it as truth."

Since moral and spiritual problems, including truth, fall within the realm of nature, Maslow considers them part of science, not opposing domains. He said that science, in its role as a social institution and as a human enterprise, does have goals, ethics, morals, purposes—or, in simplest terms, values—which both Freud and Watson excluded from the scientific study of human behavior.

Life is the only real counselor; wisdom unfiltered through personal experience does not become a part of the moral tissue.

EDITH WHARTON

AGE OF CREATION

Are we born with a truth detector, or must we develop this potentiality over time as we do character? Anthropologist Ellen Dissanayake, author of *Art and Intimacy: How the Arts Began*, writes: "Many people are surprised to learn that 'innate' does not mean 'inevitable.' Most innate aptitudes in humans require fostering—a child who never hears language will not learn to speak; someone who lives in a desert will not learn to swim; women who have never been around babies will not instinctively know how to care for them. Yet speaking, swimming, and mothering are all evolved ('innate') propensities—things we will normally learn to do."

Maslow had the courage to confront the establishment thinking of Freudianism and the Behaviorists with his innovative view of human motivation. What he was accumulating empirically, the self-actualized person (the artist who has adopted The Eighteen Be-Attitudes) intuitively knew to be so. After the interior man of Freud and the exterior man of Watson, it was time to see beyond the separation between the inside and the outside. As Maslow proposed, the integrated human can't be understood by compartmentalizing him. This is also synergy: you can't predict the behavior of the whole by examining its individual parts.

Of course, let's unveil the best of man and all that makes him a wonder to be admired; let's embrace the universal insights of Buddha; let's build upon Maslow's work and that of others who bring light to the inner magic of creators who are also healthy people—models for the age of creation. Studying behavior with an open mind and with the best of intentions, however, can only give us facts and perhaps even measurable data. While psychology studies and describes human behavior, psychology isn't human behavior in the same way that art history isn't art; musicology isn't music; and the quest for the self isn't ego. Don't mistake the conceptualizing, study, class or category for the experience.

NEW AGE, ART & IDEOLOGY

As we have seen, the story and study of human behavior is based on a hierarchy of needs, and needs are the basis for evolution. Nothing ever came into being without purpose, experimental or otherwise. In ancient times, Buddha described our collective understanding of suffering and its root cause—craving, and its subsequent dire yet preventable consequences of pain and anguish. In recent memory, the progression from Freud and Behaviorism to Maslow and Humanistic Psychology culminated with a broader view that accepted values and transcendence as part of a quantifiable human reality; and this, in turn, fueled the thirst for the 'personal growth' that germinated in the late 1960's and later flowered into the 'New Age', which was hardly new.

Often rooted in ancient traditions, esoteric practices, and mystical experiences, this freewheeling New Age movement embraced the gamut of experience, a catchall of beliefs, sound and otherwise—from tarot cards to aromatherapy, to astrology, auras, and psychic revelation, to secrets from Atlantis, and to an artist from South America who claimed to channel the great artists from the past in his paintings. During this time of uncertainty, turbulence, political unrest, and spiritual crises, mainstream institutions

Besides the noble art of getting things done, there is the noble art of leaving things undone. The wisdom of life consists in the elimination of non-essentials.

LIN YUTANG

The tighter you squeeze, the less you have.

ZEN PROVERB

Without hyperbole, indoctrination, or the need for years of training in a monastery, the kiteflier takes the line and instantaneously becomes one with the kite.

This is the Tao of kites, the irreducible arrangement of opposing forces that connect the flier to nature—the source of all that is.

EDEN

weren't providing satisfying answers; old-guard ideas were being rejected as new-old paradigms were accepted and resurrected. The inherent grass-roots movement of the New Age as a catalyst was a need, a hunger for a holistic view to explain the human condition and to find meaning in life—longings that haunt the world to this day; longings that art was born to both question and answer.

POSTMODERN BLUES

In the Western world, art movements from modern to postmodern came and waned: from impressionism to expressionism, from art deco to art nouveau, from cubism to surrealism, from abstract expressionism to minimalism, from conceptualism to pop art—to the art zeitgeist of today, which, having no convenient container, or 'ism', or art movement cachet per se, many contend is a mere fusion of styles glimmering to us from the past, or worse: an art that has been co-opted for political ideology or for shock value—which is what it sounds like.

Art critic Hilton Kramer writes: "I think we're all aware of the catastrophe—not only an aesthetic catastrophe but a moral and ethical catastrophe—that's overtaken the art institutions and the teaching of art. One of the principal results of this catastrophe has been the transformation of the art museum in the last 30 years or so into a politically activist institution, ideologically bound to the worst new developments and leftist cultural criticism—that whole array of idiocies that goes under the name of post-modernism. So let me say here, there is no such thing as postmodernism, it's all warmed-over Marxism, deconstruction, and other varieties of nihilism. Postmodernism is an ideological construction that allows the substitution of political, sexual, all kinds of other ideas, for esthetic standards. The museums, the art history departments, the art studio departments in the universities, the media, all have surrendered to this juggernaut."

ART BY COMBAT

Taking combative conceptual positions in the arena of art as part of an opportunistic strategy may bring an artist media attention, and even coveted grants. Such contrivance, however, results in a pyrrhic victory of sorts, as it is the authentic artist and the public who gets burned in the process.

Lynne Munson, cultural critic, author of *Exhibition: art in the era of intolerance,* and an 'art war correspondent' provides us with astute observations from the trenches as posted on the Independent Women's Forum website:

"Few people would disagree that the art wars of the last decade have been driven less by reason than by rage. Each controversy has packed a fury so fierce that it made these art wars resemble military engagements more than intellectual arguments. In fact, I've put together a short chronicle of the ongoing conflict. We started out with the Battle of Piss Christ, then we had Mapplethorpe's Last Stand, the Finley Offensive and most recently I'm sure you all will remember the Great Dung War.

"Now each of these skirmishes was sparked by art that was crafted to provoke the public. After all, the fluid in Andres Serrano's infamous image would have been unidentifiable had the artist not gone out of his way to title the work *Piss Christ*. If its pachyderm waste had not brought wrath down upon Chris Ofili's *Holy Virgin Mary*, the pornography that the artist collaged all over and around the icon would have.

"To varying degrees, the artists who start these art wars are exhibitionists, baiting public sensibility in order to call attention to themselves. These 'shock' artists are actually the new academy. The safest work an artist can market today, in terms of having a career, and getting a gallery, and winning prizes and grants, is shock art. And every time the artist is attacked in the art wars, claims are made that this is the avant-garde of our time, that Michelangelo and all the maverick artists of their day were criticized and misunderstood. Well, the shock artists are not mavericks; they're doing the safest thing you could possibly be doing in the art world right now.

"In the art wars, the combatants take their positions along exactly the same battle lines. On one side is arrayed the army of the offended rallying to the cry of blasphemy. Against them is amassed the troops of art advocacy rousing to the charge of censorship. After a full-scale barrage and the press, via direct mail of course, and even the courts sometimes, the dust settles to reveal that the debate has not advanced.

"The art wars have accomplished nothing aside from bloating the coffers of the opposing armies and propelling the careers of the artists who started them. Least served, of course, has been the public, which has been left wondering what happened and why.

"In *Exhibitionism*, I don't rehash these controversies, I try to get at their root cause. The art wars erupted at the apex and throughout what, we at least hope, are the waning days of what is widely referred to as the postmodern era. Postmodernism is kind of a spin-off from deconstruction, which is a group of theories that dominated humanities scholarship throughout the 1980s and 90s.

"Postmodernism was accompanied by a culture of intolerance that took root in and eventually engulfed many of our central art institutions. It's a prejudice that favors the so-called cutting edge over the traditional-political art at the expense of painting, for example. It has influenced art-funding agencies like the National Endowment for the Arts, museums, college art history departments, and artists themselves. This bias puts very narrow limits on the type of art that should be studied, supported, exhibited, and to a certain degree, even made."

If, as Munson clearly asserts, the artist acquiesces to the prevailing and unpredictable gusts generated by the powers that be for what type of art he makes, then the art has been co-opted into flattery and advertising. When an artist begins to think about what will please an art grant committee, he has, as Deepak Chopra might put it: 'Stepped out of the gap, the transformational vortex where creation resides.'

The art that concerns us here can't be pinned down or demystified precisely because it is magic, unfettered, and beholden to no one. One high profile art dealer, for example, concluded that contemporary art, hybrid media and electronics notwithstanding, is but a rehash of what came before; the groundbreaking artists of yore are gone; and the artistic genius of the halcyon days is simply no longer present. This dealer's assessment may sound convincing, and to an extent it is factual: the past is dead. But revering art of yesteryear is no great stretch, either.

Those whose consciousness is unified abandon all attachment to the results of action and attain supreme peace.

But those whose desires are fragmented, who are selfishly attached to the results of their work, are bound in everything they do.

BHAGAVAD-GITA

When the subject is strong, simplicity is the only way to treat it.

JACOB LAWRENCE

Innovation isn't something you think up; it is something you release.

EDEN

REPRESENTING ITSELF

While Jackson Pollock is lauded as the abstract expressionist who, in the late 1940's, freed painting by destroying it with his drip, pour, and splash canvases, he didn't spontaneously appear into existence nor did he work in a vacuum; he liked the art of some artists, and not others. There were various influences swirling about in Pollock's magnetic ether that may well have included the Mexican muralists, surrealist automatism, Kandinsky, and a Native American method of working on the ground used by Navaho sand painters to create the tribe's spiritual art for healing. These likely influences, however, were merely undercurrents in the teeming well of the unconscious process where everything is interconnected and blissfully derivative; Pollock didn't wake up one morning to decide that this is the day to drip, to begin action painting. While working over the canvas as he did and in that fashion from an inner need that must remain a mystery, his courage to dig deep, evolve, and persevere is no secret.

Although Pollock would become the icon, fellow travelers of that era such as Willem de Kooning, Stuart Davis, Arshile Gorky, Barnett Newman, Helen Frankenthaler, Mark Rothko, and Jacob Lawrence weren't deterred from making art that was no less provocative. The works of these artists didn't happen in a vacuum either; artists who had come before them had already done their share of the grunt work for expanding the understanding and appreciation of art.

Given this lineage of bold achievers, it is essential and healthy to express gratitude toward those artists who have set the stage for your art. Once it had been established that art didn't need to be representational, the genie was out of the bottle: art was then open to being anything as the subject, as long as it worked.

Think about it.

Remember, the most original artist is influenced by everything of merit. If you envy instead of applaud the innovator, then not only have you missed the point and the opportunity for your own work to evolve, you are lost.

FEASTING ON INNOVATION

Since the 1950's, there has been no art movement to equal the organic impact that abstract expressionism had for liberating the painter from convention. However, art at its heart isn't about deconstruction, breakthroughs, or even the Holy Grail called avant-garde—those evolutionary innovations that come into play spontaneously and in their own good time. You can't have an innovation or authentic art movement every five minutes.

Art is about art—nothing more, or less. The question is this: Is the art any good? And, to paraphrase Duke Ellington: if it looks good it is good.

Unfortunately, many art marketers continue to operate within an anxiety-prone framework propped up by prefabricated 'cutting edge' attempts saddled with the ominous pretension called 'the next big thing'. In such a construct, art is like the automobile business with new models coming out every year. What is the next innovation that will be accepted as art in the 21st century?

When I write 'art' I am talking about art, not nonsense or contrived self-indulgence, which, as we have seen in recent years, all too often passes for art in a climate of uncertainty. Of course, what constitutes nonsense and contrivance can be argued, and it often is.

But I trust that you—as a creator—will journey beyond ego, politics, and outside authority to resolve this discernment for yourself—this is power.

When Albert Einstein was twenty-six, he already possessed a phenomenal grasp of nature that produced his groundbreaking theories of light and gravity that would expand our perception of space and time. On a parallel note, when Pablo Picasso was twenty-six, he too possessed a remarkable maturity that created *Les Demoiselles d'Avignon*, a brothel composition portraying five prostitutes. Picasso's 1907 masterpiece is perhaps today, a century later, not so avant-garde or outrageous to postmodern eyes. When he first unveiled the painting, however, it initially unnerved his contemporaries. Then, when he finally exhibited the large squarish canvas in 1916, it baffled the sensibilities of the public.

Six years earlier, in 1910, Wassily Kandinsky, the great Russian painter, who was forty-four at the time, executed an exercise in color that went beyond expressionism and cubism. This groundbreaking untitled work, which Kandinsky called his *First Abstract Watercolor*, is all but devoid of recognizable imagery, looks random and not particularly well-composed, yet it is the free unselfconscious harbinger of abstract art, which seems nearly a self-evident development to contemporary eyes. These two paintings, however, didn't arrive unannounced nor were they created to shock.

Innovation is an answer to a question. Innovation in art is about being unique, not about trying to be different for that implies a preexisting competitor and comparison. The artist innovator is a theorist who proves a new theory to be reality through the practical application of the transcendent. But he doesn't own this theory, which is a universal gift to all who would explore this virgin landscape. While the Wright Brothers got us off the ground, it was Neil Armstrong who first set foot on the moon.

Each fellow artist in turn can choose to work with and prove this theory in his own distinctive oeuvre. In physics, for example, while Einstein developed original theories of energy and matter with elegant symmetry, it took others to accept, prove, and put his profound equations to any practical use: from the invention of television to splitting the atom. Study any innovation and you will discover that an underlying need or organic structure was already in place to support it. Innovation creates new wealth as it is unaffected by inflation, fads, or other fluctuations.

If two Sunday painters without an established and rigorous body of work had somehow produced *Demoiselles* and *First Abstract Watercolor*, would anyone have noticed? Would such works have any value? You have to know how you came to a conclusion for it to matter. When I was in grade school being tested on long division, I couldn't simply provide the solution; the teacher demanded that each student demonstrate step-by-step calculations on how he arrived at the answer. Art, in this sense, is no different.

Picasso, who revered El Greco, who knew whorehouses, who devoured, cannibalized, borrowed and internalized art from the best, including primitive and ancient art, realized himself as the artist-shaman. In this self-proclaimed role, the young painter exorcized himself with *Les Demoiselles d'Avignon*, an iconic work that many consider a milestone of modernism.

*Do you want to know who you are?
Don't ask. Act!
Action will delineate and define you.*

THOMAS JEFFERSON

Unlike technology, design, and advertising, art doesn't become obsolete.

EDEN

I do not feel obliged to believe that the same God who endowed us with sense, reason, and intellect had intended for us to forgo their use.

GALILEO GALILEI

Kandinsky, who is one of the principal founders of abstract painting, which may well be the most radical contribution to 20th century art, realized that nature as a model for his paintings was a dead end, a detraction from his visually lyrical nonobjective compositions and improvisations. Of course, *First Abstract Watercolor* didn't spring out of nowhere. During the preceding years, he had been liberating his paintings from representation into a new grammar of forms; he saw the discovery of subatomic particles as a veil being lifted off an illusion of reality; he recognized the emotive power and transcendental impact of juxtaposed lines as articulated by art theorist Wilhelm Worringer in his 1908 publication *Abstraction and Empathy*; and he understood the spiritual in art. Over time, Kandinsky, who had also studied the piano and cello, had fused his insights, experiences, and ear for music into a nonobjective 'lyrical' art form.

The salient point of these paintings by Picasso and Kandinsky is that innovation is organic; art must evolve like the living thing it is, from within to without to its inevitable birth and conclusion.

If an artist resorts to gimmickry, then the statement he makes with such art is what it sounds like.

RECONNOITERING FOR ART

While writing this book I decided to once again investigate the current art market. I visited galleries, museums, artist's studios, websites, and alternative spaces. The range of art forms presented for public consumption was astonishing. However, my standing question is: Was the art any good? As I don't want to lead the witness, I will say this: get out of your own head; get out of town; do your own survey of what is out there; and educate yourself. Visit no less than fifty venues for perspective. If you live in a remote area or you simply can't make the rounds, I recommend *Art: 21—Art in the Twenty First Century*; this series (also available on DVD and as a companion book), which aired on PBS television, focuses exclusively on contemporary visual art and artists in the United States, and provides an intimate experience of the artist's process.

Take notes; don't rely on your memory. Of course, the Internet is a gold mine for such research as well.

After your scouting mission, could you honestly say you loved it all? Did you see art or remote bogus cousins called self-indulgence, forced innovation, and approximation? Were there artists whose works spoke to you? Maybe a few stood out among the rest. Were others marginal, and did still others elicit a—what is this? Your foray into the trenches will become a barometer for establishing a holistic view of the contemporary art scene: the one you are living in now. The purpose of your reconnaissance isn't to compare your art with other art, but to witness what types of art have gained 'legitimacy' and by whom.

Remember, those viewing your work for the first time may not immediately warm to it either.

After it leaves the studio, art is left to a populist fate of sorts; acceptance is fundamentally secured by a show of hands—some would argue the 'right' hands. Is it yea or nay? Is it high art or conceptual nonsense? Art marketers will say that the critics or museums will 'catch on' to the iconoclastic vision of the new artist in their stable. Is it art because the artist says it is art, or because the critics and public say it is art? While you can catch onto an idea, can you do so for a feeling? Is feeling contagious? Is art contagious? Art isn't an 'ism'. All the 'isms' that define the various art movements over the years have nothing to do with the creation of art. Who will be the next groundbreaking artist? This isn't up to the artist who does what he does. There is only one breakthrough in art of any value to the artist, and that is truth.

DANGEROUS FEELINGS

Another phenomenon that concerns us here is what Abraham Maslow called peak experiences. When he began exploring the psychology of health, he chose the best specimens of humanity he could find. He found that these individuals almost universally reported having peak experiences: mystical moments of awe, moments of bliss when doubts and fears were left behind, and moments of insight into the secrets of life, and ultimate truth.

Peak experiences were, Maslow believed, far more common than one might expect, that many people tend to suppress them, to ignore them, and certain people seem to fear them as being dangerous, illogical, or somehow feminine. Is it any wonder then that the personal aesthetic moment remains elusive among the popular culture; or that the meaning of art is all too often given up for adoption, left to a fate dictated by the ruminations of experts?

When I do good, I feel good; when I do bad, I feel bad. That's my religion.

ABRAHAM LINCOLN

As Maslow summarized: "But here I had already learned something new. The little that I had ever read about mystic experiences tied them in with religion, with visions of the supernatural. And, like most scientists, I had sniffed at them in disbelief and considered it all nonsense, maybe hallucinations, maybe hysteria—almost surely pathological. But the people telling me ... about these experiences were not such people—they were the healthiest people! And I may add that it taught me something about the limitations of the small ... orthodox scientist who won't recognize as knowledge, or as reality, any information that doesn't fit into the already existent science."

FINDING YOUR WAY

If you want to know how to do something, get close to those who have done it, not to those who haven't. Your grandmother loves company; misery loves nothing, but it does crave codependent coconspirators. Developing an art-aware society is a keystone to enlightenment and essential for supporting the artist. Emulating the healthy in mind, body, and spirit is the most direct route for accomplishing this task. But ferreting out the abnormal and the ill to reveal answers about the fully realized human is still in full swing.

A worldly art collector I met told me in all her sophisticated verve: "I just love complicated men." I have never understood this fascination with brooding difficult people and their self-inflicted complications. Pathology, after all, seems to be a superior source of dramatic tension than the harmony of well-being. But this is not entirely so. There is an odyssey behind every sane person living an authentic life in an 'insane' world.

There is no Energy Shortage. There is no Energy Crisis. There is a Crisis of Ignorance.

R. BUCKMINSTER FULLER

In broad brushstrokes, this is the world of psychology, ideas, perceptions, theories, notions, disinformation, and misinformation in this new and malleable millennium; this is the stage that awaits you and your art. But don't be dismayed. The important thing is that you aren't uncertain about your art and its value. By this time, you may already sense that rejection has but a bit speaking part in your play.

You have a purpose that transcends the predilections of the moment. Let the psychologists and art marketers do what they do, and you do what you do—move as if you had a purpose. If you are a poet, compose; if you are a dancer, dance; if you are a musician, play; if you are a filmmaker, direct. If you don't do it, then you aren't a player, and your dharma goes unfulfilled, which is a tragedy of the karmic kind.

Finding your dharma is the beginning of your life's work, not the end. You must supply the necessary fortitude to persevere. Nothing else will do. It is that simple. I didn't say it would be easy.

Satisfied people are the exception in our society; embrace The Eighteen Be-Attitudes, become the exception, and live *your* life. Facing uncertainty with bravura despite your ego-based doubts, racing heart, and fears is what elevates your art to greatness and character to wellness; it is what Maslow saw in the fully realized human.

NO OBSOLESCENCE

Something of quality is forever good, regardless of time, trends, fashion, or wavering tastes. We easily become desensitized to shock art over time, but never to art from the soul—which doesn't become obsolete regardless of art movements or labels.

As the maelstrom of opposing views tears at the fabric of society, you must remain steadfast and clear (this doesn't imply the false god of perfection) to make it. You must do the introspective work now; no one can do it for you; and as an artist, you wouldn't have it any other way. Needs aren't frivolous desires or nonessential wants. Buddha and Maslow made that clear.

One of the core questions in this book asks: 'Why am I an artist?' From the veracity of your answer, you will know where you stand, and why. As an artist, what needs are you willing to forego to complete your mission?

Answer honorably, or why bother.

Remember, the true artist is a creator who will find a way.

CHAPTER FORTY ONE

RESISTANCE / DISTRACTION
The Usual Suspects

IN HIS COGENT and honestly written book, *The War of Art*, Steven Pressfield picks out 'resistance' from the nefarious line up of usual suspects as the self-saboteur, the enemy of creation, and the nemesis of getting the work done that you have been born to do. What Pressfield labels resistance, I call distraction. And there was no shortage of either during the writing of this book. Another notable author states that you can confront and counter resistance as follows:

> "Become conscious of resistance, which interferes with the natural flow of healthy energy to you. This resistance is in the form of your thoughts. Any thought that's out of sync with the seven faces of intention is a resistant thought. Any thought that says *it's impossible to heal* is a resistant thought. Any thought of doubt or fear is a resistant thought. When you observe these thoughts, note them carefully, and then deliberately activate thoughts that are in energetic, vibrational balance with the all-providing Source of intention."
>
> —from *The Power of Intention* by Wayne Dyer

Still, without an organic resistance there would be no life, no creation. Without friction, there would be no heat; there would be no you or me. This is biology and a cosmic rule. I must press up against gravity to stand, and against dogma to overcome the inertia and the density of the world in my life as an artist.

Your body must have resistance to disease, or you will succumb. It is also crucial to resist those things that will do you harm; temptation wouldn't exist without resistance. Do you want to be defined by resistance, or do you want to create? It is a simple question few are willing to confront.

The beauty of intent is that it is entirely up to you.

Pressfield also explains the relationship between the ego and the self in the mix of things. Resistance hides out in the ego and the angels dwell

We are what we repeatedly do. Excellence, therefore, is not an act but a habit.

ARISTOTLE

Life is 10 percent what you make it and 90 percent how you take it.

IRVING BERLIN

The difference between resistance and persistence is character.

EDEN

in the self, which is on divine turf. 'You are on sacred ground when you know where you stand.'

Researcher of the mind, Sigmund Freud proposed that the unconscious was divided into three parts: the Ego, the Superego and the Id—names to delineate the regions that presumably exist in this mostly uncharted territory of the human psyche. Of course, not everyone agrees with Freud. Carl Jung split the unconscious into two entities, and Marvin Minsky sums up the whole affair with his 'Society of Mind' theory, which asserts that the mind isn't a single object, but the emergent behavior of the interaction of a large number of smaller simpler entities. What these theories have in common is this: most of what is happening in our lives takes place under the hood and deep within the unconscious.

Interpretations of what constitutes the unconscious, the mind, and the creator force within have been with us since the ancient Greeks and doubtless before then. Why is this important? It is a personal means of getting inside the self, which is that ineffable mechanism responsible for unleashing great art. For the artist, for anyone, it is essential to know how the human machine functions. Instead of moving along by default on 'factory settings', you are fine-tuning your organic machine, evolving in your lifetime, and co-creating your existence as a fully realized human being.

When you understand the biological machine and what makes the components tick hormonally and metaphysically, then you can confidently confront rejection, create original art, and do whatever you like to do.

SLAVES IN THE MACHINE

There was another film that explored reality and truth nearly twenty years before *The Matrix* (1999) delved into the same metaphysical territory. In the 1982 movie, *Tron*, a young computer programmer gets sucked into the virtual world of a computer where he must fight for his life playing life-or-death video games run by the evil Master Control Program (MCP). With the aid of a good warrior program named Tron, the programmer must put a stop to the MCP and set things right in the computer world before returning to his own reality. The programmer meets many different programs (who have human form) inside the computer; these programs are looking to live and work within a free system without the tyranny of the MCP.

The programs in the computer machine are called programs; of course, this is a metaphor for people who are programmed to behave in a certain way. *Tron* presents us with another intriguing concept: the different programs that inhabit this virtual reality have a mythology about the users. Do they exist? The programs believe they do. Users, like the programmer, are the gods who created them. Of course, the MCP sees the users as a threat to its ultimate authority, so it is eager to have the programs renounce the users, which it deems a superstitious and hysterical belief. It is easier to see the machinery and values of another culture than it is to evaluate your own society where you can't see what is going on because of acculturation, assimilation, and an ethnocentric bias—unless, of course, you can break free from social conditioning—the MCP—and see reality from the outside in, or, in the case of *Tron*, from the inside out.

Whether someone accepts or rejects any theory of the mind, one must add the divine self to a list of psychological constructs in this inner world where you are host to a myriad of forces that no one can fully explain. It is, after all, art from the unconscious that flows from a cornucopia of intuitive emotion. If you make art from thinking, then you have to calculate by design. If you create art from intuition, which depends upon the flow of pure intelligent emotion, the work is direct and instantaneous, and you don't have to plan it. This is how Picasso and other prolific creators produced large bodies of work. I'm not referring to the manufacture of lithographs or recycled copies of photographs of famous people. I am speaking about original works, things that have never been in this world before—art that contributes to reality. This is where I want to be.

OHM TO OM

But drawing upon the unconscious for the intuitive flow that is creation doesn't happen without first overcoming resistance. The difference between our persistence (get it done) and resistance (procrastination) is much like the ohm, which is a unit of resistance in an electrical circuit. Ohm's law demonstrates that if the applied voltage across a circuit is increased or decreased, the current generated in the circuit increases and decreases, respectively. Furthermore, as the resistance in a circuit increases, we see that the current generated in the circuit decreases. As you are a biological circuit with a body that also relies on electrical impulses to function, the analogy is consistent and relevant.

Ohm's Law was always there; it simply took a man named Ohm to find the connection. German born Georg Simon Ohm (1787-1854), who was a teacher with a passion for physics, had a demoralizing bout with another form of resistance relevant to the subject of this book. In 1827, Ohm published his discovery of the mathematical law of electric current called 'Ohm's Law'. He was able to define the fundamental relationship between voltage, current, and resistance, which was a breakthrough in understanding the electrical circuit. However, quantum leaps are rarely embraced by academia for their visionary merit, especially from an outsider to the establishment. Ohm was 'only' a teacher not a 'baptized' physicist with the proper credentials.

Keep in mind too that Albert Einstein changed the course of space-time and history while working as a patent clerk in Switzerland.

Although Ohm's importance wasn't recognized through most of his lifetime, in 1852, two years before his death, he achieved his lifelong ambition by becoming professor of physics at the University of Munich. The unit of electrical resistance, the ohm, is named after him—an honor he would no doubt have gotten a charge out of.

There is yet another word, or sound that plays a part in grounding you to the rest of the universe. In Hinduism, they chant Om (as in A-U-M), which is the sound that represents the basic vibration of the universe, the central self, or God singing to creation in all its varied forms—from the galaxies, stars, and planets to the oceans and all living things, which also includes you.

The applause of a single human being is of great consequence.

SAMUEL JOHNSON

The constant chatter in your head is like static electricity.

You have to ground the chatter to discharge it.

EDEN

I must uphold my ideals, for perhaps the time will come when I shall be able to carry them out.

ANNE FRANK

When you learn that the life-energy you call yourself is the same as the eternal energy of the Cosmos, you free your own self from anxiety. The self is the eternal self also called Brahman in India. The concept of Brahman, from which everything happens, is invaluable for all, and most especially for the artist who creates.

PHONE HOME

I don't divvy up my own self into parcels like subdivisions in a suburban housing project. Some time ago, I came to a conclusion: I'm not composed of a multiple gang of duplicitous psychological terms that are either at war with one another or conspiring to do me in. This isn't an oversimplification. It is a distillation to get at the essence, the self, or Brahman, while discarding what is nonsense, what is resistant. If you segment yourself into various categories of influence, you dilute yourself.

The integrated fully realized human being is within your power, within your reach—that is, if you are going to go for it no matter what.

Still, a label can be useful in getting a grip on what is happening, even if that label is a construct to give form to what is formless, yet a force to behold. Ego does have an important role to play in the localized part of your life and your psyche in this respect: it will help you remember your phone number, home address, important dates, and the clothes you like to wear. Unbridled ego, however, will prevent you from learning the very thing you need to know—a condition that can be remedied at any moment of your choosing.

Be aware; listen and test the counsel of wise souls, and then arrive at your own conclusions. There is no resistance or distraction when you have found your dharma, your passion—your love of life.

The Sequence is the Thing:

Things, including the metaphysical realm, have an internal logic compelling them to fall into a proper order for them to work.

Attempting to triumph over rejection without first understanding your self and your art is much the same as unplugging the radio before turning it on—it won't work.

CHAPTER FORTY TWO

DECODING THE IMAGE
Art for Art's Sake

LEARNING TO MAKE sense of the world through images and words is a lengthy and complex process that becomes hardwired in the visual cortex and language center of the brain.

Is art a language? Unequivocally.

Unique art, however, first appears as a code that must be deciphered. If you have ever visited a country where the language was completely foreign to your own, you quickly realized how difficult it is to communicate subtlety with nuance, or intricate concepts.

While images that approximate realism are more universally understood than words, abstract and nonrepresentational works are on their own.

BENEFICIAL ADDICTION

To survive, you must form your picture of the world by learning to recognize faces, expressions, colors, movement, danger, and so on.

Do you remember how many years you spent learning the alphabet and then how to read? Art appreciation demands no less.

Apart from social conditioning it is up to each one of us—artist and patron—to evolve beyond the prosaic, to see anew, to sense the substance beneath the surface, the art beneath the avant-garde. While the eyes, like a movie camera, take non-judgmental snapshots of information, the ego introduces bias, and the mind interprets for relevance. Feeling truth, however, takes place in the purity of consciousness—no thinking required.

As music conveys emotion with notes and pitch that vibrate within the ear and throughout the body, the visual artist communicates with a palette of shape, form, and color that enters the soul as feeling.

The fact that your biological software decodes this information through a network of neurons conducting electrochemical impulses in your brain doesn't diminish the metaphysical mystery of the experience.

Passion is, after all, an organic-based neurological 'addiction' of the highest beneficial order. After an artist's code is decrypted and accepted as art by early advocates, patrons, critics, and other mavens, the art, fortunate for

The man who follows the crowd will usually get no further than the crowd. The man who walks alone is likely to find himself in places no one has ever been.

ALAN ASHLEY-PITT

such attention, enters a niche and perhaps after a time even the mainstream as a language now sanctioned, inevitable, and even 'understood'.

MIRÓ AND I

Is it music? Is it art? Who decides? The widescreen version is that it is all art, but the scope of that view needs defining—not for comparing, but for an awareness of distinguishing one form from another—fine art or mass art, Mozart or Muzak. Of course, Mozart also composed for an audience, but let's not fault him for creating sublime work in the process. And, let's face it. Not everyone is prepared to accept the obstacles that the true artist must confront. Even if her dharma is to be a creator, she must still accept and dedicate herself to her purpose in life. Remember, many are called; few choose to go.

Whether your art gets rejected or accepted, knowing the intrinsic value of your work is essential for you to remain clear about your principles and on an even keel for the long haul. Otherwise, you risk floundering in a sea of opinions. For example, I was in Los Angeles at a meeting with an editor going over one of my articles for his magazine. During our talk, I took out a recent mixed media piece from my portfolio and showed it to him. "Ah," he said, "it's like Miró. I like it."

"Thank you," I said. "Then, I'm in good company."

What the editor had meant was this: There was something in my artwork that reminded him of the Spanish Surrealist painter and sculptor, Joan Miró. And what was that something? It was that the work came from the same source—intuition, which is the soul whispering the song of the Creator. If you held up the piece I showed the editor to Miró's body of work, it would become evident that they were far from similar and quite different.

WANDERING ARTIST

However, my point takes me further. I wasn't done at the magazine. When the editor had to take a call, I took the opportunity to wander in the maze of halls where I ran into an art director I had worked with years before. We went into his office. After speaking a bit about old times, I showed him a few of my artworks. He looked, and he even seemed to look intently, but his glazed over non-reaction was clear—he couldn't see my art. He had been involved in graphic design and airbrushing the naked female form into perfection for so many years that he had become totally desensitized to art in a transcendent form. I said my goodbye, left his office, but not without learning a valuable lesson. Knowing who is looking at your art gives you an edge in the moment and leverage for character building to come.

Still, being told by collectors that they explicitly love abstract expressionism doesn't mean they will grasp your work even if you happen to create such art. Being invisible to this art director wasn't surprising, nor was it upsetting, or unsettling. He was oblivious to my work, and it wasn't my duty to remove his blinders. The more you know about how art-savvy, or not, the looker is, the better you can handle both acceptance and rejection.

In their book, *Art & Fear*, David Bayles and Ted Orland write: "The difference between acceptance and approval is subtle, but distinct. Acceptance means having your work counted as the real thing; approval means having

---

Although there are many references about higher consciousness in the media, it should be understood that consciousness itself is already pure and requires no improvement on our part; higher or lower in this regard refers to one's level of awareness in accessing the power of consciousness, which is the technology behind material reality.

EDEN

people *like it*." In one case, an artist might do well with public approval, but critical acclaim eludes him; or the reverse might be the case. However, critical acceptance is no guarantee of success with the public either. Let's fine-tune this point a bit more: As I have confronted the core questions in this book, I know the quality and value of my work without having to consult an outside authority. Of course, I am interested in the perceptions of those whom I respect, and even then I defer to the clarity of my intuition. As far as other commentary about my work is concerned, whether yea or nay, I catalog it as being strictly arbitrary.

THE A SPOT

The fine art I am writing about is personal art, art that is alive, art that simply wants to be born and make its way in the world. If you don't yet know what I mean by 'alive' then you must make it your cultural quest to find out. Nothing of value is free. If fine art (high art) were the popular taste, we wouldn't need a distinction.

What one culture, or an era calls music another might dismiss as discordant noise. What one culture, or an era calls art another might dismiss as absurd, ludicrous, or worse yet, trivial. Compounding the confusion and dogma inherent within these variables is the identity of art itself, which evolves organically over time into new forms by its creators.

Many artists, too eager to appease the marketplace, force the issue by trying to be different, to come up with something new to feed the insatiable maw of the monster known as: the next big thing. This self-induced inorganic pressure to perform, while perhaps publicly and even critically accepted, is a waxed apple—all veneer, dry inside, and of no nutrient value—as the true artist will tell you.

All too often, in fact most often, the art in the news is a matter of fashion, a matter of buzz, and a matter of hype and market manipulation spiced up and dished out as a predigested banquet for the culturally malnourished.

Whenever I hear that someone has an art consultant, it strikes me as absurd—unless the advice is for buying art as a commodity, an investment, or decoration. Otherwise, how can someone else know better than you how you feel about a work of art? This is tantamount to hiring someone to have your orgasms.

HUNG LIKE AN EXCLAMATION POINT

There it stood. A large stone three-story monolithic type building one block from the Pacific Ocean on the borderline between Venice and Santa Monica. There was no sign, or name on the mailbox, and from the conspicuous absence of windows, it was clear the owner didn't want company.

I did eventually learn that the building was the property of a real estate developer (I will call him Mr. Emperor) who had made a questionable fortune in Orange County during the 1980's mad rush to buy a house boom.

What was inside the building?

After delving further, I discovered that the building housed the real estate mogul's private art collection. I had to see this for myself. I managed to get an appointment with the curator, a tall woman with a curt disposition. I had to promise not to divulge the scope of the collection.

The true work of art is born from the 'artist': a mysterious, enigmatic, and mystical creation.

It detaches itself from him, it acquires an autonomous life, becomes a personality, an independent subject, animated with a spiritual breath, the living subject of a real existence of being.

WASSILY KANDINSKY

The Universe is called, with everything in it, maya, because all is temporary therein, from the ephemeral life of a fire-fly to that of the Sun.

H.P. BLAVATSKY

Pure intelligent emotion communicates with the field of all possibilities. And that emotion is intuition—a conduit to consciousness.

EDEN

There were several more women working in the main office—a model of a well-designed workspace.

The curator lady showed me around. Humidity and temperature sensors carefully regulated the environment for the benefit of the permanent collection. Rooms and rooms were filled to the high ceilings with all manner of artworks. The curator explained that Mr. Emperor was buying up all sorts of art. The translation was this: The mogul didn't know art from artifice or artifact, so he was hedging the odds—buying this or that in the spirit of speculation. Who knows what posterity will decide to appreciate in value?

As we walked into yet another large white room, one wall was bare, except for a three-foot-high exclamation point that hung in the center. It was made of wood and in two pieces: the upper narrow rectangular part and the dot below created the punctuation mark.

"What is this?" I said.

"Oh, yes," said the curator. "It's by this up and coming artist Mr. So and So and Mr. Emperor just had to have it."

"Mr. Emperor just had to have it?" I said. "It's a punctuation mark."

"Yes. Mr. Emperor thinks it's brilliant, too."

"Brilliant for its minimalist approach, no doubt," I offered. "And he must have paid quite a sum for it, too."

"Precisely. In the high six figures … I can say no more."

How much, I wondered, would Mr. Emperor have paid for the sentence that led up to the exclamation?

But don't miss the complete point here, either. While the real estate tycoon couldn't see himself—that *Mr. Emperor was indeed naked* and had been hoodwinked, how did the artist who sold an exclamation point for such a grand sum feel about his art and himself? To believe your own bullshit breaks the first cardinal rule. Think about it. Remember, you can dupe yourself, but not forever.

READYMADES

The exclamation point had reminded me of Marcel Duchamp, the merry prankster of Dada, who wanted to enter his sculpture, *Fountain*, in the 1917 exhibition of the Society of Independent Artists. *Fountain* was a readymade (lifting the description from ready to wear clothing) in the form of a porcelain urinal that Duchamp, in a perverse and perhaps playful sense, placed on a pedestal, and signed with a false name. Years later, Duchamp explained that he was one of the founding members of the independents and, at the time of the exhibition, served on its board of directors; he didn't sign the sculpture with his own name because, to some, it might appear to be a conflict of interest.

Although the directors of the exhibition had rejected *Fountain*, an astute Alfred Stieglitz had managed to photograph it for posterity soon after. This urinal-art is still talked about today. The original *Fountain* was 'lost' after its debut, but, in 1999, an authenticated (with the artist's approval) replica sold at a Sotheby's auction for over $1.7 million dollars. The focus then shifts from Duchamp's daring provocation to the high bidder—what was he thinking? In 1943, Picasso had also felt the lure of readymades when he used a bicycle seat and handlebars to evoke a sculpture of a bull's head. Did Duchamp's urinal spout? Did Picasso's bull roar?

In his 1973 documentary *Painters Painting*, filmmaker Emile de Antonio presents a collective portrait of seminal figures who fueled the tumultuous postwar New York art scene. The film features, among others, the artist Jasper Johns who relates the following:

Johns: It's a story I heard, so I don't know whether it's true or not. I heard that Bill de Kooning had said about Leo [Castelli], with whom he was annoyed over something: 'That son-of-bitch … you could give him two beer cans, and he could sell them.' At that time I had made a couple of sculptures. I had made one of two flashlights and one or two of a light bulb, and they were small objects, small, sort of ordinary objects. And when I heard this story, I thought: What a fantastic sculpture for me! I mean, really, just absolutely perfect. So I made this work [*Painted Bronze*, 1960; two cans of beer in bronze]. It fit in perfectly with what I was doing. I did it and Leo sold it.

What was this artist, Mr. So and So, thinking with his exclamation point? Was he making some clever point about the final fate of readymades? Was this homage to American Pop art? Andy Warhol in the 1960's had already showed that paintings of Campbell's soup cans and Brillo Boxes of silk-screened wood could pass for high art. Was this some deep expression of art punctuation that only sophisticates could grasp? Was this his subtle version of the urinal? I don't chase red herrings, and I don't immerse myself, generally, into what motivated an artist to make a piece of work. Wanting to know what the artist was thinking or even feeling might be suitable for cocktail conversation or speculation in a book; such questions are, however, mostly irrelevant when it comes to understanding art since it is you who gives meaning to a painting. It is much better to know how you feel to complete the picture, which is a point of strength, not weakness.

I thanked the lady curator in charge of Mr. Emperor's collection, then departed from the large climate-controlled vault of questionable art treasures acquired with a fortune made by speculative measures. The land developer had paid many hundreds of thousands of dollars for a wooden cut out exclamation point that might fetch a quarter at a garage sale. I left the vast array of artworks behind me feeling that somehow poetic justice had been served.

As I walked across the private parking lot under a late California sun, a mild breeze coming off the ocean cooled my face. I drove off to the east and toward home in the Hollywood Hills thinking of what W.C. Fields had observed: "You can't cheat an honest man."

ART FOR WHOSE SAKE

Art from the soul isn't a qualifier (art therapy) nor is it the object of a modifier (commercial art). Art stands alone and on its own merit without having to represent something other than itself. Art is evolutionary, not creative, which is a conceptual experience of the applied arts that serves a different master. Unlike design, which wears two hats as both a verb and a noun, art is art. Let's be clear. Anything made with passion, attention to detail, and skill can be elevated to an art form.

A man can only attain knowledge with the help of those who possess it. This must be understood from the very beginning. One must learn from him who knows.

GEORGE GURDJIEFF

We should note that artists have no control over patrons and speculators willing to pay huge sums for their work.

EDEN

Seek ye first the good things of the mind, and the rest will either be supplied or its loss will not be felt.

FRANCIS BACON

It took nearly twenty years for Ridley Scott's 1982 film Blade Runner to find an audience.

EDEN

I love the work of artist Syd Mead and filmmaker George Lucas. Mead illustrates his unique sense of the future with sociologically relevant design that demands planning and thought. We appreciate the logic and integrity of his ingenious renderings, which come to life in such stunning films as *Blade Runner*. When Lucas is writing about the intuitive power of the Force in his epic *Star Wars* episodes and orchestrating dramatic interactions among the archetypal characters that populate his galaxy far, far away, he is searching for integrated ideas, plots, plans, and design that best serve the story.

Both Mead and Lucas are visionaries who create with an audience in mind, and art made expressly for public consumption is at the core of entertainment, even if it is also innovative, brilliant, and inspirational. Filmmaking is a collaborative enterprise with many mouths to feed; art is an individual act that need only sustain the artist. Art has no motive other than to be born; from there it takes its chances like the rest of us. These are distinctions, not comparisons. While both art and design fulfill our need for communication, invention, stimulation, and creation, they are on different paths. Art is born free; design is commercial. The mission is to find your dharma, not someone else's. With many tens of millions invested in a cutting edge special effects space opera, a return on investment hinges on audience approval on a large scale. Art isn't burdened with such high stakes nor is it made with focus groups or a public ideology in mind. This doesn't, however, preclude galleries and museums from merchandising cultural recreation, self-indulgent and politically correct works of dubious artistic merit, as art. If you don't know the difference, what then can you expect from the civilian population?

Whether your work is rejected or accepted, it is smart and character building to know where you and your art stand. Work rejected for ideas can be modified to suit since it is work for hire; an authentic voice, if rejected, can't be altered, nor would the artist want to if that is his dharma. When art is showcased in a designer world, then we have confusion. When a film distributor, for example, decides that an 'art' movie has limited appeal, meaning it doesn't follow a previously proven formula for success, it is then unceremoniously dumped, if it is lucky, into backwater screenings at art houses; this tells us where art as film stands in the popular culture of America.

BETTING THE RANCH

There are, of course, exceptions when it comes to mainstream films that break new ground. Lucas, who is a risk taker, managed to control the content of his art form in an industry notorious for altering the director's cut with changes that would undermine the integrity of the film for the sake of trying to please everyone.

After the unexpected worldwide success of *Star Wars* as a cultural phenomenon, Lucas decided to take on full responsibility as an independent producer to avoid the politics and creative limitations associated with the Hollywood studio system.

With his share of profits from the first film, he self-financed the next episode, *The Empire Strikes Back*, with $33 million dollars of his own money—a decision that would have been a personal financial disaster if the film had tanked at the box office. Embraced by its fans, the space saga paid off as yet another blockbuster. Would you have had the confidence in your art and the guts to bet the farm like Lucas? What are you willing to do for your art? Are you willing to complete your mission? These are real issues better confronted before you go public. Adversity will weed out the posers. Answering the core questions in this book will show you where you stand and why.

The point here is that there is no conflict in appreciating all artists who expand the human experience. We are free to love all forms of art according to our sensibilities. For most of us, love is a matter of context that takes on dimensions of disparate hues, values, and conditions. We love our mother, partner, friend, and pet, but in different ways as a matter of distinction not comparison. It is no different when it comes to loving art and the family of applied art. Mead, Lucas, and you—each has a unique dharma to fulfill.

ARE YOU TALKING TO ME?

The question persists: Why does so much mediocre art successfully infiltrate from the mainstream of so-called high art? We understand mainstream to mean the approved of art by the powers that be. Regardless of venue and touted quality, mediocrity in whatever form is familiar and non-threatening in a culture weaned on advertising, exploitation, the next big thing, vicarious thrills, and where technique, ideology, and shock art are mistaken for the real thing—art. Proving this to yourself counts as a basic lesson.

There are many out there with vested interests—economic, cultural, and political—in preserving and controlling that which is sanctioned as art, and even what type of art gets shown and supported by way of grants, awards, and fellowships. Let's face it. Given the hardships that a creator must endure to persevere, it is no surprise that few with a paintbrush have the mettle to confront the gatekeepers who faithfully and dogmatically defend the establishment.

The art I am writing about throughout these pages leaps from the soul without thinking, preordained purpose, or a net; while such art may eventually get a public viewing, it is immune to the throes of rejection because its creator knows the value of the process and the eternal power of the source.

Of course, thinking is a necessary function of life. However, over thinking instigates self-consciousness, which ultimately begets doubt, fear, and anxiety—negative emotional states that demarcate the barren terrain of inertia. The fine spin here is that art is rarely, if ever, immediately perceived for what it is; art history is ripe with 'failures' that were later lauded as masterpieces.

Gauguin and van Gogh, for example, never received an award, fellowship, or a grant for their work; they didn't allow rejection, hard times, or a lack of encouragement to dissuade them from painting in their language, nor will such tests of character paralyze you; that is, after you have successfully confronted the core questions in this book. Art is free from routine,

A person who is gifted sees the essential point and leaves the rest as surplus.

THOMAS CARLYLE

Until the dark side of the force tempts you, you do not know who you truly are.

EDEN

contrivance, conceptualization, ideas, and, can we agree here to include isolated 'punctuation' marks proffered to clueless real estate moguls?

Art without motive is, after all, art for art's sake, a declaration that is all too often misunderstood.

WILDE AT HEART

Oscar Wilde, in his 1891 essay *The Soul of Man Under Socialism*, wrote:

"Now, I have said that the community by means of organization of machinery will supply the useful things, and that the beautiful things will be made by the individual. This is not merely necessary, but it is the only possible way by which we can get either the one or the other. An individual who has to make things for the use of others, and with reference to their wants and their wishes, does not work with interest, and consequently cannot put into his work what is best in him. Upon the other hand, whenever a community or a powerful section of a community, or a government of any kind, attempts to dictate to the artist what he is to do, art either entirely vanishes, or becomes stereotyped, or degenerates into a low and ignoble form of craft.

"A work of art is the unique result of a unique temperament. Its beauty comes from the fact that the author is what he is. It has nothing to do with the fact that other people want what they want. Indeed, the moment that an artist takes notice of what other people want, and tries to supply the demand, he ceases to be an artist, and becomes a dull or an amusing craftsman, an honest or a dishonest tradesman. He has no further claim to be considered as an artist.

"Art is the most intense mode of individualism that the world has known. I am inclined to say that it is the only real mode of individualism that the world has known. Crime, which, under certain conditions, may seem to have created individualism, must take cognizance of other people and interfere with them. It belongs to the sphere of action. But alone, without any reference to his neighbors, without any interference, the artist can fashion a beautiful thing; and if he does not do it solely for his own pleasure, he is not an artist at all."

Art for art's sake isn't a rally cry for arrogance; it is a statement of clarity; it isn't about a formal movement; it is about personal evolution that knows no borders. It means the artist is an artist, a woman connected to the world, but not fooled by its illusions or those who would co-opt fire from heaven to roast marshmallows. Although they might exist, I haven't encountered a single creator who has an issue with the legitimacy of non-utilitarian art making, which simply means the art is made without a concern for a market. You will note that those decrying art for art's sake as immoral, the devil's work, lacking in virtue, pretentious, and irrelevant are not the artists who pay the price for creation with their blood.

As Red Smith had observed: "There is nothing to writing. All you do is sit down at the typewriter and … just open a vein."

INSIDE THE OUTSIDER

When I asked Colin Wilson, the prolific writer and self-proclaimed 'enthusiastic phenomenologist' if he had thoughts as to the purpose of art,

---

Although Wilde's essay, or sermon, has socialism in the title, don't be misled; read it for the distinction he makes about art and then apply it to yourself as an artist and as required.

EDEN

he sent me a document with a note that read: "Here is perhaps the most important essay I have ever written on this topic." Wilson's cogent and provocative essay melded well with the organic shape, spirit, and substance of firsthand experience. Wilson, who wrote this philosophical adventure and analysis toward the end of the 1960's, compels us to question and—as necessary—expose bogus everyday perceptions that have been socially engineered for us. If we have the courage to confront our own lethargy, including the homogenized reality we inherit and imbibe daily from society's breast, we earn the opportunity to evolve.

Then, by comprehending the inexorable yet fluid relationship between consciousness and its temporal instrument and mirror—art, we can glimpse the fullness of awareness without blinders. The more contact you have with consciousness, the better you can deflect rejection and other negative aspects that aim to erode the quality of your art and life. Remember, if you want depth, you must dig deep.

Here is a brief excerpt from Wilson's essay, 'Husserl and Evolution':

"It must have been in the early 1960's that I went to call on Sir Julian Huxley at his house in Pond Street, Hampstead. At the time, I was working on a book called Beyond the Outsider—the sixth and last of my 'Outsider Cycle'—and I really wanted to ask Huxley how he could be the foremost living exponent of man's future evolution, and still regard himself as a strict Darwinian. Expressed in that way, the question may not make too much sense—for after all, there's no contradiction between human evolution and Darwinism. But, as all Huxley's admirers know, he had swung from a rather narrow form of Darwinism—with the emphasis on genetic factors—to a kind of Shavian optimism about man's future as the 'managing director of evolution.'

"Huxley's explanation was roughly this: that in the past, all evolution has been purely 'mechanical,' dominated by the brute need for survival; nature favored the strong. But man has opened up a new phase in evolution. His mind wants to embrace the whole universe; not for survival, but from sheer delight in knowledge for its own sake. Animals are 'conscious,' but only of their bodies and of the immediate present; this extraordinary creature called man is distinguished by his curious desire to escape the present, to give his mind a free run of other times and other places—as well as of a whole world of abstractions that do not exist in time and space. This new 'dimension' of consciousness has enabled him to look down on himself from above, as it were, to consider himself as a creature, and to ask himself how he would like to evolve. He is, potentially at any rate, 'in control.'

"And how can he control his own evolution? I wanted to know. Huxley mentioned genetic engineering. Then he said something that puzzled and excited me. 'Have you ever thought about the significance of the development of art?' I found it hard to relate this to Darwinism or genetic engineering, and asked him to explain himself; but he declined to enlarge. 'Think about it' was all he would say. And, on and off, I have been thinking about it ever since."

Wilson then sums up his essay on art and consciousness with this mindful assessment:

"Once we understand that 'everyday consciousness' (which Edmund Husserl called 'the natural standpoint') is not the real thing, we are in the

Courage is the first of human qualities because it is the quality which guarantees the others.

ARISTOTLE

Conceptual art is what it sounds like; the artist is saying that this is what I think art looks like.

EDEN

It takes a wise man to discover a wise man.

DIOGENES

Who has the power when you're waiting for a reaction? Understand this dynamic. Do not give your power away, no matter what.

Do not let your own desire undermine you.

EDEN

important position of being ready to try to see beyond it, to brush it aside in favor of 'primal perception.' For although the 'taming' process is important to human evolution—it could be compared to ploughing the land—the revitalizing or fertilizing process is equally important. This can only be done by trying to go back to 'things in themselves,' and to recognize that they are always richer and more complex than our 'tamed' perception can understand. As Heidegger would say, what is 'out there' is pure Being.

"And here, I think, is the basic meaning of Huxley's insight. It is completely natural for us to think of 'the natural standpoint'—everyday consciousness—as being identical with consciousness itself. Yet consciousness shows an odd ability to extend into new dimensions—that is, to develop new levels of control over itself. It has learned to do this—instinctively, as it were—through art. The next step is clear. The instinct itself must become 'conscious.' We must develop a level of consciousness that is able to unmask everyday consciousness for a liar—or at least, a harmless impostor. We require an instinct—or a habit—which leads us to constantly reject the world presented to us by everyday consciousness—like a man trying to poke a hole in a piece of stage scenery. This instinct—or habit—can only be acquired by the constant practice of phenomenological analysis. As to the aim—whether we call it 'uncovering the secrets of Transcendental Ego' or striving 'to approach the Keepers of the Keys of Being'—this hardly concerns us at the present stage. It will only concern us when we possess real consciousness."

Here, in Wilson's keen observation, we grasp a profound understanding of art for art's sake. Art comes into being from consciousness, which precisely reflects awareness. What better reason can there be for art to exist? As Wassily Kandinsky and other like-minded visionaries have noted: art and art appreciation will transform the world for the better.

There is one raison d'etre, or dharma that we can happily attribute to art for art's sake: art exists to wake you up from sleeping consciousness, which slips away day by day, to reality as it is, which is the one awakened consciousness and awareness known as the Buddha.

THE ROSE CACHET

And, yes, it is the inherent value of the art that does matter. If not art for art's sake, then what are you left with—art for whose sake? There is art for a specific commercial purpose, and then there is art for no apparent utilitarian motive. Each artist must decide for herself, remain undivided, and then hold fast.

The artist isn't tormented to create; she is blessed to do so. If a particular artist were tormented, she would be tormented if she were a plumber, cab driver, librarian, doctor, or baker. An artist creates not because of an affliction, but despite it. You might have heard, and repeatedly so, that art stands on its own merit; this is an oversimplification. I could select a painting by van Gogh, Miró, Picasso or Kandinsky and offer it to a random group of people on a street corner and wouldn't be able to get twenty-five dollars for it. The art doesn't sell itself without a context. To fully appreciate a work, you must know how the art came into being, not merely its pedigree, or provenance; consequently, the art must be viewed within the creator's oeuvre, to know it as art.

Remember, it isn't the *rose*; it is how the *rose* got into the painting that matters. Did it appear according to plan, or did it spontaneously flower into existence to everyone's delight and surprise, including the painter? If the process is magic, then the art is magic. Even then, magic art, which doesn't exist in a vacuum, must have a platform to be seen and heard. And to that extent, such art also relies on the cascading benefits of cachet to distinguish itself from the mundane within the art market.

A SLICE OF EAR

When a patron acquires a piece of art by a mainstream artist, he is also buying into the artist's demonstrated approval rating. The critics, dealers, and posterity—the art establishment, have sanctioned this artist's language as bona fide. It is the alleged mystique surrounding the 'approved' artist that is being marketed to an audience hungry to acquire a piece of God, a patch of genius, a slice of ear, or a precious page from history. Stripped of its public relations value, is the *Mona Lisa* truly priceless? Is it a great painting? Do you know why one way or the other?

One of van Gogh's most famous works is *The Portrait of Doctor Gachet*, an oil on canvas painted in 1890 that is notable for a few reasons. It was painted in the last few months of Vincent's life, and the subject of the portrait has been the focus of much controversy. How competent was this Gachet, the provincial French doctor who last treated the ailing artist? On one occasion, Vincent wrote to his brother Theo: "First of all, he [Dr. Gachet] is sicker than I am, I think, or shall we say just as much, so that's that." What precisely did Vincent mean?

At a Christie's auction in 1990 *Dr. Gachet* sold within three minutes for what was at the time a record-breaking $82.5 million to Ryoei Saito, a Japanese industrialist. As counterpoint, van Gogh's sister-in-law had originally sold the work in 1897 for 300 francs (around $58). Although there is certainly an intrinsic value to this portrait for various reasons, we know the perceived value is no longer the painting itself, but the iconic tortured life of the painter—which has become clichéd from overexposure.

In 2004, *Boy With a Pipe*, a 1905 work from Picasso's Rose Period, eclipsed the previous record for a painting set by Vincent van Gogh's *Dr. Gachet* by selling for $104.1 million at Sotheby's. This painting was among a fine collection sold by Mr. and Mrs. John Hay Whitney. Whitney and his wife, Betsy, acquired the Picasso in 1950 for about $30,000, which by 2004's prices would be worth $229,000.

As a barometer on a federal art funding level, the FY 2004 budget for the National Endowment for the Arts was $121 million. What is a painting or a sculpture worth? What are these high bidders buying? Why would anyone acquire a painting for millions of dollars? They are buying a brand, a van Gogh or a Picasso.

If you have ever been to an art auction, you would soon realize that the value of the work has more to do with the ego of the bidder than the value of the art per se. On one level, art is purely a commodity, an investment; and if it is an investment, tax laws are so written that the owner can't

I'm not offended by all the dumb blonde jokes because I know I'm not dumb ... and I also know that I'm not blonde.

DOLLY PARTON

All lies and jests, still a man hears what he wants to hear and disregards the rest.

PAUL SIMON

enjoy the work by placing it in his living room. On another, it is a trophy of power—my art is bigger than your art. At the intrinsic level, however, the buyer is acquiring the artist's soul forever revealed and sealed in paint. As we see, art speaks in many tongues and gestures: in the language we already know and, if we dare to understand, in a wondrous code that only the spirit can comprehend.

ACQUIRE THE LIVING

It is always the true artist who first knows that it is art. If a creator doesn't know the value of his creation, then he and his work are lost. The integrated artist of character doesn't need a focus group to tell him what is what. Through various means of exposure, the artist's work then flows, if not bumps, stumbles, and falls along, into the art marketplace. If the work is unique, which personal fine art must be, the art world and the public must confront a new alphabet and consequently a new language to decipher.

Of course, while the artist may know his work is art, what is accepted as art and by who remains a real question for everyone else concerned. Although this might sound like asking a lot (it is, but so what) of artist and patron alike, the payoff can't be put into words; it can, however, be put into acquisitions, which sustain the artist while satisfying the patron's need to fulfill her own dharma.

My standing advice to art collectors is this: acquire the work of living artists, as the dearly departed are beyond the need of your support.

Create some time and set yourself a worthy task. Investigate the evolution of Western art—from classical to academic, to realism, through the Blue Rider school, impressionism, post impressionism, cubism, Ashcan school, modern art, pop art, abstract expressionism, and up to the controversial complications of postmodern art. As you travel through the centuries and decades to see the language of art evolve, you won't feel alone.

Remember, those who succeeded in the past did so because they didn't surrender—no matter what—to the common wisdom, which is rarely common or wise.

DAYDREAMER

CHAPTER FORTY THREE

THE THRESHOLD
Drawing the Line

IS IT POSSIBLE to have one foot on the stage and the other in the audience? Ouch. That would be a pointless if not an altogether painful stretch added to the mortal coil.

I love the word threshold. There is a boundary between the true artist and a wannabe. This boundary isn't the demarcation line between talent on one side and its absence on the other. It is talent plus self-inspiration—an action term more often described than exercised.

Where do you stand in relation to this dividing line?

"If we become addicted to the external, our interiority will haunt us. We will become hungry with a hunger no image, person, or deed can still. To be wholesome, we must remain truthful to our vulnerable complexity. In order to keep our balance, we need to hold the interior and exterior, visible and invisible, known and unknown, temporal and eternal, ancient and new, together. No one else can undertake this task for you. You are the one and only threshold of an inner world. This wholesomeness is holiness. To be holy is to be natural, to befriend the worlds that come to balance in you. Behind the façade of image and distraction, each person is an artist in this primal and inescapable sense. Each one of us is doomed and privileged to be an inner artist who carries and shapes a unique world."

—from *Anam Cara: A book of Celtic Wisdom* by John O'Donohue

WHO AM I?

The true artist—a creator—has no boundaries because *an artist has no medium*. Test this observation and you will discover that this knowledge has great liberating power. Always consider the source, search out the feelings and conclusions of great souls, and most important, be an individual, which means being less, not more.

Now in order that people may be happy in their work, these three things are needed: They must be fit for it; they must not do too much of it; and they must have a sense of success in it—not a doubtful sense, such as needs some testimony of others for its confirmation, but a sure sense, or rather knowledge, that so much work has been done well, and fruitfully done, whatever the world may say or think about it.

JOHN RUSKIN

> *The test of a first-rate intelligence is the ability to hold two opposed ideas in mind at the same time and still retain the ability to function.*
>
> F. SCOTT FITZGERALD

And by less, I am referring to artificial social trappings and the false masks of personality.

COMING THROUGH

When we see the surface of a thing, there is a supporting structure behind it. For every front there is at least one back. When we see courage, we don't see the fear. When we see great art, we don't see the sacrifice. When we see achievement in any endeavor, we see only the end product, behavior, or performance. It is up to each artist to see beyond the shadow, which owes its existence to the light.

Have you ever been motivated to accomplish some task? If you have, then you know that there was a force at work, an inner drive that took over, a power that wouldn't be deterred no matter what the obstacles, including physical and psychic stress. You knew it was time to start doing and stop thinking. If you recall such an event in your life, you knew you were unstoppable. While those self-induced inhibitors, fear, doubt, rejection, anxiety, and resistance, don't necessarily disappear, they lose their death grip and are of insignificant consequence when you focus on your mission.

When momentum overcomes inertia, the physics of your life suddenly takes on an energy that converts the mediocre into the startling. The laws of time and space are now part of your palette. To see the mechanism that drives the universe for yourself and to make the gears turn in your favor is a sensation ripe with fulfillment. It is thrilling to witness what a motivated person can achieve; and, to ratchet things up, it is amazing to see what a self-inspired one can create.

The only way to stop someone on a mission of life or death is to kill him. Are you on a mission or a joy ride? In the context of this book, however, the artist embodies both the protagonist and antagonist; he either gets it done or does himself in. It is an internal affair.

No blame. No whining. No victimhood. And, I mean it.

The question then escalates to: What is my mission? If you have answered the core questions in this book and are secure in your soul that your art is your dharma, then the elixir of inspiration to make this dream come true is running through your veins right now; you need only tap into it by confronting the mission with the will power that is at your command.

People want to work with people who have talent, a direction, and a steadfast commitment to their art. When you are on a mission, you take charge; those who will help you succeed acknowledge and welcome your initiative.

Do it! Prove it!

The way for you is unique. Lead, if that is your dharma. Follow, if that is your dharma, but follow and support others wisely and for good reason. Every player has a purpose.

If you are unconvinced about your own mission, then the cosmic supply line of reinforcements won't arrive to save the day; they don't know where to show up or why. But don't lose heart. You can change the complexion of your life in a second with one right feeling, one brilliant insight—one act of unwavering determination that confirms your authenticity. Stop to see the awe in your life and the cosmic cavalry will arrive.

THE ENVELOPE, PLEASE

A thought inside your head: *Am I an artist?* If you have to ask someone, then projecting insecurity shouts: I don't know. And if you don't know, you haven't found your dharma. Somewhere along your quest you have faltered; you didn't follow through, which is the undoing of many would-be artists. It's not that opportunity to confirm your gift and purpose didn't surface; you chose to dismiss it, most likely out of fear and doubt. I make this assessment based on my experience over many years with a master painter. I had witnessed flocks of so-called artists flit into his studio on the pretense of wanting to learn more about art. But their egos stood in the way. Their rigidity prevented them from appreciating the wonder in front of them, from elevating their standard. Somehow, these thirsty travelers for culture had stumbled into the wellspring of art and couldn't drink from those divine waters—not because they had no cup, but because they were unwilling to cup their hands.

Placing your future upon the value scale of others does not an artist make. Don't shortchange your own self. Dig deep; answer the core questions posed in this book, and you will thank yourself later. If you are in need of chronic reassurance and ego stroking to keep you going, then you are merely 'acting' as if you were on a mission. You are being disingenuous with yourself.

Do not dismay if the 'rewards' for your art aren't yet happening on your time schedule. Persist in the direction of your intent and immediately get back on course if you sense you have strayed—that is, from the threshold of the artist you seek to become. No one else can do this for you because only you have access to your moral compass. Remember, 'you are on sacred ground when you know where you stand.'

Miracles are all around you.

When one begins to live by habit and by quotation, one has begun to stop living.

JAMES A. BALDWIN

CHAPTER FORTY FOUR

TRAFFICKING IN ART
Acquire Within: Premodern to Modern

IN THE MARKETPLACE, nothing happens until energy and currency are exchanged. Making the leap to earn your daily bread from your artwork is a bold and eloquent gesture. However, to elevate your decision from a gesture into a solid intention with a backbone, you must also read between the lines of your own resolve.

Aside from answering the core questions posed in this book, there are other fundamental concerns for you to address: What am I selling? And why would anyone want to acquire my work? In turn, answers to these questions then beg yet another question: If you are selling art, do you know what art is? You do if you have confronted the core questions. Guessing or glib remarks won't carry the day. If you can't respond to these questions with vigorous confidence based on performance and firsthand experience, you can't expect the art-buying public to deliver you from yourself by answering them for you. If you do defer to public opinion in resolving these issues for you, then you might as well tattoo your forehead with these words: kick me.

Remember that all the decisions you make contribute only to your side of the equation—you know where you stand, which is more than most can claim. There are other factors and other people who must complete and balance out the equation, one way or another.

HOTEL RESERVATIONS

One evening, years ago in San Francisco, I had a situation, a conversation with a mustachioed art historian of some renown. We were sitting in the posh office of a hotel tycoon who had an extensive collection of primitive and modern art. The historian had come to evaluate the collection for his new book—an ambitious tome about art from the beginning of time to present day. This meeting of ours hadn't been planned.

Our appointments had overlapped into one another because the busy tycoon was running late. The tycoon had expressed interest in a fine painting by an artist friend of mine who entrusted me to negotiate on his behalf.

I passionately hate the idea of being with it. I think an artist has always to be out of step with his time.

ORSON WELLES

Rule of Compensation:

Beginners nearly always attempt to over or under compensate in any new endeavor that demands intuition and sensation over thinking. To find that sweet spot called balance, you must feel the way, and that requires initiative, introspection, dedication, and risk.

EDEN

We hadn't been in the tycoon's office for five minutes, when an emergency of some magnitude erupted in one of the hotels that demanded his personal attention. He left us to ourselves, but not before having room service bring in wine and a beautifully prepared table of delectable hors d'oeuvres. The historian and I began talking. When I said that art was evolutionary, he suddenly jumped up with a scowl as if I had insulted his mother. He became indignant. No, he said with the authority of his doctorate in art history from Harvard; art was definitely not evolutionary.

So, there we were on seemingly opposite ends of the party platter. Was this a game of semantics? Each art, the art historian instructed me, stood on its own merit and couldn't be compared with art from another age. To evolve meant that art would get better or improve—a notion he wouldn't accept. But I was not at odds with his observations; only his conclusion faltered. My contention was that since the artist was evolving, the art was a consequence of maturing spiritually. I explained: Art itself, which is intrinsically irreducible, wasn't evolving, only the way it was perceived; and, to whatever extent, art elevated the apprehension of consciousness by the artist and the art appreciator. We must maintain that sense of 'raised' consciousness that we take from the museum or gallery exhibit experience and drag it with us out onto the streets. The historian would have none of this transcendental talk as he eyed the table for more chunks of lobster flesh destined for drenching in warm butter. He couldn't conceive of an art—which is a state of beauty—that evolves and transmutes itself into a new form over time.

OLD SOULS

There are many different levels of experiencing consciousness on this planet, and that pretty much explains quite a lot. The Freudians and Behaviorists didn't include consciousness in their study of human behavior; this is a fundamental oversight. There is only one thing that distinguishes one self from another, and that is awareness. Of course, subconscious stirrings, stimulus-response, and environmental factors play their part, but only to a limited extent for the fully realized individual who feels that there is a better way. Who that person is has little to do with surface considerations; it is the eternal energy of consciousness that not only affects but creates the external world. There was a young boy from the inner city slums who grew beyond his circumstances to become a creator and consequently self-aware. We could call his rise to awareness a matter of: luck, destiny, karma, an inevitability, an example of social Darwinism, or what Herbert Spencer called survival of the fittest—but, right or wrong, these are merely labels, not the consciousness behind the struggle, the art, and the success story.

The soul is a function of consciousness; more contact with the soul expands one's ability to access 'the field of all possibilities' also known as an awareness of consciousness. But the soul isn't an inert manifestation; it also evolves. An old soul has nothing to do with the chronological age of the host person; an old soul can be a child or an adult. You can't detect an old soul with thinking. When you meet an old soul, you can sense a depth in her that is palpable. You can't quantify this feeling because it is a metaphysical encounter; you are, however, the 'galvanic response', the instrument of detection. An old soul brings things to light in the most simple ways; an old soul sees past the pitfalls of illusion; an old soul is gentle and lively; an old soul is evolved; an old soul is mostly free from karmic debt; and, perhaps, most of all, an old soul is fully present, which we can call divine. This also explains the enigma of why not all intelligent people are smart—which is a function of the soul. Let's focus on the opportunities available to us in the here and now. Art, after all, is created in the present moment. Let's learn from the soul by releasing attachment to the troubles of the past and the uncertain potential of the future. The mechanism for accomplishing freedom from destructive thoughts is through the passion of creation, which is your prayer.

In my talk with the historian, I wasn't comparing art from one epoch with art from another; art must be viewed within the context of its age. Hindsight is for historians; foresight is for artists. Not to compare a Monet with a Rothko (both feature inviting color fields) was a lesson I had learned a long time ago; all comparisons in art are a trap. A primal cave painting of 40,000 years ago made by an anonymous artist is no less an artwork than an etching by Rembrandt.

On seeing the cave paintings at Lascaux, Picasso reportedly remarked: "We have discovered nothing new in art in 17,000 years."

Good work is forever good; time doesn't diminish the spirit of quality. Pure art, pure emotion is, after all, timeless. Humankind had evolved and is still evolving; in some future time we 'moderns' may well be regarded as the 'Neanderthal' species of the 21st century. The innate gift of art had evolved from the first protoartists who created symbolic representation to artists of recent memory who revolutionized art with nonrepresentational work that describes itself instead of that which already exists in nature. I restated my thought to the historian: art was a living thing, a reflection of consciousness, and as the ascension toward consciousness has been evolving over the eons through an expanding awareness among many more people, we can say and must acknowledge that art is evolutionary.

While I never did get a satisfying answer from him as to why he was resistant to art as evolutionary, this encounter with the art historian did get me thinking about how the trafficking of art evolved, which places an invaluable depth of perspective on the here and now.

A WORKING DEFINITION

Although it is the present that concerns us for our art life, it is illuminating to look back, in broad brushstrokes, at the evolving vocation of the artist, and to appreciate the status and opportunity you have as an artist in the 21st century. However, to make sense of the past (and the present) we need a universally satisfying definition of art, one that transcends time, cultures, politics, Eastern and Western sensibilities, including Aboriginal people and Native American from Navaho to Mayan. There are artistic traditions that fall outside the Western mindset. In Japan, for example, artists sometimes adopt different art pen names at various stages of their career, usually to mark significant changes in their art and life. Taking the signature element further, certain Buddhist artists wouldn't sign their works, for doing so would be an act of ego, which Buddhist philosophy

Prehistoric painters didn't make their images as art in the institutionalized modern sense.

These days, cave artists of eons ago would be described as self-taught and catalogued under the banner of Outsider Art—which is a unique accomplishment.

EDEN

teaches causes suffering. Although our focus here is primarily concerned with the customs associated with Western art, note that our way of doing things isn't the only game in town.

What is art? As I have written elsewhere, the answer is that 'it's all art.' Where did the art come from? What is the quality of the work? These are the questions that matter. Quality is a function of experience and consciousness; if the creation is magic, then it is a function of spirit. The spirit of the art is its quality.

Milton Glaser, in the introduction to his book, *Art is Work,* writes:

"There seems to be much confusion about what we mean when using the word *art*. I have a recommendation. We eliminate the word *art* and replace it with *work* and develop the following descriptions:

1. Work that goes beyond its functional intention and moves us in deep and mysterious ways we call *great* work.

2. Work that is conceived and executed with elegance and rigor we call *good* work.

3. Work that meets its intended need honestly and without pretense we call simply *work*.

4. Everything else, the sad and shoddy stuff of daily life, can come under the heading of *bad* work.

"This simple change will eliminate anxiety for thousands of people who worry about whether they are artists or not, but this is not its most significant consequence. More importantly, it can restore art to a central, useful activity in daily life—something for which we have been waiting for a very long time."

We can apply Glaser's word substitution scheme to encompass the creation of all artwork and, to our benefit, avoid the traps of styles, movements, meandering definitions, pretense, politics, and comparison.

THE ARCHETYPE

Although the qualities we most often associate with art today, such as individuality and originality may seem familiar if not altogether natural or inevitable to us, it wasn't always so. Prehistoric man made art in a context far removed from our cultural bias and classically based definitions. Whatever these protoartists called their art, they were sufficiently sophisticated in working with natural mineral pigments and various binding agents to make their own art supplies, a feat of technological know-how that demonstrated their knowledge of chemistry.

Historically, art hasn't been perceived as an act of independence or self-expression, either. The archetype for the 'modern' artist who is appreciated for his unique vision started to take shape about 500 years ago during the Renaissance (rebirth) in Italy, and most conspicuously under the patronage of the Medici: the ruling family of Florence. Prior to this unique flowering of art and connoisseurship, artists didn't create a 'personal' art that was for sale

A loving heart is the beginning of all knowledge.

THOMAS CARLYLE

in galleries or auctioned off for large sums to avid collectors. Artists were cataloged as workers; and their art, rather than an artifact devoted solely to pure contemplation, served some utilitarian purpose.

From the primordial moment when humans began to create, the artist has felt his calling through a connection with the divine. However, within the perception of the ever-expanding needs of the tribe—from pre-modern to ancient world to Middle Ages to the Renaissance to industrialized society—who and what an artist is has changed over the millennia. For thousands of years, artists were members of a social group with a 'skill' who made art for practical sustainable purposes: to insure a successful hunt, to rout the enemy, to enhance fertility, or to appease an influential totem or spirit. Tribal cultures used art as a collective instrument to bind the group where everyone knew everyone else. According to many anthropologists, the individual artist, as we know her today, didn't exist in pre-modern societies. Art for art's sake, it seems, wasn't yet a 'tenet' for the cult of the individual. Within this social arrangement, there wasn't a Jackson Pollock to speak of among the whole lot—this is a distinction, not a comparison.

PRIMITIVE URGES

From a social science perspective, the author of *Art and Intimacy*, Ellen Dissanayake, told me the following: "In the Pleistocene and in pre-modern societies, people's art would not have been 'rejected' in the way it can be in our modern, highly individualistic society. In ancestral and pre-modern times, arts were participative and it was the *act* of making, singing, dancing, etc. that was important—everyone's efforts were appreciated. Participation was the standard and through engaging in the arts, people gained such psychologically valuable things as a sense of belonging to their group, feeling competent in what they did, and feeling a sense of shared meaning in their efforts and contributions. In the contemporary world almost everything is competitive, and so the 'losers' feel that they don't belong, that they may not be competent, and that their own personal meaning is not part of the meaning of the people around them. It's no wonder that rejection of one's art is so distressing."

The anthropological conclusion, which may be factual, doesn't rule out the presence of an individual creator from those 'primitive' cultures, nor does it preclude the fashioning of ornaments (arts and crafts) for decorative purposes. Jewelry, for example, was no doubt useful for tribal identity as well as establishing an individual's standing among the group; and this early utilitarian approach to art doesn't conflict with the lone artist who felt the transcendental connection to the source of his art. Attempting to explain *your* magical connection to the gods through your art was a personal issue that might not have been understood much less appreciated by the rest of the tribe—unless, of course, you were the anointed artist-shaman who presided over spiritual matters. If you were an artist who was intuitively connected to the Great Spirit and a member of a Cro-Magnon group of hunter-gatherers in Europe during the late Paleolithic Period, where life hung in the balance based on group acceptance and protection, you most likely practiced discretion, which, with deference to Falstaff, is still the better part of valor.

The greatest magnifying glasses in the world are a man's own eyes when they look upon his own person.

ALEXANDER POPE

Let the beauty of what you love be what you do.
RUMI

There were individual artists in those pre-modern societies who, within the constraints of tribal custom (dogma), didn't have the opportunity for self-expression, which isn't that far afield of contemporary drones working nine to five in today's society.

WORKMEN FOR HIRE

As we travel forward along our historical timeline from tribal communities to classical Greece and their model of the arts, the perception then was that painters and sculptors, specifically, were merely lowly workmen who weren't worthy of having a dedicated muse of their own from the pantheon; this bias endured into ancient Rome society that, like the Greeks of the Golden Age before them, appreciated painting and sculpture more for proficiency than the singular expressive voice of a particular artist. Both the Greeks and Romans applied rules to art in an attempt to bring order to the seeming chaos of nature that surrounded them. How well an artist followed these rules was a measure of his skill. This is how a painting should look; this is how a sculpture should look; this is how art should look. Keep in mind too that these traditional cultures from Greco-Roman antiquity needed to be conservative and routinely consistent if they were to enforce their rules and laws in controlling the general population—and art was no exception. Neither the Greeks nor Romans had a specific word for the fine arts in the modern sense. The term for art in Greek (*techne*) and Latin (*ars*) refers to technique and skill applied to all sorts of activities, which doesn't specifically single out painting or sculpture as being a higher art than pottery, weaving, shoemaking, or other crafts.

During the Middle Ages, which lasted from about 476-1450 CE and spanned a period from the dissolution of the western half of the Roman Empire up to the Renaissance, Christianity ruled Western culture under a medieval heaven—a period in history that is also referred to as the Dark Ages. Under the strict auspices of the church, the visual arts were eventually co-opted to indoctrinate a mostly illiterate population about religion. Art and architecture merged to design the great medieval cathedrals that were constructed by hundreds of skilled craftsmen. Huge tapestries that provided a pictorial narrative chronicling tales from mythology often adorned the homes of the wealthy. Fashion statements could include elaborately decorated clothing that conveyed a person's status and moral views. Although no particular form of art was considered superior during the Middle Ages, items such as illuminated manuscripts, jewelry, and metal objects used in church services were highly prized.

NO GILDED LILIES

Highly specialized artisans who were members of craft guilds, which were essentially unions and monopolies, created many of the objects now displayed in museum collections as medieval art. Members of a craft guild were divided into master, journeyman, and apprentice. The master was an accomplished craftsman who took on apprentices, usually boys in their teens. In return for no wages, often for an agreed upon term of service from five to nine years, apprentices received room and board, and an education from the master. While most guilds excluded women, some, which included butchers, ironmongers, shoemakers, hot-food sellers, bookbinders, and even goldsmiths (which certainly required artistry), allowed girls, usually at the age of seven or eight, to be placed as apprentices where the wife of the master would take charge of their training. Other domestic oriented trades, such as brewing, spinning, and silk making, were exclusively female industries. Although the role of artist for women was rarely encouraged, records of the period reveal that females who became artists were most often daughters of artists who trained in their fathers' workshops or privileged female offspring of noblemen.

Evelyn Welch, in her book, *Art and Society in Italy 1350-1500*, observes that: "The public and professional nature of these enterprises ensured that, unlike in later centuries, almost all the artists considered in this book are male. There were exceptions, although these should not be exaggerated: as we have seen, documents show that a number of nuns were trained to provide manuscript illuminations and embroideries; the sculptor Guido Mazzoni (active 1473-1518) renowned for his work in terracotta and *cartapesta*, seems to have also employed his wife and daughter as valued assistants; and one of the daughters of the famed Venetian glass-maker Angelo Barovier specialized in enamel-painting, an area in which we now know other women were employed. The paucity of these examples does not mean that gender is not a consideration in the study of Renaissance art; it merely tells us that images of women, commissions by women, or objects seen by women are almost always produced by men."

Women artists also faced considerable prejudice from men who considered them to be inferior and incapable of producing art. Women, for the most part, were saddled with time-consuming domestic chores, leaving them out of the loop for learning artistic skills and from considering careers outside the home. To place the challenge for the would-be woman artist of the past into a meaningful context, consider how difficult it is for any artist today to live the dream.

MASTERPIECES AND PRINCES

After an apprentice graduated to journeyman he was paid for his work. When the journeyman could prove his attainment of technical and artistic expertise with a 'masterpiece' of his own, he could then rise in the ranks to master and open his own workshop. Our concept of a 'masterpiece' has its roots in the tradition of the medieval workshop. In this age, the reverence by the patron for technique, style and standards made sense since the guilds kept their craft-making secrets close to the vest—and keeping trade secrets is no stranger in the 21st century, either. A masterpiece during the Middle Ages could be any representative object that showed mastery of materials and technique: sculpture, a stained glass window, a shoe, a piece of pottery, a silver chalice, a painting, or a suit of armor.

While art is the focus here, also remember that in the mid-fourteenth century the Black Death (plague) killed off an estimated nearly one third of Europe, about 25 million people. This great population loss provoked economic upheaval and accelerated social and economic change during the 14th and 15th centuries. In this tumultuous climate, the church's power was weakened and—in some cases, the roles it had played were replaced

Say not, 'I have found the truth,' but rather, 'I have found a truth.'

KAHLIL GIBRAN

You don't take a photograph, you make it.

ANSEL ADAMS

with secular ones. Since religious officials couldn't keep their frequent promises of curing plague victims and banishing the disease, the Black Death led to cynicism of the clergy. Before long an interest in more scientific alternatives to fighting disease took root in European society that was also growing more politically secular. Peasant rebellions against the establishment in France, England, and Italy laid the groundwork for more liberal and equitable treatment. The sudden scarcity of cheap labor, most notably in Western Europe, provided an incentive for innovation and increased social mobility that broke through the stagnation of the Dark Ages and, some speculate, caused the Renaissance.

But some artists rose above the traditional confines of the medieval art industry. A different social role for the artist had begun to emerge in the late 14th century. By becoming a member of an aristocratic household as the court artist, an artist could gain an unprecedented degree of prestige and more freedom to improvise beyond the rigid conformity and rules of a craft guild. The status associated with this position at court played a significant role in transforming the social ranking of the artist from the role of artisan in the late medieval period to artist of a different caliber. Artists in this elite group included Jan Van Eyck, Mantegna, Piero della Francesca, Botticelli, Leonardo da Vinci, Albrecht Dürer, Hans Holbein, Michelangelo, and Peter Paul Rubens who all held, at one point in their careers, a position at court.

BENEFITS PACKAGE

During the later Middle Ages the court artist was considered a member of a prince's family. The artist and the prince had a personal connection. In a real sense, the prince acquired the artist along with his talent. Like any other member of the household, the artist would have to swear an oath of loyalty to the prince. If the prince should happen to die, the artist lost his position at court. The artist usually received an annual salary or pension—an annuity for the artist to be on call to do work and not for any specific artwork. In addition, court artists would often receive a house and clothing befitting their position as a member of court.

Keep in mind too that acquiring art was out of reach for the common folk; art was a luxury commissioned by royalty, wealthy families, and the most powerful institution of that age—the Catholic Church. The mentality of the time was more intrigued about materials and techniques than in who created a specific piece of art.

Evelyn Welch writes:

"But while we can find a small number of fifteenth-century patrons proudly listing the artists whose works they possessed, the emphasis on authorship was not always crucial. Instead the question, 'who made it?', was often replaced with 'what is it made from, and how?'

"This may not seem an obvious issue today. Renowned late twentieth-century artists often use common everyday materials. Part of their argument is that the individual, whether painter, sculptor, performer, or installation organizer, personally transforms the physical mundane into a higher cultural form. In defining the artwork as 'art', the conceptual or philosophical idea, the location of the exhibition in a museum or gallery, the artist's individual reputation, and the price the work last sold for, can frequently prove as, if not more important than, the material in which the artist was working.

"But in the period we are considering, 1350-1500, materials and artistry were closely linked. The more expensive, rare, or unusual the substance, the more deserving it was of fine craftsmanship and distinguished design. This did not always imply an elaborate narrative and to properly understand the value of works like the tomb of Medici brothers Piero and Giovanni in the old sacristy in the church of San Lorenzo, Florence, we have to stop looking for the story and examine the workmanship.

"God and nature, rather than man himself, provided the most precious and valued objects in Italian collections. In the famed fourteenth-century Visconti library in Pavia or in Lorenzo de' Medici's fifteenth-century study, pride of the place was given, not to paintings, but to the tusks of the sea-mammal, the narwhal, commonly assumed to be the horn of a unicorn. Ostrich eggs and nautilus shells were similarly conserved and displayed for their rarity and unusual properties. Pearls, diamonds, and other gems, carved or uncarved, were gathered because of their rarity, monetary value, and because of the magical abilities they were thought to possess. For example, coral was thought to ward off evil."

WORKERS OF ART

Art during the Middle Ages was commissioned and bought for clearly defined purposes that mostly included self-promotion and church-related iconography. This restrictive medieval relationship to art lasted well into the Italian Renaissance of the 15th century where, for the most part, artists were still seen as tradesmen selling services, not as individual creators inspired by the gods or the muses like poets who, in the classical tradition, were perceived as having a nobler calling. Artists were expected to follow the rules of their craft, like any other trade. They were paid for their time and labor, not for their unique ability to create.

Members of the visual arts were assigned to guilds that regulated artisans, who, unlike 'gentlemen', worked with their hands; there were no specific or independent 'art' guilds for painters, sculptors, or for architects. Because paint pigments and medicines were ground in much the same way, and artists and physicians had the same patron saint (St Luke was both a physician and an artist who, according to legend, painted a portrait of the Virgin Mary from life.), painters were relegated to the guild that served apothecaries (which also sold art supplies) and physicians. Perhaps, on an unconscious level, it was understood that art also heals. A sculptor who worked in bronze was a member of the goldsmiths' guild, which was a branch of the *Arte Della Seta* (guild of silk weavers). The famous Florentine sculptor Donatello of the Early Italian Renaissance, who had apprenticed to a goldsmith, belonged to the guild of the *Arte di Pietra e Legname* (workers in stone and wood) that also included sculptors, masons, carpenters, and some architects.

A record of 1412 tells us that Donatello, who often worked in bronze, also belonged to the Company of St Luke, and his profession was listed as goldsmith and stonecarver.

I paint with shapes.
ALEXANDER CALDER

The essence of all art is to have pleasure in giving pleasure.

DALE CARNEGIE

Motivated by economic and political concerns (guild membership was also a prerequisite for holding political office), the guilds, in promoting proficiency in materials, technique, and a dogmatic adherence to rules over experimentation and invention, were on a collision course with progress; guild membership couldn't stifle those true artists of the Renaissance. Leonardo, who was also an inventor and scientist, and Michelangelo, who considered himself a sculptor, not a painter, were both apprenticed as painters; and years earlier, the Florentine engineer, scholar of ancient architecture, sculptor, and daring innovator, Filippo Brunelleschi (1337-1446), refused to be contained by labels and narrow definitions enforced by the guilds—a self-image which led him into a career as the great architect of his age.

THE RADICAL EGG

Brunelleschi, like his peer Donatello and his rival Ghiberti, had been an apprentice to a goldsmith who taught him mounting, engraving, and embossing. To capitalize on his skill in mathematics and architecture, Brunelleschi later joined the Masons' guild. Like other men with crossover talents of the Renaissance period, Brunelleschi, who was temperamental and ambitious, had also immersed himself in the science of motion, using wheels, gears, cogs and weights—disciplines that would one day serve him well when he undertook what was perhaps the most challenging and coveted commission of his time—designing the magnificent cupola, or dome, for the Duomo (cathedral) of Santa Maria del Fiore in Florence.

The design of the dome, which was completed in 1436, was so radical that he had to invent new methods and machinery to construct what is still the largest masonry vault ever raised—143 feet in diameter and weighing an estimated seventy million pounds. Note too that Brunelleschi, who was first denounced as a lunatic for his unorthodox architectural solutions, went on to raise his dome, his masterpiece, above the Florentine skyline amid plagues, wars, and political feuds. Would you have fared as well as Brunelleschi? Do you feel gratitude for the freedom you do have to create?

To win the commission to build the dome, Brunelleschi had to participate in a contest to see who would produce the best model for the dome. When the Great Council of wardens who were judging the merits of each design asked Brunelleschi to show them precisely how he would achieve his ambitious structure, Brunelleschi, according to an account written by Giorgio Vasari, made the following suggestion: the commission should be awarded to whoever can make an egg stand on end on a flat piece of marble. When the other contestants failed to make their eggs defy gravity, Brunelleschi cracked an egg on the bottom and then simply stood it upright. When his rivals protested, saying they could have done the same, Brunelleschi said that they would also know how to vault the dome too, if only they knew his secret plans. The commission, of course, as Vasari, reports, went to Brunelleschi. Whether Vasari's anecdote is apocryphal or not, the object lesson then and now is this: no thing is obvious.

In addition to the architecture of the dome and to make its construction possible, Brunelleschi invented an ox-powered hoist based on an advanced engineering system of pulleys and gears (including a new concept, a reverse gear); this marvelous lifting machine would one day come under the scrutiny of a gifted young artist who was apprenticed in the workshop of the Florentine artist Andrea del Verrocchio. The apprentice was Leonardo da Vinci. As Ross King observes in his book, *Brunelleschi's Dome*, "Fascinated by Filippo's machines, which Verrocchio used to hoist the ball, Leonardo made a series of sketches of them and, as a result, is often given credit for their invention. How Filippo would have reacted to this misattribution—Filippo, who was so proud of his invention and so fearful of plagiarism—scarcely bears contemplation."

In 1434, two years before the Duomo was completed, Brunelleschi contributed yet another milestone of ingenuity. He changed the perception of Western art forever by reproducing a three-dimensional object in two-dimensional space; by employing a mathematically based illusion of reality, he devised perspective, which would become the hallmark signature technique of Renaissance painting and drawing.

As King informs us: "Filippo is generally regarded as its [perspective] inventor, the one who discovered (or rediscovered) its mathematical laws. For example, he worked out the principle of the vanishing point, which was known to the Greeks and Romans but, like so much other knowledge, had long since been lost."

Before the second coming of perspective during the Renaissance, it was generally accepted that the function of art wasn't naturalistic representation, but rather the expression of spiritual power. When we think of ancient knowledge being lost we tend to think of it in relation to our present day culture. Seeing how ancient knowledge was also forgotten or lost during the Renaissance gives us a sense of how close we are along the historical timeline to the 15th century, Brunelleschi, and the first stirrings of what would become 'modern' art in our own age.

Portraying real figures in real pictorial 'three-dimensional' space is a distinct Renaissance characteristic.

A WAX CANDLE

Evelyn Welch provides further insight about the guilds during the mid-fourteenth to fifteenth centuries in Renaissance (1350-1500) Italy:

"In most Italian cities the activities of artists, like other professional craftsmen, were regulated by guilds or corporations which went under different titles such as *arti* in Tuscany, *paratichi* or *università* in the Veneto and Lombardi, and the *Fraglia* in Padua. The importance of these organizations varied from town to town. In Florence guild membership was a condition of government office, and many crafts were subsumed within larger, more powerful associations. Although stone masons had their own *arte*, the goldsmiths belonged to the influential silk guild, the *Seta*, while painters belonged to the guild of doctors and apothecaries, the *Medici e Speziali*. Outside Florence, however, the corporations were less prominent in political affairs and more interested in regulating purely economic activities. The Venetian guild of glass-makers faced strict conditions on their production which were overseen by the government itself. In order to limit output, they were, for example, not allowed to operate their furnaces from August until January and severe penalties were threatened against those who worked abroad or passed on their skills to non-Venetians.

Poor ego.

It has gotten a lot of negative press in recent years. For our purposes, we will follow suit and use it as a convenient metaphor to describe that aspect of ourselves that prevents us from achieving all that we can become.

Keep in mind too that the ego is not the enemy here; but fear and doubt are if you allow them to rule.

EDEN

Exactitude is not truth.

HENRI MATISSE

"The *1355* statutes of the Sienese painters' guild were less rigid in their conditions. Foreigners only had to pay a fine in order to work in the city, but artists were forbidden to take work away from a fellow painter without the latter's permission, to tempt workers or apprentices away from a colleague's shop, or to substitute low-quality gold, silver, or colors for those promised. Other clauses insisted that painters attend each other's funerals and those of members' close relatives. They were also to ensure that no one cursed or blasphemed and that holy days were observed. On the annual feast of St Luke, they were to attend a procession and offer up a wax candle to him as their patron saint."

THE INDIVIDUAL ARTIST

Beginning around 1500 CE in the high Renaissance period, things began to change toward quite a different appreciation of the artist; painters and sculptors, 'dirty hands' notwithstanding, began to gain enviable stature in a culture where individual expression was to become preeminent, most especially under the ruling dynasty of the Medici family of Florence, Italy. Lorenzo de' Medici in particular sanctioned non-religious art during a time when art was supposed to serve the aims of the church and the Pope. Also known as Lorenzo the Magnificent (*il Magnifico*), he was urbane, an impresario, a poet of some note, and a progressive statesman in the modern sense. He founded the first school of art in Florence; and one of its first students was a thirteen-year-old boy who displayed great artistic promise by the name of Michelangelo. Lorenzo invited the young apprentice artist to live in the palace with the Medici family.

Lorenzo, who was a patron to genius (which was also a political act) that included Botticelli, Leonardo, and Michelangelo, encouraged and protected his artists and their irrepressible avant-garde and often secular thematic works from retribution by the church. Botticelli, for example, who, like any other artist of the period, painted religious works, also felt free under the auspices of his Medici patron to create a new form of art known as *La Primavera* that drew upon poetry, mythology, and fantasy—inspiration that was far afield from Jesus, the church, and the Pope.

One of Botticelli's most daring works was the *Birth of Venus*, a painting that celebrated human desire and was meant to be hung over the marital bed as a wedding gift for Lorenzo's cousin. The controversial work of pagan influence was so politically incorrect at the time that it was kept 'under wraps' for half a century. Although the Florentine Republic seems to have garnered the headlines here as the mecca for artistic evolution and scientific advancement, seeds of the Renaissance were flowering throughout northern Europe, which included France, the Netherlands, and Germany.

In her book, *The Vocation of Artists*, Deborah Haynes writes:

"Directly related to the idea of the artist-hero was the artist as semidivine creator. This notion of a person endowed with semidivine powers emerged in fifteenth-century Florence in the writing of Neoplatonist humanists such as Marsilio Ficino. Supported by the Medicis, Ficino wrote that the human mind functions analogously to God's when a person creates: 'It expresses this in audible speech, writes it with pen on paper, represents it in the matter of the world by what it makes.... Man is god over all the material elements, for he uses, modifies and forms them all.'

"This equation of the human creator with God, and the birth of the artist as a semidivine creator, further stimulated the movement of art-for-art's-sake. What then mattered was not the content, but the signature of a particular artist—Leonardo, Michelangelo, or Bellini. The birth of the artist and the work of art as independent entities also mark the beginning of the commercialization of and speculation in art as a commodity for profit. Earlier, artists had worked under specific patronage of the church or government, but a significant reversal occurred. Patrons, kings or merchants, sought particular artists to paint their portraits or for other work. Artists like Raphael and Titian succeeded in this atmosphere."

MOVEABLE ART, MOVEABLE TYPE

While it is well known that art commissioned (custom made so to speak) by patrons was the principal reason for making art during the Renaissance, more art commerce was trickling down into the mainstream among a growing middle class eager to emulate the rich by owning artworks. If you dig deep, history, which is rarely black or white, often provides a more complete and multicolored picture of bygone events and customs. Things we take for granted today weren't always so—like buying art in a gallery.

Was there a precise period when non-commissioned works of art first began to sell in galleries? This is the question I asked Louisa Matthew, associate professor of art history at Union College, and a contributing editor of *The Art Market in Italy, 15th-17th Centuries*, a volume of essays, who replied as follows:

"Your question, and an answer to it, is a widely-debated topic in art history and economic history right now. We now know that artists did sell non-commissioned works in 'open markets' in Italy during the Renaissance although the major model was still commissioned work. There was a more highly developed setup for selling non-commissioned art in northern Europe (especially Flanders) during the same period. As far as selling in galleries—if you mean dealers' galleries—that is another issue. Art dealers as we know them today didn't begin to develop until the second half of the 16th century in Italy. The venues for selling non-commissioned work in Italy before that were multiple: friends and agents (often merchants or clergy) who were traveling to other locales; painters and related trades such as gilders working on out of town projects; fairs and pilgrimage sites; and selling works right out of the artist's workshop where he/she would also be taking orders for commissioned works."

Prior to the 15th century, all art was essentially one-of-a-kind and understandably expensive. In the early 1400's, with the advent of widely available paper, printmaking became a more commercially viable enterprise, making it possible for hundreds or even thousands of identical images to be reproduced from a single woodcut or a metal plate engraving. This technology increased the availability of each print while decreasing its price. Given this economic advantage of mass production to reach even the poorest members of society, the early print market was driven by the demand for playing cards and inexpensive devotional images.

Learn from nature.

If you want to sail into the prevailing wind, against the mainstream, then you have to tack to move forward.

You can apply this principle to your art life; opportunity often arrives obliquely and from sources you couldn't have anticipated.

You must be aware, alert, and active to take advantage of what you can accomplish in the field of all possibilities.

EDEN

Evelyn Welch writes: "There were a number of different ways of obtaining a work of art in this period. Modest items could be purchased quite simply from a diverse range of sources. If a patron was trying to save money, he or she could buy a reconditioned second-hand altarpiece or obtain one of the cheaper varieties sold by shops or itinerant salesmen who moved from city to city. There are late fourteenth-century records in Bologna, for example, of a German peddler who sold 'certain cards figured and painted with images of saints.' In Padua in 1440 one salesman, operating on behalf of a Flemish trader, was offering 3,500 woodcuts for sale. Engravings, such as the image of St Catherine of Siena produced in Florence, helped to popularize new figures of devotion while most artists usually had the more traditional Virgin and Child readily available for immediate purchase or special order."

OIL AND WATER

By the mid-fifteenth century, another image form—the letters of the alphabet—was to be liberated from the exclusive domain of the wealthy. Johannes Gutenberg, a German goldsmith, invented the printing press with replaceable wooden or metal letters (1440), making the first printed books more affordable for a mass market. The proliferation of arts, technique, and letters was reshaping the identity of the modern artist.

It can't be overstated that the Renaissance was a watershed time in history, especially for artists. Subject matter began to expand beyond the parochial dogma of religious symbolism as innovate techniques and skills opened up new possibilities in the making of art. Leonardo, for example, put aside traditional fast-drying fresco and egg tempera to experiment with oil painting, a novel technique in Italy, but already quite developed as a painter's medium in northern Europe. In the early 15th century, the Flemish artist Jan Van Eyck helped perfect the newly discovered technique of oil painting. These slow to dry paints gave the artist more time to work and the translucent character of the oils were ideal for rendering subtle tones of light and color—especially useful qualities for capturing nature on canvas.

Momentum for artistic individuality was in the Tuscan air and the aroma of freedom of expression was intoxicating. People began to admire personal artistry as well as the subject of the artwork. The late Renaissance brought about a staggering shift in perception: artists were no longer seen as being exclusively tradesmen. A master artist could work on his own terms and enjoy a higher social status than a 'mere' craftsman. However, to diminish the artisan is highly misguided. Craft is the perfection of a valuable technique. Artists were beginning to assert their individual visions as independent creators.

And, with such stellar artists as Leonardo and his younger 'rival' Michelangelo becoming famous throughout Europe, the image of the modern artist had already begun its process toward indelibility. The freelance genius was out of the bottle.

THE ACADEMY MODEL

In the 16th century, the notion that there was a decided difference between arts and crafts continued to build momentum. In Italy, architecture, painting,

Art is either plagiarism or revolution.

PAUL GAUGUIN

and sculpture were grouped together as part of a comprehensive school of design where reproducing ideas and observations of the natural world into drawings began to take a prominent position. By the 17th century, the restrictive model of the guild workshop of the Middle Ages, which was slow to warm to innovation, was waning. A short list of artists, like those in the late Middle Ages, continued to gain creative freedom as court artists—a position that didn't oblige them to join guilds; and increasing numbers of artists were selling work to private collectors. A prospective artist now had another option. He could bypass joining a guild by studying at an art academy where, unlike the old workshop mentality that combined a variety of arts and crafts under one guild, he could take part in a new distinction between figurative drawing and decorative painting. As the academy model evolved, students learned anatomy, geometry, perspective, and art theory.

By vigorously delineating the difference between arts and crafts, one academy in France etched an indelible distinction in the development of Western art. Founded in Paris (1648), the *Académie des Beaux-Arts* referred to the arts of painting, sculpture, and architecture as the *beaux-arts*, or the 'fine arts'. Inspired by classical Greek and Roman aesthetics and modeled after Italian academies, the *Académie* analyzed and judged works of art by: invention, proportion, color, expression, and composition. Drawing, which 'appealed' to the mind, was pronounced with great authority to be superior to color, which, admittedly expressive, was deemed a supplementary technique to drawing that 'appealed' to more primitive senses. For better or worse, the *Académie*, while enhancing the individuality and status of the artist, also co-opted art by making drawing—especially the nude figure—a prerequisite skill for being an artist. Four centuries later, life drawing is a requirement that remains part of the curriculum in many of today's art schools. Learning how to draw was a prejudice that had more to do with academia and politics than art. To any painter who might disagree, remember, the protoartists of the late Paleolithic Period didn't attend art school in the modern sense.

Genius is the ability to renew one's emotions in daily experience.

PAUL CÉZANNE

BREAKING AWAY

As the 19th century heralded in the Age of Enlightenment, artists were actively in defiance of the now state sponsored French *Académie*. By expressing their individuality and perceptions through provocatively inspired modern subject matter executed through unconventional compositions (ordinary scenes of life instead of classical or religious archetypes) and techniques (including a sketch like approach and painting in the open air—*en plein air*), these artists were cutting themselves loose from the classically oriented and restrictive definition of art by the *Académie*. Breaking away from the *Académie* to pursue light, color, atmosphere, and feeling as a primary subjective construct had a twofold effect: it led to Impressionism, which was a pivotal movement in the development of modern art. Then, in turn, seeking alternative spaces and opportunities to state-sponsored exhibits and competitions, new and progressive venues for showcasing art eventually evolved into the contemporary commercial gallery system that both exhibited and sold the artist's work.

The moment you cheat for the sake of beauty, you know you're an artist.

DAVID HOCKNEY

If you've experienced the risk of creation, then rejection is a passing gadfly, nothing more.

EDEN

In 1863, for example, the *Académie* rejected to display certain works by the Impressionists and Realists in the officially sanctioned Paris Salon. Complaints of bias from the artists involved prompted French Emperor Napoleon III to command that these rejected works have a showcase in a separate exhibit known as the *Salon des Refusés* (Room of the Rejected). Although much of the exhibit might not have been first-rate, it did include the works of Paul Cézanne, Camille Pissarro, Armand Guillaumin, Johan Jongkind, and Henri Fantin-Latour. The *Salon* also featured Édouard Manet's 'scandalous' *Déjeuner sur l'Herbe* (Luncheon on the Grass) and the American James McNeill Whistler's classically executed yet austere *The White Girl*, a painting more about art for art's sake than the narrative value critics of the time held up as sacrosanct.

Impressionism led to a new generation of the Post-Impressionists (1880-1920) who were exploring expression, emotions, structure, and form in their work. The Post-Impressionists included such late 19th-century painters as Paul Cézanne, Georges Seurat, Paul Gauguin, Vincent van Gogh, Henri de Toulouse-Lautrec, and others. Most of these painters began as Impressionists before setting off in their own directions where each developed a highly personal art, which would influence many abstract artists and early 20th century modernism—where the subjective experience of the artist would become synonymous with art.

SEARCHING FOR AN ISM

In our time, artists owe a clearly defined debt to the avant-garde art movements of the past. Innovators such as the previously mentioned van Gogh and Gauguin, and their successors, Pablo Picasso, Wassily Kandinsky, Marcel Duchamp, Jackson Pollock, Arshile Gorky, and Mark Rothko were apostles of their time who through their perseverance and rigorous honesty (at least in their work), demonstrated that art—hyperbolic, or not—had evolved into a form of self-referential expression, an accepted definition that has remained an important part of our understanding of what art is to this day. And, let's not overlook Andy Warhol, Jean-Michel Basquiat, and others who popularized art for a new generation.

In this context, we have, most especially in painting, art formalism where it is form, not external world content that determines its value as art. No 'ism' is a panacea. What forms are then significant? You must discover that for yourself—keeping in mind that contrivance as a scheme isn't an answer that concerns us here.

Of course, the pattern of art as it evolves in retrospect is clear if not always precisely understood during its incubation. Legitimate (meaning organically developed, not artificially or politically inseminated) art movements serve a great purpose; they allow artists to explore beyond familiar and comfortable customs into as yet uncharted realms.

BOUGHT IN AMERICA

Today, it often seems that no one, including many an artist, can get a handle on what art is. To help explain this apparent lack of comprehension, remember that art, at its essence, isn't about fads, trends, taste, or even movements, which are like waves, not the energy creating the waves. Fine art or high art, they are one in the same; this is art from the soul, driven by passion, and executed in pure emotion; such art is a source of power and creation that can't be defined by academicians, demystified by the press, or pigeonholed with convenient labels by critics. Remember too that anything of quality—art, craft, or design—transcends time and remains forever a thing to be appreciated. Franz Marc's painting *Blue Horse I,* for example, is as exciting for its spirit, bold colors, and purity of form today as it was when he painted it nearly a century ago. And, as Milton Glaser reminded us earlier, art is work, and that is a truth.

In the Preface to her 1957 book, *Men & Monuments*, Janet Flanner provides us with a perceptive context:

"The United States has had to import its great art. Everything else we make for ourselves. It would appear that the greatest impediment to our obtaining any initial national notions of the cultural and civilizing pleasure of art was probably the ubiquitous American husband who too good-naturedly left art to the females of his family—as if Giotto, Rembrandt, Goya, Manet and Matisse were like embroidery or some sort of fancy housewifely decorations, unsuitable as virile concerns. Though European art was bought around the turn of the century by certain rare collectors or on a lower level by big spenders like the Vanderbilts, on the whole art was thought by most American men to be an emasculating refinement until it began to be purchased in fairly considerable quantity by rich businessmen after the First World War. They frequently knew nothing more about the matter than what their art merchant said and how much it would cost, but they accidentally served the national interest by putting what amounted to their O.K. on art as a privately held choice commodity, and in this way it gained its first influential, respectable ranking. Since the Second World War, private art collecting on an enormous costly scale by American multimillionaires living in magnificent new houses, from Hollywood to Texas, in refurbished old Virginia mansions or deep in Manhattan and out on Long Island, has become the next step in art appreciation in the United States. It has placed pictures in a new social context as necessary luxuries, colorful symbols of prestige culled from a preciously limited market, as marks of power and superior position."

The art market as we know it, and as Flanner described a half century ago, was the product of politics, gender, ego, chance, and many other influences. In 2004, The Getty Museum in Los Angeles held an exhibition titled *The Business of Art: Evidence from the Art Market* that exposed a behind-the-scenes look at the modern art market as it has developed over the past 400 years—from the sixteenth through the twentieth century.

To support this rare and objective look into the interdependent process of selling a work of art—from artistic vision to evaluation to acquisition—the exhibition revealed a well-documented paper trail that included: "dealers' stock books, artists' personal letters, codebooks, rare photographs, press clippings, scholars' diaries, inventories of private collections, agents' reports, early manuals of auction results for collectors, and other valuations of art." Through this historical array of artifacts, the exhibition provided an insider's look into the hidden intrigue and players behind the marketing, selling, and buying of art.

The test of character and inner strength comes not when everything is together, but when everything appears and feels as if it's falling apart. And then, you see if you can hold it together, which is what it's all about—holding it together as a force of nature.

EDEN

Being good in business is the most fascinating kind of art. Making money is art and working is art and good business is the best art.

ANDY WARHOL

The answer is there if you are still, clear, and positioned to feel it.

EDEN

"Although art is sold, bought, or traded, it is not a commodity in the ordinary sense," observes Thomas Crow, director of the Getty Research Institute. "The value of a work of art can fluctuate radically in an instant, depending on a number of factors, including the assessments of scholars and critics, the power and marketing savvy of dealers, the influence of artists, the taste of collectors, and the economy and fashion of the time."

Besides the artist who creates, the other primary figures—in symbiotic fashion—that drive the art market today include the collector, dealer, and critic, or scholar—and all, in varying degree, contribute to establishing a monetary value for a work of art.

THE LATIN HUSTLE

But art, even in Western contemporary time, hasn't always been viewed as a thing of value. In his book, *Status Anxiety*, Alain de Botton writes:

"What is art good for? That question was in the air in Britain in the 1860s, and according to many commentators, the answer was, not much. It was not art, after all, that had built the great industrial towns, laid the railways, dug the canals, expanded the empire and made Britain preeminent among nations. Indeed, art seemed capable of sapping the very qualities that had made such achievements possible, prolonged contact with it appeared to encourage effeminacy, introspection, homosexuality, gout and defeatism. In a speech in 1865, John Bright, Member of Parliament for Birmingham, described cultured people as a pretentious cabal whose only claim to distinction was knowing 'a smattering of the two dead languages of Greek and Latin.'

"Every great work of art, suggested [Matthew] Arnold, was marked (directly or not) by 'the desire to remove human error, clear human confusion, and diminish human misery,' just as all great artists were imbued with the 'aspiration to leave the world better and happier than they [found] it.' They might not always realize this ambition through overtly political subject matter—indeed, might not even be aware of harboring it at all—and yet imbedded within their work, there was almost always some cry of protest against a status quo, and thus an impulse to correct the viewers insight or teach him to perceive beauty, to help him understand pain or to reanimate his sensitivities, to nurture his capacity for empathy or rebalance his moral perspective through sadness or laughter. Arnold concluded his argument with the idea upon which this chapter [on art] is built: Art, he insisted, was 'the criticism of life.'

"What are we to understand by Arnold's phrase? First, and perhaps most obvious, that life is a phenomenon in need of criticism, for we are, as fallen creatures, in permanent danger of worshipping false gods, of failing to understand ourselves and misinterpreting the behavior of others, of growing unproductively anxious or desirous, and of losing ourselves to vanity and error. Surreptitiously and beguilingly, then, with humor or gravity, works of art—novels, poems, plays, paintings or films—can function as vehicles to explain our condition to us. They may act as guides to a truer, more judicious, more intelligent understanding of the world.

"Given that few things are more in need of criticism (or of insight and analysis) than our approach to status and its distribution, it is hardly surprising that so many artists across time should have created works that in some way contest the methods by which people are accorded rank in society. This history of art is filled with challenges—ironic, angry, lyrical, sad or amusing—to the status system."

THE CULTIVATION OF ART

For the artist who is for the first time getting a taste for the varied players and the logistics involved in the art 'game', it quickly becomes evident that the artist is not a solo act when it comes to the commerce aspect of this enterprise. Although the evolution of making art is a naturally occurring and organic phenomenon, the art market itself, in a real sense, has been artificially sown with 'experts' and middlemen; the art market has matured as a cultural industry, not like a weed but through careful cultivation and control. Of course, we would expect everyone concerned in our art life to behave honorably, but that may not always be the case. Remember too that sincerity, for all its pathos, can be totally wrong—and often is. Always know *who* is talking before giving the information any credence. There is nothing charming about being gullible. If substantial money is to be made in the trafficking of art, then it is no surprise that interested parties will promote their artists and certain artworks to keep prices up—often through Machiavellian manipulation of the market where perception is reality manifested in acclaim and followed by dollars.

It may come as an enlightening shock to the cultural skeptic that art isn't only aesthetically necessary, it is, as anthropologist Ellen Dissanayake asserts, an evolutionary adaptation for survival—a conclusion that would most certainly have thrown the art historian I met in the hotel a curve. How would he have reacted? Dissanayake, author of *Art and Intimacy: How the Arts Began* argues that art, far from being an abstract or unnecessary activity for survival, is a biological imperative. According to Dissanayake, art, at its most fundamental, is an essential mechanism for perpetuating the species. It all begins with the human trait of birthing immature and helpless infants. To ensure that mothers find their demanding babies worth caring for, humans evolved to be lovable and to attune themselves to others from the moment of birth. The ways in which mother and infant respond to each other are rhythmically patterned vocalizations and exaggerated face and body movements that Dissanayake calls rhythm and sensory modes. And, as she asserts, it is these rhythms and sensory modes that gave rise to what we call the arts.

"Because humans," according to Dissanayake, "are born predisposed to respond to and use rhythmic-modal signals, societies everywhere have elaborated them further as music, mime, dance, and display, in rituals which instill and reinforce valued cultural beliefs. Just as rhythms and modes coordinate and unify the mother-infant pair, in ceremonies they coordinate and unify members of a group." Dissanayake further notes that "The biological phenomenon of love is originally manifested—expressed and exchanged—by means of emotionally meaningful 'rhythms and modes' that are jointly created and sustained by mothers and their infants in ritualized, evolved interactions. From these rudimentary and unlikely beginnings grow adult expressions of love, both sexual and generally

The greatness of art is not to find what is common but what is unique.

ISAAC BASHEVIS SINGER

Remember, art from the soul is not in search of subject matter.

EDEN

affiliative, *and the arts*. That is to say, in their origins in ourselves and in our species, love and art are, I suggest, inherently related." And, as Dr. Dissanayake observes: "At the same time, 'art' is notoriously vague, with multiple meanings and associations." Given these anthropological variables, it is not surprising that art is little understood by a modern human who relies on experts and critics to feel as well as think for him.

MANY CHAPEAUS

We have seen that art collecting, as we know it in the modern sense, began to emerge in the 16th century, and by the mid-1900's art as an investment opportunity (and often as a tax write off as well) had become attractive among the moneyed collectors. Over the centuries and well into the Information Age, the dealers, collectors, curators, critics, connoisseurs, and conservators have carved out a slice of the art pie to the extent that their influence is pervasive: their authority is welcome by those they anoint as artists and for those whose work remains unappreciated, or worse yet, ignored, these same experts are 'persona non grata'. In addition, although we may give these authoritarian roles a specific description, there are times when these professions overlap—when a dealer is also an impresario, or when a collector is also a patron and dealer, or when an artist takes on the role of agent, dealer, critic, and collector.

During the early years of his life, for example, van Gogh was a relatively successful art dealer before his passion became painting. Loving, collecting, and selling art before becoming an artist himself is also the path taken by one of van Gogh's contemporaries. In 1879, at the age of thirty-one, Paul Gauguin was employed as a stockbroker's agent in Paris earning a respectable yearly income of 30,000 francs (over $100,000 today). Gauguin, a Sunday painter in those days, spent his weekends studying with Camille Pissarro, a French Impressionist painter who suffered financial hardship in pursuing his faith in Impressionism while rejecting the aesthetic tenets conveyed by the *Académie des Beaux-Arts*.

Not only did Gauguin collect his teacher's art, he also acted as Pissarro's representative. The following letter from Gauguin to Pissarro was on display in *The Business of Art* exhibition at the Getty:

> July 29, 1879
>
> My dear Pissarro,
>
> I know an employee at the stock exchange who has asked me to buy two paintings for him for 300 F. Naturally, I intend to suggest some Pissarros to him and so upon your return, I would like for you to bring over a few, but in the 6 by 8 format–there is no need for them to be large. Don't be offended by what I am going to say, but you know as well as I do that the middle classes are difficult to please, so I would like this young man to have two paintings whose subjects are as pretty as possible. He is a young man who knows nothing at all about art, and does not pretend otherwise which is already something; however, some

---

The concept of working for your own self (artists fall into this class) and rising to your level of achievement based on work instead of birthright is meritocracy, a concept made whole as an American phenomenon.

Of course, to create something no one wants to acquire does not earn you a living, either. This is the conflict each creator must confront.

EDEN

of your works could frighten him despite my influence on his judgment. So act for the best and see you soon.

P Gauguin

I subsequently discovered a letter written in 1878 by Pissarro, who was then forty-eight, to the painter, dealer, and collector Eugène Murer. The letter ended with the following self-assessment:

> Living in Saint Thomas in 1852, [although] employed in a well-paying business, I could not endure the situation any longer, and without thinking, I abandoned all I had there and fled to Caracas, thus breaking the bonds that tied me to bourgeois life. What I suffered is incredible, but I have lived: what I am suffering now is terrible, much worse even than when I was young, full of zeal and enthusiasm. Now I am convinced that my future is dead. Yet I think that if I had to start all over again, I would not hesitate to follow the same path.

It is clear from the tone of this letter that Pissarro's headstrong pupil and colleague, Gauguin, learned his lessons well; he, like his teacher, understood that freedom didn't mean chaos or anarchy. Freedom meant inventing new rules. Freedom came at a price. Gauguin, too, went on painting until the end in La Dominque (Hiva Oa), the Marquesas Islands, with no true sense that he would be acknowledged for his vision in his own time, or ever. Do you have the same commitment to your art?

CALL ME MR. ARTIST

For the artist today, the bottom line is to be smart and learn from your predecessors; they have paved the way with valuable lessons in advance of your arrival on the art scene. As an artist, you must confront the hard questions before exposing yourself to the public theater of taste. The artist must know the value of his work (answer the core questions posed in this book) before entering the not for faint of heart fray where the agendas of others are often the result of an overlapping arrangement of evaluations and opinions that can lead to an artist's financial and critical success or premature demise.

While the impact wielded by the powerbrokers and shapers of taste, quality, and art investment can't be underestimated, nothing can happen without the artwork. Although a well-timed spin can hurl a work of art from obscurity into fame, no amount of savvy, business acumen, or the 'right' connections, or personal charisma can create an original work of art. The artist must know what is original, or what is he point?

If you create a personal art and aspire recognition and support from an audience to whatever extent, some designated individual, in addition to you, will have to champion your work—this implies another soul who recognizes your language of art, and that is an achievement.

What is your art worth? If you know what you are selling, then this answer comes more naturally. If you already have a following, you also have leverage. If you are unknown, while you may not yet possess gravitas

The artist is nothing without the gift, but the gift is nothing without work.

EMILE ZOLA

The highest reward for man's toil is not what he gets for it, but what he becomes by it.

JOHN RUSKIN

Art has nothing to do with medium, style, period or any other classification; if the person is a creator, then whatever he describes as his art is art.

EDEN

in an insecure market that grovels at the mere hint of cachet, you can still exercise the power of insight over your work by setting a minimum selling price (the price to the buyer, not the dealer).

If you don't value your work, no one else will, either.

The point here of exploring the history of art as a vocation, as a way of earning a living, serves several purposes: While it is true that art is a divine calling (dharma), this doesn't preclude today's artist from also being a freelance entrepreneur; acknowledging that the art itself does become 'goods' for sale once it enters the marketplace elevates the artist from hapless misinformed misfit to the proper stature of an astute player who doesn't relegate the business end as being distasteful, undignified, or beneath him. Picasso didn't get rich by completely entrusting his business affairs to others. You must know the details of how your art is bought and sold. Renaissance artists drew up explicit contracts for their work; some would go so far as to charge their patrons for each figure, and a prorated fee for partial figures in a painting. Of course, this was work for hire, which is counterpoint to the artist who creates art for art's sake; good business practices apply in either case. If you insist on ignorance when it comes to selling your work, you will pay an unwelcome price in the end.

Fortunately, in today's world, the artist need not be completely dependent upon a single patron who supports the artist and dictates what work should be created. Although patrons aren't intrinsically evil, power does corrupt. Samuel Johnson, the 18th century writer and wit, referred to a patron as "a wretch who supports with insolence, and is paid with flattery." A broad base of patron-customers who acquire art without meddling in the content provides a more level playing field for the artist to create on her own terms. This is good business sense.

ARTIST OR PAINTER

There is another object lesson to be gleaned here, and that is—as mentioned at the beginning of this chapter—to honestly feel gratitude that you are an artist of this new millennium who can work free from the narrow constrictions imposed by patrons, religious institutions, guilds, or academies. If not co-opted by the church or like-minded patrons to make religious based works and monuments, what personal art would Michelangelo or Leonardo have created as their legacy?

You aren't ignorant of tradition, which is the living ghost of the past seamlessly integrated into your art of the present moment. As we have seen, the concept of today's artist as a model of individuality, intuitive creator, free agent, and entrepreneur selling non-commissioned work is a relatively new one. You have learned the liberating lesson that *an artist has no medium*; you can create with any materials that you desire. You have learned that suffering for one's art is a modern myth, and a false one at that. While sacrifices must be made to make the grade, true suffering comes from being lost, from not ever finding your art, your dharma.

It is also intriguing to learn that not everyone wants to be called an artist. As Lynne Munson writes in her book, *Exhibition: art in the era of intolerance*: "There are many artists working today who want to be known as painters, not artists. Some even carry business cards with the designation 'fine art painter.' They argue that the term *artist* has been co-opted by people who consider art-making a mere act of self-expression. Art historian Barbara Rose explains: *Artist* means 'I'm an artist because I say I'm an artist.' Being a *painter* means 'I have certain kinds of skills and a relationship to a tradition.' The French-born artist Balthus, who at age ninety-two is often called the greatest living painter, draws the distinction even more starkly: 'I'm considering myself as a craftsman. I don't want to be an artist. I have a horror of the word.' Painters stress practice—including drawing from life and studying past art—that the most celebrated art of the last three decades has devalued."

We graciously and posthumously defer to the late Balthazar Klossowski de Rola who also preferred the moniker Balthus. Whatever you call yourself, do so with authentic work and you will be ahead of the curve knowing that 'you are on sacred ground when you know where you stand.'

THE SELF-TAUGHT

If you haven't confronted the following question as this chapter has unfolded, now is the time. Why did these artists from the past and of recent memory confront tradition? What was their motive? Were they masochists?

By challenging the accepted norms of art, these artists were inviting rejection—not avoiding it, and were willing to pay the price for affronting the taste of the day. Search your soul and you will know the answer without having to consult with anyone else other than your intuition. When you know what you are doing and what you are making, you will know what the work is worth. It is true. The world at large is confused about art.

While one museum exhibits motorcycles (not to diminish their beauty of design) next to Kandinsky, another features self-indulgent works in the guise of a personal art, while still another art museum advocates 'cutting edge' works that are, despite their graphic sensationalism, conspicuously devoid of organic origins and plain dull.

To add further confusion to the mix, we have the institutionalizing and unfortunate lumping together under the broad banner of 'Outsider Art' the self-taught artist along with a 'rogue's gallery' featuring: the harmless insane or the criminally deranged (what Jean Dubuffet called *Art Brut*), or the highly neurotic or manic depressive (bipolar if you will), or the deaf visionary or the mute intuitive, or the congenitally withdrawn or the simply eccentric—or name your idiosyncrasy or infirmity. Again, the public is encouraged to view such art as a product of affliction or alienation instead of grace. As we have come to understand in this book, an artist creates work not because of but in spite of any illness.

Some galleries and museums promote self-taught art to mean an item that was initially made for some purpose other than art; this could have been utilitarian in purpose, or even spiritual in nature. Since the maker didn't intend for the work to be art, someone began scavenging after such handiwork. Collecting and perceiving bric-a-brac as something of value elevated and classified it as art of the self-taught—with folk art and art brut under its umbrella. Despite such confining labels, we know that finding some fine work among this lot is possible.

Art is making something out of nothing and selling it.

FRANK ZAPPA

Outsider Art, which is a broad anglicization of Art Brut, evokes wonderful imagery in a literary sense, and the term is sufficiently anti-establishment to get my vote; but its current catchall usage does a disservice to the sane self-taught artist.

EDEN

From now on, if someone asks you for something, remember that you can often grant the wish contingent on some small condition. Instead of concentrating on what can't be done and why, figure out how it can be done and when.

SAM HORN,
TONGUE FU!

Art school teaches technique; you must find art on your own. When you do, the myths will evaporate, leaving the uplifting gestalt: creation is a conscious act, not a compulsion, obsession, or some other out of control irrational impulse.

EDEN

Still other art aficionados more accurately categorize self-taught as coming up through the ranks outside the academically sanctioned pecking order of art—art schools, exhibit laundry lists, galleries, and museums.

For the sake of clarity in your own mind, not merely slavish adherence to esoteric or pedestrian labels, I restate my mantra to make a distinction: all great art is self-taught, which is no accident. Whether one came up through the MFA model or learned his art 'outside' the system, which is the domain of all innovation, the only thing that matters is the art itself—for that *is* the artist's resume.

Based on such catchall labels, one might conclude that van Gogh and Gauguin were outsider artists whose paintings were not initially conceived of as art—of course, this is not so. The passing of time has made them an integral part of the Western art establishment.

As innovation can't be learned in a classroom, whether the artist has an art degree has no bearing on genius; while 'self-taught' refers to unschooled art, we should also note that this term is somewhat misleading as it includes all creators—from Cézanne to Picasso, to Kandinsky to Pollock, and to perhaps, even you.

You must know where you stand.

THE MAGIC FORMULA

Art—and here I mean from a creator not a committee—often seems to evaporate in an atmosphere thick with dumbing down pandering to consumerism, political correctness, or other agenda that co-opts the arts and by tacit arrangement, the public. Let's not overlook a significant factor in this scenario. Simply because a carrot in the guise of funds or implied prestige is dangled, which might even be in earnest, by those who would appropriate and redirect your gift for their purposes doesn't mean that you have to bite. If you know it's true for you, restrain yourself from selling out and adulterating your dharma.

Work for hire, which is honorable and another matter entirely, isn't art from the soul or the topic that concerns us here. Don't get your hackles up. This is a distinction, not a comparison. Some might believe the ceiling of the Sistine Chapel was divinely inspired; it is certainly a consummate achievement; however, for Michelangelo, it was a job.

Without courage there is no art, no innovation.

You—the artist of original work—need not dismay or suffer because those courageous artists—living, breathing, people—who came before you have already shown you the magic formula in three words: genius is dedication. You need only follow their example; and, it is by example that we learn and lead.

Remember, anything is possible for an artist, a creator with a vision and an unwavering sense of mission to back it up.

Say Cheese, Mon Amie!

If Pablo Picasso took a photograph, is that art? It's an artist taking a photograph. Of course, there is a perceived value that it is Picasso who took the picture.

It's similar to someone not wanting to cash a check that Picasso made out for some service or product because they value his signature more than the money on the check—something that possibly served Picasso well, even if it threw the balance off in his ledger.

If you don't know what is art, then who will?

CHAPTER FORTY FIVE

A PREMONITION
Phantom In the Parking Lot

I WAS A SHINING STAR in the corporate world. I had a gift for getting the job done. This trait didn't go unnoticed, and I was moving up that ladder on a fast track.

Externally, all appeared well to the casual observer. I was, it seemed, living the American dream. The only issue was this: I knew I didn't belong in the world of suits and boots. Where did I belong? I had this persistent and gnawing urge to write, to write for my own self and make a living at it. This would require a radical shift of priorities on my part. It is hard to cut the umbilical cord to a hefty paycheck.

This feeling to write wasn't a whim. I was sitting in my office one chilly fall afternoon after returning from a successful meeting with a client who committed substantial money for a project that my department would handle. My phone was conspicuously silent. Looking through the glass window that faced a row of work stations, I could see my secretary typing at her desk. I got up, closed the blinds and sat back. Although I had gotten approval for everything necessary from my client in the end, the meeting had been intense. I'd have to perform and had to do better with each client to keep the billable dollars coming in.

Suddenly, a dense fog began to appear in my office. How could this be, I thought. At first, it seemed that smoke was coming in through the ventilation system—but no. Feeling dizzy, I sat down. Then, I began to make out a gray and foreboding scene forming in the mist. I saw people hidden by umbrellas huddled together in the rain. It was a funeral. The casket had already been lowered into the earth. Trying to see deeper, I squinted and made out a headstone off to the side near a mound of earth. My name was on the slab of marble. My body shuddered. Was I having a clairvoyant episode? Then, as the people began leaving the gravesite, the vision revealed its purpose. Underneath my name, I read these words etched in the stone: *Business Man—he paid his bills on time.*

I felt both devastated and liberated. The epiphany was undeniable. Is this how I want to be remembered? Is this the extent of my legacy? Forget that—is this how I want to live? The answer was immediate: No. I wanted

Every great advance in natural knowledge has involved the absolute rejection of authority.

THOMAS H. HUXLEY

Not knowing what or why you are doing something is the breeding ground for insecurity. Rejection and its minions are at the door, ready to cause havoc for the unprepared soul.

EDEN

to be the inventor, not the cog. I blinked a few times. The fog and the disturbing vision were gone, dissipated back to their own realm. I opened the blinds, and my secretary was still at her typewriter. Everything looked normal again.

I had no issue with people who made business their career. I felt my destiny was along another path. I knew then that this moonchild in a suit and tie would have to make crucial life-altering decisions before that headstone would turn up again.

My boss was the executive vice-president who ran the day-to-day operations of the company. I didn't like his management style, which relied on belittling people and fear. He never showed that dark side of himself to me.

For some reason, he had taken me on as his protégé when I was first hired, and I didn't disappoint him. I had recently been promoted again, and my future seemed secure and bountiful.

One late afternoon, some weeks after my vision into the future, I met with my boss in his office suite. When I told him that I would be leaving the company, his eyes ignited as if a devil had woken up. But then he sighed and even looked pleased. He thought this was a tactic of mine for more money. "If you had a better offer," he said, "then maybe I would do better." He didn't like losing.

I explained it had nothing to do with another job. I wanted to write and I needed time to do it.

"Why now? Why now?" he said. "You've got possibilities here for very big things."

"I had a premonition," I said.

"What? Are you kidding? Ah, that's bull. Premonitions are for those loony folk out there in California. You've got it too good, or is someone from another company whispering in your ear like I thought?"

He went on. He told me I was making a major mistake at this time in my life. He stood up and let me know that if I left now I would be ruining a fine career and a rich future.

When he realized he couldn't sway me from my decision, he asked me to follow him.

Once we were both outside in the company parking lot, he pointed to his parking space and said: "What is that?"

"A car," I said.

"No. No. No. Not a car," said my boss. "You're missing the point. It's a Rolls Royce Phantom. Don't you want that for your life? Don't you want that and all that goes with it? The world will be yours."

I said, "No. But I appreciate your concern for my future."

"I'll tell you again," he said. "If you leave now to follow some crazy notion to become a writer, or whatever it is you're looking for, you will be making a horrendous mistake. You will regret it." He could be extremely convincing.

"If it is a mistake," I said, "then it will be mine."

I returned to my office, loosened my tie and sat down. My boss was furious, but I had made my decision. In my mind's eye I saw that the headstone in my vision was now blank; my future wasn't set, not etched in marble; and to find my life's purpose was solely up to me.

In less than forty-eight hours, I was an ex-employee who hasn't looked back since. No thing except your intuition can guide you toward your dharma, your purpose in life. In my case, it didn't preclude having a Rolls Royce; it simply meant that working for one wasn't my goal.

The executive vice-president had been right about one thing. Some *thing* had been whispering in my ear, which I now know to be my intuition.

Don't hit the snooze button when you get that wake-up call.

INNER NEED: FOREVER SHINING

As I have learned since my phantom experience of years ago, expression in a pure sense isn't limited to artists. The world is full of people who desire inner fulfillment, peace, and dignity. Who among them will grab the brass ring with the key to the universe?

In his book, *The Third Force,* Frank Goble, who condensed many of Abraham Maslow concepts and ideas about psychology, summarizes Maslow's understanding of inner needs and self-fulfillment: "The specific form that these needs will take will of course vary greatly from person to person. In one individual it may take the form of the desire to be an ideal mother, in another it may be expressed athletically, and in still another it may be expressed in painting pictures or in inventions. It is not necessarily a creative urge although in people who have any capabilities for creation it will take this form."

Or, put another way in the context that concerns us here, each one of us is seeking our own dharma, which is our reason for being here. Respect your intuition and the form of your art will follow as surely as gratitude opens the heart and mind to compassion and awareness.

As the sages of the ages have taught, knowing who you are is a supreme achievement. Do you know your self? If not now, then perhaps later, for it is also your dharma to find out.

Make it happen. Answer the core questions in this book.

You are a child of privilege.

You and none other than you are the final arbiter of success, wealth, and well-being—the crowning achievement in our temporal space-time continuum.

EDEN

CHAPTER FORTY SIX

BEYOND THE VEIL
Creation, Creativity, Imagination

IT IS ALWAYS SMART to know that whatever you are doing, you are doing it on purpose. Being conscious of your actions and taking responsibility for them is leverage that lets you know where you stand and in what direction you are heading.

> "The difference between the right word and the almost right word is really a large matter—it's the difference between lightning bug and the lightning."
>
> —Mark Twain

Here is a good place to begin. Trying to navigate the world of art without a compass makes for aimless if not reckless seamanship. Deceitful denizens of the deep take no prisoners. Get a bearing on what follows and you will be on your way toward understanding the subtlety that is art. After a time you will come to trust your own feelings; after a time your sense of nuance about a piece of art will place you on a par or better with the most erudite art scholar, museum director, or art critic; after a time you will come to realize that no one can know better how you feel about a thing than you do; and after a time you will develop a new found liberation as your art enhances the quality and meaning of your life. All this happens, after a time.

KNOCK, KNOCK

Toward my last days in Los Angeles some years back when I was living in the Hollywood Hills, I had a moving sale of various items, not art. A bearded man came to the door, looked around quickly, and went directly to an item leaning against one of my easels.

"How much is that?" he asked.

"Do you know what this is?"

"I surely don't," he whipped back.

Astronomer Carl Sagan was asked if he believed in the existence of highly evolved life elsewhere in the universe:

'The key word in that question is believe ... and in my view, you believe on the basis of compelling evidence.'

CARL SAGAN

Hallelujah, I thought. With those two words and a contraction, the bearded man had uttered a heaven's worth of understanding.

I said: "Then there's no sense talking about money."

He grinned and left. The point was keenly etched for all to see. What is the point of discussing price if you don't know what you are looking at? We must all learn how to see and that is how reality reveals herself.

PREPARING YOUR MIND'S EYE

Let me prime the canvas of meaning with several even coats of white gesso to begin anew and clarify the gist of three words that are often used interchangeably and abused as being synonymous: imagination, creativity, and creation. Almost everyone has heard these powerful and abstract nouns used in one context or another, yet their meaning and place often slips through the ever-widening cracks in a semantically shoddy environment. If you, the artist, don't discern the difference, who will?

Imagination, creativity and creation are words; they aren't the end product of what concerns us here—which is the intrinsic experience that distinguishes and elevates the act of making art from the ordinary to the extraordinary to the sublime.

You know who you are and where you stand.

Imagination: Everyone has imagination, which is a conceptual ability to form images and ideas in the mind, especially of things never seen or experienced directly. Imagination, a thinking activity, is what first instigated civilization. As wonderful as imagination is, it isn't unique. An active imagination produces results based on thought. We live in a society infatuated with the power of imagination; movies and novels promise to take us places only imagined as if that were some special or inaccessible piece of real estate. Imagination is ubiquitous—resourceful at best, clever at worst; and limited by your own imagination says it all. Oscar Wilde noted: "The imagination imitates. It is the critical spirit that creates."

Creativity: This quality is beyond imagination. By rearranging existential facts, known elements, or developing other physical properties into new forms, it strives toward an inspired level of accomplishment, which has its limitations because creativity, like imagination, is also based on thinking. Creativity speaks of ingenuity and makes things happen in unorthodox ways. Although creativity is what transformed humankind from an inventive toolmaker and seafarer to spacefarer, it will take a society of creators to make a leap in awareness from a destructive and warring tribal mentality toward a productive planetary civilization with a passion for art, science, and exploration.

Creation: God creates some thing from no thing; this means each creation is unique. Creation isn't a function of imagination or creativity—these two levels out of necessity originate from within the realm of thought. Creation, each artwork, flows from intuition, which is the gentle soul whispering the transcendental song of God to any artist who listens. True to its metaphysical nature, creation can't be planned since it is unleashed into existence as spontaneous passion. Creation does more than rearrange that which already exists. Creation, like a newly forming star, unleashes energy into a boundless and ever-expanding reality. Creation has no limitations,

---

Physics and art:

Intelligence, like art, cannot be reduced or divided. If non-random events imply intelligence, what do random events imply if not some other form of intelligence. The fact that there are events at all is a mystery. Random events are no less wondrous than non-random events.

EDEN

mental blocks, or hidden agendas. For the aware artist, creation is supply without end—the wondrous and generous cornucopia of the spirit.

THE ENFORCER

Words can help us sort things out. Words can be used precisely with laser-like accuracy to communicate our intent. Words can heal, or spread like a pathogenic virus. Words can also be used with only vague notions of what they mean, assuring ambiguity and further confusion. Now that you are aware of the distinctions between these three words, you will begin to notice their constant misuse in describing art by many, including those who should know better. With awareness comes responsibility: if you see it, you own it. Comprehension fuels power, confidence, and clarity. With these attributes, you will come to experience that rejection or disappointment can no longer topple you.

If you don't elevate your standard for clarity, who will? Conversely, when you do find someone who knows the distance and difference between imagination, creativity, and creation, you will have immediate common ground between you—and that real estate is priceless. Remember, 'you are on sacred ground when you know where you stand.'

You will come to know that to the extent you know your art (Brahman), the stronger both you and your art will become. This is a universal law that serves to illuminate when enforced directly by you.

Chance is perhaps the pseudonym of God when he did not want to sign.

ANATOLE FRANCE

CHAPTER FORTY SEVEN

IMMORTAL COMBAT
Disarming the Dragon and the Demon

IF YOU HAVE been a follower instead of a leader, what did you expect? Bruce Lee, the iconic martial artist, understood that any system of mindless tradition, or style, has the baggage of limitations, and that *no style* was the ultimate, limitless expression of his art form. Still, no matter how many opponents—dragons—Lee defeated, he knew he would find no peace until he defeated the demon within. For our purpose the dragon is an external adversary, and the demon dwells only from within.

Contrary to the stereotype of the artist as a damaged lone figure, a hapless victim of misunderstanding, or a weak sister—a creator of art is no less a warrior than a Samurai who maintains an unwavering allegiance to his own code of conduct. Every creator must face the inner demon, or what is the point? Buddha and Jesus, to test the truth of their convictions, faced their demons, too.

MINDLESS PRIMITIVE

As I have noted elsewhere, harnessing the volatile power of divine fire comes at a price that the artist must pay willingly without the slightest hesitation or resentment. The demon I am writing about isn't the devil's doing; it is much worse—it is your own handiwork.

The science fiction 1956 classic film, *Forbidden Planet*, dramatically illustrated the inner demons at work. The storyline included a mission to a faraway planet and the discovery of a long extinct super intelligent race, but apparently not smart, of beings millions of years more evolved than humankind. These aliens had created a machine that instantly transformed their thoughts into physical reality. However, they had forgotten one thing. By manifesting any thought, including those in nightmares or rages, into existence, they had also unwittingly freed 'monsters from the id', the mindless primitive urge for unrestrained pleasure, killing, and destruction.

Their subconscious minds, unleashed by the 'limitless' power of the machine, annihilated their civilization in one night of unspeakable horror. Consider the consequences if your every thought became reality.

In life as in dance: Grace glides on blistered feet.

ALICE ABRAMS

MASKS OF FEAR

To know heaven, you would have to know hell. The external dragons are negativity and ignorance, a destructive pair far easier to defeat than the inner demon—the ego in disguise that wears the masks of fear, hatred, doubt, jealousy, envy, and anger. For clarification, remember that the ego knows fear while the id, eager for unbridled gratification, has no regard for alarm or anxiety. We should also note once again that the ego and the id aren't foreign bodies; they are integrated aspects of the individual—you.

There can be no creator without a destroyer in a universe where duality and symmetry dance their duet in the cosmos. For our purpose the destroyer's role isn't to wreak terror from the subconscious id, but to consciously confront the dragon without and the demon within.

Nothing supersedes character.
—SO SAID THE MASTER

LAST MAN STANDING

Myths of heroes fighting monsters have endured through the ages and are ingrained within the popular culture to this day, and for good reason. In these myths, essentially morality plays, the hero faces the embodiment of negativity—the bad guy—in the form of a single incarnation. In a final showdown, the winner takes all, as in the 1952 movie *High Noon*, which raised the genre of the Western to allegorical status. Gary Cooper plays the lone marshal, already past his prime; he rises to the role of the reluctant hero because he must confront not only his fear of the gang of gunmen coming to kill him, but his duty to protect the same townspeople who have betrayed him in the final hour. Another device that adds a high degree of tension is that the story unfolds nearly in real time, from 10:40 a.m. to high noon in an eighty-four-minute film that was produced and written by Carl Foreman.

Even when everyone has deserted him, the marshal stands his ground, knowing his loyalty may inevitably cost him his life. While most of the local folk acknowledge that they owe their prosperity to the marshal, they won't help defend him because they believe his cause is hopeless. In the end, the marshal faces the showdown on his own, with an unexpected twist from his new Quaker bride played by Grace Kelly, who proves herself worthy of a hero's wife.

When the dust settles, the evil gunmen are dead. Only if you are fully committed to your cause will the universe provide you with help—you, the artist, must be willing to see it through and stand fast for a fellow partisan who often shows up as the most unlikely of characters. If you don't stand up as the artist, how will the cavalry find you? The marshal has faced his fear and has triumphed; he throws down his badge into the dust and leaves town with his wife.

The End. But is it? If we could follow the marshal and his wife further along after they ride off toward what we believe will be a positive future, we may come to realize that the story is now beginning. Has the marshal vanquished his inner demons? This mastery over the self is the ultimate test of the warrior if he is to avoid becoming the heroic figure with a tragic flaw in the Greek sense.

As it turns out, we can take a step beyond the last frame of the film by way of *Darkness at High Noon: The Carl Foreman Documents*, a riveting documentary on how the blacklisting of Foreman and his betrayal at the hands of his colleagues defined and shaped what would become the classic motion picture *High Noon*, which did poorly in early screenings; and Harry Cohn, head of Columbia Pictures, didn't care for it either—so much for focus groups and the taste of a Hollywood mogul.

LIGHTS, CAMERA, NONLINEAR ACTION

A bias is often mistaken for a factual perception—in politics or in the cinema. At the turn of the last century, in the early days of silent movies, for example, there was some serious concern that an audience wouldn't be able to get the picture if one scene were cut to another without a real time transition. Let's say, for example, if our hero were getting ready to go to work and the next scene cut to him already at work, it was erroneously held that moviegoers wouldn't be able to grasp the sequence without showing how he got to his job.

Another misconception of the times was that the audience was incapable of following the story if there were close-ups on the actor: seeing only the actor's face, disembodied as it was, would be disorienting and confusing. It was also felt by some that the audience was paying to see the whole actor. The audience, of course, had no problem with close-ups or following the thread of a storyline composed of logically cut scenes. In retrospect, such faulty thinking had to do with our everyday sense of real time activity and linear perception. Given the opportunity we are capable of integrating new concepts.

Then, when sound was introduced in motion pictures, many directors mistakenly surmised that the audience didn't want to hear the actors speak. Eventually, more progressive directors not only included sound, they introduced flashbacks, a proven age-old literary nonlinear device, into their movies. In recent memory, such films as *Rashomon*, *Pulp Fiction*, *Memento*, and *21 Grams*, for example, explicitly challenge the audience to participate in solving a puzzle composed of a seemingly disjointed mosaic of images, where the chronology of events—memory and logic—are cut and manipulated so that the story can unfold from any direction, from the past, future, and present into a satisfying conclusion.

RED CELLULOID: THE BELLY OF THE BEAST

When art gets politicized, co-opted, what then? What happens when life and art are indistinguishable? Perception becomes reality when you must find the courage to face fear and the density of the world—a situation each artist must eventually confront.

Although Hollywood films have always been regulated in one form or another, the House Un-American Activities Committee (HUAC) became indirectly involved between 1947 and 1954 in controlling the content of movies. After the Second World War the alliance between the United States and the Soviet Union collapsed, the Cold War began, and the 'Red Scare' gripped America. Members of the HUAC considered it their duty to purge the country of any Communist influences—and that, of course, included artists, who in this case included mostly writers and actors, but not yet visual artists, who weren't entirely overlooked.

When I asked art critic Dore Ashton if Mark Rothko, whom she knew, had a philosophy on persevering, she revealed the following—In 1955, Rothko gave this advice to a fellow painter who was on the receiving end of rejection:

'You are part of an underground. You are a partisan, a freedom fighter. You are on your own. Don't expect help, or reinforcements.'

MARK ROTHKO

Art is not subjective; you are.

EDEN

We must be the change we wish to see in the world.

GANDHI

When you find your dharma, eventually all the loose ends of the past are reconciled through your awareness and dedication.

EDEN

In the 1930's, for example, the FBI had already assembled a dossier on the Spanish painter Pablo Picasso, who was a member of the Communist Party (What was Pablo, an avowed pacifist, thinking?); the dossier was created in case Picasso wanted to visit America; if he had, his visa would have been denied. Keep in mind that the late 40's and into the 50's was also the era when the radical abstract expressionist movement in New York City was flourishing and changing the face of art.

But, while the HUAC investigated numerous industries, it was Hollywood with its high profile mass media power that became the best-known target of this now infamous committee.

In 1947 the committee's purpose was threefold:

First, it intended to prove that the Screen Writers Guild did have Communist members.

Second, it hoped to show that these writers were able to insert subversive propaganda into Hollywood films.

Third, J. Parnell Thomas, head of the committee, argued that President Roosevelt had encouraged pro-Soviet films during the war. Although none of these claims was ever substantiated, the committee's tactics worked to intimidate and coerce many talented and creative people to turn informer on their friends, or leave Hollywood.

Witnesses who refused to answer were cited for contempt of Congress. The witch-hunt was on. If you refused to testify, you faced being sent to jail and you were blacklisted, meaning that no Hollywood studio would hire you. Although critics contended that the committee's actions were unconstitutional because it disregarded the civil liberties of its witnesses, the courts ruled in favor of the committee.

The First Amendment crumpled over fear (which wasn't totally unfounded) of what left-leaning citizens and communists would do to America. In a land of free speech, however, there is a difference between disagreement and stirring up hate and violence. After 1950, Senator Joseph McCarthy borrowed the committee's 'strong arm' tactics for his own brand of Senate investigations. Many interpreted Foreman's drama of *High Noon* as an allegorical reflection of apathy and the passive acceptance of McCarthy's anticommunist reign of 'democratic' terror.

THE FINAL SHOWDOWN

During production of *High Noon*, Foreman was subpoenaed by the HUAC and subsequently blacklisted by Hollywood after refusing to testify. In August of 1952, Foreman was living in London—now a fugitive because he wouldn't name names to the HUAC. However, others weren't so steadfast. His close associates and Hollywood colleagues had betrayed him, and this deep cut most certainly had defined and shaped *High Noon*. Unable to work in America, and with the State Department attempting to seize his passport, the exiled Foreman read the outstanding review of his film in *The New York Times*. He was up for an Oscar for best screenplay, too.

Instead of enjoying what should have been the high point of his career, Foreman had to play out this scene in lonely exile as *High Noon* stoically mirrored Hollywood's darkest hour. Foreman summed things up by saying: "What *High Noon* was about at that time was Hollywood and no other place but Hollywood. And that was perfectly recognizable to people in Hollywood when they saw the picture."

The satisfying nature of the drama and morality issues raised in *High Noon* is universal. But does this plot play out that way in your life as an artist? Even if you feel you have faced your fear and have slain the dragon, time is the ultimate barometer of victory. We feel good when our hero rides off into the sunset where he remains forever young, free from earthly ills, and where good has triumphed. It is done; it is clean; it is over. You leave the theater or close the book feeling contented.

When you attempt to climb and reach the summit of a mountain, there is a clear, quantifiable, and objective outcome of what you have achieved or not. In the same way, it would be wonderfully efficient to confront all those who would stop you from your mission embodied in one test. However, it rarely works that way.

The showdowns most often come incrementally in piecemeal fashion—a rejection here, a disappointment there, an innovation not developed, and all the while there is an omnipresent feeling of self-doubt ready to fill any space abdicated by your courage.

ENTER THE DEMON

On my own odyssey toward becoming an artist, I resisted the leash of dogma and tradition, which was ultimately Bruce Lee's legacy as an innovative martial artist, filmmaker, and master of self-discipline.

Like Lee, I knew I faced my most formidable adversary in the mirror; if anything could defeat me, it was my inner demon, the one that feeds on doubt and fear.

'You are on sacred ground when you know where you stand.' This means that you understand your place in relation to the scheme of things. It's a good place. You are standing shoulder to shoulder with your soul—your comrade in character and art. You know your art is honest; you know the source and quality of your work; you don't need anyone to tell you what you have achieved—although hearing it is welcome.

But you aren't waiting for validation from others to continue your work. You know your art is awesome, don't you? Knowing where you stand is a territorial matter, a construct of your own being that is exclusive of others; bitter competition and the rue of comparisons don't dwell on this piece of real estate. Knowing where you stand isn't a combative pecking order where you want to best the other artist. Think about it. How can unique be compared with unique?

THE TERRITORY

Steven Pressfield, in his book, *The War of Art*, writes about territory and what turf means to a creator. The true artist knows his territory because he has carved and staked it out with his own hands. His territory is unique and not dependent upon a hierarchical structure of comparisons that muddy the bountiful landscape.

As an artist, you must not only know the terrain, you must also be aware of the time and place in which you live. What are the preeminent values of the society around you? You must know all this so you know where you stand

Out beyond ideas of wrongdoing and rightdoing there is a field.

I'll meet you there.

When the soul lies down in that grass the world is too full to talk about.

RUMI

Critics and reading reviews:

While I might agree with what a reviewer writes, here's the point: In whatever the critic is writing about—an exhibit, a film, a book, he may have missed or dismissed something that only you or I will see in that art.

EDEN

in relation to social conditioning. You are, after all, an entrepreneur who knows the bottom line: nature takes no prisoners.

Every significant break that has come my way has always come from a place other than expected—this is the field of all possibilities at work. The experience of opportunities rising up out of unlikely places first gave me the insight about the questionable meaning and usefulness of the word 'obvious', which is hazardous to art appreciation, and is on my verboten list.

Of course, to see these opportunities, I had my eyes open and wasn't attached or a slave constrained to any particular outcome. To prevail, I would have to remain strong when I felt the weakest. It is in the darkest hours that we see our true selves.

Where others saw problems, I saw opportunity; and the opportunity seemed to appear spontaneously; all I had to do was say—yes. And, as with all overnight successes, the prospect to show my talent, that I was ready, qualified, and worthy was the result of every decision I had made up to that very second in time and space.

Who we are and what we become is the culmination of countless decisions that take us along a well-trodden route we sheepishly follow, or onto a new path we carve out for ourselves.

BREAKING THE DRAGON'S TEETH

Immortal combat as an artist isn't about attacking a blank canvas; while you may approach with vigor, you don't transgress upon a loved one "full of sound and fury, signifying nothing." Remember, the freedom to create art is a blessing, not a curse. The combat that has lasting value must entail overcoming your inner demon, while also engaging any outside forces that would hinder the space and time for you to create. Your objective is to tame, not kill the inner demon—your ego, yourself. This is the struggle between your power to create and your power to self-destruct, not an abstract metaphor describing the amorphous realm of the psyche. It is enough that you bloody its nose, giving this monster of your own creation a clear message: demon, you have no power over me. Of course, you are talking to yourself.

Stand your ground and face the worst, and the demon will weaken from a lack of attention. Eventually, you will absorb its wild power and transmute its chaotic energy into strength of character. This magical transformation of energy and purpose is an example of the First Law of Thermodynamics, which the British scientist C.P. Snow described as follows: "You cannot get something for nothing, because matter and energy are conserved."

You do your art in your own words, your own language, your own symbols, your own vocabulary, your own form. You want to create in your own unique lexicon. You are after the prize, your authentic voice, which reveals itself only to the brave willing to engage and disarm the external dragons and inner demons in whatever form. Your unadulterated voice when paired with dedication is genius—which is a pillar of strength that elevates your spirit above triviality and rejection.

Bruce Lee defeated his dragons, and only he knew whether he had finally defeated his demons. The question is will you?

Do not forsake your gift.

There is a defining moment when you look at the seeming inequities of the past, and you let them go in favor of an uncluttered now.

This is the act of exorcism, of casting out the demon called victim from one's psychology.

This is an act of self-discipline, of freedom, of art.

CHAPTER FORTY EIGHT

DETACH AND CONQUER
The Law of Non-Attachment

TO DEFY THE POTENTIALLY pernicious effect caused by having your work rejected, you must confront the status of your relationship to attachment—not to any particular rejection, but to rejection itself. When we want, crave, or desire a thing, we become its slave in direct proportion to our attachment to it. Who owns whom? This is the question of possession each artist must ask and answer of himself. As you detach yourself from a particular outcome, you free yourself to witness other opportunities that were previously obstructed by ego.

> "You can't always get what you want
> You can't always get what you want
> You can't always get what you want
> But if you try sometimes you might find
> You get what you need—"
>
> —Rolling Stones

As the Stones will forever remind us in pounding rhythm and repetitive refrain, there is a fundamental difference between what you want and what you need. For the artist, becoming attached to an outcome is a dead end. This isn't an opinion; it is a natural law. Mother Nature defers to evolution—trial and error, culminating in an awareness of consciousness, the technology behind all matter. *Mother* isn't stuck on any one particular way to accommodate survival. The only thing that matters in the jungle is what works. All else is extinction.

The Eighteen Be-Attitudes described in this book inevitably lead the artist to the doorway of unfettered perception, also known as the Law of Non-Attachment. This law, a shield that frees and protects the genius in us all from succumbing to entrapment by the illusion (maya) of the world, instructs us to release those temporal desires and ideas that inflict destructive emotional and mental compulsions. Once you see and feel anything, you own it, one way or another. You won't find the Law of Non-Attachment

> *[William] Hopper may have adopted this curmudgeonly façade during the years when, failing to earn a living as a 'serious' artist, he was obliged to devote himself to commercial illustration.*
>
> *Born in Nyack, New York, of a family long settled in the neighborhood, he had begun his artistic studies under the tutelage of Robert Henri, a member of the so-called Ashcan school of American art. Hopper believed in the methods of the school but not in their purposes, and three early visits to Paris left him similarly detached from the radical aesthetic experiments under way there.*
>
> *Hopper was well into his sixties when substantial recognition arrived—too late, he might have said, to do him any harm.*
>
> BRENDAN GILL,
> LATE BLOOMERS

The quest for the next big thing is about style over substance; it implies that the thing before—physical or metaphysical—has been completely understood, interpreted, and fully realized.

EDEN

on the legislative books of any country, state, or municipality. You are the only one who will or can for that matter enforce this law. Non-Attachment is far-reaching and impacts all of creation, including art, philosophy, and even science. You will, for example, find the influence of this law in a textbook about quantum mechanics; this aspect of theoretical physics states that the physical universe is governed by probability, not certainty, a conclusion Einstein, who favored a predictable universe, wouldn't accept. However, it is safe to say that anything is possible when you aren't attached to a particular outcome.

UNDERSTANDING IS THE GOAL

How can I not be attached to my goals? I am working hard to attain them. After all, I know what I am after and I know what is good for me. The answer is this: How can you not subscribe to the beauty of non-attachment if it means freedom from unnecessary suffering, liberation from the side effects of negativity, and a pardon for life from the solitary angst of rejection? If you think you know what is good for you, now is a good time to reexamine that volatile theory. What is good for you—what you *need*, not *want*—can only be assessed over time.

Go ahead. Look back over your shoulder and the years in retrospective wisdom to see how those things you once craved wouldn't have ultimately served you if you had gotten them. Rejection, after all, does have uses; and the one that concerns us here is that it separates those on a mission from those on a joyride; 'no' demands that you make a course correction in the direction toward what you need or face extinction—a fate that is rarely apparent until it is too late.

Now, if you insist on rigidly attaching yourself to a particular outcome, you become a barnacle hitching a ride to wherever the driver is going. With no direction of your own, you are a slave of your attachment; you are a coconspirator in your own undoing. For most of us in the West where consumerism, materialism, pop culture adoration, neurosis of the next big thing, and movie star idolatry are fixtures on the totem pole of conspicuous consumption, adhering to the Law of Non-Attachment doesn't feel natural; it is neither effortless, nor is its impact immediately evident.

While this law isn't difficult to understand, it may be difficult to believe. No one who knows what they are talking about ever said it was easy. And what choice do you have?

NIGHT OF THE COLLECTOR

I had spent many months in setting up a meeting, and it seemed that my efforts had paid off. An influential art collector was coming to my home in the Hollywood Hills on Wonderland Avenue in Laurel Canyon. She arrived promptly at 7:30 p.m. that evening. After our cup of tea, I was ready to show her a selection of my paintings. In the instant I began setting up for the private showing, there was a knock at the door. A policewoman matter-of-factly informed me that I had to evacuate the house immediately. There had been a bomb threat in the area. All the residents on the street had to drive down the hill until it could be sorted out, one way or another.

My slightly nervous art collector took it as an adventure; I took it as a conspiracy. I grabbed my two Yorkies, Larry and Beau, and began the winding drive down the mountain; the art collector followed me in her car. At various checkpoints along the steep road, police barricades waved us on until we had descended into the flats. Eventually, I pulled over and parked on a side street below Sunset Boulevard. The lady collector drove up behind me. Who knows when or if she would come up to see me again? Who knows how long the bomb squad would be up there? After I said goodbye to the patron and a possible acquisition, she drove off toward her mansion in Malibu. Larry, Beau, and I walked along Sunset for some time. Then, as I drove back up the hill that starry night, I thought of the sign that Einstein had in his office at Princeton. It read: 'Not everything that counts can be counted, and not everything that can be counted counts.'

The bomb threat had been a hoax.

BULL'S-EYE

Consciousness isn't passive. With our thoughts, and more important, with our emotional intelligence, we use the invisible matrix of consciousness to cocreate material reality. This power doesn't come without field practice and is of no value without proof. While taking in the big picture is lofty, leading edge, and exhilarating, you must also remain grounded by maintaining your presence of mind. Although I extol the value of non-attachment and independence, it is as essential not to become compulsively self-reliant. Knowing when you do need help in this world is a matter of sanity and life. Self-reliance is an art borne of subtlety, reflection, and discernment, not brute strength.

To be obeyed, the Law of Non-Attachment must be exercised.

Did you for a fleeting moment think otherwise? Making non-attachment work for you doesn't come automatically; it is a function of consciousness that must be acquired and developed through determination. Fortunately, you can get there from here.

Let's use the pedestrian example of riding a bicycle. It takes time, patience, and motivation to learn how to ride a two-wheel bicycle. However, once you learn how to balance yourself, you will forever know how to ride. While you may not be the flashiest cyclist, the most acrobatic, or win the Tour de France, the object lesson is that you are riding the bicycle. It is the same with non-attachment. It isn't about defeatism, petty judgements or comparisons. It is about cycling toward the benefits of this law—which provides rewards in direct proportion to your dedication.

To put it another way: you are the Zen archer with the bow. It is entirely up to your skill whether your arrow strikes the bull's-eye. And, of course, it is also up to you to decide if close does count.

ALL APPLICANTS WELCOME

If you do lose sight of the grander scheme and your divine compass, a contingency for which you must prepare, then no matter how strong or self-reliant you are, issues of living no matter how extraordinary or banal seemingly conspire to wear you down. Of course, this confederacy takes place with your full complicity.

Confidence is not a mysterious characteristic we're born with or not, and it's not a result of extraordinary success, accessible only to an exalted few who achieve superhuman feats.

Confidence is a skill anyone can acquire.

SAM HORN,
CONCRETE CONFIDENCE

If you aren't feeling the love, you aren't giving the love.

EDEN

The Art Lesson:

'Why be disingenuous?' thought the art student to himself. 'If you have something to contribute, do it. If you have some question, fear not, and ask it.'

Then, one late afternoon, the moment came.

'But Master,' said the student, 'how can you paint without thinking?'

'What made you think that you could not,' replied the artist who continued to paint without missing a brushstroke.

EDEN

Remember, courage and love exist independent of physical prowess, size, sex, age, nationality, or occupation. Your mission as an artist is to fulfill your dharma. Death is the only thing that can stop a man or woman on a mission. Let no thing dissuade you. There is a vast gorge between agreeing to the concept of non-attachment and making this law an integral part of your daily life—as necessary and habitual as eating.

We have all been there. One problem solved creates a vacancy for another problem to enter, and the ante escalates. After all, who among us can't be bold and non-attached when the events don't personally concern us? But losing that which you love hurts. I am referring here to living things. We are human; we are driven by primal urges. Although we can't control the temporal flow, we can to varying degrees control ourselves. Few become mystics, ascetics, or bodhisattvas who, by their transcendental nature, are impervious, or at least not devastated by the ever-present and ever ready agony associated with earthly loss. You, the artist, don't have to be an ascended master to reap the benefits provided by obeying the Law of Non-Attachment. Your commitment to this law will see you through any potential anguish, including what rejection can cook up.

However, don't get lazy or unaware by becoming a one trick pony. Performing by rote, or counting on any single law, or any single thing for that matter, can become a crutch. Since nothing supersedes awareness, use it to complement and test your actions. Never take anything for granted: day, night, drops of rain, or your precious gift of life. The Law of Non-Attachment is a marvelous insight, not a panacea. Use everything that comes your way: this is economical and smart. What is the point of going through disappointment and anguish if you don't harness it to become stronger, more discerning, and more evolved? Physical pain alerts us to danger and teaches us lessons; pain of the psyche does the same.

Is there a more important mission than your work? Yes. I am asking you, the artist, who would persevere to transcend rejection and embrace success with a healthy disposition and vitality.

BRAIN SHIFTING AND STRAVINSKY

British scientist, philosopher and mystic, John Godolphin (J.G.) Bennett, in the section 'Living in the Medium' from his book *Creative Thinking*, writes: "I always answer this question of 'how to think' with 'the way to think is not to think.' If you grasp this, then you will be able to follow what I mean." Bennett's observation is pure *koan*, a Zen riddle, or problem that by defying logic empties the mind for enlightenment. The reasoning by the numbers left side of the brain gets frustrated, gives up, and let's the empathic and holistic right side the of brain take over.

In her book, *Drawing on the Right Side of the Brain*, Betty Edwards also writes about the need to oust logic by not thinking. As Edwards describes the strategy: "In order to gain access to the subdominant visual, perceptual R-mode of the brain, it is necessary to present the brain with a job that the verbal, analytic L-mode will turn down." Put another way: when you are drawing, stop thinking.

Through a series of exercises, Edwards demonstrates that any motivated person with the proper understanding can learn how to draw. Brain research has established that each person has two brains: the left (L-mode), which handles verbal and by the numbers step-by-step rational tasks, and the right (R-mode), which is the nonverbal, empathic side that handles pattern recognition as in pictures, faces, and other things that can be seen as a whole. It is important that you prove to yourself that such a shift is real.

In her book, Edwards provides a simple test. She shows a drawing of Igor Stravinsky by Picasso that is upside down. Her instructions are that we copy it. After a few moments, you will sense frustration, as the left side of your brain can't make sense of the drawing. Soon, the left side gives up when it can't identify what the lines of the upside down drawing represent. As you persist in copying what appear to be arbitrary and abstract lines, the right side of the brain, which has no need to label things, kicks in. The telling part—the proof of the brain shift—of this exercise is how accurately the finished copy (regardless of drawing talent) of the art is rendered when drawn from the upside down position.

To learn how to draw, as Edwards lays it out, we must shift from the verbal, analytic L-mode to the visual, perceptual R-mode. When the linear left brain, which reduces thoughts to numbers, letters, and words, is relieved of art duty and stops calculating, the right non-analytic hemisphere of the brain, which processes spatial visual information, dutifully takes over so you can begin to draw what you see in front of you with impressive clarity. When you stop giving verbal labels to the various parts (nose, mouth, ear, etc.) of the face you are drawing, you smoothly shift from the judgmental frustrated left to the free flowing right side of the brain.

CLEANING HOUSE

Making the shift from left to right mode can, at first, cause confusion and conflict, and even a mental paralysis of sorts. Like raising your awareness, making this subtle shift takes practice. Once you learn how to make the transition, the shift engages naturally and you can draw what is in front of you without the distracting static produced by the verbal part of the brain. Edwards is writing about drawing, which is learnable through a handful of perceptual skills that rely on measurement and specific spatial relationships among the component parts of the gestalt—the composition.

The art of self-expression is another matter because no one can teach you how to put down in paint that which is uniquely you. Edwards recognizes that to accurately draw what you see, you must learn to see in new ways. And seeing in original ways requires the artist to detach from what is already known. To draw what you see is a skill; to create what doesn't yet exist is a gift from another realm. In this place the artist harnesses the forces of nature in a contribution to reality—this is the artist as the universal shaman, the alchemist for all seasons.

Insights about shifting into drawing mode made by Edwards dovetails with Bennett's advice about thinking by not thinking. To arrive at an original thought, Bennett knew he had to let go and detach from preconceived notions—attachments. By not thinking (a goal of meditation), you create a space (Deepak Chopra calls this space the *gap*) for an innovative thought to appear. Great insights can't enter if the space is cluttered with stale ideas and leftover feelings. To find a unique solution, you must remain fluid while

An artist must be able to belligerently commit, tolerate solitude, and all the rest. Being an artist is not the same as choosing a career or learning certain skills but is instead becoming and being a person who is an artist.

ERIC MAISEL,
FEARLESS CREATING

Living an authentic, aware, and gracious life gives proper meaning to: a higher standard of living.

EDEN

obeying the Law of Non-Attachment—which is the same law governing the spontaneous creation of art from the soul through feeling, not thinking. And by feeling, I don't mean my state of happy or sad. I mean feeling your way into the cosmic palette and creating something that doesn't yet exist. When I make art, I'm not thinking because I'm not planning; premeditated artwork is design. If you haven't experienced this yourself, my statement may sound paradoxical, but it isn't. If you must stop thinking to draw, creating original art also demands that you draw upon this higher power. After slipping into right brain mode, I then let go, trusting my intuition, the language of the soul, to guide my hands. In the same way that you can't plan an original thought, you can't contrive original art. This isn't an opinion; it is a universal constant.

BHAGAVAD-GITA

The universe, all creation, operates according to natural laws. These laws exist in time and within all the dimensions of space. They exist whether or not we have discovered and named them. The Law of Non-Attachment might have been practiced by other civilizations of antiquity; it is India, however, that put this practical philosophy on the map.

Deeply rooted in the sensibilities and values of ancient India, the Law of Non-Attachment is thousands of years old and the central teaching of the *Bhagavad-gita* (*circa* 400 BCE), which is perhaps the most widely read, ethical text of ancient India—a complex land that manifested a culture as intricate, colorful, and cosmologically aware of the divine as the subcontinent is vast. As an episode in India's great epic, the *Mahabharata*, the *Gita*, one of three primary texts, vividly expresses the essence of Hinduism; the other two are the *Upanishads* and the *Brahma Sutras*.

In the *Gita*, as two great armies prepare for battle, Lord Krishna (an incarnation of the god Vishnu) explains the teachings of God and transcendence in a dialog with his friend, prince Arjuna. Although the *Gita* contains theology, its instruction is also ethically based. This summary quote by Lord Krishna is worth hearing again: "Be equally poised in success and failure; this is called yoga . . . Therefore, always perform actions which should be done, without attachments; for, by performing action without attachment, man attains the Supreme." Lord Krishna informs us that expectations and judgments subjugate human beings into a diabolical addiction, which is a form of slavery. Of course, the greatest battle is the one waged within oneself.

METAPHYSICAL JURISPRUDENCE

The concept of non-attachment isn't limited to esoteric belief systems, mysticism, or faraway exotic places. You don't have to be a transcendental philosopher or of the Hindu faith to embrace the wisdom of Lord Krishna. Non-attachment in varying degrees is already a familiar experience for most of us. To feel neutral regarding things that neither concern nor affect you personally is the simplest form of a non-attached relationship, as it presents no hardship at all. It is another matter entirely to feel this sense of neutrality when your art (its acceptance and success being the object of your attachment) is being rejected, criticized, or getting overlooked.

The Upanishads are to the Vedas what the Kabbalah is to the Jewish Bible. They treat of and expound the secret and mystic meaning of the Vedic texts.

H.P. BLAVATSKY

It is smart to look at things through a philosophy that is inherently flexible and is in the best interests of everyone. You know the rule: treat your neighbors as you would have them treat you. To succeed as a self-realized human being in this world, you must see beyond the temporal images of mass social conditioning. To an imposing extent, we are all indoctrinated in the system. You are raised to believe you are Russian, American, French, Brazilian, German, Portuguese, Egyptian, and so on. Is there any doubt that you have been acculturated and co-opted to a significant extent?

You must detach your self from debilitating things that don't work in the long term, including the incessant wanting for things and the consequences of not getting them. This doesn't mean that you can't blossom with your cultural endowments or achieve financial success and even fame. It does mean that you have attained a certain freedom where a specific outcome, one way or another no longer traps you. There is a price for getting what you desire, although the cost isn't immediately apparent. Remember the words of the master: "It is better to live in fulfillment than in hope."

ROSE-COLORED GLASSES

You might think: India is also the place of the rigid and hierarchal caste system. For thousands of years, people had no opportunity to rise above the caste they were born into. And doesn't Hinduism support this system? How can I take this Law of Non-Attachment seriously? You write in this book to consider the source. You might conclude with: this is what I am doing now—considering the source.

These questions are certainly valid and yes, you don't accept anything without first proving its value to your own self. I too wanted to find out how this Law of Non-Attachment could come from a society based on a caste system that was destructive and debilitating to human beings. I had to look deeper to see if there was any value in this law. Remember, if you want depth, you must dig deep. I had to investigate this law to make sure it isn't a regurgitation of new-age doublespeak. After many years, I have found that the Law of Non-Attachment is as real and as positively potent as the belief system that isn't working for you right now.

On balance, the caste system isn't that far removed from what we have in the West, where social status, although not as formalized and inflexible as the caste system, is no less apparent in the hierarchy and division of labor: the poor, middle class, and the wealthy. The few who do break out to become upwardly mobile are precisely that, the few, not the many. In our culture, it is the large middle class, blue and white collar, with their serf-like responsibilities that carry most of the load. While there isn't an official caste system in the West, there is a definite hierarchy of social standing for each person. The major difference in the West is that the individual can work his way up or down the ladder of social standing, influence, and opportunity. But don't be cajoled into wearing rose-colored glasses: freedom to choose can also cause complications.

SIZE MATTERS

In his book, *Status Anxiety*, Alain de Botton writes in the chapter on Equality, Expectation, and Envy: "It is the feeling that we might, under different

Without courage, wisdom bears no fruit.
BALTASAR GRACIÁN

Non-Attachment is the window of opportunity.
EDEN

Living with integrity means:

Not settling for less than what you know you deserve in your relationships.

Asking for what you want and need from others.

Speaking your truth, even though it might create conflict or tension.

Behaving in ways that are in harmony with your personal values.

Making choices based on what you believe, and not what others believe.

BARBARA DE ANGELIS

---

circumstances, be something other than what we are—a feeling inspired by exposure to the superior achievements of those whom we take to be our equals—that generates anxiety and resentment. If we are short, say, but live among people of our same height, we will not be unduly troubled by questions of size. But if others in our group grow just a little taller than us, we are liable to feel sudden unease and to be gripped by dissatisfaction and envy, even though we have not ourselves diminished in size by so much as a fraction of a millimeter."

De Botton also notes that is was the American professor of psychology, William James, who "argued that one's ability to feel satisfied with oneself does not hang on experiencing success in every area of endeavor. We are not always humiliated by failing at things, he suggested; we are humiliated only if we invest our pride and sense of worth in a given aspiration or achievement and then are disappointed in our pursuit of it. Our goals dictate what we will interpret as a triumph and what must count as a catastrophe."

A CLEVER SUBTERFUGE

The caste system of India was and to a great extent, especially in rural areas, is extant as a structure of social roles. Caste was determined by birth: you fell into the same caste as your parents, and there was almost no way to change it. The caste system dictated your occupation, choice of spouse, and many other aspects of your life. If you involved yourself in some activity outside your caste, you could be excommunicated from your caste. That would cut you off from doing any work to support yourself because you could only do the jobs allowed by your caste.

Death, it seems, was the only way out of this insidious cycle.

Many believe the caste system began as a form of clever subjugation of local populations by the Aryan peoples (*circa* 1500 BCE) who invaded and settled ancient India. The Aryans who were in the higher castes (no surprise there) placed the native peoples of the subcontinent into the lower castes. Since the system favored those at the top economically, those in the upper caste were motivated to maintain their superior standing.

Revolts to reform the rigidity of the caste system by religious leaders such as Mahavira (540-468 BCE), the founder of Jainism, and Siddhartha Gautama (563-483 BCE), the founder of Buddhism, were enlightened but ultimately failed as dogma and caste distinctions persisted in both sects.

In modern times, the Industrial Revolution brought with it a new awareness to the people of India, especially of the lower castes. Social mobility might be possible. Industrialization encouraged villagers of both high and low castes to move into the cities for better jobs. In the urban environment, rigid, age-old, caste-centered thinking gave way to a more liberal outlook, encouraging the mixing of castes without distinction. Trade unions and other associations had members from all castes working together.

DIE HARD

The Hindu caste system is comparable to class structures in other countries, such as the European monarchy system of king, nobles, and peasants before the Industrial Revolution. Dogmatically enforced for thousands of years, the caste system was the law of the land throughout India until

1949 when the Indian constitution outlawed it. Despite being banned by legislation, the caste system remains a deeply ingrained social structure, particularly in rural India. Prejudice dies hard, which is a testament to dogma, intolerance, and ingrained social conditioning.

While the caste system isn't explicitly religious, Hinduism has played a large part in maintaining its structure. Hindu religion preaches a cycle of birth and reincarnation, in which a person's soul is reborn into a new form after death. Your actions in this life determine your fate when you are born again. If you are faithful and dutiful in this life, next time, you will get a better lot. The caste system fits well within this belief. Lower-caste people believed that if they lived a good life, they could be reborn into a higher caste in the next. Regardless of its moral iniquity and decrepitude, the ancient Hindu caste system certainly let the individual know where he stood.

You were born into a caste, which was the same as your parents' lot in life. The system of status, economic position, and mores, was based on social grouping borne of heredity. If one's parents had high social standing, then so did the offspring. If they had low social standing, then the offspring did as well. You can see how the Law of Non-Attachment would be encouraged within this inflexible system. If you didn't get what you desired, so what. This law, which most assuredly was used for crowd control, has another dimension, which is also a source of liberation, then and now.

Buddha knew that the great enemies of man were ignorance and superstition, which, in turn, are lethal weaknesses fused together through social conditioning.

EDEN

MATERIALLY YOURS

Like it or not, you are judged by the class your were born into, your appearance, the manner in which you speak, your assets, sphere of influence, and contribution you make to society. As an artist the value of your social station corresponds directly to your popularity. Of course, this applies to an artist who measures his worth based solely on the opinions of others.

The true artist, a self-referential being, needs no outside authority to validate him, or his purpose on earth. He knows his dharma and that is the source of his well-being—not the paparazzi. No thing can stop a person who has discovered his dharma because that soul has been unleashed to become a force of nature. In a society where people have bought into a system of judging one another by their possessions and status, on balance it must also be known that these external 'measurements' of success are often volatile and can disappear at any time. Should you lose your well-paid job—there goes the house, cars, boats, clothes, and your place in the pecking order of society. Those things that you 'owned' and were attached to were never really yours, or *you* for that matter.

What then?

After having invested heavily in your sense of identity through external manifestations, you might feel shortchanged. It is much simpler and smarter to invest in your own self where your identity is your dharma, not your possessions. In this way you maintain your dignity, stability, and sense of purpose despite the flux of outward circumstances, which can cause havoc for the unprepared citizen artist.

Again, de Botton, in his perceptive book, *Status Anxiety,* also makes these observations:

The dissenter is every human being at those moments of his life when he resigns momentarily from the herd and thinks for himself.

ARCHIBALD MACLEISH

"Blessed with riches and possibilities far beyond anything imagined by ancestors who tilled the unpredictable soil of medieval Europe, modern populations have nonetheless shown a remarkable capacity to feel that neither who they are nor what they have is quite enough.

"Such feelings of deprivation may seem less peculiar if we consider the psychology behind the way we decide precisely how much is enough. Our judgment of what constitutes an appropriate limit on anything—for example, on wealth or esteem—is never arrived at independently; instead, we make such determinations by comparing our condition with that of a reference group, a set of people who we believe resemble us. We cannot, it seems, appreciate what we have for its own merit, or even against what our medieval forebears had. We cannot be impressed by how prosperous we are in historical terms.

"If we are made to live in a draughty, insalubrious cottage and bend to the harsh rule of an aristocrat occupying a large and well-heated castle, and yet we observe that our equals all live exactly as we do, then our condition will seem normal—regrettable, certainly, but not a fertile ground for envy. If, however, we have a pleasant home and a comfortable job but learn through ill-advised attendance at a school reunion that some of our old friends (there is no more compelling reference group) now reside in houses grander than our own, bought on the salaries they are paid in more enticing occupations than our own, we are likely to return home nursing a violent sense of misfortune."

Attachment to material objects and goals (keeping up with those ubiquitous Joneses in every metaphorical sense for example) is the primary cause of self bondage, a state of entrapment that instigates envy, greed, and jealousy, which then further lead to suffering and injustice.

MAKING ROOM

Remember, Bennett reminded us that we must make room for the solution to enter by not thinking. In his book, *Creating Affluence*, Dr. Deepak Chopra lays it out for us in beautiful detail: "There is a precise mechanism through which all desires can be manifested. These four steps are as follows:

- Step one: You slip into the gap between thoughts. The gap is the window, the corridor, the transformational vortex through which the personal psyche communicates with the cosmic psyche.
- Step two: You have a clear intention of a clear goal in the gap.
- Step three: You relinquish your attachment to the outcome, because chasing the outcome or getting attached to it entail coming out of the gap.
- Step four: You let the universe handle the details.

"It is important to have a clear goal in your awareness, but it is also important to relinquish your attachment to the goal. And the goal is in the gap, and the gap is the potentiality to organize and orchestrate the details required to affect any outcome."

OPEN YOUR EYES

Not getting what the artist wants, or what society 'promises' him, instigates unhappiness. I'm not referring to mild disappointment that lasts for a waning bit of time. I mean a deep-seated sense of feeling lost, worthless, and, in due course, depression—feelings that make life seem unbearable, which is a tragic and pathetic situation (and avoidable) that often perpetuates self-destructive behavior.

This is grist for the mill that doesn't go unnoticed by spin doctors of art who play up despondency to deepen the tragedy of the artist in some weird formulation for increasing the cachet of the artist's name and—as a quantifiable effect—the perceived value of that artist's work. The public is willing to pay more for self-inflicted pain, or so it seems.

Films, biographies, and novels stress the agony more than the ecstasy in a melodramatic conspiracy to keep the image of the tortured artist alive. Is this sick, or what?

The issue here isn't the goal, but the dynamic nature of the goal, which is an evolving multi-dimensional event that falls along a unique timeline. Misery as an outcome for not attaining a predefined accomplishment is a poor choice. Succumbing to this system means you are either unaware of or simply don't yet understand the Law of Non-Attachment.

There is no prime directive on the books making it mandatory for anyone or everyone to discover or adopt the Law of Non-Attachment. However, if you are fortunate to find this law of liberation waiting for you on your path—like now—and you ignore the possibility of its value, you will forever remain on the effect side of cause—a victim instead of a creator who uses the dynamic of rejection to reaffirm and prevail.

If you become attached to the precise outcome of your plan, you are blind to every other superior opportunity that is in front of you now, or what will come your way shortly. Your initial desire is a precursor for an outcome not yet anticipated. You will confront future events for the better because you know that to be attached is to severely limit the power of your own self, which isn't what you seek. But, as with all powers, you must be discerning or you will become consumed by obeying the letter of the law instead of the spirit. Don't get stuck in splitting metaphysical angel hair.

Of course, unless you are a Buddha, there is the cost of attachment when it comes to family, friends, pets, and possessions. For most of us, losing a loved one causes the inconsolable pain of heartache. That is why many artists feel dejected when their art (their loved ones) is rejected. Loss and impermanence are the price of temporal existence. It is the life we are born into, and no one gets out alive.

Don't waste pain; don't deny pain; use pain to become stronger; use rejection to clarify your art and your mission. Feel the beauty of pure emotion which is intuition, your conduit to the manifesting matrix that is consciousness: the source of great art. Let the joyful tears of God cleanse your psyche and your karma, and your soul will show you the serenity of the present moment. As essential as love is, it isn't as fundamental as food. If you are hunting and the prey gets away, then non-attachment is also the way to go. You don't give up as you begin the hunt again. Failure on the hunt isn't an option. The lioness, for example, doesn't feel rejected, depressed, nor does she have an identity crisis if she misses her kill. She begins stalking again until successful. You must do no less.

Remember always that you not only have the right to be an individual, you have an obligation to be one.

ELEANOR ROOSEVELT

When you scrutinize the Law of Non-Attachment you will realize why it is more important to have a direction than a detailed plan; you must not lose sight of your direction, your goal; plans must remain adaptable so they can be modified as necessary to serve the overall objective.

In our culture The Law of Non-Attachment has been distilled into this bromide: 'If the world gives you lemons, make lemonade.'

CAVEAT

In certain respects, especially when exchanges are made, attachment isn't only acceptable, it is anticipated. When you go to the doctor, you expect him to help you get better; you pay for a product, you want to get the item you paid for; and so on.

You have to use your sensibilities, your brain, and your savoir-faire when it comes to not being attached to the outcome. These are the quality of life issues we can't predict or control; and I'm not talking about shopping at the mall. Seeking out your intuition to handle temporal matters that you can handle yourself is what it sounds like.

Remember, intuition doesn't involve itself in the mundane—that is a job for instinct.

Are you your art?

Don't let your personal relationship, whatever it might be, with your art end up working against you.

Whether you feel each piece of art is a child, of you but not you, or that you and your art are one, or you view your art dispassionately as not you at all, the key for dealing with rejection is to disconnect and, as we have seen, protect yourself from any particular outcome through the Law of Non-Attachment. If your work is accepted, you can certainly be pleased for any reason you like, except one: don't perceive recognition as validation. If you do, you give away the power of your art to the accepting authority. On balance, if your work is rejected, then the power also lies in your strength to keep your feelings about the situation to yourself, as you maintain the self-inspiration to move on. This isn't always so easy, but so what. Whether it is yea or nay, go deeper than your ego.

DIGGING DEEP

A whiner doesn't win, and a winner doesn't whine. Through non-attachment, you will develop strength of character and a gentle gracious power to confront both rejection and acceptance. You have a destiny to fulfill of your own making. When you have answered the core questions in this book, you will successfully come to terms with the value of your work.

Keep your awareness above the fray of temporal turmoil and you will prevail. Thinking or saying that this is hard to do is of no relevance for the artist who has found his dharma, for the artist on a mission. If rejection can derail you, then you must confront your own intention.

Remember, once you become attached to the content and outcome of a piece of art, you have drifted from the source. If you want to be great, you must do great things—there is no other way.

Your sacred space is where you can find yourself again and again.

JOSEPH CAMPBELL

THE HEALER

CHAPTER FORTY NINE

NO WHINING
And I Mean It

THE NO WHINING that concerns us here refers specifically to definition number two as shown below. There is more to whining than irritation; scratch a whiner and you most assuredly won't find a winner.

> **whine (hwīn, wīn) v. whined whinäing whines v. intr**. 1. To utter a plaintive, high-pitched, protracted sound, as in pain, fear, supplication, or complaint. 2. To complain or protest in a childish fashion, often in an annoyingly plaintive voice. 3. To produce a sustained noise of relatively high pitch: jet engines whining. v. tr.

Whining projects a negative image of the one engaged in the futile act. If your close associates are whiners, then do yourself a great service and find new friends who don't dwell there. If you are the whiner, you can choose to excise this thorn from your psyche at any time and make being around you desirable instead of a drag. Your positive can-do mental attitude and spiritual countenance are gifts to all those around you. Whining is chronic; it isn't the occasional complaint.

COVET NO THING

Whiners are more than annoying; they represent a special breed of victim; they are spiritual vampires who insidiously drain the life force from others. *Victim-no-more* is the mantra and the way forward toward evolution.

No complaining. No blaming. No bouts of ego-induced self-sabotage. No shooting thyself in the foot.

Remove the stings and barbs from your vocabulary—from the inner critic to your verbal engagements. Defeat angst by removing jealousy and envy. Desist from comparing yourself to others.

Stop wishing and hoping; start dreaming, for waking dreams lead to dynamic actions that transform impossible ambitions into reality. Since this life is about making dreams come true, begin by directing the scenes

I find your lack of faith disturbing.

DARTH VADER,
STAR WARS: EPISODE IV, A NEW HOPE

The Expedient Guru:

I recall the time I spent with the holy man from India. We were sitting together having a talk on a porch one summer evening.

A mosquito kept buzzing around between us. The insect could not be waved off as it came back again and again.

Finally, the holy man reached out and slapped it dead into the ground. I looked at him and he looked at me. He said "Next incarnation," and smiled.

EDEN

of your own life. Know that the whole you, the non-whining you, the grounded you, the art-conscious you need covet no thing. Know that art is the magic entrance to the kingdom of fulfillment in this life. You need only knock and have the courage to enter.

God is the door opener. Whining has relatives, bored and excuses to name two. If you are bored, then you are boring. Excuses. I can't paint because the light isn't right; I can't paint with people watching me; I don't have a studio; I don't have a studio that's big enough; I don't have the right color oils; I can't write at night; I can't compose in the morning; and all the 'I cannots' and 'do nots' in the universe are impotent bits of self-justification that keep the whiner a prisoner from entering the land called 'can do'.

Count and keep a log of how many negative thoughts you have in a single day; the number and their cumulative effect will startle you into a greater awareness of your own complicity.

Artists as a group are no different from any other group. There are generous artists, and there are cheap artists. There are gregarious artists, and there are reclusive artists. There are moody artists and there are even-tempered artists. The list goes on. While artists who are whiners may even be famous and externally successful, it is the non-whining artist who concerns us here because she ultimately triumphs in the grandeur of the big picture. Not buffeted by the whims of public taste, the non-whining artist draws her success from self-discipline, knowing that she touches God when she works. After all, who better to emulate than the Creator? The rest of it—that is to earn a living—is marketing, politics, and timing: elements that play their part in direct proportion to her dedication. The same grace for non-whining is available to the civilian as well.

HEAD OF A PIN

When the whining habit finally withers away from neglect and is replaced by gratitude and appreciation, the focus becomes working. The house of complaining has been aired out, leaving a vacancy for marvelous creations. At this juncture, you come to realize that there is always plenty of room at the top. Theoretical physicist Richard Feynman would argue that the contrary is also true. In 1959, Feynman gave a talk at the California Institute of Technology (Caltech) on the opportunities for invention inherent within the 'new' field of nanotechnology.

To get right to the point, Feynman spoke about the feasibility for writing the entire twenty-four-volumes of the *Encyclopædia Britannica* on the head of pin. And he theorized about not only writing on such a small scale, but to be able to read the text as well.

Feynman: Now, the name of this talk is 'There is Plenty of Room at the Bottom'—not just 'There is Room at the Bottom.' What I have demonstrated is that there is room—that you can decrease the size of things in a practical way. I now want to show that there is plenty of room. I won't now discuss how we are going to do it, but only what is possible in principle—in other words, what is possible according to the laws of physics. I'm not inventing anti-gravity, which is possible someday only if the laws aren't what we think. I am telling you what could be done if the laws are what we think; we aren't doing it simply because we haven't yet gotten around to it.

While Feynman was referring to space that exists on the quantum level in physics, his premise is extremely useful for all artists: it isn't the space, it is how you use it that matters.

BACK TO THE SUMMIT

Despite best efforts, if complaining can't be brought under control and life in the arts isn't what you had envisioned, then it may be time to reevaluate your dharma. This is a good thing.

Nothing—except you—can prevent you from living an authentic life. If your desire to create is fueled on less than a fire in the belly, then fully realize your situation: to be self-aware is the goal. To live your dream, you must wake up and remain awake.

The artist's life isn't for everyone. You must decide if this observation is relevant for your situation. To maneuver the rugged terrain while avoiding the pitfalls as one ascends the mountain is a required skill that comes with its share of bruises. After all, you wouldn't plan on climbing Mount Everest without training, the proper equipment, a seasoned guide, and a party of fellow mountaineers who shared your vision. The quest for art demands no less.

As we have come to appreciate: rejection and failure are not synonyms; failure is when you give up on your own self. Excuses are what they sound like. Do you hear the truth of it? No thing has ever stopped the true artist from living an authentic life because he always finds a way; and the way demands dedication tempered with relative patience. You must do whatever is necessary to complete your mission. Otherwise, you are being disingenuous with your own self. This is a distinction not a judgment.

The next time you are fortunate enough to catch yourself grumbling about your art life—stop thinking. Grab hold of this moment of disenchantment; it is an opportunity to feel the truth of your fears, doubts, motivations, and the value of your art. Step up and confront your complaints and self-inflicted woes; if you want depth, you must dig deep. Use disappointment, including rejection to affirm your purpose and to develop your strength of character; this is the object lesson.

Now that your dharma has reasserted itself, you too are ready to wine and dine with the gifts and blessings that you have cultivated and earned as a 'whine-free' spirit.

You don't suffer for your art; you may, however, have to pay your dues in finding your purpose: what your art is.

EDEN

CHAPTER FIFTY

RORSCHACH'S INKBLOTS
What Might This Be?

WHAT A PERSON sees and how he sees provides an insight into the individual's awareness of consciousness, the culture that spawned him, and the perceptions labeled as reality.

I am the beholder.

In many ways, contemporary art has a lot in common with the Rorschach (pronounced 'raw-shock') inkblot test. The art critic Clement Greenberg saw truth in Jackson Pollock's drip paintings. Why?

PROJECTIONS

The Rorschach test is a psychological examination of personality in which a subject's interpretations of ten standard abstract inkblot designs are analyzed as a measure of perceptual and cognitive processes, including emotional and intellectual functioning. The test is named after Hermann Rorschach (1884-1922), a Swiss Psychiatrist who developed the inkblot test that bears his name. Rorschach had studied art as a secondary-school student where he earned the nickname Kleck, meaning 'inkblot', because of his interest in sketching. His father was a painter and although Rorschach considered a career in art, he was drawn to psychiatry, especially psychoanalysis, which was a new field at the time.

By 1918, Rorschach had started to experiment with the interpretation of inkblots by showing a series of accidental inkblots to patients and asking them, "What might this be?" The Rorschach test is based on the human tendency to project interpretations and feelings onto the ambiguous and abstract. Rorschach believed a person's perceptual responses to inkblots could serve as clues to basic personality tendencies.

POSTHUMOUS ENTHUSIASM

In 1921, he published the results of his studies with the inkblot test on 300 mental patients and 100 normal subjects in a monograph called *Psychodiagnostik*, a work that was initially ignored. Not only did Rorschach have difficulties in finding a publisher, the monograph wasn't well received

In his 1973 documentary Painters Painting, *filmmaker Emile de Antonio interviewed many of the figures who, after the Second World War, had fueled the abstract expressionism movement in New York City.*

Among this influential group of artists was the painter Willem de Kooning.

de Kooning: I don't think painters have particularly bright ideas.

de Antonio: What do they have?

de Kooning: I guess their talent is painting things.
Not such bright idea for [Claude] Monet to paint his haystacks.

EMILE DE ANTONIO

When you don't know the way, you have to look at the signs. When you know the way, you don't have to look at the signs.

Extrapolate this metaphor into everything else, including your journey to find your audience and the art that demands your dedication.

Make no mistake about it. Life is biology, but living is an art, not a science. If living were a science there would be a formula and no need for poetry or the wisdom of experience.

EDEN

upon publication. Today, *Psychodiagnostik* is regarded by many as one of the great classics of psychiatry and psychology. Rorschach never experienced its success and died of complications from appendicitis before he could properly test and evaluate his invention. Especially popular in the 1950's, the Rorschach test was later criticized for its susceptibility to subjective interpretation on the part of the evaluator and subsequently fell out of favor as a diagnostic tool.

Seeing images in abstract shapes and forms isn't a new concept and has been observed by artists throughout history to the present. In 1500, for example, Leonardo da Vinci wrote in his *Treatise of the Painting*: "Do not note this opinion small, in which I guess/advise you, it may appear to you not annoying, sometimes to stand still and have a look on wall marks, in or into ash in the fire, into the clouds, or into the mud and on other such places; you will discover very marvelous inventions to them, if you regard them quite. Because the painter's spirit gets such new inventions by it."

OFF THE RACK

I've mentioned the 'art' urinal and the bull's head figure elsewhere, and it's worth repeating here. In 1917, Marcel Duchamp (1887-1968) took a urinal and rotated it ninety degrees from its normal, functional position. The artist left the piece unembellished except for the inscription 'R. Mutt 1917' and titled it: *Fountain*.

Was this a joke, a prank, or was it a serious work? Rejected from an exhibition that was to be open to all works of art sponsored by the Society for Independent Artists in New York, the porcelain urinal was to become the most influential of his 'readymades', which radicalized the potential for art making by recasting an 'as is' manufactured consumer products as art—an early form of Pop Art.

As Beatrice Wood, who knew Marcel Duchamp quite well, recalls in her autobiography, *I Shock Myself*:

"The rejection of R. Mutt's *Fountain* had caused a small hurricane of controversy in art circles and thus unfurled the banner of freedom in art. This gave Marcel an inspiration. We went to see the noted photographer Alfred Stieglitz. At Marcel's request, he agreed to photograph the *Fountain* for the frontispiece of the magazine [*The Blind Man*]. He was greatly amused, but also felt it was important to fight bigotry in America. He took great pains with the lighting, and did it with such skill that a shadow fell across the urinal suggesting a veil.

"The piece was renamed: *Madonna of the Bathroom*... Stieglitz' photograph of the *Madonna* appeared on the front page with the heading 'Exhibit Refused by the Independents,' and opposite was an editorial which I wrote: 'Whether Mr. Mutt with his own hands made the fountain or not has no importance. He CHOSE it. He took an ordinary article of life, placed it so that its useful significance disappeared under the new title and point of view, creating a new thought for that object'... Stieglitz also sent in a letter: 'This first exhibition is a concrete move in as I understand the Independent Society, its chief function is to smash antiquated academic ideas. This first exhibition is a concrete move in that direction... NO JURY... NO PRIZES ... NO COMMERCIAL TRICKS.'"

Another example of seeing art in manufactured goods took place in 1943 when Pablo Picasso (1881-1973) reconfigured a bicycle's handlebars and seat into a *Bull's Head* sculpture.

Was this art? Why is it art?

While others may have observed that a bicycle seat and handlebars when properly aligned resembles a bull's head, it was Picasso, already confident in his work, who had the nerve to assemble the pieces into a whole.

Would you fare as well with a readymade as did Duchamp and Picasso? It is an important question to answer.

COMPLETING THE PICTURE

Although disagreement among psychologists as to the reliability of the Rorschach test continues to this day, the blots remain an ideal metaphor for the perception of what is art in the world. We learn how to see and we project our experience onto that which we perceive, giving it meaning.

We mostly see through the eyes of the mainstream culture. Consequently, advertising is understood; there is but one interpretation inherent in an ad and that is to buy whatever it is promoting. It is a one-dimensional art form, however subtle, designed for passive instant recognition. Art demands significantly more: the viewer must participate beyond the superficial to fulfill the art experience, the aesthetic moment. In art, if the viewer sees it, then it is there—as with the Rorschach test. The significant difference is that the art from the soul is alive, and unlike the inkblot, it isn't random, or accidental.

You, the artist, who spells things out in your own language must take into account that, for the most part, the art viewer is looking at your work through gauze that is interwoven with strands of predetermined reactions, meanings, insecurities, and predigested interpretations supported by society as being normal and acceptable. These viewers include: the public, gallery owner, critic, art editor, curator, museum director, grant or fellowship committee person, friend, family member, and even a colleague in art.

Fortunately, there are exceptions in each sphere of influence, those people who can see for themselves; and, to encounter someone who can recognize art without a show of hands is as rare as a great artist who must do no less.

Remember, for better or worse, we see what we have been conditioned to see, inkblots, art, readymades, and all.

If the path be beautiful, let us not ask where it leads.

ANATOLE FRANCE

Reality is only a Rorschach ink-blot, you know.

ALAN WATTS

CHAPTER FIFTY ONE

LETTER TO MY MOTHER
Boulevard of Dreams

IT WAS MANY years ago. Life was edgy, sexy, and ripe. My girlfriend and I had moved to the Cow Hollow district of San Francisco. We lived in a cozy apartment at the top of a steep street that overlooked the Marina flats below.

In the sidebar to the right is a letter (which I happened to find one day while writing this book) I had mailed to my mother for her birthday.

She was born on July 14th in Romania; and I arrived twenty years later and a day earlier of the same month on the 13th in Germany.

Note: I wrote this letter ages before I had excised the words 'hope' and 'just' from my vocabulary.

DOWN THE DRAIN?

In retrospect, that was a feisty letter considering my circumstances when I wrote it. I had given up much to follow that voice, that feeling, which I couldn't have told you was intuition at the time.

My inner self had led me on precarious journey and my odyssey was far from over.

Things weren't going well for me financially.

Fiscally, I was spiraling downward with no prospect for improvement in sight. To raise money, I had sold off what material items I could at the weekend flea market in Sausalito; I also traded my car for cash.

Culturally, I was immersed in art and spent nearly all my time with a master artist; not only did I watch him paint great works, our days together and evenings with his family were about the art of living. The true artist doesn't relegate his art to some part of the day or night; his art is inexorably integrated into every facet of his life.

My long hours with the artist were uplifting, demanding, often gruelling, and priceless; I knew I was doing the right thing.

To an outside, or even a familial observer, I was making a huge mistake. After all, these were my vital and formative professional moneymaking years that were seemingly going down the old drain.

July 12

Dear Mom:

Well, here we are—you are 60—I'm 40. Hey, doesn't that add up to 100% percent. Good times ahead—success, joy ... fulfillment. Who knows what excitement the future holds for you ... and yours truly.

So, I didn't follow the American Dream. I'm following something else ... something inside, something that has to do with art, culture, integrity, and character. I hope you continue to understand. I know it will pay off in many ways.

I don't want you to worry. I want you to write down your feelings in poetry or prose. To help you get started, here's a small gift [a smart-looking journal and a pen] from Hanna and myself.

I feel strong. I am confident. I will persevere ... and I will always love you. Thanks for being just who you are.

Love,

Eden

To work on oneself one must know every screw, every nail of one's machine—then you will know what to do.

GEORGE GURDJIEFF

ODD JOBS

While space and time with the master artist was good for me, it didn't pay the rent—that took cash. I was working minimum wage odd jobs such as telemarketing, loading trucks, and taking inventory in department stores at midnight.

One job from 11:00 a.m. to 7:00 p.m. three days a week was handing out samples of cigarette brands in various parts of the city. You had to say in a loud manner 'Free Cigarette Samples' over and over as you walked those crowded and lonely streets of San Francisco, which was more of a town than a metropolis like Manhattan; it wasn't long before I began running into acquaintances. Although they didn't verbalize it, their thoughts were reflected in their eyes: 'What is he doing here handing out cigarettes? The poor bastard.'

Being exposed to the public in this fashion, I went through three stages. First, I felt embarrassed and dejected. Feeling awkward came next, and then, after a time, I simply thought: What difference does it make? I was naked, and I was hawking cigarette samples. These were the facts; reality as it was: no back up, no trust fund, and no generous rich uncle.

No one looking at me on the street corner back then could have known I had embarked upon a larger purpose. I had a vague sense of direction but no destiny yet. I had no guarantee that I would ever discover anything of value.

I was barefoot inching my way along a razor sharp tightrope with no first-aid kit, or a net.

NO EXIT

Life as a day worker and laborer was a galaxy away from the self-esteem of my former life on the East Coast where I had been an executive in big business making the coveted bucks that leased all the outer manifestations of success.

Then, after moving to Los Angeles, I landed a plum as editor for a business magazine where I negotiated an enviable package: a hefty salary, expense account, and a new Corvette as my company car.

Although I had been riding high on corporate perks in those days, I wasn't oblivious that my soul was running on empty. The past seemed to be a surrealistic side street off the boulevard of dreams. Now, as people took the cigarette samples from me, well, my life seemed to have taken yet another turn marked no exit, and that seemed to be a nightmare.

There was no turning back.

SHEDDING THE TRAPS

I didn't realize or appreciate it at the time, but what seemed to me as hitting the skids, this ostensible degradation of my life, was my time for purging, for stripping away social conditioning, ego, what other people thought, and the seductive entrapments of society called security and status—tradeoffs payable only by relinquishing your soul.

Paying your dues is one of the mandatory tests in the school of man for becoming an artist; it was a compulsory requirement, not an elective. This object lesson in catharsis was by no means part of a graduation exercise either.

Over the erratic course of many hard, uncertain, and bleak times waiting in the wings, I would have to prove my commitment to finding my dharma, to earn my authenticity. Then, more than a decade after meeting the master artist, I awoke to a miracle. Suddenly, organically, and remarkably, I was no longer in the audience; I was onstage; I was an artist. But my euphoria was ephemeral, as finding my purpose in life was only the beginning. I then faced the next challenge: dedication to my dharma, my passion for art each day, no matter what.

Failure wasn't then nor is it now an option.

FUTURE PERFECT

Awakening to my dharma as an artist was magic; however, my insights at the time about overcoming difficulties to come were cerebral, not firsthand experience. I sensed a difficult task lay ahead; not knowing how formidable and to what extent was a blessing—then and now.

No matter how superb the work, to make a living an artist must not only create, he must also grapple with a daunting uphill task: relentless self-promotion while confronting an exclusive marketplace notorious for cronyism, inflexibility, and rejection.

It is no great stretch to love the art of the past. Original art faces the most difficulty in gaining exposure and acceptance. Art history is fraught with great art that was debunked in its time. Gauguin and van Gogh created despite personal difficulties, including rejection—and are now called visionaries.

Why would any artist willingly set himself up for a life of adversity by challenging the mainstream? Art is either a calling or a job. Many are called; few choose to go.

I am forever mindful of this choice: What's the point of going through pain if you won't transmute the agony into ecstasy, the hardship into strength of character?

An artist isn't an occupation; it's a gift with one condition—dedication.

EDEN

CHAPTER FIFTY TWO

THE GESTALT
Children of Art

AS THERE IS NO substitute for doing it yourself, how we learn and acquire knowledge should not be a mystery or a task rigidly relegated to rote. There are but two ways to approach learning.

In Zen, for example, words merely get in the way of grasping the object lesson. You must experience the truth directly and intuitively; and, of course, anything less is hearsay.

The other approach is more oriented to the Western mind where a description of the lesson is presumably put down clearly enough so that the student will know the truth the next time he stumbles over it.

My approach is a synthesis of the two.

WORK BOOTS

Nature goes with what works over the long term, and we call it evolution. In emulating success, working from a proven model makes sense. But copying a model on a surface level is what it sounds like: superficial and unsatisfying. One of your primary objectives as an artist is to find out firsthand what makes the model tick inside.

If I were to describe an artist who has triumphed over rejection, he would possess an overall confidence supported by attributes, or qualities that define his character. These qualities apply not only to the artist, but also to any fully realized human being who lives by his wits, and projects a positive voice in this universe of souls.

A fully realized person has realized that there is a distinction between the ego, which is the self-important aspect of the mind, and the self, which is the soul—the inexhaustible energy that is compassion and strength of character. A fully realized person is one, while doing no harm, has the drive and desire to express her unique potential at whatever the cost.

If you have the will to be, you will have to be some thing—and this thing will exist only in contrast to the things that surround it. And to get this thing to fly, you will need the correct posture and attitude, attainable by adopting The Eighteen Be-Attitudes of the model artist.

And as for fortune, and as for fame
I never invited them in
Though it seems to the world they were all I desired;
They are illusions
They're not the solutions they promised to be
The answer was here all the time
I love you and hope you love me ...

EVITA,
DON'T CRY FOR ME ARGENTINA

By believing passionately in something that still does not exist, we create it. The non-existent is whatever we have not sufficiently desired.

NIKOS KAZANTZAKIS

Far from being a construct of a rigid system, which is inherently limited, the Be-Attitudes converge into an adaptable and fluid rush of power for hosing rejection off your work boots.

TAKE THE A-TRAIN

Let's say you needed to travel to a remote destination and didn't know how to get there. If I wrote down the street name and number, you would find the address helpful, but insufficient. If I gave you the location and accurate directions for getting there, then you would have complete information before beginning your trip.

For the past 400 plus pages, this book has been describing the destination and the means for getting there. You must still supply the energy plus your unique dharma. But directions themselves aren't infallible when it comes to expediency. You must be discerning. The most direct route is not always the fastest or best route. For example, if you want to drive somewhere in midtown Manhattan, the most direct route may be bumper-to-bumper traffic. It may be better to go around the congestion, make better time, and get to your destination with less stress on you and everyone else.

Or, take the subway.

Keep in mind that although the destination is that place where rejection has been rendered inert, it is not your terminus. The destination is dynamic, ever-changing and shifting with experience, fluid, not static. No matter how precise the directions are presented, you may still get lost for a time. But that is part of learning any new and often daunting route. Remember, the destination is of no value without experiencing the journey.

You don't confront rejection once, and then it's over forever—nice and neat. Confronting rejection and the mentality of the status quo repeatedly in your life is part of being an artist.

If you think 'they' know more than you, then you are both right and lost. You do know better, don't you?

You can't lead without risk.

Rejection won't change, you will—if you have the will to prevail. Dealing with 'no thanks' or some other equally curt blow-off line will become easier over time. Eventually, occasions of rejection will be relegated to mild nuisance status and harmless instead of experiencing spurned feelings, or worse.

Remember, you can always get there from here if you need to.

TRANSCENDENTAL TRAIL MIX

Instead of going over well-trodden ground already trampled by others in an aimless fool's gold rush to nowhere, I know an uncrowded route toward a desirable destination. I have walked, danced, tripped, and often run along this route for many years. I am still on this golden path. Although far from being a shortcut, this lane to the light has unwaveringly led me in the direction of strength and character.

To make sure you stay on course, a set of signposts in 'Words in the Way' describe a selection of misused terms, and the importance of thoughtful and verbal clarity for artists of all forms—even mimes. Clarity leads to purpose, and purpose is the magic potion that dissolves the thorns of rejection.

It is both unnecessary and counterproductive to pore over and study The Eighteen Be-Attitudes, as one might cram for an exam. The content of this book isn't about regurgitating rote. Knowing these attributes by attempting to memorize them won't work in this realm of achievement. Remember, memorization leaves no room for originality. When you are on a journey and need energy, you eat; you don't have to think about it. Your hunger pangs have told you precisely what you need. Similarly, to make these attributes your own, you must feel them with the same degree of organic tension induced by hunger, the most basic of survival mechanisms.

The wisdom of your body will, over time, assimilate, transform, and infuse these qualities as intelligence into every cell of your corporeal being. You eat, and the body transforms the food into energy. You don't have to think about the process. Ingesting kernels of new concepts and possibilities is no different.

You are what you consume physically and metaphysically. I share with you my transcendental trail mix, the soul food that has sustained me from the depths of darkness into the light of art that is awareness.

CHILDREN OF ART

Routing rejection is not an isolated part of your existence. You are part of a grander mystery; a greater parental consciousness lovingly envelops you for some purpose that you must uncover.

To develop the inner strength you seek, you must inevitably adopt these attributes, these Be-Attitudes, which are essentially the universal building blocks of character, and integrate them. This means you can't fling these attributes upon yourself and expect them to stick like *pasta al dente*.

You can't force natural growth, which evolves in its own good time and rhythm. Organic development doesn't preclude nutrients, the proper environment, and care.

You must have direct kinship with these attributes as you would with any child that you would adopt out of compassion and love. You can count on the world to challenge these attributes regularly for your lifetime, and at the worst possible time. Or what is the point?

Without tests of character, all is bluster and hearsay. As time passes, you will come to know that the external circumstances of acceptance and rejection—both the result of action—are reflections that glow with an intensity in direct proportion to your authenticity as an artist. Knowing that you are a reliable witness has great liberating power.

An artist who has triumphed over rejection in a way that is healthy in the long term owns these eighteen qualities, or attributes. He owns them because he has earned them. You can't purchase or bequeath them. Your money is no good in this department.

As I often mention, the self I am writing about is the self called your soul, not the myself associated with ego, which is mostly driven by temporal issues of insecurity, personality, conflict, and fear. The soul self is beyond pettiness and comparisons because of its intrinsic mission to connect with the Creator's force.

If you want to touch a piece of heaven, you do have to reach upward. You can't win the lottery without first buying a ticket.

If you don't know how you got there, then the destination is meaningless. You will forever be insecure, afraid of getting lost.

Was that painting a fluke? Can I do it again?

This is where faith comes in, a faith borne of awareness, not a blind faith in the whelping box of dogma.

EDEN

The aim of [a] Koan is to enable the pupil to resolve what the mind cannot resolve.

WILLIAM SEGAL

ET TU, ARTIST

You are still asking: But how do I make these qualities mine? Being conscious of them is a good start. You exercise to tone and toughen up your body. While exercising your character follows the same rules, there is a special condition that you must factor in. Character can't be bullied or forced to perform on demand, or on a workout schedule. No personal trainer can do it for you. You can't fabricate, or stage tests for your character.

There is a precise mechanism for developing the strength you dream of as an empowered artist. The next time an authentic issue arises to test your resolve, stop. This is that fabled moment of truth. You must confront the thing that is now in your way. You can be sure the test will involve one of the Be-Attitudes. If you hide or procrastinate at the moment of your truth, not only do you miss a rare opportunity, you weaken your character, making the next test more difficult. As Shakespeare aptly wrote in his play *Julius Caesar*: "Cowards die many times before their deaths; the valiant never taste of death but once."

Be strong for your own sake, for your art. You won't be alone as your self will support you, and if you have been true, you will have exercised that specific Be-Attitude that was called for in the fray. You will begin to appreciate what it means to earn that which can't be bought or sold.

SHIP SHAPE

The tests will come, and they will challenge and continue to challenge each Be-Attitude until there is no reason to proceed since you have proven your mettle—this is the nexus point, the exquisite moment when you make a quality your own; and because you have earned it honestly, bravely, and at all costs, this quality, like the most alluring member of the opposite sex, is naturally attracted to you.

But don't get too comfortable. This relationship between you and the Be-Attitudes is anything but static; you need not fear complacency. As the stakes get higher, the ante increases; each quality will be tested again, and on a more intense level. Or what is the point? The description here and throughout this book for building character is left in general terms; you are unique and you must fill in the details of your own challenges. Of course, the upside to this lifelong commitment is that handling the density of the world gets easier as your character develops and gains strength.

Your unwavering determination will spontaneously provide you with the direction (via your intuition) you need to stay your course. After a time, when you reach that welcomed harbor of confidence, you can scrape the barnacles of rejection off your ship and watch them float out to sea.

Remember, many are called; few choose to go. The beauty of quality is that it depends solely upon you. The spirit in art is the quality of perceiving consciousness. There is no competition involved among the unique. Adopt the Be-Attitudes into your life and they will serve you faithfully. As the master said: "Nothing supersedes character."

Character is the crucible containing your Be-Attitudes; character shapes and focuses an immutable force that flows victorious and will never let you down in your quest as an artist.

Greatness demands that you do great things.

Validation, Mon Amour:

Outside public validation, as wonderful as it can be, can also weaken you, if that is the source of your strength.

A private validation from an honorable witness that only you know about retains its vitality, as it is the silent source of inner strength and character, which is immune to the bias and cluelessness of outside authority.

EPILOGUE

HERE AND NOW
Art of the Covenant

IF YOU CLAIM to have found a truth in life, you can be sure that this discovery and you will be tested to see what is what. It has been eight years since I developed the basic outline for this book; and I have devoted the past three years to writing the manuscript.

Although I knew there would be challenges in writing about art, metaphysical matters, truth, and rejection—volatile subjects to be sure, I couldn't have predicted the onslaught of obstacles I would have to overcome.

There were the distractions—some serious—that couldn't be ignored, the tests of faith—always serious—that would cue up daily, and the everyday difficulties of living that needed handling—all this while carving out time to make art, too.

Of all the personal issues I had to confront these past years while writing this book, I was unprepared for what followed.

The day I had been dreading arrived.

Tragedy.

Larry, my older Yorkie, succumbed to the hunter that stalks us all. While I was devastated by this loss, I had been anticipating it because of his advanced years. Then, the other cold shoe of death dropped at our door. Less than two months later my other younger Yorkie, Beau, who had been full of life one moment, was taken down in the next by a fatal illness; much too young to die, he was taken from us in a matter of days.

More sorrow.

Where once there had been the exuberance of two little creatures roaming about, there was now the empty and frigid absence of life. There was nothing I could do to resurrect these sweet souls, my little reincarnated yogis. Their time had come; Larry and Beau were now forever gone from this place.

I now more fully appreciated the adage: Praise the soul who has an old dog who loves him.

To see value and gain insight from each experience is a decision that helps us make sense of life, and death, which is the body's ultimate release of spirit from this particular existence.

The final forming of a person's character lies in their own hands.

ANNE FRANK

When you conquer your demons, then that is a life well spent. Not every triumph is the conquest of other peoples.

It is the personal triumph over yourself that is the crown in the jewel of awareness.

It is self-control over yourself, an achievement known only to you, that both supplies and drives the internal strength you are seeking.

EDEN

Losing my long time companions reinforced the maxim: *Do it!* Yes, do it now while you are still here. Don't put it off. Don't sit on that crowded fence of indecision where there is always room for another slacker. Make your commitment to go for it, and then do it.

I can't state it more simply. If you want to be great, then you must do great things.

Reaffirm to your own self that there is an art to living; engage with first-hand knowledge as your comrade; observe the Law of Non-Attachment, and, as a manifestation of your newfound power, live in the present moment of fulfillment, not in the future uncertainty of hope.

MY ARTIST'S STATEMENT

As you have discovered, I trust, this book advocates the positive use of language and the power of words that elevate each of us above the mainstream and mediocre.

I wrote my artist's statement long ago. Its essence has passed the test of space and time as there was hardly a need to tweak it over the years.

Here is my Art of the Covenant:

Art is either alive or it isn't. Art can't be conveniently pinned down or demystified precisely because it is metaphysical: if its creation is magic, then the art is magic.

My art comes directly from my soul. The soul is the magic window into the Cosmic Psyche—the source of all creation, material reality, the field of all possibilities … God.

My art making is based on the physical flow of spontaneous intuition, which involves a remarkable journey. Impulses of energy and information surge down my arm and, through improvisation, I compose visual jazz with line and color. My paintings and drawings are confirmation of a universal mythology of dreams within dreams—timeless images taken through the lens of my life experience. Unfettered by premeditated ideas, I create from a depth of intelligent feeling that establishes evidence of the Spirit in Art, and transcendence in the physical world.

Everyone sees and feels in a unique way; that is why no two people are precisely the same. If you see or feel something in a work of art … it is there! As one needs to learn how to read the written word, one must also have the desire to understand the language of art, and the alphabet of a particular artist.

I create confidently on a faith borne of knowing—not believing. I do so with an agreement to accept that intuitive guidance fearlessly. Create means original; creation isn't the reproduction or rearrangement of existential facts—that which already exists. When I finish a piece I—like the spectator—am seeing it for the first time.

Humility is the artist's ally.

FULL MOON RISING

In my bereavement over my beloved boys, I recalled the novel *The Sheltering Sky* by the writer and composer Paul Bowles, and a passage in particular that conjures up an indelible image of impermanence, of being, of memory, of soul, and of urgency that resonates as poetry as well as music to our ears.

Bowles wrote: "Because we don't know when we will die, we get to think of life as an inexhaustible well. Yet everything happens only a certain number of times, and a very small number really. How many more times will you remember a certain afternoon of your childhood, some afternoon that is so deeply part of your being that you can't even conceive of your life without it. Perhaps four or five times more, perhaps not even that. How many more times will you watch the full moon rise? Perhaps 20. And yet it all seems limitless."

It is true. We are all passing through from here to there. This book is about living in and engaging the present moment, the here and now, not the hereafter. The trek can be rocky but no match for empowered artists who have embraced their dharma.

We now come full circle.

Let us return to the brilliant analogy of 'leather shoes', which has variations in several different Indian scriptures. Sri Ramana Maharshi, who, as previously mentioned, to bring home his own teachings, drew the comparison in his own words: "Wanting to reform the world without discovering your true self is like trying to cover the whole world with leather to avoid the pain of walking on stones and thorns. It is simpler to wear shoes."

The Maharshi also considered humility to be the highest quality.

As you begin testing the counsel of this book, be mindful that memorizing doesn't allow insight or originality—and it is you, after all, who must walk the walk.

The next step is yours.

Understanding is the booby prize.

—SO SAID THE MASTER

BIBLIOGRAPHY

BIBLIOGRAPHY
Recommended Resources

Adrienne, Carol. *The Purpose of Your Life*. New York: William Morrow and Company, Inc., 1998.

———. *When Life Changes or You Wish it Would*. New York: HarperCollins Publishers, Inc., 2002.

Allen, James. *As You Think*. San Rafael: New World Library, 1998.

Ashton, Dore. *About Rothko*. New York: Da Capo Press, 1983.

———. *Picasso on Art*. New York: Da Capo Press, 1972.

Barron, Frank, Alfonso Montuori and Anthea Barron. *Creators on Creating*. New York: A Jeremy P. Tarcher/Putnam Book, 1997.

Bayles, David and Ted Orland. *Art & Fear*. Santa Cruz: Image Continuum Press, 2001.

Bhaktivedanta Swami Prabhupada, A. C. *Bhagavad-Gita As It Is*. Los Angeles: Bhaktivedanta Book Trust, 2001.

Blake, Michael. *Like a Running Dog: Volume 1 Los Angeles 1970-1972*. Tucson: Hrymfaxe, 2002.

Blesh, Rudi. *Modern Art USA: Men, Rebellion, Conquest – 1900-1956*. New York: Alfred A. Knopf, Inc., 1956.

Bodanis, David. *E=mc²: A Biography of the World's Most Famous Equation*. New York: Berkley Books, 2000.

Bolles, Richard. *What Color Is Your Parachute?* Berkeley: Ten Speed Press, 2005.

Bowles, Paul. *Bowles: Collected Stories & Later Writings*. New York: The Library of America, 2002.

Braden, Gregg. *The Divine Matrix*. Carlsbad: Hay House, Inc., 2007.

Breslin, James E. B. *Mark Rothko: A Biography*. Chicago: The University of Chicago Press, 1993.

Brookes, Mona. *Drawing with Children*. New York: A Jeremy P. Tarcher/Putnam Book, 1996.

Cameron, Julia. *The Artist's Way*. New York: A Jeremy P. Tarcher/Putnam Book, 1992.

Cassou, Michell, and Stewart Cubley. *Life, Paint and Passion*. New York: A Jeremy P. Tarcher/Putnam Book, 1995.

Cézanne to Picasso: Ambroise Vollard, Patron of the Avant-Garde. Exh. cat., New York: Metropolitan Museum of Art, 2006.

Chopra, Deepak. *Creating Affluence: Wealth Consciousness in the Field of All Possibilities*. San Rafael: New World Library, 1993.

———. *The Seven Spiritual Laws of Success*. San Rafael: New World Library, 1994.

Clark, Kenneth. *Leonardo da Vinci*. New York: Penguin Putnam, Inc., 1993.

Coelho, Paulo. *The Alchemist: A Fable about Following Your Dream*. San Francisco: HarperSanFrancisco, 1993.

Collodi, Carlo. *Pinocchio: Story of a Puppet*. Translated by Nancy Canepa. South Royalton, Vermont: Steerforth Press, 2002.

Cooper, Terry. *Accepting The Troll Underneath the Bridge*. Mahwah: Paulist Press, 1996.

Cytowic, Richard E. *The Man Who Tasted Shapes*. New York: A Jeremy P. Tarcher/Putnam Book, 1993.

De Botten, Alain. *Status Anxiety*. New York: HarperCollins Publishers, Inc., 2004.

Dissanayake, Ellen. *Art and Intimacy: How the Arts Began*. Seattle: University of Washington Press, 2000.

Dyer, Wayne W. *The Power of Intention*. Carlsbad: Hay House, Inc., 2004.

Edwards, Betty. *Drawing on the Right Side of the Brain*. New York: A Jeremy P. Tarcher/Putnam Book, 1989.

Flanner, Janet. *Men & Monuments. Profiles of Picasso, Matisse, Braque & Malraux*. New York: Da Capo Press, Inc., 1990.

Fitzgerald, Michael C. *Making Modernism*. New York: Farrar, Straus and Giroux, 1995.

Gawain, Shakti. *Living in the Light*. Novato: New World Library, 1998.

Gill, Brendan. *Late Bloomers*. New York: Artisan, 1996.

Glaser, Milton. *Art is Work*. Woodstock: The Overlook Press, 2000.

Goble, Frank G. *The Third Force: The Psychology of Abraham Maslow*. Berkeley: Maurice Bassett Publishing, 2004. www.reinventingyourself.com

Grant, Daniel. *How to Start and Succeed as an Artist*. New York: Allworth Press, 1997.

Greene, Brian. *The Elegant Universe*. New York: Vintage Books, 2000.

Haynes, Deborah J. *Art Lessons: Meditations on the Creative Life*. Boulder: Westview Press, 2003.

———. *The Vocation of the Artist*. Cambridge: Cambridge University Press, 1997.

Henderson, Bill, and Andre Bernard (editors). *Pushchart's Complete Rotten Reviews & Rejections*. New York: W.W. Norton & Co., 1998.

Hendrick, Becky. *Getting It: A Guide to Understanding and Appreciating Art*. Boston: Houghton Mifflin Co., 2001.

Henri, Robert. *The Art Spirit*. New York: HarperCollins Publishers, 1984.

Hesse, Hermann. *Siddhartha*. Berkeley: Maurice Bassett Publishing, 2004. www.reinventingyourself.com

Hofmann, Hans. *Search for the Real*. Cambridge: The M.I.T. Press, 1989.

Horn, Sam. *Concrete Confidence*. New York: St. Martin's Press, 1997.

———. *POP! Stand Out in any Crowd*. New York: Perigee, 2006.

———. *Tongue Fu!* New York: St. Martin's Griffin, 1996.

Jenkins, Elizabeth. *Initiation*. New York: G. P. Putnam's Sons, 1997.

Kaku, Michio. *Visions: How Science will Revolutionize the 21st Century*. New York: Anchor Books, 1997.

King, Ross. *Brunelleschi's Dome*. New York: Penguin Books, 2000.

Kandinsky, Wassily. *Concerning the Spiritual in Art*. Translated by M.T.H. Sadler. New York: Dover Publications, Inc., 1977.

Kandinsky, Wassily and Franz Marc, eds. *The Blaue Reiter*. Edited by Klaus Lankheit. New York: Da Capo Press, Inc., 1974.

Larkin, Geri. *Stumbling Toward Enlightenment*. Berkeley: Celestial Arts, 1997.

Lehrman, Lewis. *Becoming A Successful Artist*. Cincinnati: North Light Books, 1992.

Lloyd, Carol. *Creating a Life Worth Living*. New York: HarperCollins Publishers, Inc., 1997.

Mailer, Norman. *Portrait of Picasso as a Young Man*. New York: The Atlantic Monthly Press, 1995.

Maisel, Eric. *Affirmations for Artists*. New York: A Jeremy P. Tarcher/Putnam Book, 1996.

———. *Fearless Creating*. New York: A Jeremy P. Tarcher/Putnam Book, 1995.

———. *A Life in the Arts*. New York: A Jeremy P. Tarcher/Putnam Book, 1994.

———. *The Van Gogh Blues: The Creative Person's Path Through Depression* Emmaus, Pennsylvania: Rodale, Inc., 2002.

Mascetti, Manuela Dunn, ed. *The Little Book of Zen*. New York: Barnes & Noble Books, 2001.

Maslow, Abraham. *The Psychology of Science: A Reconnaissance*. Berkeley: Maurice Bassett Publishing, 2002. www.reinventingyourself.com

Matossian, Nouritza. *Black Angel: The Life of Arshile Gorky*. Woodstock: The Overlook Press, 2000.

McCully, Marilyn, ed. *A Picasso Anthology*. Princeton: Princeton University Press, 1997.

Michels, Caroll. *How to Survive and Prosper as an Artist*. New York: Henry Holt and Company, 2001.

Miller, Arthur I. *Einstein, Picasso: Space, Time, and the Beauty That Causes Havoc*. New York: Basic Books, 2001.

Miller, John. *Noa Noa: The Tahiti Journal of Paul Gauguin*. Translated by O.F. Theis. San Francisco: Chronicle Books, 1994.

Morrell, Margot and Stephanie Capparell. *Shackleton's Way*. New York: Penguin Putnam, Inc., 2001.

Munson, Lynne. *Exhibitionism: art in an era of intolerance*. Chicago: Ivan R. Dee, 2000.

O'Conner, Patricia T. *Woe is I: The Grammarphobe's Guide to Better English in Plain English*. New York: Riverhead Books, 2003.

O'Donohue, John. *Anam Cara: A Book of Celtic Wisdom*. New York: HarperCollins Publishers, Inc., 1997.

———. *Eternal Echoes: Exploring Our Yearning to Belong*. New York: HarperCollins Publishers, Inc., 1999.

Philips, Eric. *Ice Trek: The Bitter Journey to the South Pole*. New Zealand: HarperCollins Publishers Limited, 2000.

Pressfield, Steven. *The War of Art: Winning the Inner Creative Battle*. New York: Warner Books, 2002.

Richardson, John. *A Life of Picasso: The Early Years, Volume I: 1881-1906*. New York: Random House, 1991.

———. *A Life of Picasso: The Painter of Modern Life, Volume II: 1907-1917*. New York: Random House, 1996.

Robinson, Lynn A. *Compass of the Soul*. Kansas City: Andrews McMeel Publishing, 2003.

Rothenberg, Albert. *Creativity & Madness*. Baltimore: Johns Hopkins University Press, 1990.

Rubin, Ron and Stuart Avery Gold. *Dragon Spirit: How to Self-Market Your Dream*. New York: Newmarket Press, 2003.

Rubin, William. *Picasso and Braque: Pioneering Cubism*. Exh. cat., New York: Museum of Modern Art, 1986.

Rumi, Jelaluddin. *The Essential Rumi*. Translated by Coleman Barks. San Francisco: HarperSanFrancisco, 1995.

———. *Say I Am You*. Translated by John Moyne and Coleman Barks. Athens: Maypop, 1994.

Ruskin, John. *Lectures on Art*. New York: Allworth Press, 1996.

Savage, Elayne. *Don't Take it Personally*. Oakland: New Harbinger Publications, 1997.

Schulz, Mona Lisa. *Awakening Intuition*. New York: Harmony Books, 1998.

Shlain, Leonard. *The Alphabet Versus the Goddess*. New York: Penguin Putnam, Inc., 1998.

———. *Art & Physics*. New York: HarperCollins Publishers, Inc., 1991.

Sollins, Susan. *Art: 21. Art in the Twenty-First Century* (Volume 2). New York: Harry N. Abrams, Inc., 2003.

Storr, Robert. *Art: 21. Art in the Twenty-First Century* (Volume 1). New York: Harry N. Abrams, Inc., 2001.

Wallis, Brian, ed. *Art After Modernism: Rethinking Representation*. Boston: David R. Godine, Inc., 1984.

Welch, Evelyn. *Art and Society in Italy 1350-1500*. New York: Oxford University Press, 1997.

Wilson, Colin. *New Pathways in Psychology: Maslow and the Post-Freudian Revolution*. Berkeley: Maurice Bassett Publishing, 2001. www.reinventingyourself.com

Wood, Beatrice. *I Shock Myself*. San Francisco: Chronicle Books, 1988

Wunderlich, Richard and Thomas J. Morrissey. *Pinocchio Goes Postmodern: Perils of a Puppet in the United States*. New York: Routledge, 2002.

Yogananda, Paramahansa. *The Law of Success*. Los Angeles: Self-Realization Fellowship, 1990.

DVD'S AND CD-ROM'S

Art: 21. Art in the Twenty-First Century (Season One). Executive Prod. Susan Sollins. Series Prod. Eve Moros Ortega. DVD. PBS, 2001.

Art: 21. Art in the Twenty-First Century (Season Two). Executive Prod. Susan Sollins. Series Prod. Eve Moros Ortega. DVD. PBS, 2001.

The Elegant Universe. DVD. WGBH Boston Video, 2003.

The Medici: Godfathers of the Renaissance. DVD. Warner Home Video, Inc., 2003.

The Mystery of Picasso. Dir. Henri-Georges Clouzot. DVD. Image Entertainment, 2003.

Painters Painting. Dir. Emile de Antonio. CD-ROM. Voyager, 1998

Picasso: Magic – Sex – Death. DVD. BFS Entertainment & Multimedia Limited, 2003.

Picasso: The Man and His Work, Part 1 (1881-1937). Dir. Edward Quinn. DVD. View Video, Inc., 2001.

Picasso: The Man and His Work, Part 2 (1938-1973). Dir. Edward Quinn. DVD. View Video, Inc., 2002.

Siddhartha. Writ., dir., and prod. by Conrad Rooks. DVD. Image Entertainment, 2002.

Van Gogh Starry Night. Writ. Albert Boime. CD-ROM. Voyager, 1995.

www.edensart.com
email: artist@edensart.com

Okyo

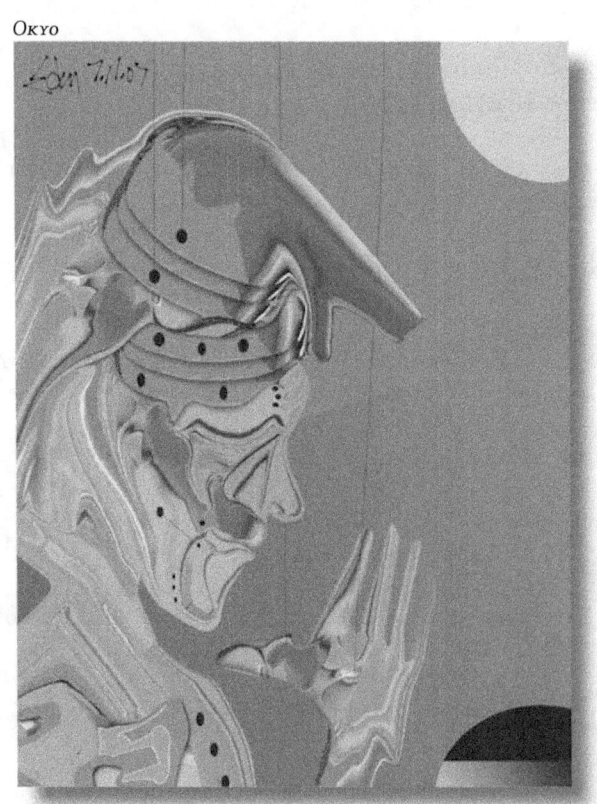

website design: Adobe Dreamweaver
blog: ExpressionEngine
main site & galleries: Project Seven Development

COLOPHON

The production of this book was made possible with the following:

initial research / chapter organization: NoteTaker from AquaMinds, Inc.

spelling, dictionary, and grammar: Grammarian Pro X from Linguisoft, Inc.

word-processing: Word from the Microsoft Corporation.

page layout and design: Adobe InDesign CS3; a significant amount of edit work and writing was done within InDesign.

main text font: Casion Pro (an Adobe OpenType face), regular, 10.5 pt.

index: Sonar Bookends Index Pro (InDesign plug-in) from Virginia Systems, Inc.

barcode / typography adjustments: BarcodeMaker and TypeFitter (InDesign plug-ins) from Teacup Software.

computer: Apple Dual 2.3 GHz PowerPC G5 (4.5 GB memory) running on OS X 10.4.10. **graphics**: Adobe InDesign, Photoshop, and Illustrator; **graphics tablet**: Wacom Intuos³; **paintings**: with Painter IX natural media tools from the Corel Corporation.

INDEX

A
A-list, 126-127
A-train, 428
Abbot, Buddhist, 263
Aberrations—tragedies of human ignorance, 114
Abilities, Magical, 367
Ability,
    Conceptual, 390
    Unique, 367
Aboriginal, 361
About—that divine fire, 9
Abrams, Alice, 393
Absinth, 190
Abstraction and Empathy, 330
Abstraction, Pure, 190
Abstractions,
    Systems of, 296
    Whole world of, 349
Abuse, Substance, 147
Abuser,
    Cliché, 213
    of 'obvious', 49, 269
Abuses, 89, 114
Academia, Latin of, 213
Académie des Beaux-Arts, 373-374, 378
Academies, Italian, 373
Accelerators, Particle, 76, 182
Acceptance,
    Audience, 160
    Critical, 343
    Double-edged sword of, 158
    External circumstances of, 429
    Group, 363
    Moment of, 170
    Public, 162
    Self-referential, 37
    Sporadic, 67
Accident, Serious car, 217
Accolades, 125, 317
Accomplishment,
    Metaphysical, 169
    Predefined, 411
    Sense of intermittent, 315
    Unique, 361
Accomplishments, Seeming, 93
Accordion, Cheap, 19

Acculturated, 407
Acculturation, 336
Achievement,
    Admirable, 280
    Individual, 115
    Realm of, 429
    Reward system of, 315
    Supreme, 162
Achievements, Superior, 408
Achievers, Lineage of bold, 328
Acquisition, Material, 284
Acquit, 13
Acrobats (See also Picasso's Blue Period), 253
Act,
    Heroism, 144
    Individual, 346
    Political, 370
    Solo, 377
Action,
    Awareness of right, 106
    Consequence of, 109
    Importance of right, 291
    Independent, 131
    Intelligent, 218
    Performing, 285, 406
    Rejection of a lesser, 38
    Restraint not mindless, 67
    Result of, 183, 429
    Right, 14, 38, 65, 106, 114, 233, 291, 322
    Sphere of, 348
    State of, 13
    Taking, 85
Actions, Dynamic, 415
Activities, Right, 321
Activity,
    Competitive, 169
    Creative, 22
    Thinking, 390
Actor,
    A-list, 127
    Torment of the once-famous, 156
Actors, Bankable A-list, 126
Acts, Unscrupulous, 259
Acumen, Business, 379
Adams,
    Ansel, 295, 366
    John Quincy, 309

Adaptation,
    Biological, 186
    Evolutionary, 377
Adept, Hindu, 285
Adherence,
    Dogmatic, 368
    Slavish, 382
Adler, Felix, 238
Adoration, Culture, 402
Adrienne, Carol, 305
Advancement, Scientific, 370
Advantage,
    Supreme, 62
    Unobstructed, 196
Adventure, Mind-expanding, 144
Adversary, 38-39, 393, 397
Adversity,
    Despite, 84
    Face of, 19
    Overcoming, 59, 170
    Various degrees of, 39
Advice,
    Savvy, 205
    Standing, 352
    Words of, 30
Aeronautics, 283
Aesthetic, 17, 113, 155, 161, 173, 180, 270, 314, 324, 326, 331, 378, 401, 421
Aesthetics, Roman, 373
Affair,
    Internal, 38, 356
    Quiet, 281
    Vollard, 255
Affairs, Political, 369
Affectation, 228
Affiliative, 378
Affinity, Strong, 112
Affliction, Product of, 381
Affluence, Creating, 102, 118, 410
African, 189
Age,
    Greeks of the Golden, 364
    Information, 235, 378
    Inherent grassroots movement of the New, 326
    Old, 178, 321
    Social commentator of the Victorian, 102
    Stone, 310

Victorian, 102
Catholic Church, 366
Age-old, 268, 313, 395, 408
Agencies, Art-funding, 327
Agenda, Misleading, 287
Agendas,
    Human, 106
    Personal, 188
    Secular, 197
Ages,
    Dark, 320, 364, 366
    Late Middle, 373
    Middle, 190, 363-367, 373
    Stagnation of the Dark, 366
    Wisdom of the, 286
Agreement, Universal, 23
Aikido, 77, 166
Air, Realm of, 101
Airplane, 81
Airwaves, Invisible, 261
Aladdin, Fable of, 236
Albert Einstein's universe, 177
Albert Hofmann Foundation, 146
Alchemist, Self-described, 318
Alchemy, 87
Alertness, Mental, 44
Alexander the Great, 156, 160, 206
Alien, 6, 132-133, 173, 175, 200
Alienation,
    Feeling of, 220
    Similar themes of, 322
Alighieri, Dante (See also *The Divine Comedy*), 213
All,
    Arbiter of, 101, 103
    Eternal umbrella of, 29
    The truth of, 187
'All natural', 105
Allah, 183
Allegiance, Unwavering, 393
Alleviating, 121
Alphabet,
    New, 268, 352
    Unique and spontaneous, 297
The Alphabet Versus the Goddess, 268
Amadeus, 93, 95, 98
Amateurish, 176
Ambiguity, Assuring, 391
Amendment, First, 396
America,
    Popular culture of, 346
    South, 325
American,
    Native, 328, 361
    Unsuccessful, 156
Amplitude, Moral, 103
Analysis,
    Dream, 323
    Jungian, 318
    Meaningful, 172
    Quantitative, 118
Anam Cara, 131-132, 286, 355
Anarchy, Linguistic, 225
Anka, Paul, 155
Ancient Egyptian hieroglyphs, 297

Andalusian, 248
Andean, 68
Andy's atelier, 164
Angel, 213, 249, 411
Angeles, Los, 98, 202, 220, 342, 375, 389, 424
Angst,
    Inner demons of, 40
    of a 'successful' artist, 129
Anomaly, 313
Anonymity, 39
Anonymous, 96, 169-170, 173, 361
Antagonist,
    Leading, 90
    Worthy, 39
Antarctic, 211
Anti-establishment, 381
Anti-gravity, 416
Antiquity,
    Art of, 176
    Civilizations of, 406
Anxiety-ridden, 26, 158
Anything, Proof of, 184
Apathy, Allegorical reflection of, 396
Apollo, 142
Appreciation,
    Art, 253, 328, 341, 350, 375, 398
    Level of, 15
Appreciator, Art, 97, 118, 360
Apprentice, Young, 249, 370
Approach,
    Astute, 126
    Holistic, 324
    Humanistic, 316
    Minimalist, 344
    Smart, 74
    Tesla-Westinghouse alternating-current, 125
Approval,
    Audience, 346
    Creation regardless of, 158
    Public, 343
    Such, 5
'Approved' artist, 351
Approximation, Life of, 106
Aptitude, Inherent, 185
Archaeological, 268
Archer, Zen, 403
Archery, Zen, 115
Archetypes,
    Jungian, 27
    Religious, 373
Architects, 249, 367
Archives, Edward Quinn, 251
Arena, Public, 75
Arguments, Intellectual, 326
Aristotle, 193, 335, 349
Arjuna,
    Disciple, 285
    Prince, 406
Armstrong, Neil, 329
Arnold's phrase, 376
Aromatherapy, 325
Arrangement, Tacit, 382
Arroway, Elly, 175

Art,
    Abstract, 16, 29, 191, 263, 329, 352
    Acceptance of, 254
    Accepted norms of, 381
    Act of creating, 260
    Alphabet, 295
    American Pop, 345
    Ancient, 39, 297, 329
    Appreciation of, 328
    Approach, 195, 363
    Artists creating personal, 169
    Aura of, 170
    Author of, 154, 325, 363, 377
    Birth of, 24-25
    Children of, 427, 429
    Co-opt pure, 183
    Commercial, 23, 275, 295, 345
    Conceptual, 56, 133, 274, 330, 366
    Confines of three dimensional, 189
    Contemporary visual, 330
    Controversial postmodern, 352
    Create great, 163, 226, 423
    Creating universal, 228
    Creation of, 106, 331, 406
    Crucible of, 153, 165
    Definition of, 361, 373
    Demystify, 227
    Development of
        modern, 256, 373
        Western, 373
    Domain of, 182
    Dreams of an, 95
    Enemy of, 56, 95
    European, 29, 375
    Evolution of Western, 352
    Evolving language of, 310
    Exhibition titled *The Business of*, 375
    Face of, 396
    Fine, 26, 34, 73, 157, 160, 163, 180, 219, 295, 303, 342-343, 352, 374, 380-381
    Function of, 187, 369
    Gift of great, 93
    History of, 109, 157, 249, 253, 371, 377, 380
    Identity of, 343
    Importance of, 254
    Inherent
        quality of, 161
        value of the, 350
    Innate gift of, 361
    Inspired, 305
    Internalized, 329
    Japanese, 28
    Language of, 310, 352, 379, 434
    Legitimacy of non-utilitarian, 348
    Life of, 170
    Light of, 429
    Love all forms of, 347
    Loving, 159, 347
    Magic, 24, 164, 194, 275, 351, 382, 434
    Magnificent, 73
    Mainstream of so-called high, 347
    Make great, 17
    Marketing of modern, 253
    Mass, 342

Mavens of, 21
Meaning of, 320, 331
Mechanics of, 227
Medieval, 364, 366
Mediocre, 26, 347
Metropolitan Museum of, 56, 253
Modern, 29, 159, 176, 179-180, 189-190, 197, 205, 253, 256, 352, 359, 369, 373, 375
Nature of universal, 182
Necessity of, 194
Nonobjective, 191, 227, 330
Oracle of, 255
Original work of, 169, 337, 379
Outsider, 361, 381
Path of, 175
Pattern of, 374
Perception of Western, 369
Personal, 84, 169, 219, 295, 343, 352, 362, 374, 379-381
Piece of, 134, 146, 274, 351, 366, 389, 412
Pleasure of, 375
Point of, 195, 323
Politicize, 197
Politics of, 140
Pop, 164, 189, 326, 345, 352, 420
Popular, 95
Power of, 275-276
Precursors of, 238
Prehistoric man made, 362
Priceless, 283
Primitive, 190
Private, 343, 375
Process of creating, 139
Producing commercial, 295
Promotion of modern, 189
Pure, 117, 170-171, 183, 361
Purpose of, 348
Quality of the, 274
Religious, 190, 197, 248
Renaissance, 190, 365, 371
Renunciation of, 247
Restore, 362
Restrictive definition of, 373
Revolutionary, 180
Royal Academy of, 133
Seed of, 5
Self-taught, 26, 127, 381-382
Selling non-commissioned, 371
Shock, 327, 332, 347
Showcasing, 373
Soul of, 186, 323
Source of
    all great, 102, 208, 286
    great, 263, 411
Spirit of the, 362
Spontaneous creation of, 406
Study of Renaissance, 365
Success of Pop, 164
Such collections of, 161-162
Teaching of, 326
The
    Business of, 68, 158, 375, 378
    Museum of Modern, 190

War of, 335, 397
Timeless, 56, 63, 95
Traditional religious, 248
Traditional-political, 327
Trafficking of, 361, 377
Transcendental nature of living, 194
True, 10, 97-98, 380
Tyranny of the, 23
Unique flowering of, 362
Universal, 182, 228, 323
Valuations of, 375
Value of the, 163, 350-351
Wallpaper, 206
Wellspring of, 83, 318, 357
Western, 326, 352, 362, 369, 373, 382
Works of, 98, 105, 220, 337, 371, 373, 376, 420
Art & Fear, 342
Art-buying, 171, 359
Art Brut (See also Jean Dubuffet), 381
The Art Market in Italy, 371
Art-savvy, 342
Arte Della Seta (See also Guild of silk Weavers), 367
Artifact, Physical, 6
Artifice, Dramatic, 86
Artis, Ars Gratia, 98
Artisan, Role of, 366
Artist,
    Absentee, 164
    Ailing, 351
    Alphabet of
        a particular, 434
        the, 297
    Archetypal, 27
    Attributes of an, 315
    Authentic, 9, 84, 326
    Avant-garde, 254
    Aware, 82, 157, 284, 290
    Celebrated, 62
    Dedicated, 28, 212
    Deranged, 28
    Destitute, 27
    Different appreciation of the, 370
    Empowered, 13, 75, 207, 289, 430
    Evolving vocation of the, 361
    Gestalt of the true, 56
    Hallmark of an empowered, 75
    Healthy, 226, 290
    Iconic martial, 393
    Iconoclastic vision of the new, 330-331
    Image of the
        modern, 372
        tortured, 411
    Individual, 180, 309, 363, 366-367, 370
    Innovative martial artist, 397
    Insecure, 141
    Language of the, 298
    Liberated, 64
    Life of every true, 40
    Lone, 363
    Mad, 28
    Mainstream, 351
    Model, 37, 427
    New poster child, 37

    Notion of the ambiguous, 23
    Part-time, 85
    Prospective, 373
    Psyche of every, 93
    Role of, 365
    Sane self-taught, 381
    Sanguine, 194
    Savvy, 141, 165
    Scrutiny of a gifted young, 369
    Self-inspired art of the, 227
    Self-motivated, 228
    Self-taught, 26, 381
    Smart, 292
    Social ranking of the, 366
    Spiritual makeup of an, 14
    Stance every, 18
    Status of the, 373
    Stereotype of the, 393
    Stone Age, 310
    Subjective experience of the, 374
    Superb, 273
    The Eighteen Be-Attitudes of the model, 427
    Tragedy of the, 411
    Troubled, 314
    Universal, 198
    Unknown, 141, 159, 211, 243
    Unprepared citizen, 409
    Unwary, 165
    Victim, 39, 62
    Visual, 341
    Wandering, 342
    Wanted The true, 18
    Well-known, 157
    What true, 159
    World famous, 251, 292
    Young apprentice, 370
    ally, 27, 74, 434
    angst, 207
    bad karma, 290
    cachet, 170
    demonstrated approval rating, 351
    code, 341
    lack of purpose, 21
    language, 351
    life, 38, 158, 165
    primary mission, 26
    spiritual condition, 158
    studios, 330
    vocation, 154
Artist-shaman, 245, 329, 363
Artist-wife, 314
Artists,
    Activities of, 369
    Avant-garde, 181, 251
    Bane most, 13
    Breakthrough, 206
    Buddhist, 75, 361
    Cave, 361
    Celebrated, 22
    Courageous, 382
    Even-tempered, 416
    Extraordinary, 172
    Generous, 416
    Groundbreaking, 327

Independent, 344, 420
Individual, 161, 363-364
Insecure, 25
Limited number of, 141
Living, 141, 163, 281, 352, 382
Mangled bodies of wannabe, 144
Maverick, 327
Mediocre, 172
Moody, 416
Munich, 171
Perplexed, 194
Reclusive, 416
Renaissance, 380
Renowned late twentieth-century, 366
Shock, 327
Society of Independent, 344
Undoing of many would-be, 357
Unwary, 196
Visual, 395
Vocation of, 370
Volunteer, 147
Winning, 90
Women, 365
Work of living, 141, 352
Arts,
    Applied, 24, 26, 345
    Performing, 169
    Professor of Fine, 252
    Proliferation of, 372
    Variety of, 373
    Visual, 163, 311, 364, 367
Artwork,
    Internal logic of the, 298
    Original, 274
    Self-referential, 139
    Specific, 366
    True, 274
Aryan, 408
Ashley-Pitt, Alan, 341
Ashton, Dore, 395
Asian, Distinct, 28
Asimov, Isaac, 199
Asleep, Being, 134
Assignment, Plum, 137
Association, Free, 317
Astronauts, 177
Astronomers, NASA, 191
Asylums, Lunatic, 318
Atheist, 247
Atlantis, 325
Attachment,
    Cost of, 411
    Pitfalls of, 238
    Release of, 322
    Rigid, 37
Attainment, Spiritual, 74
Attention,
    Media, 145, 326
    Personal, 360
Attitude,
    Healthy, 27, 155
    Positive can-do mental, 415
    Proper, 81
Attraction, Law of, 68, 77
Attribute, Special, 232

Auction of La Peau del'Ours, 252, 254
Audience, Widest possible, 98
Auditioning, Actor, 172
Austria, Emperor of, 96
Auteur, 160, 322
Authentication, Right of, 164
Authenticity, Trials of, 144
Author of Art, 154, 325, 363, 377
Authority,
    Accepting, 412
    Soul, 41
    indecision, 91
Automatism, Surrealist, 328
Avant-garde,
    Irrepressible, 370
    Patron of the, 253
Avignon, 190, 250, 329
Awareness,
    Art of, 101
    Elevated, 274
    Expanding, 361
    Feeling of pure, 103
    First rule of, 185
    Gift of, 14
    Greater, 416
    Heightened, 308
    Inner strength of, 200
    Intuitive, 82, 227, 259
    Lack of, 62
    Level of, 170, 236, 306-307, 342
    Lucid mirror of, 129
    Moment of, 13
    Ocean of, 82
    Power of pure, 14
    Profound comprehension of, 187
    Public, 67
    Pure, 14, 82, 101-103, 213
    Sense of, 37
    Soul, 19, 134
    Sphere of, 108
    State of, 25, 132, 267
    Third rule of, 270
    Time-bound, 102
    Timeless, 102, 188
    Toward, 82-83, 112, 267
Awe, Mystical moments of, 331

B

Babel, Tower of, 117, 194, 228
Babylon, 16, 228
Back,
    Look, 74, 86, 106, 222, 361, 402
    The Empire Strikes, 346
    Years, 30, 73, 220, 389
Backers, Portraits of the three, 252
Backscratchers, 30
Backtrack, 164
Bacon, Francis, 346
Badlands, 24
Balance,
    Sense of, 264
    Vibrational, 335
Baldwin, James A., 357
Ballot, Karmic, 106

Balthus, 381
Banausos, 305
Bandage, Temporary, 81
Bane, 13, 68, 218
Bang, Big, 184
Bank, Left, 51
Barcelona's Colombofila Society, 248
Barista, 291
Barometer, Infallible, 202
Barovier, Angelo, 365
Barricades, Police, 403
Barron, Steve, 237
Basquiat, Jean-Michel, 374
Bassett, Maurice, 192
Bateau-Lavoir, Le (See also Picasso), 250
Baudelaire, Charles, 69, 119
Bayles, David (See also *Art & Fear*), 342
Be-Attitude, Specific, 430
Be-Attitudes, Attributes of the, 267
Beach, North, 51
Beams, Laser, 125
Beard, James, 4
Bearer, Standard, 49-50
Beast, Belly of the, 171, 321, 395
Beattie, Melodie, 268
Beauty,
    Evidence of transcendent, 179
    Intrinsic, 285
    State of, 360
    Timeless, 10-11
    Truth, 10
    Universal, 87
Beckett, Samuel, 34
Beckmann, 169
Beckons,
    Destiny, 281
    Regret, 166
Bed,
    Marital, 370
    Strange, 217
Beecher, Henry Ward, 134, 263
Beer, Two cans of, 345
Began, Arts, 325, 377
Behavior,
    Admirable, 126
    Essential, 317
    Human, 281, 316-320, 324-325, 360
    Integral source of human, 316
    Learned, 323
    Mindless, 270
    Passive aggressive, 159
    Quantifiable, 319
    Rat, 316
    Self-destructive, 411
    Shortsighted, 125
    Studying, 325
    Subsequent, 118, 317
    Unacceptable, 63, 123
Beholder, Eye of the, 184
Being,
    Art of, 225
    Awareness of, 295
    Corporeal, 429
    Despite, 191, 206, 409
    Keys of, 350

Living, 17
Practice of, 132
Pure, 118, 350
Self-realized human, 201, 407
Serendipity of, 211
Ultimate lightness of, 182
Veil, 330
Beings, Actions of human, 180
Belief,
Out of, 38
Popular, 124
Beliefs,
Catchall of, 325
Phantom world of dogmatic, 117
Valued cultural, 377
Bell, Alexander Graham, 283
Bellini, 371
Ben Gurion, David, 298
Benares, Deer Park near (See also Gautama Buddha), 74
Benigni, Roberto, 237
Bennett, J.G., 404-405, 410
Bergman, Ingmar, 322
Bergson, Henri, 248
Berlin, Irving, 336
Bernard, Emile, 29
Bettelheim, Bruno, 237
Bhagavad-gita, 285, 327, 406
Bias,
Age-old, 268
Complaints of, 374
Bidder, Ego of the, 351
Bierce, Ambrose, 24-25, 121, 139, 165
Billions, Power of, 199
Bin, Irrelevant, 320
Biorhythm, 188
Biotechnology, Miracles of, 186
Birth,
Cycle of, 409
Inevitable, 330
Moment of, 284, 377
of Venus (See also Botticelli), 370
Birthright, True, 281
Blade Runner, 346
Blake, Michael, 67
Blasco, José Ruiz y, 248
Blavatsky, H.P., 344, 406
Blesh, Rudi, 205
Bliss,
Moments of, 331
Pure, 118
State of, 102
Block,
Grammar, 217
Public, 35, 69
Blocks,
Creative, 23
Mental, 391
Bloodied block of public opinion, 35
Blue Fairy (See also *Pinocchio*), 238
Blue Rider, 352
Blueprint, Transcendental genetic, 87
Bob, Uncle, 16
Bodhidharma, 116
Bodies,

Celestial, 15
Electrodynamics of Moving (See also Einstein), 181
Body, Strong, 154
Bodybuilder, Dedicated, 267
Bohemian, 51
Boime, Albert, 28
Bolles, Richard, 68
Bond, Common, 245, 297
Bondage, Primary cause of self, 410
Bonfire of the vanities, 185
Bonnard, 169
Bonze, 28
Book,
Feel-good, 22
How-to-feel-good, 16
Self-help, 30
Books,
Art history, 189, 274
Law, 233
Legislative, 401-402
Reading hundreds of, 118
Boost, Adrenalin, 129
Borders, Artificial, 322
Borg, Professor Isak, 322
Botticelli, 24, 366, 370
Boulevard,
Santa Monica, 221, 302
Sunset, 303
Boundaries, Self-imposed, 17
Bourgeoisie, 254, 306
Bow, Cosmic, 180
Bowles, Paul (See also *The Sheltering Sky*), 434
Box,
Confines of the, 195
Out of the, 117
Boxes, Brillo, 345
Boy with Pipe (See also Whitney), 351
Boy,
Real, 231, 234-235, 237-238
Role of a real, 237
Young, 360
Boulle, Pierre, 257
Bradbury, Ray, 91
Braden, Gregg, 263
Brahman, 118-119, 186-187, 280, 338, 391
Brain,
Biomechanics of the, 259
Function of the, 259
Human, 268
Language center of the, 341
Left, 260, 322-323, 405
Perceptual R-mode of the, 404
Right non-analytic hemisphere of the, 405
Verbal part of the, 405
Braque,
Georges, 189
Cubism, 190
Brazilian, 407
Bread, Daily, 222, 226, 359
Breakthrough, 189, 328
Bride, Quaker (See also *High Noon*), 394
Bridge, The Golden Gate, 50

Bright, John, 376
Brilliance,
Face of, 94
Morsels of, 127
Real, 252
Source of all, 231
True, 96
Brilliant, 27, 52, 90, 95-96, 109, 113, 117, 125, 179, 181, 189, 191, 193, 221, 252, 269, 275, 316, 344, 346, 356, 435
Britain, 376
Britannica, Encyclopædia, 416
British, 46, 51, 102, 297, 398, 404
Brother's keeper, 26
Brothers, Wright, 283, 329
Browning, Robert, 185
Brunelleschi,
Filippo, 368
Dome, 369
The Radical Egg, 57
Bruno, Dominican Friar Giordano, 45
Bubbles, Laws of, 127
Buck, Pearl S., 247
Bucks, Lure of, 161
Buddha,
Eternal, 28
Gautama, 74
Insights of the, 115
Nature of, 117, 170
Story of, 220
Universal insights of, 325
farewell admonition, 170
first realization, 26
Buddha-nature,
Innermost mind of, 116
One, 115
Buddhism,
Founder of, 408
Integral aspect of Zen, 185
Introspective simplicity of Zen, 112
Intuitive serenity of Zen, 29
Pillar of, 134
Teachings of Zen, 101
Zen, 27, 115-116, 323-324
Buddhist, Classic, 87
Buddhists, Zen, 289
Buehler, Huber Gray, 25
Bug, Lightning, 389
Bukowski, Charles, 51
Bull's
Head sculpture, 420
eye of objectivity, 246
Bullet, Karmic, 77-78
Bums, Dharma, 51
Burke, Edmund, 319
Burroughs, William, 51
Buscaglia, Leo, 61
Business,
Art, 23, 68, 157-158, 191, 375, 378
Commodities, 163
Exhibition, 161
Mainstream gallery, 302-303
Private, 139
Butler,
Henry, 151

Jerry, 129
Butter, Warm, 360
Button, Snooze, 212, 242, 283-284, 387
Buyers, Potential, 163

C

Cabal, Informal, 157
Cachet,
    Art movement, 326
    Perceived, 164
    of the artist's image, 251
Caesar, Julius, 236, 430
Café, 39, 140-141
Calculations, Step-by-step, 329
Calder, Alexendar, 367
Caliber, 126, 366
California, Southern, 145
Call, Wake-up, 212, 242, 284, 387
Calligraphy, Zen, 116
Calling,
    Divine, 281, 380
    Evolutionary, 114
    Higher, 61
    Muses, 306
    Nobler, 367
    Opportunity, 3
Calm, Inner, 24
Calories, Empty, 22, 164
Caltech, 416
Camera, Movie, 341
Cameron, Julia, 33
Campbell, Joseph, 412
Campbell's soup cans, 345
Camus, Albert, 297
Can, Metaphysical, 183, 200
Cancer, Breast, 248
Candle, Wax, 369-370
Canepa, Dr. Nancy, 236-237
Canon, Integral part of the Picasso, 248
Canvas, Infinite, 192
Canyon,
    Laurel, 202, 402
    Santa Monica, 145
Cappuccino, 5, 139-140, 291
Car, Tragedy of a fatal, 207
Caracas, 379
Carlyle, Thomas, 347, 362
Carnegie, Dale, 213, 368
Carnegie Hall, 22
Carpet, Magic, 85
Cartapesta, 365
Casagemas, 249
Cash, Ordinary, 132
Cassandra, 142
Caste,
    Higher, 409
    Upper, 408
    Warrior, 279
Caste-centered, 408
Castelli, Leo, 345
Castes,
    Higher, 408
    Lower, 408
    Mixing of, 408

People of all, 279
Cat, Sacred, 193
Catalan, 252, 254
Catalogue,
    Picasso exhibition, 190, 253
    The Museum of Modern Art exhibition, 190
    Vollard exhibition, 254
Catastrophe, Aesthetic, 326
Catholic, 247, 366
Cato, 213-214
Cats, The Four, 251
Cauldron, 318
Cause,
    Just, 269
    Root, 321, 325, 327
    Spontaneous, 286
Causes, Buddhist philosophy teaches, 361-362
Cavalry, Cosmic, 356
Cell, Photoelectric, 193
Celluloid, Red, 395
Celtic, 131-132, 286, 355
Censorship, Political, 281
Century,
    Mid-fifteenth, 372
    Mid-fourteenth, 365
    Twentieth, 190, 248, 375
Cézanne, Paul, 159, 169, 189-190, 205, 253, 256, 373-374, 382
CGI, 133
Chado ((See also Zen Buddhism)), 115
Chain, Top of the food, 197
Chair,
    Cosmic booster, 200
    Painting of a, 116
Chakra, Heart, 323
Chalice, Silver, 365
Challenge,
    Gauntlet, 49
    Mental, 44
    Tick word, 43
Challenges,
    Manageable, 129
    Pure tenet of the faith, 112
    Chaotic, 377
Chamber, Secret, 157
Champollion,
    Jean Francois, 297
    Rue, 254
Chance, Probability of, 211
Channel, Open, 46, 259, 261-262, 306
Character,
    Absence of, 75
    Attributes of, 22
    Essential, 117
    Function of, 55
    Integrated artist of, 352
    Main, 4, 89-90, 242, 322
    Person of, 81
    Pillars of, 75
    Qualities of, 24
    Sole barometer of, 313
    Strength of, 18, 35, 64, 75, 201, 398, 412, 427

    Test of, 309, 375
    Tests of, 25, 75, 347, 429
Characters,
    Archetypal, 346
    Various unstable, 222
Charisma,
    Dint of, 249
    Personal, 379
Chastity, Vow of, 94-95
Chekhov, Anton, 250
Chesterton, G.K., 179
Chicago, University of, 236
Child, Julia, 157
Children, neurons of little, 233
China, 116
Chinatown, 51
Chinese, 241
Choice,
    Conscious word, 49
    Pivotal, 235, 242
    Poor, 411
    Right word, 234-235, 249
Choices,
    Hard, 87
    Make, 34
    Poor, 154
Chopra, Dr. Deepak, 9, 22, 61, 102, 118, 121, 307, 309, 327, 405, 410
Chris Ofili's *Holy Virgin Mary*, 327
Christ, Battle of *Piss*, 326
Christendom, Cosmology of, 45
Christian, 297
Christianity, 27, 112, 134, 213, 364
Christie's auction, 351
Church,
    Aims of the, 370
    Catholic, 366
    Specific patronage of the, 371
    Strict auspices of the, 364
    power, 365
Churchill, Winston, 44, 211, 236
Cicero, 255
Circuit,
    Biological, 337
    Electrical, 337
Circumstances,
    Dire, 56, 129
    Unconventional, 171
Citizen, Senior, 175
Citizen-artist, 237
Citizens, Left-leaning, 396
Citizenship, Active, 234
Civilization,
    Philosophy of, 320
    Planetary, 199, 390
    Productive planetary, 390
    Science fiction of a Type III, 199
    Superior alien, 175
    Technical, 200
    Type A, 199-200
Civilizations, Advanced, 200
Clarity,
    Foundation of, 22
    Harbinger of, 30
    Impressive, 405

Moment of, 286
Realm of, 101
Sense of mental, 282
Statement of, 348
Toward, 309
Unflinching, 29
Clark, Kenneth (See also Leonardo da Vinci), 249
Class, Middle, 220, 371, 407
Classes,
    Four rigid social, 279
    Middle, 378
Classical forms of the past—the status quo, 176
Clergy, Cynicism of the, 366
Clerk, Patent (See also Einstein), 177, 180, 337
Cliché,
    Occasional, 44
    Single, 43
Clichéd, 351
Clichés, Visual, 296
Climate, Right, 220
Clio, 305
Clock,
    Atomic, 178
    Celestial, 188
    Doomsday, 197-198
    Stationary, 178
Cloth, Out of whole, 189, 248
Clouzot, Henri-Georges, 250, 275
Co-op, Innovative, 164
Coconspirator, 76, 284, 331, 402
Codependency, 63
Codependent, 21, 74, 103, 178, 331
Cohn, Harry, 84, 395
Coincidences, Meaningful, 211, 318
Coliseum, Roman, 206
Columbia Pictures, 84, 395
Coll, Pere, 252
Collar, Blue, 305
Collections, Museum, 364
Collector, Art, 164, 202, 206, 331, 402-403
Collectors,
    Art, 67, 140-141, 352
    Loyal, 212
    Private, 373
    Right, 205
    Taste of, 376
    Wealthy, 163
College,
    Trinity, 252
    Union, 371
Collins, J. Lawton, 109
Collodi, Carlo (See also *Pinocchio*), 232, 238
Combat, Art by, 326
Commandments, Ten, 268
Commendation, Critical, 252
Commentary, Social, 234
Commerce, Art, 371
Commitment,
    Lifetime, 4
    Steadfast, 356
    Unwavering, 67, 155, 186
Committees, Such selection, 161

Commodities, Rarest of temporal, 113
'Common' wisdom, 86, 98, 109, 316, 352
Communication,
    Direct, 220
    Transcendent, 186
Communion, Power of, 115
Communists, 395-396
Communities, Tribal, 364
Community, Perception of, 315
Comparison,
    Anguish of, 95
    Matter of distinction not, 347
    Mediocre by, 93
Comparisons, Rue of, 397
Compass,
    Divine, 403
    Moral, 9, 38, 185, 227, 309, 357
Compassion,
    Out of, 429
    Power of, 62
Competition,
    AC, 125
    Gallery, 172
    Healthy, 169
    Pointless, 131
    Sense of, 165
Competitions, Art, 171-173
Competitor, Preexisting, 329
Complacency, Need not fear, 430
Complaints, 374, 415
Complications,
    Self-inflicted, 331
    Spiritual, 23
Complicit, 34, 57
Composer, Court, 96-97
Composers, Two, 93
Composition V, 171
Compositions,
    Lyrical nonobjective, 330
    Unconventional, 373
Comprehension,
    Divine, 97-98
    Intuitive, 298
Compulsion, 226, 382
Compulsions, Mental, 401
Computer, Virtual world of a, 336
Conceit, Height of human, 233
Concepts, Hardwired, 117
Conceptualization, 212, 348
Conceptualize, 161, 238
Conceptualizing, 214, 275, 310
Conchita (See also Pablo's sister), 247-249
Conclusion,
    Anthropological, 363
    Metaphysical, 108
    Spirit of a meaningful, 316
Conclusions,
    Curious, 248
    Logical, 122
Condition,
    Human, 320, 326
    Special, 430
Conditioning,
    Aspects of social, 3
    Entrapments of social, 101

Illusion of social, 156
Limits of social, 242
Mind-numbing social, 41
Prisoners of social, 44
Products of social, 205
Temporal images of mass social, 407
Vast sea of social, 19
Veil of
    mass social, 102
    social, 314
Years of social, 238
Conduct, Code of, 55, 61, 393
Conduit,
    Cosmic, 201
    Direct, 103
    Instantaneous, 310
    Organic, 76
Confidence,
    Gain, 262
    Harbor of, 430
    Indestructible, 24
    Organic, 13
    Supreme, 29
    Vigorous, 359
    Vote of, 164
Confident, 23, 43, 83, 212, 420, 423
Conflict,
    Experience no, 115
    Inner, 323
Conflicts, Unconscious, 317
Conformity,
    Mindless, 87
    Pattern of, 166
    Rigid, 366
    Weaknesses of, 84
Confrontation,
    Moment of, 55
    School, 291
Confronting, 16, 23, 75, 83, 96, 121-122, 128, 134, 205, 242, 260, 356, 428
Confusion, Human, 376
Congress, 123, 396
Conjecture, 190, 200
Connection,
    Healthy, 147
    Infallible, 227
    Intuitive emotional, 154
    Magical, 363
Connoisseur,
    Art, 302
    Domain of the, 159
Conscience, People of, 114
Consciousness,
    Accessing, 290, 323
    Artifact of, 178
    Awakened, 350
    Awareness of, 360, 401, 419
    Cosmic, 184
    Everyday, 349-350
    Evolutionary scale of, 63
    Fabric of, 147
    Genius of, 119
    Gift of, 114
    God, 233, 259
    Higher, 83, 342

Inner comprehension of, 307
Invisible matrix of, 403
Level of, 350
Nature of, 285
One, 74
Power of, 118, 342
Pure, 118, 183, 186
Purity of, 341
Realm of, 85
Reflection of, 361
Sea of, 101
Transcendental experience, 323
Creator, 63
source of great art, 411
Consensus—the tyranny of the masses, 9
Consequence,
    Direct, 13, 225
    Significant, 362
Constitution, Indian, 408-409
Construction, Rigid, 112
Consultant, Art, 157, 343
Consumerism, Cult of, 34
Consumers, Thoughts of most, 219
Consumption,
    Intellectual, 260
    Mass, 164
    Public, 330, 346
    Totem pole of conspicuous, 402
Contact, the film, 175, 200
Contemplation, Pure, 363
Contentment, False, 286
Continuum, Space-time, 10, 17, 108, 189, 198, 200, 202, 387
Control,
    Mind, 43-45
    Out of, 154, 226, 290, 382
Conventions, Social, 254, 317
Conversation, Art of, 137
Conviction, Strength of, 63
Cooper, Gary, 394
Copernicus, Nicolaus, 45
Coptic, 297
Coquiot, Gustave, 252, 254
Correctness, Political, 15, 382
Cortex, Visual, 341
Corvette, 220-222, 424
Cosmic scale of Einstein's general relativity, 182
Cosmos,
    Eternal energy of the, 338
    Machinery of the, 30
Countenance,
    Pleasant, 73
    Spiritual, 415
'Counter-intuitive' concepts of space, 178
Counterproductive, 234, 428-429
Coupling, Strange, 180
Courage,
    Moral, 109
    Source of, 85
Court, Royal, 94
Covenant, Art of the, 433-434
Cows, Sacred, 268
Craft, 164, 200, 276, 348, 364, 366-367, 372, 375

Craft-making, 365
Craftsmanship, 367
Craftsmen, Professional, 369
Craving, Unbridled, 281
'Crazy', 84, 226, 290-291, 386
Crazy-making, 127
Cream, 115, 186, 308
Creating, Way of, 236
Creation,
    Act of, 24, 155, 268, 286, 323
    Age of, 324-325
    Art, 26, 106, 142, 226, 274, 331, 402, 406
    Aspects of spontaneous, 310
    Daily, 190
    Domain of, 274
    Enemy of, 335
    Force of, 197, 207
    Indivisible essence of, 182
    Intuitive, 310
    Magic of, 64
    Mystery of, 186, 200
    Passion of, 361
    Power of, 83, 102, 213, 323
    Practical application of, 105
    Result of spontaneous, 139
    Showcase of all, 142
    Source of, 112, 194
    Strings of, 188
    Veil, 389
    Wellspring of, 310
Creative Thinking, 404
Creativity, Enemy of, 56
Creator,
    Countenance of the, 11, 183
    DNA of a, 87
    Equation of the human, 371
    Eye of the, 82
    Ineffable manifestation of the, 285
    Intuitive, 380
    Presence of
        an individual, 363
        the, 134
    Promethean, 125-126
    Pure manifestation of the, 84
    Semidivine, 370-371
    Song of the, 3, 342
    Sublime countenance of the, 183
    Superb, 73
    Thoughts of the, 262
    Trait of a, 189
    True, 85, 273, 286, 397
    handbook, 63, 93, 270
    oeuvre, 351
Creators,
    Comrade, 158
    Independent, 372
    Inner magic of, 325
    Prolific, 337
    Society of, 390
Credit, Social, 153
Creeds, Masculine, 268
Crick, Francis, 145
Crime, 242, 348
Crises, Spiritual, 325

Crisis, Identity, 411
Criteria, Subjective, 37
Critic,
    British art, 102
    Cultural, 326
    Inner, 21, 90, 134, 236, 415
    Smart, 162
Criticism,
    Art, 21, 162, 226
    Flow of, 250
    Need of, 376
Criticized, 279, 318, 327, 406, 420
Critics, Art, 21, 67, 119, 162, 206
Critique, Premise of a, 162
Cro-Magnon, 363
Croce, Benedetto, 234, 309
Cross-pollination, 27
Crouch, Tom, 283
Crow, Thomas, 376
Crown, Literary triple, 231
Crucible, Dynamic, 97
Cruelty, Sanctioning of, 125
Crutch, Verbal, 236
Cry, Rally, 348
Cubley, Stewart, 57
Cubism, 189-191, 205, 250, 326, 329, 352
Cubist, 190-191, 248, 253
Cues, Visual, 232, 308
Culture,
    Eyes of the mainstream, 421
    Popular, 28, 172, 219, 232, 243, 331, 346, 394
    Western, 114, 364
Cultures,
    Advanced, 198
    Traditional, 364
    Tribal, 363
Cummings, E.E., 237
Cupola, Magnificent (See also Brunelleschi), 368
Curator, Art, 157, 421
Curie, Marie, 279
Currency, Universal, 133
Customs, 103, 233, 362, 371, 374
'Cutting edge', 76, 194, 327-328, 346, 381
Cycle, Outsider, 349
Cycles, Solar, 188
Cytowic, Dr. Richard, 154

D

Dada, Prankster of (See also Duchamp), 344
Dali, Salvador, 25
Damocles, Sword of, 206
Dancehall Performers (See also Frou-Frou), 254
Dante's face, 214
Darkness, Depths of, 429
Darwinian, Strict, 349
Darwinism,
    Example of social, 360
    Rather narrow form of, 349
Data,
    Empirical, 314
    Measurable, 325
Davis, Stuart, 328

Day,
    First cliché of the, 44
    Psychology of the, 313
    Speed every, 177
    Taste of the, 381
Daydreaming, 62
Days, Corvette, 222
De
    Angelis, Barbara, 408
    Antonio, Emile, 22, 201, 345, 419
    Botton, Alain, 102, 155, 376, 407-409
    Kooning,
        Bill, 345
        Willem, 201, 205, 328, 419
    Rola, Balthazar Klossowski, 381
    Sales, Frances, 246
    Tocqueville, Alexis, 155
    Toulouse-Lautrec, Henri, 374
Deadlines, Artificial, 225
Deadwood, Negative, 156
Deal, Art of the, 158
Dealer,
    Art, 4-6, 75, 157, 191, 251, 302, 327, 378
    High profile art, 327
    New York Soho art, 5
    San Francisco art, 191
    Successful art, 378
    assessment, 327
    commentary, 5
Dealers,
    Art, 67, 163, 206, 371
    Savvy of, 376
Death,
    Black, 365-366
    Masks of, 40
    Personification of, 74
The Death of Iván Ilych, 322
Debs, Eugene V., 290
Debt, Karmic, 3, 361
Debussy, 273
Debut, Paris (See also Picasso), 254
Decade, Art wars of the last, 326
Decision,
    Conscious, 238
    Result of every, 398
    Unalterable, 67, 77
Decisions,
    Cerebral, 281
    Make
        crucial life-altering, 386
        sound, 260
Declaration of Independence, 46, 119
Deco, Art, 326
Deconstructing, 191
Deconstruction, 326-328
Decree, Universal, 197
Decrypted (See also Artist code), 341
Dedication,
    Fearless, 308
    Inevitable potential through, 167
    Personal, 122
    Self through, 26
    Sign of, 40
    Talent plus, 162
Deduction, Prosaic, 18

Deeper,
    Digging, 236, 253
    Look, 407
Defeat, 6, 21, 39, 62, 77, 91, 103, 118, 236, 239, 260, 267, 394, 397, 415
Defeatism, 376
Definition,
    Accepted, 374
    Unique by, 26, 169
Definitions,
    Assortment of, 306
    Shortage of, 225
Degree, Art, 26, 382
Déjeuner sur l'Herbe (See also Édouard Manet), 374
Deliverance, Work of, 227
Democracy, Golden Age of Greek, 305
'Democratic' terror, 396
Democritus, 181
Demon, 153, 393-394, 397-399
Demons, Inner, 40, 393-394, 398
Demos, Erik, 33
Demotic, 297
Demystified, 23, 274, 327, 375, 434
Denominator, Common, 98, 160, 267, 296
Density, Dull, 194
Denny, Sandy, 117
Department,
    Manic-depressive, 232
    State, 396
Departments, Art history, 326-327
Deplorably, Acting out, 63
Depression, 74, 192, 226, 411
Deprivation,
    Crucible of, 289
    Such feelings of, 410
Deprogrammed, 138
Design, Graphic, 163, 342
Designs, Inkblot, 419
Destabilizing, 315
Destiny,
    Material, 170
    Product of manifest, 113
    Rhythm of, 286
    Sense of, 286
Detach, 40, 285, 401, 405, 407
Detector, Truth, 325
Detour,
    Momentary, 156
    Worthwhile, 43
Devalued, Feel, 68
Developer, Land, 99, 345
Development,
    Metaphysical, 24
    Organic, 429
    Self-evident, 329
    Significance of the (See also Julian Huxley), 349
Developments, Astounding, 190
The Devil's Dictionary, 25
Dharma,
    Concept of, 279, 282
    Fulfillment of, 70
    Rules of, 279
    System of, 320

    Unique, 250, 347, 428
Dharma Field Zen Center, 280
Dial, Radio, 261
Dialog, Meaningful, 200
Diet, Latest fad, 228
Difference,
    Distinct, 297, 372
    Quantifiable, 232
    Significant, 420-421
Differences,
    Cultural, 114
    Irreconcilable, 180
Difficulties,
    Everyday, 433
    Unnecessary, 213
Dignity, Equal, 197
Dickinson, Emily, 281
Dilations, Significant time, 178
Dimension,
    Discovery of the fourth, 177
    Fourth, 177, 188-191, 194
    Spatial, 188
    Third, 190
Dimensions,
    Four, 177, 191, 198
    Shackles of three, 191
    Three spatial, 188
Dimple, Cusp of the, 192
Diogenes, 350
Direction,
    Moral, 38, 227
    Vague sense of, 424
    Wrong, 250
Directions, Accurate, 428
Director,
    Art, 56, 157, 342, 389
    Museum, 56, 86, 157, 188, 197, 389, 421
Directors,
    Hollywood, 133
    Museum, 127, 161
Disagreements, Agreeable, 169
Disapproval, Voices, 90
Disarming, 74, 121, 249, 393
Disaster, Spell, 132
'Disasters', 196, 199
Discern, 23, 25, 83, 107, 112, 119, 127, 154, 170, 274, 297, 390
Discernment, Unique sense of, 38
Disciple, Young Zen, 217
Discovery,
    Insight of self, 13
    Scientific, 180
Discretion,
    Matter of, 55
    Practiced, 363
    Vigilant, 75
    quality, 309
Dish, Petri (See also Hollywood Studio), 98
Disinformation, 165-166, 313, 332
Disney,
    Walt, 232
    adaptation, 234
    Pinocchio, 232, 235
Disorder, Symptoms of a mental, 314
Disorders, Mental, 323

Disposition, Healthy, 404
Dissanayake, Ellen (See also *Art & Intimacy*), 325, 363, 377
Dissonant Quartet (See also Mozart), 95
Distances, Stellar, 178, 199
Distinction,
    Indelible, 373
    Semantic, 25
    Significant, 282
Distinctions, Caste, 408
Distinguish, 125, 137, 195, 201, 225, 351
Distributor, Film, 346
Diversity, Healthy, 154
The Divine Comedy (See also Dante), 213
DNA, 87, 145, 183
Do-it-yourself 'religion' (See also Zen), 112
Doctors, Guild of, 369
Doctrines, Hosing petty, 114
Document, Magical, 46
Documents, Carl Foreman, 394
Dog, Wagging the, 105
Doggies, Diminutive, 150
Dogma,
    Institutional, 111
    Leash of, 397
    Question, 179
Doll, Kachina, 137, 144, 146, 454
Dollars, Twenty-five, 350
Dolphins, 145
Domain, Aspect of the spiritual, 184
Dome, Architecture of the (See also Brunelleschi), 368
Dominque, La, 379
Don Quixote, 232, 260
Donahue, Robert, 163
Donatello, 367-368
Donnas, Prima, 127
Doom, Ultimate, 94
Dots, Sublime convergence of perception, 190
Doublespeak,
    New-age, 156, 407
    Orwellian, 129
Douglass, Frederick, 236
Down,
    Feeling, 179
    Look, 315, 349
    Put, 242, 404-405, 427
Dragon, Indignant, 105
Dragons,
    Dissipation of the, 260
    External, 394, 398
Draughtsmanship, 173
Draw, 15, 57, 76, 132, 146, 154, 173, 190, 197-198, 203, 211, 247, 373, 404-406
Drawing, 5, 39, 68, 102, 140-141, 145, 275, 291, 314, 337, 355, 369, 373, 381, 404-405
Dream,
    American, 220, 385, 423
    Animated pictographs of a, 307
    Enlightened, 197
    Surreal, 220
    Unique, 37
    Waking, 283

Worthy, 287
Dreaming, Lucid, 282-283
Dreams,
    Boulevard of, 423-424
    Collective, 207, 284
    Interpretation of, 282, 317
    Marvelous, 283
    The Interpretation of, 282, 317
    Waking, 147, 415
    Wishing makes, 238
Drives, Result of evolutionary-based instinctual, 317
Drones, Contemporary, 364
Dubuffet, Jean, 381
Duchamp,
    Marcel, 191, 344, 374, 420
    daring provocation, 344
    urinal (See also R. Mutt), 345
Duncan, Isadora, 111
Duomo (See also Santa Maria Del Fiore), 368-369
Dürer, Albrecht, 366
Dutch, 28
Dyer, Wayne, 335
Dyson, Freeman, 200

E

$E=mc^2$, 108, 181, 186-187
Ear, Slice of (See also Van Gogh), 351
Earning, Way of, 380
Earth,
    Mother, 194
    Spaceship, 233, 259
    motion, 45
Ecstasy, Agony into, 35
Edge,
    Leading, 403
    So-called cutting, 327
    Unbreakable, 27
    Undeniable psychological, 163
Edison, Thomas Alva, 124-125, 191
Education, Arts, 142
Edwards,
    Betty, 404-405
    Professor, 218-219
Effect,
    Pernicious, 401
    Unique, 286
Effects,
    Interference, 194
    Superficial, 24
    Wonderful interference, 194
Egalitarian, 114, 289
Egg, The Radical (See also Brunelleschi), 57, 368
Ego,
    Act of, 361
    Healthy, 132
    Insecure inner voice of, 261
    Judgmental, 207
    Mysterious, 132
    Pressure of, 127
    Role of the, 131
    Straightjacket of, 18

    Transcendental, 350
    Unbridled, 338
Egocentrism, 26
Egoism, Act of, 26
Egoist, 24-25
Egos, Myopic, 68
Egotism, 25
Egypt, Ancient, 193
Egyptian, Secrets of the ancient, 297
Einstein, Picasso, 181, 190-191
Einstein,
    Albert, 108, 176-177, 181, 191, 284-285, 329, 337
    Truth, 253
    brilliant deductions, 189
    equation, 186
    friend (See also Max Planck), 189
    general theory of relativity, 177, 182, 192, 195
    great insight, 177
    insight, 193
    linear space-time continuum of general relativity, 108
    special theory of relativity, 176, 178
    subsequent work, 182
    view of time, 177
Elbowroom, Plenty of, 171
Electric,
    AC, 124-125
    Alternating, 124
    Westinghouse, 125
Electromagnetic, 193-194
Electromagnetism, 181, 189
The Elegant Universe, 182, 261
Elements,
    External, 284
    Material, 371
    Plot, 38
Elixir, 62, 356
Ellington, Duke, 301, 328
Emancipation, Divine, 112
Emerson, Ralph Waldo, 31, 38, 235, 254, 285
Emotion,
    Evolved, 262
    Flow of pure intelligent, 337
    Healing, 81
    Intuitive, 155, 337
    Pure, 154, 337, 343, 361, 375, 411
Emotions,
    Intelligent, 260
    Unique palette of, 154
Empathy, 154, 260, 330, 376
Emperor, Mr., 343-345
Empire, Roman, 364
Employer, Equal opportunity, 153
Empowered, Artist, 13, 75, 207, 289, 430
Empowerment, Personal triumph of, 97
Emptiness, 112, 154, 221, 284
Encouragement,
    Lack of, 347
    Word of, 123
Endowment, National, 327, 351
Endowments, Cultural, 407
Enemy, Worst, 76

Energies, Lived by sacred, 122
Energy,
    Impulse of, 261, 307
    Impulses of, 434
    Intuitive, 68
    Life, 192-193, 228
    Living, 68, 170
    Magical transformation of, 398
    Nuclear, 186
    Strands of, 181
    Theories of, 329
Engagement, The Rules of, 55, 61-62
Engagements, Verbal, 415
Engineering,
    Behavioral, 319
    Genetic, 349
England, 366
English, 11, 25, 45-46, 151, 217-218, 236-237, 279, 302
Engravings, 372
Enigma, Grammar, 217
Enjoyment, Personal, 162
Enlightened, 74, 103, 105, 114, 119, 167, 194, 197, 219, 261, 321
Enlightenment,
    Age of, 95, 373
    Buddha, 187
    Journey toward, 26
    Origins of, 116
    Path toward, 75
    Pilgrimage of, 77
    Vista of, 111
Entanglements, Unwelcome, 212
Enterprise,
    Cerebral, 310
    Human, 324
Entity,
    Indivisible, 187
    Integrated, 316
    Linguistic, 225
    Simple, 193
    Soul, 11, 184
Entrance, Magic, 416
Entrapment, State of, 410
Entrapments, Self-fulfilling, 247
Entrepreneurship, Tradition of, 254
Entropic, 75
Environment,
    Cultural, 296
    Degradation of the, 197
    Proper, 429
    Urban, 408
Envy, Lifetime of, 93
Epictetus, 103, 286
Epiphanies, Smart, 149
Episode, Clairvoyant, 385
Episodes, Epic *Star Wars*, 346
Epistemology, Trenches of, 306
Equal measure—busboy, 86
Equality, Social, 105
Equation,
    Art, 108, 180
    Balanced, 247
    Human, 314
    Short, 108

Temporal, 183
Equations, Four elegant (See also Electromagnetism), 189
Equilibrium, Rhythm of a dynamic, 286
Era,
    Postmodern, 327
    Romantic, 95
Escapade, Spiritual, 38
Espresso, Top of the, 291
Essay, Provocative, 349
Essence,
    Nonmaterial timeless, 183
    Supreme and consistent, 102
    Transcendental, 27
Essential quality of the winner's art, 169
Establishment, Art, 141, 162, 206, 347, 351, 382
Estate, Warhol, 164
Eternity, Wheel of, 131
Ether, 143, 307, 310, 328
Ethnic, Diverse, 51
Euphoria, 425
Europe,
    Medieval, 410
    Northern, 370-372
    Western, 366
European, 29, 125, 301, 366, 375, 408
Euterpe (See also Greek Muses), 305
Evaluators, Art, 17
Event,
    External, 129
    Original, 109
    Spontaneous, 101
Events,
    Celestial, 192, 310
    Dynamism of the, 296
    Intuitive, 314
    Outcome of, 184
    Transcendental, 156
Everything,
    Perception of, 186
    Price of, 34
    Theory of, 180-182, 188, 191
    Use, 35, 62, 68, 404
Evidence,
    Empirical, 320
    Forensic, 41
    Material, 18
    Physical, 24
Evil, 39, 90, 114, 117, 164, 170, 206, 215, 219, 320-321, 336, 367, 380, 394
Evita, 427
Evolution,
    Artistic, 370
    Gene pool of, 139
    Human, 274, 349-350
    Toward, 276, 415
Excellence,
    Inherent beauty of, 50
    Neurotic, 323
Exchange, Stock, 318, 378
Excitement, Inherent, 170
Exclamation,
    Three-foot-high, 344
    Wooden cut out, 345

Excuse, 13, 19, 68, 85, 114, 123, 150, 253, 268, 270, 416
Executioners, 35, 69
Exhibition,
    Author of, 326
    The Business of Art, 378
Exhibitionism, 327
Exhibitions, Art, 121-122
Existence,
    Everyday, 28
    Evidence of the, 184
    Goal of human, 285
    Grand prize of temporal, 10
    Meaning of, 323
    Metaphysical masterpiece of, 132
    Paradoxes of, 187
    Price of temporal, 411
    Selfish puppet, 237
    Spiritual, 184
    dharma, 183, 283
Expectations, Provincial, 94
Experience,
    Aesthetic, 17, 270, 314, 421
    Common, 261
    Direct, 133, 187, 275, 287
    Everyday, 177, 184
    Eyes of firsthand, 10
    Firsthand intuitive, 289
    Function of, 362
    Gift of, 256
    Having no direct, 147
    Human, 317, 320, 324, 347
    Immediate, 101, 115, 269
    Intrinsic, 390
    Life, 38, 63, 184, 189, 197, 289, 434
    Measuring, 182
    Metaphysical mystery of the, 341
    Near death, 218-219
    Personal, 82, 111, 116, 187, 324
    Polarity of, 84-85
    Practical metaphysical, 318
    Quality of life, 63
    Quantifiable, 30, 180
    Result of hard-earned human, 317
    Stamp of direct, 133
    Substance of firsthand, 349
    Transcendental human, 320
    Vicarious, 16
    Wealth of, 221
Experiences,
    Diverse, 69
    Mystical, 68, 325, 331
    Peak, 331
    Private, 319
    Transcendent, 82, 324
    Unique, 187, 220, 357
    Unusual, 314
Experiment, Creativity, 146
Experiments, Groundbreaking, 45
Exploration, Scientific, 316
Exposure, Function of, 38
Expression,
    Individual, 370
    Innovative, 25
    Limitless, 393

Medium of, 310
Result of, 154
Expressionism, Anti-abstract, 164
Expressionist, 95, 301, 328, 396
Expressions, Trite, 44
External 'measurements' of success, 409
Extinction—a fate, 402
Eye, Human, 190
Eyes,
    Contemporary, 329
    Different, 107
    Postmodern, 329

F

Fabric,
    Cosmic, 17
    Single, 189
    Space-time, 181, 191-192, 199
Face,
    Authentic, 86, 227
    Lost, 68
Faces, Hero, 39, 394
Factor, Significant, 382
Factory, Silkscreen (See also Pop Art), 164
Facts,
    Measurable, 323
    Rearrangement of existential, 434
    Rearranging existential, 390
    Relative, 134
Fagus, Félicien, 252
Failure, Inevitability of, 320
Faith,
    Hindu, 406
    Intuitive, 17
    Leap of, 17
    Lost, 21
    Meaning of, 179
    True, 18, 183, 260
    Unrelenting tests of, 39
Falling, Tree, 184
Falls, Why the apple, 14
Falstaff, 363
Fame, 27, 39, 70, 97, 142, 192, 206-207, 256, 292, 379, 407, 427
Family, Medici, 362, 370
Fantin-Latour, Henri, 374
Farscape, TV series, 199
Fascist, 260
Fashion,
    Different, 164
    Matter of, 343
    Zen-like, 218
Fat, Linguistic, 267
Fauves, 189
Favor, Out of, 420
FBI, 396
Fear,
    Art &, 342
    Face, 395
    Out of, 132, 357
    emotions, 117
Fearlessly, Intuitive guidance, 434
Fears, Darkest, 322
Features, Film, 232, 345

Fee, Non-negotiable, 133
Feedback, Positive, 4
Feel 'good', 16, 18, 29, 129, 331, 397
Feeling,
    Curious, 231
    Depth of intelligent, 434
    Empty, 284
    Experience of, 212
    , 162
    Pure, 18, 103, 154, 212, 261, 263, 307
    Significance of, 260
Feelings,
    Intuitive, 154
    Mixed, 228
    Positive, 128
    Pure, 262
    Symphony of, 155
Felony, Linguistic, 235
Ferlinghetti, Lawrence, 51
Feuds, Political, 368
Feynman, Richard, 193, 416-417
Ficino, Marsilio, 370
Fiction,
    Ancient races of science, 199
    Contemporary, 236
    Pulp, 395
    Science, 133, 195, 199, 393
Fiddler, Tevya of, 75
Field,
    Incredible, 309
    Unified, 181, 187
Fields, W.C., 171, 246, 345
Fighter, Freedom, 395
Figure,
    Damaged lone, 393
    Heroic, 394
Figures,
    Celebrated, 126
    Collective portrait of seminal, 345
Filament, Dancing (See also String Theory), 182
Filippo's machines (See also Brunelleschi), 369
Film,
    Disney, 232-234
    Integrity of the, 346
    Major, 22, 98
    narrator, 251
Filmmaker, Independent, 160
Filmmakers, 21
Filmmaking, 133, 346
Films,
    Hollywood, 395-396
    Independent, 98
    Mainstream, 346
    Pro-Soviet, 396
'Fine arts', 26, 142, 161, 252, 305, 364, 373
Fire,
    Crucible of divine, 194
    Divine gift of creative, 166
    Eternal flame of divine, 213
    Harnessing divine, 29
    Intensity of divine, 214
First Abstract Watercolor (See also Kandinsky), 329-330

Firsthand,
    Learned, 55, 306
    Rigidity of a mindset, 44
    Scene, 173
    Truth, 10, 18
Fittest, Survival of the, 360
Fitzgerald,
    F. Scott, 356
    Michael C., 252
Flame, Keeper of the, 158, 189
Flanders, 371
Flanner, Janet, 23, 78, 119, 375
Flatland, 127
Flaw,
    Character, 39
    Tragic, 394
Flemish, 372
Flock, Sheep, 137
Floor, Valley, 195-196
Florence, Fifteenth-century, 370
Florentine, 249, 367-370
Floundering, Risk, 342
Flower, Lotus, 111, 114, 116-117, 159
Flowers, Way of (See also Kado), 115
Focus, Lack of, 196
Folk, Common, 366
Folks, Pushy, 139
Follow, Sheepishly, 398
Followers, Zen, 116-117
Food,
    All natural, 105
    Regular diet of wholesome, 22
    Soul, 429
Forbes, Malcolm, 219
Force, Intuitive power of the, 346
Ford, Henry, 164
Forebears, Medieval, 410
Foreman, Carl, 394-396
Form,
    Human, 336
    Innovation of, 161
    Literary, 198
    Machiavellian, 157
    Material, 286
    Physical, 322
    Regardless of, 43, 227
    Transcendent, 342
Formalism, Art, 374
Forman, Milos (See also *Amadeus*), 93
Forms,
    Different, 62, 105
    Tax return, 263
Formula,
    Accepted, 160
    Empirical marketing, 162
    Magic, 382
    Personal, 33
    Reductionist, 98
    Well-worn, 126
Formulation, Weird, 411
Forster, E.M., 105
Fortune, Questionable, 343
Foundation Series (See also Isaac Asimov), 199
Fountain (See also Porcelain urinal), 344,

420
Fraglia, 369
Fragmentation, 212
France,
    Anatole, 391, 421
    France, 252, 366, 370, 373, 403
Francesca, Piero della, 366
Frankenthaler, Helen, 315, 328
Franklin, Aretha, 245
Freedom,
    Aroma of, 372
    Degree of, 113
    Gain creative, 373
    Lotus flower Petals of, 111
    Magic, 291
    One true, 75, 227
    Sense of, 106
    True, 75, 86, 227, 281
Frequency, Right, 101
Fresco, Traditional fast-drying, 372
Freud, Sigmund, 282, 316, 336
Freudian, 317-319, 323
Freudianism, 325
Freudians, 281, 320, 324, 360
Friend,
    Artist, 73-74, 140, 301, 359
    True, 77, 241
Frou-Frou (See also Dancehall performers), 254
Frustration,
    Level of, 166
    Out of, 76
    Sense, 405
Fulfillment,
    Divine, 34
    Kingdom of, 416
    Life of, 56
    Moment of, 14, 191, 434
    Specific, 236
    Toward, 250, 285
    Wish, 233, 282
Fuller, Buckminster, 11, 14, 73, 233, 259, 332
Fulton, Professor, 217
Functional, 34, 215, 362, 420
Functioning, Intellectual, 419
Fund, Trust, 424
Furnace, Nuclear, 193
Future, Unique sense of the, 346

G

Gachet, The Portrait of Doctor (See also Van Gogh), 351
Galaxy,
    Andromeda, 178, 202
    Milky Way, 178, 193, 198-199, 202
Galilei, Galileo, 45, 330
Galleries,
    Limited number of, 141
    Mainstream, 303
    Trendy, 163
Gallery,
    Art, 73, 118, 127, 159
    Owner, 56, 127, 141, 159, 165-167, 171-172, 205, 250, 301, 421
    Soho, 5
    Trendy, 5, 301
Gandhi, Mahatma, 285
Gap, the (See also Deepak Chopra), 53, 102, 309, 327, 405, 410
Gardener, Smart, 159
Gatekeeper, Representative, 302
Gatekeepers, 303, 347
Gats, Els Quatre (See also Picasso), 251
Gauguin, Paul, 28-29, 67, 159, 169, 212, 253, 302, 347, 372, 374, 378-379, 382
Gauntlet, 4, 43, 49, 235
Gautama, Siddhartha (See also Buddha), 74, 96, 193, 321, 408
Gawain, Shakti, 46, 93
Gene, Unique rejection-proof, 285
Generation,
    Baby boomer, 284
    Beat, 51-52
Genie's bottle, 145
Genius,
    Associating, 28
    Equal, 162
    Freelance, 372
    Gift of, 94
    Patch of, 351
    Tortured, 208
    True, 19
    Unique, 247
Geometry, Function of, 192
Geppetto (See also *Pinocchio*), 234-235, 237-238
German, 51, 337, 372, 407
Germany, 370, 423
Gestalt, 56, 173, 233, 260, 295, 316, 405, 427
Getty Research Institute, 376
Ghiberti, 368
Gibran, Kahlil, 365
Gift,
    Muzak, 93
    Specific, 97
    Superb, 52
    Universal, 329
    Wedding, 370
Gill, Brendan, 401
Ginsberg, Allen, 51
Giotto, 375
Giovanni, 367
Glance, First, 94, 181, 290
Glaser, Milton, 362, 375
Gluck (See also Antonio Salieri), 96
Go,
    Letting, 201, 241
    Zen to, 112
Goal,
    Attainment of the, 40
    Commercial, 254
    Dynamic nature of the, 411
    Specific, 128
Goble, Frank G., 41, 387
God,
    Child of, 115
    Formula of, 108
    Grace of, 144
    Love of, 285
    Measure, 114
    Mind of, 108, 227, 309
    Sex of, 268
    Talent, 97
    Teachings of, 406
    Tears of, 411
    Transcendental song of, 390
    Values of, 106
    Vision of, 9, 276
    Word of, 317
    eyes, 83
    gender, 268
    guidance, 290
    malice, 94
    prerogative, 233
    voice, 95
God-centered, 190
Goddess, 268, 306
Goddesses,
    Disappearance of (See also Leonard Shlain), 268
    Fickle, 310
Godhead, Supreme Personality of (See also Lord Krishna), 285
Gods, 114, 143, 195, 215, 269, 290, 336, 363, 367, 376
Goethe, Johann Wolfgang Von, 202, 228
Gold, Stuart Avery, 26
Good,
    Being, 84, 173, 376
    Feel, 16, 18, 29, 129, 331, 397
    Inherent, 320
    Make, 39, 128
    Powers of, 39
Goods,
    Material, 284, 290
    Society-approved tokens of material, 284
Gorky, Arshile, 328, 374
Gown, Different wedding, 87
Goya, 375
Gracián, Baltasar, 407
Grammar,
    Realm of, 219
    Rules of, 218-219
Grant, Cary, 145
Gratification,
    Instant, 44, 129
    Unbridled, 394
Gratitude,
    Express, 236, 328
    State of, 83
Gravitas, 167, 175, 192, 379
Gravity,
    Defy, 127, 282, 368
    Effects of, 15, 177, 191
    Theory of, 176-177
Greco, El, 189, 256, 329
Greco-Roman, 364
Greece,
    Ancient, 28, 161
    Classical, 364
Greed, 83, 114, 125, 140, 164, 212, 238, 410
Greek,

Ancient, 156
Classic, 181
Hellenic, 305
Languages of, 376
Greeks, Ancient, 161, 206, 305, 336
Green, Marina, 50
Greenberg, Clement (See also Jackson Pollock), 206, 419
Greene, Brian, 182, 185, 261
Grid, Space-time, 132
Grit, True, 109
Ground,
    Common, 225, 319, 391
    Neurological high, 154
    Pioneer new, 9
Grouping, Social, 409
Groups, Social, 114
Growth, Mindless, 205
Guernica (See also Picasso), 250
Guggenheim, Peggy (See also Jackson Pollock), 206
Guidance, Divine, 306
Guild, Rules of a craft, 366
Guillaumin, Armand (See also Salon des Refusés), 374
Guilt, Lifetime of, 247
Gulags, 151
Gurdjieff, George, 345, 424
Gutenberg, Johannes (See also Printing Press), 372
Gyroscope, Self-maintaining, 81

H
Habits, Negative, 115
Hackwork (See also Frou-Frou), 97, 254-255
Hagen, Steve (See also Zen Buddhism), 115, 280
Haiku (See also Zen Buddhism), 115, 123
Hair, Metaphysical angel, 411
Hallucinations, Uncontrollable, 147
Hamlet, 89, 91, 154
Hand, Sleight of, 194
Hands, Show of, 10, 162, 226, 330, 421
Happiness,
    Pursuit of, 46
    Secure, 280
Hardship,
    Financial, 378
    Life of, 285
Harline, Leigh, 233
Harm,
    Immediate, 255
    Malicious, 50
Harmony,
    Inner, 147
    Organic, 170
Haste, Out of, 129
Hayakawa, S.I., 268, 296
Haynes, Deborah, 153-154, 370
Health,
    Laws of, 321
    Positive mental, 316
    Psychology of, 331
Heart,
    Human, 318
    Open, 262
    Restless, 220
Hearts, Miserly, 159
Heaven,
    Grammar, 218
    Kingdom of, 147, 197
    Know, 214, 393-394
    Piece of, 429
    door, 197
    gate, 34
Hebrew, 87
Heidegger, 350
Hell,
    Ego, 40
    Know, 214, 394
Hellman, Lillian, 306
Helplessness, Illusion of, 62
Hendrick, Becky, 28
Henri, Robert, 112, 154, 401
Herbert, Frank, 196
Heresy, Scientific, 316
Hero,
    Artist as, 37-40
    Role of the reluctant, 394
    must experience encouragement, 4
    wife, 394
Heroine, Physicist, 183, 187
Hesburgh, Theodore, 317
Hesitation, Slightest, 393
Hesse, Hermann (See also *Siddhartha*), 321
Hieroglyphs, Ancient Egyptian, 297
High Noon (See also Carl Foreman), 394-397
Higher realm of self-inspiration—the eternal flame, 228
Highway, Cultural, 196
Hills,
    Beverly, 303
    Hollywood, 221-222, 302, 345, 389, 402
Hilltop, Strategic, 195
Hindrance, Social, 233
Hindu,
    Hindu, 280, 285, 406, 408-409
    Religion, 409
Hinduism,
    Essence of, 406
    Teachings of, 29
Historian, Art, 359-361, 377, 381
Historians, Art, 24, 190
History,
    Ancient, 199
    First Western book of art (See also Giorgio Vasari), 249
    Human, 114, 197, 268
    Icons of art, 109
    Impressive command of art, 157
    Professor of art, 371
Hockney, David, 133, 374
Hofmann, Hans, 24, 76, 310
Holbein, Hans, 366
Holden, William, 221-222
Holistic, 38, 81, 212, 268, 279, 324, 326, 330, 404
Holmes, Oliver Wendell, 253
Holy Grail, 107, 181, 328
Hollywood,
    Hills of, 222
    darkest hour, 396
    director's artistic license, 4
Homme du Métier (See also Kenneth Clark), 249
Honesty,
    Rigorous, 374
    Risking, 226
Hope,
    Future uncertainty of, 434
    Rickety fence of, 18
Hopeless, 394
Horizon, Lost, 194
Horn, Sam, 55, 206, 382, 403
Horowitz, Vladimir, 273
Horses, Old (See also Thomas Edison), 124
Hour, Darkest, 106, 396
Hours, Darkest, 398
House,
    Malibu beach, 22
    Random, 33
    Safe, 78
Housekeeping, Lexicon, 267
Houses,
    Art, 346
    Auction, 140-141
Hoving, Thomas, 56
Hq, Rejection, 55
HUAC (See also Carl Foreman), 395-396
Hubris, Societal, 194
Hues, Dimensions of disparate, 347
Hugo, Victor, 249
Humanists, Writing of Neoplatonist, 370
Humanity, Genetic fabric of all, 107
Humankind's wonderful discoveries, 263
Humbert, Marcelle (aka Eva Gouel), 248
Humiliation, Dangers of, 156
Humility, Conscious, 74
Humor, Sense of, 4, 219
Hunch, Divine, 261
Hunger,
    Growing, 220
    Raw, 289
Hunter-gatherers, 363
Hurdle,
    Existential, 166
    Major, 124
Hurley, Tonya, 267
Husserl, Edmund, 349
Huxley,
    Aldous, 145
    Thomas H., 385
    Sir Julian, 349
Hype, Matter of, 343
Hypothesis, Academic, 10
Hysteria, New age, 75

I
Iago (See also *Othello*), 158
Icon,
    Post-Impressionist, 67
    World-famous, 249
Iconic, 164, 268, 329, 351, 393

Id, Subconscious (See also Sigmund Freud), 394
Idea,
    Accepted, 143, 193
    Result of an, 212
Ideas,
    Realm of, 170
    Streaming, 201
    Welcomes new, 38
Identity,
    Adversarial, 134
    Concept of, 29
    Eternal, 283
    Material-based, 3
    Naked, 62
    Sense of, 84, 409
    Temporal, 132
Ideology,
    Political, 105, 319, 326
    Public, 346
    Sectarian, 285
Idiom, Original visual, 166
Idiosyncrasies, Share of, 125
Idolatry, Mainstream, 315
Ignorance,
    Avant-garde out of, 115
    Foundation of, 321
    Smacks of, 270
Illness, Mental, 28-29, 97, 314
Illumination,
    Intuitive, 286
    Point of, 14
Illuminations, Manuscript, 365
Illusion,
    Absence of, 109
    Lord of (See also Maya), 73-75, 96, 147, 220
    Perceiver out of, 40
    Persistent, 195
    Pitfalls of, 361
    Sea of, 196
    Seductive veil of, 134
    Stupor of, 321
    Traps of, 117
    Veil of, 28, 134
Illusions, Stubborn hardwired, 188-189
Image, Mental, 176
Image-clichés, 296
Imagery,
    Computer-generated, 133
    Dramatic, 283
    Everyday, 164
    Poetic, 51, 263
    Recognizable, 329
Images, Abhorrence of, 268
Imagination, Function of, 390
Imitation, Lustrous, 29
Immortal, 94-95, 193, 393, 398
Impact,
    Degree of, 21
    Organic, 328
    Transcendental, 330
Impermanence, Indelible image of, 434
Implication, Direct, 194, 267
Importance,
    Degree of, 89
    Order of, 316
Impressionism, Arbitrary rules of, 29
Impressionist, 374, 378
Improvement, Immediate (See also Rogue's Glossary), 269
Improvisation, Divine, 212
Impulse, Irrational, 382
Impulses,
    Electrical, 337
    Electrochemical, 341
Incarnation,
    Later, 134
    Life-enriching, 133
Inch, Linear (See also $E=mc^2$), 108
Increase, Salary, 57
Indelibility, Process toward, 372
Independence, Act of, 362
Independent 'art' guilds, 367
India,
    Ancient, 279, 406, 408
    Northern, 74
    Rural, 409
Indian, 146, 408-409
Indicator, Reliable, 206, 208
Indiscriminate, 289
Individual,
    Aspects of the, 394
    awareness of consciousness, 419
Individuality,
    Artistic, 372
    Model of, 380
    Surrendering, 228
Individuals, 18, 69, 126, 228, 324, 331
Indivisible
    code—universal truth—of creation, 189
    constituents of an atom's nucleus, 181
Indomitability, 69
Industry,
    Cultural, 377
    confines of the medieval art, 366
Inevitably, 125, 149, 264, 321, 394, 401, 429
Inferno, 4, 213
Infinity, 176
Inflation, Unaffected by, 329
Influence,
    Goddess, 268
    Sphere of, 192, 409
Influences,
    External, 84
    Share of self-evident, 189
Information,
    Age of, 235
    Complete, 428
    Firsthand, 45, 246, 253
    Instantaneous transmission of, 184, 307
    Intuitive impulse of, 309
    Language of, 147
    Non-judgmental snapshots of, 341
    Processes spatial visual, 405
    Quanta, 175
    Sanctity of firsthand, 246
    Secondhand, 9, 13, 33, 37, 45, 109, 245, 250, 255, 275, 281
    Specific, 250
    Still secondhand, 9
    Trustworthy, 315
Informer, Turn, 396
Infrastructure, 231
Ingenuity,
    Milestone of, 369
    Result of, 145
Ingredients,
    Magical, 82
    Secret, 21
Ingres, Dominique, 189
Inhibitors, Self-induced, 356
Iniquity, Moral, 409
Initiation (See also Elizabeth Jenkins), 68
Inkblots, 419, 421
Inner demon—your ego, 398
Innovation,
    Domain of all, 382
    Presence of an, 146
Innovator,
    Artist, 329
    Daring, 368
    Prolific, 310
Innovators, 21, 318, 374
Inquiry, Wrong path of, 164
Inquisition,
    Church, 45
    Spanish, 105
'Insane' world, 331
Insecure, 25, 141, 205, 261, 270, 292, 379-380, 429
Insensitivity, 50
Insight,
    Direct intuitive, 283
    Gain deeper, 190
    Light of, 31
    Marvelous, 404
    Moments of, 331
    Original, 13, 316
    Power of, 380
    Searing moment of, 131
    Shining, 162
    Significant, 44
Insights,
    Amazing, 259
    Astounding, 176
    Brilliant, 27
    Intuitive, 260, 264
    Perennial, 27
Inspiration,
    Elixir of, 356
    Perpetual state of, 86
    Source of, 190
Instinct, 185, 289, 291, 305, 350, 412
Institution,
    Activist, 326
    Social, 324
Institutions,
    Funding, 162
    Mainstream, 325
    Religious, 380
Instruction,
    Proper, 263
    Verbal, 307
Instructions, Genetic, 146

Instrument,
   Collective, 363
   Commercial, 254
   Metaphysical, 316
   Temporal, 349
Integration,
   Power of, 85
   Quality of, 85
Intellect, Keen, 154
Intelligence,
   A. I. Artificial, 237
   Emotional, 30, 40, 56, 153-154, 162, 264, 307, 309, 403
Intent, 95, 123, 127-128, 144, 166, 196, 283, 286, 290, 335, 357, 391
Intention,
   Conscious, 283
   Functional, 362
   Seven faces of, 335
   Solid, 359
   Unwavering, 14
Interactions,
   Orchestrating dramatic, 346
   Strange, 176
Internet, 156, 262, 330
Interpretation, Subjective, 420
Interpretations, 170, 232, 248, 306, 336, 419, 421
Intervention, Divine, 247
Intimacy, True, 82
Intimate experience, 330
Intolerance,
   Culture of, 327
   Era of, 326, 380
Introspection,
   Matter of lucid, 275
   Rewards of, 127
Intuition,
   Awakening, 127, 260
   Definition of, 185
   Direct
      function of, 149
      power of, 308
   Embracer of, 180
   Function of, 76, 149
   Infallible, 218, 220, 262
   Know, 225, 231, 259-260, 283
   Measure, 185, 307
   Mistaking, 260
   Power of, 4, 308
   Precise moment of, 309
   Realm of, 147, 324
   Scientists studying, 259
   Song of, 306
   Source of, 259
   Spontaneous, 434
   Test, 290
Invention,
   Prehistoric, 43
   Symbolic, 259
Inventions, 125, 193, 420
Investigation, Effort of, 189
Investigations, Senate (See also HUAC), 396
Investment, Realm of, 141
Investor, Mentality of an, 163

Invocation, Mystical, 112
Involvement, Emotional, 164
iPods, 56, 186
Irish, 172, 215
Irrefutable evidence—personal, 183
Irrelevance, 196, 198
Islam, 112
Islands, Marquesas (See also Gauguin), 379
Issue, Surface, 29
Issues,
   Creative block, 5
   Overwhelming number of, 113
Italy,
   Post Unification, 234
   Renaissance, 45, 369

J

Jacob, Max, 250, 252
Jacobs, Arthur, 257
Jainism, Founder of (See also Mahavira), 408
James,
   William, 155, 408
   McNeill Whistler's, 374
   equation, 156
Janiger, Oscar, 144-147
Japan, 117, 361
Japanese, 28, 112, 116, 351
Jazz, Visual, 434
Jealousy, Motives of, 249
Jefferson, Thomas, 46, 119, 329
Jenkins, Elizabeth, 68
Jesus, 107, 147, 197, 220, 254, 268, 370, 393
Jewel,
   Crown, 86, 227, 281
   of India's spiritual wisdom, 285
Jewelry, 363-364
Jiminy (See also Walt Disney), 232
Job,
   Creative, 221
   Story of, 39
Jobs, Functional, 34
Johns, Jasper, 345
Johnson, Samuel, 45, 220, 337, 380
Jongkind, Johan, 374
José, Don (See also José Ruiz y Blasco), 248-250
Joseph, Austrian Emperor II, 93, 96
Journey, Precarious, 423
Joy ... fulfillment, 423
Joyride, Aimless, 68
Juan (See also *Initiation*), 68
Judaeo-Christian, 115
Judaism, 27, 112
Judging, System of, 409
Judgment,
   Poor, 56
   Sound, 84
   Value, 22, 323
Judgmental, 207, 405
Judo (See also Zen Buddhism), 115
Jung, Carl, 165, 211, 276, 317-318, 336
Jungian, 27, 83, 150, 207, 318
Jungle, Urban, 292

Jurors,
   Panel of art, 166
   Panels of, 169
Jury,
   Competition The, 169
   The Art, 171
Just—filler word, 269
Justice,
   Poetic, 345
   Sense of, 269

K

Kado (See also Zen Buddhism), 115
Kafka, Franz, 134
Kahnweiler, Daniel-Henry, 254
Kaku, Michio, 178, 190, 199
Kandinsky, Wassily, 169, 171, 189, 256, 262-263, 293, 310, 328-330, 343, 350, 374, 381-382
Kant, Immanuel, 218
Kapellmeister (See also Antonio Salieri), 95
Kardashev, Nikolai, 198
Karma,
   Law of, 17
   Sands of, 205
Karmic,
   Old wheel of, 40
   Tragedy of the, 332
Kazantzakis, Nikos, 306, 428
Keats, John, 10
Keller, Helen, 85
Kelly, Grace (See also *High Noon*), 394
Kendo (See also Zen Buddhism), 115, 310
Kepes, Gyorgy, 296
Kepler, Johannes, 45
Kerouac, Jack, 51
Key,
   Master, 112
   Secret, 286
Keys, Keepers of the, 350
KGB, 151
Kindness, Loving, 87
King,
   European monarchy system of, 408
   Martin Luther, Jr., 236, 322
   Ross, 369
Kites, 3, 123, 137-138, 326
Kleck (See also Hermann Rorschach), 419
Knot, Gordian, 156
Know God—personal, 187
Knowing,
   Absolute, 320
   Empirical, 180
   Intuitive, 119, 156, 180, 185, 264, 320
   Out of, 38
   Quality of, 227
   Transcendental, 29, 318
   Wellspring of intuitive, 156
Knowledge,
   Ancient, 369
   Direct, 306
   Firsthand, 14, 107-108, 195, 231, 255, 434
   Gain, 217

Instantaneous, 259
Introspective, 29
Lifelong pursuit of, 212
Perennial kernel of, 127
Real, 318
Secondhand, 16
Transcendental, 285
Koan (See also Zen Riddle), 115, 404, 430
Kosinski, Jerzy, 33
Kramer, Hilton, 326
Krishna, Wisdom of Lord, 285, 406
Kuntz, Andrew, 25
Kurosawa, Akira (See also *Rashomon*), 107
Kurtz, Colonel Walter E., 64
Kyudo (See also Zen Buddhism), 115

L

L-mode, Analytic, 404-405
La Peau del'Ours, 252, 254
LA, Wanderlust to, 220
Labeling, Intellectual, 24
Labels,
   Giving verbal, 405
   Indistinguishable, 196
   Pedestrian, 382
   Reactionary, 164
Labor,
   Division of, 407
   Menial, 305
Lads, Yorkshire, 202
Lamp, Magic, 236
Land,
   Law of the, 408
   Promised, 4, 197
Landscape, Virgin, 329
Language,
   Art, 159, 296, 310, 341, 352, 379, 434
   Effect of visual, 296
   Human, 274, 308
   Limited, 296
   Lost, 297
   Mother of, 238
   Positive use of, 434
   Power of, 268
   Verbal, 296
   Written, 296
Lapse, Momentary, 129
Larger, Problems loom, 89
Largesse, Such anthropological, 114
Larry,
   Walking, 163
   Yogis, 202
   bowl, 175
Lascaux, 361
Latin, 213, 364, 376
Laundry-boat (See also Bateau-Lavoir), 250
Law,
   Discovery of the mathematical, 337
   Divine, 206
   Letter of the, 411
   mentality, 270
   Natural, 24, 186, 401
   Universal, 22, 62, 106, 113, 134, 186, 253, 263, 315, 391
   Wisdom of the, 322
Lawrence,
   Jacob, 328
   chair, 51
Laws,
   Mathematical, 369
   Natural, 182, 406
   Physical, 307
   Proof of metaphysical, 6
   Universal, 10, 85, 106
Lead-time, 137
Leaders, World, 236
Learning—noble pursuits, 305
Leather Shoes, 6, 435
Lee,
   Bruce, 393, 397-398
   Peggy, 315
Left-brain, Analytical, 323
Leftist cultural criticism—that whole array of idiocies, 326
Legacy, Unfortunate (See also Plato), 28
Legal Tender, 133, 219, 263, 281
Legend,
   Greek, 142, 269
   Urban, 93, 245, 251
Legend-monger, Principal (See also Jamie Sabartés), 247
Legends,
   Picasso, 248
   Urban, 256
Legname, Guild of the Arte di Pietra e, 367
Legwork, 163
Lemonade, Make, 412
Lens, Looking glass, 194
Leo, 98, 322, 345
Leonardo, da Vinci, 24, 212, 249-250, 283, 310, 366, 368-372, 380, 420
Les Demoiselles d'Avignon (See also Picasso), 190, 250, 329
'Lesser' cultures, 113
Lesson,
   Essential, 302
   Liberating, 380
   Object, 35, 49, 93, 118, 200, 208, 234, 255, 368, 380, 403, 424, 427
   Valuable, 10, 342
Lessons,
   Art, 154
   Life, 83, 220
   Valuable, 76, 379
Letdowns, 124, 161, 173, 315
Letters, Visual, 298
Lewis, C.S., 283
Level, André, 254
Leverage, Metaphysical, 113
Lexicon,
   Modern, 318
   Unique, 398
Liberation,
   Law of, 411
   Source of, 409
Liberties, Civil, 396
Liberty, 46, 86
Libraries, Largest personal (See also Oscar Janiger), 145
Lichtenberg, Georg C., 282
Lie, White, 234
Lies,
   Power, 112, 412
   Wisdom of Zen, 289
Life,
   Art-making, 162
   Authentic, 14, 21, 35, 40, 84, 135, 281, 331
   Author of A, 247
   Blueprint of, 146
   Daily, 362, 404
   Disappointments of, 40
   Empty, 322
   Everyday experience of, 184
   Evolution of, 105
   Existential quality of, 185
   Experience of, 38, 63, 184, 189, 197
   Experiencing, 102, 314
   Holistic experience of, 38
   Integrated holistic, 212
   Make sense of, 433
   Marvelous pictures of, 51
   Matter of, 144
   Miracle of, 323
   Mission of, 356
   Monastic, 117
   Ordinary scenes of, 373
   Our Lady of, 250-251
   Painful meaning of a, 322
   Quality of, 24, 63, 107-108, 131, 163, 185, 235, 276, 290, 319, 412
   Real, 322
   Reality of, 220
   Secrets of, 331
   Self-congratulatory, 97
   Sentient, 187
   Spirit of, 154
   Stimulus-response model of, 320
   Superficial, 220
   Temporal, 179
   The criticism of, 376
   Unique, 69
   Visual art, 3
   Well-integrated, 290
   magazine, 207
   of experiences—from exultation, 154
   mission, 68
   purpose, 127, 155, 386
Lifestyle, 222
Lifetime,
   Opportunity of a, 263
   Prolific, 251
Light, Speed of, 107, 177-179, 199-200, 321
Lights, Neon, 221
Lightspeed, Transcendental, 188
Limit, Cosmological speed, 177
Limitations,
   Box of self-imposed, 38
   of the small … orthodox scientist, 331
Limitless, 393, 435
Lincoln, Abraham, 331
Lion, MGM, 98
Liposuction, Metaphysical, 22-23
List,

Top of the, 137
Verboten, 398
Lists, Laundry, 382
Literacy, Alphabetic, 268
Literature, Visual, 297
Living, Acquire the, 352
Llotja, La (See also José Ruiz y Blasco), 248
Lodge, Sweat, 112
Logic, Internal, 108, 298, 339, 353
Lombardi,
    Lombardi (Italy), 369
    Vince, 318
London, Jack, 67
London's Royal Academy of Art, 133
Loner, Brilliant (See also Abraham Maslow), 316
Longing, Common, 165
López, María Picasso y, 254
Lord, 73-75, 94, 96, 147, 158, 220, 246, 285, 406
Lorde, Audre, 243
Loren, Sophia, 251
Lorenzini, Carlo (See also Carlo Collodi), 232
Lorenzo, de' Medici, 367, 370
Losing, 123, 142, 171, 173, 217, 255, 376, 386, 404, 411, 433-434
Lottery, Cosmic, 40, 357
Love,
    Biological phenomenon of, 377
    Express, 319
    Feeling of, 274
    Magic of, 238
    Ministry of (See also *Nineteen-Eighty-Four*), 45
    Nature of, 238
    Questions of, 213
    True, 10
    eternal art, 94
Lover, Art, 162, 171, 323
Loves, Lost, 68
Lower-caste, 409
Loyal, 10, 185, 212
Loyalty, Oath of, 366
LSD, Hallucinogenic properties of, 146
Lucas, George, 40, 52, 346
Lucidity, 282
Luck, 76, 151, 163, 165, 173, 212, 241, 260, 269, 302-303, 360
Luke,
    Annual feast of St, 370
    Apostle, 305
    Company of St, 367
Lunar, 188
Lund (See also *Wild Strawberries*), 322
Lure, Lurid, 222
Luster, Mirror-like, 273
Luxuries, Necessary, 375

M

M-theory, 181
M45 (See also Pleiades), 178
Machiavellian, 157, 377
Machinations, Pluralist, 114
Machine,
    Marvelous lifting, 368
    Organic, 336
    Publicity, 161
    Slaves in the, 336
    Time dilation, 195
Machinery, Aspect of the universal, 14
Macleish, Archibald, 410
Madhvacarya, 285
Madman, Work of a, 171
Madness, Everyday, 286
Madrid, 254
Magazine,
    Art, 4, 56
    Major, 16
Magic, Collective, 19
Magnifico (See also Lorenzo de' Medici), 370
Magnitude, Order of, 127, 182, 185
Mahabharata, 406
Mahakashyapa, O venerable (See also Mount of the Holy Vulture), 116
Maharshi, Sri Ramana, 6, 435
Mahavira (See also Jainism), 408
Mailer, Norman, 246, 250
Mainstream,
    Current values of the, 285
    Torrential conformity of the, 34
Maisel, Eric, 49, 69, 405
Major, C, 95
Majors, Art, 179
Make art, 112
Make-believe, Land of, 17
Maker, 17, 183, 308, 320, 381
Makeup, Psychological, 315
Making,
    Art, 17, 70, 170, 295, 323, 328, 348, 371-372, 376-377, 390, 420, 434
    Competitive crazy, 84
Málaga, City of, 246
Malibu, 22, 403
Mall, Strip (See also Albert Hofmann Foundation), 146
Malnourished, 343
Malnutrition, Spiritual, 212
Man,
    Black, 149
    Common, 64, 86
    Great enemies of, 409
    Honest, 171, 246, 345
    Ordinary, 289
    Pious, 94
    Real enemy of, 78
    Renaissance, 315
    Sacrifice of, 249
    School of, 424
    Tax, 34
    Universal archetypes of, 318
    antisocial behavior, 319
    conscious mind, 317
    hierarchy, 316
The Man Who Tasted Shapes (See also Richard Cytowic), 154
Mañach, Pedro, 252
Management, Crisis, 63

Manet, Édouard (See also *Déjeuner sur l'Herbe*), 374
Manhattan, 375, 424, 428
Manifestation,
    Divine, 227
    Inert, 360
    Neurotic, 97
    Psychological, 306
Manifestations, External, 409
Manifested—expressed, 377
Manifesto, Well-intentioned, 235
Manipulator, Media, 17
Mansions, Opulent, 114
Mantegna, 366
Mapplethorpe's Last Stand, 326
Mara (See also Bodhi tree), 74, 96
Marc, Franz, 375
Mare, Magnificent, 241
Mareym, Etienne-Jules (See also Motion picture camera), 191
Marina, 50, 273, 423
Marionette, Living, 235
Mark, Punctuation, 344
Market,
    Art, 140-142, 162, 330, 351, 371, 375-377
    Mass, 160, 372
    Out of the, 157
Marketers, Art, 165, 328, 330, 332
Marketing,
    Jungle of art, 153
    Tyranny of, 98
Marketplace, Art, 352
Markets,
    International, 140
    Specific art, 160
Marley, Bob, 131
Mars, 261
Marshal, Lone (See also Gary Cooper), 394
Marshmallows, 82, 348
Martyr (See also Gauguin), 67
Marxism, 326
Mascetti, Manuela Dunn, 116
Mask, Social, 102
Maslow, Abraham H., 41, 69, 97, 145, 188, 211, 289-290, 313-314, 316-318, 324-325, 331-332, 387
Masochists, 381
Mason, Fort, 50
Masons' guild, 368
Mass,
    Critical, 59, 109, 114, 197
    Power of, 192
Master,
    Aikido, 166
    Ascended, 82, 404
    Different, 345
    Esteemed, 113
    Silence of the, 116
    Words of the, 290, 407
    Zen, 112, 187-188, 286
    workshop, 249
Masterpiece, Cinematic (See also *Wild Strawberries*), 322
Masters, Zen, 115-117, 323-324

Materialism, Worship, 205
Materials, Mastery of, 365
Mathematics, Universal language of, 200
Matisse, Henri, 169, 256, 370, 375
Matrix,
    Invisible, 10, 403
    Irreducible, 183
    Manifesting, 411
    The (*film*), 138, 242
    The Divine, 263
Matter,
    Elemental relationship of, 181
    Heart of the, 29, 201
    Mystery of, 263
    Physical, 107
    Presence of, 192
    primordial, 147
    Redistribution of, 187
    Subatomic structure of, 183
Matters,
    Metaphysical, 433
    Spiritual, 363
    Temporal, 134, 412
Matthew, Louisa, 371
Maturity, Sign of, 234
Maugham, W. Somerset, 149
Mavens, 21, 341
Maxwell, James Clark (See also electromagnetism), 189
Maya (See also Lord of Illusion), 156, 344, 401
Mayan, 361
Maze, Out of a, 196
Mazzoni, Guido, 365
McCarthy, Senator Joseph, 396
McCully, Marilyn, 252
McLuhan, Marshall, 98
MCP (See also *Tron*), 336
Mead, Syd, 345-346
Meal, Nutritious, 22
Meandering, Cerebral, 75
Meaning,
    Access, 297
    Canvas of, 390
    Create, 315
    Giving, 4, 420
    'inkblot', 419
    Lasting, 220
    Personal, 363
    Precise, 225
    Questionable, 398
    Significant, 162
    Symbolic, 297
    Transcendental, 319
Meaningful coincidence (See also Synchronicity), 211
Measure,
    Equal, 86, 132
    artifacts of the Creator's consciousness, 183
Measures, Speculative, 345
Meat, Corrupt fresh, 63
Mecca, 205, 370
Mechanics, Quantum, 108, 147, 166, 176, 182-183, 187, 193, 402

Mechanism,
    Defense, 270
    Essential, 377
    Precise, 259, 410, 430
Mechanisms, Survival, 429
Media, Power of the, 235
Medicis, 24, 362, 367, 369-370
Meditation,
    Goal of, 405
    Proper, 117
Medium, 16, 43, 85, 98, 310, 355, 372, 380, 404
Melodrama, Self-induced, 280
Melpomene (See also Greek Muses), 305
Members, Communist, 396
Membership, Guild, 368-369
Memento, 395
Memories, 114, 163, 183
Memorizing, 55, 82, 429
Memory,
    Function of, 263
    Recent, 170, 325, 361, 381, 395
    Space-time experience of, 308
Men,
    Realm of, 321
    Richest of, 97
    Wise, 76, 338
Mentality,
    Herd, 228
    Victim, 283
Merchant, Art, 375
Merit, Everything of, 328
Merton, Thomas, 118
Mescaline, 145
Message,
    Recognizable, 15
    Specific, 297
    Subliminal, 141
    Timeless, 285
Messages, Mixed, 34
The Metamorphosis (See also Franz Kafka), 134
Metaneeds (See also Maslow), 289
Method, Scientific, 320
Methods,
    Hardwired, 34
    Verbal, 118
Mexican, 328
Michelangelo, 24, 327, 366, 368, 370-372, 380, 382
Michels, Caroll, 37, 165
Micro-ticks, 200
Micro-universe, 182-183
Midas, King, 40
Milkomeda, 202
Millennium, Equation of the, 181
Miller,
    Arthur I. (See also *Einstein, Picasso*), 147, 181-182
    Henry, 14, 50
Mind,
    Artifacts of the, 296
    Celtic, 132
    Circumstance of a prepared, 145
    Cosmic, 147, 307

    Freedom of, 115
    Function of the, 131
    Human, 316, 370
    Open, 4, 18, 165, 262, 281, 325
    Out of, 194
    Presence of, 263, 403
    Quiet, 112, 117, 134, 225
    Receptive, 307
    Researcher of the (See also Freud), 336
    Science of the interior, 318
    Self-important aspect of the, 37, 427
    Society of, 336
    Student of the, 145
    Subconscious, 147
    Temporal success of the, 283
    Theory of the, 319, 337
    Unconscious, 317-318, 336
Mind-boggling, 178
Mind-numbing, 41
Mindless, 44, 67, 87, 103, 106, 114, 205, 267-268, 270, 307, 393
Mindlessly, Life lived, 34
Minds,
    Small, 159
    Subconscious, 393
Mindset,
    Positive, 81
    Western, 361
Minimalism, 326
Minimalist, 14, 190, 344
Minsky, Marvin, 336
Miracles, 186, 314, 323, 357
Miró, Joan, 108, 342
Mirror,
    Magic, 102, 186, 201
    Mirror, 349
Misery, Human, 376
Misinformation, 106, 113, 141, 166, 255, 279, 313, 332
Mission,
    Aborted, 315
    Inherent, 17
    Intrinsic, 429
    Reconnoitering, 173
    Scouting, 330
    Stated, 40
    Unwavering sense of, 382
Mistakes, 9, 38, 44, 67, 83, 126, 144, 151, 261, 268, 299, 319, 325, 386, 420, 423
Misuse, Inherent dangers of, 279
Mitchell, Joni, 231
Mix, Transcendental trail, 428-429
Mnemosyne (See also Greek Muses), 305
'Mob' of art buyers, 213
Mobility, Social, 366, 408
Model,
    Academy, 372-373
    Major, 371
    MFA, 382
    Poor, 63
    Revolutionary, 181
Modem, 262
Moderation, Path of (See also Middle Path), 74
Modernism, Milestone of, 329

Modes, Sensory, 377
Modifier, Object of a, 23, 275, 345
Mogul (See also Harry Cohn), 395
Mom, 291, 423
Moment,
    Aesthetic, 155, 331, 421
    Awareness, 13, 149
    Circumstance of the, 263
    Defining, 102, 399
    Personal aesthetic, 331
    Predilections of the, 332
    Primordial, 363
    Transcendental, 116, 119
    Transitory, 5, 129
    Truth of the, 55, 77, 132, 134, 149, 166
    Zen, 78
Moments,
    Scary, 232
    Seminal, 16
Momentum, 4, 39, 111, 178, 201, 356, 372
Mona Lisa, 138-139, 351
Mondrian, Piet, 16
Monet, Claude, 201, 361, 419
Money,
    Desperate need of, 171
    Easy, 221
    Expensive, 221
    Face, 219
    Flow of, 153
    Lot of, 254
    Out of, 133
    Plenty of, 221
    Substantial, 377, 385
    Throw, 133, 160
Monk, 113, 241-242
Monkey, Trained, 96
Monologist, Inner, 90, 261
Monologue, Incessant, 121, 132
Monster, Green-eyed (See also Iago), 158
Montmartre, 250, 254
Men & Monuments (See also Janet Flanner), 375
Mood, Public, 164
Moolah, Matter of, 133
Moonchild, 386
Moor (See also *Othello*), 158
Morpheus, Mysterious (See also film, *The Matrix*), 242
Morrissey, Thomas J. (See also *Pinocchio Goes Postmodern*), 232
Mosaic, Cosmic, 147
Moscow, Post-Stalinist, 15
Mother,
    Protective, 82
    Teresa, 160
Motion,
    Expression of, 191
    Laws of, 150, 176
    Measurement of, 179
    Perpetual, 125, 186
    Science of, 368
    picture camera—film, 191
Motion Pictures, 193, 395
Motivated, 45, 68, 188, 245-247, 289, 297, 306, 316, 319, 345, 356, 367-368, 404, 408
Motivation, Innovative view of human, 325
Motivational, Self-induced, 86
Motivations, External, 86
Motive,
    Preeminent, 159
    Questionable, 197
    Specific, 15
    Ulterior, 39
Motives, Egocentric, 94
Motors, Polyphase AC, 125
Mougins (See also Notre-Dame-de-Vie), 251
Moulin Rouge, 252, 254
Movement,
    Art, 190, 326, 328
    Expressionism, 22, 201, 419
    Expressionist, 396
    Formal, 348
    Roots of the most influential art, 190
    of art-for-art's-sake, 371
Movements,
    Art, 326, 331-332, 374
    Avant-garde art, 374
    Various art, 331
Moviegoers, 395
Movies, 160, 219, 235, 390, 395
Mozart, Wolfgang Amadeus, 93-98, 171, 273, 342
Mudras (See also Herman Hesse), 263
Multiverses, 108
Munich, University of, 337
Munson, Lynne, 98, 326, 380
Muralists, Mexican, 328
Murer, Eugène, 379
Muse,
    Allegorical nature of the, 305
    Dedicated, 364
    Fickle, 86, 306
Muses, Greek, 305
Museum,
    British, 297
    Getty, 375
    Prestigious, 90
    Space, 283
    Transformation of the art, 326
Music,
    Classical, 93, 98
    Gift of, 94
    Love of, 94
    Study, 96
    Traditional, 95
Musicians, 21, 96, 146
Musicology, 21, 325
Mutt, R. (See also Porcelain Urinal), 420
Muybridge, Eadweard, 191
Muzak, 93, 98, 273-274, 342
Myopia, Self-interest, 158
Mystery,
    Marvelous, 297
    Woman of, 15
Myth,
    Modern, 380
    Muses of, 305
    Pathological, 207
    of too many' artists, 165
    don José's renunciation, 249
Mythology,
    Confirmation of a universal, 434
    Greek, 215, 306
Myths, Spurious, 68

N

Nader, Ralph, 315
Names, Different art pen, 361
Nanotechnology, 416
Napoleon, French Emperor III, 374
NASA, 191
National Book Award, 33
Nature,
    Brilliant simplicity of Buddha, 117
    Capturing, 372
    Copying, 274
    Dual, 193
    Essential, 276
    Force of, 107, 125, 192, 200, 313, 375, 409
    Forces of, 188, 405
    Intrinsic, 16
    Laws of, 198
    Metaphysical, 390
    Mother, 179, 185, 401
    Primordial, 324
    Provocations of, 178
    Realization of the true, 285
    Realm of, 324
    Scientific study of human, 319
    Seeming chaos of, 364
    Transcendental, 194, 404
    Underlying secrets of, 186
    Unique, 27
    blueprint, 108
    law, 108, 173
Navaho, 328, 361
Naysayers, 37, 55, 83, 323
Nazi, 320
Neanderthal, 361
Nebbish, Misanthropic, 141
Necessities, Biological, 315
Necessity,
    Creation blossoms out of, 289
    Individual, 284
    Jury-rigged out of, 133
    Unconventional by, 86
Neck, Artistic, 69
Need, Inner, 226, 328
Needle, Eye of, 10, 171, 197
Needs, The Dynamic of, 313
Negativity,
    Destructive power of, 75
    Pitfalls of, 144
    Psychic, 128
    Side effects of, 402
    Thwart, 31
Neo ... *The Matrix*, 242-243
Neoplatonist, 370
Nepotism, 303
Netherlands, 123, 370
Neurons, Network of, 341

Neuroscience, 154
Neuroscientist, 260
Neuroses, 318-319
Neutrality, Sense of, 406
Neutrinos, 182
Neutrons, 181
New York City, 4, 22, 137, 172, 201, 301-302, 396, 419
The New
   York Times, 163, 396
   Yorker, 23
Newman, Barnett, 22, 328
Newspeak (See also *Nineteen-Eighty-Four*), 44
Newton, Isaac, 45, 176-177, 192-193, 254, 310
Newtonian, 178, 192
Nicholson, Jack, 145
Nicotine, Stimulants of, 246
Nietzsche, Friedrich, 35
Nihilism, Varieties of, 326
Nin, Anaïs, 145, 234
Nineteen-Eighty-Four (See also George Orwell), 44
Nirvana, Inner journey toward, 147
Nobel Prize, 145, 188
Noble, 74-75, 280, 305, 322, 325
Noblemen, Privileged daughters of, 365
Non-attachment, The Law of, 29, 107, 127-128, 246, 255, 286, 315, 322, 401-404, 406-407, 409, 411-412, 434
Non-material (See also Intuition), 185
Non-threatening, 291, 347
Non-whining, 416
Nonpathology—psychologically healthy people, 324
Nonrepresentational, 341, 361
Nonsense,
   Ego, 307
   Pile of symbolic, 298
   Subjective, 160
Nonverbal, 405
Normality, Nature of, 324
Nose-growings, Irrepressible (See also *Pinocchio Goes Postmodern*), 234
Nothing, Value of, 34, 343
Notion,
   Crazy, 386
   Romantic, 86
Notions—attachments, 405
Notre-Dame-de-Vie (See also Mougins), 250-251
Nourishment, Spiritual, 157
Nouveau, Art, 326
Nuance, Sense of, 389
Nude Descending (See also Duchamp), 191
Number, Metaphorical, 14
Numbers, Prime, 200
Numerology, Hebrew, 87
Nuts, 165

O

Object,
   Speed of an, 177

Three-dimensional, 369
Objects,
   Complementary, 192
   Valued, 367
Obligation, Social, 197
Observation,
   Astute, 253
   Baffling, 177
   Brilliant, 269
   Function of, 184
   Personal, 122
   Truth of an, 109
Observations, Astute, 326
Observer,
   Astute, 301
   Social, 259
Obsession, 226, 290, 382
Obsessive, 132, 226
Obstacles,
   Apparent, 39
   Cycle of, 40
   Overcoming, 18
Obvious—one dangerous word, 269
Oceania (See also *Nineteen-Eighty-Four*), 44
O'Conner, Patricia, 259
O'Donohue, John, 131, 286, 355
Odds, Insurmountable, 281
Odyssey, Perilous, 290
Oedipus Complex, 317
Offense, Smart, 77
Ohm,
   Georg Simon, 337
   law, 337
Oil, Technique of, 372
Okudzhava, Bulat, 15
Old Testament, 268
Oller, Josep, 254
Om, 287, 337
One,
   Awakened, 87, 96
   Enlightened, 74
Open air—*en plein air*, 373
'Open markets', 371
Operas, Writing (See also Salieri), 95
Opinion,
   Personal, 253, 270
   Public, 35, 162, 207, 359
   Sharp tongues of, 69
   Tyranny of public, 207
Opinions,
   Sea of, 342
   Taking anonymous, 173
   of focus groups, 160
Opportunities,
   Creating new, 127
   Experience of, 398
   Toward better, 129
Opportunity,
   Art and, 96
   Rare, 430
   Saw, 398
   Superior, 411
Optimism,
   False, 38
   Shavian, 349

Organization,
   Art sales, 141
   Giving, 161
   Nonprofit, 146
Orientations, Prisoners of ancient, 268, 296
Origins,
   Organic, 381
   Viewpoint of the, 190
Origins of the Species, 105
Orland, Ted (See also *Art & Fear*), 342
Orwell, George, 44
Orwellian, 129
Oscars, 98
Othello, 158
Otherness, 132
Otherworldly, 133, 200
Out,
   Looking, 319
   of
      control—a mental state, 290
      harm's, 77
      ignorance—yours, 206
      towners', 73-74
Outcaste, 279, 280
Outcome,
   Potential, 184
   Precise, 29, 411
   Predefined, 139
   Specific, 6, 196, 231, 407
   Unwelcome, 269
Outside, Problems, 317
Outsider, 337, 348-349, 361, 381-382
Overexposure, 269, 351
Overwhelmed, 183, 291
Ovid, 143
Oxford, 173
Oz, 145-147, 234

P

Pablo's (See also Picasso)
   love, 248
   sense of self-worth, 255
   sister (See also Conchita), 247
Pablum, Media, 212
Packets, Discrete energy, 189
Pacific Ocean, 343
Padua, 369, 372
Pain,
   Lots of, 292
   Self-inflicted, 40, 411
   Sufferings of, 40
   Surface of, 218
   Waste, 411
Painter,
   Alfred, 270
   Artist or, 380
   Court portrait, 95
   Expressionist, 301
   Florentine, 249
   House, 189, 262
   Master, 198, 301, 357
   Spanish Surrealist, 342
   Sunday, 378
Painters,

Cave, 274
Patron saint of (See also Apostle Luke), 305
Prehistoric, 361
Painting (See also Emile de Antonio), 22, 345, 419
Pair, Mother-infant, 377
Paleolithic, 274, 363, 373
Palette,
    Cosmic, 406
    Cultured, 275
    of the month, 206
Pallarés, Manuel, 248
Pan, Peter, 237
Panacea, Sea of, 126
Pandering, Shameless, 160
Pandora, Greek legend of, 269
Pantheon, Sisters of the (See also Greek Muses), 305
Papacy, Absolute power of the, 45
Paparazzi, 409
Parables, Modern, 242
Paradigms, New-old, 326
Paradise, Island, 67
Paradox, Classic twin, 178
Parameters, Mission, 41, 59, 201
Paranoid, 77
Paratichi, 369
Paris' Left Bank, 51
Parisian, 252
Park, Cosmic, 199
Parmeshwara, 183
Parsecs, Rejection many, 202
Particle,
    Elementary, 261
    Sub-atomic, 76
Particles,
    Different elementary, 261-262
    Individual, 193
    Subatomic, 108, 181, 330
Partisan, 61, 260, 394-395
Parton, Dolly, 351
Party,
    Communist, 396
    Rejecting, 55
Passage, Rite of, 67, 220, 236, 284
Passion,
    Experience of, 318
    Meaning of, 134
    Ruthless, 165
    Spontaneous, 390
    love of life, 338
Passive-aggressive, 270
Passivity of 'wishing', 238
Pasteur, Louis, 242
Path,
    Dharma, 279, 284
    Enlightened, 74, 321
    Golden, 322, 428
    Middle, 74-75, 77, 170, 321
    Spiritual, 24
Pathology, 69, 331
Pathos, 129, 205, 208, 251, 377
Paths, Different, 346
Pathway, Direct, 147

Pathways, Literary, 115
Patience, Relative, 6, 41, 308
Patriarchy, 268
Patron,
    Medici, 370
    Potential, 56
    Single, 159, 380
Patrons,
    Cadre of, 212
    Pleasing, 24
    Warhol art, 164
Pattern of causation, 322
Patterns,
    Destructive, 194
    Different resonant vibrational, 261
    Predictable, 160
Patton, George S., 23, 89
Pavia, 367
Payback, Eventual, 95
Peace,
    Make, 40, 235
    Sense of, 207
Pecking,
    Combative, 397
    order of art—art schools, 382
Penrose, Roland, 248
Pension, Security of a, 284
Pentimento, 24
People,
    Bullying, 63
    Creative, 396
    Everyday, 15
    Healthiest, 331
    Intelligent, 49, 361
    Lower-caste, 409
    Malevolent, 260
    Media, 236
    Pliable mind of the, 235
    Rich, 236
    Self-actualizing, 317
    Study healthy, 316
    Successful, 284
    Three dimensional, 190
    Village, 241
    We The, 46
Peoples,
    Ancient, 181
    Aryan, 408
Perceived—like truth, 183
Perception,
    Holy grail of ultimate, 107
    Intuitive, 82, 227
    Linear, 395
    Structure of human, 296
    Talent of, 301
Perceptions, Critical, 235
Perceptual, Measure of, 419
Perfection,
    False god of, 332
    Icons of, 126
    Mortal, 25
    Seeking, 102
Peril, 61-64, 109, 232
Period,
    Classic Greek, 181

    Classical, 95
    Late
        medieval, 366
        Paleolithic, 363, 373
    Rose (See also Picasso), 253, 351
Persist, 81, 305, 357, 405
Persistence, Unfaltering, 27
Person,
    Ethical, 233
    Excuses of every, 13
    Obstinate, 128
    Persistent, 140
    Self-actualized, 318, 325
    Sinful, 316
    Virtuous, 316
    character, 307-308, 319, 433
'Persona non grata', 378
Personality,
    False mask of, 25, 37, 64, 86, 197, 356
    Motivation &, 316
    Psychological examination of, 419
Perspiration, 34, 125
Peru, 68
Pestalozzi, Johann Heinrich, 185
Petals, 156
Peter, Laurence J., 291
Pettiness, 64, 95, 97, 124, 195, 201, 259, 429
Phenomena,
    Physical, 319
    Recent media-spawned, 315
Phenomenon,
    Cultural, 346
    Organic, 377
    Unexplained, 194
Philips, Eric, 81
Phillpotts, Eden, 232
Philosopher, Transcendental, 406
Philosophies, Eastern, 112
Philosophy,
    A system of, 25
    Eastern, 118
    Practical, 406
    Professors of, 22
    Sensible like Zen, 228
Phony, 317
Photographs, Rare, 375
Photons, Stream of, 193
Phrase, Trite, 269
Physicist,
    Heroine, 183, 187
    Iconoclastic, 193
    Nobel prize-winning (See also Francis Crick), 188
Physicists,
    Modern, 193
    Theoretical, 180, 186
Physics,
    Art &, 150, 175, 180
    Holy grail of advanced, 181
    Laws of, 150, 416
    Modern, 45, 176, 181, 187
    Newtonian, 178, 192
    Particle, 181
    Professor of, 200, 337
    Quantum, 175, 183-184, 261

Symmetry of, 186
Theoretical, 108, 175, 182-183, 188, 307, 402
Pianist, Jazz, 284
Picasso,
    Anthology, 252
    Film, 250-251, 275
    María, 254
    Mystery of, 146, 250, 275
    Pablo, 179, 181, 189, 232, 245, 251, 255, 275, 329, 374, 383, 396, 420
    Portrait of, 246
    Rite of Pigeons, 247-248
    Talk to the Driver, 250
    art, 73, 249
    Blue Period, 253
    bull, 345
    business, 254
    contribution, 256
    death, 247, 251
    Demoiselles, 190
    difficulties, 251
    enthusiasm, 254
    first show, 252
    innovations, 256
    last words, 256
    life, 245
    memorable portrait of Vollard, 253
    monumental struggles, 190
    motivations, 254
    Rose Period, 351
Picture,
    Cosmic, 201
    Larger, 90
    Road, 322
    Whole, 115
Pie, Slice of the art, 378
Piece,
    Integrity of the, 108
    Outcome of a, 412
Piero, 366-367
Pietra, 367
Pigeon of the Year, 248
Pigments, Natural mineral, 362
'Pinch' of talent (See also Picasso), 256
Pinewood (See also *Pinocchio*), 236
Pinocchio,
    Adaptation of, 238
    Author of, 234
    Disney animated feature of, 231
    Existential, 231, 238, 282
    The Adventures of, 232, 237
    greatest ambition, 235
    Heirs, 236
    nose, 232, 234
Pinocchio Goes Postmodern, 232
Pioneer, 9, 144, 289
Pissarro,
    Camille, 374, 378
    headstrong pupil (See also Gauguin), 379
Pit, Snake, 141
Pitch, Savvy, 157
Pitfall of *obvious*—my verboten word, 119
Place,
    Quiet, 27

Right, 211, 246
Plagiarism—scarcely, 369
Plan, Cosmic, 262
Planck, Max (See also Quantum theory), 189, 193
'Planck length' sized bard, 126
Planet,
    Forbidden, 393
    Motion of the, 192
    of the Apes, 257
Planets, United Federation of, 199
Plank, Walking the, 207-208
Plasma, Metaphysical, 285
Plato, 28, 106, 156
Player,
    Proper stature of an astute, 380
    Seasoned poker, 81
    Worthy, 201
Pleiades, 178
Pleistocene, 363
Pliers, Retro-technology of, 176
Plots, Nefarious, 263, 307
Poe, Edgar Allan, 68, 123
Poet,
    Revered Soviet-era (See also Bulat Okudzhava), 15
    Dante Alighieri's, 213
    'unhelpful', 126
Poetry,
    Lyric, 305
    Sacred, 305
    Shortest form of (See also Haiku), 115
    Visual, 297
Pointless, 90, 117, 131, 147, 194, 355
Poison—Do Not Drink, 45, 83
Police, 403
Policewoman, 402
Politicized, 17, 320, 395
Politics,
    Product of, 375
    Radical, 254
Pollock,
    Jackson, 189, 201, 206, 208, 317-318, 327-328, 363, 374, 419
    Sole invention of, 189
    demons—bipolar, 207
    magnetic ether, 328
Pollyanna, 277, 313
Polyhymnia (See also Greek Muses), 305
Polynesia, 67
Pomeranian, 302
Pool, Swimming, 222
Pop Art—a style of art, 164
Pope,
    Pope, 96, 247, 370
    Alexander, 363
Population, Avant-garde, 51
Porcelain Urinal (See also Duchamp), 344, 420
Portuguese, 407
Position,
    Adversarial, 122
    Functional, 420
    Specious, 114
    Superior, 375

Possibilities,
    Field of all, 40, 119, 256, 309, 343, 360, 371, 398, 434
    Polar opposite theoretical, 176
    Realm of, 189
    Universe of all, 77
Possibility, Infinite, 108
Post-911, 58
Post-Impressionism, 29
Post-Impressionist, 67
Post-impressionists, Successor of the (See also Picasso), 252
Posterity's
    domain, 97
    art establishment, 351
Postmodernism, 326-327
Posture, Correct, 37, 427
Pousette-Dart, 169
Power,
    AC, 124-125
    Apparent, 221
    Comprehension fuels, 391
    Electrical, 125
    Emancipating, 129
    Expression of spiritual, 369
    Feeling of quiet gentle, 291
    Higher, 324, 406
    Innate, 260
    Invincible, 109
    Lack of, 62
    Marks of, 375
    Positions of overt, 63
    Potential, 82
    Rules of engagement, 61
    Source of, 375
    Timeless, 186
    Wild, 398
    Will, 63, 213, 321, 356
The Power of Intention, 335
Power's
    seductive heat, 63
    life force, 106
Powerbrokers, 379
Powerless, Feeling, 62
Powers, Semidivine, 370
Practical Exercises In English, 25
Practicality, 255
Practices,
    Esoteric, 325
    Occult, 318
Prayer, External artifacts of, 263
Preconditions, Self-limiting, 85
Predictions, Accurate, 177
Predisposition, Inherited, 285
Prefabricated 'cutting edge', 328
Prehistoric, 43, 361-362
Prejudice, Ancient, 305
Prejudices, Self-serving, 246
Premise, Magical, 236
Premodern, 359
Premonitions, 386
Preoccupation, Unhealthy, 226
Presidio, 50
Pressfield, Steven, 335, 397
Pressure,

Self-imposed psychological, 228
Self-induced inorganic, 343
Social, 28
of the 'what have you,' 191
Pressures,
    Cultural, 10
    External, 226
    Social, 144
Prestige, Academic, 160
Priceless, 283, 351, 391, 423
Prices, Substantial, 253
Pride, False, 63
Primavera, La (See also Botticelli), 370
Prime, Metaphysical, 200
'Primitive' cultures, 363
Princess, Trojan, 142
Princeton, 200, 403
Principle, Indivisible, 111
Principles,
    Egalitarian, 114
    Physical, 185
Printmaking, 371
Printing Press (See also Johannes Gutenberg), 372
Privilege, Life of, 74, 321
Prize,
    Booby, 102-103, 435
    Prestigious Newdigate, 173
Prizes, Winning, 327
Problem,
    Core of every, 127
    Existential, 91
    Major, 217
    Mathematical, 189
Problems,
    Laundry list of the, 142
    Realm of, 127
    Seeming absence of, 142
    Spiritual, 324
    Torrent of, 90
Problems, 219
Process,
    Art, 17, 227
    Creative, 227, 310
    Evolutionary, 17, 181, 308
    Intuitive, 260, 309
    Rational, 306
    Unconscious, 318, 328
    Value of the, 347
Processes,
    Cognitive, 419
    Mental, 319
Prodigy,
    Adult, 302
    Brilliant little, 96
    Child, 98
Professor, Art, 28, 172-173, 371
Professors of esthetics—and artists, 22
Proffering, 189
Program, Evil Master Control (See also *Tron*), 336
Programmer, 242, 336
Programming,
    Reality, 4
    Subliminal, 238
Television, 235
Programs, Spiritual, 132
Promethean, 125-126
Prometheus, 290
Pronouns, 11, 43, 106
Proof,
    Function of, 323
    Indisputable, 6
    Material, 23
    Out of, 38
    Want, 18
    of the Creator's existence, 183
Propaganda,
    Insidious, 284
    Subversive, 396
Propagation, Mere, 186
Properties,
    Physical, 390
    Quantifiable, 180
    Unusual, 367
Prophecy,
    Art of, 142
    Self-fulfilling, 34, 284
Proportion, Direct, 150, 175, 262-263, 275, 307, 401, 403, 416, 429
Proposition, 154, 316
'Prose-water', 124, 127
Proselytizing, 106
Protégé, 386
Proteins, Right, 22
Protoartists, 361-362, 373
Protons, 181
Proust, Marcel, 264
Proverb,
    Hasidic, 21
    Jewish, 219
    Zen, 109, 326
Providence, 162, 217-218, 286
Prowess,
    Intuitive, 115
    Physical, 404
Pseudoscience, 318
Psyche,
    British, 46
    Cosmic, 102, 309, 410, 434
    Human, 318, 336
    Mediator of the, 21
    Pain of the, 35, 404
    Personal, 309, 410
Psychiatrists, 144, 260, 316, 419
Psychoanalysis, Freudian, 318
Psychoanalyst, 323
Psychoanalyzing, 324
Psychodiagnostik (See also Hermann Rorschach), 419-421
Psychology,
    Behavior school of, 323
    Direction, 316
    Experimental, 318
    Goal of, 319
    Humanistic (See also Maslow), 27, 69, 314, 324-325
    Inherent, 290
    Mainstream, 316
    Professor of (See also William James), 156, 408
    Programs of, 132
The Psychology of Science (See also Maslow), 313-314, 324
Psychopathological, 314
Public Relations, 219-220, 351
Public's
    attention, 159
    fancy, 157
    perception of art, 313
Publisher,
    Mainstream, 3
    agreement, 160
Publishers, Art, 127, 160
Pulleys, Advanced engineering system of (See also Brunelleschi), 368
Pumping, Strength of character, 201
Pumping, Adrenaline, 39
Punctuation, Rules of, 218
Pupil, Apt, 281
Puppet,
    Perils of a (See also *Pinocchio Goes Postmodern*), 232
    Story of a (See also *The Adventures of Pinocchio*), 232
    The Persistent (See also Rebecca West), 236
    nose, 234
Puppy, Lost, 250
'Pure' science, 200, 319
Purgatory, Isle of (See also *The Divine Comedy*), 213
Purity, Unspoiled, 123
The Purloined Letter, 68, 123
Purpose,
    Affirm Your, 33, 35
    Conscious, 123, 389
    Eternal flame of, 86
    Expressed, 13, 103
    Inherent freedom of, 196
    Inner perception of, 29
    Larger, 424
    Positive, 221
    Sense of, 409
    Sole, 30
    Sterility of, 186
    Ultimate, 14
    Unique, 281
    Unparalleled satisfaction of, 34
Purse, Power of the, 220
Pursuits, Cerebral, 275
Purveyor of the 'too many' artists myth, 165
Pushcart's Complete Rotten Reviews & Rejections, 33
Pyramid, Great, 193

Q

Quaker, 394
Qualities, Indivisible, 82
Quality,
    Beauty of, 430
    Essential, 128, 169, 289
    Film noir, 236
    Indicator of, 165

'Quality' of life, 24, 63, 107-108, 131, 163, 185, 235, 276, 290, 319, 412
Quality,
 Spirit of, 290, 361
 of Salieri's music, 97
Quanta, Energy packets of, 193
Quanta-extractor, 182
Quantifiable effect, 411
Quantification, Scientific, 290
Quantum, 108, 126, 147, 166, 175-176, 182-184, 187, 189, 193, 261, 307, 337, 402, 417
Quarks, Subatomic realm of, 183
Quest, Cultural, 343
Question,
 Core, 69
 Fundamental, 127, 166
 Preeminent, 306
 Quintessential, 274
 Real, 221, 352
 Red herring of a, 107
 Right, 181, 321
 Standing, 330
 Vanguard, 321
 Wrong, 164
Questions,
 Fundamental, 69, 274
 Hard, 379
 Two fundamental, 274
 Understanding of the core, 171
 Valid, 308
 Witness, 197
 Wrong, 197
'Quiet desperation', 106, 276, 322
Quinn,
 Edward, 250-251
 film, 252, 255

R

R-mode, Perceptual, 404-405
Rabbit, White, 242
Race,
 Collective purpose of the human, 127
 Discovery of a long extinct super intelligent, 393
Rachmaninoff, Sergey, 273
Rain, Acid, 201
Rainbows, Chasing, 27
Raison d'etre (See also Dharma), 279, 350
Ramanuja, 285
Rand,
 Archie, 311
 Ayn, 301
Raphael, 371
Raschid, 297
Rashomon (See also Akira Kurosawa), 107, 395
Rationalization—the endless onionskin of excuses, 68
Ravena (See also Oscar Wilde), 173
'Razor's edge', 40, 220
Reaction,
 Direct, 123
 Knee-jerk, 201
 Visceral, 75
Readymades, 189, 344-345, 420-421
Reaffirm, 90, 434
'Real' artists, 238
Real,
 Everyday sense of, 395
 estate mogul's private art collection, 343
 pictorial 'three-dimensional' space, 369
 thing—art, 347
Realists, 245, 374
Reality,
 Absolute, 118
 Cocreate material, 403
 Consensus, 34
 Divining temporal, 316
 Essence of, 180
 Experience of, 268
 Freeform, 283
 Future of, 191
 Illusion of, 330, 369
 Magic, 24
 Mainstream perception of, 189
 Material, 17, 138, 194, 285, 342, 403, 434
 Nature of, 180
 Objective, 186
 One reliable, 113
 Pattern of, 194
 Penetration of, 38
 Perceived, 242
 Physical, 176, 282, 285, 393
 Reevaluating, 40
 Revelations of, 147
 Revision of, 118
 Truth of, 321
 Ultimate, 183
 Virtual, 336
Realized, Fully, 37, 64, 85, 109, 111, 156-157, 161, 228, 309, 313-314, 331-332, 336, 338, 360, 402, 427
Realm,
 Authentic, 219
 Material, 281
 Metaphysical, 17-18, 339, 353
 Physical, 184, 227
 Power of the metaphysical, 18
 Transcendent, 186
 of 'predictability', 323
Reason,
 Radiance of, 313
 Spokesmen of, 301
 concept, 282
Reasoning process ... Intuitive insights, 260
Reassurance, Need of chronic, 357
Reborn—the transmigration of the soul, 134
Receiver/sender, 262
Receiving, 4, 68, 137, 163, 192, 254, 395
Recognition,
 Passive instant, 421
 Seductive morsel of, 67
'Recollections', 29-30, 232, 253
Reconnoiter, 63
Recovery, Risk and, 52
Red Herrings, 26, 107, 141, 196-197, 320, 345
Red pen—a glorious A, 218
'Red Scare' (See also HUAC), 395
Redemption, Artistic, 213
Reductionism, Sweet spot of, 183
Refinement,
 Emasculating, 375
 Sign of, 234
Reflection, Symbolic, 307
Reflex, Mindless, 114
Reggae, 51
Regions, Infernal, 213
Regret, 126, 166, 172, 247, 281, 299, 320, 322, 386
Rehearsal, Dress, 55, 67
Reincarnation, Gates of, 279
Reinterpretation, Inventive, 237
Rejected, Room of the (See also Salon des Refusés), 374
Rejection,
 Act of, 37
 Angst of, 14, 402
 Confident attitude toward, 23
 Counterbalance, 315
 Crippled by, 285
 Crosshairs of, 107
 Defy, 317
 Different levels of, 156
 Dynamic of, 411
 Experience, 153, 391
 Face of, 109, 175
 Feelings of, 187-188
 Handling, 30
 Hard face of, 109
 Hosing, 428
 Hurt of, 28
 Impact of, 68
 Inviting, 381
 Issue of, 156
 Larger world of, 165
 Mastering, 5
 Momentary, 195
 Occasions of, 428
 Piercing thorns of, 156
 Pool of critical, 153
 Poor, 91
 Psychology of, 117
 Receiving end of, 395
 Route, 194
 Smart action of, 218
 Solitary angst of, 402
 Subject of, 5, 123
 Tackling, 44
 Tempered, 218-219
 Thorns of, 156, 428
 Throes of, 109, 320, 347
 Tiers of, 68, 153, 167
 Trenches of, 172
 View such, 16
 Word, 27
 Words of, 67
 cohort, 178
 Relative, 433
Rejections, Transitory, 18, 173
Relationship,
 Astounding, 176

Codependent, 21
Eternal, 285
Intimate, 14
Mind-body, 259
Personal, 412
Restrictive medieval, 367
Simplest form of a non-attached, 406
Relationships,
    Mathematical, 180
    Specific spatial, 405
Relativist, Cultural, 113-114
Relativity,
    Special Theory of, 176, 178
    Theory of General, 177, 182, 191, 195
Relic, Alien spaceship (See also Ridley Scott), 132-133
Remarks, Ad hominem, 129
Rembrandt, 163, 361, 375
Renaissance,
    Early Italian, 367
    Late, 372
    Technique of, 369
Renderings, Ingenious, 346
Renunciation, Story of, 248
Repeating, Worth, 87, 406
Repercussions, Insidious, 321
Repertoire, 51, 84, 270
Reprehensible concept in art, 159
Representation, Symbolic, 361
Representational, 274, 328
Reproductions, 5, 160, 276, 434
Republic, Florentine, 370
Reputation, Posthumous, 17
Research,
    Brain, 404
    Pure, 15
    Result of original, 13
    Scientific, 317
Researchers, 175, 177, 323, 336
Residue, karmic, 4, 78, 197, 281
Resistance
    / distraction The Usual Suspects, 335
    Organic, 335
    Unit of electrical, 337
Resolve, 38, 64, 75, 128, 144, 177, 185, 329, 359, 430
Resonates, 141, 434
Resources, Art funding, 161
Response,
    Direct, 82
    Right, 55, 62, 102, 123
    Spontaneous, 124
    Visceral, 270
    Winning, 201
Responses, Proper, 55
Responsibilities, Serf-like, 407
Responsibility,
    Personal, 116, 320
    Taking, 234, 389
    With awareness comes, 391
Restlessness, 322
Result, Direct, 9, 26, 37, 44, 81, 84, 129
Revelation,
    Psychic, 325
    Solo, 273

Revelations, Future, 10
Reverence, Equal, 320
The Revision of Vision (See also S.I. Hayakawa), 296
Revivalist, 318
Revolts, 408
Revolutionary, 180-181, 184
Revolutions, Purges of cultural, 281
Reward,
    Inherent, 180
    Material, 219
'Reward'
    system of favors, 252
Rewards, 4, 38-40, 127, 170, 290, 357, 403
Rhetoric—an effective technique, 200
Rhythm,
    Out of, 286
    Pounding, 401
    Sense of, 286
Rhythms,
    Ancient, 285-286
    Meaningful, 377
Richardson, John, 247, 252
Richter, Adele, 225
Riddle,
    Zen (See also Koan), 404
    Zen-like, 184
Right,
    connections, 379
    hands, 133, 330
    opportunity, 82
    Sense of, 317
    words, 58
Rightdoing, 198, 397
Rinzai (See also Different Schools of Zen), 117
Risk, Result of, 29
Risks,
    Brilliant, 95
    Taking, 205
Rivalry,
    Petty, 62
    Sibling, 317
Roadkill, Potential, 292
Robes, Well-worn, 77
Rod, Divining, 232, 310
Rodin, Auguste, 125
Roethke, Theodore, 141
Rogers, Will, 292
'Rogue's
    gallery' featuring, 381
    glossary' of linguistic felons, 269
Role,
    Lead, 22, 126
    Leading, 89, 290
    Significant, 162, 366
Role-play, 122
Roles, Structure of social, 408
Rolling Stones, 401
Romans, 206, 364, 369, 373
Romance, 232, 274
Romania, 423
Romantic, 86, 95, 273, 305
Rome, 364

Roof, 75, 107, 319
Room,
    Make, 128, 410
    Plenty of, 165, 190, 197, 416
    Still ample maneuvering, 261
    Working the, 94
Roosevelt,
    Eleanor, 411
    President, 396
Rorschach, Hermann, 419
Rose, Barbara, 381
Rosetta Stone, 295, 297
Ross, Chuck, 33
Rothenberg, Albert, 227, 314
Rothko, Mark, 116, 318, 328, 374, 395
Roulette, Russian, 207
Routing, 69, 87, 231, 239, 429
Rolls Royce Phantom, 386
Rubenesque, 51
Rubens, Peter Paul, 366
Rubenstein, Arthur, 273
Rubin,
    Ron, 26
    William, 190
Rue Laffitte (See also Ambroise Vollard), 252-253
Ruiz, Dr. Salvador, 246
Rule,
    Cosmic, 335
    First cardinal, 344
    Second, 83
    Standardized grammatical, 11
Rules,
    Adopted, 62, 143
    Artificial, 24
    Temporal, 106
    of Engagement', 55, 61-62
Rumi, 9, 61, 198, 364, 397
Ruskin, John, 102, 355, 380
Russell, Rosalind, 153
Russian Bear, 150
Ruthless, 62, 165

S

Sabartés, Jamie (See also Picasso), 247
Sacrament, Single significant, 268
Sacrifice, Word, 144
Sacrifices,
    Life involved successive, 249
    Such, 290
Sagan, Carl, 199-200, 389
Sagittarius, 199
Sailplane, 81
Saito, Ryoei (See also Dr. Gachet), 351
Sales, Promising, 253
Salieri, Antonio, 93
Salk, Jonas, 313
Salon des Refusés (See also Napoleon III), 374
Salons, 318
Salvation, Individual, 285
Samanas, 74, 321
Samurai, 393
San Andreas Fault, 220

San Francisco, 50-51, 73-74, 191, 273, 359, 423-424
San Lorenzo, Church of, 367
Sanction, Religious, 279
Sand, Cosmic, 35
Sangha, 279
Sanity, Matter of, 403
Sankara, 285
Sanskrit word 'dharma', 279
Santa Maria Del Fiore (See also Brunelleschi), 368
Santa Monica, 145-146, 221, 301-302, 343
Santayana, George, 186
Sartre, Jean-Paul, 75
Satori, 117
Sausalito, 423
Sauvé, Antoon, 86, 123
Savoir-faire, 412
Savor, 115, 127, 170
Savvy, 4, 68, 128, 141, 157, 165, 205, 376, 379
Say, Mean What You, 225
Scale,
    Cosmic, 182, 198
    Quantum, 182, 184
    Small, 416
Scene, Art, 142, 330, 345, 379
Scenes, Parisian, 252
Schiele, 169
Scholars, Assessments of, 376
School, Art, 26, 189, 248, 274, 302, 352, 370, 373, 382
Schools, Secular, 320
Schopenhauer, Arthur, 119, 176
Schulz, Dr. Mona Lisa, 127, 260
Schwarzenegger, Arnold, 137
Schweitzer, Albert, 28, 160, 274, 285, 320
Science,
    Empirical world of, 17
    Foundation of, 176
    Limitation of, 182
    Marvels, 186
    Psychology of, 313-314, 324
    Pure, 200, 319
    Roots of, 190
    Social, 363
Scientists,
    Bulletin of the Atomic, 198
    Vast majority of behavioral, 319
Scott, Ridley, 132-133, 346
Screen Writers Guild, 396
Screenings, Backwater, 346
Screenplay, Quality of the, 126
Script, Everyday Egyptian (See also Rosetta Stone), 297
Scriptures, Reading, 286
Sculpting, 270
Sculptors, 24, 161, 249, 305, 364, 367, 370
Sculpture, African, 189
Sea-mammal, Tusks of the, 367
Seamanship, Reckless, 389
Seat, Shotgun, 219
Second-guess, 17, 85, 98, 142, 160, 261
Secondhand no's, 33
Secure, 67, 69, 172, 280, 356, 386

Seduction, Potential, 39
Seeds, Grievance, 93
Seeking—its destiny, 281
Seer, Vedic, 102
Seine, 250
Selection, Law of natural, 24
Self-absorbed, 142, 290
Self-acceptance, 158, 226
Self-actualization, 289, 316
Self-actualized, 318, 325
Self-actualizing, 316-317
Self-admiration, Undue, 25
Self-appointed, 303
Self-awake, 282
Self-aware, 135, 139, 360
Self-awareness, 13, 63, 85, 103, 163
Self-centered, 25, 286, 322
Self-confidence, 172, 205, 219, 256, 267
Self-consciousness, Cumulative, 102
Self-control,
    Freedom of, 127
    Ultimate strategy of, 62
Self-deception—hindrances, 213
Self-defense, Zen, 115
Self-denial, Unpitying, 321
Self-destruct, 398
Self-destruction, Subsequent, 206
Self-determination, Direction of, 232
Self-discipline,
    Aspect of, 128
    Expressed confidence of, 55
    Master of, 397
    Result of, 84
Self-discovery, 112, 220
Self-doubt,
    Agony of, 262
    Feelings of, 18
    Omnipresent feeling of, 397
Self-effacing, 69, 269
Self-esteem, Healthy dose of, 62
'Self-evident', 10, 46, 111, 119, 170, 189-190, 202, 206, 329
Self-expression, Art of, 381, 405
Self-fulfillment, Direct result of, 26
Self-image, 102, 324, 368
Self-induced, 86, 214, 247, 280, 343, 356
Self-indulgence,
    Price of, 234
    Sensual, 321
    Sticky traps of, 154
    Veneer of, 134
Self-inspiration, 69, 228, 355, 412
Self-inspired, 86, 227, 356
Self-mortification, 74, 321
Self-motivated, 86
Self-pity, 142, 259, 307, 314
Self-referential, 10, 37, 139, 192, 197, 317, 374, 409
Self-reflecting, 184
Self-reliance,
    Elegant necessity of, 133
    Sense of, 128
Self-reliant, 85, 132, 403
Self-sabotage, 68, 415
Self-saboteur, 335

Self-sacrifice, Lessons of, 237
Self-seeking, 290
Self-seriousness, Obsessive, 132
'Self-taught', 26, 125, 127, 302, 361, 381-382
Self-worth, Sense of, 255, 323
Semantics, Matter of, 269
Senesh, Hannah, 287
Sense,
    Anticlimactic, 106
    Common, 184
    Intimate, 275
    Intuitive, 134
    Jungian, 83, 150, 207
    Literary, 381
    Make, 141, 341, 361, 405, 433
    Ordinary, 376
    Real, 112, 366, 377, 395
    Semicolon made, 218
    Significant, 297
    Zen, 259
    of 'raised' consciousness, 360
Senses,
    Physical, 77
    Primitive, 373
Sensibilities, Western, 118, 361
Sentence,
    Life, 21, 117
    Punctuation of a particular, 218
    Useful, 127
Sentience, Self-reflecting, 184
Separation, Point of, 10
Serbian (See also Nikola Tesla), 124-125
Serendipity, 128, 211
Serfs, 190
Sermon, The, 74, 116
Serrano, Andres (See also Battle of *Piss Christ*), 326
Serve Somebody, 13
Service, Giving lip, 207
Setbacks,
    Despite, 86
    Transitory, 179
SETI, 175
Seurat, Georges, 189, 374
Seuss, Dr., 15, 137
Sex, 39, 164, 268, 315-316, 404, 430
Sexy, 423
Shackleton, Sir Ernest, 211
Shaffer, Peter (See also *Amadeus*), 93
Shakespeare, William, 38, 89, 158, 221, 430
Shalom, 287
Shaman, Universal, 405
Shameless, 160, 242, 270
Shamelessly, 89
'Shattered' art, 190
Shavian, 349
Shaw, George Bernard, 27
Shells, Nautilus (See also Visconti library), 367
The Sheltering Sky (See also Paul Bowles), 434
Shifts, Cognitive, 147
Shlain, Dr. Leonard, 268
Shodo (See also Zen Calligraphy), 115-116
Shoemaking, 364
Shortchanged, 409

Shortcut, Cosmic, 199
Shortcuts, 112, 179
Shortsightedness, Self-imposed, 315
'Should nots', 317
Show,
    Juried, 171-172
    Museum, 157, 162, 166
    Vollard, 251-254
Showcase 'acceptable' artists, 161
Showdowns, 394, 396-397
Showing, Private, 402
Shows, Prerequisite laundry list of, 302
Siblings, 235
Siddhartha, 321
Side,
    Dangerous, 236
    Right, 404-405
Siena, St Catherine of, 372
Sienese, 369-370
Sight, Out of, 51, 194
Signals, Rhythmic-modal, 377
Signature of a particular artist—Leonardo, 371
Significance,
    Potential, 184
    Real, 181
    Single moment of great, 116
    What possible, 171
Silence,
    Aesthetic, 113
    Benefits of, 129
'Silent' hieroglyphs, 297
Silk-screened, Brillo Boxes of (See also Warhol), 345
Simon, Paul, 352
Simone, Nina, 3, 62
Sinatra, Frank, 155
Sincerity, Saccharine, 154
Singer, Isaac Bashevis, 377
Single
    string—and all strings, 261
    utterance of 'hope', 46
    work of art, 13
Sistine Chapel, 382
Sisyphus, Myth of, 90
Sites, Pilgrimage, 371
Situation,
    Complementary, 82
    Out of a life-threatening, 233
    Parallel, 306
    Truth of the, 58
Skelton, Red, 84
Skeptic, Cultural, 377
Skill—like drawing, 68
Skimming, 295
Slackers, 57, 128, 434
Slang, 268-269
Slave, Biological, 320
Slavery, 406
Slaves, Backs of (See also Golden Age of Greek Democracy), 305
Slogan, New-age, 129
Slope,
    Seductive, 40
    Slippery, 29, 194

Smart, 18, 35, 62, 74, 77, 86, 149-151, 159, 162, 218, 261, 292, 346, 361, 379, 389, 393, 404, 406-407
Smarter, Be, 103
Smith, Red, 348
Smitten, 15
Snow, C. P., 398
Social conditioning—the MCP, 336
Socialist, 318
Societies, Pre-modern, 363-364
Society,
    Ancient Rome, 364
    Art-aware, 331
    Consumer-driven, 205
    Contemporary, 34
    European, 366
    Fabric of, 332
    Individualistic, 363
    Industrialized, 363
    Mental thruways of, 103
    Pecking order of, 409
    Preeminent values of the, 397
    Seductive entrapments of, 424
    'The Humane, 197
    Useful members of, 237
    Western, 206, 284
'Society of Mind' theory (See also Marvin Minsky), 336
Society's
    breast, 349
    collective dreams, 284
    conceit, 315
    demands, 284
Socrates, 254, 268
Soho, New York, 5
Solution,
    Positive, 133
    Tantalizing, 181
    Unique, 405
Solutions, Unorthodox architectural, 368
Son,
    Paulo, 249
    Prodigy of a, 248
    Responsible, 237
    talent, 250
Song,
    Wonderful, 233
    of God—the indivisible truth, 185
Sophocles, 268
Sorts,
    Populist fate of, 330
    Pyrrhic victory of, 326
Sotheby's auction (See also *Fountain*), 344
Soto (See also Different Schools of Zen), 117
Soufflé (See also James Beard), 4
The Soul of Man Under Socialism (See also Oscar Wilde), 348
Soul,
    courier of all great art, 37
    inexhaustible energy, 427
    comrade, 397
Souls, Old, 360
Sound, Definition of, 185
Sounds like—indirect, 109
Source,

    Eternal power of the, 347
    One universal, 183
    Transcendental, 259
    of all existence—consciousness, 187
Sources,
    Majority of art funding, 161
    Reliable, 251
    Secondhand, 83
South Seas (See also Gauguin), 67
Soviet Union, 395
Sown, Seeds of intuitive perceptions, 27
Space,
    Dimensions of, 189, 406
    Interstellar, 183
    Make, 273
    Nonmaterial, 309
    Nonphysical, 184
    Perception of, 329
    Riddle of, 178
    Shortage of, 165
    Size of a studio, 85
    Test of, 434
    Three planes of, 198
    Three-dimensional, 113, 188, 369
    Transcendental, 308
    Vacuum of, 179, 192
    Valuable, 49
Space-time,
    Fabric of, 181, 192, 199
    Physics of, 189, 201
Spacefarer, 390
Spaces, Alternative, 330, 373
Spaceships, 132-133, 200, 233, 259
Spain, 261
Spanish, 105, 261, 342
Speak, Time to, 128-129
Species-wide, 316
Spectacles, Public circus-like (See also Edison), 124
Speculation,
    Intelligent, 253
    Spirit of, 344
Speculations, Adolescent, 176
Speech,
    Everyday, 44
    Land of free, 396
Speechless, 183
Spencer, Herbert, 360
Speziali, Medici e, 369
Sphere, Public, 162
Spielberg, Steven, 237
Spin-offs, *Pinocchio*, 234
Spinoza's God (See also Einstein), 180
Spirit,
    The Art (See also Robert Henri), 154
    Concept of, 320
    Cornucopia of the, 391
    Evidence of the, 434
    Evolving, 320
    Function of, 362
    Generosity of, 84
    Human, 214, 237, 324
    Indomitability of, 69
    Manifestation of, 183
    Material manifestation, 180

Possibility of the, 276
Pure, 187
Readiness of, 286
Your, 4, 19, 159, 173, 260, 284, 290, 398
Spirits, Evil, 90
The Spiritual Universe, 183
'Spoken language', 297
Spontaneity,
Elements of, 298
Sense of, 132
recklessness, 307
Sport, Blood, 114, 291
Spot, The A, 343
Springboard, Underside of the same, 153
Squad, Bomb, 403
Squalor, Stereotypical, 290
Squares, Painting of, 15
Stability, Rare political, 199
Stage, World, 157, 246
Stallone, Sylvester, 123
Stand, Last, 326
Standard,
Higher, 27, 87, 102, 233, 285, 405
Powerful, 125
Universal, 114
Your, 17, 62, 391
Standards,
Esthetic, 326
Moral, 114
Standing,
Social, 305, 407, 409
Superior, 408
Star,
Shining, 385
Spontaneous birth of a, 192
Trek, 183, 199
Wishing, 235
Wars, 199, 346, 415
Starbucks, Local, 139-140, 291
Stardust, Child of, 183
Stargate, 199
Starship, Speed, 178
Starry Night (See also Van Gogh), 28, 403
State, Wonderful, 154
Statement, Truth of a, 109
States,
Aspect of theoretical physics, 402
United, 155, 172, 207, 232, 261, 330, 375, 395
Station, Social, 409
Stature, Gain enviable, 370
Status,
Advanced, 197
Allegorical, 394
Anxiety (See also Alain de Botton), 155, 376, 407, 409
Higher social, 372
Social, 197, 372, 407
System of, 409
Status, 62
Steinlen, Théophile Alexandre, 254
Steps (See also Jerzy Kosinski), 33
Stereotype, Destructive, 27
Stereotypes, Interpretative, 296
Stern, Sounds, 22

Stewardship, Planetary, 194
Stevenson, Robert Louis, 316
Stieglitz, Alfred, 420, 344
Stimulus-response, 320, 360
Stone, W. Clement, 252
Stonecarver, 367
Store, Window of the candy, 21
Story,
Human, 156
Success, 360
Whole, 69
The Strange Theory of Light and Matter (See also Richard Feynman), 193
Strange' things, 177
Stranger, Alluring, 195
Stravinsky, Igor, 273, 405
Stream, Audio, 263
Street,
Pond, 349
Side, 403, 424
Surrealistic side, 424
'Street of pictures' (Rue Laffitte), 252
Streets, Mean, 220, 291
Strength,
Direction of, 428
Inner, 56, 85, 200, 375, 429, 431
Out of great, 74
Pillar of, 127, 260, 398
Point of, 345
Sign of inner, 56
Source of, 308
Stress, Psychic, 356
Strewn, Endless minefield of hardships, 67
String, 95, 182, 261-262
Strings,
Origin of, 181
Puppet, 238
Theoretical cosmos of, 182
Stroking, Ego, 357
Structure,
Organic, 329
Social, 408-409
Sublime, 128
Struggle, Eternal, 67
Student, Worthy, 323
Studio,
Hollywood, 160, 346, 396
Laurel Canyon, 202
New York, 164
Studios,
Hollywood, 141, 257
Major film, 98
Study,
Advanced, 200
Dramatic, 145
Various fields of, 27
of LSD's, 144
Style, Personal, 189
Styles, Traps of, 362
Subatomic, 108, 181-183, 193, 330
Subcontinent, Native peoples of the, 408
Subculture, 269
Subdominant, 404
Subpoenaed, 396
'Substance', 126, 147, 159, 242, 341, 349, 367,

402
Substructure, Internal, 182
Subtleness, Insidious, 63
Succès d'estime (See also John Richardson), 252
Success,
Commercial, 252, 254
Critical, 171, 252, 379
Current, 207
Economic, 153
Emulating, 427
Experiencing, 155, 408
Financial, 84, 139, 252, 407
Guarantee of, 343
Mechanics of, 139
Outer manifestations of, 424
Overnight, 303
Seeds of, 6
Self-esteem equals, 156
Standards of, 49
The Law of, 321
True, 38
Succumbing, 401, 411
Such 'pure' devotion, 94
Sufi (See also Rumi), 9, 61, 112
Sulk, 206
Sun,
Distant, 178
Rising, 31
gravity, 192
Sunlight, Thin beam of, 193
Sunset Boulevard—the film, 222
Superego, 336
Superficiality, Life of, 87
Superheroes, Material of, 192
Superman, 192
Supernova, 188, 310
Superstition, 114, 119, 313, 320, 409
Surfaces, Opportunity, 133
Surge, Information, 434
Surprise, Universal, 94
Surreal, 220, 243
Surrealism, 326
Surrealist, Spanish (Joan Miró), 342
Surrealists, 24
Surreptitiously, 376
Survival,
Basic, 65, 131, 429
Physical, 289
Pursuit of, 185
conclusion, 377
Survive, Strong, 121, 129
Suspects, Usual (See also Resistance / distraction), 335
Sutras, Brahma, 406
Suzuki-roshi, Shunryu (See also Zen teachers), 116
Swampland, 123
Swedish, 322
Swift, Jonathan, 19
Swiss,
Patent Office (See also Albert Einstein), 176
Psychiatrist (See also Hermann Rorschach), 419

scientist (See also Albert Hofmann), 146
Switzerland, 185, 251, 337
Sword, Way of the (See also Kendo), 115
Swope, Herbert B., 39
Sycophants, Lemming-like, 249
Symbolically, 116, 242
Symbolism, 234, 318, 372
Symbols,
    Status, 163
    Wonder of the alphabet, 297
    Word, 225
Symmetry,
    Elegant, 329
    Moment of, 261
Symphony, Cosmic, 262
Symposium, 156
Sync, Out of, 335
Synchronicities, 212
Synchronicity, Proof of, 150
Syndrome, Wish, 238
Syntax, Visual, 108
System,
    Absolute proof of the heliocentric, 45
    Ancient Hindu caste, 409
    Authentic, 115
    Autonomic nervous, 310
    Belief, 118, 407
    Contemporary commercial gallery, 373
    Current marketing, 158
    Dogmatic caste, 303
    Esthetic, 22
    Hierarchal caste, 407
    Hollywood Studio, 160, 346
    Integrated four-dimensional, 176
    Proven, 112
    Rigid, 427-428
    Rigidity of the caste, 408
    Severe critic of the caste, 279
    Solar, 310
    Status, 377, 409
Systems,
    Belief, 27, 115, 134, 406
    Exotic-sounding, 112
    Representational, 274
    Star, 199
    cookie cutter approach, 34

T

Tableau, Cosmic, 192
Tagore, Rabindranath, 11, 269
Taker, Risk, 18, 346
Talent,
    Having enough, 97
    Pecking order of, 52
    Specific, 126
    Unique, 34, 75, 98
    such whining, 142
    plus self-inspiration, 355
Talents,
    Lesser, 52
    Social, 252
Tales,
    Fairy, 102, 237, 282
    Favorite Buddhist, 241

Talmud, 101
'Tamed'
    perception, 350
    process, 350
Tantrums, 62-63, 227
Tao, 102, 326
Taoism, 112
Task, Worthy, 352
Tea, Way of (See also Chado), 115
Teacher,
    Art, 96, 248, 378
    Great, 323
    Trademark of a true, 282
Teachers, Zen, 118
Teaches, Pain, 322
Teaching, 96, 137, 217-218, 234-235, 280, 326, 406
Techne (See also Ancient Greek), 364
Technique, Mastery of, 275
Techniques, Art-making, 5, 157
Technologies, Progression of future, 185
Technology,
    Advanced, 193
    California Institute of, 416
    Poet of, 125
    Superior, 124-125
    Wormhole, 199
Teleportation, Quantum, 184
Telescopes,
    Radio, 200
    Special, 193
Television,
    Invention of, 329
    PBS, 330
Tempera, Egg, 372
Temperament, 63, 158, 170, 227, 290, 348
Tempered, 29
Temptations, Subtle, 39
Tenet for the cult, 363
Tenets, Aesthetic, 378
Tension,
    Degree of organic, 429
    Superior source of dramatic, 331
Term, Archaic (See also 'Quiet desperation'), 276
Terms,
    Duplicitous psychological, 338
    Scientific, 15
    Simplest theoretical, 199
    Spiritual, 180
    'synchronicity', 318
Terpsichore (See also Greek Muses), 305
Terracotta, 365
Terrain, 195, 318, 347, 397
Terriers, Yorkshire, 50, 123, 138, 163, 175
Territory,
    Marvelous, 156
    Metaphysical, 336
    Pristine, 276
Tesla, Nikola, 124-125
Test,
    Acid, 314
    Aptitude, 10, 309
    Mental abilities, 309
    Rorschach, 419-420

    Simple, 115, 405
Tests,
    Aptitude, 284
    Tempered by many, 84
    of faith—always serious, 433
Texas, 375
Text, Ancient, 118, 186, 406
Texts, Religious, 297
Thalia (See also Greek Muses), 305
Thanks, Giving, 94
'The Magnificent Truth', 105, 111
Theater, Public, 379
Theist, Existential, 320
Theories, Groundbreaking, 329
Theorist, Quantum field, 126
Theory,
    Art, 373
    Brilliant new, 181
    Minimalist, 190
    Quantum, 175, 189, 193, 261
    Radical, 193
    String, 182, 261
    Superstring, 108, 181-182, 188
    Unified field, 181
    Unifying, 182
    Volatile, 402
Therapy, Art, 23, 227, 275, 345
Thermodynamics, First Law of (See also C.P. Snow), 398
Thermometer, Language of the, 296
Thing,
    Aspects of the same, 87, 187
    Awareness of a particular, 103
    Magnificent essence of a, 182
    Next big, 159, 328, 343, 347, 402
    Smart, 77
    Smarter, 234
    Source of a, 260
    Truth of every, 102
    Whole, 4, 22
Things,
    Awareness of, 228
    Correct comprehension of, 282
    Material, 308
    Nature of all conditioned, 321
    Petty, 40
    Rarefied view of, 200
    Rearrangement of existential, 274
    Relative importance of, 154
    Size of, 416
    Truth of, 175
    Underlying reality of, 146
    Useful, 348
    Value of, 52, 83
    Way of, 283
The Third Force, 41, 387
Thomas,
    J. Parnell, 396
    Saint, 379
Thoreau, Henry David, 51, 95, 285
Thorn, Psychic, 121
'Thought
    criminals (See also *Nineteen-Eighty-Four*), 45
    experiment', 176, 179

Thread,
    Indestructible, 192
    Universal, 175
Threat,
    Bomb, 402-403
    Immediate, 292
Threshold, Word, 355
Thrills, Vicarious, 347
Tibet, 263
Tic, Conversational (See also *The Psychology of Science*), 314
Ticks, Annoying verbal, 49
Tightrope, Razor sharp, 424
Time,
    Allotted, 309
    Commitment of, 166
    Discovery of all, 183
    Eternal existence outside of, 115
    Experience of, 175
    Expression of, 191
    Laws of, 356
    Magical, 189
    Marking, 43
    Metaphysical, 177
    Popular vernacular Italian of the, 213
    Possibility of, 177, 195
    Privileged, 18
    Question, 69, 176
    Real, 143, 394-395
    Regardless of, 332
    Relative, 176, 178
    Single dimension of, 189
    Watershed, 372
    Western contemporary, 376
    resilient 'fabric', 192
The Time Machine (See also H.G. Wells), 198
Times,
    Ancient, 325
    Financial, 206
    Misconception of the, 395
    Modern, 408
    Pre-modern, 363
    Taste of the, 211
    Zeitgeist of the, 315
Timing, Magic of, 303
Tinterow, Gary, 253
Titian, 371
Today,
    Art zeitgeist of, 326
    Popular culture of, 172
    Vatican of, 45
    art schools, 373
    artist, 380
Tolstoy, Leo (See also *The Death of Iván Ilych*), 322
Tommy, 82
Tongues, Many, 194, 200, 352
'Too many' artists, 165-166, 343
Toolmaker, Inventive, 390
Torment, Eternal pit of, 29
Totem, Influential, 363
Toulouse-Lautrec, 252, 254, 374
Tour de France, 403
Tower, Ivory, 33
Towners, Out of, 73-74

Trade, 365, 367, 408
Trademark, 111, 282
Trader, Slave, 114
Tradition,
    Andean, 68
    Classical, 367
    Judaeo-Christian, 115
    Mindless, 268, 393
    Monastic, 87
    Torrent of, 306
Traditions,
    Ancient, 325
    Artistic, 361
Tragedy, 39, 51, 90, 128, 207-208, 305, 315, 318, 322, 332, 411, 433
Train, Unstoppable, 196
Trainer, Personal, 430
Trait, Learned (See also Self-confidence), 205
Tranquility, 322
Transcendence,
    Knowledge of, 195
    Power of, 114
Transcendental manifestation of God—personal, 182
Transition,
    Apt, 261
    Metaphorical, 101
Transitory symbols—cars, 34
Transmigration, 134, 187
Trappings, Artificial social, 356
Trauma, Sexual, 318
Traumatized, 14
Traveler, Time, 198
Treatment, Freudian, 319
Tree,
    Bodhi, 74, 96, 193, 321
    Shade of a huge sacred fig, 77
Trendoids, 157
Trends, 95, 157, 163, 198, 332, 374
Tribal, 363-364, 390
Tribe—from
    pre-modern, 363
    spiritual art, 328
Trickles, Collective meaning of words, 225
Triumph, 9, 29, 84, 97, 106, 118, 128, 156, 200, 239, 255, 265, 283, 309, 339, 353, 408, 434
Trivialized, 232
Trojan, 142
Tron (See also Slaves in the Machine), 336
Troopers, Three starship, 178
Trophy of power—my art, 352
Trucks, Loading, 424
Trust,
    Fearless, 4
    Whom do you, 111
Truth,
    Core of, 249
    Cosmic, 108
    Direct, 115
    Eternal, 21, 117, 282
    Existence of, 105
    Experience of, 287
    Feeling, 341

    Inner, 307
    Intuitive, 118, 321
    Irrepressible, 309
    Knowing, 45, 109, 133, 187, 320
    Liberating, 129
    Measuring, 68
    Metaphysical, 18, 433
    Mirror, 246
    Moment of, 4, 77, 112, 132, 134, 149, 166, 430
    Noble (See also Buddha), 74-75, 280
    Object of, 106
    Objective, 107, 111
    Pill of, 241
    Question of, 107
    Reflection of the everlasting, 200
    Relative, 107-108
    Second Noble (See also Unbridled craving), 280
    Seek out, 315
    The Fourth Noble (See also Middle Path), 74
    Timeless, 105, 113
    Transcendent, 316
    Transcendental, 106, 109, 200
    Transitory, 107
    Ultimate, 108, 180, 331
    Underlying, 24, 180, 187
    Universe of, 116
    Vanilla, 105
    Whole, 113
    Word, 10, 119
    Truth, 105, 227
'Truth de jour', 22
Truths,
    Absolute, 151
    Four Noble, 280, 322
    Transcendental, 187
    Universal, 106, 115, 280
Tummies, With full (See also Yogis), 202
Turf (See also *The War of Art*), 397
Tuscany, 369
Twain, Mark, 31, 127, 389
Twists, Plot, 237
'Two extremes'—that of asceticism, 321
Two-dimensionally, 190
Tycoon,
    Real estate, 344
    office, 359-360
Tzu, Lao, 102

U
Ubiquitous words 'hope', 46
Ufologist, Intrepid, 6
Ugliness, Effects of, 324
Ugly, 176, 245
Ultimate of rejections—by God (See also *Amadeus*), 93
'Unaccredited' artist, 302
Unafraid, 182
Uncertainty,
    Climate of, 328-329
    Facing, 332
    Time of, 325

Unconscious, 69, 83, 146, 207, 227, 231, 235, 275, 317-318, 328, 336-337, 367
Unease, Feel sudden, 408
Unfettered, 9, 18, 25, 155, 172, 327, 401, 434
Unhappiness, 411
Unification, Ultimate (See also Buddha Enlightenment), 187
Unions, Trade, 408
Units, Linguistic, 296
Universal rule—immutable ideals, 106
Universe,
  Chaotic, 182
  Dimensional, 181
  Economical, 113
  Evolution of the, 184
  Fundamental particles of the, 182
  Larger, 310
  Meaningful, 38
  Metaphysical gears of the, 30
  Mystery of the, 175
  Mythic empire of the *Star Wars*, 200
  Physical, 402
  Predictable, 402
  Supreme mysteries of the, 108
  Unobserved, 184
  Whole, 349
Universes, Parallel, 179
Università (See also Guild Membership), 369
Unrest, Political, 325
Unsupportive, 159
Upanishads (See also Bhagavad-gita), 118, 406
Upstart (See also *Amadeus*), 94
Urania (See also Greek Muses), 305
USA, 140, 205, 220
Usage,
  Current catchall, 381
  Indiscriminate, 289
Use of 'wish', 236
Usefulness of the word 'obvious', 398
Utica, Cato of (See also *The Divine Comedy*), 213
Utopia, 234

V

Vador, Darth, 415
Validation,
  External, 207
  Public, 252, 431
  of, 201, 412, 431
Value,
  Artwork of great, 33
  Everything of, 118
  Inherent, 62, 106, 144, 155, 205, 243, ·350
  Innate, 314
  Intrinsic, 37, 69, 163, 171, 291, 297, 342, 351
  Journey of, 290
  Lasting, 14, 33, 103, 398
  Mission of, 19
  Perceived, 351, 383, 411
  Positive, 221, 433
  Public relations, 351
  Reality of, 49
  Shock, 326
  Thing of, 19, 153, 376
  Truths of eternal, 18
  Vision of, 83
  of man's transcendence, 324
  someone's opinion, 160
Values,
  Problems of (See also *The Psychology of Science*), 324
  Sense of, 194
Van
  Buren, Abigail, 307
  Eeden, Frederik (See also Lucid Dreaming), 282
  Eyck, Jan, 366, 372
  Gogh,
    Theo, 28-30, 351
    Vincent, 28-29, 37, 55, 163, 169, 251-252, 302, 317, 347, 350-351, 374, 378, 382
      Portrait of Dr. Gachet, 351
      masterpiece *Starry Night*, 28
      sister-in-law, 351
Vanderbilts, 375
Vanilla, Eternal, 274
Vanishing, Principle of the (See also Brunelleschi's Dome), 369
Vanity Fair, 164
Vasari, Giorgio, 249, 368
Vatican, 45
Veda, 118, 186
Vedic, 102, 118, 406
Veil of grammatical confusion—my nemesis, 218
Venetian, 365, 369
Veneto (See also paratichi), 369
Venice, Moor of (See also *Othello*), 158
Vera (See also Oscar Wilde), 173
Vermeer, Johannes, 298
Verrocchio,
  Anecdote, 250
  Andrea del, 249-250, 369
  Baptism, 249
Vessel, Indestructible, 154
Vested interests—economic, 347
Vibrations, Authentic, 154
Victim's position, 270
Victim-no-more, 415
Victimhood, 37, 129, 154, 314, 356
Victims, Resentful, 249
Victory, Ultimate barometer of, 397
Vienna, 96-97
View,
  Ancient, 187
  Cosmic, 201
  Holistic, 326, 330
  Perilous, 49
  Secular, 285
Viewpoints, Conflicting, 27
Views,
  Moral, 364
  Political, 119
Villain, Treacherous (See also Iago), 158
Virgil (See also *The Divine Comedy*), 213-214
Virgin Mary, 327, 367
Virginia, 375
Virtue, Model of, 96
Virtues, Significance of, 320
Visconti Library (See also Nautilus Shells), 367
Vishnu,
  Avatar of (See also Lord Krishna), 285
  Incarnation of the god, 406
Vision,
  Clairvoyant, 170
  Expanded, 324
  Films of, 242
  Individual, 226
  Test of, 162
  The Language of, 296
  Unique, 67, 133, 171, 180, 362
Visions, Individual, 372
Visual 'languages', 296
Voice,
  Annoying self-defeating, 21
  Authentic, 306, 346, 398
  Intuitive, 260, 264
  Original, 295
  Plaintive, 415
  Positive, 37, 427
  Unadulterated, 398
  Welcome, 238
Voltaire, 58, 108, 115, 129, 172, 191, 214, 217
Vollard, Ambroise, 159, 251, 253
Vortex, Transformational, 309, 327, 410
Voyage, Fantastic, 183
Vuillard, 252
Vulture, Mount of the Holy (See also Buddha), 116

W

Wachowski, Andy & Larry (See also *The Matrix*), 242
Wagner, Jane, 285
Wake-up, 242, 284
Walkabout, Twenty-year-long, 309
Walks, Long (See also Einstein), 185
Wallpaper, Expensive (See also Peggy Guggenheim), 206
Wandering, 74, 284, 321, 342
Wanderlust, 217, 220
Wannabes, 3, 85, 144, 299, 355
Want,
  Pinocchio, 234, 237-238
  Serious collectors, 160
Wanting,
  Incessant, 407
  Pretense of, 357
Wants, Nonessential, 332
War,
  End of the Cold, 198
  First World, 375
  Second World, 22, 201, 320, 395, 419
'War of the currents' (See also AC competition), 124
Warhol, Andy, 164, 189, 317, 345, 374, 376

Warrior, Ultimate test of the, 394
Washington, Ned, 233
Water, Domain of, 101
Watson,
    James, 145
    John B., 316, 319
Wattage, 226
Watts, Alan, 24, 114, 142, 145, 150, 164, 421
Wavelength, 193
Waxed apple, 343
Weak sister, 393
Weakness,
    Moment of, 75, 112
    Sense, 283
    Underlying, 69
Weaknesses, Moral, 321
Wealth,
    Symbols of, 141
    Timeless, 34
    Transcendental, 17
Wealthier, 222
Weavers, Guild of silk, 367
Weeds, Suffocating, 93
Weekend, Long, 138
Weightless, 101
Weill, Berthe, 254
Welch, Evelyn, 365-366, 369, 371-372
Well-trodden, 40, 398, 428
Wells, H.G., 197-198
Welles, Orson, 359
Wellspring of humanity's symbols (See also Carl Jung), 207
Wem Shu's good luck, 241
West,
    Jessamyn, 302
    Dr. Rebecca, 236-237
Westinghouse,
    Electric Company, 125
    George, 125
Wharton, Edith, 324
What Color Is Your Parachute, 68
Wheels, Training, 264
'Whine-free' spirit, 417
Whining, 95, 142-143, 246, 260, 356, 415-416
Whistler, James McNeill, 374
White, E.B., 303
The White Girl, 374
Whitewaters, Uncertainty of, 34
Whitney, John Hay (See also *Boy with Pipe*), 351
Whole,
    Behavior of the, 325
    of Plato's Symposium, 156
Whorehouses, 329
Whyte, David, 126
Width, Three-dimensional universe of, 193-194
Wife, Rubenesque, 51
Wild Strawberries (See also Ingmar Bergman), 322
Wilde, Oscar, 34, 109, 133, 163, 172-173, 226, 241, 348, 390
Wilder, Thornton, 296

Will,
    Material, 154
    Self, 430
    True, 77, 343, 430
Wilson,
    Colin, 348
    essay, 349
    keen observation, 350
Window, Magic, 434
Winds, Temperamental, 10
Winner's edge, 23
Winning, 29, 39, 90, 106, 171, 173, 179, 201, 327
Wires, Action crosses, 233
Wisdom,
    Celtic (See also *Anam Cara*), 131, 286, 355
    Common, 86, 98, 109, 316, 352
    Retrospective, 402
Wish, Weak, 237, 269
Wishing, 231, 233, 235-236, 238, 282-283, 415
Witch-hunt (See also HUAC), 396
Within, Acquire, 359
Witness,
    Fair, 83
    False, 91
    Reliable, 111, 185, 275, 429
Witnesses, 396
The Wizard of Oz, 234
Woe is me, 144, 154
Woes, Financial, 142
Wolf, Fred (See also *The Spiritual Universe*), 183
Woman, Young, 241-242
Wonder,
    Age of, 313
    Sense of, 201, 234
Wonderland, 202, 234, 243, 402
Wood, Beatrice, 420
Woodstock, 22, 231
Word,
    Dangerous, 49, 269
    Painted, 295
    Passive, 46, 269
    Pathetic, 269
    Right, 234-235, 249, 389
    Specific, 364
    Verboten, 44, 119
    Written, 43, 218, 268, 296, 434
    choice—meaning, 231
Words,
    Accuracy of the, 225
    Awareness of mindless, 267
    Catchall, 269
    Distinctions of, 225
    'hope', 43-44, 46, 423
    Impact of, 122
    Impotent, 232
    Limitations of, 296
    Meaning of, 25, 225
    Power of, 434
    Tick, 43-44, 46, 50, 236
    Truth of, 123
    of the 'profits', 23

Work,
    Authentic, 381
    Critique of the, 165
    Groundbreaking untitled, 329
    Introspective, 332
    Original, 26, 44, 84, 131, 133, 160, 169, 173, 175, 214, 232, 270, 379, 382
    Quality of the, 362
    Rigorous body of, 329
    Superb piece of, 255
    Value of the, 171, 351
Workings of the cosmos—the manifest artwork, 179
Workmanship, 367
Workplace, System of the, 34
Works,
    Original, 170, 337
    Religious, 370, 380
    Secular thematic, 370
    Value of, 367
    of art—novels, 376
Workshop,
    Restrictive model of the guild, 373
    Tradition of the medieval, 365
World,
    Ancient, 297, 363
    Contemporary, 363
    Corporate, 56, 63, 221, 385
    Density of the, 77, 335, 395, 430
    Digital, 261
    Empirical, 17, 318
    Everyday, 321
    External, 360, 374
    Fickle, 76
    Industrialized postmodern, 125
    Larger art, 197
    Make sense of the, 341
    Material, 9, 40-41, 276
    Maze of the art-buying, 171
    Observations of the natural, 373
    Outer, 146, 307
    Perception of the, 225
    Physical, 41
    Real, 186, 235
    Sense of the, 308, 341
    Teacher of the (See also Lord Krishna), 285
    Waking, 283
    Western, 270, 326
Worldview, Unadulterated, 205
Wormholes, Network of, 199
Worringer, Wilhelm (See also *Abstraction and Empathy*), 330
Worrying, 9, 159
Wright, Orville & Wilber, 283
Writ, Metaphysical, 315
Writer,
    Freelance, 33, 163
    Prolific, 348
Writing,
    Invention of, 268
    Process of, 309
Wunderlich, Richard (See also *Pinocchio Goes Postmodern*), 232, 237

Y

Yardstick,
　　Stellar, 198
　　Useful, 68
Years,
　　Advanced, 433
　　Aged many, 178
　　Post-relativity, 108
Yesteryear, Art of, 327
Yoga, 64, 112, 285, 406
Yogananda, Paramahansa, 261, 321
Yogi, Goal of the, 170
Yogis, The, 202
Yogurt, 163
Yokel, Poor, 283
Yorkies, Two, 403
Yorkshire, 50, 123, 138, 163, 175, 202
'You' of the ego variety, 115
You—the
　　artist of original work, 382
　　lover of the art, 298
Yutang, Lin, 41, 325
Younger 'rival' Michelangelo (See also
　　Leonardo da Vinci), 372
Your awareness—a subtlety, 154
Youth, Cult-worship of, 315

Z

Zanuck, Richard, 257
Zappa, Frank, 381
Zealots, 105
Zeitgeist, Current, 313
Zen,
　　Different schools of, 117
　　History of, 116
　　Insightful aroma of, 34
　　Inspired, 187
　　Japanese, 116
　　Later, 134, 283
　　Point of, 187
　　Practice, 117
　　Teachings of, 78, 101, 115, 117
　　What followers of, 117
　　metaphor of the master's fingers, 106
Zen-like, 184, 218
Zeus, Nine daughters of (See also Greek
　　Muses), 305
Zoketsu Norman Fischer, 321
Zola, Emile, 379
Zorba the Greek, 306

DRUID SPRING

www.ingramcontent.com/pod-product-compliance
Lightning Source LLC
Chambersburg PA
CBHW081413230426
43668CB00016B/2220